THE URBAN TRANSPORTATION SYSTEM

A Publication of the Joint Center for Urban Studies of the Massachusetts Institute of Technology and Harvard University

MIT Press Series in Transportation Studies
Marvin L. Manheim, editor
Center for Transportation Studies, MIT

1. *The Automobile and the Environment: An International Perspective,* edited by Ralph Gakenheimer, 1978

2. *The Urban Transportation System: Politics and Policy Innovation,* Alan A. Altshuler with James P. Womack and John R. Pucher, 1979

THE URBAN TRANSPORTATION SYSTEM
Politics and Policy Innovation

Alan Altshuler

with
James P. Womack
John R. Pucher

The MIT Press
Cambridge, Massachusetts, and London, England

Third printing, February 1980
Second printing, October 1979

This book was set in IBM Baskerville by To the Lighthouse Press and printed and bound by The Alpine Press, Inc., in the United States of America.

Library of Congress Cataloging in Publication Data

Altshuler, Alan A   1936–
   The urban transportation system.

   Bibliography: p.
   Includes index.
   1. Urban transportation policy—United States.   2. Local transit—United States.   I. Womack, James P., joint author.   II. Pucher, John R., joint author.   III. Title.
He308.A63   388.4′0973   78–25805
ISBN 0–262–01055–0

CONTENTS

SERIES FOREWORD

The field of transportation has emerged as a recognized profession only in the last ten years, although transportation issues have been important throughout history. Today, more and more government agencies, universities, researchers, consultants, and private industry groups are becoming truly multimodal in their orientations, and specialists of many different disciplines and professions are working on multidisciplinary approaches to complex transportation issues.

The central role of transportation in our world today and its recent professional status have led The MIT Press and the MIT Center for Transportation Studies to establish The MIT Press Series in Transportation Studies. The series will present works representing the broad spectrum of transportation concerns. Some volumes will report significant new research, while others will give analyses of specific policy, planning, or management issues. Still others will show the interaction between research and policy. Contributions will be drawn from the worldwide transportation community.

The Joint Center for Urban Studies of MIT and Harvard University joins the Transportation Studies series in the publication of *The Urban Transportation System.* The Joint Center's purpose has been to encourage interdisciplinary research among faculty at the two universities. Its book series has been designed to reflect this multifaceted approach to urban problems.

This book deals with the broad range of factors—economic, technological, political, and cultural—that must be considered in the analysis and evaluation of urban transportation systems and that ultimately dictate urban form. As such, it adheres to the spirit of the Joint Center's research and exemplifies one of the styles of work that is presented in the transportation series.

Marvin Manheim
Center for Transportation Studies

Arthur P. Solomon
Director, Joint Center
for Urban Studies

To Julie, Jenny, and David, with love

Policy debate and analysis in the field of urban transportation have traditionally proceeded from the concerns of key institutions and occupational groups in the field. These in turn have been organized around specific technologies and services. Thus analytic activities have tended overwhelmingly to focus on the appraisal, advocacy, and/or incremental adaptation of these technologies and services—which we term *preselected solutions*—rather than on laying bare the character of the problems generating demands for public action or on searching with a fresh eye for effective remedial strategies. Paramount among these preselected solutions have been highway and transit improvements, and policy discussions have typically proceeded as if these were the only options available for addressing sources of dissatisfaction with the urban transportation system.

This is not to suggest that urban transportation actors and policy analysts have been unaffected by shifting public problem perceptions. It is to note, however, that with rare exceptions they have sought to accommodate such shifts within the framework of an ongoing dialogue about the roles and relationships of a rather narrow range of preferred policy instruments, and that they have had little to say about the problems except as they could be related to these instruments. Illustratively the question has been; How much energy might be saved by implementing various types of transit improvements? rather than; What means of reducing urban transportation energy demand are likely to prove most cost-effective and compatible with other public and private objectives?

Policy practice frequently races ahead of policy analysis, and in fact a high proportion of the most significant policy developments affecting urban transportation in recent years have been outside the traditional mold—involving, for example, regulation of the auto manufacturers rather than highway or transit improvements. These have emanated primarily from agencies, legislative committees, and pressure groups concerned primarily with other issues (energy and air pollution, for example), and only derivatively with transportation activities. The consequences have included a significant expansion, de facto, of the realm of urban transportation policy, together with a forging of critical new linkages between urban transportation and several other policy arenas. But these developments have occurred to date in relatively ad hoc fashion, unaccompanied by systematic efforts to achieve a coherent reappraisal of the problems and plausible policy options of urban transportation.

The urban transportation literature is characterized, finally, by a paucity of serious political analysis. The vast preponderance of scholarship in the field has been by engineers and economists who have tended to ignore political variables or merely to note their relevance as contextual constraints. Social scientists writing about urban transportation have generally focused on the psychology of modal choice or on specific project controversies. When dealing more broadly with the forces shaping urban transportation policy, they have typically slipped into a polemic vein and been content to espouse simplistic theories of political causality.

Contemplating these deficiencies in the existing literature, my colleagues and I resolved to undertake a review of the field and to develop an analytic framework for the appraisal of policy options with the following characteristics:

• Oriented toward clarifying thought about the problems of urban transportation and only thereafter toward search for effective policy instruments.

• Open to a considerably broader range of potential strategies than those traditionally discussed under the rubric of urban transportation policy.

• Alert to the roles of politics and culture in shaping distinctive American features of the urban transportation system (and policies bearing upon it).

• Equally sensitive to the importance of technical and economic variables as sources of opportunity, threat, inducement, and constraint.

• Respectful of the complexity of relationships among political, cultural, economic, and technical variables, hence resistant to single-factor explanations.

This has proved to be a much taller order than we imagined at the outset, and we make no pretense of having filled it adequately. We judge that we have carried the analysis about as far as we can on our own, however, and we have been encouraged by some of our early readers to believe that it merits wider exposure. We hope that it may contribute in some measure to the enhancement of public and scholarly discourse about urban transportation issues and represent a useful addition as well to the growing literature on public policy evolution in American society.

In a genuinely collaborative work, it is always difficult to assign precise credit (or blame). Roughly, however, the distribution in this case was as follows. Alan Altshuler provided overall project direction and wrote all but a few pages of the text. James Womack shared fully in the research and conceptualization of chapters 5, 6, 7, 9 and 10, wrote all of the appendixes and made significant contributions to virtually all other portions of the manuscript. John Pucher shared fully in the research and conceptualization of chapter 8, bearing particular responsibility for the original research on the distribution of transit subsidy benefits and tax contributions among income groups; additionally, he assembled the data on the price elasticity of demand for gasoline and automobile travel reported in chapter 5, drafted the summaries of chapters 5 through 10, and made numerous useful comments on early drafts of chapter 5, 9, and 11.

The preparation of this book was supported by the Office of University Research, U.S. Department of Transportation, which, we hasten to add, bears no responsibility for our findings or interpretations. Ron Fisher, director of the Office of Service and Methods Demonstration, Urban Mass Transportation Administration, served as our project monitor. Without his consistent encouragement and frequently invaluable advice, our task would have been much less pleasant and the result far less sensitive to the concerns of potential critics. Michael Rabins, director of the Office of University Research during most of the period of our study, demonstrated unfailing confidence in the value of our work and brightened our days whenever we had occasion to interact with him. Jim Bautz, Doug Gurin, Kevin Heanue, Don Morin, Sandra Rosenbloom, Jerry Ward, Ray Weil, and Eldon Ziegler met with us as an informal advisory committee on several occasions and provided extremely constructive criticism. Kenneth Orski read drafts of several chapters and provided valuable encouragement.

Reid Ewing, Chris Hendrickson, Michael Meyer, and Peter Van Doren made significant contributions to the analysis as research assistants and provided us as well with critical readings of individual chapters. We are indebted to our M.I.T. faculty colleagues Ralph Gakenheimer, Nigel Wilson, Jerome Rothenberg, and William C. Wheaton for numerous insights and references. Among scholars elsewhere, Charles Lave merits special note as a source of encouragement, thoughtful feedback, and provocative suggestions for improvement.

Scores of individuals employed by several dozen agencies at the federal, state, and regional levels generously took time—on occasion, substantial amounts of it—to assist us in gathering and interpreting data. Although they are too numerous to list separately, and most of them doubtless prefer anonymity in any event, we wish to express our gratitude and to acknowledge that the task we set ourselves would have proved impossible but for their help.

Appreciation is due as well to Diane Drapeau, who served as project secretary, and to Myra Musicant and Kathy Huber, who provided additional typing assistance.

Alan Altshuler

THE URBAN TRANSPORTATION SYSTEM

The aims of this book are to elucidate the ways in which political, cultural, economic, and technological factors have combined to shape the American system of urban transportation, to appraise the significance and potential for durability of the most salient policy themes that have emerged since World War II, and to provide a broad foundation for evaluating proposed innovations in urban transportation policy during the years immediately ahead. Our primary focus will be on the personal travel components of the urban transportation system, although a brief discussion of trucking appears in appendix A.

In the evaluative phase of our analysis, we shall strive particularly to identify measures that appear to combine technical cost-effectiveness as a means of addressing important problems with a reasonably high potential for political adoption. Such measures tend in practice, we shall argue, to be of the "technical fix" variety that entail little or no behavioral change for urban travelers (for example, requirements that the auto manufacturers produce more fuel-efficient cars), and to be available with reference to only a subset of urban transportation problems. In other periods, when resources have seemed more ample, the American political system has been disposed as well toward strategies involving the distribution of largesse, such as increases in highway and transit spending. These appear cost-ineffective with respect to most of the significant current problems of urban transportation, however, and in any event the predominant public mood of the late 1970s is one of fiscal austerity. There remain various strategies of behavioral constraint, whether by direct regulation or by the manipulation of price disincentives; but these generally provoke intense political resistance even when, in the judgment of most technical analysts, their cost effectiveness has been demonstrated.

In the shifting constellation of perceived problems and potential strategies, of course, the range of possible combinations and permutations is extraordinarily great. Public attitudes, priorities, and expectations are far from fixed, and the precise bounds of political feasibility are ever uncertain. The sense of uncertainty is particularly great in the late 1970s, because the decade has been one of unusually rapid change. The time seems appropriate for a fresh look at the problems, the available policy instruments, and the new strategic opportunities that may be emerging in the field of urban transportation.

The Problems of Urban Transportation

Although the major features of the urban transportation system have displayed considerable stability in the postwar period—remarkable stability, if one counts among its features the continuous trend toward automobile dominance—public perceptions of the main problems associated with the system, and government policy priorities, have been characterized by fairly rapid change.

The concept of an urban transportation problem first emerged in the early 1950s. Throughout the remainder of that decade and the first half of the next, the "problem" was perceived almost exclusively as one of highway congestion. The overwhelming priority was to accommodate rising traffic demand by constructing new and improved expressways. Gradually since the mid-1960s, however, the following viewpoints have gained wide acceptance: the urban transportation problem is in fact a complex set of problems; in aggregate these problems touch vitally on national security, the overall state of the economy, public health, equity, and environmental amenity, as well as motorist convenience; many (some would say all) of these problems are closely linked to features of the auto-dominant system of urban transportation that most Americans find highly congenial; and measures proposed to enhance mobility are properly judged in terms of their implications for a wide variety of other values as well.

In considering this evolution of viewpoints, we find it convenient to distinguish among conditions, problems, and values. *Conditions* are objective phenomena, such as the number of homes in the path of a proposed highway or the quantity of polluting emissions per mile of automobile use. Conditions become *problems* only when they are perceived as grounds for dissatisfaction and remedial action, and they become *public* problems only when they are widely perceived as grounds for *governmental* action. *Values* are the normative criteria against which actors measure change, to determine whether it is for the better or worse.

Problem perceptions may emerge because conditions have recently changed for the worse with reference to the values of substantial numbers of people, because new information has come to light about the harmful consequences of long-standing conditions, because expectations have risen, or because values have changed. In practice new problem perceptions are frequently rooted in a combination of these causes. So are changes in priority among pre-existing problem perceptions and changes in attitude toward programs. The greater the number of problem perceptions and of value criteria for appraising change, the greater the potential for controversy about government programs and priorities. Thus the growth in complexity of the urban transportation policy agenda has entailed a dramatic increase in the potential for disagreement, and at times stalemate, among the relevant actors as to what government should do.

After congestion, the next conditions to gain widespread recognition as public problems were the continuing precipitous decline of mass transit, the disruptive impacts of urban expressway construction, and the large numbers of people killed and injured each year in automobile accidents. The first two of these were closely linked, and they emerged as public issues during the 1960s from a base of numerous local controversies. The last emerged full-blown and virtually overnight at the national level, spurred by the publication of Ralph Nader's book, *Unsafe at Any Speed,* in 1965 and by his subsequent appearance before a U.S. Senate subcommittee chaired by Abraham Ribicoff.[1]

The safety issue was addressed politically by national regulation of the automobile manufacturers, with no significant role opportunities for state and local actors; it thus had no immediate impact on thought about urban transportation policy options. The growth of concern about transit decline and the disruptive effects of highway construction did, on the other hand, gradually have profound consequences for urban transportation policy. These conditions did not stir controversy and give rise to sharply defined problem perceptions everywhere simultaneously. Rather, concern emanated outward from areas characterized by the highest urban densities and the greatest historic reliance on transit. In these the disruptive impact per mile of new highway tended to be most severe,[1] and transit decline was most likely to be viewed as a major problem by political and business leaders.

The local officials of these areas found it far more attractive to join the campaign for the revival of transit than that against proposed expressways, because the former did not entail any conflict with business or construction interests. Thus numerous localities and a few of the most urbanized states commenced transit subsidization during the middle and late 1960s; those few that had previously begun to subsidize transit sharply increased their spending levels; and Congress enacted a modest program of transit capital assistance in 1964. (Transit did not become a major urban spending priority until the 1970s, however.) By contrast local highway protest movements achieved very few clear-cut victories in the 1960s. They did, however, contribute to a climate of opinion in which, during the latter half of the decade, Congress authorized substantially more generous compensation for those dislocated to make way for new highways and mandated consideration of environmental effects in the planning of highways. As interpreted by the courts beginning in 1971, the latter provisions in particular were to have profound consequences during the 1970s.[2] During the early 1970s, moreover, the environmental movement was riding a tidal wave of public support and political success, and anti-highway activity enjoyed a prominent place on the environmental agenda. The result was a decisive shift in the local political balance against disruptive highway construction in numerous urban areas, including many with low-density settlement patterns.

In the 1970s new problem perceptions have emerged with be-

[1.] The most controversial miles, it bears note, tended to be those that threatened university areas, affluent or cohesive ethnic neighborhoods, and/or sites of regionwide historic or environmental importance. As highway planners operated under severe locational constraints—they needed wide swaths of land, straight or gently curving, connecting throughout the region at points where interchanges could be built—they found it virtually impossible to avoid impinging on such zones of extreme sensitivity in the course of laying out freeway networks in dense urban areas.

wildering rapidity as central focuses of urban transportation concern. More or less in chronological order, these have included the air pollution effects of motor vehicle usage; the high levels of energy demand associated with predominant reliance on the automobile for urban mobility; the special constraints on mobility experienced in the auto-dominant system by those who, because of age or physical disability, are unable to drive; the rapidly growing fiscal demands of mass transit; and sharply reduced rates of revenue growth for all public purposes at the state and local levels.

On the whole, these new problem perceptions have simply been added to the urban transportation policy agenda. Of those that emerged earlier, none have really been solved, although the social and environmental consequences of urban expressway construction have sharply diminished as the most disruptive projects have either been completed or been dropped in the face of citizen protest, environmental lawsuits, and/or fiscal shortages. Moreover this list of problems does not by any means include all of the issues around which controversy has swirled. In practice public debate and mobilization have typically focused far more on proposed remedial measures than on the problems themselves. This pattern commenced with the battles over expressways. More recently controversy has focused on such proposed measures as new rail rapid transit systems, sharp increases in transit operating subsidy appropriations, authorization for urban areas to use their highway aid allocations for mass transit purposes, and restrictions on auto use to reduce air pollution.

Though popular attention tends to focus on the proposed solutions, the problem perceptions are generally the key stimuli providing impetus for their development and enabling them to command prominent places on public agendas.[3] In this respect, one may properly speak of the problem perceptions as the fundamental engines of policy change.

Proponents of measures to alleviate urban transportation problems have had to exercise their persuasive skills in recent years within the context of a dramatic shift in the atmosphere of policy debate on domestic issues generally. The sense that resources are abundant has given way to a sense of austerity. The growing perception of environmental, energy, and revenue limits has led to a sharp decline of interest in problems associated with rapid growth and of receptivity to demands for new public services. Attention has increasingly focused on the challenge of how to maintain existing amenities and public service levels in a period characterized by modest rates of population, personal income, and public revenue growth—and quite possibly by periodic shocks due to energy and other shortages as well.

If there was a specific turning point, it was the Arab oil embargo of 1973–1974. The embargo itself was relatively brief (five months) and only partially effective, but it jolted American complacency about the long-term reliability of the auto-dominant mobility system. It also raised serious questions about the compatibility of this system with the nation's national security and economic (balance of payments, inflation, employment) objectives, and it triggered the intense "stagflation" (a steep national recession accompanied by high inflation) of 1974–1975. The stagflation in turn played a major role in triggering the New York City fiscal crisis, which reached a peak of intensity in 1975 and which greatly heightened public awareness throughout the country of the potential risks associated with high levels of public spending.

These broader shifts in political orientation have had a marked effect on policy debate and planning in urban transportation. Most notably, they have led to a dramatic reduction in emphasis on the need for proposed new expressways and rapid transit systems and toward much greater concern with means of improving the utilization of existing highways, with allocating scarce resources among multiple claimants, and with devising low-cost strategies that promise to serve multiple objectives simultaneously. Stated another way, the focus has shifted significantly (though by no means entirely) from high-cost, capital-intensive, facility-oriented strategies toward relatively low-cost, and particularly low-capital, management and service strategies. Because capital-intensive strategies tend to require long lead times, moreover, and once implemented to be essentially irreversible, whereas management and service strategies are generally susceptible to rapid implementation and easy reversal, there has also been a notable shift in planning orientation from the long term (twenty to twenty-five years) to the short term (one to five years).

One final point. We have suggested that fresh problem perceptions on the part of significant sectors of the public are the most fundamental engines of policy change in urban transportation. It bears emphasis, however, that within the framework of adopted policy, specific activities are often undertaken primarily for other reasons than alleviating urban transportation problems. For want of better terms, we shall refer to stated policy objectives that entail the enhancement of mobility or the alleviation of harmful external effects directly related to the functioning of the urban transportation system as transportation objectives, and we shall refer to all other objectives as nontransportation in nature.

The most typical nontransportation objectives of government transportation activities are economic: the promotion of employment and the encouragement of desired real property investments. Highway spending, for example, is often advocated principally as a means of generating employment for construction workers, and specific highway improvement projects frequently jump to the top of priority lists when there is reason to believe that they would facilitate business investments desired by state and/or local officials. Similarly, key arguments typically used to sell rapid transit projects are that they will bring about massive private investment adjacent to stations (especially in the downtown core) and that their construction will provide a great deal of local employment. Since most large-scale highway and transit investments are undertaken with 70 to 90 percent federal assistance, moreover, both are often urged by state and local actors as means of maximizing the flow of federal aid into their jurisdictions.

The $1.2 billion Westway project in Manhattan provides an outstanding illustration. The Westway is a planned stretch of interstate freeway—depressed and largely covered—that would run four miles from the Battery to Forty-Second Street along the Hudson River. After the U.S. secretary of transportation announced federal approval of funding for the project in January 1977, Governor Hugh Carey of New York quipped that as the secretary spoke, "I could hear the money flowing." Emphasizing in his formal statement that the project would be financed 90 percent by the federal government and 10 percent by the state, he maintained that it was "a milestone in the effort to revitalize [New York] City" that would cost the city taxpayers nothing.[4]

Nine months later the Westway was again prominently in the news as Congressman Edward Koch, the Democratic nominee for mayor, labeled it "an economic and environmental disaster." Labor and business criticism instantly rained upon him. His leading opponent, Mario Cuomo (whom Koch had narrowly defeated in the Democratic primary, and who was running as a third-party candidate), claimed that this demonstrated Koch was less of a "traditional Democrat" than himself. Koch quickly moved to qualify his position. Without retracting his substantive assessment of the project, he stated that he would support construction if it developed that the alternative was loss of the federal aid involved. (Federal law permits a transit transfer only when the governor and affected local governments apply jointly. Thus the key question was whether Governor Carey would go along.) "If I'm not successful in persuading the Governor," Koch said, "there is no alternative but to go ahead with the Westway. This city cannot afford the loss [of this federal aid]." Governor Carey (who had himself labeled the project "a planning and ecological disaster" while campaigning for election in 1974) made clear that his main concern as well was to ensure that the federal aid was not lost. "I have an open mind [on Koch's proposal]," he said; "I want to create jobs, and jobs are just as available in mass transit as in building the highway."

In April 1978, Governor Carey and now-Mayor Koch announced that they had reached agreement on joint support of the Westway, along with a commitment by the governor to seek additional state appropriations for mass transit assistance.[5]

System Evaluation: The Contours of Debate

Controversy about whether the urban transportation system should be considered a success or a problem tends to be rooted in the differing value priorities of those taking part in the debate rather than disputes about fact. These priority differences in turn tend to correlate highly with the individual circumstances assumed (often implicitly) as the appropriate vantage points for evaluation. The system looks quite a bit better from the standpoint of an automobile owner-driver than from that of a low-income household without a car or a handicapped person unable to drive. Similarly the pros and cons of highway construction look considerably different from the perspective of a commuter or construction worker than from that of a resident along the planned right-of-way.

As the agenda of perceived problems has become more crowded, debate about the proper valuation to be placed on the overall system of urban transportation has become more heated. In part this debate has focused on the normative weights that should be attached to the problems by comparison with the attractive features of the system. In part as well it has focused on the question of whether the main problems are linked inextricably to the basic pattern of automobile dominance, so that effective attacks on them must necessarily entail a fundamental modification of that pattern. For the most part, however, the contestants have simply talked past each other, spotlighting quite different features of the system.

Critics of the auto-dominant system have stressed its prodigious energy requirements; its air pollution impacts; the large numbers of fatalities and personal injuries associated with it; its facilitation of urban sprawl and thereby its devastating impact on the quality, coverage, and unit cost of mass transit service; its high private cost, and the quasi-compulsory nature of automobile expenditures in urban areas that have adapted to the automobile; the inconvenience and frequent hardship it imposes on those unable to afford cars and/or to drive; and the disruptive consequences of highway construction.[6]

By contrast, defenders of the auto-dominant system have argued that the automobile has enabled the vast majority of adult Americans to achieve unprecedented mobility (as measured in terms of speed, flexibility, reliability, immediate availability, and comfort); that it has enabled large numbers of urban households to satisfy their desire for single-family home ownership; that Americans have demonstrated that they are willing to bear the costs of automobility; that four-fifths of American households now own automobiles and that some at least of the others (for example, young people who have deliberately chosen central city life-styles or who are students living close by their colleges) do not experience significant hardship in consequence of being without cars; and that in any event the United States has progressed so far down the path of auto reliance—in its predominant life-styles no less than its land use patterns—that attempts to reverse the trend are quixotic.[7] If and when the automobile is partially replaced, in this view, it will be by some future technology offering even greater individual mobility, not by anything resembling current forms of mass transit. Additionally defenders of the system frequently note that the production, marketing, and servicing of motor vehicles, and the production and maintenance of highways, have come to account for a very substantial part of the nation's economic activity. While it would doubtless be possible to achieve high employment in the face of major cutbacks in these sectors over a period of decades, the short-run effects of any significant declines would be highly disruptive. And, for very good reasons, most voters as well as elected officials are predominantly concerned about the short run.

Until recently these themes of evaluation have rarely met head-on. System critics have recognized that the automobile is here to stay, and system defenders have generally acknowledged some continuing role for transit as a minority mode. Having made these concessions, they have simply focused on different aspects of the system.

The debate has taken on a sharper tone in the mid-1970s, however. As the agenda of recognized problems associated with the urban transportation system has grown, critics have become increasingly bolder in calling for fundamental change. Supporters of the auto-dominant system, in turn, have increasingly sought to establish that its main deficiencies—which they have perceived as relating to energy, air quality, and safety—can be remedied by requiring the auto manufacturers to improve their product. They have differed widely as to whether government should in fact engage in performance standard regulation and, if so, what the standards and deadlines should be. But most have accepted in principle that government has a legitimate role to play—as long as it confines itself to mandating performance targets that are technically feasible at modest cost and, in particular, avoids requiring changes in personal travel behavior. Most have also accepted the idea that transit subsidization is appropriate in high-density urban settings and for the benefit of specific mobility-deprived groups, notably, the handicapped, the elderly, and the very poor.

Critics of the auto-dominant system tend to disparage these concessions as grudging tokens; to dismiss the view that the energy, air quality, and safety problems of urban transportation can be ameliorated adequately by technical improvements alone; to emphasize that the problems of urban sprawl, central city decline, and hardship for those without cars would remain even if all of the other deficiencies of the system were fully amenable to technical fix remedies; and to demand in practice considerably tighter standards and deadlines, and much larger transit appropriations, than system defenders deem reasonable.

Political Responses

Though individual actors, scholarly critics, and media commentators typically stress a single priority or evaluative theme, the political system as a whole seems to strive for inclusiveness and broad support rather than for theoretical consistency or elegance. That is, it seeks to accommodate new demands as they emerge by means, insofar as possible, that leave previous settlements (programs and administrative arrangements) undisturbed, that involve the least possible disruption for private enterprises, and that involve the least possible inconvenience and annoyance for individuals who have built their life-styles around the expectation of system stability.

Though almost never stated explicitly, these decision rules are vital keys to understanding the urban transportation policy sys-

tem. Their main function is simple. They tend to confine new issues within the narrowest possible bounds and thereby to minimize conflict. They maximize the capacity of decision makers to
define the policy game as one of winners without losers, and thereby
to produce the greatest possible ratio of satisfied to dissatisfied
constituents.

Another way to put this is to say that the political system strives
to maintain the security of its key institutions and personnel as it
responds to outside change stimuli. Virtually all institutionalized
systems exhibit such security-oriented behavior in high degree.
Systems vary widely in the strategies that they utilize to pursue
security, however, and in the priority that they accord it relative
to other key objectives.[8]

The American political system in this respect is something of a
paradox. On the one hand, its task is to manage an extraordinarily
dynamic society, which throws up a constant stream of new demands and opportunities. Numerous officials in the system, moreover, are highly attuned to the need for constant adaptation in the
face of changing conditions. On the other hand, the organization
of the political system itself is such as to generate an extreme
orientation toward caution. The system is most notably characterized by fragmented authority, weak party organization, and
minimal ideological coherence. It affords numerous opportunities
for veto and/or delay during the life of any bill and subsequently
during the implementation of any policy.[9] With party organization rudimentary in most locales, with party identification weak
among the electorate, and with nomination by direct primary rather than by the favor of party leaders, moreover, individual elected officials feel highly vulnerable (even when representing sup-
posedly safe districts) and very much on their own.

In such a system, a great many people must agree before any
policy initiative can be adopted and effectively implemented;
elected officials as a group are about as prone to disagree among
themselves on the merits of any initiative as are the potentially
affected parties; political timidity is the individual norm; and
weak leadership is the institutional norm. Specific officials, of
course, are frequently driven by conviction, ambition, and/or a

taste for publicity and risk to champion bold policy departures. In order to achieve some measure of legislative success, however, they must secure the freely given consent of many others who are less impressed with the need for change, who feel more protective toward existing programs, and/or who have little taste for political risk.

From time to time, on the other hand, circumstances do arise that permit the adoption of policies requiring substantial shifts in existing program and institutional arrangements. These circumstances tend to consist, in varying degree, of crisis (war, depression, oil embargo), the emergence of powerful new demands (such as for environmental protection circa 1970), and/or the accession to key leadership positions of individuals with both the disposition to innovate and remarkable coalition-building gifts. Not surprisingly, however, the system's normal pattern of policy evolution, only rarely breached, is by cautious accretion—designed at each step to disturb as little of the existing policy landscape as possible—rather than by fundamental rationalization.[10]

In practice, then, the paradox between rapid social, economic, and technological change on the one hand and a political system oriented toward cautious, value-inclusive incrementalism on the other tends to be resolved as follows. First, the political system appears to have a weak commitment to any particular value. Policies in any sector of public activity, such as urban transportation, often seem to contradict rather than reinforce one another. At the same time, the system is highly open to innovative ideas and technologies that can be injected into the ongoing stream of activity with minimal disturbance to existing programs, institutional arrangements, and behavior patterns. Stated another way, the system does not treat apparent tensions among policy objectives as inescapable sources of conflict. Rather it seeks politically to blur the tensions and technically to find ingenious new means of reconciling the objectives.

Problems, Programs, and Priorities

In general it is highly misleading to think of societies and governments as having goals. And it is particularly misleading to think of the American social and political systems, with their extreme pluralism, as having goals. It is far more useful to think of them as having an enormous number of values and a constantly shifting set of priorities among them.

Public policy priorities emerge from the interplay of objective conditions (reality), perceptions as to the feasibility of altering some of these conditions (opportunity), and values for appraising the desirability of change (decision criteria). There is no abstract consensus on the ultimate level of societal performance to be sought with respect to any particular value, nor on the weight that should be accorded it in situations of conflict with other values. From time to time, however, practical agreements do emerge that societal performance on a given dimension is highly inadequate and that government should act to improve it.

We have labeled such agreements *problem perceptions*. From them frequently emerge programs. Programs typically include statements of goals, and we shall devote significant attention in part II of this volume to examining those that have been adopted in the field of urban transportation. But most program objectives are stated in highly general fashion. Viewed collectively, the objectives of public policy (in all their varying precision) are incredibly diverse and so weakly related as in some circumstances to seem directly at odds with one another. They are weighted in the context of actual budget and administrative practice but not in the framework of any comprehensive policy plan.[11]

This lack of an authoritative statement severely complicates the task of determining public priorities—whether overall, or merely within a single policy arena such as urban transportation. Thus we turn to the relative emphasis among programs for the best available statement of societal priorities at any time. In order to read this statement with any degree of reliability, one must focus on what actually occurs in the implementation of programs as well as on their formal articulation. One must also bear in mind significant omissions from the text—that is, programs that have been proposed and rejected, and programs that have been adopted in other political settings but that have been unable even to get on the American political agenda.[12] Those who wish to grasp causality must seek to disaggregate the elements of reality, opportunity, and decision criteria that have given rise to existing priorities. Finally those who wish to prognosticate must seek to determine the extent to which these key components of priority choice are changing.

Our efforts to perform these tasks in the ensuing chapters will necessarily be incomplete and our interpretations open to dispute. We are hopeful, nonetheless, that they will help to clarify thought about the nature of, the relationships among, and the outlook for the problems, programs, and priorities of American society in the field of urban transportation.

I THE POLITICS

The most striking feature of the American system of urban transportation is the predominance of private market choice within it. Nearly 90 percent of urban transportation spending is in the private sector. (See table 2.1 and appendix B.)[1] It should come as no surprise that government, with direct control over only 10 percent of spending, has had great difficulty shaping and steering the remainder, even when it has tried. Bearing in mind that the American political system is highly responsive to interest group and popular desires, it should come as no surprise, either, that the 10 percent has rarely sought deliberately to steer the 90 percent, but has far more typically sought to accommodate it.

It is imperative, therefore, in considering the choices and activities that have shaped the American pattern of urban transportation, to distinguish the following categories: individual choices in the marketplace; public investment, subsidy, and service (distributive) activities[2]; and public constraint activities, aiming to influence private market choices by direct regulation and/or price (including excise tax) increases. Most discussions of urban transportation policy focus exclusively on public distributive activities. This is quite understandable because it includes the vast preponderance of what government has actually done in the field of urban transportation. This is far from saying, however, that government policy has been the predominant force shaping the urban transportation system or that it can effectively be reshaped in future by the use of distributive measures.

Individual Choices in the Marketplace

Acting as individual consumers, Americans have shifted in over-

[1.] Another 7 percent consists of highway user tax payments, which are built into the market prices of privately produced goods and services but which are received by governments rather than by the private producers. The main participants in the highway policy arena have traditionally viewed these taxes as part of a quasi-market system, in which highway users were implicitly purchasing the public provision of highway services rather than simply contributing to the general pot of revenues available for political allocation. This perception, though dubious in principle and increasingly controversial in practice, has been of central political importance during most legislative efforts to enact and allocate user taxes, and it has deeply influenced highway planning and administrative practices.

[2.] Theodore Lowi has coined the term *distributive* (as part of a more general policy typology) to denote programs that most obviously entail the distribution of benefits by government.[1]

TABLE 2.1
Cost of the Urban Transportation System, 1975 (in Billions of Dollars)

Automobile	
Vehicles (capital and operating; excludes excise taxes and registration fees)	93.1
Public highway expenditures attributable to auto use	7.5
	100.6
Local Transit (bus, rapid transit, and commuter rail)	
Operating revenues	2.3
Public operating subsidies	2.0
Current capital expenditures (all public)	1.7
	6.0
Truck	
Vehicles and Terminals (capital and operating; excludes excise taxes and registration fees)	44.1
Public highway expenditures attributable to truck use	2.8
	46.9
Other	
Taxi	1.6
School and other nontransit bus	1.1
	2.7
Total	156.2

Sources and notes: appendix B.

whelming numbers from transit to automobile travel in the period since World War II. As of 1975, estimated auto passenger mileage in urban areas stood at 559 percent of the 1945 level, transit passenger mileage at 29 percent. (The 1945 figures were, of course, reflective of special wartime conditions. Thus 1950 is frequently used as the base year for comparison. Urban auto passenger mileage in 1975 stood at 333 percent of the 1950 level, transit passenger mileage at 42 percent.) Transit, which had accounted for 35 percent of total passenger mileage in 1945 and 18 percent in 1950, accounted in 1975 for only 3 percent.[3] (See table 2.2.)

In the course of achieving this overwhelming dominance, the automobile appears to have become the less expensive mode for most purposes, as well as the more rapid, convenient, and flexible. As near as we have been able to estimate, expenditures for urban automobile and transit travel in 1975—public and private, capital and operating—totaled $106.6 billion. The transit share of this combined total was 5.6 percent (table 2.1), and its share of urban passenger mileage was 2.8 percent (table 2.2). On average, then, transit cost about twice as much per passenger mile as urban automobile travel.

This finding must be qualified with reference to the specific travel functions performed by transit. Most transit travel occurs

3. The growth of automobile dominance did not occur simply at the expense of transit. Even more significantly, it entailed rapid growth in the total amount of travel and shifts from walking to mechanized modes of travel. Boris Pushkarev and Jeffrey Zupan have recently made the following estimates.[2] (Their transit totals include taxi.)

Urban Passenger Miles of Travel (PMT) per Urban Resident

Year	Total	Transit	Transit (%)
1900	500	499	99.7
1929	3,700	877	23.7
1944	3,600	1248	34.7
1960	4,600	344	7.5
1974	6,300	241	3.8

Pushkarev and Zupan estimate that the absolute level of transit PMT in 1974 was nearly two and one-half times as great as in 1900. Total urban population, however, was five times as great, and overall PMT was nearly twelve and one-half times as great. The Pushkarev and Zupan estimates for the period before World War II are based on extremely fragmentary data. As approximations, however, they are persuasive.

TABLE 2.2
Trends in Urban Transit and Automobile Travel

Year	Transit Passenger Miles[a] (in billions)	Auto Passenger Miles (in billions)	Percent Transit[a]
1945	130	240	35.1
1950	90	403	18.3
1955	60	515	10.4
1960	48	627	7.1
1965	43	786	5.2
1970	41	1,089	3.6
1975	38	1,341	2.8

Sources and notes: appendix C.

[a] Includes transit bus, rapid rail, and commuter rail.

during peak hours along the most heavily traveled corridors of large urban areas. Though precise figures are unavailable, it is clear that automobile travel is at its most expensive in such circumstances. Thus it by no means follows that because automobile travel is less expensive on average nationally, it is also less expensive in the corridors where most transit service is currently provided. These figures do suggest, however, that careful analysis is in order before concluding that major expansions of transit service, and diversions of current automobile travelers to the transit mode, would reduce the real dollar cost (public and private combined) of the urban transportation system.

Though acting separately, consumers have made their modal choice decisions over the decades within a common framework of culture and public policy. Culturally American urban residents have always sought, within the limits set by their incomes and the speed of available modes of commutation, to combine key elements of the rural life-style with their urban means of earning a livelihood. In particular, they have sought low-density living in single-family homes on generous, privately owned plots of land. The poor, who in many cultures squat on the fringes of urban development, have tended to occupy the older, high-density areas close to the core.[3]

Technological factors have strongly reinforced these cultural factors in recent decades. Since at least the 1930s changes in materials-handling techniques have been driving manufacturers to seek out sites large enough, and cheap enough per square foot, to permit the development of single-story factories. Improved power transmission technologies have enabled companies with large electrical requirements to locate as easily in the open countryside as in central cities. The availability of trucking services has reduced the incentive for goods-handling businesses of all types (industrial, wholesaling, and so forth) to locate near railheads, and as their reliance on trucking has grown, so has their incentive to locate away from central city traffic congestion. Improvements in communications have been rapidly increasing the locational freedom even of office activities traditionally viewed as downtown captives.[4]

Just as powerful cultural and technological forces tending toward urban dispersal were well established before 1945, so was the popularity of the automobile. Between 1910 and 1930, when the nation's road system and its consumer credit mechanisms were both primitive, automobile registrations grew from under 0.5 million to 23 million—from one for every two-hundred Americans to nearly one for every five. By 1975, the number of auto registrations had risen to nearly five times the 1930 level, but the ratio had risen by only two and one-half times since 1930, from 1:5 to 1:2 (table 2.3).

There is much to be said, then, for the view that the explosive dispersal of urban activities in the postwar period, accompanied by an equally dramatic shift in travel patterns, was a product of consumer preferences and changing technologies, delayed in the 1930–1945 period by the Depression and then by wartime shortages, but waiting to burst forth as soon as these restraints were removed.

Public Decisions and Consumer Preferences

Public policy played a significant reinforcing role in the quarter-century following World War II, years of rapid urbanization and population growth. Consequently the pattern of new development during this period was able to establish itself as the predominant

TABLE 2.3
U.S. Auto Registrations and Population (in millions)

Year	Auto Registration[a]	Population[b]	Ratio
1910	0.46	92.0	1:200
1930	23.0	122.8	1:5.3
1950	40.4	150.7	1:3.7
1970	88.8	203.2	1:2.3
1975	106.1	213.0	1:2.0

Source: Federal Highway Administration, *Highway Statistics*, (various years), table VM-1; U.S. Bureau of the Census, *Statistical Abstract of the United States* (1976), p. 2.

[a] Includes private and commercial vehicles but not publicly owned or military vehicles.

[b] Does not include U.S. nationals overseas.

form of American urbanization. From 1950 to 1970 (precise 1945 data are unavailable), urbanized area population increased by 71 percent, from 69.2 to 118.4 million. During this same period, urbanized land area increased by 176 percent, from 12, 733 square miles to 35,081 square miles.[5]

In considering the explosion of motor vehicle usage and of urban sprawl in the decades that followed World War II, it is useful to ask whether any public policies or institutions deliberately sought to create the patterns of urban sprawl, transit decline, and automobile dominance. As near as one can tell, these were not deliberate public objectives. Government did not act pursuant to a conscious urban development policy. Rather it responded in a wide variety of policy arenas to organized pressures, to conventional wisdom, and to widespread public aspirations. In practice, the result was consistently to accommodate and reinforce the majority taste for low-density living and for automobility.

Yet during the period in which postwar patterns were most decisively shaped—1945 to 1960—urban highway construction was extremely limited. The interstate program was enacted by Congress in 1956, but it did not provide many new facilities that motorists could drive on until the 1960s. The most important urban development policies between 1945 and 1960 were those that affected housing. The federal government, acting as regulator of the banking industry, as buyer and seller of mortgages, and as direct insurer of mortgages, became the most important factor in the credit structure of the housing industry. Its objectives were to relieve the postwar housing shortage, to satisfy the widespread desire for home ownership, and to maintain a high level of activity in the home building industry. Within the framework of these objectives, the primary motive of federal housing officials was to minimize risk. Delay, red tape, poor planning, even charges of racial and economic discrimination were unlikely to get officials in trouble; but to be perceived as responsible for high default rates was a very serious matter indeed.

The conventional wisdom of the period, shared by bankers, economists, and all others professionally concerned with urban real estate markets, was that property values were generally most secure in areas characterized by resident-owned single-family homes, inhabitants who had stable incomes adequate to support these homes and who were racially and ethnically homogeneous, locations distant from concentrations of lower-class and racial minority population, and adequate parking space for family automobiles.[6] If these were in fact the safest areas in which to lend and invest, and they probably were, the reason was that most Americans with money wanted to buy these amenities. A more aggressive set of public policies might have tapped certain minority markets. The government might, for example, have introduced and encouraged condominium development in the older parts of urban areas. But it did not. It did what government and industry do most characteristically in the United States: aim at the heart of the mass market.

Similarly federal tax policies had an enormous impact on the calculations of housing investors and consumers. Most notably they permitted home owners to deduct their mortgage and real estate tax payments from taxable income. In addition they provided developers of new structures with considerably more favorable treatment than renovators of old. Because it is generally cheaper to build new structures on vacant land and because the idea of condominium home ownership within the framework of multifamily buildings did not come into widespread fashion until the 1970s, these provisions as well were significant spurs to dispersal. Again, however, there is no evidence that this was a matter of deliberate intent.[7]

Land use planning and regulation were viewed exclusively in this period as local government functions, and they rarely functioned effectively until after development was far advanced—when property owners had acquired a sense of collective economic interest, and when both government and citizenry had acquired some sophistication in dealing with the complexities of urban life. In urban as well as rural areas, moreover, the proper objective of government in regulating land use was viewed as the protection of property values, not the achievement of collective community visions. It was one thing to prevent commercial or industrial users from invading a stable residential neighborhood. It was quite another to prevent a farmer from making a large profit by selling land to a developer.

In this situation, though individual localities might hold the line against development pressures. their resistance had almost no significance within the broad emerging pattern of urban sprawl.[8] What impact such resistance did have was generally to *accelerate* sprawl. Developers were likely to find land beyond the urban fringe less subject to regulation, as well as much cheaper, than vacant parcels within the zone of existing development. And, having opted for leapfrog development, they could generally count on public agencies to provide schools, utilities, and improved highway access for the citizens to whom they made their sales.

Public Investment Decisions, I: The Great Era of Highway Building

In this context, the great era of highway building got underway in the late 1950s. Both this policy, and the neglect of mass transit by American governments until very recent years, were squarely in the American public tradition of following the private market. The highway program in particular was consistently defended by its supporters on the ground that it served a visible public demand, as demonstrated in the marketplace, on the highways, and in the voting booths.

There were, of course, great political forces at work. A program as massive as construction of the interstate highway system does not secure enactment merely because it seems likely to be popular. A great campaign to mobilize, direct, and translate into law the latent public support for highway construction was successfully undertaken by the industries and labor unions with the most to gain. It is important to keep in mind, however, that there was widespread public support and that the market forces to be served by highway construction were already sweeping the field in the marketplace. Thus those who lobbied successfully for increased highway construction were able to operate within a highly congenial framework of popular taste, market behavior, and apparent political predisposition.

The best evidence of support at the ballot box is that constitutional amendments earmarking highway user tax revenues for highway-related purposes were adopted in more than half the states by referendum in the late 1940s and early 1950s. In Massachusetts, for example, voters approved the so-called good roads amendment by a ratio of six to one in 1948. In 1974, they voted by a substantial margin to authorize expenditures from the highway trust fund for mass transit purposes, but it would be highly misleading to read the popular sentiments of 1974 into interpretations of the events of the 1940s and 1950s.

By the early 1950s, the automobile industry was intensely concerned that motor vehicle sales, which had been on a steeply rising curve since 1945, would stagnate or decline unless the highway system were expanded to keep pace with the growth of motor vehicle usage. Along with such major allies as the oil, steel, rubber, and trucking industries, together with their labor unions, the auto industry began to orchestrate a public clamor for vigorous public action to deal with congestion. The media of the time indicate the apparently uncontroversial nature of the campaign. The material generated by the auto industry and its allies was printed in every popular journal of general circulation, month after month. Dissent was virtually nonexistent. The same pattern prevails in the record of congressional hearings on the interstate highway program. There were disputes about financing but none about the desirability of the program itself.[9]

The Eisenhower administration came into office in 1953 with particularly close ties to the automobile and oil industries. Its central domestic policy was to roll back the size of the federal government. In line with this aim, it announced a policy of "no new starts" in the domestic public works field during 1954 and 1955. During this same period, nonetheless, it prepared and submitted to Congress the enabling legislation for the largest domestic public works program in the history of the world: the interstate system.

As of 1955, the year prior to enactment of the interstate program, combined federal and state expenditures for urban highway construction totaled $718 million. By 1962, this figure had nearly tripled, to $2.07 billion. Most of the increase involved expressway construction on new rights-of-way, and substantial highway investment was being focused for the first time on the densely developed portions of large urban areas. (The urban share of total federal and state expenditures for highway construction increased from 22 to 35 percent during this period.)[10]

Highway interests were generally viewed in the 1950s and 1960s as constituting one of the two or three most powerful lobbies in American politics. The most significant assets of this lobby (or, more precisely, network of allied lobbies) were as follows:

First, it represented a large sector of the American economy. Roughly one-sixth of all American businesses, employing one-seventh of all American workers, were (and are) involved in the production, marketing, service, and commercial use of automobiles, trucks, and highways. Second, it had geographic distribution. These businesses and workers were spread fairly evenly across every congressional district. By contrast, 61 percent of all transit patronage as of 1975 was in ten metropolitan areas. New York and Chicago alone accounted for 42 percent, including 88 percent of all rapid transit and 85 percent of all commuter rail patronage. (See table 2.4.)

Third, it had leadership. Not only were its small businesses and groups of employees spread throughout every congressional district; it also included a significant proportion of the nation's largest companies. In 1976, all of the top seven, and twelve of the top fifteen, in *Fortune*'s annual ranking of the largest industrial com-

Table 2.4
Transit Patronage in the Ten Largest U.S. Metropolitan Areas, 1975 (in
Thousands of Passengers)

Place	Rank	Bus[a]	Rapid Rail Transit	Commuter Rail	Total
New York	1	972,120 (18.4)	1,120,497 (79.2)	145,609 (56.0)	2,238,226 (32.2)
Chicago	2	514,316 (9.7)	121,931 (8.6)	71,000 (27.3)	707,247 (10.2)
Philadelphia	3	190,761 (3.6)	68,695 (4.9)	29,813 (11.4)	289,269 (4.2)
San Francisco	4	172,885 (3.3)	27,877 (2.0)	4,720 (1.8)	205,482 (3.0)
Los Angeles	5	200,000 (3.8)	0	0	200,000 (2.9)
Boston	6	81,078 (1.5)	62,422 (4.4)	7,461 (2.9)	150,961 (2.2)
Washington	7	126,805 (2.4)	0	1,214 (0.5)	128,019 (1.8)
Baltimore	8	111,140 (2.1)	0	0	111,410 (1.6)
Pittsburgh	9	110,818 (2.1)	0	328 (0.1)	111,146 (1.6)
Detroit	10	85,469 (1.6)	0	331 (0.1)	85,800 (1.2)
Total top ten		2,565,662 (48.5)	1,401,422 (99.0)	260,476 (100.0)	4,227,560 (60.7)
Total national		5,286,000	1,415,657	260,476	6,962,133

Source: John Pucher, "Losses in the American Transit Industry: An Analysis
of the Variation in Operating Expenses, Revenues, and Ridership Levels by
Mode and Urban Area, 1973–1976," technical report 2 (MIT Center for
Transportation Studies, May 1977), table 2-1, 2-2-1 to 2-2-6, and 2-3-1 to
2-3-4.

Note: Figures in parentheses represent percentages of the national totals in
each category.

[a] The bus category includes motor bus, trolley coach, and light rail (streetcar)
except for Boston, where light rail was included in the rapid transit category.

panies were automobile, oil, and steel companies.[11] These figures have been essentially stable since the 1950s.

Fourth, the lobby was excellently equipped to forge strong ties between its national and local business components. A substantial percentage of the latter—particularly the automobile dealerships, the service stations, and many roadside businesses—were franchisees of the major national firms. Others were suppliers. The 1972 Census of Manufacturers reported that the automobile manufacturers directly purchased $16.1 billion worth of goods annually from other companies.[12] Numerous other large institutions—among them banks, insurance companies, and pension funds—had major investment stakes in the highway-related sectors. Indeed, it was an article of faith among business people that any slowdown in automobile production tended quickly to generate recession and unemployment throughout the economy.

Fifth, the highway lobby included organized labor. The construction trades, of course, have historically been among the most powerful of unions and the most active in state and local politics. National behemoths such as the Teamsters, the Auto Workers, and the Steel Workers unions perceived a major stake in the highway program as well. In labor as in business, moreover, the universal sentiment was that prosperity for the highway-related sectors was a requisite of prosperity for all other sectors.

Sixth, the highway lobby had money. The oil and automobile industries were among the largest financial factors in national politics. The highway contractors and automobile dealers everywhere were among the largest contributors to state and local campaigns. Nor should it be forgotten that the enormous advertising expenditures of the national companies and of auto dealers in every locale were bound to be of help in securing both prominent and favorable media coverage. As Gary T. Schwartz has documented, media enthusiasm for the interstate highway program was virtually unanimous across the entire political spectrum.[13]

Finally, the highway lobby had a receptive popular audience. The American romance with the automobile was in floodtide, and few had yet begun to associate highway development with such negative consequences as community disruption, air pollution, and vulnerability to international oil embargoes. Far more simply, new highways were associated with the economic benefits of congestion relief and the pleasurable experience of free-flow driving. Individual Americans, of course, also had substantial investments in their cars and were amenable to the suggestion that good roads were essential to their full utilization. It is commonly remarked that the second largest investment made by the average American household is in cars, after housing. In fact, if one includes depreciation, automobiles clearly rank first. Over the past forty years most American households have seen their homes appreciate in value. Their cars, by contrast, depreciate rapidly and must be replaced.

Public Investment Decisions, II: The Growth of Mass Transit Capital Assistance

As one reviews these factors that made the highway interest so powerful, it is difficult to imagine how the recent policy shift away from expressway construction in urban areas and toward dramatically increased support for mass transit could have occurred. In practice as well, the shift caught virtually all observers by surprise. Even as the 1960s drew to a close, such a sharp policy reorientation appeared all but inconceivable.

Throughout the 1950s, when the interstate highway program was getting underway, the conventional wisdom was that all transit costs, capital as well as operating, should be financed by users. This wisdom held in the vast majority of American urban areas, not merely in the White House and the halls of Congress. There were exceptions—most notably New York City, Boston, and San Francisco—but they were very few. Even in Chicago, Philadelphia, and Cleveland, all of which had rapid transit systems, the doctrine of finance from the farebox held sway. (In 1950, the transit industry as a whole had operating revenues after taxes $66 million greater than its operating expenses. In 1960, though patronage had declined by almost half, the industry still had after-tax operating revenues $31 million above its operating expenses. Moreover it paid $87 million in taxes.) [14]

At the national level, it was considered sufficient justification for the federal neglect of mass transit to note that few transit trips crossed state lines. Federal disinterest in the precipitous decline of transit was reinforced by the general conviction that transit was a dying industry, rooted in obsolescent technologies and land use patterns. A popular analogy was that subsidization of mass transit would be akin to public spending for the revival of horse-and-buggy travel. Like the active effort to accommodate rising traffic demand, of course, this passiveness in the face of transit decline reflected the national disposition in transportation policy and planning to facilitate rather than seek to shape or resist market trends.

Whereas transit was viewed as purely local in character, federal aid for highway construction was justified on the ground that an integrated national system was required. Historically even farm-to-market secondary roads had been viewed as of interstate significance because they carried agricultural products to railheads for national and international distribution. By the 1950s, even the most hidebound conservative could accept the case for a national line-haul expressway network developed pursuant to the traditional federal responsibility for promoting interstate commerce. It was widely accepted as well, though without much critical analysis, that an improved highway system would be of great value for national defense purposes. Thus the new expressway system authorized in 1956 was justified in terms of federal responsibility for national security as well as for interstate commerce, and it was officially labeled the National System of Interstate and Defense Highways.[15]

Moving forward a decade to the mid-1960s, the period in which the Urban Mass Transportation Act of 1964 was enacted, the predominant view was that transit had a continuing, though minor, role to play in the nation's urban transportation system. Transit continued to be of central importance in a few metropolitan areas, but it served a shrinking minority of trips even in these. The role of government, it was generally believed, should be to provide capital for needed transit expansion and modernization, while continuing to impose fiscal "discipline" by requiring that all operating costs be covered by farebox revenues. Even in areas where existing transit already required operating subsidies, the prevailing ideology was that new transit investments should be confined to those that would not increase the operating deficit burden.

Thus, when the voters of the San Francisco Bay Area were presented with the BART proposal in 1962, they were assured that no operating subsidies would be required. Similarly when the Massachusetts legislature in 1964 created the Massachusetts Bay Transportation Authority (reorganizing a predecessor agency and expanding its jurisdiction from fourteen to seventy-nine localities), it also authorized a major program of rapid transit extensions into the Boston suburbs. The advocates of this program forecast that the extensions would generate adequate operating profits to offset the deficits (then about $21 million annually) incurred on the older portions of the system. This conventional wisdom guided the development of the Federal Urban Mass Transportation (UMT) Act as well. Enacted in 1964, the UMT Act provided only for capital assistance (along with planning, research, and development activities related to transit capital investment).

Even in the 1970s numerous rapid transit proposals have been placed before the voters of urban regions with assurances that construction would be financed predominantly with federal grants and that no operating subsidies would be required thereafter. Such forecasts were central components, for example, of the successful Denver and Atlanta referendum campaigns. A new wrinkle in some of the recent rapid transit campaigns, in areas already accustomed to substantial bus operating deficits, has been to promise that required transit operating subsidies with rapid transit will be lower than without it. Such, for example, is the current official forecast in Miami.

In a closely related field, Congress set up Amtrak in 1971 with a mandate to become self-supporting and sought to deal with the Northeast rail crisis in 1973 by means (mainly reorganization and start-up capital assistance) that it claimed would avert the need for continuing operating assistance.

Though implausible to most dispassionate observers, each of these forecasts has obviously played a significant part in mustering the support required to get its program approved.

A Further Distributive Step: Transit Operating Subsidies

The promises of operating self-support for new and reorganized systems often do not seem terribly different in the 1970s from those of the 1960s. But predominant ideologies with respect to transit and the public treasury have changed profoundly over the past decade. Public acceptance of the need for transit operating as well as capital subsidies has become general. Large-scale federal operating assistance for mass transit was authorized in 1974, though highway assistance is still confined to capital investment purposes. Transit aid has been one of the most rapidly growing of all federal programs since 1970. And indeed, even the promises made on behalf of new systems in recent years generally seem intended more to establish a tone, to communicate a hope and a recognition of taxpayer concerns, than to convey firm guarantees.

How can one account for the crumbling of public resistance to transit operating subsidies and for the meteoric growth of public transit budgets in the 1970s? Moreover, how can one account for the decisive shift away from expressway construction that has occurred in most of the nation's large urban areas?

The federal transit program was first proposed by big city, liberal Democrats in the late 1950s; the first president to champion the cause was Kennedy; and the UMT Act of 1964 was viewed as a major liberal triumph when enacted under the auspices of President Johnson. It was a new spending program for the big cities, and it was generally viewed as conferring its greatest benefits on relatively disadvantaged groups. Yet the greatest flowering of the transit program has occurred in the 1970s, primarily under two Republican presidents, both drawn from the conservative wing of the party. In fiscal 1970, federal transit obligations totaled $108 million. The estimate for fiscal 1978 is $3.2 billion, an increase of more than thirty times in eight years (and roughly nineteen times in constant dollars).[16]

By contrast, the highway program, which grew rapidly in the late 1950s and early 1960s has declined in real dollar terms since then. Federal highway obligations in 1964, the year the transit program was first enacted, were $4.3 billion. The estimate for fiscal 1978 is $7.9 billion, an increase of 84 percent. During this period, however, consumer prices doubled and highway construction prices rose by two and a half times.[17]

Federal Highway Administration data indicate that about 38 percent of federal highway spending is in urban areas. Thus combined federal highway and transit obligations in urban areas will total $6.2 billion in fiscal 1978. The transit share will be about 52 percent, though transit accounts for under 3 percent of urban passenger travel and for 0 percent of urban freight movement.[18]

These figures tell only part of the story, because the nature of highway expenditures in urban areas has changed dramatically in recent years. As resistance to new expressway construction has spread across the country, the focus of highway spending has shifted to the improvement of existing streets and highways. The antihighway revolt has by no means been limited to older, high-density urban areas in the 1970s. Plans for new expressways have been killed and future construction planning has been curtailed in many of the newer, auto-oriented metropolitan areas as well, regions as diverse as Denver, Miami, Tucson, Atlanta, and Portland (Oregon). Although long-committed expressway projects are still moving forward in many regions, particularly in suburban corridors that have not yet experienced intense development, few new expressways are being planned, and it seems apparent that the era of major urban highway expansion is drawing toward a close.[19]

Causes of the Recent Changes in Urban Transportation Policy

No definitive explanation of these shifts in urban transportation policy emphasis seems possible at the present time. In seeking a rough understanding of how they came about, however, we believe that it is most fruitful to focus on the following factors.

First, there have been major changes in national domestic preoccupations from the 1950s, when the great period of highway expansion began, to the 1970s. The urban problem was defined in the 1950s in terms of traffic congestion, downtown decline, the alleged cultural sterility of suburbia, and so on.[20] Few were disposed in this period to focus on the nation's more profound domestic problems, such as racial discrimination, poverty, crime, and environmental degradation.

Attention shifted dramatically in the early 1960s, however, to issues of race, poverty, and urban violence. And during the 1970s, environmental, energy, and fiscal issues have claimed increasing attention. The Nixon-Ford years witnessed a turning away from many of the antipoverty and antidiscrimination priorities of the 1960s, and nowhere was this deemphasis more striking than in the priorities of the national administration. Yet the same administration, while often preferring a bit more fiscal restraint than the Congress, played a key role in bringing about the shifts in urban transportation policy with which we are here concerned.

The explanation, we judge, lies in the fact that transit proved to be a policy for all perspectives on the urban problem. Though its direct constituency was relatively small, its ideological appeal proved to be extremely broad. Whether one's concern was the economic vitality of cities, protecting the environment, stopping highways, energy conservation, assisting the elderly and handicapped and poor, or simply getting other people off the road so as to be able to drive faster, transit was a policy that could be embraced. This is not to say that transit was an effective way of serving all these objectives, simply that it was widely believed to be so. Additionally, because the absolute magnitude of transit spending was so meager at the beginning of this period, it was possible to obtain credit for rapid program growth with quite modest increases in the absolute level of expenditures.

Thus the Nixon administration, while striving to distance itself from the big city, pro-black, welfare state image of the Johnson administration in domestic affairs, felt comfortable promoting sharp increases in mass transit spending and substantive provisions enabling states and localities to utilize highway aid entitlements for mass transit purposes. Transit turned out, in short, to be an ideal centerpiece for the urban policy of a conservative administration. Though clearly of high priority to urban spokesmen, it did not stir class and racial antagonisms. Quite the contrary; it attracted support from every portion of the urban ideological spectrum.

The main weakness of the transit program in Congress was its narrow geographic base. As table 2.4 indicates, ten metropolitan areas account for three-fifths of the nation's entire transit patronage. The Urban Mass Transportation Administration (UMTA) has carefully sprinkled buses upon nearly every urban area in the country, but this alone cannot account for the remarkable flowering of the mass transit program. The vast preponderance of aid has still gone to a very few regions. From the beginning of the federal transit program in 1964 through September 30, 1977, five urban regions received 61 percent of all capital grant dollars committed, and ten regions received 80 percent.[21]

Perhaps the single factor most responsible for the rapid growth of the transit program has been the growing strength of antihighway sentiment among liberals and "good government" supporters generally, rather than simply among active environmentalists and neighborhood residents directly threatened by highway interests. Numerous highway advocates in Congress and the state legislatures, traditionally contemptuous of transit, have found it prudent to adapt. Reflecting the orientation toward inclusiveness of the American political system, they have judged advocacy of increased transit spending to be an effective means of protecting their own vital interests.

At the national level, the most significant landmark in this process of adaptation was enactment of the Federal Aid Highway Act of 1973. During its evolution the Senate and House public works committees succeeded in adding transit to their long-standing jurisdiction over highway legislation. Their main argument to highway interests in favor of this jurisdictional expansion was that it would facilitate the reestablishment of near-unanimous congressional support for the highway program, and they proved correct. Their main argument to transit advocates was that it would be a vehicle for dramatic increases in the level of spending for transit; and here again they proved as good as their word. The 1973 act provided state and local officials plagued by urban expressway controversies with a highly attractive instrument for resolving them—the option to trade in their federal aid entitlements for these highways in favor of equal transit aid entitlements from the general fund. By specifying that the transit aid would be financed from the general fund, they ingeniously managed to reconcile urban demands for flexibility with the insistence of pro-highway groups that the Highway Trust Fund continue to be reserved for highway uses. In 1974, the same committees produced legislation substantially increasing the overall level of federal transit assistance, providing a firm six-year commitment with respect to funding levels, and authorizing federal operating assistance for the first time.[22]

The senator (Jennings Randolph) and congressmen (Jim Wright) who played the key roles in forging the new strategy were from West Virginia and Texas, respectively. Along with nearly all of their committee colleagues, they were perennial champions of the highway program who had minimal interest in transit. Their central concern was that urban expressway controversies and transit aid demands had become significant threats to the consensual and veto-proof dominance of the highway coalition in Congress. By extending the program concept to include (and provide major new benefits for) transit and to return disputes about highway-transit tradeoffs firmly to the local level, they not only reestablished congressional harmony in the highway policy arena, but they also enhanced their own reputations as legislative statesmen. (Congressman Wright became House majority leader in January 1977). This is by no means to minimize the victory achieved by urban transit and antihighway interests in the 1973 and 1974 acts. But it is to emphasize that they were minority actors who achieved influence largely by maximizing their nuisance potential. Their triumph occurred when a few farsighted leaders of the highway coalition, which remained politically dominant, discerned that a mutually beneficial solution was possible and persuaded the rest of the coalition to accept it.[4]

4. One of the present authors, Altschuler, was Massachusetts secretary of transportation from 1971 through 1974 and, in this role, lobbied actively at the federal level. The Greater Boston area stood to gain more from flexibility than any other region in the country because Governor Francis W. Sargent had recently rejected all further interstate expressway construction within it. Faced with charges by business and labor interests that it had thereby caused the state to lose nearly $700 million in federal aid, the Sargent administration proposed and lobbied intensively during 1972 and 1973 for the so-called interstate transfer provision—subsequently codified as 23 U.S.C. 103 (e)(4). Our account of the maneuvering and argumentation that surrounded the forging of the highway-transit coalition during these years is based on Altschuler's observations and conversations at the time.

Transit has never ranked as a high priority for groups represent-ing the poor, racial minorities, the elderly, and other disadvan-taged groups. Doubtless part of the reason is that transit subsidies do not go predominantly to the very poor. The income distribu-tion of transit patrons in the urban areas where most transit rider-ship occurs is not very different from that of highway users. (The situation is different in urban areas where few employees commute by transit and where transit patronage is therefore confined over-whelmingly to the very poor and children.) Further, most federal transit aid has gone to finance the construction of new rapid transit systems and extensions intended to serve the most affluent end of the potential transit market spectrum. It is also true that spokes-men for blacks, the poor, the elderly, and the handicapped have generally had more urgent priorities than transit, among them wel-fare, health programs, nutritional support programs, and antidis-crimination efforts. Nonetheless they have supported transit aid, and it is a rather unusual program that unites downtown company presidents, construction workers, environmentalists, and spokes-men for the various disadvantaged groups of urban society.

In short, shifting national priorities and the ideological breadth of the transit coalition provide a significant part of the explana-tion for recent shifts in urban transportation policy. Several other factors, however, deserve close attention as well. One is the gradual maturation of a learning process about the impact of programs that entail large-scale eminent domain. One of the most striking characteristics of the American pattern of government has always been its profound respect for private property. Eminent domain on more than a spot basis is a post–New Deal phenomenon. Urban renewal, beginning in 1949, and the interstate highway program, beginning in 1956, were the first two national programs ever to involve massive eminent domain. In aiding construction of the turnpike, canal, and railroad systems of the nineteenth century, American governments had for the most part granted rights to land that was already in the public domain. For reservoirs, toll roads, and other public facilities, large takings had more recently been made in rural areas. But major takings in highly developed urban areas were extremely rare until the enactment of the re-newal and interstate programs.

Not surprisingly, both began to encounter vigorous resistance as their eminent domain activities spread.[23] Of the two, the urban renewal program proved far more amenable to adaptation. Initially a clearance and redevelopment program, it gradually became a rehabilitation program and subsequently produced offshoots in the antipoverty and Model Cities programs.[24] Originally designed to remake neighborhoods for new populations, it became a series of programs intended to improve neighborhoods and economic opportunities for their existing residents.

The highway program, with its interstate centerpiece, was far more resistant to change. As long as most federal aid was for interstate construction, the program inevitably had an enormous appetite for property. And its requirements were inflexible. Land had to be taken in straight or gently curving corridors that connected with one another throughout each region. Highway planners could seek to minimize political resistance by searching out corridors with substantial amounts of public open space and/or corridors in which the residents (particularly, racial minorities and the very poor) were relatively powerless. This strategy conserved highway dollars as well as political resources. But there was no way that highway planners could avoid stepping on an extraordinary number of toes.

The federal highway program was able to ride roughshod over the growing opposition to its eminent domain appetite for substantially longer than the urban renewal program because its base of support throughout the nation was far more powerful. The 90 percent federal matching ratio was irresistible to most state and local officials; in controversial cases affirmative local approval could generally be dispensed with (though the laws of some states permitted local veto); and an essential part of the program ideology was the alleged need for system connectivity throughout the nation. Thus project controversies normally sufficient to paralyze the governmental process typically had little impact on the highway program. And its national scope, with 87 percent of interstate system mileage outside of urban areas, tended to dwarf the significance of controversies in a few big cities.

In the 1970s, however, even the highway program has had to

adapt. The federal funding emphasis, particularly in urban areas, has gradually shifted away from expressway construction toward improvements within existing rights of way. The Federal Aid Highway Act of 1973 provided additional flexibility by authorizing the use of urban highway aid allocations, including those for interstate expressway construction, for mass transit purposes. The Federal Aid Highway Act of 1976 liberalized these provisions even further; it provides for inflationary adjustments during the period required to bring substitute projects to the point of construction, and it permits the use of interstate allocations for alternative highway, as well as mass transit, projects.

Another factor meriting attention has been the growing militancy and mobilization of aggrieved groups in American society. The immediate origins of this trend were in the civil rights activities of the late 1950s and early 1960s. It quickly spread to numerous other groups, so that by the mid-1960s even civil disobedience by organized public employees, including law enforcement officials, had become commonplace. In consequence of this development, and also of various statutory provisions requiring citizen participation that have been enacted over the past decade, it is now essential for transportation planners to win the support of citizens at the neighborhood level before projects can be viewed as serious candidates for implementation. In the 1950s and early 1960s, by contrast, it was generally enough to consult with key local elected and public works officials and with the professional representatives of large enterprises that might be affected by transportation investment decisions (such as businesses, hospitals, and universities).

Citizen participation has been a humanizing and democratic, but also an extremely conservative, influence. We use the term conservative here in its classic sense: resistant to change. Established institutions participate in politics almost as much to serve their expansion needs as to avert threats. In the field of urban transportation, for example, business and labor interests typically press for increased construction activity. The primary mobilizing incentives for individual citizens who participate in transportation planning, on the other hand, tend to be fear and indignation. The objective of improved service is rarely sufficient to motivate sustained or energetic participation. Citizens expend the time and energy required for effective participation mainly in order to protect their homes and immediate community environs. The result has been to challenge development agencies to figure out ways of implementing their mandates without destroying neighborhoods or public open spaces, and where this is not feasible, as with respect to urban expressway construction, to rethink the very nature of their missions.

The Emerging Fiscal Crisis of Transit

Though a wide variety of political factors appear to be militating in favor of expanded mass transit spending and against urban expressway investment, transit in some respects is as endangered today as in the 1950s and early 1960s. A more sophisticated opposition to transit spending increases is developing, and one that may prove more difficult to deal with. There is a growing perception that the fiscal appetite of public transit is voracious and extremely difficult for elected officials to control. There is also a growing awareness that the recent shifts in public spending emphasis in favor of transit have not significantly altered urban travel behavior and are unlikely to do so in the future.

The transit industry as a whole first fell into operating deficit in 1963. Even in 1965, the national operating deficit was still only $11 million. But thereafter it rose rapidly to $288 million in 1970 and $1.7 billion in 1975.[25] The rate of increase from 1970 through 1975 was 43 percent a year. During this same period consumer prices rose by 7 percent a year and overall public spending by 11 percent a year.[26] (Spending on urban highways by all levels of government increased by less than 6 percent a year during this period.)[27]

Transit advocates note that the high rate of deficit increase has in part been a statistical aberration, and one that will gradually dissolve over time. When the deficit is small relative to total expenditures and revenues are static, a modest expenditure increase can

generate a large percentage increase in the deficit.[5] Thus, in looking ahead, the key point to note is that transit operating expenditures increased by 13 percent a year from 1970 to 1975, while
operating revenues rose at an annual rate of 3 percent. Should
these trends continue to 1985, revenues in that year would cover
only 22 percent of operating expenditures (versus 86 percent in
1970 and 54 percent in 1975) and the national transit operating
deficit would be $9.95 billion. The average rate of deficit increase
in this scenario would be 22 percent between 1975 and 1980 and
17 percent between 1980 and 1985. While well below the recent
rate of increase, these projections are still far in excess of the
recent rate of inflation, and their realization would entail rapidly
growing absolute dollar commitments (even as the percentage rates
of increase gradually declined).

There is fragmentary evidence that the rate of deficit growth
has been sharply curtailed since 1975. The trend of service expansion, which increased transit vehicle mileage by 13 percent from
1972 to 1975[28], appears to have ended and quite possibly has
been reversed. Labor settlements, always deeply influenced by experience in New York City, appear to have become somewhat more
modest in the wake of the New York fiscal crisis. And numerous
areas that held fares stable or actually reduced them during the
early 1970s (average fares nationally rose by only 1 percent from
1971 to 1975, and bus fares actually declined[29]) have been
opting for fare increases as one method of holding down subsidy
requirements.

The recent intense pressures to hold down the rate of transit
deficit growth seem likely to remain dominant for many years to
come—given the overall shift in political balance toward austerity,
the sharply enlarged absolute dollar amounts now associated with
any given rate of transit budgetary increase (by comparison with a
few years ago), and the fact that state and local transit spending
are heavily concentrated in declining urban regions with particu-

[5.] Assume, for example, that a system has revenues of 90 monetary units in each of two
successive years, whereas its expenditures total 100 units in the first year and 105 in the
second. Its expenditures have risen only 5 percent from one year to the next, but its
deficit has risen 50 percent.

larly severe fiscal problems. It bears emphasis, however, that government involvement in the public transportation industry has tended overall to be a force of spending acceleration. The politicization of transit has strengthened the hand of organized labor, has regularly tipped the balance in favor of maintaining (and even inaugurating new) lightly patronized routes, and in many areas has promoted fare stability to the status of a sacred cow. The disciplines imposed by the farebox have been replaced, in short, by those related to the maintenance of broad political support.

An illustrative case, recently examined in detail by Reid Ewing, is Portland, Oregon (1970 population: 1.0 million).[30] Portland, which was formally cited by the UMTA administrator in 1976 as one of the nation's outstanding transit success stories, established its regional transit authority and commenced public operation in 1969. During the transition from private to public operation, expectations ran high that public ownership would yield substantial cost savings. It was estimated that the benefits of tax exemption alone would cover the next round of transit wage increases.

In its first year, however, the new regional transit authority—known as Tri-Met—proposed a budget four times that of the private operator in the most recent year. Asked by the *Oregon Journal* to explain the increase, Tri-Met responded that the private operator had paid substandard wages and provided inadequate service. "Tri-Met," it wrote, "will be service-oriented. It will pay a fair wage scale. It will upgrade service in the metropolitan area and expand service to the suburban areas." Though it failed to receive approval of this requested first-year increase, Tri-Met did over the next seven years increase vehicle mileage by 178 percent, reduce the average age of the bus fleet from sixteen years to five, implement selective (but quite significant) fare reductions, raise the wages and fringe benefits of transit employees from well below average to near the top of the national scale, and nearly double ridership. The private transit company had earned a small operating profit through its last full year; Tri-Met's revenues fell below 40 percent of its operating expenses during the first half of 1976. The private operator had held the rate of expenditure increase to 2 percent a year between 1963 and 1968 (its last full year of operation); Tri-Met's operating expenses in 1976 were more than five times those of 1968, representing a 23 percent annual rate of increase. In July 1976, faced with a deficit that was continuing to rise rapidly after having increased by 57 percent (to $13.5 million) in 1975 alone, Tri-Met implemented modest fare increases—five cents a ride for those paying cash, a dollar a month for those using passes—and placed a moratorium on further service expansion. Thus the era of rapid transit budgetary expansion has ended for the time being even in Portland. But it seems amply clear that government involvement to date, for better or worse, has been an extremely powerful stimulus for increased spending.

Broadly, the following specific policy elements appear to have played particularly significant roles as spending stimuli on a nation-wide basis:

• In order to obtain federal transit aid, local transit authorities must convince the Department of Labor that no employees will have their circumstances adversely affected. Generally, the department will grant certification only if all potentially affected unions concur.[31] The result has been to minimize labor saving as an objective of transit modernization programs and to help embed obsolete work practices ever more deeply into the fabric of the industry.

• The Davis-Bacon Act requires that highest prevailing union wage rates be paid to workers on federally aided construction projects.[32] Numerous states and localities, moreover, have enacted "little" Davis-Bacon acts, which apply even when federal aid is not a factor.

• Competitors who are threatened by publicly aided service improvements are generally entitled to be compensated or bought out. UMTA has accepted the view, furthermore, that even bankrupt enterprises with no hope of earning a profit should be paid for their assumed value as going businesses in addition to the market value of their tangible assets.

• William Tye and George Hilton have presented evidence that the availability of federal capital assistance has led many transit agencies to overcapitalize.[33] Although their thesis is controversial in some respects, it is certainly true that new rapid transit systems and major rapid transit extensions would in most cases be politically unthinkable at the state and local levels except for the prospect of federal aid to cover 80 percent of their cost. (Prior to 1974, the federal matching ratio was 66 2/3 percent.) In Greater Boston, for example, state and local officials are moving forward enthusiastically, despite a general atmosphere of extreme fiscal austerity, on two rapid transit projects—one an extension, the other a relocation—with a combined estimated cost of $1.1 billion for eleven miles. The package has been sold to the state legislature primarily on the ground that it will create construction jobs at relatively little cost to state and local taxpayers.[6]

• Many observers anticipate that federal operating subsidies—first authorized in 1974 and distributed in 1975—will reduce the pressure on local officials to hold down operating costs. Appraisal of this hypothesis is severely complicated at present by the fact that the inauguration of federal transit operating assistance occurred more or less simultaneously with the broad shift in national mood toward austerity. Insofar as it does prove to be valid, one would expect the impact to be greatest where the overall transit subsidy

6. Lest transit be singled out unduly, it bears note that an even more expensive highway project (per route mile) is going forward simultaneously in Boston. If ultimately approved by federal officials, this will entail the reconstruction and depression of three miles of the existing Central Artery, a predominantly elevated route through downtown Boston, at an estimated cost of $1 billion. The special attraction in this case is that the Federal Highway Administration will pay 90 percent.

The mileage in question was constructed in its present form prior to the interstate program, but it is on the interstate system. Thus the reconstruction project would not add any mileage to the system—a critical factor, as the mileage authorized by Congress has long since been parcelled out. At the same time, because the project has not been included in past interstate cost estimates, the funding for it is not available for reallocation to transit projects.

This case effectively highlights one of the more peculiar features of the interstate program. Congress, in choosing to express the long-term program ceilings in terms of mileage rather than dollars, and in specifying that each state's annual allocation shall be based on its share of the estimated nationwide cost of system completion, has provided a powerful set of incentives for each state to run up its costs per mile. Federal highway administrators can endeavor to control costs by refusing to approve unusually expensive state proposals, but they are extremely sensitive to political pressures generated by the states, and in any event they are indisposed to reject projects that conform to legal standards and command broad local support. The Central Artery project may be the boldest state effort yet to exploit these inflationary incentives, but as such it illustrates their direction of impact with particular clarity.

cost per capita is relatively low, so that federal assistance is adequate to cover a substantial share of annual deficit increases.[7]

• In order to utilize federal operating assistance, transit operators must permit riders over sixty-five to ride at half-fare during off-peak hours.[35]

• Extremely stringent federal requirements for accessibility by the physically handicapped are requiring the addition of substantial sums to public investment in fixed route (especially rapid transit) systems—though virtually all students of transit agree that those with serious mobility limitations can be served better and less expensively by subsidized taxi or dial-a-ride services.

• The tendency of federal administrators to insist on local consensus before grants are approved, and the need in most local circumstances to establish a regionwide constituency for tax and spending authorizations, provide powerful stimuli to logrolling and gold-plating—the first to ensure that all parts of the urban region receive acceptable shares of the benefits for which they are sharing the cost, the latter to placate specific groups of potential objectors with expensive design or service solutions.

Until recently the potential conflicts between taxpayer forces and those pressing for transit expenditure increases have been obscured by several factors. As noted previously, the absolute level of transit subsidization was quite low until the mid-1970s, so that—except in a few urban regions—large percentage increases still entailed very modest dollar amounts. Second, the political triumph of Keynesianism during the 1960s removed the stigma from budget deficits, and—for roughly a decade beginning in the

---

[7.] Each urbanized area is eligible for an absolute dollar amount determined by formula within statutory spending ceilings. If the funds are utilized for operating subsidy purposes, the maximum rate of federal participation is 50 percent. As this applies to pre-1975 spending levels as well as future increments, however, the federal assistance has enabled many areas to reduce their local transit budgets while permitting their transit deficits to increase at a relatively rapid rate.

If urban areas utilize their formula assistance for capital projects, the federal participation rate is 80 percent. As capital assistance is also available under a separate discretionary grant program, however, few areas have chosen to utilize formula assistance for capital projects unless their operating deficits were too small to absorb their formula entitlements completely.[34]

Fiscal Years	Average Federal Budget Deficit per Annum (billions of dollars)	Budget Deficit as a Percentage of Gross National Product
1960–1962	3.4	0.66
1963–1965	4.1	0.66
1966–1968	12.5	1.61
1969–1971	7.5	0.78
1972–1974	14.3	1.16
1975–1977	52.2	3.17

mid 1960s—made it possible for presidents and Congress to enact major increases in benefits without raising taxes. Third, national defense outlays declined in absolute dollar terms from 1968 through 1974, as the Vietnam War wound down. As a percentage of GNP, defense spending fell from 9.7 to 5.9 percent during this period.[37] Fourth, at the state and local levels, where operating budgets are still generally required to be in balance, outstanding debt quintupled from 1955 to 1975 (from $44 billion to $221 billion).[38]

These special opportunities for rapid and relatively painless expenditure growth all reached exhaustion, however, in the mid-1970s. The absolute level of transit budgetary requirements has now reached a point at which large percentage increases are a cause for deep concern in most jurisdictions. A broad consensus has developed among federal policy makers that substantial further increases in the federal deficit are likely to be inflationary. In a major anti-inflation address on April 11, 1978, President Carter singled out the mass transit program as one of five bearing particular responsibility for the recent burgeoning of federal expenditures, adding that he would vigorously resist pressures for significant further transit spending growth over the near term. A similar consensus has developed on the need for defense spending to grow at least as rapidly as GNP over the foreseeable future. In the wake of the New York City fiscal crisis, investor and voter skepticism have placed tight new constraints on state and local officials anxious to bond expenditures, leaving most of the burden of payment to their successors. Finally the economic slowdown since 1973 has sharply curtailed the automatic growth of tax receipts at all levels of government and has severely intensified voter resistance to increases in tax rates.

It remains to be seen whether these tensions between the newly invigorated forces of fiscal austerity and those fueling transit cost inflation will prove susceptible of resolution in the years ahead on terms compatible with a continuing transit revival. The alternative, if it does not, would appear to be a new spiral of transit decline, consisting of widespread service cutbacks and fare increases intended to hold down transit budgetary requirements even at the cost of significant patronage losses.

Innovative Alternatives

In response to the growing sense of the limits of conventional highway and transit programs, there has recently been an upsurge of interest in more innovative means of alleviating the problems of urban transportation. Some of these are essentially service strategies, falling within our category of public distributive activities. Others are regulatory and pricing strategies, falling within our category of measures aiming to constrain private market choices.

As used in this volume, the term *innovative* refers to policies and service concepts that would, if widely implemented, significantly alter the performance characteristics of the urban transportation system. It follows from this definition that an option need not be original in the intellectual sense to be classified as innovative. Our concern, rather, is to highlight the distinction between those types and levels of government activity that are likely to perpetuate the current system of urban transportation unchanged in its essential features and those that would significantly alter it.

Thus, we classify nearly all current public activity in the field of urban transportation as noninnovative. This is not to disparage ongoing highway and transit programs, but it is to emphasize that they are themselves aspects of the existing system of urban transportation. They provide mainly for the operation, maintenance, periodic renewal, and routine expansion (to accommodate travel demand trends) of the public portions of the system. They also, of course, include a limited number of projects intended to alter the system significantly in particular corridors. For the purposes of our discussion in this book, however, we shall categorize existing levels of highway capacity expansion and (fixed route) transit service expansion activity as noninnovative, and focus on what the potential effects might be of major increases in spending levels for these purposes. Overall we shall seek to appraise eight broad system-changing options:

1. Highway capacity expansion.

2. Fixed route transit service expansion.

3. Widespread implementation of demand responsive transit (such as dial-a-ride and shared-ride taxi).

4. Government efforts to promote increased private ride sharing (carpooling and vanpooling).

5. Traffic management techniques giving preference to high-occupancy vehicles (such as exclusive bus and carpool lanes).

6. Business regulation focused on product performance character-istics (for example, fuel economy).

7. Regulatory measures aimed directly at consumers (such as gaso-line rationing and seat belt use laws).

8. Price, including tax, increases designed to bring about reduc-tions in vehicle miles of travel and/or in gasoline consumption.

The first four of these measures are clearly distributive in nature, whereas the last three overwhelmingly entail constraint. Preferen-tial traffic management measures, on the other hand, generally entail a mixture of benefit distribution and constraint. They are regulatory in nature, but their aims are to improve transit service and (frequently) to increase highway person-carrying capacity. In analyzing public attitudes toward specific management techniques, it is essential to consider the distribution of these elements that they are perceived to entail.

A word is in order about the relationship between our list of innovative options and the list of measures that urban areas have been required since 1975 to consider under the official rubric of "transportation system management" if they desire federal highway and transit aid. Until September 1975, federal planning regulations in the field of urban transportation required only that each area have a long-range (twenty to twenty-five year) capital improvement plan. In that month the Federal Highway Administration (FHWA) and the Urban Mass Transportation Administration (UMTA) jointly issued a new planning regulation mandating that urban transportation plans should henceforth deal explicitly with short-term as well as long-term, and with operational as well as capital improvement, alternatives.[39] The new regulation required each metropolitan area to submit two short-range plan elements in addition to its long-range plan. One of these, the transportation improvement program (TIP), was to be a staged three-to-five year capital improvement plan. The other was to be a transportation system management (TSM) plan, aimed at bringing about more effective usage of the existing transportation capital stock, private as well as public. The TSM portion of the regulation included an extensive list of actions to be considered, subdivided into the following categories:

(A) Actions to ensure the efficient use of road space through (1) traffic operations improvements . . . , (2) preferential treatment for transit and other high occupancy vehicles . . . , (3) appropriate provision for pedestrians and bicycles . . . , (4) management and control of parking . . . , [and] (5) changes in work schedules, fare structure, and automobile tolls to reduce peak period travel and to encourage off-peak use of transportation facilities and transit service.

(B) Actions to reduce vehicle use in congested areas through encouragement of carpooling and other forms of ride-sharing; diversion, exclusion, and metering of automobile access to specific areas; [and] area licenses, parking surcharges, and other forms of congestion pricing . . . .

(C) Actions to improve transit service through provision of better . . . services (including route-deviation and demand responsive services) within low density areas, provision of express bus services in coordination with local collection and distributions services, . . .

encouragement of jitneys and other flexible paratransit services and their integration in the metropolitan public transportation system, . . . [and] better passenger information systems and services.

(D) Actions to improve internal transit management efficiency such as . . . developing cost accounting and other management tools to improve decision making [and] establishing maintenance policies that assure greater equipment reliability.[40]

In brief, then, the TSM concept embraces a wide variety of operational measures, including most of those that we have classified as innovative along with many that we have not. Some readers may wonder why we have not chosen to build on this familiar set of TSM categories. The answer is that our purposes have differed sharply from those of the federal officials who drew up the TSM regulation. They sought to communicate with practicing highway and transit officials throughout the nation in immediately recognizable terms. Thus they organized their discussion around the theme of how more effectively to pursue several objectives—improved traffic flow and transit service, for example—that are consensual, familiar, and of immediate concern to such officials in every metropolitan area. By contrast, we are concerned primarily with the interplay among political, economic, cultural, and technological factors in shaping the urban transportation system. Our political focus, in particular, led us quickly to zero in on compliance mechanisms as central differentiating characteristics among potential public actions.[41] It makes a great deal of difference, we judged, whether measures primarily entail positive or negative inducements and, if the latter, whether constraints are in the form of rules for the use of public systems, of regulations applicable to businesses, of regulations impinging directly on the lives of consumers, or of higher prices. Additionally we found the TSM definitions of transportation policy purpose inadequate for our purposes. In considering such immediate aims as improved traffic flow, we wished to focus on their linkages to more fundamental conceptions of the problems and policy priorities of urban transportation. Thus we chose to develop our own typology of policy objectives to keep it distinct from our typology of innovative policy methods and to organize the latter in substantial part around the compliance variable noted above.[8]

Demand Responsive Transit (DRT) and Private Ride Sharing

These two categories are typically grouped together under the label *paratransit*, a term that has come into widespread use only within the past several years.[42] Although universal agreement on a definition is lacking, essentially it denotes organized ride-sharing activity in the range between (but not including) pickup carpools organized solely at the initiative of their individual members and fixed route bus services. The unifying characteristics of services within this range are use of rubber-tired vehicles and the highway system, ride sharing by unrelated passengers with different origins and/or destinations, flexible routing to serve specific rider origins and destinations rather than simply high demand corridors, and some measure of formal organization to facilitate the ride-sharing arrangements and/or to operate the shared-ride services directly. The route flexibility may be as complete as that of conventional taxi service or, at the other end of the spectrum, it may involve only minor deviations from fixed bus routes when requested by patrons. The formal organization may be as limited as a carpool matching service or as extensive as that of a regional transit authority.

There are two main bases for distinguishing between DRT and private ride-sharing services: whether the drivers are paid and the relationship of the service providers to the patrons. In the case of private ride sharing, the drivers are unsalaried[9] and the providers are employers or fellow employees of the passengers. In the case of DRT, the drivers are typically on salary and the providers are third parties (neither employers nor fellow employees of the patrons).

[8.] These typologies are not intended to be logically comprehensive. The typology of innovative methods, moreover, is quite partial in practice. Its purpose is to distinguish among sets of policy techniques considered throughout this volume, and to do so in a way that reflects both common usage and the compliance variables that we have found useful for purposes of political analysis. No further implication is intended.

[9.] They may, however, receive nonsalary compensation such as use of the vehicle nights and weekends. And some companies encourage vanpool drivers to solicit patronage by permitting them to keep fare revenues above a specified level.

Some paratransit service configurations do not fall neatly into one or the other category, but in practice these are extremely rare.

The focus in this book will be on two relatively pure service types in each category, with the following characteristics:

Demand Responsive Transit: dial-a-ride service (available on phone request to provide door-to-door service or some close approximation thereof, typically provided in a van or minibus but operated about as frequently by taxi companies as by transit agencies directly); and shared-ride taxi service (basically similar to dial-a-ride except for vehicle type, usually provided as an adjunct of exclusive-ride taxi service, more likely to be responsive to street hails, never provided by a transit agency).[10]

Private Ride Sharing: vanpool service (by subscription, usually in vans or minibuses that are owned or leased by employers for commutation use by their own employees; the drivers are themselves commuters who receive no direct wage compensation), and carpools, when organized with the aid of public agencies, employers, or other institutions.

Current law and public policy have been shaped decisively by a bimodal image of personal travel options within the urban transportation system, and paratransit options do not fall neatly into either of the categories that make up this image. They are neither "mass" in the sense of being fixed route transit services primarily geared to operate in high-density corridors, nor are they so highly individualized as most private automobile and exclusive-ride taxi travel. Thus, uncertainties exist in most jurisdictions with respect to at least several of the following:

• the division of responsibility among public agencies for planning, promoting, subsidizing, and regulating paratransit services;

[10.] We shall have little to say in this book about a third significant type of DRT, subscription bus service. Although they involve paid drivers and third-party providers, subscription bus services more closely resemble vanpools in their primary function (commuter subscription service) and in their performance characteristics (peak period operation only, high load factors, excellent fuel economy) than they do the other types of DRT service. Thus, when we do on occasion touch upon subscription bus service, we shall do so in conjunction with vanpooling. By the same token it should be clear that when we speak of DRT without further elaboration we have dial-a-ride and shared-ride taxi services in mind.

• appropriate mechanisms for coordinating paratransit activities with fixed route transit programs;

• whether local transit operators or taxi companies should be assigned primary responsibility for the provision of subsidized DRT services;

• whether taxi operators should be permitted, or indeed even encouraged, to offer shared-ride services on an unsubsidized basis as a means of increasing their productivity and holding down fares;[11]

• whether privately owned common carrier (including taxi) providers and their employees are entitled—legally and/or morally—to protection from publicly subsidized DRT competition, or to compensation if they are harmed by such competition;

• whether vanpools should be granted tax benefits, subsidies, and/or other forms of public policy preference on the ground that they perform transit functions;[12]

• which, if any, common carrier regulatory provisions should apply to vanpools, and which insurance law (motor vehicle or workmen's compensation) should apply in determining liability for accidents involving harm to commuters in company-owned vans; and

• whether federal and state minimum wage laws, including overtime rate provisions for work in excess of eight hours a day, apply to vanpool drivers (are they, in short, receiving a fringe benefit or performing overtime work? Those raising this question have mainly been representatives of transit labor).

Despite these uncertainties, government involvement in para-

[11.] Shared-ride taxi service has been prohibited in most localities since at least the 1920s–originally as part of the campaign against jitney competition with fixed route transit, more recently in part on personal security grounds.

[12.] Company vanpool program expenditures are already deductible as business expenses, and vehicle purchases are eligible for the investment tax credit. A proposal by President Carter that the federal government purchase six thousand vans for commutation use by its own employees reached the floor of the House of Representatives in 1977, but it was soundly defeated. Whereas the administration billed this proposal as an energy conservation measure, House members apparently viewed it as little more than a new fringe benefit for federal employees.[43]

transit activities has burgeoned during the 1970s. At the federal level, agencies involved as of 1977 in the subsidization or promotion of paratransit included the Urban Mass Transportation Administration (UMTA), the Federal Highway Administration (FHWA), the Environmental Protection Agency (EPA), the Federal Energy Administration,[13] numerous units within the Department of Health, Education and Welfare (HEW), and the Veterans Administration (VA).

UMTA has been interested, within the framework of its research and development program, primarily in the development of DRT services, though it has also funded four vanpool demonstration projects.[44] Additionally since 1973 it has administered a program of grants to private nonprofit organizations for the purchase of buses to provide special DRT services for the elderly and handicapped. And, since 1976, it has permitted urban areas to use their transit formula assistance funds for DRT as well as fixed route transit purposes.

EPA became the first federal agency to promote private ride sharing by virtue of its responsibility for administering the Clean Air Act Amendments of 1970—which required the achievement of specified air quality standards throughout the nation by mid-1977. Pursuant to this requirement, EPA promulgated transportation control plans in 1973 for thirty-eight metropolitan areas that it found could not achieve the standards simply by controlling stationary source (such as factory and power plant) emissions and benefiting from the cleaner engines on new cars. Twenty of these plans called for reductions in vehicle miles of travel (VMT) to be achieved primarily by combinations of pricing, regulatory, and ride-sharing methods. (Seventeen of the twenty contained ride-sharing elements.) EPA's plans to impose pricing and regulatory measures were gradually withdrawn in the years that followed, however. Left without authority to do more than urge states and urban regions to undertake VMT-reduction measures, by 1975 EPA let them slip to the bottom of its overcrowded agenda. Inso-

---

[13.] In October 1977, FEA was merged into the newly created Department of Energy (DOE). We shall refer to FEA when discussing federal energy activities prior to October 1977 and to DOE when discussing more recent and ongoing activities.

far as it did press states and localities to pursue VMT reduction, though, the strategy on which it focused was the promotion of private ride sharing.

FHWA activity dates from the enactment of the Emergency Highway Energy Conservation Act of 1974, which authorized the use by states of regularly apportioned highway aid funds for car-pool demonstration projects. Although programs were initiated in eighty-six urbanized areas within the next eighteen months, enthu-siasm quickly waned in most of them as memories of the oil embargo faded; by 1976, only a handful of programs were still functioning in more than token fashion. A provision of the Federal Aid Highway Act in that year, however, placed the program on a permanent footing and eliminated any suggestion that programs had to be of a demonstration nature. FHWA also administers the Rural Highway Public Transportation Demonstration Program, first enacted in 1973, which provides grants-in-aid for DRT as well as fixed route transit services in rural areas. (UMTA's mandate is to assist urban areas only.)

If the ride-sharing activities of FHWA date from the oil embargo, FEA is itself a product of the embargo. It was created in 1974 with a mandate to plan and implement the emergency oil alloca-tion program and to promote energy conservation.[14] By early 1975 it concluded that commuter ride sharing offered one of the nation's best opportunities for oil conservation. Over the next two years it sponsored a series of workshops for major employers in about 150 metropolitan areas. Funding limitations prevented FEA from doing much beyond this to promote ride sharing, though, and its vanpool promotional authority was transferred to the Department of Transportation upon the creation of DOE in Octo-ber 1977. DOE continues, however to administer $35 million a year in grants to the states for state energy conservation activities. States may use these funds for the promotion of ride sharing, though not for the purchase or operation of vehicles. Only two

[14.] Responsibility for promoting the development of new energy sources and technolo-gies was assigned to the Energy Research and Development Administration (ERDA). Both FEA and ERDA were brought within the framework of the Department of Energy as it came into being in October 1977.

states as of late 1977 (California and Massachusetts) had chosen to use substantial amounts of state energy conservation funds for this purpose.

HEW and VA support transportation services as adjuncts to their social service and medical care programs. The primary trips served are to and from social service centers and medical care facilities. Some payments are made in the form of reimbursement for transit and exclusive-ride taxi trips, but with increasing frequency human service agencies are contracting with DRT service providers or are themselves providing DRT services directly (often with volunteer drivers or with drivers who perform nontransportation duties as well).[45] A 1976 HEW study counted more than fifty separate federal programs contributing to the cost of transportation services for "special needs" groups in connection with human services and estimated that at least several thousand special human service transportation systems were currently operating around the country.[46] Though data are extremely fragmentary, it appears that human service agency expenditures on client transportation were in the range of $400–500 million by 1973[47], prior to the recent upsurge of interest in paratransit.

Though paratransit services are in practice highly diverse, several key features that they share in common go far toward explaining the surge of interest in them during the mid-1970s. Specifically:

1. They promise to address some of the central criticisms of the auto-dominant system of urban transportation while avoiding the rigidities of fixed route, fixed schedule transit. The spatial and temporal flexibility of paratransit services makes them suitable for application in low-density settings and as a means of carrying out nonradial trips, whereas conventional transit is primarily effective as a carrier of radial trips in high-density settings.

2. Both DRT and private ride sharing have low capital requirements, and the latter have low operating costs as well (which are borne almost entirely in the private sector). Thus both are highly suitable for a period in which authorizations for major capital projects are difficult to obtain, and ride-sharing services in particular are attractive in a period of fiscal austerity.

3. Paratransit services rely on state-of-the-art technology—a signi-

ficant advantage in the current period, when transit officials are acutely consciousness of several recent efforts to apply advanced technologies that have taken far longer to perfect and have ended up costing far more than originally anticipated. (The most frequently cited examples are UMTA's Morgantown Personal Rapid Transit demonstration, the Dallas-Fort Worth Airport "peoplemover," and certain features of the San Francisco BART system.)

4. Paratransit services can be implemented quickly. Thus they mesh well with the current emphasis on short-term planning.

5. As long as usage is purely voluntary, paratransit services merely add to the range of consumer options. Thus they do not arouse controversy as infringements upon consumer freedom.

6. Paratransit initiatives do not entail any neighborhood or environmental disruption and generally do not even require the preparation of environmental impact statements.

7. Although DRT does raise significant issues of transit-taxi competition in some settings, and ride-sharing programs are potentially competitive with transit in serving core-oriented commuter trips, no other interests are threatened by paratransit. In practice, moreover, transit-taxi and transit-pool competition have rarely become active political issues. Many taxi companies are fatalistic about transit competition; others have managed to secure contracts to serve as the providers of dial-a-ride service. And public efforts to promote ride sharing have typically focused on employment sites outside the core.

In short, paratransit initiatives tend to mesh well with both the special policy themes of the mid-1970s in urban transportation and the general orientation of the American political system toward choices that leave existing arrangements undisturbed. Consequently the main issue likely to arise in connection with them is their potential budgetary impact.

The several types of paratransit service in fact have very different budgetary implications. We have found it most useful to distinguish three broad categories in this regard: private ride-sharing arrangements, DRT serving the general public, and DRT serving "special needs" groups.

Carpooling and vanpooling entail the use of unpaid drivers and private vehicles. Public expenditures in connection with ride-sharing programs are almost exclusively for publicity and limited technical assistance to cooperating employers. Both categories of DRT service, on the other hand, normally entail the use of paid drivers and vehicles purchased with public funds, and they typically require operating subsidies far in excess of those incurred in the same urban areas for conventional bus transit. While both DRT categories are expensive, the difference in their clienteles provides an important basis for distinguishing them politically. Large per-trip subsidies to enable human service recipients to reach service facilities and to enable the elderly and handicapped more generally to make short local trips without having to ask neighbors for rides appear to command wide acceptance as priority public obligations. When required per-trip subsidies are large, however, the proposition that DRT should be made more broadly available is often highly controversial. Thus DRT has proliferated to date mainly as a special service mode.

As fiscal austerity has become a more central preoccupation of transit officials during the mid-1970s, interest has been growing in potential means of controlling DRT subsidy requirements. It has become apparent that per-trip costs tend to be greatest where service is immediate (rather than by subscription or by advance notice of individual trip demands), fully demand responsive (rather than oriented toward major traffic generators and/or around generally defined routes), and provided by a public mass transit agency (by comparison, in particular, with a private taxi company). The last of these appears likely to become increasingly salient as a political issue in the years ahead. Organized transit employees command high wages—38 percent higher as of 1975 than the average for all manufacturing employees[48] —and are important political forces in many states and localities, as well as at the federal level. Taxi employees, by comparison, are quite poorly paid.[15] Historically they have also been weakly mobilized as a

15. Taxi employment has nonmonetary features that are important to some members of the labor force, however: availability during intermittent periods of unemployment, potential as a moonlight activity, lack of direct supervision, and human contact with patrons, for example.

political force, but there is reason to believe that they will join taxi owners with increasing effectiveness in protesting publicly sponsored DRT competition and in demanding a substantial share of the work generated by public DRT expenditures.[49]

Overall it appears that transit employee wages average about two and one-half times those of urban taxi drivers. In 1970, when transit wages nationally averaged $4.94 an hour, a survey of taxi-cab fleet operations in twenty-seven large cities revealed that driver commissions averaged $1.79 an hour.[50] Moreover transit work rules often add significantly to the number of man-hours required per unit of DRT service.[51] As labor costs generally constitute 75 to 80 percent of DRT operating costs[52], the choice between transit and taxi providers will normally have an extraordinary impact on subsidy requirements. On the evidence to date, however, many public officials will find it preferable to forego DRT service entirely than to risk disputes with transit labor unions asserting jurisdiction over this work. And it seems likely that the more significant DRT becomes, the more aggressive transit labor will be in pressing such claims.

Traffic Management[16]

The first U.S. traffic signal was installed in 1912. During the 1920s the position of traffic engineer was established in most American cities.[53] And until enactment of the interstate program in 1956 it was taken for granted in all but a handful of cities that the only available methods of alleviating congestion were those involving traffic regulation, law enforcement, and physical improvements within existing rights-of-way. New expressways might be desirable in principle, but they were far too costly in practice to be feasible in developed urban corridors at state or local expense.

The interstate program greatly relaxed financial constraints and

[16.]This section is based in part on an M.I.T. doctoral dissertation in civil engineering by Michael Meyer titled "Organizational Response to a Federal Policy Initiative in the Public Transportation Sector: A Study of Implementation and Compliance" (1978).

for almost two decades after 1956 the focuses of attention in the urban transportation policy arena were major capital projects. By comparison traffic engineering measures seemed almost insignificant. During the mid-1970s, however, the pendulum has swung back as the result of several developments: the growth of intense citizen resistance to urban expressway construction, the shift in political mood toward fiscal austerity, and the recent surge of interest in measures promising visible benefits in the near term.

Traffic engineering in the 1920s and 1930s consisted primarily of maintaining and determining new locations for traffic signals and signs. Traffic regulations were quite rudimentary in this period, and little attention was paid to the benefits that might be gained by altering the geometric designs of existing streets. The decade following World War II, however, was a period of rapid traffic engineering innovation. As traffic burgeoned and public concern with traffic congestion became intense, traffic engineers achieved substantial increases in traffic flow by the widespread application of improved channelization techniques, one-way street systems, staggered traffic signals, street widenings, parking restrictions, and intersection improvements. They also pressed transit operators (with great success) to replace their streetcars with buses, which could operate more flexibly in traffic and which could pick up and discharge passengers at curbs rather than in the middle of streets.

Local traffic engineers continued to apply these techniques in the years following 1956, but public interest in traffic engineering languished and, with the attention of highway engineers focused elsewhere, few new techniques were developed. Early in the interstate period, however, at least a few officials in the U.S. Bureau of Public Roads (BPR) became concerned that limitations on local street capacity would prove the weak links in the emerging "modernized" urban road systems that would have the interstates as their centerpieces. The freeways could bring great amounts of traffic to core area interchanges, but if local streets could not accommodate it, much of the projected benefit of urban interstate construction might be vitiated. As early as 1959 BPR financed a study to estimate the ultimate capacity increase that could be achieved on an existing urban arterial with a combination of operational improvements.[17] In 1966, the bureau issued an instructional memorandum stating that major investments in new capacity on existing streets and highways should be made only after a study of less expensive—including operational—alternatives. Early in 1967, the bureau, now renamed the Federal Highway Administration, adopted the Traffic Operations Program to Improve Capacity and Safety (TOPICS), designed to encourage the use of noninterstate highway aid funds in urban areas for the capital elements of traffic engineering projects (such as channelization improvements and new traffic signals). Congress formally authorized this program in 1968. (TOPICS was merged into the new Federal Aid Urban System, FAUS, program in 1973.)

During the late 1960s as well, the concept of the exclusive bus lane emerged as a potentially exciting path toward the reconciliation of highway and transit interests. The first American bus lane on a city street was implemented in Madison, Wisconsin, in 1966, but the concept did not attract wide national attention until two bus-lane-on-freeway demonstrations got underway in 1970 (on the Shirley Highway outside Washington, D.C., and on the I-495 approach to the Lincoln Tunnel in northern New Jersey). In the same year Congress authorized the use of federal highway funds for bus lane construction.

The bus lane idea represented a major turning point in the history of traffic engineering. The entire previous orientation of the discipline had been toward improving the flow of vehicles on any given right-of-way. Now highway officials began to adopt the posi-

17. Most federal and state highway officials at the time were uninterested in this question. Their standard position was that local street improvements in the vicinity of interchanges were a local responsibility, and that they had no doubt well-managed local street networks could handle the projected flows. They frequently emphasized as well that the expressways would take a great deal of through traffic off currently congested local streets.

The study focused on Wisconsin Avenue in the District of Columbia. It concluded that a combination of the simplest traffic control measures—parking restrictions, turning movement controls, one-way regulations on cross-streets, and reserved curb space for bus operations—could bring about roughly a 40 percent increase. The addition of more expensive and complicated techniques—such as physical division of the Wisconsin Avenue roadway and limitations on access—could bring the overall increase (on different parts of the avenue) to the range of 100–200 percent, it estimated.[54]

tion that, at least in some circumstances, the unit of analysis should be the person. Where the aim of improved person flow conflicted with that of maximizing vehicle flow, and where it was feasible to channel high- and low-occupancy vehicles into separate traffic streams, preference should be accorded the former. In the early days of the bus lane concept, this view was a subject of intense controversy among highway engineers. Arguing that it was inequitable, even "undemocratic," those who were critical noted that the highway system was supported by user taxes, that these were paid almost entirely by private motorists, and that indeed most transit operators already enjoyed tax exemptions. Bus lane advocates retorted that highways were a public service and that the American tradition was for governments to pursue the greatest good of the greatest number—counting people, not machines.

In 1973 and 1974, as air quality and energy issues rose to the top of the urban transportation policy agenda, an even more radical idea emerged: that traffic engineering in some circumstances should not aim at maximizing any kind of flow, but that, instead, it should aim at times to curtail automobile travel demand so as to reduce emissions and energy consumption. When the Environmental Protection Agency sought to apply this concept in its Transportation Control Plans during 1973 and 1974, it proved to have far less political than intellectual appeal. But the idea that in some circumstances traffic should be managed rather than simply facilitated caught on. It appeared increasingly unlikely that many large-scale highway investments would be undertaken in the congested sectors of large urban areas during the next several decades; citizens' groups and the media were increasingly demanding that government concentrate on improving the quality of life rather than simply pursuing growth; and the news was beginning to spread of exciting developments in Europe.

During the 1960s, European traffic engineers—unconstrained by the long American tradition of accommodating the automobile, and overwhelmed by traffic growth on street systems that long predated the motor age—had begun to pioneer along new paths of traffic management. In particular they had devised numerous ingenious techniques for encouraging transit usage and enhancing urban pedestrian amenity by prohibiting or discouraging auto usage on selected urban streets. During the early and mid-1970s large numbers of these schemes—more than three hundred by 1976—were implemented.[55] In some cases—Munich and Copenhagen, for example—substantial portions of the downtown area were closed off to automobiles in order to create an attractive pedestrian environment.[56] This represented an extreme application of the view that streets should be managed for people rather than for vehicles. By 1976, however, it was possible for the U.S. federal highway administrator to devote much of an address to a major conference of urban transportation officials to praise of the auto-restricted zone concept.[57]

In brief, then, the concept of traffic engineering has evolved into that of traffic management during the past decade. Initially this simply entailed a partial shift in orientation from the improvement of person-flow. Since about 1973, however, the idea has gradually taken hold that traffic managers should aim at enhancing a wide variety of values—most notably energy conservation, air quality, and pedestrian amenity—in addition to (and sometimes at the expense of) mobility.

These developments, however, are still reflected far more clearly in the language of the federal TSM regulations than on the roads of U.S. urban areas.[58] At present, the new management approaches to dealing with traffic growth and multiple demands for road space are still initiatives of the professionals. By contrast with the highway and transit construction programs, they lack any significant business-labor constituency motivated by the prospect of profit and employment. (In this respect their most striking virtue, parsimony, may be viewed as a source of political weakness.) By contrast with transit operating subsidy programs, they lack a constituency of fiscally desperate elected officials, operators, and employee unions as well as of users who are perceived—at least potentially, when fares are raised and services curtailed—as a significant political force. Moreover whereas transit service improvements rarely antagonize any voters by taking away personal options, some categories of traffic management improvement do. Finally the new traffic management concepts have not yet caught the

imagination of activist citizens' organizations in the way that transit improvements did in the late 1960s and early 1970s.

Thus, although the emergence of traffic management as a central theme in urban transportation planning is indisputably of
great significance, two important sets of questions remain to be
answered. First, what types of traffic managment measures are feasible at all in the American environment, and which of these are
feasible in more than just a few isolated circumstances? Second,
how great is their potential if adopted to alleviate the major
problems of urban transportation, and how does their cost-
effectiveness compare with other measures available to serve the
same ends?

Market Constraint Measures

The unifying characteristic of most public policy bearing upon
the urban transportation system has been an orientation toward
accommodating rather than shaping market trends. The most conspicuous exception, developing modestly in the 1960s and burgeoning in the 1970s, has been mass transit assistance. The surge
of government spending on transit has—with some aid from the oil
embargo and subsequent gasoline price increases—brought about a
reversal in the long decline of transit patronage. It has not enabled
transit to increase its relative share of urban passenger mileage,
however, nor does it seem likely to do so in future. (From its low
point in 1972, transit ridership rose by 8 percent through 1976.
The 1976 figure, however, was still 3 percent below 1970.)[59]

Politically the most significant feature of the transit program is
that it relies exclusively upon the deployment of positive incentives. It seeks to influence travel behavior by offering improved
service of a preferred type, but it does not threaten any penalties
for failure to utilize this service. When they enact such distributive
programs, politicians are in the happy position of handing out
benefits to constituents. Someone must pay for these benefits, it
is true, but the question of payment is typically blurred—because
the money will be obtained from a wide mix of tax sources and
diffused over a very large number of households, because decisions
to enact new programs are generally treated as separate from deci-

sions to enact new taxes, and because there is frequently hope that much of the funding will come from higher levels of government.

Distributive policies tend to be highly attractive for claimant groups as well as for politicians. They enable groups with relatively narrow bases of support to seek public aid without arousing the ire of potential antagonists. In the early years of the transit program, for example, proponents often took great pains to emphasize that they had no quarrel with the highway program and that they laid no claim to highway user taxes. Rather, they maintained, all they wanted was some modest assistance from the general fund to preserve and modernize existing services, to help stem the decline of central cities, and to provide an alternative to the automobile for those unable to drive and/or employed in congested downtown areas. Indeed, they frequently argued, the two programs were symbiotically related. The highway program was most vulnerable to attack if it claimed to be a cure-all for every problem in urban transportation, and improved transit services would, by drawing some people out of their cars, alleviate congestion for those who continued to drive.

Distributive programs, as Theodore Lowi has noted, are particularly attractive to politicians in a highly pluralistic system. Where power is fragmented, it is most feasible to act where potential beneficiaries are clamoring for assistance and the rest of the political universe is indifferent. When financing demands reach highly conspicuous levels, or fiscal constraints heighten public consciousness of the competition for scarce resources, even distributive programs are likely to become intensely controversial. But on the whole they are the easiest to enact, and at relatively stable levels of funding their political paths tend to be smooth.

Contrasting with programs that seek to influence behavior by distributing benefits are those that aim to do so by levying (or threatening) penalties. The distinction, as Robert Salisbury has pointed out, is not always clear. Many regulatory programs—such as restrictions on entry and price cutting in the trucking, airline, and taxi industries—are in fact sustained politically by the support of the regulated parties and are widely understood to be for their benefit. Salisbury terms such programs *self-regulatory* and notes that they are essentially distributive in nature though regulatory in form.[60]

Leaving aside self-regulatory policies, programs that seek to influence behavior by levying penalties have a far greater inherent potential for arousing conflict than those involving the distribution of benefits. If they wish to secure the enactment and vigorous implementation of such programs, proponents normally must face the prospective victims head-on. Where political power is highly fragmented and opportunities for veto are numerous, the cards are stacked for the defense. Thus, until quite recently, few regulatory programs opposed by the prospective regulated parties have ever been enacted except in the wake of scandal or some other source of intense public and media indignation.[61]

Since about 1960 this pattern has been altered dramatically. Charles Schultze has recently noted that as of the mid-1950s, the federal government played a major regulatory role in only four areas: antitrust, finance (banking and securities marketing), transportation, and communications. During the following two decades the scope of regulation vastly expanded, and its nature became far more complex. By the mid-1970s, about a hundred thousand federal employees distributed among eighty-three agencies were engaged in regulatory activity, and interlocking, often overlapping, regulatory policies reached deeply into every sector of the nation's economic activity.[62]

It is far from apparent what changes in the character of American politics have occurred since the 1950s to make possible this remarkable expansion of regulatory activity—which has focused primarily on issues of health, safety, environmental protection, and civil rights rather than such traditional economic issues as entry, exit, pricing, and fraud. In search of an explanation, one can cite the growth in citizen activism that got underway with civil rights activity in the late 1950s and early 1960s and that soon spread to numerous other areas, giving rise, in particular, to vigorous consumer and environmental movements. One can also hypothesize that as the proportion of voters whose attitudes were shaped prior to the New Deal has diminished, public resistance to welfare state proposals has sharply eroded over the past two decades.[18] Even in combination, however, these developments do not seem adequate to explain the change that has occurred.

There is substantial room for dispute about the extent to which these recent policy changes have been translated into actual changes in business and consumer behavior. The new regulatory programs have frequently been premised on assumptions of implementation capacity that have proven far off the mark in practice. As Schultze has written:

The single most important characteristic of the newer forms of social intervention is that their success or failure depends upon affecting the skills, attitudes, consumption habits, or production patterns of hundreds of millions of individuals, millions of business firms, and thousands of local units of government. The tasks are difficult not so much because they deal with technologically complicated matters as because they aim ultimately at modifying the behavior of private producers and consumers. The boundaries of the "public administration" problem have leapt far beyond the question of how to effectively organize and run a public institution and now encompass the far more vexing question of how to change some aspect of the behavior of a whole society.[64]

If policy ambition has frequently outstripped capability, it is clear nonetheless that some momentous changes have occurred, and they have been reflected in the field of urban transportation as well as elsewhere.

Let us now turn to an examination of recent experience and controversy with respect to the three types of measures that fall within the market constraint category: business regulation, direct consumer regulation, and price (including tax) increases.

Business Regulation
As of the early 1960s, the urban transportation marketplace was essentially free from government regulation and from price structure elements designed explicitly by government to influence

18. This has been a period of burgeoning social expenditure as well as social regulation. Social program expenditures by all levels of government combined more than quintupled between 1960 and 1975. In so doing they rose from 11 to 20 percent of GNP and from 35 to 52 percent of total public spending.[63]

behavior. Governments did impose highway user taxes, but these were reserved almost everywhere for highway construction and operation, and they were held to the lowest levels compatible with providing these services to motor vehicle users.

The first significant breaks in this pattern occurred in the mid-1960s when Congress enacted the Motor Vehicle Air Pollution Control Act (1965) and the National Traffic and Motor Vehicle Safety Act (1966).[65] The Air Pollution Control Act emerged within the context of more general developments in pollution control legislation, and received far less attention at the time. Thus, we shall comment first on the background of the Safety Act.

Safety regulation came to the auto industry with an absolute minimum of warning, following the publication of Ralph Nader's best-selling book, *Unsafe at Any Speed*,[66] and a series of well-publicized hearings orchestrated by Senator Abraham Ribicoff. [67] Several features of this episode bear special note. *First*, the targets of regulation were to be large corporations, not consumers directly. *Second*, the technology to achieve significant improvements in automobile safety was well in hand. This is by no means to deny that great scope existed for progress beyond the current state of technological art, but simply to emphasize the point that was critical at the time. Automobiles could be made much safer right now, and the companies had not bothered to make them so. *Third*, the immediate trigger for regulatory action was a scandal—two in fact. The first was the lamentable safety record of the Chevrolet Corvair, to which Nader devoted the opening chapter of his book. The second occurred as the Ribicoff hearings progressed, with Nader as star witness. General Motors hired a private detective to look into Nader's private life. The detective found nothing, but Nader discovered who his employer was and brought suit against GM. Media condemnation of this GM effort to discredit its critic rather than argue the merits of his criticisms was virtually universal, and the president of GM felt compelled to apologize publicly. *Fourth*, regulatory action did not appear to pose any threat to the prosperity of the industry. The auto companies maintained that they had been prevented from offering safety features by competitive pressures, which in turn simply reflected consumer preferences. Faced with a market choice, most consumers preferred styling to safety, and indeed would not even pay a few dollars for seat belts. No one claimed, however, that sales would go down if all new cars were required to meet certain minimal safety standards. Thus it appeared that auto safety features were likely to become available to consumers who desired them only if government acted to eliminate market pressures for their neglect. Such regulation would, of course, constrain the options of the majority who apparently preferred to buy unsafe cars. Either their market preference was a weak one, however, or it failed to translate well into politics, because virtually nothing was heard from such consumers during the legislative history of the act.[68]

The Motor Vehicle Air Pollution Control Act emerged from a rather more prosaic background but one that had several key features in common with that of the Safety Act. Ever since the 1951 discovery that auto emissions were the primary source of Los Angeles smog, awareness of the motor vehicle contribution to air pollution had gradually been spreading. California had adopted a motor vehicle air pollution control program in 1959, federal legislation had been enacted in 1960 directing the U.S. surgeon general to study the effects of motor vehicle emissions on public health, and Congress in 1963 had enacted the first federal air pollution law conferring any enforcement powers. The Clean Air Act of 1963 dealt only with stationary sources such as factories and power plants. In 1964, the Senate Subcommittee on Air and Water Pollution, chaired by Senator Edmund Muskie, conducted hearings that highlighted auto emissions as the major remaining gap in federal air pollution law. Early in 1965, Muskie introduced what became the Motor Vehicle Air Pollution Control Act.[69]

In brief, then, air pollution regulation came to the auto industry in fairly routine fashion as an extension of an economy-wide regulatory policy previously adopted with respect to the other main emission sources. In common with the Safety Act, however, the targets of regulation were the car manufacturers rather than auto users directly, the technology appeared to be in hand (the companies had already agreed to meet California standards beginning in 1967), and regulatory action did not appear to threaten industry prosperity.

The act itself conferred authority on the secretary of Health, Education and Welfare to establish emission control standards and deadlines. He did so simply by requiring the companies to meet the 1967 California standards on a nationwide basis beginning in 1968. The fact that California, which accounted for 10 percent of the national market, had already begun successfully to implement a strong regulatory law apparently did a good deal to ease passage of the federal act. It provided compelling evidence that regulation could bring about improved performance by the industry, and it undermined the will of the companies to resist. Though reluctant to be regulated by the federal government, the companies were even more concerned at this point about the prospect of having to satisfy a wide variety of state standards. [70]

By the beginning of the 1970s, then, the only market constraint measures that had been undertaken in the field of urban transportation involved available technology and the regulation of only a few large companies. A number of programs adopted more recently, however, have gone beyond available technology; the two most salient examples are the Clean Air Act Amendments of 1970 and the Energy Policy and Conservation Act of 1975.[71]

The Clean Air Act Amendments, enacted at the height of American environmental fervor, required auto manufacturers to reduce carbon monoxide and hydrocarbon emissions, by the 1975 model year, 90 percent below the levels that the secretary of HEW had previously mandated pursuant to the 1965 act.[19] The act also required that nitrogen oxide emission levels (previously uncontrolled) be reduced 90 percent between the 1971 and 1976 model years.

The Energy Policy and Conservation Act, enacted in the wake of the Arab oil embargo, required the manufacturers to double the average fuel economy of automobiles marketed in the United States by 1985. Whereas the Environmental Protection Agency (EPA) estimated that the average fuel economy in the 1974 model year had been 14 miles per gallon (mpg), the target established for 1985 was 27.5 mpg.

[19.] By comparison with the average emissions of uncontrolled pre-1968 vehicles, the two standards required 95 percent and 96 percent reductions.

What both these acts had in common, though in varying degree, was that they established statutory standards—rather than following the more usual practice of leaving some discretion to administrators—and that these standards exceeded current technological capability. In the case of the Energy Act, there was room for disagreement about what should be considered present capability. The companies could certainly make cars that averaged 27.5 mpg, but given the current state-of-the-art, these would have to be extremely small and lightly powered. The question was whether Congress anticipated forcing the public into such cars. Clearly it did not. It hoped and expected that the manufacturers would find new ways to meet the mpg standard while simultaneously offering consumers most of the amenity and acceleration features to which they were accustomed. In the case of the Clean Air Act, the issue was simpler. The companies did not know how to meet the standards as of 1970, and no one claimed otherwise.

In describing the history of the Clean Air Act Amendments, Charles Jones has coined the term *policy beyond capability.* [72] He emphasizes that the predominant feature of the political atmosphere at the time was the rapidly spreading influence of passionate, activist environmental groups. The result was, in another of Jones's phrases, *policy escalation* throughout the legislative process—rather than the more familiar pattern whereby controversial elements of proposals are whittled away during the course of building successful legislative coalitions. President Nixon submitted a bill that in any previous year would have been considered extremely strong. The house passed an even stronger version by a vote of 374 to 0. And then the Senate, by a vote of 73 to 0, passed a version that was considerably stronger still. The conference committee adopted the Senate version, and the president affixed his signature with apparent enthusiasm.

There was a widespread view in 1970 that the manufacturers could do virtually anything if simply told that they had to. Illustratively three members of the House Commerce Committee, which had jurisdiction over pollution legislation, issued a statement in which they said:

We are not impressed by the wails of the auto industry that meaningful improvements in their product pose insurmountable cost and engineering problems. We listened to the same complaints back in 1967, when Congress agreed to permit California to depart from national auto emission norms in setting and enforcing more stringent controls. The industry demonstrated then that it has the expertise and the know-how to make just about any change for the better when the public demand is great enough.[73]

The other side of the coin was that congressmen knew the law could be amended later if it proved to be leading toward sharply higher car prices or a shutdown of the industry. When pressed by Senator Griffin (R.-Mich.) on the Senate floor for having neglected to hold hearings on whether the industry could meet the 1975 emission standard deadline, Muskie responded: "The deadline is based not, I repeat, on economic and technological feasibility, but on considerations of public health. We think, on the basis of the exposure we have had to this problem, that this is a necessary and reasonable standard to impose upon the industry. If the industry cannot meet it, they can come back."[74]

In the event, of course, it proved easier for congressmen to vote with the environmentalists in 1970 than to secure compliance in 1975. By 1977, the companies had been granted three one-year extensions. In the summer of that year, with the industry threatening to shut down unless further extensions were authorized, Congress relaxed the 1970 targets on a more wholesale basis. Bowing to company estimates of what targets were achievable at reasonable cost, it extended the hydrocarbon and carbon monoxide deadlines to 1980 and 1983, respectively. Additionally it increased the ultimate nitrogen oxide standard from 10 to 25 percent of the 1971 level, extended the deadline for meeting it to 1982, and empowered the EPA administrator to authorize still higher emission levels (up to 37.5 percent of the 1971 level) through 1984 for innovative technologies promising fuel economy benefits.[75]

Notably the key issues stressed by the industry and its allies in seeking Clean Air Act modifications during the mid-1970s have been jobs and energy. The companies have concluded, apparently, that arguments about their own economic circumstances and technical capabilities cut little ice politically. Arguments about potential layoffs of workers and about inescapable tradeoffs between fuel economy and air quality objectives, on the other hand, command respectful attention. The United Auto Workers Union, which joined with environmentalists in demanding the toughest possible standards in 1970, has been the industry's most valuable ally in more recent years, stressing the threat of layoffs and their potential widespread ramifications throughout the economy. The result has been to confuse the question of whether insistence on tight deadlines should be viewed as a liberal issue. Ironically the major source of funding for environmentalist lobbying during the legislative history of the Clean Air Act Amendments of 1977 was the catalytic converter industry, a group brought into being by the Clean Air Act Amendments of 1970.[76]

There were no citizens' groups demanding energy conservation in 1975 with the same fervor or degree of public support enjoyed by the environmental groups as of 1970, but energy had become the hottest issue on the domestic policy agenda. And criticism of the federal government for its failure to adopt energy conservation measures since the Arab oil embargo was rife. In this situation Congress again opted for the strategy of regulating the auto companies. Taking account of the emission standard experience, however, it deferred the target date for achievement of the energy act's only difficult standard for ten years. The act required the companies to achieve sales-weighted fuel economy averages of 18, 19 and 20 mpg during the 1978, 1979, and 1980 years, respectively. These were, even industry spokesmen agreed, quite feasible targets—indeed, targets that were likely to be achieved even in the absence of legislation. The secretary of transportation was authorized to determine interim standards for the model years 1981 through 1984. Only in 1985 was the tough statutory standard of 27.5 mpg to come into play.

In brief, then, the auto industry, essentially free from regulation until 1965, has been subjected to an increasingly complex mix of standards since then. As the requirements have become stiffer and grown in number, potential conflicts among them have become increasingly significant. In addition to trade-offs between fuel economy and emission standards, there are also significant trade-offs between fuel economy and safety aims—as most safety features add weight and, more generally, as the occupants of smaller cars tend to be more vulnerable to injury when accidents occur. We shall defer substantive discussion of the choices that have been adopted to later chapters. Suffice it here to say that business regulation has become demonstrably a feasible political approach to dealing with urban transportation problems that attract wide public attention and that, indeed, the product development and design priorities of the auto industry are today dictated mainly by government standards and deadlines.

Consumer Regulation and Pricing

Serious public discussion of constraint measures that would bear directly on consumers did not get underway until 1973, although a key statutory provision was enacted as early as 1970. The framework of this discussion has been a growing perception that service improvements and price cuts are unlikely to lure many Americans into transit or other forms of ride sharing unless there are also major changes in the larger framework of urban transportation incentives. Through 1977, all proposals to bring about such changes have foundered on the shoals of public resistance. The two most serious efforts have involved air pollution and energy conservation.

The Clean Air Act Amendments of 1970, in addition to establishing new-car emission standards, required the EPA administrator to establish ambient air quality standards for each pollutant that he found to have an adverse effect on public health and welfare. These standards were to be achieved in each air quality control region (AQCR) by May 31, 1975, though the administrator was authorized to grant extensions of up to two years where he found that full compliance by the 1975 deadline was unfeasible.[20] It was understood as the legislative language was drafted that it would bring into play a set of standards suggested in a recent report by the Department of HEW. On the basis of current estimates, it appeared that the automobile contribution to meeting

20. EPA has divided the nation into 247 AQCRs, which together cover the entire U.S. land area except for a small portion of Alaska. AQCRs generally include at least one Standard Metropolitan Statistical Area (SMSA) and never divide an SMSA, but they include substantial amounts of nonmetropolitan land area as well.

these standards could be achieved in twenty years simply by waiting for cars meeting the new-car emission standards to be marketed and for older models to complete their useful lives. This was deemed much too long to wait, however, and thus provision was made for the development and enforcement of supplementary measures in AQCRs that would otherwise be in violation of ambient air quality standards after May 31, 1975. Implementation plans were to be prepared by the states, subject to EPA approval, and were to include such measures as might prove necessary to achieve the standards by the statutory deadline. This provision attracted little attention in 1970, doubtless because there were no peacetime precedents for government efforts to constrain individual travel behavior and because there were no detailed forecasts of what it might mean in specific AQCRs.

The implementation plan requirement first attracted widespread public attention in 1973 when the first draft plans surfaced for discussion and public hearings. Early in 1973, moreover, a blanket two-year extension that the EPA administrator had granted to all AQCRs requiring implementation plans was disallowed by a U.S. court of appeals.[77] Thus although the administrator was subsequently able to grant extensions on a case-by-case basis, regions were faced for a time with the prospect of full compliance by May 31, 1975. Even more significantly, public officials, the media, and the public at large became sharply aware for the first time that achievement of the Clean Air Act targets would, in a number of the nation's largest metropolitan areas, involve restrictions on personal travel by automobile.

Eventually, after case-by-case extensions to 1977 had been granted by the administrator to all of the areas threatened with personal travel restrictions, plans calling for reductions in vehicle miles of automobile travel (VMT) were promulgated for eighteen regions. In every case but one, EPA had to promulgate the plan itself because state officials refused to do so. In four of the areas affected, EPA estimated that an auto use reduction of more than 50 percent was required to achieve full compliance by 1977. In another nine, reductions of 10 to 50 percent were needed.[78]

While proposing to spur transit and carpool use by a variety of positive incentives—for example, bus service improvements and carpool matching services—EPA concluded that significant reductions in auto use were likely to be achieved only by the application of tough disincentives. Basically two approaches were identified to bring about reductions in auto travel: pricing and the creation of shortages (most notably, of parking space and/or gasoline) by direct regulation.

More specifically EPA proposed three disincentives in its 1973 plans, sometimes in combination:

1. Parking surcharges were to be utilized in seven AQCRs: Boston, the District of Columbia, Los Angeles, San Francisco, San Diego, Sacramento, and Fresno.

2. Reductions in parking space availability were elements of most of the VMT-reduction plans. The methods utilized ranged from the prohibition of nonresident parking on streets near commercial areas to requirements that specified vacancy rates be maintained in for-hire parking facilities until after most people had to be at work.

3. Reductions in gasoline availability were included as a contingent, last-resort strategy in several plans, most notably that of Los Angeles (where the required VMT reduction was 84 percent). The EPA administrator stated even as he promulgated these plans, however, that he considered them too drastic and would recommend that Congress authorize further extensions for the regions in question.[79]

The initial public outcry against the EPA transportation control plans focused on the parking surcharges. Late in 1973, the conference committee on an emergency energy bill adopted a provision prohibiting EPA from imposing any regulations involving price disincentives—on the ground that only Congress could impose taxes. Though the bill in question died (because of a controversy over an unrelated provision) in the rush to congressional adjournment, [80] EPA judged that similar language would be adopted in 1974 unless it rescinded its pricing orders. Thus, in January 1974 it did so, ordering that replacements be found to bring the affected plans into technical compliance with the law. (A prohibition on parking surcharges was nonetheless enacted in June 1974.)[81]

The replacement for surcharges that EPA came up with in a

number of regions was intensified parking regulation. In Greater Boston, for example, the original plan had included numerous surcharge and parking regulatory elements, all focused on the core of the region. With the surcharge elements removed, parking regulation was extended regionwide. All employers of more than fifty people were to be required to reduce their employee parking by 25 percent. Congress responded in December 1974 by enacting, as part of the EPA appropriation bill for fiscal 1975, a prohibition on the use of any funds for the promulgation or implementation of parking regulations.[82] Thereupon, EPA suspended the parking regulatory elements of all transportation control plans indefinitely. Congress did not enact a specific prohibition on the use of the third disincentive proposed by EPA in 1973—reductions in gasoline supply—but EPA officials had no doubt that it would if they reminded anyone that such reductions could be ordered.

There matters stood until July 1977. The May 31, 1977, "final" deadline under the 1970 legislation (with the maximum two-year extensions that it empowered the EPA administrator to grant) came and went without a single plan that would entail travel disincentives going into effect. The standards and deadlines mandated in 1970 remained the law of the land, but the main techniques identified by EPA for reducing VMT had effectively been eliminated by Congress.

This stark discrepancy between statutory goals and authorized means was finally rectified by the Clean Air Amendments of 1977. Its method was to extend the final deadline for achievement of the ambient air quality standards by ten and a half years, to December 31, 1987. Additionally, in listing measures that should be considered in the preparation of implementation plans, it conspicuously omitted any mention of automobile travel disincentives.

Since the oil embargo and abrupt quadrupling of world oil prices in 1973–1974, the debate about whether and how to shape consumer incentives has increasingly focused on energy. Here the root concerns are the strength of the national economy, the balance of payments, and national security. The United States is today more dependent on imported oil than just prior to the embargo. Whereas 36 percent of the nation's oil was imported in 1973, 47 percent was imported in 1977. The nation's oil import bill in 1977 totaled $45 billion (up from $3 billion in 1970), and its balance of trade deficit totaled $31 billion.[83]

The economic consequences of these trends have been somewhat muted, at least until 1977, for the following reasons.

• Most of the other noncommunist industrial nations, which produce little or no oil themselves, were even harder hit initially than the United States by the oil price increases. The American advantage has gradually eroded, however, because its consumption per capita is uniquely high and it has lagged in adopting conservation measures.

• The United States has been successful in building exports of real wealth—goods and services—partially to offset the increased dollar outflow for oil. In the immediate aftermath of the embargo, the most dramatic growth involved arms and agricultural products. More recently, however, concerns about the destabilizing effects of uncontrolled arms sales have led to a leveling off in this sector, and improved harvests elsewhere in the world have curtailed the growth of agricultural exports. Moreover American imports surged during 1976 and 1977 as the U.S. economic recovery led that of most other nations.

• The oil nations have invested most of their foreign exchange surpluses (which grew by an estimated $157 billion between January 1, 1974, and June 30, 1977) in dollar-denominated assets.[84] Additionally, because most of the world's oil trade is transacted in dollars, the quadrupling in value of that trade led initially to increased requirements for dollar reserves on the part of oil importers.

• These factors in combination actually reinforced confidence in the dollar during the two or three years immediately following the embargo. Consequent decisions by financial managers throughout the world to hold large portions of their discretionary reserves in dollar form provided a powerful additional fillip to its strength in world currency markets.

During 1977, however, ominous signs began to emerge. As the American economy enjoyed a vigorous expansion, imports grew rapidly, the nation's trade balance (positive in 1974 and 1975) swung into severe deficit, and the confidence of financial managers in the future strength of the dollar began to erode. The consequence was a sharp downward trend in the value of the dollar relative to the other leading world currencies. Between January 1977 and October 1978, for example, the dollar declined 37 percent against the Japanese yen, 38 percent against the British pound, and 23 percent against the German mark.[85] With another very large trade deficit projected for 1978, there seemed to be little prospect of a near-term reversal of these trends. Even more seriously, the nation's still-growing dependence on oil imports meant that it was becoming ever-more vulnerable to potential shock from a future oil embargo.

There has been a great deal of talk among American policy makers since 1974 about the need for energy conservation, and several measures have in fact been adopted—most notably the new-car fuel economy standards—that are likely to yield significant energy savings after 1980. The only regulatory constraint on personal travel behavior that has been adopted, however, is the fifty-five mile per hour speed limit.

In 1975, chairman Al Ullman of the House Ways and Means Committee proposed legislation that would have permitted each licensed driver nine gallons of gasoline per week at the current federal tax level, with higher taxes being levied on additional purchases. The surtax would have been a percentage excise, rising gradually over a four-year period from 5 to 40 percent.[86] Despite the support of key House leaders, this legislation was defeated overwhelmingly when it came before the House in June.[87] In 1977, President Carter determined to make energy the main domestic priority of his first year in office and likewise recommend a gas tax increase. In order to sweeten his proposal, he recommended that the entire revenue yield of the tax—which might have risen to fifty cents a gallon by 1987 unless overall gas consumption fell below specified target levels—be returned to the public in the form of cash rebates. (The result would have been to raise the relative price of gas without reducing the overall consumer income.) This time congressional leaders made clear from the outset that they viewed the proposal as quixotic, and it was quickly buried in committee.

Why has there been such apparent resistance by the American political system to market constraint measures bearing directly on urban transportation consumers? The core of the answer, we believe, is readily apparent. Given that the life patterns of most American households are built around the automobile, any program designed to reduce its use will inconvenience a large share of the electorate. Any program, moreover, will visit its impact differently on different regions of the country and different types of households, in ways that many people are bound to consider inequitable. Tax schemes, for example, even though in theory they can be designed to avoid doing so, tend in practice to affect rural and low-income households most painfully. Additionally they compound inflation over the short run.[21] Rationing schemes tend to become bureaucratic nightmares as they seek to accommodate special needs.[22] [89] Restrictions on downtown parking not only inconvenience one group of employees by comparison with all

[21.] The U.S. Bureau of Labor Statistics (BLS) has long included sales, excise, and property (though not any other) taxes as prices.[88] The incomes of numerous groups, in turn, are explicitly linked to the consumer price index. Many other groups who do not have a legal claim to automatic adjustments base their equity claims on the price index. Increases in income for some groups, of course, entail increased costs for others, and thus added pressures for price and tax increases. Overall, then, tax increases counted as prices by the BLS appear to have significant short-term inflationary effects, even if they contribute to curbing inflation over the longer run by absorbing consumer purchasing power.

[22.] The essence of rationing is allocation by bureaucratic decision. Thus a considerable bureaucracy is required to operate any rationing system. And though it normally begins by proposing allocations in accord with simple rules of thumb (historic usage for institutional users, so many gallons per adult for personal usage), it is inevitably overwhelmed in short order by claims of need for special treatment. The users who desire supplemental allocations must devote a great deal of time, energy, and often money as well (for the employ of professional advocates) to dealing with the bureaucracy. They may likewise seek to evade or corrupt it, and both black marketeering and official corruption are endemic in most mature rationing systems. Even if the system remains pristine and fully effective, it is bound to generate capricious patterns of resource allocation. Given their inescapable ignorance of which claims genuinely merit economic priority, rationing officials necessarily respond in large measure to well-presented stories and to political influence. The claimants themselves have little incentive to curtail their demands because they typically find negligible correlation (within broad categories) between the level of effort required to deal with the bureaucracy and the magnitude of special need being claimed. Equity tends to suffer, finally, because the most aggressive and effective in pursuing special allocations are, in general, quite different from those with the most acute needs. Ultimately, it is much easier to rebate tax revenue to the poor (thus dealing with general needs for purchasing power) than to determine each user's level of need for specific products within the context of a rationing system.

others; they may also harm the central area economy by diverting travelers with discretionary destinations (such as restaurants and department stores) to outlying locations. To the extent that this occurs, the long-term outcome may be more auto travel as the pace of urban dispersal is accelerated. Broader restrictions, such as the 25 percent reduction in employer-provided parking proposed for Greater Boston, are more even-handed in their economic and land use effects. but they disproportionately inconvenience employees in locations poorly served by mass transit. Moreover by threatening so many (like gas tax increases), they generate near-universal opposition.

Conclusion

We are faced with a fascinating paradox. The American public, expressing itself collectively, has brought about a remarkable shift in government spending, promotional, and regulatory policies affecting urban transportation since the 1960s—most notably from expressway construction to transit assistance, to the promotion of carpooling and vanpooling, and to product performance regulation of the auto manufacturers. Individually in the marketplace, however, Americans continue to resist the lures of both transit and organized pooling. Finally, the same public, speaking collectively again, appears throughly hostile to any scheming by government to reduce automobile use by restructuring market options and incentives.

Is there a constant theme running through these apparent contradictions? We believe there is. Citizens press their public officials to alleviate "problems," and they are receptive to being provided with improved services. But insofar as their own environs and life-styles are concerned, the status quo appears to be the objective. New highways are resisted as disruptive of existing neighborhoods, social patterns, and natural ecologies. Automobile travel disincentives are resisted as disruptive of established behavior patterns. Urban Americans can and do adjust to inconvenience when they must. But they are likely—or, at very least, politicians deem them likely—to take out their annoyance on elected officials whom they judge might have averted the need, or, even worse, deliberately created it.

In short, American governments can spend great sums to provide carrots, even when these appear to be relatively ineffective in serving their announced objectives. But they find it extremely difficult to apply even gentle and highly cost-effective sticks when these would discomfort large numbers of voters. This disposition toward serving rather than controlling constituents is perhaps the most significant charm of the American political system, but it also accounts for its weakness as a shaper of travel patterns.

To say that contemporary patterns of urban travel are overwhelmingly the product of market forces—accommodated but not substantially molded by public activity—is quite different, however, from saying that government has invariably been ineffective as an urban transportation problem solver. It is more accurate to say that the capacity of American governments to act effectively has tended to vary with the nature of the problem and with the nature of the means required to address it effectively.

At times, for example, the most significant problems perceived by American officials and interest groups have involved failures adequately to accommodate market trends. Traffic congestion in the 1950s and 1960s was such a problem, and it lent itself readily to the energetic undertaking of remedial public actions. If problems vary in their mesh with the capabilities of American public institutions, so do solutions. Not only is it far more congenial to distribute benefits than penalties—to spend than to regulate—but it also seems to have become far more feasible to regulate large corporations than the average American voter.

The American political system strives to accommodate new political demands with minimal disturbance to existing policies, institutional arrangements, and individual behavior patterns. At the same time, it is accustomed to dealing with rapidly evolving conditions and voter priorities. In short it has certain political maintenance requirements of a conservative nature, but it is oriented as well toward dealing with the radical nature of modern reality. These characteristics result in piecemeal, but constant and relatively adaptive, policy accretion. If they impair the clarity and consistency of policy outcomes, they tend also to maximize their broad acceptability. Additionally they render the system unusually open to innovative ideas and technologies that can be injected into the ongoing stream of activity without substantially disrupting entrenched public programs, private economic interests, and personal life-styles. In short the system does not treat apparent tensions among policy objectives as inescapable sources of conflict; rather it seeks by political means to blur the tensions and by technical means to find ingenious new means of reconciling the objectives.

It follows that, other things being equal, change strategies will vary in political acceptability in accord with the degree to which they inconvenience powerful institutions and large or well-organized blocks of voters. To this basic proposition we would add, as a corollary, that the visibility of the connection between the public action and the private discomfort is a key desideratum. It matters a great deal to elected officials whether the linkage is clear and immediate or blurred and deferred.

With these features of the political system in mind, we postulate that policy and technical innovations will be found attractive politically in accord with the fit between their own imperatives and the maintenance imperatives of political decision makers. Specifically, innovative options can usefully be categorized and ranked in order of acceptability as follows:

1. *The ideal innovation is one that consumers will buy voluntarily in the marketplace at a price high enough to cover its cost.* Where such an innovation requires public implementation, its advocates will be greatly strengthened if they are able to contend that con-

sumer decisions on its use will be voluntary and that any required public expenditures will be financed by user charges.

Public highway programs were long promoted and defended on this basis. Decisions to use the highway system were perceived as voluntary, payment was roughly proportional to use, and the system appeared to pay its own way. More recently of course, resistance has developed as large numbers of constituents have perceived that highway programs have major external effects that are far from adequately covered by user payments; that highways influence the spatial distribution of activities and thus tend to compel their own use; that decisions to use the existing highway system are not properly interpreted as votes in favor of future expansion; and that the highway revenue-expenditure system includes major cross-subsidies.

Among currently fashionable options, government efforts to promote voluntary carpooling and vanpooling fall most notably in this first category. The uncertainty surrounding them is whether they can elicit substantial consumer response. Many state and local officials who otherwise support such promotional efforts hesitate to expend substantial energy on them for fear of wasting their time and of visibly failing. Commitment is also impeded in most locales by the fact that such activities do not mesh easily with the traditional responsibilities or capabilities of existing transportation agencies. Finally many transit officials fear that increased carpooling and vanpooling would be significantly at the expense of mass transit usage.[1]

2. *Among measures that entail some compulsion, the most attractive are those that alleviate widely perceived problems at little or no cost and that either operate on corporate enterprises rather than individual travelers (for example, new-car performance standards) or entail the exercise of traditional governmental powers in relatively unobtrusive ways (such as traffic management improvements).*

At their best, performance standards for new cars induce the auto manufacturers to find means of providing the public with better products at lower or essentially unchanged prices. At second best, they lead to higher purchase prices, which are more

than offset by reductions in average lifetime cost both to purchasers and society at large: for example, by improving fuel efficiency, by reducing accident damages, or by reducing health and
property expenditures attributable to air pollution. Even when
such requirements are not themselves cost-effective, they may be
defensible on the ground that they have diverted manufacturer
energies from even less cost-effective activities, such as annual
style changes.

Traffic management innovations also vary widely in obtrusive-
ness and in the extent to which they force painful trade-offs. At
the least obtrusive and most consensual end of the range are traffic
signal improvements that reduce congestion and increase overall
highway carrying capacity. Such measures tend to improve service
for all users, to generate a sense of enhanced individual freedom
rather than increased compulsion, and to operate by the inexpensive exercise of a long-accepted governmental function.

Management innovations that entail more explicit choices among
users have tended to be ignored until the past several years. The
record of their neglect is highly revealing of the political system's
historic preference for expending resources over managing them
efficiently—where the latter would entail explicit trade-offs among
categories of voters and thereby risk antagonizing some. Interest in
highway management innovation has grown rapidly in the 1970s,
however, as public resistance has made it increasingly difficult to
alleviate congestion by the physical expansion of highway capacity, and as an acute new sense of resource limitations—fiscal, environmental, and material—has evolved.

Among the management innovations that have recently gained
easiest acceptance are traffic signal systems that give priority to
transit vehicles, exclusive high occupancy vehicle lanes, and wrong-
way bus lanes. All of these entail discrimination in favor of one or
more categories of vehicles. As implemented, however, this
discrimination has generally entailed little or no inconvenience
for other users. Priority signal systems have generally not impaired
the overall traffic-carrying capacity of the streets affected. Wrong-
way bus lanes have been implemented only where it has been possible to do so without causing significant congestion delays for

those highway users moving in the off-peak direction. And exclusive freeway lanes have been developed only as features of new or expanded facilities.

Acceptance of the need for explicit trade-offs has progressed farthest in connection with the management of central business district street systems. As early as 1965, Minneapolis established a pedestrian mall and transit street on its main shopping thoroughfare, Nicollet Avenue. The planning rationale was straightforward and was actively promoted by Nicollet Avenue business interests.[2] In order for the avenue to thrive as a regional shopping center, it had to have amenities at least comparable to those of the largest suburban shopping centers. It could not be provided with comparable amounts of free parking, but it could be given far better transit access and a comparably attractive pedestrian environment. Shoppers arriving by automobile were already accustomed to parking on other streets because no parking was available on the affected portion of Nicollet Avenue itself; and in any event, motorists had been conditioned at suburban shopping centers to expect a sharp distinction between automobile access areas and auto-free zones in the immediate vicinity of the shops. Finally the concentration of bus traffic on Nicollet Avenue promised to improve traffic flow on parallel streets, leaving many private motorists using the downtown street system even better off than before.

Despite the widely publicized success of the Nicollet Avenue transit-pedestrian mall, imitations have to date been few and very modest in scale—generally confined to a single street and no more than a couple of blocks in length.[3] However, the Federal Highway and Mass Transportation administrations have been energetically promoting the idea of auto-restricted zones and publicizing the most ambitious foreign applications as part of their transportation system management (TSM) initiative announced late in 1975. Overall the notion that a tiny segment of the street system in any metropolitan area—within the congested heart of downtown—may properly be managed with priority for pedestrians and buses seems likely to prove an idea whose time finally arrived in the latter half of the 1970s. This is by no means to suggest that it will be applied in all downtowns but simply that it will be deemed a conventional alternative meriting serious consideration as a matter of course.

Just as private shopping center developers pioneered in demonstrating that auto-free commercial zones could be economic assets in the auto age, private housing developers led the way toward demonstrating that consumers preferred their residential streets to be quiet and safe for children rather than optimally efficient as traffic carriers. The basic idea that residential access traffic should be segregated from through traffic was central to the neighborhood unit concept articulated by urban planner Clarence Perry and first demonstrated (by Clarence Stein and Henry Wright) in the privately developed new town of Radburn, New Jersey, toward the end of the 1920s.[4] During the 1930s, the concept was applied by the federal government in three small greenbelt suburbs constructed on the fringes of Cincinnati, Milwaukee, and Washington, D.C., but it was first applied on a mass scale by private developers in the years following World War II.[5] Residential subdivisions since that time have been designed almost universally to exclude through traffic. This has been noncontroversial, apparently for two reasons: first, the layout planning and construction have occurred in the private sector; and second, new streets in new subdivisions, like new lanes on expressways, can be designated for uses other than optimal traffic service without taking away from motorists anything to which they have already become accustomed.

During the 1970s, residents of older neighborhoods with grid pattern streets have increasingly pressed for measures to provide them with some of the freedom from traffic noise and risk enjoyed by residents of more recently developed neighborhoods. The methods typically proposed include closing certain streets, developing mazelike one-way street systems, adding numerous stop signs and traffic lights, and placing bumps at intervals to deter travel at high speeds. Although national surveys are lacking of the frequency with which such demands have been pressed and the degree to which they have been satisfied, casual observation suggests that they have been pressed with great frequency and quite substantial success—varying with the effectiveness of neighborhood mobilization and the local strength of environmental forces.

Measures to assign existing with-flow lanes on expressways and
arterial streets for high occupancy vehicle (HOV) use remain, however, at the highly controversial end of the traffic management
spectrum. These do not lend themselves to justification in terms of
the vital interests of abutting land users, and they suffer from a
lack of active constitutency support—HOV travelers being far less
prone than land users to mobilize politically.

The most notable effort thus far to reassign existing lanes for
exclusive HOV use was that of the ill-fated Los Angeles diamond
lanes. These were lanes, one in each direction, on the Santa Monica
Freeway, the most heavily traveled artery in the Los Angeles area.
On an experimental basis, state authorities in March 1976 set aside
the diamond lanes for exclusive use by buses and carpools with
three or more occupants during peak travel periods. The result in
the early weeks was severely intensified congestion for those
denied access to the HOV lanes. The storm of public protest and
media ridicule surrounding the experiment continued unabated
even as traffic conditions settled down and as the state claimed
that the diamond lanes were providing HOV users with substantial
time savings at no cost to other travelers. When, after five months,
a federal judge ruled that the project required a full-scale environmental impact statement, state officials, judging that the experiment had been a technical success but a political disaster, decided
to abandon it. The message was duly noted by transportation officials throughout the nation.

Such experiences, along with the availability of federal capital
assistance, help to explain why in recent years it has been politically more feasible in numerous urban areas to propose spending
decades and billions of dollars to develop new rail rapid-transit
systems than to spend several years and, at most, tens of millions
of dollars to develop bus rapid-transit systems using reserved lanes
on existing streets and highways. Altshuler made a statement
along these lines during a speech at Georgia Tech in Atlanta several
years ago. As the discussion period got underway, the moderator
noted that one of the chief planners of Atlanta's rapid transit system was in the audience and asked him to comment on how, if at
all, this generalization applied to the Atlanta case. (Atlanta ranked

twenty-fifth in density among the nation's thirty largest urbanized areas in 1970, lower than such regions as San Diego and Houston.)[6] The planner's reply was concise: "It fits the Atlanta case perfectly."[1]

3. *In the next broad category of acceptability are measures that entail significant public or private cost for the benefits they confer but in a manner that permits substantial diffusion and deferment of the blame.* Examples include certain automobile performance standard regulations, transit spending increases, and infrastructure spending decisions.

The case of auto performance standard regulation illustrates that placement in one category or another may be at least as much a matter of voter and official perception as of objective reality. Price increases for mandated hardware improvements may often be defended on the ground that they will be offset by lower vehicle lifetime costs or that they are mere replacements for increases that the manufacturers would otherwise impose to pay for cosmetic style changes. Even in cases where the costs of regulation are undeniably significant, however, they will normally show up in the marketplace years after enactment of the statutes generating them, appear as prices charged by the auto companies rather than as publicly imposed taxes, and be merged indistinguishably with all other elements of the private cost of car ownership. Thus elected officials who vote for such regulations may reasonably hope to enjoy immediate credit for supporting the merit objectives (such as clean air) toward which they are directed, to defer the cost issue until years later, and to deflect any voter resentment at that time toward the companies. In the meantime, of course, they can hope that the companies will manage to meet the standards

[1.] Altshuler had a similar experience in Washington, D.C., in 1963 during an early phase of planning for the D.C. Metro. In the course of research interviews with key officials, he noted that Washington was famed for its wide, straight streets and asked if a busway system on them was receiving consideration. All replied that such a removal of general-purpose lane capacity from the street system would be unthinkable. The D.C. Metro now seems likely to cost at least $6 billion if completed and to become fully operational about two decades after the interviews just cited. Unlike Atlanta, the D.C. area is characterized by relatively high density—it ranked eighth on this dimension among the thirty largest areas in 1970—and core area employment. The city core, however, is extensive rather than high rise, leading many observers to judge that it would probably be better served by a mix of express and local buses on reserved lanes than by a subway system with only a few lines and with stations a half-mile or so apart.

without raising prices and take comfort in the thought that if all other calculations go awry, they can vote for extensions as the deadlines for compliance approach.

Analogously local elected officials have sought quite successfully in recent years to deal with rising transit costs by securing increased state and federal assistance. (From 1973 to 1975, for example, as the nationwide transit operating deficit rose by 130 percent, the local operating subsidy increased by only 66 percent. The combined federal-state contribution rose in the same period by 281 percent.)[7] Their success has been facilitated by the fact that federal taxes at constant rates (and particularly during periods of inflation) yield revenue growth more rapid than national income growth and by the growing public acceptance of federal budget deficits. Combined, these factors have enabled Congress to vote vastly increased benefits in recent years without having to face the unpleasantness of votes for new taxes.

Even at the state and local levels, it has frequently been possible to defer tax decisions until several years (and at least one election) after voting benefits. Individual legislators may hope, moreover, to have the luxury of voting for the benefits but against the subsequent tax increases. Or they may judge that periodic tax bills will have to be enacted in any event and that the contribution of any particular vote for transit benefits to the magnitude of the required tax increases will have little or no impact on the political penalty to be paid. (This line of reasoning becomes gradually less compelling as the transit share of the overall budget in any jurisdiction increases. It was highly persuasive in most jurisdictions during the late 1960s and early 1970s, however, when the transit share was miniscule.) Finally legislative leaders have numerous means at their disposal to blur tax votes so as to confuse constituents with a taste for judging their representatives on the basis of roll call records. In Massachusetts, for example, a $400 million tax increase, the largest in the state's history, was enacted in 1975 as part of an omnibus bill including the state budget. Legislators could maintain that they had to vote for the omnibus bill in order to avoid an interruption in popular spending programs (distributing more than $3 billion in benefits) even though they disliked the tax provisions. In the state senate, moreover, the omnibus bill was enacted without a roll call vote. Senators were first permitted to speak against the tax provisions and indeed to vote overwhelmingly against them in a roll call. Then, on "reconsideration," they adopted the bill by voice vote. In short, though the tax package passed handily, most Senators were clearly on record against it.

Infrastructure investments have long been popular at the state and local levels in large part because their costs can be diffused over long periods of time by bonding and over large geographic areas by the use of federal aid.[2] Combined, bonding and federal aid frequently make it possible to undertake capital projects while having to face the immediate prospect of funding only 1 or 2 percent of the total cost per year. At the same time those responsible can take 100 percent of the credit right away for providing the jobs, contracts, and user benefits associated with the projects.

Despite these attractions, urban transportation infrastructure investments have lost a good deal of their glamor in recent years as attention has shifted from their user benefits to their nonuser costs. In the case of urban expressways, the most salient nonuser costs are social and environmental. Major investments in fixed guideway transit entail much less disruption, but they leave permanent and (on the evidence of recent experience) rapidly growing commitments to the support of operating deficits in their wake. Even they often stir intense neighborhood opposition, moreover, because of the traffic and development pressures they attract to the vicinity of stations. Finally transit is most acceptable when it is out of sight, but the prohibitive cost of below-ground construction tends to be unacceptable in all but the most densely developed locations.

Because infrastructure investments generate jobs, contracts, and highly visible evidence that the governmental process does yield some tangible products for the taxpayers' money, they are not about to go entirely out of style. Decision makers are especially prone in the current period, however, to ask whether they can be

[2.] Until the enactment of formula transit assistance, available for either capital or operating purposes, in 1974, federal aid for urban transportation had always been available exclusively for capital investment purposes.

implemented without community and environmental disruption and whether they can be financed predominantly with aid from higher levels of government.[8] Typically the question of whether the projects will efficiently serve to alleviate priority problems is treated far more casually.

4. *The least acceptable innovations are those that entail substantial costs or interference with established patterns of behavior, imposed in such a manner that the blame will fall clearly and inescapably upon the public officials who adopt the innovation.* Even within this category it is important to distinguish among innovations on the basis of the degree to which blame is truly inescapable by the responsible officials, the intensity of public support for the objective, the degree of public understanding and acceptance of the method as an efficacious means of serving the objective, and the extent to which the established patterns that would be affected are entrenched in law or formal contractual agreements. A few examples may serve to illustrate these distinctions.

Market constraint strategies to reduce vehicle miles of auto travel generally entail clear responsibility for the inconvenience and/or cost visited upon the public. A decision to raise the gas tax, to restrict parking availability, to impose a parking surcharge, or to curtail gasoline supply calls forth protest as clearly focused upon the responsible decision makers as political blame ever is. By contrast, efforts to restrain auto travel by improving mass transit service, though relatively ineffective, are far more attractive politically because those affected in the first instance (transit users and employees, contractors, downtown merchants) are appreciative, and the only negative feature is the prospect of future tax increases. The transit spending vote may occur at a time when it is uncertain whether new taxes will be needed; and even if the spending increases do eventually necessitate tax increases, the latter are likely to occur a good deal later and in the context of much larger taxation decisions.

Public support is generally far more intense and consensual for objectives that entail the preservation of life, health, and/or current patterns of behavior than for those that simply entail improved amenity or prosperity. Thus the public will accept major tax increases and the rationing of key commodities in the midst of a popular war (such as World War II), and it will accept some cost and inconvenience in peacetime to deal with a clear and immediate danger (such as airplane hijacking). As threats are perceived more diffusely or as low statistical probabilities for each individual, however, resistance to inconvenience appears to grow very rapidly. Thus the ignition interlock system, mandated by the U.S. Department of Transportation for all cars produced after September 1, 1973, provoked widespread voter outrage as an infringement upon personal liberty. The result was a congressional override of this regulation in October 1974. Similarly Congress prohibited the department in 1976 from requiring states to mandate helmet use by motorcyclists. And EPA's proposals in 1973 and 1974 to restrain motor vehicle travel in selected metropolitan areas so as to achieve congressionally mandated air quality improvements met a similar fate.

As one seeks to recall peacetime public actions that have threatened direct interference with established patterns of individual travel behavior and that have actually been implemented, only one of significance comes to mind: the imposition by federal statute in 1974 of the national 55 mph maximum speed limit. It was adopted at the height of the Arab oil embargo, in response to widespread calls upon Congress for vigorous conservation action and widespread fear that major changes in American travel behavior would soon prove necessary.[3] Among the numerous conservation proposals considered during the embargo, the speed limit reduction was surely the mildest. It left most automobile travel, which already occurred at speeds lower than 55, unaffected, and it entailed only minor delays for other travelers except on long trips. In return for this inconvenience the reduced speed limit offered the individual traveler dollar savings (at a time when consciousness of gasoline cost was unusually high because prices had just risen

[3.] Nor was this entirely a peacetime measure. The oil embargo was an act of economic warfare, embarked upon by the Arab oil-producing nations while a Middle Eastern war was in progress for the express purpose of compelling world support for one side in that war. As the United States was the leading diplomatic supporter and military supplier of the non-Arab side, a central issue for many American opinion leaders was the capacity of the United States to remain an autonomous actor in world affairs.

sharply), improved safety, and a sense of patriotic action. This action also fit comfortably within the framework of a traditional government responsibility—for the establishment and enforcement of speed limits on public highways.

The enactment of the speed limit entailed two significant innovative features: it was a national rather than a state measure, and its primary purpose was other than for safety. The speed limit soon proved to have major safety advantages, however; it appears to have been the primary cause of a 17 percent reduction in traffic fatalities that occurred in the first year following its adoption— this despite the fact that most driving has always occurred at lower speeds than 55 and that enforcement of the new limit was quite spotty. (Indeed spotty enforcement may have contributed significantly to the lack of protest against permanent adoption of the 55 mph limit a year after the end of the embargo. Those who disliked it sufficiently could, in most of the country, ignore it with relatively little risk of being ticketed.)

The most surprising thing about this episode, it may be argued, is that the 55 mph speed limit had to await the oil embargo. Why had traffic safety officials and professional associations failed to alert the nation previously to the possible benefits of lower expressway speed limits or to campaign for their adoption? The reason, it appears, is that they deemed it unfeasible to enforce speed limits below those self-imposed by at least 85 percent of drivers on their own. The conventional wisdom (incorporated in the official handbook of the Institute of Traffic Engineers) was that lower speed limits would merely lead to widespread violation, generate disrespect for traffic regulations generally, and overwhelm the enforcement process.[9] In consequence speed limit determination was viewed as an exercise aimed at standardizing normal driving practice rather than maximizing safety—or even at achieving some explicit balance between normal and optimally safe driving practice. Good enforcement practice, in turn, was viewed as that which focused on the lunatic fringe of violators. These judgments on the part of traffic management officials, continue to prevail in the establishment of other limits than expressway maxima today, and public discussion of the criteria that should guide speed limit determination on lesser facilities is as lacking today as prior to the embargo.

The adoption of the 55 mph limit, however, serves as a useful reminder that public resistance to measures that interfere with established patterns of behavior varies in strength. It tends to be weakest when a crisis has shaken public expectations and generated intense pressure upon public officials to find and adopt solutions. In the presence of such an "action mood," when events seem frighteningly out of control, strong measures that would otherwise be rejected out of hand may successfully be justified as essential to the avoidance of even less pleasant alternatives. Change, in short, may be presented as the necessary path to preservation, and action may entail less risk for elected officials than passivity.

Even when crisis conditions have greatly weakened resistance to measures that entail interference with established travel behavior, and an action mood has clearly been established, the political system tends to seek out those measures that entail the lowest risk of voter backlash. Measures will tend to be more acceptable as the restraints they impose seem relatively trivial, as they fit comfortably within existing areas of public jurisdiction, as their efficacy has been established beyond controversy, and as they are inexpensive.

Further, these characteristics of potential measures frequently interact in dynamic fashion. If, for example, a measure entails behavioral change that is widely perceived to be difficult or unpleasant, public resistance to believing that it is efficacious may be all but impossible to overcome. The ignition interlock system again provides an excellent example. The public, finding it highly unpleasant, fastened upon every argument that might discredit it— such as the large numbers of automobile owners who had found ways of disconnecting it. Those who noted that seat belt use in cars with the interlock system averaged much higher than in cars without it and that it would very likely save thousands of lives a year were quickly overwhelmed. The impression became widespread that it had been a useless as well as unpopular measure, a classic case of bureaucratic bungling.

Finally, measures that threaten established behavior patterns

tend to be least feasible where the existing arrangements are entrenched in law, long-standing regulations, or formal contracts. It
is often maintained, for example, that the taxi industry could
serve the public more effectively if current restrictions on the number of licensed taxis were removed.[10] Because these restrictions
are typically rooted in local ordinances and regulatory practices
dating back several decades, however, the opportunities for current
license holders to resist change are far greater than they would be
if the existing pattern of competition were simply rooted in
custom and past economic forces. In many localities, the government-imposed scarcity of licenses has conferred substantial market
value on those that are outstanding—which are bought, sold, and
even mortgaged like other tangible business assets. Thus deregulation is viewed as a form of property taking, calling for public compensation at fair market value no less than the taking of a home or
factory. The longer that present limits have prevailed and the
higher the capital values that have accrued, the more persuasive
the arguments of current permit holders sound to regulatory and
political authorities and the more likely these arguments are to
find protection even in the courts.

Similarly proposals for transit innovation are frequently premised on the assumption that current work rules, union jurisdictions, and patterns of labor compensation can be modified. Again,
however, these practices are rooted in much more than custom.
They have been incorporated into formal labor-management contracts and frequently into public laws and regulations as well. The
result, in nearly all cases, is that change can come about only by
formal agreement between labor and management. Such agreement is frequently possible, but invariably at much higher cost
than the innovators originally anticipated.[11]

Conclusion

In light of the foregoing discussion, that is little reason for surprise
that it has proven much more feasible over the past several decades
to increase public spending programs (for highways in the 1950s
and early 1960s, for transit more recently) than to shape the

market framework within which consumers make their travel decisions. Nor does it seem remarkable that as policy has begun to move beyond conventional highway and transit spending in recent years, the most feasible innovations have been those entailing the provision of new or improved services, to be used or not on a purely voluntary basis; traffic management improvements intended for the benefit of all highway users equally or, if discriminatory in favor of high occupancy vehicles, designed to avoid any degradation of service for other motorists; and regulatory measures directing the auto manufacturers to produce more energy efficient, safer, less polluting cars. By contrast, measures entailing the direct regulation of consumer behavior or the imposition of selective price increases to influence consumer behavior have remained outside the realm of political acceptability.

These findings illustrate our central contention that in striving to reconcile the conservative characteristics of the American governmental system with their sensitivity to the radical nature of modern reality, American politicians are drawn inexorably to technical and service innovations as potential means of satisfying new public demands with minimal disruption to existing social arrangements and behavior patterns. Where innovations with these characteristics are unavailable to do the job, the system often appears woefully ineffective. Where they are available, it is able to act with impressive vigor—even if typically in fits and starts and at times with little respect for technical constraints.

II   THE PROBLEMS

We sought in part I to identify the main political factors that have shaped (or permitted to be shaped) the American system of urban transportation and that currently influence public choice among innovations proposed to alter it. In part II our focus will be on the substantive issues in urban transportation policy debate. Specifically we shall appraise the available evidence and endeavor to clarify thought about the substantive criteria most frequently utilized to evaluate urban transportation options, and indeed the system of urban transportation itself; the nature and significance of the main alleged problems of urban transportation; the remedial targets that have in fact been adopted as elements of national policy and the potential cost-effectiveness of leading innovative options.

This chapter will review the main criteria that are frequently mentioned as relevant to evaluation of the urban transportation system and efforts to alter it. Those with respect to which current system performance is widely viewed as deficient we shall label the problem criteria or, more simply, the problems of urban transportation. In so labeling them, we do not mean to imply that they are consensually viewed as problems. There is some controversy, for example, about whether current levels of traffic congestion ought to be viewed as a significant problem. And there is particularly intense disagreement about whether contemporary land use configurations and trends add up to a problem. In each case many people perceive the existence of a serious problem, however, and thus we have classified it as such for the purposes of discussion. Each of the remaining six chapters of part II will focus on one of these problems of urban transportation, with particular reference to the current state of knowledge and controversy with respect to its nature (that is, its causes and identifying symptoms, future prospects in the absence of innovative public action, and consequences for human welfare); the targets for remediation (goals) that have been established by federal law or regulation; and available evidence on the remedial cost-effectiveness of the policy options under review.

Perspectives

People experience the urban transportation system from a wide variety of role perspectives: as users and nonusers, as taxpayers and beneficiaries of subsidies, as recipients of construction contracts, and as residents dislocated from their homes. We shall strive to portray the most significant ways in which the system's characteristics tend to differ as it is experienced from different vantage points. Similarly, in appraising potential innovations, we shall endeavor to distinguish the effects felt by people in different circumstances and responding in different ways. For example, congestion pricing would tend to divert some current auto users to different origin-destination patterns, to provide those who continued to drive in the affected zones with improved mobility (due to reduced congestion) but at increased dollar cost, and to provide bus patrons passing through the affected zones with time savings, possibly even at lower dollar cost (due to increased driver and vehicle productivities).

Although we deem it essential to keep the variety of urban transportation experience clearly in view, we have found it equally essential to organize our discussion around a particular assumed vantage point. We have chosen that of the private automobile user. Our reason is not that we favor auto user interests over those of other urban residents; it is, rather, that the predominant experience most people have of the system is as automobile users and that its most frequently remarked aggregate consequences (such as high energy use and urban sprawl) are products most notably of automobile dominance. Thus we shall label the system a success with respect to such criteria as speed, comfort, and reliability. It is not notably successful, of course, in providing these values to urban residents who lack regular access to automobiles. Because theirs is a minority problem, however, we label it one of equity rather than of general system failure to provide urban residents with adequate experiences of travel speed, comfort, and reliability. To say that we have organized our discussion around the most common perspective on the system is by no means to suggest that we shall deemphasize the experiences of those in significant minority roles, such as transit users and those who do not manage to travel much by any mode. We shall in fact strive for equal clarity about majority and significant minority experiences. But it is to recognize that the choice of organizing perspective is a critical one, and to encourage readers to think about how alternative choices might have influenced the analysis.

Evaluation Criteria

We have identified nineteen criteria that are frequently mentioned as bases for evaluating the current system of urban transportation and strategies for improving it. All are "transportation" criteria as defined in chapter 2: that is, they entail aspects of personal mobility or external effects directly related to the functioning of the urban transportation system. They do not include such "pork barrel" criteria as the number of jobs generated by transportation investment expenditures. Although the latter are often of great political importance, we have not found them cited anywhere as bases for evaluating the urban transportation system itself. Nor, we judge, do they have much legitimate bearing on the evaluation of policy options. The inclusion of pork barrel effects as benefits normally involves double counting; it will amost always lead to the conclusion that public expenditures should be increased—since, by definition, they yield their worth in jobs and contracts, in addition to whatever other benefits they produce. This is, of course, a recipe for public make-work.[1]

We have arranged the nineteen criteria into three categories:

1. Those with reference to which current system performance is viewed by many people as a serious problem calling for public remedial action:

[1.] The logical fallacy is a simple one. Public expenditures entail transfers of money from the private sector. Thus their stimulative effect is precisely balanced by an antistimulative effect on the private sector. Similarly, federal aid entails transfers among geographic areas. Thus while it may make sense for a local politician to pursue an economic stimulus in the form of federal aid, the price of this stimulus is typically a depressant of equal total magnitude spread over all the jurisdictions from which the money has been taken.

It is true, of course, that aggregate economic activity may be depressed by inadequate expenditures. The need is not specifically for public expenditures in such cases, however. Economic activity can be expanded by reducing taxes (not to mention other techniques for stimulating the private sector) as well as—and, in general, quite a bit more rapidly than—by public works spending. The one careful study that we know bearing directly on this point concluded that, for any given dollar amount, tax relief would generate 7 percent more jobs (while absorbing 23 percent less energy) than highway construction.[1]

Energy consumption
Air quality
Equity
Safety
Congestion
Land use impact
Noise

2. Those with respect to which system performance in the steady state tends to be accepted grudgingly, but that frequently become major focuses of controversy when potential improvement actions threaten to generate significant increases in their magnitude:

Public dollar costs
User dollar costs other than tax payments
Neighborhood and environmental disruption incidental to public works activity

3. Those with respect to which current system performance is generally considered good, or at least sufficiently adequate as to be low-priority justifications for new public initiatives:

Reliability
Speed
Convenience
Flexibility
Personal security
Comfort
Consumer freedom
Privacy
Recreation

A full chapter will be devoted to each of the criteria in the first category, with one exception: noise. It will be treated more briefly because even though it is widely agreed to be a problem, it has commanded little attention in urban transportation policy debates. As we discuss innovations that might improve system performance with reference to the "problem" criteria, we shall also consider their most significant consequences for the criteria in the two other categories. It is important to know, for example, whether an innovation that promises improved air quality (category 1) would raise the dollar cost of travel to consumers (category 2) or significantly constrain their freedom of choice (category 3).

Category 1: The Problem Criteria

Current system deficiencies with respect to the criteria in this category are what people generally have in mind when they speak of "the urban transportation problem." There is far greater consensus on the nature and significance of some of these deficiencies than others, of course. On the whole, however, major policy initiatives in urban transportation tend to focus on ameliorating these perceived deficiencies.

Energy Consumption

Never a significant policy criterion prior to the 1973–1974 Arab oil embargo, this has since commanded greater attention in urban transportation policy debates than any other. Alone among the criteria by which the system is evaluated, it is thoroughly intertwined with issues of national security and international economic policy. It is typically measured in terms of barrel of oil equivalents utilized for all urban travel purposes combined or per passenger mile of travel. The former, more comprehensive, formulation has the advantage of giving credit for innovations that reduce the demand for travel. The latter is more useful in analyzing the amount of energy required to serve any given level of travel demand by alternative modes.

Air Quality

This is also a relatively new theme in public discussions of urban transportation, having moved into the front rank among official policy priorities with enactment of the 1970 Clean Air Act Amendments. Despite more recent policy retreats, as the costs of meeting the original Clean Air Act deadlines have become apparent, the objective of improving air quality remains among the highest priority and most consensual in the field of urban transportation.

Air quality is measured with reference to the ambient level of pollutants in the atmosphere. Although there is significant room for dispute about which pollutants should be included within the definition and about how they should be weighted in seeking to arrive at a single measure of air quality, public attention and federal policy have to date focused on six: carbon monoxide (CO), hydrocarbons (HC), nitrogen oxides (NO_x), lead, sulfur dioxide (SO_2), and particulates. Mobile transportation sources are insignificant as emission sources of SO_2 and particulates. Thus discussions of air quality with reference to urban transportation normally focus on the remaining four. HC and NO_x combine under specific conditions of sunlight and warmth to create photochemical smog, which is in turn a more serious problem than either component alone.

Equity

A philosophic concept denoting fairness and justice, the equity criterion tends to resist consensual definition or precise measurement. There has been a growing sense since the mid-1960s, however, that the American system of urban transportation entails more inequality than it should. Providing unparalleled mobility for those with ready access to motor vehicles, the system provides poorer service to those who lack such access than it did thirty, fifty, or seventy years ago. Such widening inequality is unusual in modern American society, and it gives a special flavor to discussions of equity in the context of urban transportation policy. Key groups on whose behalf equity claims (for improved services and increased subsidies) have been pressed in recent years include the handicapped, the elderly, the poor, those too young to drive, and transit users generally.

Safety

Long an explicit and consensual policy priority, safety was until the mid-1960s addressed by government solely in the enforcement of traffic laws and the design of highways. Since then, however, a substantially more activist climate has emerged. Congress has moved vigorously to regulate motor vehicle safety, to accelerate the development of improved safety technology, and to increase the emphasis on safety in highway design and investment allocation.

The primary measure of safety is the fatality rate per hundred million passenger miles of travel. Secondary measures, with respect to which data are far less reliable, include nonfatal accident rates, days lost from work due to accidents, and rates of economic (dollar) loss due to accidents.

Congestion

The concept of congestion refers to the symptoms of facility overcrowding. It can be measured in terms of frequency, duration, and/or intensity. As experienced during peak hours on highways, the most significant consequence of congestion is user delay (often the more exasperating because highly variable from day to day). For business users, it entails direct monetary costs as well. As experienced during peak periods on transit systems, congestion tends to entail personal discomfort rather than the more tangible forms of performance degradation. Indeed it may even be associated with higher performance in some respects, such as energy efficiency and cost per passenger mile.

The relief of existing highway congestion and the avoidance of projected future highway congestion were the highest priorities of federal, state, and local public policy in the field of urban transportation for many years. As other priorities have come to the fore since the mid-1960s, however, the degree of priority that congestion relief merits has come in for fresh, often highly skeptical scrutiny. Critics note that congestion tends to be associated with high land use densities and high transit usage and that congestion relief measures tend to undermine both of these values. They emphasize as well that efforts to relieve congestion by constructing additional highway capacity frequently entail significant environmental harm and community disruption. Congestion relief remains an important policy priority, however, because most people continue to find it an exasperating phenomenon. And those who use the highways for business continue to find it expensive. Public highway agencies continue to view congestion relief as one of their two or three highest priorities. And highway expenditures (capital and operational combined) continue to account for the lion's share of government spending for urban transportation purposes.[2]

Land Use Impact

The measure of this criterion is the effect of current or proposed transportation system characteristics upon the spatial distribution of urban activities. Such effects are difficult to measure, and in many circumstances there is intense disagreement about whether they exist at all. More significantly there is no consensus at the national, state, or regional levels on what urban form should be pursued. Critics of present land use and urban transportation policies generally favor vigorous measures to revitalize downtown areas and to increase urban densities more generally. Although central city officials have at times succeeded in obtaining grants-in-aid for revitalization (termed renewal in the 1950s and 1960s), these have not represented overall public commitments to the objective of high density. They have rather been minor elements in the overall mix of urban distributive policies, each designed to satisfy particular constituencies but not at the obvious expense of any others. For every dollar spent to promote downtown revitalization, at least several have been spent in ways conducive to urban sprawl.

Noise

In recognition that given sounds may simultaneously please some listeners and annoy others, noise is commonly defined as undesired sound. As such, it is unusually complicated to measure, but its extreme manifestations have long been subject to state and local regulation as nuisances. With enactment of the Noise Control Act of 1972, noise regulation became a federal priority as well, and the focus of regulation expanded from requiring the prompt replacement of worn-out engine mufflers by motor vehicle users to requiring that the manufacturers equip new vehicles with improved muffling systems. To date, however, noise control policy has

[2.] Table 2.1 and appendix B indicate that urban highway expenditures by all levels of government totalled $10.3 billion in 1975 and that mass transit expenditures (excluding those costs covered by transit fares, which we have counted as private consumer expenditures) totaled $3.7 billion.

remained low key. Few have maintained that the aim of hastening progress in motor vehicle noise reduction is of such priority as to warrant the imposition by government of large dollar costs or significant behavioral constraints on urban travelers. (For additional detail, see appendix D.)

Category 2: Other Key Evaluation Criteria

Steady state performance of the urban transportation system with respect to the criteria in this category tends to be perceived in relatively neutral terms as neither a basis for boasting of the success of the system nor a major target for remedial action. Impacts upon these criteria by change strategies proposed for other reasons are frequently perceived, however, as highly significant problems indeed. Consequently there is broad agreement that these criteria merit great weight in the evaluation of potential programs and projects—with the primary aim being to avert change in harmful directions rather than to alleviate existing deficiencies.

Public Dollar Cost and User Dollar Cost (Exclusive of Tax Payments)

Together, public and user dollar costs comprise total direct expenditures on urban transportation. They do not include indirect costs, however, such as those imposed on nonusers by the external effects of urban transportation activities, except as these have been internalized (for example, by insurance) as part of the urban transportation fiscal system.

Current levels of public and private cost, though widely viewed as high, are not substantial political issues. There is no expectation that costs can be reduced, though frequent efforts are made to shift particular items from the private into the public sector (for example, by reducing transit fares). Nor do increases that are in line with overall inflationary trends frequently become political issues. (The exceptions are invariably with reference to prices charged by government itself, such as transit fares and gasoline taxes.) If steady state costs are relatively noncontroversial, however, cost increases that substantially exceed the general rate of inflation (and/or that are imposed on private users by explicit political decision) have a high potential for igniting controversy. And the question of whether proposed new public activities will accelerate the rate of public and/or user cost inflation is invariably central to their appraisal.

Neighborhood and Environmental Disruption Incidental to Public Works Activity

This heading includes takings of homes, places of employment, public open space lands, and historic sites; harmful effects on the activities of residents, open space users, and businesses in the immediate vicinity of transportation arteries; and harmful effects on natural ecological systems.

Though some neighborhood and environmental groups believe that high priority should be given to reducing the neighborhood and environmental impacts associated with ongoing transportation activities and existing facilities, such positive improvement efforts have rarely been accorded high priority by governmental bodies. Two notable exceptions to this rule come to mind, but they do not rank as major transportation issues. First, there has been a good deal of recent agitation in many northern states for the reduction or elimination of road salting. The primary reason is that road salt drainage has been raising the sodium content of drinking water supplies, with potentially significant harmful effects on public health, particularly for those on low salt diets for medical reasons. This is a situation in which a long-standing practice has recently come to be recognized as a significant health hazard. Second, neighborhood groups have often mobilized in recent years to secure the adoption of traffic control measures reducing through traffic on their residential streets.

By contrast with the relatively low-key nature of debates about proposals for the amelioration of existing disruptive effects, passions generally run high when new projects are proposed that would entail major neighborhood and/or environmental disruption. In response to widespread criticism of interstate expressway construction projects during the 1960s, Congress enacted a spate of statutory provisions between 1966 and 1970 designed to reverse the perceived public bias toward locating facilities on alignments composed largely of public open spaces, to ensure that decisions to implement disruptive projects would be taken only after full and explicit consideration of the available alternatives, to provide property owners and tenants dislocated to make way for new facilities with full compensation for their indirect expenses as well as for their tangible property losses, and to ensure potentially affected citizens the right to participate in decision-making processes that might result in such disruption.[3] A great deal of similar state legislation followed within several years, affecting state and local projects undertaken without federal assistance. As background factors driving transportation agencies toward solutions that entail facility management and service improvements rather than major construction, the importance of these developments can hardly be overestimated.[3]

Category 3: The Success Criteria

The American system of urban transportation affords extraordinary mobility to most users while permitting them to live at the relatively low densities they seem to prefer, and it does so at costs that, though high, they seem quite willing to bear. By all historic and comparative standards, and from the standpoint of those with ready access to an automobile, the system is probably the best the world has known. The criteria in category 3 are those with reference to which it most clearly excels: from the standpoint of those with high levels of automobility, who constitute a large majority of the adult population.

Numerous studies have reported on the relative weights attached by urban travelers to the criteria in this category, primarily in order to explain and forecast levels of transit usage under varying circumstances. Their predominant conclusion has been that service

---

[3.] Key legislative landmarks include section 4(f) of the Department of Transportation Act of 1966, which dealt with takings of open space lands and historic sites; the National Environmental Policy Act of 1969, which established the requirement for environmental impact statements; and the Uniform Relocation and Real Property Acquisition Act of 1970, which established unprecedentedly generous principles of compensation for those dislocated by federal or federally aided programs.[2]

characteristic preferences are highly congruent among the varying socioeconomic groups within the American population. The desire for reliability, flexibility, travel time minimization, guaranteed seating, and personal security are essentially universal, though the precise weighting of each relative to the others varies among travelers.

The more significant differences among travelers are in their circumstances (as opposed to their preferences). Some can afford cars, others cannot. Some are able to drive, others are not. Some live and work near well-served transit routes, others do not. Some must face severe congestion if they choose to drive to work, others need not. Some have free parking at their workplace destinations, others do not. What seems clear, however, is that in general, at present, for the vast majority of trips, and with respect to the preferences of most users, the private automobile provides substantially better service than mass transit. The result is that those who are able to afford cars and to drive for the most part do so, and that even most households of modest means somehow manage to own and operate at least one car.

Michael Johnson recently surveyed 213 employed adults in the San Francisco area, all having home and work locations well suited to commutation by transit. He found that the most powerful explanatory variables with respect to mode choice were nonattitudinal: auto tolls and parking charges, household income (above or below $6,000), modal differences in travel time, and proportion of auto trip time in congested traffic conditions. Adding attitudinal factors to a mode choice model compiled on the basis of these nonattitudinal variables added no explanatory power whatever.[4] Similarly in a recent survey of 471 travelers, David Hartgen of the New York State Department of Transportation found that affluence and car ownership accounted for 80 to 90 percent of the variance in mode choice. All other factors combined accounted for only 10 to 20 percent.[5]

As their affluence has increased since World War II, Americans have opted overwhelmingly for lower-density living and for automobile travel. In 1975, 35 passenger miles were traveled by automobile in urban America for every mile traveled by mass transit (see table 2.2). Although numerous factors have contributed to the evolution of this remarkable degree of automobile dominance, the overriding causes have certainly been the high values that most Americans place on low-density residential alternatives and on the service criteria listed below.

Reliability

The basic measure of reliability is the predictability of arrival time. Numerous studies have found that this is one of the very few most significant criteria influencing modal choice, yet a recent survey of transit travel forecasting methods found that it was not among the thirteen variables frequently utilized by transportation planning agencies.[6] A market survey of potential demand for dial-a-ride carried out by H. J. Bauer of General Motors found the variable "arriving at destination when planned" to be the single service attribute weighted most heavily by respondents. (The survey involved 1,100 home interviews in a single medium-sized American city with 200,000 population.)[7] Martin Wachs, having reviewed the literature on consumer attitudes toward transit service, recently summed up as follows: "Attitudinal studies show repeatedly that perceptions of travel time depend upon travel time reliability as well as elapsed travel time. Arriving on time at an intended destination is often seen by travelers as more important than minimizing elapsed travel time in both work and nonwork trips."[8] Reid Ewing, in a review of surveys bearing specifically upon demand responsive transit services, arrived at the same conclusion.[9] Travelers assign greater weight to reliability in choosing their travel modes for work than for nonwork trips, but it ranks at or near the top of the list of user concerns with reference to all trip types.

Speed

The basic measure of speed is door-to-door travel time. It has long been axiomatic among travel analysts, and it has been confirmed by innumerable surveys of both attitudes and actual travel behavior, that travelers value time and will pay to save it. Estimating the precise values that commuters place on time in selecting their travel modes and routes was one of the main transportation priori-

ties of the 1960s—because travel time savings were the main benefits relied upon to demonstrate that interstate expressway (and,
more recently, transit) investments were justified. The leading
studies all sought to relate the value of potential travel time
savings to respondent levels of compensation at work. Those conducted in the United States and England produced estimates of
the average value of commuter time ranging from 20 to 61 percent of mean hourly income.[10] A commonly accepted standard by the end of the decade was that commuters value travel
time at one-third to two-thirds of their hourly rates of income.
The studies also showed wide variations in travel time values
among income groups and trip types, however. Notably those with
lower incomes tended to value their time at higher proportions of
their wage rates (though at lower absolute levels) than more affluent commuters, and people at all income levels tended to value
time savings more on longer trips.[11]

Much less attention has been devoted to determining the values
that people place on time devoted to nonwork travel. This is a
particularly important subject since 73 percent of urban person
trips as of 1970 were for other than commutation purposes.[12]
It is also a particularly difficult one since a high proportion of
travelers have no wage rate and since many noncommutation trips
have a substantial recreational component. On the assumption that
new urban facilities are required primarily to serve peak period
commutation demands, however, urban transportation planners
have typically assigned values to time savings for all travelers on
the basis of averages derived from studies of commuters. This practice has dovetailed nicely with agency desires to secure approval
for expensive capital projects.

Given that travelers value time in rough proportion to their
wage rates, it follows that low-income people will accept substantially greater time penalties than the more affluent in order to conserve money. Numerous studies have also shown that consumers
value off-vehicle travel time (access, waiting, transfer) two to three
times as highly as on-board time.[13] Once on board, presumably,
a traveler is protected from the elements and can relax to some
degree.

While noting that travel time variables are the most frequent and significant bases of transit demand forecasting efforts, Wachs concluded in his review of the literature on consumer attitudes that if anything they should be weighted even more heavily. Specifically he judged that consumer aversion to walking, waiting, and transferring appears to be greater than most forecasters have assumed, and he endorsed a proposal (by Peter Watson) that a new measure called the *journey unit* should be utilized in estimating the impact of out-of-vehicle time on modal choice. Thus journeys would be measured in terms of numbers of units as well as elapsed time. A typical transit trip might consist of access, waiting, transfer, riding, and distribution units. Citing a study by Gerald Brown, Wachs suggested that there may be threshold effects, with journey units taking fewer than two to four minutes not being perceived as significant by most travelers.[14] These suggestions strike us as highly plausible, with the qualification that travelers are bound to consider substantial numbers of two-to-four-minute journey units on a single trip significant, even if they tend to ignore a couple of them. (Notably even trips by automobile require brief access and distribution units on foot; since these are viewed as the irreducible minimum, travelers may well ignore them as encountered on other modes.)

Studies that weight travel time by its various components—usually weighting off-vehicle travel time at about 2.5 times the value of on-board time—generally conclude that the automobile advantage over transit with respect to trips actually made by both modes tends to be a factor of between two and three. That is, trips that are in fact made by transit take two to three times as long (weighted time), on average as the same trips by automobile.[4] Pre-

4. Michael Johnson, in his survey of the San Francisco Bay Area commuters, selected only those whose home and work locations were such as to make transit a likely possibility. The Bay Area has extremely good transit service, and the trips sampled were predominately made during the peak hours (when transit is most competitive). Nonetheless average work trip travel times for the study sample were fifty-four minutes (unweighted) by transit, twenty-five minutes by car.[15]

In a study of sixteen demand responsive transit (DRT) systems, Reid Ewing found a median ratio of DRT to auto on-board travel times of 2.1. Counting wait as well as ride times, the median ratio was 5.9.[16] (As DRT patrons normally wait indoors and frequently at home, they presumably find waiting less onerous than do fixed-route transit patrons. No estimates more precise than this of their wait versus ride time perceptions are available, however.)

sumably the automobile advantage throughout urban America is far greater because transit trips are concentrated on the routes where (and at the times when) transit service can compete most favorably.

Convenience and Flexibility

A mode is convenient to the extent that it is available when the user wishes to travel. It is flexible to the extent that it will take him wherever he wishes to go in the region and to the extent that it permits intermediate stopovers in the course of making longer trips.

Among the greatest advantages of the private automobile are that it provides optimal convenience and flexibility (except as it may break down from time to time, as it may have to be shared among the members of a household, or as it may be difficult to park at congested locations). Conventional transit provides frequent (that is, convenient) service during peak periods on specific heavily traveled corridors, but it tends to be extremely constrained in areal coverage. Private carpooling offers good areal coverage but tends to be temporally inflexible (that is, inconvenient for trips that occur at irregular times) and awkward in accommodating intermediate trip purposes. Demand responsive transit typically offers complete areal coverage within a specified service area, but this (except in very small regions) is normally much smaller than the urbanized area. Demand responsive transit systems vary widely in convenience; some offer pickup within five to fifteen minutes after phone requests are made,[5] others require up to twenty-four hours advance notice.

In his review of numerous surveys bearing on the demand for dial-a-ride service, Reid Ewing concluded that convenience, as represented in the surveys to mean choice of pickup time and transfer-free service, ranked second (in an approximate tie with speed) among all service characteristics in importance to patrons. (Reliability ranked first.)[18]

[5.] In Ewing's sample of sixteen DRT systems offering immediate (as opposed to pre-scheduled) service, five claimed wait times of five to fifteen minutes. The other eleven reported average wait times ranging from twenty to thirty-nine minutes.[17]

Despite their obvious importance, convenience and flexibility rarely receive explicit attention in modal choice analyses. The reason, presumably, is that everyone takes for granted that transit competitiveness begins with the provision of relatively frequent service along routes that large numbers of people regularly travel. The greatest limitation of conventional transit service, however, is that only a small proportion of the trips that people actually make in contemporary urban America have both origins and destinations along such routes.

Personal Security

The term here refers to the risk that one will become a victim of crime. Though neglected in virtually all conventional modal split analyses, perceptions of the risk of crime victimization are clearly of great importance to urban travelers. Wachs reports, in his survey of the literature on consumer attitudes, that most travelers seem to assume that the risk of crime victimization is negligible. When asked explicitly about this criterion, however, they rank it extremely high.[19]

The automobile has the great advantage that it can serve as a mobile personal fortress. Trips from middle-class neighborhoods to inner-city employment locations in urban America frequently pass through low-income, high-crime neighborhoods. With reference to the criterion of equity, it is important that transit lines provide good service to these neighborhoods while traversing them. With reference to the criterion of personal security, however, and particularly of perceived personal security, the situation is quite the contrary. Though rigorous studies are lacking, most transit officials believe that the residents of middle- and high-income neighborhoods are hesitant to patronize lines providing intermediate service to low-income areas. This hesitancy seems most likely to be translated into transit avoidance by certain categories of travelers (the elderly, women), during certain periods (off-peak, especially evening), for certain types of trips (noncommutation), and where good highway options exist to facilitate high speed travel by automobile through or around the low-income districts.

If there is some perceived risk with reference to on-board travel in high crime areas, there is even greater risk associated with access, waiting, and distribution. Potential advantages of the paratransit modes include their capacity to eliminate these features of transit travel or to require them only in configurations that few patrons will perceive as threatening (such as, transfers between demand responsive vehicles at rendezvous points). In some circumstances transit or paratransit travel may actually entail a higher degree of personal security than travel by private automobile. Where the required walk between a parking location and an ultimate origin or destination is threatening, and transit or paratransit provides a less forbidding alternative, the latter may achieve an advantage. Examples, particularly at night, might include travel to or from a downtown location near a heavily used transit station but several blocks through a run-down area from inexpensive parking and a location eligible for doorstep pickup by demand responsive transit or vanpool but some distance from available parking.

In general, however, it seems reasonable to view personal security as a criterion with major threshold effects. The transit and paratransit need is not to improve upon the automobile, which provides excellent security in the vast majority of urban travel situations, but to overcome at least some of the current perceived transit disadvantage (particularly outside of peak periods) with respect to this criterion. The potential of paratransit to eliminate the lonely walking and waiting elements associated with much transit travel may prove to be of considerable significance in this regard.

Comfort

This criterion embraces a number of specific aspects of amenity, but one of these appears to outweigh all the others by far for most travelers: assurance of obtaining a seat. Secondarily climate control may become significant when threshold tolerances are violated. Most people do not demand perfect climate control on local trips, but neither will they spend long periods waiting in extremely cold, inclement, or hot weather, or riding in vehicles that are sweltering or freezing, if they can avoid it.

Surprisingly little information is available on the significance of comfort variables. What little there is however, supports the view that guaranteed seating and avoidance of extreme discomfort are the key considerations for most urban travelers, rather than any aspiration for all the comforts of home (which are, to be sure, available in some automobiles). The General Motors survey found "assurance of getting a seat" and "more protection from the weather" to be the second and fifth most heavily weighted variables by respondents. By contrast "no crowding on vehicle" ranked fifteenth, and such variables as availability of coffee and stylish vehicle exteriors were considered of virtually no importance at all.[20] Wachs concluded that the only two comfort variables found to be significant in numerous studies were air conditioning and guaranteed seating. Other comfort features such as roominess, carpeting, large windows, and absence of advertising seemed to be of negligible significance.[21] On the basis of his review of surveys bearing on DRT demand, Ewing concluded that the only comfort variables consistently ranking high among the attributes valued by patrons were guaranteed seating and protection from the weather; these ranked very close to the top of the list in most cases, however.[22]

Consumer Freedom
The measure of this criterion is the extent to which producers and consumers of service are left free by government (as opposed to blind market forces) to act in accord with their own preferences. Subsidies of one mode or another are not infringements upon consumer freedom as we utilize the concept; they may enchance the attractiveness of preferred modes, but they do not reduce the attractiveness of unsubsidized modes in any absolute sense.[6] By contrast, measures to restrict the use of a mode by regulation or to price it beyond the capacity of some travelers to pay do fall within our conception of infringements upon consumer freedom. We believe that this definition accords with popular usage.

The American system of urban transportation provides an

[6.] They do indirectly entail constraint in the form of taxation, of course, but the taxes are almost never intended to (nor do they significantly in fact) influence travel choices, our concern here. More generally, we have provided in this schema for consideration of the tax effect under the rubric of public dollar costs.

unparalleled degree of consumer freedom, and this appears to be one of its most universally valued attributes. In recent years, however, numerous efforts have been made—in the name of such high-priority objectives as energy conservation, clean air, and safety—to secure the adoption of consumer regulatory and auto-disincentive pricing measures. The uproars provoked by these proposals and their unbroken record of rejection to date provide striking evidence of the weight implicitly accorded consumer freedom by American policy makers as they evaluate potential strategy options.

Privacy

The measure of this criterion is the ability to select one's own travel companions or, if one prefers, to travel alone. There is little reason to believe that privacy is a highly significant criterion in the selection of urban travel modes, except that many people do draw back from situations in which they feel compelled to socialize, as well as simply to travel with, people with whom they do not feel a high degree of rapport, or in which they must travel with people whom they perceive as having sharply different cultural characteristics from themselves. There is some evidence that carpooling suffers from the former aversion in some degree, and conventional transit from the other.

Perhaps because the automobile provides such a high degree of privacy, this criterion is frequently cited as one of the significant reasons why Americans prefer the auto to mass transit.[23] We have found no evidence, however, that many Americans place great weight on the value of privacy in urban travel.

Recreation

The measure of this criterion is the extent to which (if at all) the traveler achieves inherent satisfaction from the activity of trip making, quite aside from the satisfaction obtained from making progress toward a destination. One recent analyst contends that driving is a form of athletics for many Americans, involving the coordination of person and machine, offering a readily available form of satisfaction in performing well.[24] The Federal Highway Administration maintains that about 4 percent of highway travel is purely recreational in nature. Even ignoring the partial recreational value of many other trips, the agency finds that each acre of American highway provides four times as many person-hours of recreation per year as each acre of national park.[25]

Though it does seem apparent that many Americans enjoy driving, it is far less clear that this goes far toward explaining commutation behavior. Michael Johnson, in his survey of San Francisco Bay Area commuters, found that whereas 44 percent of his respondents said they enjoyed driving long distances with family or friends along as passengers (17 percent responded negatively to this experience), none said that they enjoyed driving on freeways in heavy traffic (versus 80 percent negative), and only 1 percent claimed to enjoy driving on downtown city streets during the daytime (versus 64 percent negative).[26] The responses to statements about driving in light freeway traffic and about driving through well-known suburban areas were substantially more favorable (19 percent positive, 10 percent negative in both cases) but hardly such as to suggest that the recreational value of driving is an important source of automobile dominance in urban commutation travel.

Those who prefer transit frequently claim among its significant advantages the fact that one can read on it (except when crowding is too great) rather than waste time and energy driving. When surveyed, many travelers do indeed cite this as an advantage of transit (53 percent of Johnson's sample, for instance) but no studies have found such responses to have any explanatory power with respect to actual mode choice decisions.[27] Despite this lack of statistical confirmation, it seems probable that at least a few people choose transit because they want to read, just as a few choose to drive primarily because they obtain pleasure from doing so and perhaps some choose carpools because they like to socialize. To the extent that existing modal choices are based on a distribution of varied but firm consumer recreational preferences, of course, publicly sponsored efforts to alter the existing choice mix are likely to encounter significantly more intense resistance than analyses of average preferences would lead one to predict.

Nature of the Problem

The massive fuel requirements of the American motor vehicle system burst on the national consciousness as a problem only with the Arab oil embargo of 1973–1974. Until then gasoline supplies had never been perceived as problematic, and prices had been declining in real terms throughout the motor age. Recent experience, moreover, tended to reinforce the predominant attitude of complacency. Between 1955 and 1970, the average real (inflation-adjusted) price of gasoline had fallen by 13 percent, and the price per thousand gallons of gasoline had declined from 6.6 percent of U.S. median income to 3.6 percent.[1] Understandably, then, little concern was evident prior to the embargo even about the fact that American cars were becoming less fuel efficient over time—as growing affluence enabled consumers to purchase larger cars with greater horsepower and with such accessories as air conditioning, automatic transmissions, power steering, and power brakes.

The oil embargo, of course, raised energy issues overnight to the top of the national policy agenda, where they seem certain to remain for decades to come. Choosing in 1977 to make enactment of a comprehensive energy program the main legislative objective of his first year in office, President Carter referred to the energy problem as "with the exception of preventing war, . . . the greatest challenge our nation will face during our lifetimes." Addressing it adequately, he maintained, would require "the moral equivalent of war," and failure to do so might result in "national catastrophe."[2]

Viewing public debate on energy issues since the oil embargo, four key points stand out. First, there is general agreement that the era of declining prices has ended and that relatively sharp increases will be experienced over the next several decades. Second, there is a broad consensus on the objectives of energy conservation and a reduced reliance on fuel imports. Third, there is wide disagreement about the cost, environmental risk, and public inconvenience that ought to be accepted in the pursuit of these objectives. Fourth, there is equally wide disagreement about whether, in the field of urban transportation, public policy ought to aim at more than improved automobile fuel economy—at, for example, fundamental shifts in travel behavior toward greater transit usage and more carpooling.

The Pattern of Consumption

The United States, with under 6 percent of world population, accounts for 30 percent of world energy consumption.[3] The magnitude of U.S. energy demand can be explained in part by the nation's high standard of living, but the United States also appears to be uniquely profligate in its energy consumption per unit of gross national product (GNP). Crude international comparisons suggest, for example, that GNP per capita in Sweden, Switzerland, and West Germany is roughly equivalent to that in the United States, but per capita energy consumption in these nations averages only about half the U.S. level.[4]

A more detailed study of West German energy consumption was carried out for the Federal Energy Administration in 1975.[5] Its authors, Richard L. Goen and Ronald K. White, concluded that in fact per-capita income in West Germany was only about 70 percent as great as in the United States. (Simple comparisons based on international exchange rates tended to overstate West German GNP because of the strength of the German mark in world money markets.) Even so, they found, German energy consumption per unit of national income was only two-thirds as great as in the United States. And the most striking disparities were in transportation.

On a sector-by-sector basis, German energy usage per capita was 61 percent as great as American for industrial purposes, 52 percent as great for commercial purposes, and only 27 percent as great for transportation purposes.[1] German energy usage for personal transportation purposes (excluding freight) was only about 20 percent as great as American. The main sources of the German advantage in personal transportation were as follows. Living at much higher

---

[1.] German energy usage per unit of GNP was 87 percent as great as American for industrial purposes, 74 percent as great for household and commercial purposes, and 39 percent as great for transportation purposes. None of the German advantage was attributable to climate. Indeed Goen and White found that West Germany averaged 30 percent more heating degree days than the United States. When corrected for the colder weather, German energy use for space heating purposes was only half as great as American.[6]

densities than those prevailing in the United States, West Germans traveled much less. Per-capita passenger mileage for all purposes in 1972 was only 47 percent of the American level.[7] When they did travel, West Germans relied less on the automobile. The auto share of overall passenger mileage (local and intercity combined) was 81 percent in West Germany versus 91 percent in the United States.[2] Thus per-capita auto passenger mileage in West Germany was only 42 percent of the U.S. level.

Finally, West Germans used much more-energy-efficient cars. Their fuel consumption per vehicle mile in 1972 was barely more than half the American level. Thus even if they had relied proportionately as much on the automobile as Americans (while continuing to travel 47 percent as much), their energy usage per capita for personal transportation purposes would have been less than one-quarter the U.S. level.

In the United States, transportation accounts directly (1976) for 26 percent of total energy consumption. Moreover since transportation runs almost entirely on oil, and oil provides just under half of all U.S. energy, direct transportation uses account for 53 percent of total U.S. oil consumption.[8] Indirect transportation uses—such as the refining of petroleum fuels consumed for transportation purposes, the operation of trucking facilities, motor vehicle manufacturing, and road construction—accounted for another 17 percent of U.S. energy consumption in the only recent year (1967) for which detailed input-output estimates have been made.[9] Automobiles account for about half of total energy consumption for transportation purposes. Thus auto travel accounts directly for about one-quarter of U.S. oil consumption. Counting indirect uses as well, auto travel accounts for about two-fifths of U.S. oil consumption.

About 58 percent of automobile vehicle mileage occurs in urban areas.[10] The urban share of automobile fuel consumption is in

[2.] Goen and White estimated that the mass transit share of overall passenger mileage was more than three times as great in Germany as in the United States and that the railroad share was more than twenty times as great. West Germans made significantly less use than Americans did of air transportation, but their energy consumption per air passenger mile was much higher than the U.S. level—presumably because average airline trips were much shorter.

the range of two-thirds, however, because vehicle fuel economy tends to be poor while engines are warming up and in conditions of stop-and-go traffic.[11]

The Oil Import Problem

The United States became a net importer of oil for the first time in 1947, but the reasons at that time had more to do with oil industry policy than need. Domestic excess capacity continued to exceed net imports until the mid-1960s.[12] Between 1965 and 1977 however, American excess capacity was brought fully into production, and net oil imports rose from 22 percent of U.S. consumption to 47 percent.[13] Domestic oil production peaked in 1972 and then declined by a total of 15 percent over the following four years. During the same period U.S. production of natural gas, which accounts for 27 percent of U.S. energy usage, fell by 12 percent.[14]

Between 1970 and 1977, primarily in consequence of rising oil prices but also because U.S. oil imports more than doubled, the nation's oil import bill rose from $2.4 billion to $44.7 billion.[15] If the economic consequences of this increase were short of disastrous, key reasons include the following. First, the oil-producing nations greatly increased their imports of American goods and services. In 1976 (the latest year for which complete data are available as this is written), U.S. exports to the thirteen members of the Organization of Petroleum Exporting Countries (OPEC) covered half the nation's oil import bill from them—$12.6 billion versus $25.0 billion.[3] [16] Second, the oil-producing nations invested a large part of their foreign exchange surplus in the United States. In 1976, although they marketed only 20 percent of their oil output to the United States, the OPEC nations invested 31 percent of their exchange surplus in the United States (12 billion).[18] Third, the other industrialized noncommunist nations are far more dependent than the United States on imported oil; Western

[3.] Increased exports mean less available for domestic consumption. During the first two years following the oil embargo, U.S. per-capita income (in constant dollars) actually declined, and even in 1976 per-capita income exceeded the 1973 level by only 1.8 percent.[17]

Europe and Japan, for example, produced only 4.8 percent of the oil they consumed in 1976.[19] Thus increased oil import prices drove up the production costs of their industries even more than those of their American competitors, and the net impact of the oil price increases on economic competition among the industrialized nations benefited the United States.

Why, then, view the future prospect as menacing? Why alarm the American public with rhetoric about the potential for "national catastrophe" if the nation does not take firm measures to reduce its reliance on oil imports? These are not idle questions. Many intelligent observers profess optimism that no new oil embargo will occur and that oil prices will not rise significantly faster over the next several decades than the average for all other prices. They maintain that as the oil nations acquire a massive stake in the economies of the industrialized nations, they will assign an ever-increasing priority to the maintenance of world economic prosperity and currency stability. Additionally they will face an increasing threat of competition from alternative energy sources if oil prices rise substantially above current levels. The United States, finally, can well afford to spend 2 percent of its GNP (2.4 percent in 1977) for the oil imports required to preserve current lifestyles and amenities.[20] It is of course appropriate, the optimists conclude, to encourage energy conservation and to press the search for new domestic sources of energy, but it would not be cost-effective to disrupt American living and economic patterns in order to reduce imports by $10 billion or $20 billion a year.

Views such as these gained widespread credence in 1975 and 1976 as the immediate shock of the oil embargo wore off, and as leaders of the oil-producing nations sought to provide public assurances that the embargo and dramatic price increases of 1973–1974 had been a one-time, not-to-be-repeated, event. They dovetailed with the interests of elected officials who were in any event reluctant to vote for measures that would annoy large numbers of constituents. Few were so rash as to suggest that another oil embargo was impossible, but many relegated this prospect to the status of a low-probability contingency, similar to a great many others meriting some concern but not crisis levels of action.

The more alarmist view of the nation's oil situation, which President Carter sought to dramatize in his energy address, takes off from the premises that a future oil embargo and/or future sharp price increases are certainly possible, and that if the nation's reliance on imports continues to grow, they will be far more damaging if and when they do occur than those of 1973–1974. The events of 1973–1974 seemed unthinkable to most people just before they occurred, just as their repetition seems unlikely now.[21] It is true that the oil-producing nations have a stake in the prosperity and currency stability of the West, but they also have military, diplomatic, and economic objectives of their own, which may at times lead them to take steps sharply at odds with the interests of the Western industrialized nations. The central issue is not how likely they are to do so; it is how vulnerable the United States should permit itself to become.

Although coal, nuclear, solar and other alternative sources of energy will doubtless supply increasing shares of U.S. energy requirements in the decades ahead, there seems little prospect that oil demand will peak before the year 2000. The other two major sources of current U.S. energy are natural gas (27 percent) and coal (18 percent).[22] The former comes from the same fields as liquid petroleum and is itself a rapidly dwindling resource. (Supply constraints drove usage down by 11 percent from 1973 to 1976.)[23] Coal reserves are ample, but the rate at which production can be increased is highly uncertain. Moreover, dramatic expansions of coal use would likely have serious effects both on air quality and world climate.[24] Current official projections are that natural gas consumption will decline slightly in the years to 1985 but that coal usage will grow by 40 percent to 95 percent, with the result that coal and gas usage combined will grow by 13 percent to 35 percent from 1976 to 1986.[25] Stated another way, coal and natural gas, which together accounted for 45 percent of U.S. energy consumption in 1976, are expected to account for somewhere in the range of 39–49 percent as of 1985.[26]

The other notable source on which many have counted for near-term growth is nuclear power. But it accounted for only 3 percent of U.S. energy consumption in 1976, and the most optimistic estimates show it rising only to 8 percent in 1985.[27] These estimates appear increasingly implausible, moreover. Only about one-half the nuclear power plants expected as of 1970 to be on-line in 1976 were in fact operational in that year, and most analysts anticipate similar slippage in the years ahead.[28] As recently as 1975, federal energy officials were estimating that two hundred nuclear power plants would be on-line by 1985. (Sixty-three were actually in operation as of early 1977.) By mid-1977, however, the Nuclear Regulatory Commission had reduced this estimate to 106.[29]

Finally solar and geothermal energy, solid waste incineration, oil shale, and a variety of other sources will doubtless become substantially more important over the next several decades. Their relative contribution is not expected to grow appreciably before the 1990s, however.

All in all, then, U.S. reliance on oil is unlikely to decline rapidly. President Carter estimated in April 1977 that, absent the implementation of strong new conservation measures, the oil proportion of U.S. energy consumption would remain constant at about 47 percent through 1985.[30]

Even if one accepts the optimistic assumption that no oil embargoes will occur in the decades ahead and that U.S. vulnerability to an embargo will not significantly weaken the nation in world affairs, the price and supply outlooks for the late 1980s and beyond are sobering. In order to grasp the danger, it is essential to examine the overall supply-demand prospect on a worldwide basis, and in doing so there are two critical questions to keep in mind. First, to what extent is world demand likely to exceed the willingness, and perhaps even the ability, of the OPEC nations to increase their production? Second, to what extent is Saudi Arabia, which has been the principal moderating force in OPEC price deliberations since 1973, likely to remain capable or desirous of performing this function?

The leading analysts who have addressed these questions differ in their forecasts.[31] They agree that demand for OPEC oil, in the absence of further sharp price increases, will probably exceed the willingness of the OPEC nations to produce in the latter half of the 1980s and thereafter. They also agree that the Saudis will be under intense pressure from the oil-consuming nations to increase their production far beyond the levels that make sense from their own standpoint. In this economic environment, the temptation for the oil-producing nations to increase their prices may well be overwhelming, and the capacity of Saudi Arabia to serve as a moderating influence (assuming that its leaders then want to) will be highly problematic. Even if the oil-producing nations resist the temptation to raise prices dramatically, moreover, they will have to utilize some means of allocating the limited supply. The obvious alternative to price increases is some form of bureaucratic supply allocation, which would be highly amenable to use for diplomatic purposes. Even assuming that an allocation system were implemented in nonpolitical fashion, the world would have to adapt to a much lower (and eventually negative) rate of oil supply growth.

The need for such adaptation is the bottom line whichever assumption one makes about the method that will be chosen to bring supply and demand into balance. Given the long lead times required to develop new, more energy-efficient technologies and behavioral patterns (both institutional and individual), it follows that the time to begin adapting with a genuine sense of urgency is now.

One key set of projections, relied upon heavily by President Carter in 1977, was developed by the Central Intelligence Agency. It estimated that combined oil demand by the noncommunist nations would grow by about twenty-two million barrels a day (mbd) in the period 1976–1985, whereas their own production would grow by only about 8 mbd.[4] [32] If these projections are realized, the OPEC nations will be under intense pressure to increase their production by about 14 mbd. Additionally, CIA estimated, the communist nations will shift from being net ex-

[4.] The CIA estimated that noncommunist oil demand would rise from 48.3 mbd in 1976 to 70.5 mbd (plus or minus two million) in 1985. This entailed a consumption growth rate for the noncommunist world as a whole of 4.3 percent a year. By comparison, world oil consumption grew at an average annual rate of 6.6 percent a year from 1940 through 1976, with no sign of a slowdown prior to 1973.[33]

porters of oil (1.1 mbd in 1976) to being substantial net im-
porters (roughly 4 mbd in 1985). If this occurs, the OPEC nations
will be under demand pressure to increase their production by
roughly 19 mbd.[34]

How much will the OPEC nations choose to produce? On the
one hand, they will be tempted to satisfy all demand in order to
avert charges that they are undermining world prosperity and in
order to protect their own investments abroad. On the other, they
will doubtless consider that the value of their oil is rising faster in
the ground than the value of their accumulated foreign exchange
surplus is rising in world investment markets, that production
increases undermine their own price leverage, that such increases
will require very large investments, and that higher rates of production are likely to prove sustainable for only a few years in any
event.

Taking these and a number of more technical factors into
account, along with current development projections in each
of the countries concerned, the CIA estimated that the OPEC
nations other than Saudi Arabia would have a production capacity
of 28.5 mbd (plus or minus one million) in 1985. This would
leave an estimated demand for Saudi Arabian oil of 17 mbd in
1985 if one excludes the CIA's estimate of communist world
demand from the calculation, or 21 mbd if one includes that
estimate (in each case, plus or minus 2 mbd).[35] Saudi Arabian
production in 1976 was 8.6 mbd, whereas its production capacity
was 11.4 mbd.[36] This excess capacity meant, in effect, that
the Saudis had a veto over OPEC price increases. If the others
sought to raise prices without its consent, it had the ability to
increase its sales quickly at the lower price. The historic experience of OPEC has been that in such a situation of excess
capacity price cutting (often in the form of secret rebates) becomes general.[37]

CIA estimated that Saudi Arabian capacity at most would reach
18 mbd in 1985. At this level, the Saudis would earn $125 billion
annually from oil exports at current prices.[38] There is little likelihood that they could use such resources effectively, and they

would risk rapid depletion of their oil reserves.[5] Even on the assumption that they do choose to produce at this very high rate, however, CIA estimated that the oil price squeeze would arrive in 1983—or, if the projected communist world import demand fails to materialize, in 1986.[39]

A major private study of the non-communist world energy outlook appeared at about the same time as the CIA study. Carried out by the Workshop on Alternative Energy Strategies (WAES), a multinational research team led by Carroll L. Wilson of MIT, WAES projected a considerably slower rate of consumption growth than did the CIA for the decade 1976–1985: 2.5 percent versus 4.3 percent.[41] In consequence the WAES demand estimate for 1985 was roughly 10 mbd less than CIA's. The mid-range WAES production estimate for 1985, however, was 11.5 mbd lower than that of the CIA.[6] These differences provide some indication of the prodigious uncertainties that beset forecasters in this field and highlight the fact that the 1985 situation could easily prove either much better or much worse than the mid-range estimates of either report would suggest. More immediately striking, however, is that both studies arrived at essentially the same scenario for the mid 1980s: one in which noncommunist world oil consumption will be pressing hard against the willingness and capacity of the supplier nations to produce.

The CIA study did not attempt to forecast beyond 1985, but WAES looked to the year 2000 and even, in a more speculative

[5] Saudi Arabia had one-third of total OPEC proven reserves and 26 percent of total non-communist world proven reserves as of 1976. Its 1975 production rate equalled 1.7 percent of its proven reserve. A production rate of 18 mbd would have entailed usage of 4.3 percent of proven reserves each year.[40] For a discussion of the concept of proven reserves and of the prospect for future additions to them, see appendix D.

[6] The two sets of production estimates (in mbd) were as follows:[42]

	CIA	WAES
OPEC	43.5–47.4	33.0–39.0
Non-OPEC	23.8–27.0	22.0–24.7
Total	67.3–74.4	55.0–63.7
Mid-Range	70.9	59.4

way, to 2025. Its basic conclusion was that the supply-demand squeeze for oil will significantly intensify from 1985 to 2000. Thereafter conventional oil production will almost surely dwindle much more rapidly than the consuming nations would like, but it is possible that new sources of oil—such as oil shale and tar sands—will become important contributors to production (see appendix D).

As the pressure grows to curtail oil consumption, automobile usage will certainly be a priority candidate for scrutiny. It is feasible to imagine stationary energy users (such as homes, factories, and power plants) escaping the need for discipline to some degree by switching to alternative power sources. But there is no serious likelihood that the automobile—or indeed other modes of transportation, with the exception of electrified rail—will shift to alternative power sources during the remainder of the twentieth century. Thus WAES projects that by the year 2000 oil will be used almost exclusively in North America for transport and petrochemical feedstock purposes. At the same time, it estimates that U.S. gasoline consumption in 2000 will have to be 16 percent less than it was in 1972.[43]

Goals

No overall goals with respect to energy consumption, domestic production, or imports have been enacted into law, but goal recommendations have been put forward as major national priorities by the Ford administration in 1975 and by the Carter administration in 1977. Congress enacted specific goals with respect to automobile fuel economy in 1975, moreover, and a broad (if mainly symbolic) package of energy legislation in 1978.

Giving the oil issue top billing in his 1975 State of the Union Message, President Ford estimated that in the absence of government action, U.S. oil consumption would rise to 23.9 mbd by 1985 (vs. 16.7 mbd in 1974), with imports accounting for 53 percent of this total (12.7 mbd). He proposed a package of measures to stimulate domestic production and conservation that he claimed would reduce consumption to 20.1 mbd and imports to 23 percent of this reduced total (4.7 mbd).[44]

A central feature of the Ford program was a proposal that Congress enact fuel economy standards for new cars. As it submitted its plan, moreover, the administration secured a pledge from the auto manufacturers that even in the absence of legislation, they would increase the sales-weighted fuel economy of new cars by 40 percent to 1980.[45] Though not stated explicitly, the comparison was apparently with 1974 models. The Federal Energy Administration later estimated that the base figure (including imports) was 14 miles per gallon (mpg) and the target for 1980 19.6. Congress rejected virtually every other feature of the Ford program, but it enacted, as part of the Energy Policy and Conservation Act of 1975 (EPCA), a somewhat stronger set of fuel economy standards than those recommended by the administration.[46] Specifically EPCA required each manufacturer to achieve the following sales-weighted averages: 18 mpg for 1978 model year cars, 19 mpg for 1979, 20 mpg for 1980, and 27.5 mpg for 1985; the secretary of transportation was directed to promulgate interim standards for 1981-1984.[7]

President Carter took EPCA as a given, but judged that in the absence of further legislation the 27.5 mpg target for new automobile fuel economy in 1985 would not be achieved. He did not specify the degree to which he expected the target to be missed, but the Congressional Budget Office (CBO), in a careful analysis it prepared of the Carter recommendations, did. CBO estimated that, if no additional incentives were enacted, average new car fuel economy in 1985 would be 23.3 mpg and the companies would be liable for penalty payments of $2.5 billion (in 1977 dollars). Enactment of the full Carter plan, it estimated, would raise the 1985 average to about 26 mpg and cut the company liability for penalty payments to the range of $1.1-1.2 billion.[47]

[7.] Fuel economy is defined for purposes of the act as the average of the city and highway ratings arrived at by the U.S. Environmental Protection Agency. A manufacturer violating the EPCA standard in any year will be subject to a heavy fine—five dollars times the total number of vehicles sold for each one-tenth of an mpg over the standard. The fines will not be deductible as business expenses, so their impact on company after-tax earnings (if levied) will be roughly twice as great as equivalent liabilities of an ordinary business nature.

In the absence of further legislation, President Carter forecast, U.S. oil consumption would rise from the 1976 level of 17.4 mbd to 22.8 mbd in 1985. He projected further that imports would grow from 7.3 mbd in 1976 (42 percent of consumption) to 11.5 mbd in 1985 (51 percent). These were mid-range estimates. At the high end of the plausible range, demand might reach 25 mbd and imports 16 mbd (64 percent) in 1985.[48] (This worst-case estimate assumed domestic production 2.3 mbd lower and consumption 2.2 mbd higher than the mid-range projections.)

President Carter's recommendations, like those of President Ford two years earlier, sought as their highest priority to reduce U.S. reliance on oil and natural gas imports and to do so by a combination of measures designed to encourage conservation, domestic production, and increased reliance on other fuels.[8]

The President sought to reduce projected growth in U.S. oil consumption between 1976 and 1985 by 85 percent (from 5.4 to 0.8 mbd) and thereby to bring about a shift in the projection of 1985 oil imports from a growth of 4.3 mbd above the 1976 level to a reduction of 0.3 mbd.[50] CBO, in an analysis of the Carter plan that gained wide recognition as more realistic in its projections than the plan itself, judged that the recommended measures were far from sufficient to bring about such sharp reductions in oil demand, but at the same time that the Carter projections of demand in the absence of further action were too high. Thus it estimated that the Carter proposals would reduce consumption growth in the decade 1976–1985 by only 28 percent but that the resultant growth (l.5 mbd) would still be 72 percent below the level projected by the president in the absence of plan implementation. CBO further estimated that adoption of the Carter plan as submitted would yield a zero growth rate in U.S. oil consumption between 1980 and 1985, possibly setting the stage for actual reductions thereafter.[51]

[8.] Among the specific targets of the Carter plan, the most significant were to reduce overall U.S. energy consumption in 1985 by 4 percent below the level otherwise indicated (2.1 mbd equivalent); to increase reliance on coal by 22 percent above the level otherwise indicated (2.4 mbd equivalent); and to reduce reliance on oil by 20 percent below the level otherwise indicated (4.6 mbd). The plan was extremely pessimistic about the potential for increasing domestic oil and natural gas production. Its targets were simply to achieve increases of 0.2 mbd and 0.6 mbd respectively above the levels anticipated in the absence of stimulative action.[49]

The Carter plan sought to reduce projected 1985 oil usage in all sectors of the economy. Thus it estimated that the share accounted for by transportation in 1985 would be essentially unchanged from 1976. The savings projected in other sectors, however, were largely to be achieved by conversion to other fuels. By contrast the plan envisaged no prospect of fuel conversion in transportation, and it projected a need for significant growth in fuel consumption for freight and passenger common carrier services. Emphasizing the wastefulness of current automobile usage, it called for an immediate slowdown in the growth rate of gasoline consumption, leading to an actual downturn beginning in 1981 and a sharp reduction of 11 percent between 1981 and 1985:[52]

1977 (estimated actual)	7.30 mbd
1978	7.35
1979	7.40
1980	7.45
1981	7.40
1982	7.20
1983	7.00
1984	6.80
1985	6.60

CBO estimated, however, that even in the absence of further government action, the nation would experience zero growth in consumption for automotive purposes between 1977 and 1985 as the result of rising gas prices combined with the EPCA fuel economy standards.[9] [53]

In order to hold gasoline usage down to the recommended target levels, President Carter recommended three new taxes: on domestically produced crude oil, on "gas guzzler" cars, and on

[9.] A key question, to which relatively little attention had been paid over the years, was what to anticipate with respect to gasoline consumption for trucking purposes. EPCA required that the secretary of transportation set fuel economy standards for light trucks, but none had yet been promulgated. Trucks currently accounted for about one-quarter of total gasoline consumption, and one recent study for FEA had suggested that they might account for almost 30 percent by 1985. CBO estimated that if this projection were borne out, total gasoline consumption in 1985 would be 5 percent above the 1977 level. CBO in fact anticipated, however, that the EPCA standards plus market forces would lead to approximately zero growth in gasoline consumption for trucking—and thus to zero growth in total consumption—through 1985 even in the absence of further legislation.[54]

gasoline itself. The first of these was designed to raise the price of domestically produced crude oil to the 1977 world price level by 1980; all revenues were to be fully rebated to the American people on a per-capita basis. The expectation was that it would discourage consumption by raising the relative price of oil while leaving overall consumer purchasing power unimpaired. Though not aimed specifically at transportation uses of oil, its projected short-term effect on the price of gasoline was an increase in the range of six or seven cents a gallon. Second, the president recommended that purchasers of automobiles failing to meet the overall fuel economy standard in any year after 1978 be required to pay a tax based on the degree to which their cars missed the standard, and urged that these tax revenues be returned to circulation by rebates to purchasers of cars exceeding the standard. The maximum tax (on cars getting 12 mpg or less) was to rise from $449 in 1979 to $2,488 in 1985. The maximum rebate to any purchaser was to be $500. Third, the president called for a standby tax on gasoline, to be imposed in 1979 and future years if actual demand in the preceding year exceeded the Carter plan target. The tax was to be five cents for each full percentage point by which consumption exceeded the target, except that it was never to change by more than five cents in any year. Like the crude oil tax, this was to be rebated to the public (including those without cars) on a per-capita basis.

CBO, in its analysis of the Carter plan, judged that gasoline price increases attributable to the crude oil tax would yield gasoline savings of 25,000 barrels per day in 1985,[10] that the system of gas guzzler taxes and rebates would yield savings of 215,000 bd,

[10.] Later in 1977 a provocative analysis by two Rand Corporation economists, which cast doubt on the likelihood that the wellhead tax would yield any conservation benefits at all, attracted substantial attention. Charles E. Phelps and Rodney T. Smith judged that current price controls were not saving consumers any money but were simply transferring profits from domestic crude oil producers to refiners. The refiners in turn were disciplined in the prices they could charge by competitive forces, which revolved around the world price of oil rather than the price of domestic regulated crude. The implication of this analysis was that while the wellhead tax would achieve a transfer of funds from the refiners to the American people, it would not lead to increases in the retail prices of petroleum products—or, therefore, to any curtailment of demand. Critics of the Phelps-Smith theory countered that in fact the domestic market for refined petroleum products was substantially insulated from the world market, but in general they admitted that the two markets were related and that some of the current benefits of domestic price regulation were probably being captured by refiners rather than consumers.[55]

and that the gas tax would yield savings of 65,000 to 150,000 bd, depending on how early it began to be imposed. (If the remainder of the plan were adapted, CBO estimated, the gasoline tax would not have to be imposed until 1984 or 1985).[56] Adoption of the whole plan, CBO judged, would yield only about half the reduction in usage claimed by the administration (5 percent versus 10 percent).[57]

Further CBO maintained that if the entire Carter plan were adopted, it and EPCA combined would result in the following: price increases of $400–600 per car as of 1985 to pay for fuel economy improvements, fuel costs per mile of driving the 1985 cars 30 percent lower than that for 1976 cars, and a reduction of one-third in the projected growth of vehicle mileage per household in 1985. (CBO estimated that average vehicle mileage per household would rise from the 1976 level of slightly under 15,000 miles to about 18,000 miles in 1985 if the government took no further action, and to about 17,000 miles if the Carter plan were adopted intact.)

The House and Senate passed quite different energy bills during 1977 in response to the president's proposals, following which a year-long deadlock (primarily over natural gas regulation) ensued. Finally, in October 1978, the stalemate having attracted wide international attention as a symbol of the nation's inability to curb energy demand or inflation, Congress enacted an emasculated bill. The Carter proposals bearing on urban transportation fared as follows:

1. A slightly revised version of the gas guzzler tax was adopted— with the expectation that virtually no one would pay it. Because the manufacturers have been moving vigorously to phase out the worst gas guzzlers, it now appears that no model projected for the 1980 model year, the first to which the tax will apply, will be subject to it.[11]

2. The proposed rebate of gas guzzler tax revenues to purchasers of cars significantly exceeding the EPCA standards was rejected— in part because no significant revenues were anticipated but also

[11.] In model year 1980 the tax will be $200 on cars rated by EPA at 14–14.9 mpg, rising to $550 on those rated at 12.9 mpg or less. By 1986 the tax will begin at $500 on cars getting less than 22.5 mpg and rise to $3,850 on cars getting less than 12.5 mpg.[58]

because, under unternational tariff agreements, it would have had to be paid to the buyers of imported as well as domestically produced cars.

3. The gasoline surtax, having attracted massive criticism and no visible support, quickly dropped from the agenda within weeks following the president's original 1977 message.

4. The crude oil tax, which would have reached consumers indirectly via company price increases, received House approval in 1977 but died in the conference committee.

We judge that the enacted features of the Carter plan will have no measurable impact whatever on future oil consumption for urban transportation purposes.[12] Indeed the predominant view of the entire energy package as it became law was that little more could be said on its behalf than that *failure* of enactment would have been a clear signal to the world of the nation's political indecisiveness. Virtually no one claimed that its provisions would significantly affect energy demand or production levels.

The Carter plan, it should be noted, essentially ignored mass transit, and Secretary of Transportation Brock Adams reportedly was rebuffed by the president when he sought to have some of the revenues from the three proposed gasoline disincentive taxes allocated for mass transit rather than cash rebates.[58] The plan did recommend that the federal government purchase six thousand vans for use by its own employees on a nonsubsidized basis, but Congress rejected this proposal, apparently judging that it represented a new fringe benefit rather than a significant energy conservation measure.

Innovations

Among the innovations under consideration in this book (see

[12.] The Administration, it bears mention, did not provide a breakdown of the savings that it considered attributable to each of its proposed measures individually. The uncertainties were such, of course, that all estimates were highly questionable. If, for example, one accepted the Phelps-Smith conclusions with respect to the crude oil tax and judged that the auto manufacturers would achieve the EPCA standards even without additional incentives (beyond those enacted in 1975), it followed that the only efficacious feature of the original Carter plan from a conservation standpoint was the gasoline tax and that the remaining elements were of purely symbolic importance.

above, p. 50), those which might potentially serve to reduce urban transportation energy requirements are business regulation to bring about the marketing of more energy-efficient cars, pricing measures to make gasoline more expensive and energy-efficient cars relatively less expensive, supply restrictions on gasoline, with allocation by rationing, and private ridesharing. Additionally it is often maintained that fixed route transit improvements can yield significant energy savings, and so we shall devote attention to mass transit as well. (We shall, on the other hand, not discuss rationing—because our objective will be to appraise the technical potential of the measures under review to yield energy savings, and there seems little to say about rationing in this regard. Rationing involves conservation by fiat, with the degree of saving depending simply on the amount permitted by the government to be marketed.)[13]

Business Regulation

Between 1937, when official estimates began to be made, and 1970, the average fuel economy of American cars—new and old combined, in actual on-the-road performance—fell from 15.0 to 14.0 mpg.[14] [60] The high compression engine, introduced during the early and mid-1950s, did represent a substantial fuel economy advance, as did subsequent increases in compression ratios through the 1960s. These improvements were more than offset, however, by increases in automotive luxury that entailed additions to vehicle weight. The average automobile became larger, capable of

[13.] It does bear note, though, that most of the rationing systems seriously discussed in recent years (for activation in the event of embargo or war) are really two-tier price systems. They would seek to avoid the economic distortions associated with pure rationing systems by permitting consumers to buy and sell ration coupons, or else they would impose a hefty surtax on purchases without coupons.

[14.] These aggregate estimates by the Federal Highway Administration (FHWA) should be differentiated from the individual model and sales-weighted estimates made by the Environmental Protection Agency (EPA) with respect to new cars in recent years. The EPA ratings are based on simulated driving conditions and trip making patterns, whereas the historic fleetwide estimates are based on actual gasoline sales and estimates of total vehicle mileage. Although both approaches are subject to inaccuracies—EPA's due to uncertainties about the average driving cycle, FHWA's due to the difficulty of estimating nationwide travel mileage—the predominant view is that the EPA ratings predict 10–20 percent better mileage than the average motorist achieves. This suggests that, had EPA been rating new cars during the period 1937–1970, it would normally have found new-car fuel economy 1½–3 miles per gallon higher than the average fleetwide performance reported by FHWA. (The disparity would have been less, of course, during periods in which new-car fuel economy was getting worse from year to year.)

greater acceleration and higher speeds, and outfitted with such convenience-comfort features as automatic transmissions, power steering, power brakes, and air conditioning. When foreign auto makers made incursions into the American market with their compact cars, Detroit responded by scaling down its full-sized cars. The resultant American compacts were more economical in their use of fuel than larger models, but solely by virtue of being smaller. They were not more efficient in the sense of having greater fuel economy per pound or per cubic inch of passenger compartment space.

As EPA's emission control regulations became more stringent in the early 1970s, the industry found it necessary to re-tune engines for low emissions rather than fuel efficiency. The result was a significant drop in new car fuel economy during the period 1972–1974 by comparison with previous years. No detailed estimate of the degree to which fuel economy declined in these years is available because EPA did not prepare ratings until 1974. In that year, however, it found domestic new-car models averaging only 12.9 mpg on a sales-weighted basis. (Including foreign makes, the sales-weighted estimate for the 1974 model year was 13.9 mpg.)[61]

The somewhat ironic upshot of this story is as follows. Having eschewed large-scale investment in fuel economy improvements since the first half of the 1950s, the American auto industry has been able since 1974 to begin tapping a whole generation of developments from all over the world. The result is likely to be an apparent technological triumph for the industry, a doubling of new-car fuel economy within a dozen years from the time that energy conservation became a priority national objective.

In March 1975 a federal interagency task force was formed to examine the potential for motor vehicle fuel economy improvements after 1980, bearing in mind the need for compatibility with the nation's environmental, safety, and economic objectives.[15] [62] Reporting in September 1976, the task force concluded that it would be quite feasible technically to achieve the 1985 EPCA

15. The task force membership was drawn from the Department of Transportation, the Environmental Protection Agency, the Energy Research and Development Administration, the Federal Energy Administration, and the National Science Foundation.

standard of 27.5 mpg, though some change in the current vehicle mix or in engine performance would be required.

In order to maintain the current (approximate) mix of vehicles by size—50 percent six-passenger, 25 percent five-passenger, 25 percent four-passenger—it would probably be necessary, the task force judged, to accept a five second increase (from the current fifteen seconds) in the average time required for acceleration from 0–60 miles per hour. Given this sacrifice in performance, however, the 27.5 mpg target could be achieved even if the market share of six-passinger cars rose to 90 percent.

If the market share of six-passenger cars were reduced from the current 50 percent to 30 percent, numerous options were available for achieving the mpg target without sacrificing acceleration capacity. Any one of the following, the task force estimated, would suffice: "(a) the dieselization of larger cars. (b) accelerated introduction of an upgraded drivetrain, [or] (c) an improvement in Otto engine fuel economy of 10 percent."[63] Various combination strategies were also available. In one scenario, involving both the dieselization of larger cars and reduced acceleration, the task force projected an average 1985 new-car fuel economy of 28.9 mpg without any increase in the market share of smaller cars.[64]

In order to achieve the 1985 EPCA standard, the task force estimated, the auto manufacturers would have to increase their capital spending over the decade 1975–1985 from approximately $40 billion to the range of $45–50 billion.[65] It judged further, however, that even if performance eventually fell 10 percent short of the 1985 target, the EPCA-inspired effort would save nine and a half billion barrels of oil, roughly the magnitude of the Alaskan Prudhoe Bay oil field, during the two decades 1975–1995. Even discounting these future savings at 10 percent a year and assuming no future increases in the price of oil, this implied a return on investment (to the national economy) of 300–600 percent.[66] The task force estimated as well that the fuel economy standards could be achieved with at most slight air pollution and safety penalties.[67]

EPCA leaves responsibility for implementation (except for the levying of fines) to the auto manufacturers. The hope is that compliance will be facilitated by a shift of consumer demand (as gasoline prices increase) toward smaller cars, and that the manufacturers will achieve technical advances enabling them to market cars with similar size, performance, and price characteristics to those available currently as well as dramatically improved fuel economy. If these developments fail to occur or prove insufficient, the companies have four options: they can pay the fines specified by EPCA for noncompliance, either absorbing them in the form of lower profits or seeking to recover them in the form of price increases; they can accentuate the price incentives for consumers to purchase small cars by revising their price structures (a strategy that, if opposed to strong consumer preferences, could prove more expensive than paying the fines); they can ration the production of large vehicles, thus risking the loss of some sales to other manufacturers (who would, however, be faced with the same set of choices); and/or they can lobby politically for a postponement or relaxation of the standard.

The task force did not seek to estimate what mix of these developments would actually occur, but it noted that there were severe uncertainties about how consumers would respond to the changes in size, performance, and/or price characteristics that it expected to be associated with achievement of the 27.5 mpg standard on schedule. If elected officials were determined to avoid slippage, it concluded, they would be advised to enact incentive measures bearing upon consumer choices directly. The options it deemed most promising were precisely those subsequently recommended by President Carter: a gas tax increase, a tax on crude oil, and/or a system of excise taxes and rebates on new cars with below-standard and above-standard fuel economy ratings respectively.

As noted above, CBO has estimated that in the absence of further legislation new-car fuel economy in 1985 will in fact average only 23.3 mpg, with the companies paying fines in the range of $2.5 billion. (The administration has not published a comparable estimate.) Auto industry leaders, on the other hand, have consistently maintained that they anticipate meeting the targets, primarily by utilizing lighter materials and (on larger models) diesel engines, secondarily by phasing out the V8 engine and by marketing more minicompact and subcompact models.[68] And they have already made impressive progress. As this is written EPA projects that the 1978 domestic models will achieve a sales-weighted fuel economy average of 18.6 mpg—44 percent better than 1974.[69] In addition the companies have marketed numerous minicompact and subcompact models that substantially exceed the 1985 EPCA standard, and General Motors has marketed a full-size Oldsmobile diesel in 1978 that EPA rates at 24 mpg in combined city-highway driving.[70] The sales-weighted fuel economy average of all foreign makes in model year 1978 is already in the range of 30 mpg. EPA rates Volkswagen's diesel Rabbit at 45 mpg, and federal tests have recently been completed on an improved version (with turbocharger) that, if and when marketed, will carry a 51 mpg rating. Similarly Honda has marketed two models powered by stratified charge engines that EPA rates at 46 and 43 mpg, respectively.[71]

The standard measure of oil conservation strategies is the number of barrels that they would save in given target years by comparison with a baseline assumption. The Task Force on Motor Vehicle Goals Beyond 1980 used the 1975 average new car fuel economy of 15.6 mpg and fleetwide average of 14.9 mpg as its baseline for comparative purposes. Assuming a development curve entailing a 20.8 mpg new-car average in 1980 and full achievement of the 27.5 mpg standard in 1985, it estimated that the fuel economy improvements would save 1.6 mbd as of 1985. Assuming an ultimate standard of 28.5 mpg, together with a gradual phasing out of the less energy-efficient older cars, it estimated further that the daily saving as of the year 2000 would be 3.7 mbd. Other scenarios, projecting ultimate new car standards as high as 33.7 mpg, yielded savings estimates as high as 4.2 mbd by 2000.[72]

Price Disincentives

There is a widespread view that the demand for gasoline is almost totally unresponsive to changes in price. This perception is incorrect. It is true that sales are affected only moderately by price changes in the short run. But over the longer term—as consumers

take the new prices into account when making their periodic decisions about where to live and what types of cars to buy—the
elasticity of demand tends to be much more substantial.[16]

John Pucher and Jerome Rothenberg, who in 1976 reviewed
most of the leading economic studies of gasoline demand elasticity,[74] found that most econometricians had estimated the
short-term direct price elasticity of demand for gasoline to be in
the range of −0.2 to −0.3. (For purposes of comparison among
the studies, Pucher and Rothenberg defined the short term as one
year.) They found much less consensus on the magnitude of long-
term elasticity, although all studies indicated rising elasticity over
time as turnover occurred in the auto fleet. (None, unfortunately,
examined the hypothesis that large gasoline price changes might
also significantly affect locational decisions over time, thereby
further increasing long-term elasticity.) The specific long-term
elasticity estimates ranged from −0.3 to −1.4, with the long-term
being variously defined as from two and a half to twelve years.

The U.S. Federal Energy Administration (FEA) has arrived at
similar conclusions. It officially adopted the following estimates:
short-term (one year) elasticity: −0.21; long-term (ten year)
elasticity, −0.76. Assuming constant elasticity at all points FEA

[16.] A definitional note. Economists speak of the demand for any product as being price
elastic only when one or both of the following conditions are satisfied: an increase in
price will cause sales to drop so sharply that overall revenues decline, and a reduction in
price will cause sales to rise so sharply that revenues increase. In such a situation, the
degree of elasticity is said to exceed unity. At unity, cutting the price by half will double
sales, leaving revenue unchanged; and doubling the price will cause sales to drop by half,
also leaving revenue unchanged.[73] It bears emphasis that even when demand is technically inelastic (less than unity), the effects of price changes on sales are often highly
significant from the standpoint of decision makers.
   Whereas elasticities are typically stated as though they were constant at all points on
the demand curve and for all magnitudes of price change, this is far from the case. In
practice, data are rarely available to permit reliable estimation of the effects of very large
changes, or even of small changes at points on the demand curve far from those recently
experienced. Thus reported elasticity estimates tend to be solidly grounded only with
respect to modest changes from the real (inflation-adjusted) price levels actually experienced in recent years.
   In general elasticities tend to rise at higher price levels and with greater price increases,
but this depends critically in each case on the availability, price, and acceptability of
substitutes. We hypothesize that, in the case of gasoline, the short-run elasticity of
demand would probably decline at much higher price levels. Much less hardship is involved, after all, in cutting back 5 percent on vehicle mileage than in cutting back 25
percent. Large gasoline price increases would also be likely, however, to generate a
dramatic upsurge in the demand for highly fuel-efficient cars. The realization of higher
long-term elasticities, consequently, might well be accelerated.

on the demand curve, these estimates suggest the following likely effects of various price increases on gasoline demand:

	% Price Increase	% Reduction in Demand
Short term	10	2
(−0.21)	50	8
	100	13
Long term	10	7
(−0.76)	50	26
	100	40

FEA projected that an average price increase of gasoline from an assumed baseline figure of $.60 a gallon to $1.00 would (if all other prices remained unchanged) save 0.7 mbd in the first year, 1.3 mbd in the fifth year, and 1.7 mbd in the tenth year.[75]

These estimates highlight the importance of distinguishing between the elasticity of demand for gasoline and that for automobile travel. As noted above with reference to the CBO analysis of the Carter energy plan, it is quite possible for auto vehicle mileage to grow even as gasoline consumption declines—particularly over the long run, as the vehicle fleet is replaced.

Over the short run, however, gasoline and auto travel demand elasticities tend to be quite similar. Reviewing the leading studies of auto travel demand elasticity, Pucher and Rothenberg found a clustering of short-term estimates in the range of −0.4 with reference to combined gasoline and maintenance costs. (As the gasoline share of this combined total tends to be about half, this translates to a travel demand elasticity of about −0.2 with reference to the price of gasoline alone.) None of the travel demand studies explicitly estimated long-term elasticities. The predominant view, however, was that even as the direct price elasticity of gasoline rises over time, the elasticity of demand for auto travel with reference to the price of gas declines sharply over time.

The travel demand studies were unanimous, finally, in concluding that work trip elasticities are substantially lower than non-work elasticities and that auto travelers are far more likely to alter their times of travel, their frequencies of travel, and their destinations than they are to switch modes.[76] In short it is much easier to reduce auto travel demand selectively (on specific routes, at specific times, to specific locations) than to reduce auto demand overall, and it is much easier to reduce auto demand overall than to divert automobile users to mass transit.

Increased Private Ride Sharing

As of 1970, 17.8 percent of urban commuters traveled as automobile passengers, by comparison with 10.3 percent who went to work by public transportation.[77] Nationally the disparity was even more striking: 18.3 percent commuted as auto passengers, 7.5 percent as transit patrons.[78] FEA officials have estimated that an increase in average work trip auto occupancy from 1.4 to 2.0 would (as of 1980) save 0.4 mbd and that a shift of 10 percent of the U.S. labor force into vanpools would generate savings approaching 0.5 mbd.[79] (The latter projection includes savings from the additional carpooling that FEA officials believe a national vanpool program, with its emphasis on ride sharing as a patriotic and economical mode of behavior, would stimulate.)[17]

Five features of the ride-sharing approach have made it particularly attractive to officials concerned with energy conservation: ride sharing saves money as well as fuel; it is as feasible in low-density as in high-density areas; it appears to be most attractive for long commutation trips (which tend to be the least well served by transit and to consume disproportionate amounts of energy);[18] It does not require any technical breakthroughs, large public invest-

---

[17.] In October 1977 FEA was abolished as a separate agency. Most of its personnel and functions became part of the new Department of Energy, but its ride-sharing activities were transferred to the Office of the Secretary of Transportation. For purposes of exposition, nonetheless, we have found it simplest to continue referring to FEA's ride-sharing estimates (which at this writing remain the most current available) in the present tense.

[18.] Though only 16 percent of all work trips were longer than fifteen miles in 1970, these accounted for 53 percent of vehicle miles of commutation travel. Average vehicle occupancy for these trips was 1.58 compared with an average occupancy of 1.36 for work trips of five miles or less.[80] The greater attractiveness of ride sharing for longer trips is probably due to the fact that the monetary benefits of sharing increase with trip length, whereas most of the disadvantages are essentially constant over the range of trip lengths.

ments, or complicated environmental impact studies; and it is available for immediate implementation.

Unfortunately, it is far more difficult to increase the amount of ride sharing in practice than the preceding considerations might lead one to anticipate. Although large numbers of people currently ride share—often irregularly and mainly with other members of their own households, with neighbors, and/or with fellow employees—it does not follow that large numbers of additional people can be induced to do so. Efforts to model ride sharing behavior have focused on five key determinants of work-trip modal choice: dollar cost, time cost, information cost, flexibility, and amenity. What emerges clearly from these efforts is that for most commuters, the advantage of ride sharing with respect to the first (dollar cost) is more than offset by its disadvantages with respect to the others. Specifically:

• Ride sharing entails significant time losses to collect and drop off passengers.

• Ride-sharing arrangements tend to be highly inflexible with respect to travel times and inhospitable to diversions for intermediate trip purposes (for example, shopping on the way home from work).

• Substantial amounts of effort are required to find and coordinate schedules with ride-sharing partners.

• Ride sharing may require awkward or burdensome social relationships from the standpoint of some commuters (allocating financial responsibilities, for example, and reconciling different preferences about punctuality, driving caution, and amount of conversation).[81]

Without exception, general efforts to promote ride sharing by media advertising and areawide carpool matching programs have had negligible impact. The first such program in the nation was undertaken by a Boston radio station in mid-1973 and continued through the period of gasoline shortages in 1974. The station distributed about a million matching forms, but only 13,000 were returned (representing about 2 percent of commuters in the region).

Because these were spread thinly over the metropolitan area, with a high proportion representing unusual long-distance trips, the station was able to provide only 3,800 of the respondents with reasonably proximate matches. Of these, only about 10 percent actually formed carpools (about 0.07 percent of all commuters in the region).[82]

Studying this experience in 1974, pursuant to a statutory mandate it had just received to promote ride sharing, the Federal Highway Administration concluded that the Boston matching system had been too impersonal. It resolved, therefore, to concentrate on programs in which the areawide organization would assist employers to promote pooling among their own employees. FHWA funded eighty-six ride-sharing programs in 1974, most of them based on this approach. Only one, however, the Portland, Oregon, program appears to have lured as many as 1 percent of the commuters in its region into pools. Portland suffered from more severe gasoline shortages during 1973–1974 than most of the country, and its program got underway while the shortages were still current. The program enjoyed remarkable cooperation from private employers as well as public agencies. The result, Portland area officials claimed, was a remarkable shift of nearly 4 percent of all commuters into carpools, reducing vehicle miles of travel (VMT) for commutation purposes by 3.6 percent and overall regional VMT by slightly more than 1 percent.[83] Though unique, the Portland experience did indicate that ride-sharing programs can achieve much higher than normal diversion rates when all circumstances are favorable.

As the gas lines of early 1974 faded into memory, however, local enthusiasm for ride-sharing programs waned everywhere, and most of the urban area programs funded by FHWA in 1974 terminated a year or two later as their initial funding ran out. Even the Portland project was turned over to the local transit operator in late 1975 and significantly reduced in scale. By late 1977, the number of urban areas with active ride-sharing programs had declined to about fifty.[84]

No follow-up studies have been carried out to determine whether the discontinued programs have left any long-term accomplishments in their wakes, but indirect evidence suggests that they probably did not. Due to high rates of job turnover, schedule change, and residential relocation, carpool arrangements tend to be quite short-lived—with the result that ride-sharing programs, unlike infrastructure construction programs, require continuing inputs at a constant level to hold their gains. Illustratively John Attanucci, in a 1974 study of ride-sharing behavior among commuters to a major employment complex on the fringe of the Boston core, found that 69 percent of those who carpooled two or more days a week had formed their carpools within the past year; 84 percent had done so within the past two years.[85]

A question frequently asked is whether people might carpool a great deal more if measures were adopted to raise the cost of automobile commutation. No urban area has to date employed auto price disincentives as a means of encouraging commutation mode changes, but there is reason to believe that they would have to be extremely powerful in order to have much impact. Cambridge Systematics, Inc., has developed a model correlating the level of ride sharing with auto operating costs, trip lengths, auto ownership/availability, commuter income, number of workers in the household, and employment density of the work zone. The model, which has been utilized in several metropolitan areas with good results, indicates that the price elasticity of demand for ride sharing is extremely low. For example, a three-dollar regionwide surcharge on weekday employee parking in Washington, D.C., as of 1975 would (according to the model) have reduced the percentage of commuters driving to work alone from 53 percent to 45 percent; increased the percentage of those commuting by automobile with others (drivers and passengers combined) from 25 percent to 29 percent; increased the proportion commuting by transit from 15 percent to 19 percent; and reduced commutation mileage per household by an average of 5.3 vehicle miles a week, partially offset by an increase of 1.9 miles for nonwork travel (using vehicles left at home by new carpool and transit users). The overall fuel saving would have averaged one-twentieth of one gallon per weekday per household (2 percent of weekday consumption).[86]

The impact of a three-dollar employee parking surcharge on

work-trip VMT would have been more than seven times as great as doubling the price of gasoline (because the average household utilized less than a gallon of gas a day for commutation). Doubling the gas price, however, would have discouraged nonwork as well as work travel, seven days a week. Indeed it would have had five times the relative impact on nonwork travel that it had on commutation travel, and its overall conservation effect would have been four and one-half times as great as that of the parking surcharge—1.22 gallons per household per week versus 0.27 gallons.[87] The CSI analysis goes far toward explaining why the relative increase in gasoline prices that occurred in 1973–1974 had no discernible impact on the level of commuter ride-sharing nationally, even though it did have a significant effect on the demand for gasoline.

If areawide matching programs and automobile price disincentives appear unlikely to stimulate major increases in ride sharing, there is growing evidence that vigorous efforts by employers can bring about substantial shifts to pooling (and mass transit as well) among their own employees. At the Tennessee Valley Authority headquarters in Knoxville, Tennessee, for example, VMT to the work site was reduced by 51 percent between 1973 and 1976 by an employer-sponsored program entailing primarily the provision of carpool matching and improved (predominantly subscription) bus services. Though the greatest shift was to subscription buses, the increase in carpooling was also impressive. Overall the proportion of employees driving alone to work fell from 65 percent to 19 percent. The proportion carpooling rose from 30 percent to 43 percent; the proportion commuting by bus rose from 3½ percent to 31 percent; and the proportion commuting by van, bike, or on foot rose from 1½ percent to 7 percent.[88] At the 3M Company in St. Paul, a vanpool program brought about a 12 percent reduction in overall work-trip VMT to the site between 1973 and 1976 (relative to estimated VMT absent the program). Though quantitative data were unavailable, company spokesmen believed that the companion carpool program had brought about an even greater reduction.[89]

The number of employer programs is quite small, however. A

survey by the Department of Energy in March 1978 found 104 company programs in operation at 147 sites and utilizing 1,573 vans.[90]

In the course of our research we interviewed key personnel involved with each of the company programs cited most frequently as a great success. We found in every case that the impetus for undertaking the program had come from a severe parking, employee-access, or corporate image problem. Both TVA and 3M were expanding, for example, and would have had to construct multimillion dollar parking facilities except for the increases in ride sharing that they achieved. Nabisco, which sponsored another successful program, was faced with the loss of many long-time employees when it moved its headquarters from Manhattan to northern New Jersey. The ride-sharing program proved to be an attractive, low-cost way of addressing this problem. The company viewed it as transitional, however, and began to phase it out as increasing numbers of employees moved their residences to New Jersey. The Prudential Insurance Company commenced a successful carpooling program in 1964 when it consolidated a number of scattered offices (with a combined total of about 1,600 employees) into a new office tower in downtown Boston. At the old locations, free parking had been available for all who wanted it. Provision of this amenity at the new site, however, would have cost the company three dollars a day per space. As a compromise, it agreed to make 200 free spaces available for carpools with three or more employee occupants.[91] Finally, at least one large oil company, CONOCO, has undertaken a vanpool program in the context of broader efforts to cultivate its corporate image as a promoter of energy conservation.

While hardly unique, neither are circumstances such as these likely to motivate a substantial percentage of the nation's employers. Short of a national crisis like the oil embargo, it will almost surely be impossible to generate large numbers of successful company ride-sharing programs except as powerful incentives can be deployed that provide top managers with significant business reasons for undertaking them. Ride-sharing programs absorb management energy, they sharply diminish employee scheduling flexibility, and they entail placing pressure on employees to change their travel behavior. Most employers find all of these at least mildly distasteful prospects, and view the potential benefits of ride sharing as completely tangential to high-priority corporate objectives. Thus it seems unlikely that mere jawboning or even modest tax incentives would induce large numbers of additional employers to embark vigorously upon the promotion of ride sharing.

Partially in response to these considerations, interest has recently been growing among the advocates of ride sharing in third-party provider arrangements (third parties in ride-sharing parlance are any participants other than commuters and their employers). The ideal third-party provider would be a business enterprise able to make money on such operations while aggressively promoting them on a wide scale. To date, however, no such providers have emerged, and ride-sharing proponents have come increasingly to accept the view that the prospects for profit in ride sharing are slim. They are now pinning their hopes mainly on a number of government-sponsored demonstrations involving non-profit providers that have just gotten underway or that are still in the planning stages. While focused on vanpooling, all of these demonstrations will include carpool matching services as well, and some may include subscription bus services.[19]

Finally, our own estimate of the fuel-saving benefits associated with any given increase in ride sharing are significantly lower than FEA's. Specifically, we find the following (See appendix E for a statement of our estimating assumptions):

1. A 10 percent shift of current auto commuters to vanpools would have saved about 48,000 bd in 1975 and would save about 52,000 bd in 1980 (1.1 percent of U.S. auto fuel consumption in each case).

2. A 10 percent shift of current auto commutation drivers to carpool passenger status would have saved 73,500 bd in 1975 and would save 74,000 bd in 1980 (1.6 percent of auto fuel consumption in each case).

[19.] The areas in which demonstrations are planned or underway as of early 1978 are as follows (funding sources in parentheses): Knoxville, Norfolk, Minneapolis, and the San Francisco Golden Gate Bridge District (UMTA); Baltimore and Honolulu (FHWA); Los Angeles (FHWA and ARCO); and San Francisco Metropolitan Transit Commission (FEA).

3. In order to achieve a commutation occupancy rate of 2.0, it would be necessary to shift 32 percent of all drivers to passenger status; such a shift would have saved 187,500 bd in 1975 and would save 191,000 in 1980 (slightly over 4 percent of auto fuel consumption in each case).[20]

FEA has made an official fuel-saving estimate only for the third of these scenarios, and only for one target year, 1980. Its estimate for that case is slightly more than twice our own (400,000 bd). Indirect support for our lower estimate comes from an unlikely source. Eric Hirst, FEA's own former director of transportation research, has recently estimated that an increase in carpooling sufficient to reduce work trip auto travel by 10 percent would save 69,000 bd in 1980.[92] This scenario is basically identical to our second one above, for which we project a 1980 saving of 74,000 bd.

In brief, then, ride sharing conserves money and fuel simultaneously; nonetheless there seems little prospect (short of an oil embargo) that large fuel savings can be generated on a regionwide or nationwide basis by government-sponsored ride-sharing programs.

Fixed Route Transit Service Expansion
National transit patronage declined in every year from the end of World War II through 1973. Load factors also dropped sharply during this period. Between 1950 and 1973, transit patronage declined by 61 percent whereas transit vehicle mileage declined by only 39 percent.[21] With the oil embargo, however, a turnabout occurred. During 1974, transit ridership increased by 4.1 percent

[20] The projected 1980 fuel savings associated with each scenario are only slightly greater than for 1975 because the two main factors accounting for change largely offset each other during this period. Improvements in automobile fuel economy are slowly reducing the amount of fuel saving associated with any given amount of ride sharing, but at the same time the size of the labor force is rapidly increasing. After 1980, as the rate of fuel economy improvement accelerates and (if current projections prove valid) the rate of labor force growth slows, the fuel saving associated with each scenario will probably decline slightly.

[21] The figures in this paragraph refer to bus, streetcar, and rail rapid transit only. The commuter rail trends have almost surely been similar, but data on vehicle mileage are lacking for the period prior to 1971. Our estimates in subsequent paragraphs of the energy effects that various levels of increased transit usage would entail in the future, though, do include commuter rail.

and, instead of falling back after the end of the immediate fuel crisis, it rose by another 2.1 percent over the following two years (to a level 6.3 percent above that of 1973). Transit vehicle mileage increased even more rapidly: by 10.4 percent between 1973 and 1976.[93] Thus average load factors continued to decline even in this period.

FEA officials estimated during 1975 that if transit patronage could be doubled with only an equivalent increase in vehicle mileage operated, the direct energy saving would be 40,000–50,000 barrels a day.[94] This estimate evoked consternation among national spokesmen for the transit industry, particularly because it was advanced within the framework of much larger energy saving estimates for scenarios involving auto fuel economy improvements and increased ride sharing. Transit representatives contended that a substantially larger amount of energy would be saved if transit patronage were doubled, because this could be achieved with much less than a doubling of transit vehicle mileage. They did not say how such an increase could be brought about, however, nor did they publish formal estimates of the energy savings associated with any particular scenarios.

Finding that none of the published estimates were accompanied by full statements of the assumptions on which they rested, we developed our own, which turned out to be even more pessimistic than FEA's. (The assumptions we utilized are set forth and explained in appendix E.) We calculate that doubling the transit share of urban passenger mileage (from 2.8 to 5.6 percent), while simultaneously doubling transit vehicle mileage, would have saved 24,000 barrels of oil per day in 1975 and would save 25,000 bd in 1980. If it were necessary to triple vehicle mileage in order to achieve a doubling of transit modal split, fuel consumption would actually have increased by 24,000 bd in 1975 and would be 31,000 bd greater in 1980. These estimates assume that 50 percent of the new transit riders would be former auto drivers. As indicated below, this seems to be about the upper limit for recent transit service improvements and fare reductions. If the proportion were considerably lower, say 25 percent, the negative energy impact would be substantial. On this premise, doubling the transit modal split while also doubling transit vehicle mileage would have produced a net fuel loss of 12,000 bd in 1975 and would produce a net loss of 16,000 bd in 1980.

Doubling the transit share of urban travel would be a remarkable accomplishment, of course. A more modest scenario, though still an extremely ambitious one by historic standards, would entail a 6 percent rate of increase in transit patronage between 1975 and 1980. This would mean a 34 percent increase in ridership over the five-year period and—as we have assumed that new patrons will, on average, make trips one-third longer than existing patrons—a 45 percent increase in passenger mileage. This scenario would entail an increase of less than one-fifth in the transit modal split: from 2.8 to 3.3 percent. If one further assumes a maintenance of current vehicle load factors and a 50 percent auto driver diversion rate, the net fuel saving—relative to maintenance of a constant 2.8 percent transit modal split—would be 5,000 bd in 1980. If, on the other hand, a 90 percent increase in vehicle mileage were necessary to achieve this 45 percent increase in passenger mileage, the result would be a net fuel loss of 16,000 bd. Alternatively if only 25 percent of the new patrons were former drivers, the net fuel loss would be 24,000 bd.

What would be required to bring about significant increases in the transit modal split under current energy price and supply conditions? This question was addressed by a 1975 study conducted for the Office of Technology Assessment (OTA) of the U.S. Congress. It concluded that a doubling of transit vehicle mileage would generate only a 20–40 percent increase in ridership.[22] [95] If this ridership projection proved valid and if 50 percent of the new patrons were former drivers, the result would be a net fuel loss of 15,000–36,000 bd in 1980. If only 25 percent of the new patrons were former drivers, the loss would be in the range of 36,000–49,000 bd.

The study further estimated that a total elimination of transit

[22.] In comparing this estimate with actual experience since the oil embargo, it is essential to distinguish 1974—a year in which energy price and supply conditions changed quite substantially—from subsequent years. During 1974 transit ridership and vehicle mileage both increased by 4 percent. During the following two years, ridership increased by a total of 2 percent while vehicle mileage rose 6 percent.[96]

fares nationwide would generate a 50–70 percent increase in ridership.[97] In order to carry so much additional ridership, we judge,
the industry would have to add at least 1 percent to vehicle mileage for each 2 percent increase in patronage. The result would be
an estimated net fuel saving of 38,000–53,000 bd on the assumption that 50 percent of the new patrons would be drivers. If only
25 percent were former drivers—quite likely in the case of fare
elimination, as it would both induce trip demand previously suppressed by cost considerations and divert a great many walking
trips to transit—the net fuel saving would be reduced to the range
of 12,000–17,000 bd.

The OTA analysts did not estimate the impact that a strategy
combining both a doubling of vehicle mileage and fare elimination
would have on ridership growth, but it seems reasonable to specu-
late that if they had their estimate would have been in the range of
60–100 percent. Our analysis suggests that, if half of the new transit riders were former drivers, the result would be a net fuel saving
of 6,000–48,000 bd in 1980. If only one quarter of the new patrons were former drivers, however, the result would be a net fuel
loss of 4,000–25,000 bd.

As of 1975, we estimate, the taxpayer cost of this combined
strategy would have been at least $6.7 billion.[23] We are reluctant
to project a 1980 price tag because the rate of transit cost inflation has been extremely volatile in recent years. If, however, one
assumes a 10 percent rate of transit cost inflation through 1980,

---

[23.] As indicated in table 2.1, transit revenues in 1975 totaled $2.3 billion, public operat-
ing subsidies totaled $2.0 billion, and current capital expenditures $1.7 billion. If one
assumes, very conservatively, that a doubling of transit vehicle mileage would have entailed an 80 percent increase in transit expenditures, the total operating budget for the
national transit system would have been $7.7 billion—$4.3 billion for the base system,
plus $3.4 billion for the additional service mileage.

On the capital side, we have assumed that the vehicle fleet buildup could not take
place in fewer than five years. Thus we have attributed only one-fifth of the capital cost
of the required buildup to 1975. Even this rate, however, would have entailed a tripling
of the actual level of transit vehicle production (5,300 units in 1975).[98] The capital
cost of the increased production, plus necessary maintenance and garage facilities, would
doubtless have exceeded a billion dollars a year.

Very conservatively, then, the additional public expenditures required to support a
package program of doubling vehicle mileage and eliminating fares would have been
about $6.7 billion, distributed as follows: $2.3 billion to replace current farebox revenues, at least $3.4 billion to cover the operating cost of the additional vehicle mileage,
and something in excess of $1 billion for the capital cost of additional vehicles and sup-
port facilities. This is quite apart from the inflationary impact that such a sharp increase
in the demand for transit equipment and labor would have had, and from any expansion
of rapid transit route mileage that might have been undertaken as part of the program.

the implication is a $10.8 billion cost in that year and—on the optimistic assumption of 50 percent driver diversion—a cost per barrel of oil saved in the range of $600–4,900.

We have thus far assumed that all service improvements would be on existing rights-of-way. This assumption has been quite favorable to transit, because the development of new rapid transit systems or lines will normally increase energy consumption over a time frame of at least several decades. Such projects invariably take fifteen years or more to move from the stage of preliminary planning to that of carrying passengers, and their construction itself during part of this period requires vast expenditures of energy. For example, T. J. Healy, in a study carried out for the California Department of Transportation, has estimated that BART utilized 44 percent of the total energy associated with its first fifty years for construction before carrying a single passenger.[99]

Charles Lave has sought to estimate how long it will take BART to repay this initial energy investment. He notes that, of BART passengers who reported in 1975 that they had previously made the trips in question, only 34 percent had previously traveled as auto drivers. The remainder had traveled by bus or as auto passengers. Assuming that this distribution would have continued in the absence of BART and that average fuel economy would have averaged only 14 mpg over BART's entire life, Lave finds that the repayment period would be 701 years. Assuming, on the other hand, that the federal standard of 27.5 mpg for new automobiles is achieved in 1985 and prevails thereafter, Lave finds that BART will never repay its initial energy investment. Indeed, on this assumption BART falls further behind every year after 1985, utilizing about one-third more operating energy than would have been required by the previous pattern.[24] [100]

[24.] These results are so astonishing that one's immediate instinct is to ask how sensitive they are to Lave's estimating assumptions. Anticipating this reaction, Lave reports a series of sensitivity tests. They yield the same basic conclusions if one judges that no investment should be undertaken for energy conservation purposes unless it will yield a relatively certain and significant return within a fifty-year time frame. Assuming, for example, a doubling of BART's 1975 patronage, an increase in the share diverted from the auto mode (including previous auto passengers)—from 46.5 percent to 75 percent, a 33 percent improvement in BART's own operating energy efficiency, and achievement of the 27.5 mpg new car fuel economy standard beginning in 1985, the energy payback period would be 193 years. Even on the assumption of stable fuel economy at 14 mpg, together with these other developments, the energy payback period would be 48 years. [101]

One potential advantage of rapid transit is that it can utilize other fuels than oil or natural gas at the power plants that supply it with electricity. On the other hand, it seems likely that the nation will face at least as severe problems meeting electric power demand in the coming decades as it will face meeting automobile and bus fuel demand. [102] Unless new rapid transit systems generate intensive patronage, moreover, their net energy effects—even excluding fuel usage during the construction period, and future improvements in automobile fuel economy—may prove to be negative. When transit officials speak of the energy efficiency of rapid transit, they invariably refer to the average experience of existing systems (which predominantly serve land-use patterns established in the preautomobile era) or to the fuel economy achievable with fully loaded rapid transit cars. In practice, however, the average rapid transit load factor in 1975 was only one-sixth of what the American Public Transit Association (APTA) estimated to be a peak load (22.5 versus 135). Indeed it was only 64 percent of what APTA estimated to be a typical off-peak load (35).[103]

Thus FEA has estimated that although the Washington, D.C. Metro will (if its patronage estimates are borne out) save 519,000 barrels of oil each year (1,400 bd) when fully in operation, it will do so at the cost of so much coal that the net amount of fossil fuel energy consumed annually for transportation purposes in the region will increase by the equivalent of 517,000 barrels of oil (1,400 bd).[25] [104]

More generally, CBO has developed modal fuel economy estimates indicating that even the automobiles of the mid-1970s are

25. The patronage estimates, moreover, appear to be overoptimistic. A 1975 study (in which Altshuler participated) by Jack Faucett Associates, carried out for the Congressional Research Service of the Library of Congress, judged that they were too high by about a factor of two. The report concluded its patronage analysis as follows: "WMATA's ridership estimates are all in likelihood an extreme exaggeration.... If one is to believe the forecast, WMATA is suggesting that the Washington rail transit system will attract *three times more* [relative to CBD employment] than do the existing rapid transit systems in Chicago, Philadelphia, and Boston—despite the fact that these other cities have higher central city densities, more intensive and well developed cores, and better downtown and central city transit system coverage. Given the additional fact that most downtown workers (those who represent the majority of rapid transit system users) tend to live close to downtown and generally within the central city rather than in the suburbs, and that Washington's rail system will have fewer stations located in the central city (in both absolute and relative terms) than the rail systems in Chicago, Philadelphia, and Boston, the WMATA projections for 1990 rail patronage seem even less creditable."[105]

as energy efficient as new rail systems when they achieve occupancies 16 percent as great, and that they are as energy efficient as bus systems when they achieve occupancies 44 percent as great (see table 5.1). For example, automobiles with occupancies of 3.0 are equivalent in energy terms to new rapid transit systems with average vehicle occupancies of 20 and to additional bus mileage with an incremental occupancy of 7. Cars with double the average fuel economy of the mid-1970s can achieve the energy breakeven point vis a vis new rail systems in this scenario with occupancies of 1.5—roughly the current average in urban commutation travel.[26]

In practice specific local transit improvements would be likely to vary widely in their energy effects, depending on the proportion of new transit passengers attracted from the ranks of auto drivers, on the number and length of new access trips to transit made by automobile, and on usage patterns of the automobiles left at home by new transit users, as well as on the operating energy requirements of the new transit services and their incremental load factors.

The firm of De Leuw, Cather & Co. has recently carried out a review of available case study materials on recent experiences with major transit improvements.[107] Of seven cases examined, it found four that appeared to have had positive energy impacts. The distinguishing features of these four were that they had relied heavily on fare reductions and/or that they had attracted large numbers of previous auto drivers by offering high-speed express bus service in a severely congested corridor. The most successful program from an energy standpoint was that implemented in Atlanta during 1972. Atlanta lowered its base fare from $.40 to $.15 and increased its bus mileage by 14 percent. The result was a

---

[26.] Data limitations are such that these should be considered only very rough approximations. CBO itself published high and low estimates of operating energy usage per vehicle mile by mode as well as the midrange estimates reported above. The CBO range totals were as follows:[106]

Auto	9,300–20,300 BTU
Bus	26,900–40,300 BTU
Heavy rail (old)	59,700–121,000 BTU
Heavy rail (new)	72,300–133,000 BTU
Commuter rail	77,500–150,000 BTU

TABLE 5.1
Operating Energy Usage of Urban Transportation Modes, in Typical Urban Circumstances (BTUs per Vehicle Mile)

Mode	Propulsion Energy	Maintenance, Station Construction, and Vehicle Mfg. Energy	Total
Auto	11,000	3,400	14,400
Bus	30,000	2,500	32,500
Heavy rail (old)	61,000	13,500	74,500
Heavy rail (new)	75,000	20,500	90,500
Commuter rail	105,000	10,700	115,700

Source: Congressional Budget Office, "Urban Transportation and Energy: The Potential Savings of Different Modes" (Washington: U.S. Government Printing Office, September 1977), table 7.

weekday ridership increase of 13 percent (or 28 percent relative to the expected level if the previous rate of patronage decline had continued). Of the new riders, 42 percent reported that they had previously driven. The others had previously ridden as passengers, not made the trip in question, or walked. Information was lacking on the proportion of new patrons reaching the transit system by car and on additional household usage of cars left at home; thus no estimates were made of energy consumption for these purposes. Moreover, the energy impact was estimated relative to the expected level had the previous 15 percent a year rate of ridership decline continued, rather than with reference to the actual patronage increase. Even so the estimated energy saving was only 221 bd, roughly 0.5 percent of transportation fuel consumption in the Atlanta region.[108]

Between August 1972 and February 1975, the San Diego Transit Corporation reduced average fares by 39 percent and increased bus mileage by 29 percent. The result was a dramatic 61 percent increase in ridership. This was a from a very low base, however. With a population roughly 90 percent as great as Atlanta's in 1972 —before either implemented its transit improvement program— San Diego's transit ridership had been only 28 percent as great. [109] Data were unavailable on the previous modes of the new transit users and their current means of reaching bus stops. Assuming a pattern like that recorded in Atlanta, however, the De Leuw, Cather analysts estimated a net energy saving of 115–120 bd.[110]

From the standpoint of energy saving per new rider, the transit improvements associated with the San Bernardino busway in Los Angeles yielded the greatest return. The busway is a physically separated two-lane facility in the median of a severely congested freeway. During the period examined (January 1973–November 1974), the express buses using it provided service only between downtown Los Angeles and a single terminal (El Monte) eleven miles to the east.[27] Their attraction was enhanced by the use of a $.25 fare, by the assignment of contraflow lanes for exclusive bus use on downtown streets, and by the availability of ample parking at the suburban terminal. Because transit service in the corridor had been virtually nonexistent prior to opening of the busway, virtually all of the patrons were new to transit. Seventy-nine percent of those riding after twenty-two months (about 6,500 riders per day in each direction) claimed that they had previously traveled as auto drivers. Currently 72 percent of them reached the system by automobile, and about three-quarters of these parked at the terminal all day. Only about 12 percent reported that other household members were now making increased use of the vehicles freed up during the day by their shifts to transit. Overall De Leuw, Cather estimated that the busway services were producing a net energy saving of 83 bd. (This estimate did not, however, include any offset for the energy cost of constructing the busway.)[111]

The Shirley Highway busway in Washington, D.C., is likewise a physically separated two-lane facility, eleven miles in length, in a severely congested corridor. Most of the buses using it, however, pick up and drop off their passengers on local streets near their homes rather than at major stations with parkride lots. As of October 1974, five years after the busway commenced operation, only 33 percent of the riders (who totaled 11,500 per day in each direction) arrived at their transit stop by car. Roughly three-fifths had located in the corridor during the period of busway operation,

27. Subsequently two intermediate stations have been opened.

so it was difficult to measure the diversion of auto drivers. The survey on which this analysis is based, however, asked users who had recently moved to the corridor how they had commuted from their previous residences. Utilizing this information, De Leuw, Cather estimated that 40 percent of the users were former auto drivers and that the net energy saving associated with the busway was 74 bd. (Again, this figure did not include any allowance for the energy cost of constructing the busway. Nor did it include any offset for additional household usage of automobiles left at home.)[112]

The Washington Metropolitan Area Transit Authority increased bus mileage by 16 percent in 1974 as part of a regionwide transit improvement program; patronage grew in response by only 5 percent. No data were available on the prior modes of the new patrons or their means of reaching transit stops. Assuming a pattern similar to that recorded in Atlanta, however, De Leuw, Cather estimated that the consequence was probably a very slight increase in regional fuel consumption (6 bd).[113]

Orange County, California, with a sprawling population larger than that of the Atlanta region, inaugurated bus service for the first time early in 1973. By 1974, it was operating about three-fourths as many bus miles per day as San Diego had been prior to undertaking its own transit improvement program, but it was carrying fewer than half as many riders. Some of the service was demand responsive. Data were unavailable on the previous modes of the new transit riders, their current means of reaching bus stops, and even their trip lengths. Under virtually all plausible assumptions, however, the net impact of the transit program was an increase in regional fuel consumption for transportation purposes. The range of increase considered most probable was 50–100 bd.[114]

The Lindenwold rapid transit line, 14.5 miles in length, commenced service in February 1969 between downtown Philadelphia and densely populated suburbs in southern New Jersey. A year later the line was carrying about 15,000 passengers a day in each direction, of whom 47 percent had previously commuted by other transit modes (bus or commuter rail). Another 25 percent had traveled as auto passengers or had not made the trips in question, leaving 28 percent who had driven.[28] Data were unavailable on increased household usage of cars left at home, so this factor was omitted from consideration. Nor was any offset taken for the energy cost of constructing the line. Even utilizing these favorable assumptions, the De Leuw, Cather analysts found that the most probable net energy impact was a saving of only 19 bd.[116] (A separate study of the Lindenwold data, carried out by Mayo S. Stuntz and Eric Hirst for FEA, concluded that the most likely impact was an increase in fuel consumption of several bd.)[117]

All of the above estimates reflect average bus and automobile fuel economy as of the early 1970s. Looking ahead through the mid-1980s, significant improvements in transit fuel economy appear unlikely. Rapid transit propulsion systems and bus diesel engines have long been engineered for fuel efficiency, and indeed the recent trend has been toward modest reductions in fuel economy to provide new amenities (such as air conditioning). Thus the outlook is for a decline in the potential energy benefits associated with improvements in transit service as automobiles become more fuel efficient. De Leuw, Cather estimated, for example, that an increase in average automobile fuel economy to 20 mpg would have cut the net energy savings associated with the San Diego and San Bernardino busway improvements by half.[118]

In brief, then, we have identified only one transit improvement strategy that seems both applicable on a nationwide or regionwide basis and highly likely to yield energy savings: that of reducing or eliminating transit fares while holding vehicle mileage increases to a minimum. Express bus services on special lanes in severely congested corridors can at times attract sufficiently high load factors and proportions of former drivers so as also to yield net

[28.] Notably, however, traffic counts on the highway bridge serving this corridor failed to confirm the auto travel reduction suggested by this estimate. A similar phenomenon was observed after the opening of the San Francisco BART system. The implication is not that the survey respondents were lying. It is rather that, as some drivers shifted to transit, others emerged to fill up the highways. Though detailed evidence is lacking in the Lindenwold case, it is clear that in the BART case, total trip making increased sharply, permitting the transit share to rise without discernibly reducing the volume of highway traffic.[115] The indirect effect of inducing new highway travel was explicitly ignored by the De Leuw, Cather analysts in calculating the energy impact of the Lindenwold line.

energy savings; but opportunities for buses to achieve dramatic speed advantages over general purpose traffic are relatively scarce. Additionally if major new construction is needed to realize such opportunities, as in the San Bernardino and Shirley busway examples, it is far less clear that aggregate energy savings can be realized in any reasonable time frame. New rapid transit lines as well are likely to entail a net energy loss if they require major construction. Finally it seems clear that even where transit strategies do succeed in reducing urban transportation fuel usage, the cost per unit of energy saved will be extraordinarily high. This is not to advance a general argument against such improvements, but it is to suggest that the case for them should generally be made on other grounds than energy conservation.

Other Strategies

The remaining measures under review in this book—demand responsive transit (DRT), improved traffic management, and highway construction—do not appear to have significant potential as instruments of energy conservation.

DRT systems (dial-a-ride and shared taxi services) have to date operated at extremely low load factors, even relative to the automobile.[29] As DRT fuel consumption is also high relative to the automobile, DRT fuel economy tends to be very low. Reid Ewing and Nigel Wilson carried out an exhaustive study of sixteen DRT systems in 1976. In the eight for which they were able to obtain fuel economy data, fuel consumption ranged from 5 to 20 passenger miles per gallon.[119] Typical routings were quite circuitous, however, because of the need to serve multiple origins and destinations. Ewing and Wilson judged consequently that effective passenger miles (those that would have been carried had each trip involved a direct routing) provided a more relevant basis for analysis. By this measure, the eight systems ranged in fuel consumption between 4 and 10 passenger miles per gallon.[120] On average, moreover, about three-quarters of the DRT patrons were making nonwork trips. Thus comparisons with automobile travel should

[29.] In calculating load factors, we exclude DRT drivers since they are not themselves achieving any travel objectives.

assume passenger car occupancies in the range of 2.3.[30] Postulating average automobile fuel economy in urban travel to be 12 mpg, this translates to 28 passenger miles per gallon for automobile trips comparable to those served by DRT.

Additionally a considerable proportion of the DRT users had previously not made the trips in question or had made them on foot: 33–53 percent in the nine systems studied by Ewing and Wilson for which data were available; in one, moreover, 36 percent had previously used fixed route bus service.[121] Thus while these DRT systems had significantly enhanced the mobility of their users, their energy impact was even more negative than the fuel economy comparison in the previous paragraph would suggest.

Traffic management improvements that give preference to high occupancy vehicles or that alleviate stop-and-go traffic congestion normally do yield fuel savings and at quite modest cost. The savings tend also to be very small, however.

By way of illustration, the Shirley busway is probably the nation's best-known example of success in implementing the preferential HOV concept. The gas saving attributable to it is equivalent to about 0.1 percent of total daily fuel consumption for transportation purposes in the Washington, D.C., area.[122] If one could imagine multiplying the Shirley busway by ten or fifty times in each region, this technique might loom as a highly significant energy-saving measure; but in fact the Shirley busway remains one of only a handful to have been implemented and to have had a substantial effect on transit usage in the United States.

In estimating the net energy impact of more conventional traffic management improvements, designed simply to alleviate congestion, one must weigh three factors—the latter two of which tend to offset the first. Fuel consumption rises with frequent changes in speed, and most notably with stop-and-go traffic conditions. On the other hand, fuel consumption also tends to increase with speed above the range of about 40 mph. And measures that succeed in alleviating congestion frequently induce additional

[30] NPTS reported average urban auto occupancies of 1.5 per vehicle mile for work travel and 2.6 per vehicle mile for nonwork travel in 1970.

traffic.[123] At the extreme, finally, it is notable that the most congested cities generally have the least auto mileage per capita, the highest levels of transit usage, and the lowest fuel consumption levels for transportation purposes. Per-capita energy usage for transport purposes in New York City, for example, is only 47 percent of the national average.[124] (See appendix F.)

Highway construction measures are subject to most of the same energy-related criticisms as traffic management measures, with one addition: highway construction activity itself is quite energy intensive. Economists Roger Bezdek and Bruce Hannon have estimated that federal expenditures alone for highway construction account for about 0.6 percent of total U.S. energy consumption. Diversion of these funds to a program of national health insurance, they judge, would save 64 percent of this total, and diversion to a mass transit investment program would save 61 percent.[125]

In short the immediate effect of any increase in highway construction activity would be additional energy usage. As the highways came into operation, they would help to save energy only where they alleviated severe stop-and-go traffic without inducing significant amounts of new traffic or facilitating high speed travel.

Rather than ask how the nation might save energy by increasing the level of highway construction activity, FEA commissioned a study recently of what energy savings might be achieved over the period 1976–1989 by terminating the urban portions of the federal highway program. The study, carried out by Charles River Associates (CRA), did not consider the energy costs of the construction activity itself; it dealt only with the impact on fuel consumption by travelers. CRA concluded that nationwide urban road capacity in 1989, after thirteen years without a federal highway program, would be only 5 percent less than if the program had continued. The effect of this capacity loss on traffic volume, it judged, would range from zero to a 1.3 percent reduction. The impact on traffic congestion would probably be negligible, though people would shift some of their travel to nonpeak periods and relatively uncongested sectors of their regions. The increase in congestion would, however, add between 0.25 and 0.65 percent to fuel consumption per vehicle mile. Overall the potential impact ranged from a fuel saving in 1989 equal to 1.1 percent of projected consumption in that year to a fuel loss of 0.65 percent. [126] (We estimate that termination of the program would also have yielded construction energy savings during each of the years 1976 through 1989 amounting to about 3.6 percent of fuel consumption for urban travel purposes.)[31]

Summary

Automobiles account for about one-quarter of U.S. oil consumption and about one-eighth of total U.S. energy consumption. The fuel requirements of the U.S. auto-dominant system of personal transportation are quite profligate by international standards. Per-capita energy usage for personal travel purposes is only about one-fifth as great in West Germany, for example, as in the United States.

These facts have been widely perceived as a problem only since 1973. But it has been generally accepted since then that, as part of the much larger set of issues posed by increasing U.S. dependence on oil imports, they constitute the most urgent problem associated with the urban transportation system.

Four types of measures have received prominent attention as means of curbing fuel consumption for urban travel purposes: regulation of the auto manufacturers to bring about the marketing of more fuel-efficient cars, price actions to increase the relative cost of gasoline and/or of automobiles with poor fuel economy, the promotion of carpooling and vanpooling, and mass transit service expansion.

Public policy to date has focused predominantly on the first of these approaches. Congress has mandated that the average fuel economy of new cars be increased from 14 mpg in 1974 to 27.5 mpg in 1985. Though many observers are skeptical, the auto manufacturers insist that they will achieve the 1985 target, and we

[31.] The bases for this estimate are as follows. On a nationwide basis, fuel consumption for highway travel purposes accounts for 16.5 percent of total U.S. fuel consumption. Federal highway expenditures account for another 0.6 percent, or 3.6 percent as much. In the absence of an urban-rural breakdown, we have assumed that these proportional relationships hold at least roughly for urban areas.

find no reason to doubt that they can. The estimated cost of their doing so will be $5-10 billion over the decade 1975-1985, but the estimated rate of return on this investment (from the standpoint of vehicle purchasers) is expected to be in the range of 300-600 percent.

Virtually any degree of fuel conservation might in principle be achieved by raising fuel prices, and at less real economic cost than by any other method. Even small price increases for conservation purposes have proven to be politically unfeasible, however, and estimates of demand elasticity suggest that quite large increases would be needed to induce significant fuel savings. Taxes on vehicles with poor fuel economy are likely to prove more accept-able than gasoline tax increases, if only because they can be struc-tured so that few voters will end up paying them. To date, how-ever, Congress has found it more attractive simply to mandate improved fuel economy than to pursue it by tax incentives.

The attractions of ride sharing as an energy conservation mea-sure are that it is already quite prevalent, even in the absence of government promotion, and that it saves money even as it con-serves fuel. Ride sharing does entail significant nondollar costs from a consumer standpoint, however—in the forms of time loss, schedule inflexibility, and potential for awkward social relation-ships—and the level of ride sharing has proven highly resistant to direct government influence. Government might, it appears, stimu-late significant increases in ride sharing if it could induce large numbers of employers to promote it vigorously, but this in turn is likely to prove extremely difficult except in the context of a national fuel emergency.

In general, transit service improvements have negligible fuel-saving potential. The most effective transit measures from an energy standpoint are fare reductions and the provision of high-speed bus services (utilizing preferential lanes and/or access ramps) in severely congested corridors. Fare reductions tend to cost the taxpayers hundreds of dollars per barrel saved, however, and new opportunities for the provision of express bus service in congested corridors are distinctly limited. Increases in other types of bus service tend to generate low incremental load factors and frequently result in slightly greater fuel consumption than would have occurred in their absence. New rapid transit systems will normally entail quite sizable energy losses when the books are kept (as they should be) in such a way as to include the energy costs of system development and projected improvements in automobile fuel economy.

Nature of the Problem

The issue of air quality in urban transportation provides a classic illustration of several of the most characteristic themes of our times:

• The growing importance, and difficulty of controlling externalities in an economy characterized by massive scale, rapidly evolving technologies, and growing interdependence.

• The pervasive roles of science and technology in identifying as well as generating and alleviating new problems.

• The frequent tendency for official goals to be established in a highly charged political atmosphere, on the basis of inadequate scientific evidence and with little regard for the precise costs, benefits, and even technical feasibility of policy alternatives.

• The extent to which public goal commitments are inextricably tied to assumptions—which often become apparent only as they prove invalid over time—about the nature of the means required to achieve them.

• The remarkable capacity for technological response in the private sector once government has led the way in assigning specific problems clear priority.

• The capacity of highly amorphous social movements in the current era of American politics—with little in the way of economic and institutional resources—to play a dominant role at times in legislative battles that involve great economic stakes.

• The far greater obstacles to dominance that such movements face, however, in the course of detailed policy implementation and adjustment over time.

The air pollution level in any setting is a product of interaction among the following factors: source emissions per unit of area, the overall size of the area, and the climatic, topographic, and vegetative characteristics of the locale.

The degree to which any given level of pollution constitutes a human health problem depends on the numbers and levels of susceptibility of those who live or work in the affected area. The degree to which it constitutes an economic problem depends as well on the susceptibility of the particular activities and types of property that are located in the area.

The degree to which any given level of substantive health and economic effects becomes a political problem tends in turn to be a function of the following: the state of scientific knowledge about pollution levels and consequences; the levels of risk or harm that are considered acceptable in the society; the intensity of public concern; the costs associated with specific clean-up alternatives; and insofar as these costs generate annoyance among large numbers of voters, the likelihood that they will identify and blame the responsible elected officials.

Discovery and Trend Estimation

Air pollution first emerged as a significant political issue in the mid-1960s. The extent to which it has been a substantive problem at various times in the past is debatable, but it seems clear that the air quality of urban America has deteriorated significantly since World War II and that a significant portion of this deterioration is attributable to the automobile. It is clear, further, that because air pollution was not an issue prior to the 1960s, the automobile industry had never viewed it as a significant criterion in the design of automobile engines.[1]

Between 1946 and 1968, automobile vehicle mileage tripled in urban America. In pursuing increased horsepower, moreover, the auto manufacturers implemented engine modifications that increased average emissions, particularly of lead and nitrogen oxides, per mile.[1] Total lead emissions, in consequence, increased more than fivefold and nitrogen oxide emissions more than sevenfold.[2]

As air pollution entered the public's consciousness, attention concentrated initially on those pollutants whose impacts were

[1.] Nitrogen and oxygen combine to form several stable oxides. Two of these, nitric oxide (NO) and nitrogen dioxide (NO_2) have been identified as important pollutants in the lower atmosphere. As both contribute to the formation of photochemical smog, they are frequently designated in combination as nitrogen oxides (NO_x).[2]

[2.] Auto vehicle mileage increased by 200 percent. Lead and NO_x emissions per vehicle mile increased by an estimated 79 and 140 percent, respectively.[3]

most obvious: smoke (consisting mainly of particulate matter), sulfur dioxide (which has a strong, unpleasant odor), and photochemical smog. Particulates and sulfur dioxide emissions are almost entirely products of stationary sources (such as industrial and power plants); thus we shall have little more to say about them here.[3] The predominant sources of photochemical smog in most settings, however, are motor vehicles.

Photochemical smog is mainly the product of hydrocarbons and nitrogen oxides—which are themselves invisible and odorless—combining in specific ways under the influence of sunlight and warmth to form photochemical oxidants. These are perceived as a whitish haze that causes respiratory and eye irritation, coughing, exhaustion, and sleepiness.[5]

Photochemical smog first became apparent in Los Angeles during the 1940s, and the chemical reactions that produce it were first identified in 1951. Los Angeles authorities moved quickly thereafter to deal with the smog problem by regulating industrial hydrocarbon emissions and by appealing to the motor vehicle manufacturers to bring mobile hydrocarbon emissions under control. They achieved rapid success with the former strategy but none at all for more than a decade with the latter. Illustratively the petroleum industry, which was the most important source of industrial hydrocarbon emissions in the Los Angeles area, had by 1957 reduced its aggregate emission level to one-eighth that of 1940. By contrast, motor vehicle emissions were increasing rapidly and accounted for 80 percent of the region's total.[6]

Public interest in air pollution spread rapidly throughout the nation in the 1960s, as Los Angeles and California authorities continued to pioneer in the development of control strategies. Along with hydrocarbons (HC) and nitrogen oxides (NO_x), moreover, pollution researchers increasingly focused on two pollutants that are not detectable by unaided human sensory organs: carbon monoxide (CO) and lead.[4] EPA estimated that as of 1973 highway

---

[3.] EPA has estimated that as of 1972, transportation sources accounted for only 4 percent of particulate emissions and 2 percent of sulfur dioxide emissions nationwide. [4]

[4.] As noted above, HC and NO_x are not themselves detectable by human beings, but the photochemical oxidants that they produce under specific conditions are detectable and provided the initial impetus for American air pollution research.

transportation sources accounted for 47 percent of nationwide HC emissions, 35 percent of NO_x emissions, 68 percent of CO emissions, and 88 percent of airborne lead emissions.[7] In the largest urban areas the motor vehicle share varied considerably but was on average slightly higher. (See table 6.1).

Evidence with respect to trends in urban air quality remains highly fragmentary even today. Outside of Los Angeles, careful monitoring of air quality in urban regions has gotten underway only since the mid-1960s. As late as 1973, the Environmental Protection Agency (EPA) was promulgating transportation control plans for metropolitan areas that were in many cases based solely on evidence from a single monitoring station, operating for one or two years, in each area.[5]

There does seem to be ample evidence that emission levels for the pollutants of major public concern, with the exception of particulates, increased substantially between 1940 and 1970. What is less certain is the impact on human exposure, given on the one hand the dramatic increase in urban population and on the other the sharp decrease in average urban density that occurred during this period. Since 1970, on the other hand, it seems clear that emission levels of most pollutants have been declining. The known exception is NO_x; data are unavailable with respect to lead.[6]

[5.] In Greater Boston, for example, the regionwide estimate of the HC reduction needed to meet the Clean Air Act ambient air quality standard was based on one day's monitoring at one location. The CO estimate was based on readings over the course of about a year at one location.[8] The extrapolations from readings at one site to regionwide air quality estimates were carried out via computer models of regional climate, topography, traffic conditions, and so forth.

[6.] EPA's 1975 nationwide estimates compare with those for 1970 and 1940 as follows:

	1975 vs. 1970 [9]	1975 vs. 1940 [10]
Particulates	−33	−60
SO_2	−4	44
CO	15	33
HC	−9	86
NO_x	7	272
Lead	NA	NA

TABLE 6.1
Highway Vehicle Emissions As a Percentage of Total Emissions in the Twenty
Largest U.S. Metropolitan Areas, 1973

Area	NO_x	HC	CO
New York/N.J./Conn.	40	65	91
Los Angeles	51	52	89
Chicago	29	36	28
Philadelphia	39	51	79
Detroit	28	34	67
San Francisco	56	64	86
Washington	48	74	94
Boston	43	56	95
Pittsburgh	21	72	83
St. Louis	20	46	71
Baltimore	47	41	95
Cleveland	40	49	71
Houston	22	17	37
Minneapolis	37	66	81
Dallas	43	60	80
Seattle	38	59	83
Milwaukee	41	27	85
Atlanta	52	67	85
Cincinnati	29	52	46
San Diego	59	60	89
Twenty-region average	39	59	77

Source: Calculated from EPA, "1973 National Emissions Report" (Research
Triangle Park, North Carolina: EPA, 1976).

Health Effects

There is still no evidence that photochemical smog causes death or serious disease in addition to discomfort.[11] There is very substantial evidence, however, that both carbon monoxide and lead disable and kill when absorbed into the bloodstream in sufficient concentrations.[12] Evidence on the scale of entire regions is fragmentary but supportive of the thesis that air pollution matters. Los Angeles, for example, has a markedly higher incidence of chronic respiratory disease than the rest of California. When gas consumption fell by 9.5 percent in San Francisco during the first quarter of 1974, cardiovascular disease deaths reportedly fell by 17 percent.[13]

A continuing problem, however, is that knowledge of the precise effects of any given concentration level, especially over sustained periods of time, remains meager. Research on large populations is extremely difficult because of the numerous factors at work in any region that can produce statistical health and mortality variations from national norms. Experimental research tends to focus on very high exposures, and by animals or plants rather than human beings, over relatively short time periods. The main sources of public concern, however, are the effects of human beings of more moderate concentrations over long time periods. Thus Howard Margolis has recently commented:

The fact was [in 1970], and remains today, that no one could make a solid scientific case that even totally eliminating auto emissions . . . would have any detectable effect on the nation's health. . . . (The official view of the British government today, for example, is that it has yet to be shown that auto emissions seriously harm anyone.) The situation was aptly described by an OECD [Organization for Economic Cooperation and Development] expert committee in 1972 (with the U.S. represented by EPA); "Ultimately the case for limiting vehicle emissions . . . rests not on incontrovertible evidence of physical harm but rather on the growing feeling that it is in the public interest to minimize all emissions suspected of having adverse effects on man's health, well-being, and environment."[14]

Similarly J. Clarence Davies III and Barbara Davies have concluded:

We do not know the effects of most pollutants on human health, on plants and animals, or on anything else. It is one of the major characteristics of pollution politics that decisions are made in the context of serious lack of knowledge about the effects of existing pollution and about the costs and benefits of any improvement in the existing situation. . . . Power, rhetoric, and instinct must substitute for knowledge.[15]

Debates about the differences in health benefit associated with alternative air quality targets are characterized mainly by an absence of persuasive data. In this situation, positions tend to become invested with great symbolic importance, and media attention tends to focus almost exclusively on which players are winning—with virtually no regard to what difference it makes.

Goals

Pre-1970 Control Efforts[16]

In 1948, twenty deaths and more than 500 illnesses were attributed to a prolonged air pollution inversion in Donora, Pennsylvania. The U.S. Public Health Service, on the basis of its investigation, reported that the Donora incident provided the first conclusive evidence that air pollution could cause human illness, and it recommended a program of publicly supported research into this problem. Federal legislation to support an extremely modest research program was enacted in 1955—appropriations averaged $3.3 million annually over the next five years—but the act clearly specified that pollution control was to remain a state and local responsibility. The federal role was to be confined to research and technical assistance.

In practice the Public Health Service confined its attentions under the 1955 act to stationary sources. Beginning in 1958, however, Congressman Paul Schenck (R.-Ohio) pressed for legislation requiring the surgeon-general to carry out research on and publish standards for motor vehicle emissions. This initiative encountered intense opposition from the automobile industry and the national administration. The industry maintained that legislation could serve no constructive purpose in the absence of a technological breakthrough. The administration contended that scientific knowledge was inadequate to support the promulgation of standards, that the issue was in any event predominantly a local one, and that in view of variations in local conditions any national uniform standards would be inappropriate. This combined opposition prevailed in 1958 and 1959. Schenck managed in 1960, however, to secure enactment of a bill requiring the Public Health Service to carry out a study of the health effects of motor vehicle emissions. This study, completed in 1962, found that it was impossible to quantify the damaging effects of motor vehicle emissions on the basis of current knowledge. The fragmentary research findings available did add up to a persuasive qualitative case, however, that motor vehicle emissions were responsible for significant adverse effects on "human beings and other biological systems."[17]

The next major air pollution statute to be enacted, the Clean Air Act of 1963, did not deal with motor vehicle pollution, but in 1964 the Special Senate Subcommittee on Air and Water Pollution, chaired by Senator Edmund Muskie (D.-Maine), conducted extensive field hearings on the subject.[7] Finding that all of its expert witnesses judged the automobile to be responsible for at least half of the national air pollution problem and (perhaps even more significantly) that California had recently succeeded in obtaining an industry commitment to reduce HC and CO emissions beginning in 1967, the subcommittee urged enactment of a national regulatory program modeled on that of California.[18]

The result, in 1965, was the Motor Vehicle Air Pollution Control Act, the first federal statute ever enacted specifically to regulate the motor vehicle industry for any purpose.[20] Despite the landmark character of the act in this respect, the industry's opposition was tepid. It indicated that it was more than willing to meet the California standards nationally but suggested that the air pollution

---

[7.] The 1963 act authorized an expanded research program and grants to state and local governments for air pollution control. Additionally it empowered the Department of Health, Education and Welfare to conduct hearings and conferences with polluters and, where persuasion failed, to seek injunctions against them. The only provision of the act dealing with motor vehicles called on the surgeon-general to "encourage the continued efforts on the part of the automotive and fuel industries to prevent pollutants from being discharged."[19]

problem outside of California did not warrant the imposition of such an economic penalty on motorists. Scholars examining this legislative history have concluded that, in the emerging climate of public concern about air pollution, the industry's main fear was the possibility of having to comply with fifty separate state standards. If these were the options, federal regulation was clearly the lesser evil. It may also have doubted that federal standards would be very hard to live with. California's initial standards had been developed with careful attention to what was feasible and with a clear understanding that all costs would be passed on to automobile purchasers. Responding to the emergence of national concern about air pollution, moreover, the industry had already begun to reduce HC and CO emissions. The 1965 models were about 25 percent cleaner with respect to these two pollutants than those of two years earlier, and were more than halfway toward the 1967 California standards. The improvement had been achieved at negligible cost, and it was estimated that, in time, the industry could achieve about a 75 percent reduction from the uncontrolled 1964 levels at a cost of roughly twenty-five dollars a car.[8] [21]

The 1965 act authorized the secretary of Health, Education and Welfare to prescribe new-vehicle standards for any emissions found to endanger human health or welfare. The secretary had in fact opposed the legislation on the ground that inadequate information existed as to what standards were practicable.[22] Following enactment, however, he required that the industry meet the 1967 California standards on a nationwide basis in model year 1968. During the next several years the federal standards continued to lag slightly behind those of California.[9] By 1970, nevertheless, the federal standards required an HC emission level 55 percent below that of 1963 and a CO standard 62 percent lower.[23]

[8.] At the time it was generally assumed that a choice had to be made between controlling HC and CO emissions on the one hand or NO_x emissions on the other, and that the sensible strategy was to concentrate on the former. HC and CO emissions are the products of incomplete combustion, NO_x emissions of high combustion temperatures. Normally measures to achieve more complete combustion entail higher combustion temperatures.

[9.] The 1965 act was silent on the question of federal preemption, though apparently it was assumed that the states would defer to the federal government on the matter of new car emission standards. In response to subsequent controversy over this issue, Congress

The Clean Air Act Amendments of 1970[24]
During late 1969 and throughout 1970, public interest in the air pollution issue exploded. Unlike the issues of race, poverty, and the war in Vietnam, which had dominated the politics of the 1960s, environmental quality was an issue around which it seemed that Americans might unite. It also seemed to be a policy arena in which substantial progress might be made without enormous public expenditures, a matter of particular concern to the Republican administration that had come into office in 1969. The National Environmental Policy Act had been enacted late in 1969. Senator Muskie, considered the frontrunner for the 1972 Democratic presidential nomination, had indicated that he intended to press for stronger air pollution regulation in 1970. And the automobile industry had informed the administration that it could achieve dramatic further progress in the years ahead.

In this set of circumstances, President Nixon proposed (early in 1970) that the industry be required to meet the following standards by the 1975 model year:

● HC emissions: 0.93 grams per mile (89 percent below 1963 and 76 percent below the 1970 standard):

● CO emissions: 16.2 grams per mile (81 percent below 1963 and 51 percent below 1970); and

● NO_x emissions: 1.4 grams per mile (not previously controlled; 65 percent below the estimated levels of 1963 and 1970).

The president of General Motors had already indicated publicly that these standards could be met provided the oil companies marketed lead-free gasoline that would not damage the industry's pollution control devices. The administration had, moreover, recently published even more ambitious goals for 1980, and the industry had indicated that it expected to be able to meet these as well.[25]

explicitly asserted federal preemption—with a specific exemption for California—in the National Emission Standards Act of 1967. The motor vehicle industry was the primary supporter of the 1967 act, except that it would have preferred preemption with respect to California as well as the other forty-nine states. The president of the Automobile Manufacturers Association testified before the Muskie subcommittee that more than one hundred bills were currently pending in state legislatures on the subject of motor vehicle emission standards.

In the months following the president's submission, however, activist environmental pressure continued to intensify. Massive Earth Day demonstrations occurred throughout the nation in April. Early in May a Ralph Nader study group issued a report charging that Senator Muskie had "failed the nation in the field of air pollution control legislation."[26] National opinion polls were showing that the public as a whole attached very high priority to the pollution issue.[27]

In July the federal administration sponsored a conference on alternatives to the internal combusion engine, following which the United Auto Workers joined leading environmental organizations in publicly calling for "standards so strict as to ban the internal combustion engine within 5 years."[28] Shortly thereafter the California state senate, by an overwhelming vote, did pass a bill banning the internal combustion engine as of 1975.[29]

In this charged political environment, a process occurred that Charles O. Jones has labeled "speculative augmentation." Normally, Jones writes, "decision makers are expected to refine existing policy by determining what is technically and administratively feasible, as well as what is within limits of acceptability to those being regulated. In speculative augmentation, however . . . feasibility is less important than estimating what will be acceptable to a rather indistinct 'public' perceived to be demanding strong action."[30] The view became predominant that the auto manufacturers could accomplish just about any technical feat required. Thus the Muskie subcommittee decided in August, without holding hearings on the subject, to move the administration's announced 1980 goals forward to 1975. Although the industry claimed that the new deadline was technically infeasible, the act, as Howard Margolis writes, "swept through Congress virtually without debate, to be then warmly embraced by the Administration, which claimed it as the response to the President's leadership on environmental matters."[31]

The opposition of the auto manufacturers was almost as muted in 1970 as it had been in 1965. Seeking to account for this phenomenon, Margolis concludes that the industry's primary fear was legislation banning the internal combustion engine. A deadline could always be relaxed, but a policy decision to alter the basic technology of the automobile engine would be far more difficult to cope with. It seemed unlikely, moreover, that in the current political atmosphere an extremely tough bill could be averted. This being the case, it made sense for the industry to concentrate on specific provisions of little symbolic but great administrative importance. For example, while the environmentalists insisted successfully that pollution control equipment be required to last for the "useful life" of each car, the industry succeeded in having that life defined as five years or 50,000 miles, whichever comes first—in fact, slightly under half the average lifetime of each car.[32]

As enacted, the Clean Air Act Amendments left as little as possible to administrative discretion. The basic standards were in most cases mandated in the act itself or described in terms of a single criterion—leaving the administrator solely to determine the facts bearing upon that criterion rather than to balance criteria as well.[10] Not only were the ultimate deadlines for compliance set in the act, but so were numerous interim deadlines for regulatory promulgations and plan submission. Finally citizens' suits to compel enforcement were authorized, and they were subsequently to play a key role in ensuring strict interpretation of the statutory provisions.[11]

Section 202 of the amended Clean Air Act specified precise automobile emission reduction targets. CO and HC emissions were, by the 1975 model year, to be reduced 90 percent below the 1970 standard (95 percent and 96 percent, respectively, below the

[10.] Altshuler, together with Robert Curry, has elsewhere elaborated on this point, stressing that whereas all developmental agencies are currently required by statute to consider multiple values (including those that bear upon environmental quality), most environmental agencies are not. This has led, in court tests, to the appearance of judicial preference for environmental over developmental values.[33]

[11.] For example, when EPA granted the urban regions needing transportation control plans in order to meet the Clean Air Act ambient air quality standards a two-year extension, the maximum permitted by law, a citizens' suit led to judicial reversal of this action. (The U.S. court of appeals for the District of Columbia found that such extensions could be justified only on a specific showing in each case that practical means were unavailable to meet the statutory deadline.) When EPA ruled that areas with very clean air could permit degradation as long as no air quality standards were violated, a citizens' suit produced a judicial ruling that the act precluded any air quality degradation anywhere. And when the EPA administrator failed to promulgate an ambient air quality standard for lead, a citizens' suit led to a judicial determination that he must do so within twelve months (of November 12, 1976).[35]

uncontrolled 1963 levels). NO_x emissions had not yet been subjected to federal regulation; thus the amended act required that the current estimated uncontrolled emission level be reduced 90 percent by model year 1976. Margolis has noted that as of late 1976 no other country except Japan had adopted standards less than a factor of five higher than the American HC standard and less than a factor of seven higher than the CO and NO_x standards.[12] [36] (See table 6.2.)

In addition to establishing these emission control standards and deadlines, the amended Clean Air Act provided as follows: (a) that the EPA administrator could grant the manufacturers an extension of one year with respect to each pollutant if he found that technology was not available to achieve the standard on schedule (in which case he could specify an interim standard); (b) that the EPA test procedure should ensure that the emission control equipment would work effectively during the useful life of each car as defined in the act; and (c) that any manufacturer selling cars in violation of the act would be subject to a fine of $10,000 per car.

Finally the act required the EPA administrator to establish ambient air quality standards for each pollutant that he found to have an adverse effect on public health and welfare and to ensure their achievement (insofar as technically feasible) by mid-1975. States containing air quality control regions (AQCRs) expected to be in violation of any of the ambient air quality standards after mid-1975 were to produce clean air implementation plans by mid-

[12.] The 1970 amendments did not stipulate a precise lead standard. Section 211(c)(1) of the amended Clean Air Act did authorize the EPA administrator, however, to control or prohibit the use of any fuel or fuel additive he found to endanger the public health or welfare. The administrator promulgated both a standard and a schedule for phased compliance in December 1973. It called for reducing the current average level of about 2.0 grams of lead per gallon to an average of 0.5 grams by 1979. Most of the reduction was to be achieved by marketing lead-free gasoline for use by cars equipped with lead-sensitive emission control devices, but the standard was also to require a reduction in the lead content of leaded gasoline to about 1.25 grams per gallon. (The uncertainty is due to the fact that each refiner was to be responsible for achieving the overall average of 0.5 by whatever methods it chose.) When this standard was challenged in court, EPA suspended its application. Only after the litigation was finally resolved in EPA's favor in June 1976 did the compliance schedule (then in its second of five years) finally go into effect. As the lead standard and schedule have never been alleged by the oil refiners to exceed feasibility and have never attracted much public attention, we shall say no more about them here.[37]

TABLE 6.2
Auto Emission Levels and Standards

Standard (Grams per Mile)	Hydrocarbons (HC)	Carbon Monoxide (CO)	Nitrogen Oxides (NO$_x$)
1963 (pre-control) actual	8.7	87.0	4.0
1970 federal standards	3.9	33.3	not controlled
1975 proposed Nixon standards[a]	0.93	16.2	1.4
1975/1976 standards enacted 1970[b]	0.41	3.4	0.4
1977 actual	1.5	15.0	2.0
Canadian standards through 1980[c]	2.0	25.0	3.1

Source: Howard Margolis, "Another View of the Politics of Auto Emissions Control" (Center for International Studies, Massachusetts Institute of Technology, August 1977), table 1.

[a] Announced, February 1970.

[b] Clean Air Act Amendments of 1970. HC and CO intended for 1975; NO$_x$ intended for 1976.

[c] Similar to those of Sweden and Australia. Common Market is substantially less stringent. Japan is numerically identical to U.S., but differences in test procedure make exact comparison difficult.

1972.[13] If, in the course of developing these plans, they found that they could not achieve compliance simply by implementing stationary source controls, they were to prepare transportation control plan (TCP) components as well. TCPs were to include strategies for reducing vehicle miles of motor vehicle travel and/or for reducing emissions per mile of travel (for example, by retrofitting older vehicles with pollution control equipment). If the EPA administrator found any state implementation plan inadequate, he was required to promulgate an adequate plan himself. If, however, he found that the inadequacies reflected technical obstacles to compliance by mid-1975, he could grant extensions of up to two years.[38]

[13.] EPA has subdivided the nation (excluding only a small portion of Alaska) into 247 AQCRs. Nearly all AQCRs include at least one standard metropolitan statistical area (SMSA), but in virtually every case the AQCR is substantially larger than its SMSA component(s).

In April 1971, the administrator promulgated ambient standards for CO, HC, nitrogen dioxide (NO_2), and photochemical oxidants.[14] [39] All but the NO_2 standard, which referred to the annual mean concentration level, prescribed annual maxima for periods of between one and eight hours that were not to be exceeded anywhere at any time.[15] The main basis for these standards was a 1970 in-house study by the Department of Health, Education and Welfare (HEW). The staff personnel who carried out this study had sought to establish the concentration levels of automobile-related pollutants that could be tolerated by anyone, however ill or fragile, without ill effect. Finding the evidence extremely skimpy, they had adopted a conservative two-step procedure, first ascertaining the lowest levels at which any ill effects had ever been observed and then building in large margins of safety below these levels. The NO_2 standard was derived on the basis of a study showing that second-grade children and their families in a single neighborhood with high NO_2 levels had suffered above normal respiratory disease rates. The oxidant standard was based on a study showing impairment of the performance of long-distance runners. The CO one-hour standard was based on two studies, the more serious of which showed that high CO concentrations increased the frequency of heart attacks among persons already suffering from heart disease.[40]

The auto emission standards prescribed in the act itself were apparently based on the same study. Having arrived at recommended ambient standards, it had gone on to estimate the levels of emission per mile that would be compatible with them as of 1990 (given estimated travel growth to that year) in the metropolitan area with the most severe air pollution problem in the nation.[41]

The study was not a cost-benefit analysis, and its approach, while reasonable on health grounds given the limited evidence available, was extraordinarily ambitious in political and technical terms. By way of comparison, a safety standard that entailed zero

[14.] He established standards for sulfur dioxide (SO_2) and particulates as well, but since these did not have significant implications for urban transportation we shall not discuss them here.

[15.] The oxidant standard was for the highest hour in the year; the HC standard was for the highest morning peak period (6-9 A.M.) in the year; and there were two CO standards, for the highest hour and eight hours in the year, respectively.

levels of mortality and personal injury would be achieved only by a total ban on travel.

Surprisingly, however, the Clean Air standards themselves have come in for little challenge since 1970—though a great deal of controversy has occurred with respect to methods and timetables for achieving them. Official and scholarly reviewers have invariably taken the aim of perfect safety as a reasonable given and focused on whether EPA's ambient standards are unreasonably stringent with reference to it. More or less invariably, they have concluded with a puzzled affirmation that the EPA standards are as plausible as any that might be put foward on the basis of current knowledge. Thus a committee of the National Academy of Sciences concluded in 1973 that there was "no substantial basis for changing the present standards."[42] David Harrison, Jr. and John Kain have concluded a more recent review of the literature with the following observation: "Although it is difficult to find many experts who will defend the present standards, it is still more difficult to find anyone who will recommend and defend an alternative set of standards."[43]

Implementation, 1970–1977

The Clean Air Act Amendments of 1970 were enacted toward the end of a period characterized by rapid economic growth, low rates of unemployment, relatively stable prices, and cheap, plentiful energy. Beginning in the final quarter of 1973, however, every one of these circumstances changed abruptly for the worse. With the quadrupling of world oil prices and the Arab oil embargo, the nation entered its worst postwar recession, accompanied by its worst experience of peacetime inflation (see table 6.3). Meanwhile the automobile manufacturers had continued to insist that they could not achieve the Clean Air Act emission standards by 1975, and they now added that a singleminded focus on achieving the Clean Air Act standards and deadlines would entail significant energy as well as dollar penalties. Finally, as it became clear that achievement of the ambient air quality standards on schedule would require constraints on individual travel behavior in a number of large metropolitan areas, it became increasingly apparent as well: that such restraints would provoke many voters who

TABLE 6.3
Selected National Economic Indexes, 1962–1975

	Rate of Increase: Gross National Product (Constant Dollars)	Unemployment Rate	Rate of Increase: Consumer Price Index	Rate of Increase Wholesale Price Index of Fuels, Power, and Related Products
1962–1965 (annual average)	5.3%	5.2%	1.5%	−1.0%
1966–1969 (annual average)	3.9	3.7	4.3	1.4
1970	−0.3	4.9	5.5	5.3
1971	3.0	5.9	3.4	7.5
1972	5.7	5.6	3.4	3.9
1973	5.5	4.9	8.8	13.2
1974	−1.4	5.6	12.2	55.1
1975	−1.3	8.5	7.0	17.7

Source: Council of Economic Advisors, *Economic Report of the President* (Washington: U.S. Government Printing Office, 1978), tables B-2, B-29, B-54, B-55.

had hitherto been on the sidelines of the air quality issue to outrage; that the number of such voters was far greater than the number of militant, still-uncompromising environmentalists; and that when faced with choices involving confrontation between these two groups, the vast majority of elected officials would side with the former.

In this constellation of circumstances, trade-offs between the objective of perfectly safe air quality by 1975 on the one hand and the values of prosperity, energy efficiency, and consumer freedom on the other quickly came to be viewed in a more flexible light.

With the standards themselves immune from serious challenge, controversy at first focused exclusively on the timetables. Until

1974, Congress had been able to leave all responsibility for retreat to EPA. But by that year the EPA administrator had exhausted his limited discretion under the 1970 legislation. He had authorized a one-year extension for the auto manufacturers in meeting each of the three emission standards, and two-year extensions for each of the metropolitan areas threatened with the need for transportation controls in order to meet the ambient air quality standards. Although the energy crisis provided a perfect excuse beginning in 1974 for a broad reappraisal of the 1970 clean air commitments, Congress found it impossible during the next three years to muster majorities for more than year-by-year postponements. The only amendments adopted during this period were to authorize two additional extensions in the CO and HC emission standards and one additional extension in the NO_x emission standard, shifting the deadline for meeting all three to the beginning of model year 1978 (September 1977).

The strict legal implication of this failure to amend the ambient air quality standards was that urban areas would take compensatory actions to offset the negative air quality impacts of the emission standard extensions. In practice, however, a process of deliberate—if never explicitly admitted—nonenforcement of the transportation control plan requirement got underway in 1974. Congress in effect mandated this nonenforcement policy by quietly enacting prohibitions on use of the most powerful tools EPA had identified to bring about reductions in automobile travel. But it never acknowledged that in thereby crippling enforcement it was implicitly relaxing the tight deadlines adopted with such fanfare (and invested with such symbolic significance) in 1970.

Although the emission standard deadlines were the only ones formally extended, the only substantial progress that in fact occurred between 1970 and 1977 was in the emission standard portion of the clean air program. New cars in model years 1976 and 1977, according to EPA, were about 60 percent cleaner than 1970 models with respect to HC emissions, about 55 percent cleaner with respect to CO emissions, and about 50 percent cleaner with respect to NO_x emissions.[16]

[16.] By comparison with uncontrolled 1963 cars, these represented emission reductions of 83 percent, 83 percent and 50 percent respectively.

HEW's 1970 study, it will be recalled, had estimated that the requisite transportation contribution to meeting the ambient standards could be achieved by 1990 if all vehicles on the road at that time complied with the emission control standards. This target date was compatible with the Nixon administration's announced objective of achieving 90 percent reductions in new-car emissions by 1980 and with the ten-year life of the average American car.

The deadline for compliance set by Congress in 1970, however, was mid-1975. As of that date, even if the new car emission standards had been fully achieved, only about 10 percent of all cars on the road (those produced in the 1975 model year) would have been in compliance with them, and about two-fifths of the active fleet would still have pre-dated even the baseline 1970 model year.

In 1972, following receipt of the initial state implementation plans, EPA reported that sixty-six AQCRs, containing three-fifths of the nation's population, were currently in violation of at least one ambient air quality standard.[44] By mid-1975, EPA estimated, new car and stationary source emission controls would reduce the number of regions in noncompliance to twenty-seven (including twenty-nine SMSAs).

Projecting the anticipated benefits of source control progress beyond 1975, EPA estimated that twenty-one to twenty-four regions would be in noncompliance as of 1977 unless transportation controls were adopted, twelve to fourteen in 1980, and nine to ten in 1985. Thereafter, unless lower emission standards were mandated, traffic growth would tend to increase the number of regions in noncompliance.[45]

Three major sources of error in these estimates, all tending to worsen the outlook, gradually became apparent in the years following 1972. First, the emission control projections (for stationary as well as mobile sources) on which they were based quickly proved to be overly optimistic, and the divergence from actual trends has grown substantially with every passing year. Second, continued and improved monitoring gradually revealed in many AQCRs that existing levels of pollution were a good deal higher than originally estimated. Third, it became increasingly apparent that the performance of automobile emission control devices was highly variable depending on their age, vehicle use patterns, and climatic factors. An internal EPA report, completed in June 1975, concluded that "only at low mileage are any of the [interim model year] standards even approached." It found that "while compliance with, or proximity to, the standards seemingly appeared to improve from Model Year '68 through Model Year '71, thereafter (as the standards became more stringent) noncompliance appears to have increased." The report estimated that the 1974 models, over their entire lives, would in practice achieve HC and CO reductions below the 1970 levels of only 15 percent and 22 percent respectively, although the 1974 (interim) standards called for reductions of 61 percent and 62 percent respectively.[17] [46]

By mid-1975 EPA officials were estimating privately that, even without taking on-the-road performance degradation of emission control devices into account, at least sixty AQCRs would be in violation of one or more ambient air quality standards as of mid-1977 (when the two-year extensions authorized under the 1970 amendments ran out) rather than the twenty-one to twenty-four estimated three years earlier. Moreover the regions that had been identified earlier were now, in almost every case, expected to be more severely in noncompliance as of 1977 and later dates than previously anticipated.[47] If EPA was keeping these new, more pessimistic projections to itself, the reason lay in its experiences seeking to implement the TCP requirement over the previous three years.

Finding the draft state implementation plans submitted in 1972 for those AQCRs requiring TCPs inadequate, the administrator had granted two-year extensions (the maximum permitted by the 1970 legislation) in the compliance deadline.[18] During 1973 and 1974, however, as it had become apparent that the states would

[17.] The authors of the report recommended two measures to improve compliance. First, they urged that EPA shift from exclusive reliance on the testing of prototype models to the testing of large numbers of vehicles as they came off the assembly line. California already conducted assembly line tests of 2 percent of automobile engines destined for sale in that state. Second, they urged periodic inspections of all vehicles actually on the road—with the manufacturers being held responsible for compliance.

[18.] As noted previously, the D.C. Court of Appeals disallowed a blanket extension early in 1973. Subsequently, however, the EPA Administrator granted case-by-case extensions for all of the affected AQCRs.

not voluntarily adopt plans strong enough to achieve compliance even by mid-1977, he had been compelled—in every case but one among the eighteen in which it appeared that motor vehicle travel reductions would be required—to draw up plans himself. Four of these called for reduction in projected motor vehicle mileage of more than 50 percent. (In the worst case, Los Angeles, the required reduction was 84 percent.) Nine others required reductions of 10-50 percent.[48] All of these plans, moreover, were premised on the optimistic 1972 estimates on baseline air quality and future emission control progress.

In developing the plans, EPA had concluded that significant reductions in auto use were likely to be achieved only by the application of tough disincentives. Thus while the plans did include a variety of positive inducements to increased transit and carpool use (such as, expanded bus service and carpool matching programs), they depended fundamentally on disincentives to generate a substantial consumer response to them. Specifically,

1. Parking surcharges were central elements of seven plans, those for Boston, the District of Columbia, Los Angeles, San Francisco, San Diego, Sacramento, and Fresno.

2. Outright reductions in parking space availability were features of most of the plans. Particular measures ranged from commuter parking bans on streets near central commercial areas to mandatory reductions in employer-provided parking throughout the urbanized area.

3. Reductions in gasoline availability were included—as a contingency, last resort strategy—in several plans, most notably that of Los Angeles. The administrator stated even as he promulgated these plans, however, that he considered this measure too drastic. He was including it, he said, in order to be in technical compliance with the law, but he was also submitting draft legislation to the Congress that would permit extensions of the ambient air quality deadlines for the areas affected.[49]

The initial public outcry against these proposals focused on the parking surcharges. A congressional response was not long in coming. Late in 1973 the conference committee on an "emergency" energy bill adopted a provision prohibiting EPA from imposing any surcharges. Although President Nixon vetoed the bill in question for other reasons, the EPA administrator (in January 1974) removed the parking surcharge elements from all TCPs that contained them and ordered that replacements be found to bring the plans into technical compliance with the law. (The prohibition on surcharges was subsequently enacted as part of the Energy Supply and Environmental Coordination Act of 1974.)[50]

The main alternative that EPA officials came up with was intensified parking regulation. In Greater Boston, for example, the original plan had included numerous surcharge and parking regulatory provisions focused on the core of the region. With the surcharge provisions removed, parking regulation was extended regionwide. All employers of more than fifty people were to be required to reduce their ratio of parking spaces to employees by 25 percent. That is, an employer who provided one space for every employee in 1974 would have to reduce the ratio to 0.75 by 1977; an employer who currently provided an average of 0.4 spaces per employee would have to reduce the ration to 0.3.[51]

Public criticism next focused on the parking regulatory provisions. Congress responded in December 1974 by enacting, as part of an EPA appropriations bill, a prohibition on the use of any funds for the promulgation or implementation of parking regulations. Though the original prohibition applied only through the end of fiscal 1975, it soon became clear that it would be reenacted as part of all future appropriations bills. Thus in July 1975 EPA suspended the parking regulatory elements of all TCPs indefinitely.

Finally the legal authority for EPA to enforce Clean Air Act implementation plans at all was brought into serious question by a series of court decisions during the latter half of 1975. All of the plans relied on state enforcement. During 1974, a number of states brought suit on the ground that EPA lacked authority to require them to execute federal plans. In August and September 1975, two federal appeals courts decided the California and Maryland cases against EPA. Although the decisions were based on statutory grounds, both courts indicated that serious constitutional questions would arise if the statute were interpreted as EPA urged.[52] The District of Columbia case was decided in October, with an opinion only slightly more favorable to EPA. The court of appeals upheld the administrator's authority to require compliance by the states with emission standards for their own facilities and to require traffic management and service strategies intended to improve the relative attractiveness of mass transit; but even it rejected the claim that EPA could require new state regulatory activities bearing upon the private sector.[19] [53]

Thus, by late 1975, the accelerated schedule for air quality improvement that Congress had legislated five years earlier was in shambles. Taking on-the-road degradation into account, new car emissions were only about 20 percent below those of 1970 rather than 90 percent. The law still required EPA to take whatever supplemental measures were necessary to achieve the ambient air quality standards by mid-1977, but Congress had effectively repealed the agency's authority to curtail automobile travel and several U.S. appeals courts had found that it could not even require such regulatory programs as the inspection of emission control equipment. This situation with respect to Clean Air Act implementation was to remain essentially unchanged over the following twenty months as the focus of attention shifted once again to the legislative arena.

The Clean Air Act Amendments of 1977
The congressional effort to reestablish a coherent and broadly acceptable air pollution control program got underway early in 1976 and was not concluded until August 1977. The major issues with respect to urban transportation were automobile emission standards and deadlines on the one hand, and supplemental transportation controls as a means of hastening the achievement of ambient air quality standards on the other.

[19.] At issue in these cases were two types of regulatory activity: vehicle inspection and maintenance programs, and emission control retrofit requirements for older vehicles. In May 1977, the Supreme Court remanded all three cases back to the appeals courts on a technicality. Though the TCPs in question were dormant by this time in any event, EPA stated an intention to see the cases through to the end—so as to ascertain what it might be able to require of states in more favorable future circumstances.

Agreement on the latter issue proved relatively easy to achieve. Virtually no one in Congress chose to insist that the early achievement of ambient air quality standards was a goal of sufficient importance to warrant the imposition of motor vehicle travel disincentives; and even the environmental organizations, viewing this issue as a lost cause, chose to focus their energies on other provisions of the bill. The bill as enacted extended the final deadline for achieving the ambient air quality standards by a full decade, from May 31, 1977, to December 31, 1987. It required the states to submit new Clean Air Act implementation plans to the administrator by January 1, 1979, and continued the administrator's authorization to promulgate plans directly where he found the state plans inadequate. The plans were to "provide for the implementation of all reasonably available control measures as expeditiously as practicable." In defining such measures, however, the amended Clean Air Act conspicuously omitted any reference to automobile travel disincentives. Indeed the only transportation measure required—and this only in regions expected still to exceed one or more of the ambient air quality standards after December 31, 1982—was "a specific schedule for implementation of a vehicle emission control inspection and maintenance program."[20] [54] Determination of the acceptability of such schedules was left to the discretion of the administrator.

In accord with the historic preference of Clean Air Act draftsmen for tougher symbolic than actual commitments, the 1977 amendments backed up the new inspection and maintenance requirement with two penalty provisions.[55] First, a region covered by the requirement and failing to submit an acceptable plan on schedule would—unless it satisfied the administrator that

---

[20] The other required provisions all related to stationary sources. Notably, however, the 1977 amendments overruled the earlier court decision that air quality degradation could not be permitted anywhere. Indeed they explicitly permitted air quality degradation even where the standards were already being violated. They simply required that environmental impact statements be carried out with respect to proposed major new emission sources and that these not go forward except upon a determination that their benefits "significantly outweigh the environmental and social costs." In arriving at such decisions, alternative sites, production processes, and emission control techniques are to be considered. Additionally the amendments required that implementation plans provide for the adoption of "reasonably available" emission control technologies at existing stationary sources.

it was making reasonable efforts toward the development of such a plan—become ineligible for most federal highway assistance as well as for the meager grants available under the Clean Air Act itself. The only highway projects permitted to go forward in such a region would be those justified primarily by their contributions to safety, mass transit, and/or air quality improvement. Second, a region failing to implement its plan would be barred from receiving grants under the Clean Air Act but would remain eligible to receive its full quota of federal highway assistance. In short, the primary emphasis of the amended act seemed to be on securing compliance with its paperwork requirements rather than on ensuring substantive implementation.

If there was general agreement not to require much of state and local governments or of individual motorists in the pursuit of transportation-related emission reductions, there was intense controversy over what to require of the automobile companies. The companies now claimed that they could not meet the ultimate HC standard enacted in 1970 before the end of the decade, that they might need several years even beyond that to meet the CO standard, and that the NO_x standard should be relaxed substantially or deferred indefinitely. Insistence on the NO_x standard, even as a target for the mid-1980s, they argued, would severely impede their quest for fuel economy improvements. Specifically, they maintained, the most promising way to achieve the federally mandated target of doubling fuel economy between 1974 and 1985 without forcing all new-car buyers into subcompact cars would equip most larger models with diesel engines. Unless the ultimate NO_x standard were raised from 0.4 grams per mile to 1.0 or even somewhat higher, the manufacturers asserted, adoption of the diesel would essentially be ruled out. And, they stressed, no persuasive evidence existed that such an increase would have any harmful effect on the health of the American people.[21]

21. Additionally industry spokesmen argued that the emission control technology relied upon to date in the face of tight federally imposed deadlines was inherently makeshift. The technology in question, the catalytic converter, involved cleaning up the exhausts of the inherently dirty Otto cycle internal combustion engine. The converters were expensive, and they had proved highly vulnerable to degradation in on-the-road operating conditions. It was impossible to know what might occur in future, the industry maintained, but Congress should not legislate such rigid standards that the adoption of new, inherently much cleaner, and more energy-efficient engine technologies would be stymied.

The leading environmental organizations disagreed sharply with all of these industry positions. They pointed to new administration estimates that even if the current emission standards were achieved promptly some AQCRs would remain in violation of each ambient air quality standard through the year 2000,[22] and that even the 0.4 gram per mile NO_x emission standard could be achieved by model year 1983 at no fuel penalty (though at a sticker price penalty of about eighty dollars over and above that required to meet the 1.0 gram standard.[23] Concerning degradation the environmentalists argued that the answer was to supplement the current practice of testing prototype vehicles for durability by requiring company warranties that emission controls would work effectively during the lifetime of each vehicle. And in order to ensure utilization of these warranties by motorists, they maintained, Congress should provide for the periodic inspection of all registered vehicles.[58]

The legislative battle of 1976–1977 differed from that of 1970 in several very important ways. First, the issues of energy, unemployment, and inflation were now more salient than that of air pollution control. Second, the TCP experience and EPA's inability to accelerate the pace of emission control technology progress had generated substantial caution about what Congress could accom-

These arguments were distinctly secondary in the policy debate, however. The central issue was the diesel and its potential for enabling Americans to continue riding in relatively roomy cars while achieving the fuel economy targets that Congress had enacted in 1975 (see above, p. 145).

22. The administration now estimated that, even in this "most favorable" scenario, five to twelve regions would remain in noncompliance with the ambient CO standard as of the year 2000, that twenty-six to thirty-one would remain in noncompliance with the HC and oxidant standards, and that four would remain in noncompliance with the NO_2 standard. (If the ultimate NO_x emission standard were raised from 0.4 to 1.0 grams per mile, the number of regions in noncompliance with the NO_2 ambient standard as of the year 2000 would rise to seven.)

The lower bound CO, HC, and oxidant projections, together with the NO_2 projection, assumed average fleet performance in the year 2000 in full complaince with the ultimate CO, HC, and NO_x emission standards. Even the upper bound projections made only modest allowance for on-the-road degradation.[56]

23. The administration itself found this price too high and urged deferral of any decision on whether to reduce the ultimate NO_x emission standard below 1.0 gram per mile until additional research findings were available. For the time being it simply urged a one-year delay in achievement of the HC standard (to model year 1979), a three-year delay in achievement of the CO standard (to 1981), and achievement of the interim 1.0 gram NO_x standard by 1981.[57]

plish simply by legislating. Third, organized labor had now cooled toward the issue of pollution control; the United Auto Workers in particular, who had vigorously supported the tough provisions in the 1970 legislation, were now determined to head off any provisions that might reduce sales by the domestic manufacturers. Fourth, it was now clear that if a choice ever developed between shutting down domestic automobile production (however briefly) and relaxing air quality standards, elected officials would quickly and with virtual unanimity choose the latter. Finally the environmental lobbying effort was financed primarily by an industry that had been brought into being by the 1970 legislation: the manufacturers of catalytic converters.[59]

Toward the end of the 1976 Congressional session, a confrontation developed between the House and Senate on the emission control issue. The House adopted a bill providing for delays of up to four years (to model year 1982) in meeting the HC and CO emission standards, while the Senate provided for a delay of only one year (to model year 1979). Even more significantly, the House bill provided for the existing 2.0 gram per mile NO_x standard to remain in effect pending further study by EPA, and it directed the EPA administrator to promulgate an ultimate standard in time for compliance to be achieved in model year 1982. The Senate bill, on the other hand, merely relaxed the ultimate NO_x standard to 1.0 grams per mile (from 0.4) and deferred the effective date to model year 1980 (from 1978).[60]

The general assumption was that the automobile industry had to support enactment of a bill before adjournment so that it could go forward with production planning for the 1978 models, scheduled to go on sale in September 1977. (In the absence of new legislation, the ultimate standards enacted in 1970 were scheduled to become effective at that time.) The Senate conferees, led as in 1970 by Senator Muskie, capitalized successfully on this assumption in the conference committee. At the last moment, however, the industry decided that, rather than accept the conference bill, it would prefer to take its chances in 1977. In the rush to adjournment at the end of the session, one of its Senate supporters easily killed the bill by threatening a filibuster.

A similar confrontation developed in 1977, but this time with the bargaining chips more evenly balanced. The supporters of a tough bill could not afford to appear responsible for an industry shutdown—and that is precisely what industry leaders said would happen unless a bill were enacted by early September. The industry, for its part, could not afford to appear intransigent for fear of a public backlash. The result, throughout most of the session, was a cautious stalemate. As Congress prepared to recess for a month from early August through Labor Day, however, industry leaders announced daily to the media that failure to enact a bill before Congress went on vacation would mean layoffs for substantial numbers of automobile workers in September. In this context President Carter and the congressional leadership successfully brought pressure on the conferees to reach agreement, and the bill they reported was enacted by both houses with minimal debate.

The 1977 amendments gave the industry virtually all of the flexibility that it had requested. Specifically, they provided for: an increase in the ultimate NO_x emission standard from 0.4 to 1.0 grams per mile;[24] a delay of three additional model years in meeting the NO_x standard;[25] authority for the EPA administrator to authorize NO_x emissions of up to 1.5 grams per mile through model year 1984 for diesel engines or any other innovative technology with promise of eventually being able to meet the 1.0 gram standard and of providing fuel economy benefits; a delay of up to five additional model years in meeting the CO standard; and a delay of two additional model years in meeting the HC standard (see Table 6.4). In brief, then, while leaving both the general objective of perfectly safe air quality and the specific ambient standards adopted earlier intact, Congress in 1977 abandoned the notions

[24.] The act also provided for an EPA study to determine the health implications of this increase and declared as a research objective the development of new powerplant and emission control technologies that would meet the 0.4 gram standard. The auto manufacturers were to be required to carry out this research at their own expense and, "on a regular basis," to demonstrate their research vehicles incorporating this objective.

[25.] The act authorized an additional two-year delay for American Motors if the administrator found that it lacked the financial resources and technological ability to meet the standard at the same time as the other manufacturers.

TABLE 6.4
1977 Clean Air Act Motor Vehicle Emission Standards

Model Year	Standard (Grams per Mile)		
	Hydrocarbons	Carbon Monoxide	Nitrogen Oxides
1978–1979	1.5	15.0	2.0
1980	0.41	7.0	2.0
1981–1982	0.41	7.0 – 3.4[a]	1.5 – 1.0[b]
1983–1984	0.41	3.4	1.5 – 1.0
1985	0.41	3.4	1.0

Source: Sec. 202 of the 1977 Clean Air Act.

[a] The CO standard for model years 1981–1982 may be set by the EPA administrator between 7.0 and 3.4 grams per mile based on technical feasibility.

[b] The NO_x standard for model years 1981–1984 may be set by the EPA administrator between 1.5 and 1.0 grams per mile for diesel powered vehicles and for those employing innovative emission control technologies. These technologies must have been used on less than 1 percent of 1977 model vehicles and must offer a significant prospect of meeting the 1.0 gram per mile standard by model year 1985 along with the 27.5 mile per gallon fuel economy standard. All other vehicles must meet the 1.0 gram per mile NO_x standard beginning with model year 1981.

that they could be achieved throughout the nation in the near future, that any potential benefits of haste could justify the use of travel disincentive measures, and that the automobile manufacturers could achieve virtually any technical feat on any schedule if Congress simply insisted.

Deferral of the ambient air quality deadlines in 1977 for another ten and one-half years may properly be viewed as a way of deferring them indefinitely. What remains essentially is a symbolic commitment to reaching the goals adopted in 1970 at some future point. This interpretation becomes increasingly persuasive as one considers the official EPA projection that, in the absence of travel disincentive measures, several dozen regions will remain in violation of one or more ambient standards even as the twenty-first century gets underway. Finally, what is most striking about the emission control deadlines adopted in 1977 is their close resemblance to the goals announced by the Nixon administration early in 1970, arrived at in consultation with the auto manufacturers during 1969.[61]

Innovations

In considering the potential of urban transportation measures to bring about air quality improvements, it is essential to distinguish between those that would reduce vehicle miles of travel (VMT) and those that would reduce emissions per vehicle mile. Since the emergence of air quality as an issue in the 1950s, the predominant focus of policy attention has always been on measures in the latter category, although federal policy makers aspired for a time in the early 1970s to apply both types in combination—utilizing VMT-reduction measures where emission controls alone could not bring regions into compliance with ambient standards by the tight deadlines specified in the Clean Air Act Amendments of 1970.

We shall forego a discussion of VMT-reduction measures in this section, for two reasons. First, we have treated them in chapter 5, and second, even the strongest among them are likely to seem of trivial importance in the future if federal emission reduction targets can be achieved. If, for example, VMT were reduced 20 percent by 1990 relative to what it would otherwise have been and at the same time emissions per mile were reduced 80 percent from the 1970 level, the total emission reduction (relative to what would have occurred in the absence of any constraints but the emission controls in use as of 1970) would be 84 percent. All but the final 4 percent, of course, would be attributable to the emission controls.

The obstacles in the path of achieving a 20 percent VMT reduction seem considerably more formidable than those in the way of achieving an 80 percent reduction in emissions. As indicated in chapter 5, even a doubling of transit patronage would reduce auto VMT by less than 2 percent. And the air pollution (like the energy) benefits of this reduction would be at least partially offset by the required increases in transit VMT. Moreover, the predominant consumer response to gas rationing or dramatic price increases would, over a period of years, be a shift to more energy-efficient cars. Given sufficient incentive, consumers could shift by 1990 to cars with triple the average fuel economy of the mid-1970s. Thus it would require drastic measures indeed to bring about VMT reductions of more than a few percent.

The great uncertainty about emission controls is how effectively on-the-road performance degradation can be prevented. As noted previously, a 1975 EPA report found that whereas model year 1974 cars were theoretically 61 percent cleaner than the 1970 models with reference to HC emissions and 62 percent cleaner with reference to CO emissions, in fact they would achieve only 15 percent and 22 percent reductions over their lifespans because of on-the-road degradation. Moreover the gap between new-car and on-the-road performance seemed to be growing as the new-car standards became more stringent over the years.

Section 207(b) of the Clean Air Act (enacted in 1970) directs the EPA administrator to develop a "short test" for determining whether on-the-road vehicles are still in compliance with the emission standards they were required to meet when new. (A short test is defined as one that can be administered quickly and inexpensively, and that is "reasonably capable of being correlated" with the results of the full EPA testing procedure employed in the certification of new models.) As soon as he determines that a reliable short test is available, the administrator is directed to promulgate regulations giving it official status and requiring the manufacturers to warranty the "emission control device or system" on each vehicle for its "useful life." The term "useful life," it will be recalled, was defined in the act as five years or 50,000 miles, whichever came first. Though it covered only about half the actual lifetime of the average vehicle, this was in accord with the longest manufacturer warranty provisions then in effect. The warranties were to provide that the manufacturers would repair malfunctioning emission control equipment at no cost to owners so long as all prescribed maintenance had been carried out and the owner had nonetheless been subjected to a state or federal penalty for violation of an emission standard. Thus the warranties were to acquire more than symbolic value only as and when compulsory

inspection programs were established with penalties for violators.[26]

EPA did not in fact issue a draft short test regulation until May
1977. While it was still awaiting public comment, Congress enacted the Clean Air Amendments of 1977, including provisions
that necessitated a redraft of the regulation. As of mid-1978,
final promulgation of the revised regulation is expected to occur
in 1979. As section 207(b) provides for warrantying only those
vehicles produced in model years subsequent to the one in which
applicable short test regulations are promulgated, the first emission control systems to which it may be applicable (unless the
schedule slips again) will be those installed on new vehicles in model year 1980.

The Clean Air Act still does not authorize the administrator to
require periodic testing of on-the-road vehicles. His specified test
procedures are to have official standing insofar as state and local
governments establish inspection and maintenance (I/M) programs
with penalties for violators, but the act provides no mechanism
for ensuring that such programs are established. As noted above,
the 1977 amendments do require that schedules for the introduction of I/M programs be developed for regions likely to be in violation of ambient air quality standards after December 31, 1982.
But they leave the determination of acceptable schedules to the
administrator, and they provide him with only a single weak instrument (the threat of withholding grants under the Clean Air
Act itself) to bring about the effective implementation of these
programs without schedule slippage.

In brief, then, the warranty and maintenance provisions of the
Clean Air Act have been nullities to date, and the 1977 amendments contemplate, at most, the effective application of these pro-

[26.] Section 207(c), also enacted in 1970, makes the manufacturers liable for the cost of
repairs if the EPA administrator determines that vehicles of a given make and model
year are consistently failing to meet the standards during their useful lives even though
properly maintained. Recalls under this provision have grown rapidly in recent years (to
5.1 million in 1977) as EPA surveys have turned up more and more vehicles exceeding
the standards at low mileage. Owners have minimal incentive to bring recalled vehicles
in for repairs, however, because there are no legal penalties for failure to do so and because a by-product of engine retuning to reduce emissions is frequently performance degradation from the driver's standpoint. Additionally EPA has no way of ensuring that
dealers properly repair vehicles that are brought in.

visions in a few of the most polluted urban regions beginning in the middle or late 1980s.

The primary reasons why I/M strategies have been given such short shrift to date appear to be as follows. First, elected officials have balked at requiring any direct payments by motorists for the maintenance of pollution control equipment. Thus they have sought to address the degradation problem by requiring manufacturer warranties—acting on the premise that few consumers blame their elected representatives for costs built into the price of new cars. There has been a widespread recognition, however, that this premise is most valid when the costs are modest and that true lifetime warranties would probably entail very considerable costs indeed. Second, environmental organizations and the media have focused virtually all their attention on the new-car emission standards, assuming implicitly that cars meeting the standards when new would continue to do so throughout their lives. EPA, beset on all sides with demands that it is unable to satisfy, has done nothing to disabuse them of this illusion. Finally, there are serious technical problems, though these are less significant insofar as costs are borne by the manufacturers (who can deal with errors statistically) rather than by individual motorists. In particular, no "short test" inspection method has yet been devised (or probably can be devised) that correlates in near-perfect fashion with EPA's federal test procedure (FTP) for the certification of new car prototypes. As EPA has officially noted:

A short test must be performed in a short time on a fully warmed up vehicle, is limited at best to a very few vehicle speed/load conditions, and will be performed under a wide range of environmental conditions (i.e., temperature, humidity, human factors or instrument factors that are either uncontrollable or under limited control). Conversely, the FTP is performed with a cold start, includes a very large number of vehicle speed and load conditions simulating a typical stop-and-go urban commutation, and is performed under closely controlled laboratory environmental conditions.[62]

The consequence is that any short test will produce a significant number of errors in each direction; that is, some vehicles will fail the short test that would pass the FTP, and vice-versa. EPA administrators until 1977 reportedly judged that a short test run on a probabilistic basis—for example, with the passing grade set for each model year to ensure with 95 percent certainty that the average emissions of all cars certified would meet the standard for that model year—would generate intense consumer resistance (even if most repair costs were covered by warranty) and would be likely to fail a court test of fairness. It is not entirely clear why, despite this concern, EPA did finally issue a draft short test regulation in 1977, but three contributing factors bear mention. First, a new president and a new EPA administrator took office. Second, concern within EPA over the seriousness of the degradation issue had been growing for several years. Third, it was apparent that Congress would shortly, in the new Clean Air Act Amendments, bar all strategies of emission control by the use of motor vehicle travel disincentives. Thus if the EPA effort in urban transportation were to consist of more than just new-car emission certification, the most likely—indeed, the only likely—candidate was I/M. New technical developments, parenthetically, played no part in the decision. The short test procedures specified in the administrator's draft regulation of May 1977 had all been available for at least several years.[27]

As of early 1978, the expectation is that the manufacturers will accept EPA's proposed test procedure with minimal complaint. (EPA claims to be confident as well that the courts will uphold the short test procedure, despite its probabilistic nature, on the ground that no better way exists to implement the social objective of emission control enforcement. In part to reinforce this probability, it has agreed to set the passing grades so that fewer cars will need repair than if all had been run through the full FTP.) Consumers are unlikely to be heard from in substantial numbers until and unless I/M programs actually begin to be implemented

[27.] The 1977 draft regulation approved five alternative short test procedures.[63] These ranged in complexity from an "idle" test involving the measurement of vehicle exhaust with the engine idling to two alternative "transient" tests involving multiple engine speeds and sophisticated exhaust sampling equipment. The idle test, while quick, simple, and cheap, was deemed virtually useless for the measurement of NO_x emissions (because these are close to zero at idling speeds). The more complex procedures were adjudged considerably superior, but they also required much more expensive equipment and highly trained personnel. Thus the several I/M programs planned or implemented (by states and localities) to date have all relied upon the idle test.

on a wide scale. And the 1977 legislation appears to contemplate stringent I/M programs in at most a few dozen metropolitan areas beginning a decade or so hence. Thus the immediate impact of the short test regulation on manufacturer costs will be negligible. By the mid-1980s, moreover, it appears likely that the companies will be able to improve reliability to the point where their costs will remain negligible under the warranty provisions of the 1977 legislation.[28] The other side of the coin is that stringent I/M programs covering the actual life of each vehicle will, if implemented in some urban areas, probably entail quite significant out-of-pocket costs for the owners of older cars.[29]

Finally some critics of federal policy have argued that it makes little sense to require expensive emission controls on all new cars when the air pollution problem is confined to a limited number of metropolitan areas. The current policy, they maintain, provides the vast majority of its benefits to residents of the nation's most polluted areas, while imposing its highest per-capita costs on residents of the least polluted areas (which are in general characterized by low densities and high rates of automobile ownership). David Harrison, Jr., for example, contends that if the interim 1973 emission standards were made permanent everywhere except in the forty-three most polluted urban areas, consumers would save one-third of the dollar cost of the ultimate emission control requirements (as specified in the 1970 act), while sacrificing only about 4 percent of the photochemical oxidant benefits, 7 percent of the CO benefits, and 21 percent of the NO_x benefits associated

[28.] EPA engineers now believe that the main cause of degradation, at least during the early years of vehicle use, is not mechanical failure but rather the widespread tendency of owners and mechanics to alter engine settings in the hope of improving performance and fuel economy.[64] Consequently the agency has proposed that manufacturers be required (beginning with the 1981 models) to certify that engine settings observed during the FTP are the same as those motorists will actually use on the road.[65] This will be possible only if carburetors are sealed and engine timing is set permanently at the factory. (At present, since the FTP ignores driveability, manufacturers face a strong temptation to send vehicles out of the factories with engine settings they know are far from optimal in terms of driveability and fuel economy. It seems likely that many dealers routinely modify these settings before delivering new cars to purchasers.)

[29.] Estimation of these costs for future models is not feasible because emission control technology is still in a phase of rapid development. As a practical matter it is not even possible yet to make lifetime estimates for vehicles currently on the road that were subject to the interim standards of the mid-1970s when new.

with them. The magnitude of the saving, he calculates, would be about $1.4 billion annually in constant 1972 dollars.[66]

Although we believe that Harrison's estimates are overly optimistic—he appears to assume, for example, that the vehicles in each category will perform throughout their lives in conformity with the emissions standards for their model year, and that virtually all travel in the forty-three most polluted areas will occur in vehicles originally purchased therein—we mention the dual strategy here because the I/M provisions adopted by Congress in 1977 represent an analog of it. They accept implicitly that on-the-road degradation will be ignored except in the most polluted urban regions—those expected to be in violation of ambient standards well beyond 1982. The strategy of targeting these regions for strict I/M enforcement appears sensible in principle. The serious question is whether—given the weak warranty provisions of the 1977 act and the history of congressional retreat as measures involving direct consumer cost or inconvenience approach implementation —even this approach to controlling on-the-road degradation will be carried out effectively in practice.

Summary

Although percentages vary significantly from one metropolitan area to another, automobiles account for at least 80 percent of carbon monoxide (CO) and lead emissions in most large metropolitan areas, about 70 percent of hydrocarbon (HC) emissions, and about 50 percent of nitrogen oxide (NO_x) emissions. The degree to which emissions are translated into ambient air pollution in any region depends on a wide variety of factors: the size, density, topography, and climate of the area; the nature and extent of non-automotive emissions; and the degree to which auto use is concentrated by subarea, corridor, and/or time of day. Thus ambient air quality varies widely among and within metropolitan areas. Further, there is wide room for debate about what levels of ambient air pollution should be viewed as constituting problems. The sources of disagreement are twofold: experimental evidence with respect to the health effects of various levels of air pollution exposure is fragmentary, and attitudes vary about the prices worth paying to eliminate any given degree of health risk.

During 1969 and 1970, air pollution surged to the top of the nation's political agenda as part of a broader set of environmental issues. In an atmosphere of political euphoria, Congress mandated (in the Clean Air Act Amendments of 1970) the achievement of stringent emission and ambient air quality standards by 1975. The target reductions in new-car emissions were 90 percent. The ambient air quality standards were premised on the objective of perfect safety for every individual, no matter how sick or infirm, at all times and places.

In practice, it has proven impossible to achieve these goals at acceptable social and economic costs. The oil shortages and price increases of 1973–1974, followed by the severe recession and inflation of 1974–1975, highlighted these costs and sharply diminished the constituency for expensive and/or inconvenient air pollution control strategies. Additionally, whereas it had been attractive politically in 1970 to concentrate on the anticipated benefits that would flow from Clean Air Act compliance, public attention increasingly focused on implementation costs as the deadlines approached. In response to these shifts in public mood, Congress has authorized a series of delays in meeting both the auto emission and ambient air quality standards and prohibited EPA from requiring changes in urban travel behavior. The practical effect has been to postpone full achievement of the ambient air quality standards indefinitely.

While the auto manufacturers have achieved dramatic reductions in new-car emissions per vehicle mile since the mid-1960s, much of the potential benefit has been vitiated by on-the-road degradation of the improved pollution control equipment. The obvious remedy would appear to be strict inspection and maintenance (I/M) requirements, at least in urban areas that are in violation of ambient air quality standards. The 1977 Clean Air Act amendments explicitly incorporate this strategy, but with long lead times and extremely weak enforcement provisions. The main obstacle to a more vigorous attack on the degradation problem appears to be political. I/M requirements will entail some cost and inconvenience for all vehicle owners in the affected regions, plus occasional expenses of more significant magnitude as pollution control devices need repair or replacement. In the absence of clear evidence that the public will accept such requirements passively, most elected and key environmental officials have preferred to edge toward them with the utmost caution.

Nature of the Problem

Approximately 46,000 Americans are killed in motor vehicle accidents each year, and four million are injured—about 100,000 of them severely. Estimated monetary losses are in the range of $35–40 billion a year.[1] [1] Motor vehicle accidents constitute the sixth leading cause of death among Americans of all age groups, and are *the* leading cause of death among those fifteen to thirty-four years of age.[3]

While the aim of reducing these tolls has been consensual since the beginning of the motor vehicle age, controversy has been endemic on the questions of who should be blamed for them and what methods should be deemed permissible in seeking to ameliorate them. Until the mid-1960s, the general view—actively promoted by the automobile manufacturers and safety organizations financed by them—was that the source of the problem, purely and simply, was "the nut behind the wheel." Motorists were urged to "drive defensively" and to support driver-training courses for young people in their school systems, and were assured that their cars and highways were remarkably safe. Reporting on a survey of 802 drivers carried out in four cities during 1966, Leo Bogart has recently called attention to the great success of this strategy. Asked to free associate with the word "automobile," only one in eight mentioned safety. When requested to comment freely on "driving today," four out of five included some negative remarks but few mentioned accident risk except in the course of complaining about the discourtesy and recklessness of other drivers. "In short," Bogart writes, "drivers thought of themselves as being

[1] The latest comprehensive figures available as this is written are for 1975. In that year, the National Highway Traffic Safety Administration estimates the monetary loss attributable to motor vehicle accidents was $37.6 billion. This figure included the present value of future earnings by those incapacitated or killed, medical and funeral costs, litigation and insurance, administration costs, and property damage losses. It did not include any imputed value of pain and suffering, nor did it include expenditures by such agencies as fire and police departments. Thirty percent of the $37.6 billion total was attributable to the 22 million accidents that involved property damage only.

Passenger miles of motor vehicle travel in 1975 totaled about 2.9 trillion nationwide.[2] Thus the monetary loss estimate was equivalent to about 1.3 cents per passenger mile (2.8¢ per vehicle mile).

in social interaction with other drivers, rather than as potential victims of faulty mechanical design."[4]

This survey occurred, notably, a year after the publication of Ralph Nader's book, *Unsafe at Any Speed,* and the widely publicized Senate hearings at which he aired his charges about auto maker responsibility for a large proportion of motor vehicle fatalities.[5] A survey carried out a year or two earlier would doubtless have revealed even less concern about safety. As it was, the 1966 respondents ranked safety first when asked to name social problems associated with the automobile. They equated safety with car size, weight, good brakes, and good tires, however, rather than with any special safety equipment. When asked specifically, one-third said that they would be willing to pay extra for a lap seat belt, and one-fifth said that they would be willing to pay for a collapsible steering wheel. By contrast, half were willing to pay extra for air conditioning.[6]

If the general public appeared apathetic the media spotlight was intense, and Congress enacted the National Traffic and Motor Vehicle Safety Act in 1966, along with a companion Highway Safety Act. The former established the National Highway Traffic Safety Administration (NHTSA), empowering it to issue and enforce motor vehicle safety performance standards.[7]

The regulatory activities of NHTSA have provided a focal point since 1966 for public discussion and media coverage of the safety issue. During this period two central ideas have achieved general acceptance, at least among those seriously concerned with the dialogue: first, that nearly all accidents have multiple causes, and second, that accident and injury prevention are quite distinct objectives, because there are numerous means available to protect the occupants of vehicles involved in crashes. Serious debate has focused on appraising the relative cost-effectiveness and political acceptability of candidate measures. In these debates, although the auto makers have continued to urge that the primary strategy of intervention should be to alter driver behavior, the predominant view has been that the driver is probably the most difficult component of the injury-producing environment to change. Even among those sharing this negative perception, however, disagreement has been rife about the cost-effectiveness of alternative safety strategies and even about the priority that motor vehicle safety merits in view of the continuing apathy of most motorists.

Trends and Comparisons

Taken in isolation, annual statistics on the motor vehicle accident toll fail to indicate whether matters are getting better or worse, whether motor vehicle travel is unusually dangerous by comparison with other modes, or whether safety-conscious motorists can do much to reduce their individual risk. Thus, in the course of determining what policy initiatives may be appropriate, it is essential to review some other perspectives on the safety attributes of the motor vehicle-dominant system.

The death rate per hundred million vehicle miles of travel (hmvmt) has declined significantly since the beginning of the motor age. In the 1923–1927 period, the first for which data are available, the rate was 18.2. By 1956, when Congress enacted the interstate highway program, it was 6.3. In 1973, just prior to enactment of the 55 mph speed limit, it was 4.3; and in 1974, following enactment of the reduced speed limit, it was 3.6. By 1976, it had fallen to 3.3. (See table 7.1.) The U.S. rate in recent years has been the lowest, moreover, of any major nation. Quite a few of the others have rates more than twice as high. The Belgian rate is actually quadruple and the French rate triple that of the United States. (See table 7.2.)

The mileage death rate, furthermore, is a complicated indicator which tends to overstate the risk of travel by automobile relative to other modes. It encompasses travel by all types of motor vehicle (autos, trucks, buses, motorcycles, and even farm tractors) and fatalities suffered by all types of travelers (most notably, pedestrians and cyclists in addition to motor vehicle occupants).

Pedestrian deaths have typically accounted for more than one-sixth of all motor vehicle accident fatalities in recent years. Motorcyclists and bicyclists, who accounted for only 3 to 4 percent of fatalities in the 1950s (pedestrians then accounted for 20–25 percent), account for 9 percent today. Consistently, then, 25 to 30

TABLE 7.1
Motor Vehicle Accidents, United States, 1923–1976

	Vehicle Miles (billions)	Deaths	Mileage Death Rate (per 100 million vehicle miles)
1923–1927[a]	120	21,800	18.20
1928–1932[a]	199	31,050	15.60
1933–1936[a]	224	35,481	15.80
1937–1945[a]	267	31,397	11.76
1946–1950[a]	398	32,966	8.27
1951–1955[a]	543	37,351	6.88
1956	628	39,628	6.31
1957	647	38,702	5.98
1958	665	36,981	5.56
1959	700	37,910	5.42
1960	719	38,137	5.30
1961	738	38,091	5.16
1962	767	40,804	5.32
1963	805	43,564	5.41
1964	847	47,700	5.63
1965	888	49,163	5.54
1966	930	53,041	5.70
1967	965	52,924	5.48
1968	1,020	54,862	5.38
1969	1,070	55,791	5.20
1970	1,120	54,633	4.88
1971	1,186	55,624	4.69
1972	1,268	56,529	4.46
1973	1,309	55,579	4.26
1974	1,290	46,629	3.61
1975	1,332	45,515[b]	3.42
1976	1,391	46,150[b]	3.32

Source: Years 1923–1936: National Safety Council, *Accident Facts* (1976) p. 59; 1937–1976: NHTSA, *Traffic Safety '76*, p. A-10.

[a] Average.

[b] Based on fatalities occurring within thirty days of an accident. Not directly comparable to previous years.

TABLE 7.2
Comparative Mileage Death Rates by Country, 1969, 1971, and 1974

Country	Rates per 100 Million Vehicle Miles		
	1969	1971	1974
Australia	7.7	7.4	5.7
Belgium	19.8	20.1	14.9
Canada	7.3	6.7	6.0
Finland	11.9	NA	7.4
France	16.3	16.2	10.8
Germany	12.5	11.2	8.8
Italy	13.9	10.0	8.5
Japan	18.3	13.3	9.1
Netherlands	12.4	10.9	7.3
Norway	8.2	NA	6.1
Sweden	NA	4.7	NA
United Kingdom	6.4	6.3	4.9
United States	5.2	4.7	3.6

Source: Motor Vehicle Manufacturers Association, *Motor Vehicle Facts and Figures 1973/74*, p. 42; *Motor Vehicle Facts and Figures 1977*, p. 56.

percent of those killed in motor vehicle accidents over the past quarter century have been pedestrians, motorcyclists, and bicyclists rather than occupants of vehicles with four or more wheels. (See table 7.3.)

Motor vehicle fatality rates are generally discussed in terms of vehicle rather than passenger miles of travel, whereas the rates for other modes are usually discussed in terms of passenger miles. This practice doubtless stems from the period when little was known about automobile occupancies and has been perpetuated by the generally held—but false—impression that motor vehicle occupancies average little more than one. According to the Nationwide Personal Transportation Study (NPTS), however, the average occupancy for automobile travel as of 1970 was 2.2 per vehicle mile.[2] [8] Assuming that this figure still applied in 1975, the mo-

[2.] Average occupancy per passenger trip was only 1.9. The explanation for the discrepancy is that auto occupancies were considerably greater on longer trips.

tor vehicle fatality rate of 3.42 per hundred million vehicle miles in that year translated to 1.55 per hundred million passenger miles of travel (hmpmt).

Although the Federal Highway Administration estimates that 55 percent of motor vehicle travel occurs on urban streets and highways, almost two-thirds of motor vehicle accident fatalities occur on rural roads. (See table 7.4.) Taking this factor into account, we find that the motor vehicle fatality rate on urban roads in 1975 was 1.03 per hmpmt (versus 2.23 on rural roads).

Further, whereas automobile and truck travel accounted for roughly 98 percent of highway travel in 1975, only 51 percent of urban highway fatalities occurred to occupants of such vehicles (versus 84 percent of rural fatalities). The urban fatality rate for auto and truck occupants was 0.52 per hmpmt.[3]

Finally, the motor vehicle traveler has substantial latitude in determining the degree of risk to incur. The most important elements of choice are as follows:

• Alcohol is estimated to be a factor in roughly three-fifths of fatal accidents nationwide, affecting pedestrian as well as driver risk.[4] A recent study in the state of Washington, for example, found that 23 percent of all pedestrians killed in motor vehicle accidents during one recent year were themselves drunk.[10]

• Roughly 30 percent of all fatal accidents in 1975 involved vehicles that were being driven at speeds higher than the posted limits or at speeds too high for the prevailing traffic and weather conditions, according to the traffic authorities who reported the accidents.[11]

• NHTSA estimates that 28 percent of motor vehicle fatalities could be averted if all drivers and passengers utilized lap and shoulder belts (versus the 15 percent now using both and the 5 percent now using lap belts only).[12] This translates to a 49 per-

[3.] In arriving at this estimate we have assumed, given the lack of available data, that the average truck occupancy was the same as the average automobile occupancy and that the urban shares of nationwide motorcycle and auto travel were the same.

[4.] National data are unavailable because such estimates can be made only on the basis of blood and breath tests of accident victims. The estimate reported is from a special accident investigation study conducted in Maryland in 1974.[9]

TABLE 7.3
Number and Distribution of Motor Vehicle Accident Fatalities by Function in the Accident, 1950–1976

Year	Total[a] Number	Percent	Bicyclists[b] (%)	Motorcyclists (%)	Pedestrians[b] (%)	Others[c] (%)
1950	34,763	100.00	1.08	2.87	25.86	70.20
1951	36,996	100.00	0.99	2.45	24.69	71.87
1952	37,794	100.00	0.99	2.34	23.52	73.15
1953	37,955	100.00	0.98	2.09	22.99	73.95
1954	35,586	100.00	0.93	2.07	22.42	74.58
1955	38,426	100.00	0.90	1.67	21.34	76.09
1956	39,628	100.00	1.02	1.72	19.98	77.28
1957	38,702	100.00	1.11	2.02	20.34	76.53
1958	36,981	100.00	1.12	1.83	20.66	76.39
1959	37,910	100.00	1.22	2.05	20.68	76.05
1960	38,137	100.00	1.18	1.98	20.59	76.24
1961	38,091	100.00	1.27	1.89	20.21	76.62
1962	40,804	100.00	1.24	1.92	19.65	77.19
1963	43,564	100.00	1.21	2.09	18.64	78.06
1964	47,700	100.00	1.32	2.46	18.66	77.56
1965	49,163	100.00	1.28	3.18	17.83	77.70
1966	53,041	100.00	1.25	3.99	17.51	77.25
1967	52,924	100.00	1.28	3.84	17.49	77.39
1968	54,862	100.00	1.24	3.55	17.36	77.84

1969	55,791	100.00	1.24	3.51	16.45	78.80
1970	54,633	100.00	1.46	4.27	18.49	75.78
1971	54,381	100.00	1.51	4.78	18.02	75.69
1972	56,278	100.00	1.97	5.15	18.13	74.75
1973	56,056	100.00	1.95	6.03	17.87	74.15
1974	46,685	100.00	2.42	7.31	17.78	72.49
1975[d]	45,515	100.00	2.21	7.21	17.81	72.77
1976[d]	46,150	100.00	1.96	7.07	17.11	73.86

Sources: NHTSA, *Traffic Safety '76*, table A-4.

[a] These figures exclude aliens. Their inclusion would add about one-tenth of 1 percent to the total number of fatalities.

[b] Motor vehicle involvement only.

[c] Includes primarily drivers and passengers in motor vehicles other than motorcycles and motorscooters. There are a few riders of animals, occupants of animal-drawn vehicles, occupants of street cars, unauthorized riders, and others also in the category.

[d] Based on fatalities occurring within thirty days of an accident. Not directly comparable to previous years.

TABLE 7.4
U.S. Highway VMT and Fatalities, 1975

	Total VMT (Billions of Miles)	Percentage	Fatalities				
			Pedestrian	Bicycle	Motorcycle	Auto, Truck, Bus	Total
Rural	600,631	45.2	2,500	400	1,900	24,700	29,500
Urban	729,443	54.8	6,100	600	1,400	8,400	16,500
Total	1,330,074	100.0	8,600	1,000	3,300	33,100	46,000

Source: VMT data from Federal Highway Administration, *Highway Statistics* (1975), table VM-1. Fatalities from National Safety Council, *Accident Facts* (1976 ed.), p. 45, except for motorcycles. Total motorcycle fatalities are from NHTSA, *Traffic Safety '76*, table A-4. The urban/rural split is estimated by the authors based on NHTSA, National Center for Statistics and Analysis, "Highway Fatality Statistics, 1972" (mimeo., 1973).

cent reduction for auto/truck occupants killed in motor vehicle accidents.[5]

• The urban fatality rate for motorcycle, motor scooter, and motor bike riders in 1975 was 10.8 per hmvmt. No estimate of average occupancy is available, but it was presumably not much above 1.0. If one assumes an occupancy rate of 1.2, the fatality rate per hmpmt was 9.0, seventeen times the rate (0.52) for automobile and truck occupants. (See table 7.5.)

In short, travelers can sharply reduce the risk associated with motor vehicle travel by driving only when sober, by obeying speed limits, by fastening safety belts, and by keeping off two-wheeled motor vehicles. Data are lacking for precise estimation of an occupant fatality rate for those who regularly adhere to all four of these rules, but presumably they experience rates well under half those reported for the population as a whole. If for discussion purposes we assume that their risk factors in 1975 were about two-fifths those of the overall population, their occupant fatality rate in urban travel was approximately 0.2 per hmpmt.

Some have speculated that the objective experience of infinitesimal risk during any particular trip, combined with the frequency and familiarity of motor vehicle travel, account for the unwillingness of most travelers to take even the elementary precaution of fastening their seat belts. For the average (as opposed to the careful) motorist, the likelihood of being killed during an eight-mile urban trip is only about one in 19 million. While traveling 10,000 miles a year on urban and rural roads combined, the likelihood of being killed is about one in 6,400.

Transit safety statistics were, until the past several years, collected much less systematically than those for motor vehicles. Since 1975, however, NHTSA and the Federal Railroad Administration (FRA) have compiled comprehensive statistics on transit

[5.] In the base year for the estimate (1975), 45,515 motor vehicle fatalities occurred. NHTSA estimated that 27,200 of those killed were automobile occupants. The others included truck and farm vehicle occupants, as well as motorcyclists, bicyclists, and pedestrians. The estimate did not consider the potential benefits of seat belt use in motor vehicles other than passenger cars.

TABLE 7.5
Urban Auto, Truck, and Motorcycle Fatalities, 1975

Number of fatalities	
Auto and truck occupants	8,400
Pedestrians	6,100
Pedalcyclists	600
Motorcyclists	1,400
Total	16,500
Fatality rates per 100,000,000 vehicle miles	
Auto and truck occupants	1.15
Pedestrians and pedalcyclists	0.92
Motorcyclists	10.80
Overall (excluding motorcyclists)	2.07
Overall (including motorcyclists)	2.22
Fatality rates per 100,000,000 passenger miles	
Auto and truck occupants	0.52
Pedestrians and pedalcyclists	0.42
Motorcyclists	9.00
Overall (excluding motorcyclists)	0.94
Overall (including motorcyclists)	1.02

Source: Fatality data, except for motorcycles, from National Safety Council, *Accident Facts*, 1976 ed., p. 45. Urban motorcycle fatalities are estimated from nationwide motorcycle fatalities reported in NHTSA, *Traffic Safety '76*, table A-4. Estimate is based on a motorcycle fatality urban/rural split estimate in NHTSA, National Center for Statistics and Analysis, "Highway Fatality Statistics, 1972" (mimeo.), 1973. Vehicle mileage data from FHWA, *Highway Statistics, 1975,* table VM-1. Average auto/truck occupancy per vehicle mile from FHWA, Nationwide Personal Transportation Study, "Report 1, Automobile Occupancy," table 1. In the absence of data on average motorcycle occupancy, an occupancy of 1.2 was assumed. In the absence of data on the number of pedestrians and pedalcyclists killed by motorcycles, it has been assumed that all were killed by automobiles and trucks.

bus and rail rapid transit accidents.[6] We have combined these data with information available from other sources on vehicle and passenger mileage in order to generate the estimates (for urban travel in 1975) presented in tables 7.6, 7.7, and 7.8. Notably, they indicate that:

1. Overall fatalities per hmpmt were 0.58 for buses and 1.90 for rapid transit, by comparison with 0.94 for automobiles and trucks. (The transit figures exclude drivers and other operating employees.)

2. The transit modes were distinctly safer for occupants. The bus rate was 0.07 per hmpmt and the rapid transit rate was 0.25, versus a combined auto/truck rate of 0.52.[7]

3. The transit modes were more threatening to nonoccupants, however. Whereas automobiles and trucks killed 0.42 nonoccupants per hmpmt, buses killed 0.51 and rapid transit vehicles killed 1.65.[8]

4. In considering transit expansion options that are likely to generate below-average load factors, it is relevant to examine vehicle as well as passenger mile fatality rates. The overall transit bus fatality rate in 1975 was 7.59 per hmvmt, an the rapid transit rate was 12.52. By comparison, the urban auto/truck rate was 2.07. As one considers the risk factor associated with additional mileage at low incremental load factors, the relevant rates are those for nonoccupants, and here the disparities are particularly striking. Buses killed 6.62 nonoccupants per hmvmt in 1975, and rapid transit vehicles killed 10.87,[9] whereas autos and trucks killed 0.92.

[6.] Neither agency collects data on light rail systems even now. Such systems account for under 2 percent of transit patronage, however, and their safety characteristics probably lie somewhere between those of buses and rapid transit.

[7.] Further, six of the seven passenger fatalities that occurred on rapid transit during the year involved patrons falling between cars while trains were in motion. Those exposing themselves to this risk were presumably among the least safety-conscious rapid transit users.

[8.] None of the rapid transit fatalities involved collisions or derailments, and roughly one-third involved nontrain incidents altogether (falls on stairs or from platforms, contact with third rail, assaults on persons). The remainder involved people being struck or run over by trains.

[9.] It seems likely, however, that the rates are lower in settings where load factors are also below average. Where there are fewer people waiting at transit stops, and fewer pedestrians per street mile generally, there would appear to be less potential for hurting them per vehicle mile.

TABLE 7.6
Bus Transit Fatalities and Fatality Rates, 1975

Number of fatalities	
Bus occupants	
Drivers	1
Passengers	14
Overall	15
Nonoccupants	
Pedestrians	58
Pedalcyclists	8
Occupant of other vehicles	36
Overall	102
Fatality rates per 100,000,000 vehicle miles	
Passengers	0.91
Nonoccupants	6.68
Overall	7.59
Fatality rates per 100,000,000 passenger miles	
Passengers	0.07
Nonoccupants	0.51
Overall	0.58

Source: Fatality data are from the National Highway Traffic Safety Administration's Fatal Accident Reporting System (FARS) data files. FARS classifies accidents by vehicle type rather than vehicle use, so that a few fatalities may possibly involve a transit type bus used for charter or other nontransit work. Conversely a few fatalities involving transit patrons riding on minibuses or school buses may be unreported. However it is unlikely these marginal cases significantly affect the overall picture. Vehicle mile estimate is from American Public Transit Association, *Transit Fact Book, 1976–1977 Edition,* table 11. Figure includes both trolley coach and motor bus. Passenger miles are calculated by multiplying the National Transportation Study's estimate of unlinked bus trip length (3.93 miles) by APTA's "total passenger rides" on trolley coaches and motor buses. U.S. DOT, *1974 National Transportation Study: Urban Data Supplement,* tables D-23, D-30, and APTA, *Transit Fact Book, 1976–1977 Edition,* table 7.

TABLE 7.7
Rail Rapid Transit Fatalities and Fatality Rates, 1975

Numbers of Fatalities

	Occupants	Nonoccupants	Total
Collision or derailment	0	0	0
Train-related incidents			
Getting on/off train	1	0	1
Struck/run over by train	0	31	31
Miscellaneous[a]	6	0	6
Nontrain incidents[b]	0	15	15
Total	7	46	53

Fatality rates per 100,000,000 vehicle miles

Rail passengers	1.65
Nonoccupants	10.87
Overall	12.52

Fatality rates per 100,000,000 passenger miles

Rail passengers	0.25
Nonoccupants	1.65
Overall	1.90

Source: Fatality data are from Federal Railroad Administration, "Accident/ Incident Bulletin No. 144" (Washington: Federal Railroad Administration, 1977), table 101-C. Data do not cover light rail and commuter rail operations. Vehicle miles for heavy rail are from APTA, *Transit Fact Book, 1976–1977 Edition*, table 11. Passenger miles are calculated by multiplying the *1974 National Transportation Study* estimate of heavy rail passenger trip lengths (6.57 miles) by APTA's count of "total passenger rides" for "heavy rail." (U.S. Department of Transportation, *1974 National Transportation Study: Urban Data Supplement*, tables D-23 and D-30, and APTA, *Transit Fact Book, 1976–1977 Edition*, table 7.)

[a] Includes passengers falling between cars while train is in motion.

[b] Includes falls or mishaps on stairs, platforms, or elevators and assaults on person.

TABLE 7.8
Comparative Urban Fatality Rates by Mode, 1975

	Auto and Truck	Bus	Rail Rapid Transit
Rate per 100,000,000 vehicle miles			
Passengers[a]	1.15	0.91	1.65
Nonoccupants[b]	0.92	6.68	10.87
Overall	2.07	7.59	12.52
Rate per 100,000,000 passenger miles			
Passengers	0.53	0.07	0.25
Nonoccupants[b]	0.42	0.51	1.65
Overall	0.94	0.58	1.90

Source: Tables 7.5, 7.6, 7.7.

[a] Excludes drivers and other operating employees for transit.

[b] Excludes motorcycle fatality totals.

5. Since transit travel occurs predominantly during peak periods, and hardly at all during late night hours, an adjustment should be made for the distribution of motor vehicle fatalities as between these time periods. Nationwide, according to NHTSA, 41 percent of automobile passenger mileage in 1975 occurred during peak hours (6-9 A.M. and 4-7 P.M.) but only 23 percent of fatalities. By comparison, 8 percent of passenger mileage occurred between 10 P.M. and 4 A.M., but 34 percent of fatalities. Thus motor vehicle travel was more than seven times as dangerous late at night as during peak hours, and the motor vehicle fatality rate during the six peak hours was little more than half the twenty-four hour rate. (See table 7.9.)

In brief, then, intermodal safety comparisons are surprisingly difficult to make. It does seem clear that transit vehicle occupants are much safer than auto occupants. When nonoccupant fatalities are brought into the picture, however, and adjustments are made for the hours in which most transit travel occurs, the motor vehicle rate compares much more favorably. Thus the peak period auto/truck fatality rate in 1975 (0.57 per hmpmt) was virtually

TABLE 7.9
Motor Vehicle Fatality Rates by Time of Day, 1975

Time Period	Percent of Daily		Percent of Fatalities	Average Occupancy	Fatality Rate per	
	VMT	PMT			Vehicle Mile	Passenger Mile
10:00 p.m.-4:00 a.m.	7.4	8.4	33.5	2.51	9.01	4.11
6:00 a.m.-9:00 a.m. and 4:00 p.m.-7:00 p.m.	43.1	40.6	22.6	2.07	1.26	0.57
Overall	100.0	100.0	100.0	2.2	2.22	1.02

Source: Calculated by multiplying occupancies per vehicle mile by trip purpose from NPTS, Report 1, "Automobile Occupancy" table 1, by the breakout of travel purpose by time of day in NPTS, Report 10, "Purposes of Automobile Trips and Travel" (Washington: FHWA, 1974) table A-14.

identical to the overall bus transit rate (0.58), and it was less than one-third the rapid transit rate (1.90).

There are other complications as well. It seems likely, for example, that a significant proportion of both the rapid transit nonoccupant fatalities and the motor vehicle occupant fatalities were suicides, though in neither case is it possible to be more precise. Most of the rapid transit occupant fatalities occurred to people who ignored posted warnings against moving between cars while trains were in motion. And most of the auto/truck occupant fatalities occurred to people who were speeding, driving while drunk, and/or traveling with their seat belts unfastened. As noted previously, a persistent source of debate in the safety field is the priority that government should accord to protecting consumers from the consequences of their own recklessness.

Additionally, one may ask whether crime on transit systems should be considered in estimating the personal risk associated with transit use, and whether transportation improvements should be judged partially on the basis of whether they stimulate additional travel (and thus risk exposure). Our own observation is that most people include the former but not the latter in their calculations. One who is mugged while riding, waiting for, or even walking to mass transit will normally take this very much into account when making future judgments about the safety of the mode. By contrast, most people feel that travel decisions themselves are properly viewed as voluntary, and that the transportation system should not be blamed if better service induces additional consumption. Few disparage the remarkable safety record of commercial air transportation, for example, on the ground that people would make many fewer long trips in the absence of airplanes.[10] At the same time, travel decisions are very much a function of social, economic, and land use patterns. Equal amounts of mobility (defined as access to desired destinations) require considerably different amounts of travel in different settings. In assessing the impact of highway construction proposals on energy usage and air pollution, it has become standard in recent years to consider induced travel. Quite conceivably, policy makers will in the future wish to consider induced risk exposure as well when evaluating proposed transportation improvements.

If these findings leave room for a wide range of interpretations, they do clearly suggest that improved transit services are likely to enhance urban transportation safety only insofar as they generate high incremental load factors and attract a high proportion of the new patrons from the ranks of current (and preferably off-peak) travelers. The provision of lightly patronized new transit runs and the stimulation of new travel may be desirable on other grounds, but they are certainly not means of reducing the urban transportation accident toll.[11]

[10] The commercial air fatality rate during the years 1970–1976 was 0.08 per hmpmt. [13]

[11] We calculate that if bus and rail rapid transit ridership had been doubled in 1975 with no increase in vehicle mileage, if all the new riders had been attracted from autos, and if the diverted auto users would otherwise have experienced peak period fatality rates, the number of urban transportation fatalities would have declined by 110, or 0.7 percent.

If, on the other hand, we assume a doubling of bus and rail transit vehicle mileage along with the doubling of ridership, while holding our other assumptions constant, the impact would have been an increase in urban transportation fatalities of 38, or 0.2 percent.

Finally, if we assume a doubling of vehicle mileage and only a 50 percent ridership increase, the number of urban transportation fatalities would have increased by 93, or 0.6 percent.

Goals

Few if any dispute that enhanced safety ranks with the highest priority objectives of urban transportation policy. The several main components of this objective, moreover, are in high degree clear, measurable, and consistent. Measures to reduce fatalities will normally reduce nonfatal injuries and property damage as well. There is additionally a widespread consensus that safety cannot be left solely to the marketplace. Governments today mandate safety standards for all types of conveyances; they require periodic safety inspections of private motor vehicles as well as common carriers; they construct, maintain, and police virtually all (except intercity railroad) rights-of-way; and they license vehicle operators. At the federal level, Congress has moved vigorously since the mid-1960s to mandate improved motor vehicle and transit safety, to accelerate the pace at which new safety technologies are developed and marketed, and to increase the emphasis upon safety in federal highway programs.

If it seems clear that safety is a public responsibility and a consensual objective, there remain serious questions about what priority it commands relative to other public values, most notably that of consumer freedom. While displaying little reluctance since 1966 to regulate the motor vehicle manufacturing industry, Congress has consistently rejected the imposition of substantial costs or standards of behavior upon motor vehicle users. Examples include the following:

Acting pursuant to the Motor Vehicle Safety Act, the secretary of transportation ordered the manufacturers to install ignition interlocks in all automobiles produced after September 1, 1973. The interlocks prevented ignition until the combination lap-shoulder belts of front seat occupants were fastened. Though owners quickly found ways to disconnect their interlocks, all indications were that they did bring about a dramatic increase in seat belt usage. (See table 7.10.) At the same time, however, they generated cries of outrage from many motorists who viewed them as infringements upon their liberty. By a statutory provision enacted in

TABLE 7.10
Seat Belt Usage By Auto Year, United States, February 1974

	1974 (%)	1973 (%)	1972 and earlier (%)
Both shoulder and lap belts fastened	64	3	5
Lap belt only	12	24	11
Total	76	27	16

Source: Opinion Research Corporation," Safety Belt Interlock System: Usage Survey," prepared for NHTSA, May 1975, pp. xi, 12, 13.

October 1974, Congress forbade the secretary to require interlocks.[14]

In 1975 the secretary commenced sanction proceedings against three states that had failed to implement a federal standard (promulgated in 1967) requiring the enactment and enforcement of helmet use laws for motorcyclists. These states were to face the full penalties specified by the Highway Safety Act—loss of all of their federal highway safety and 10 percent of their highway construction aid allocations—unless they enacted adequate laws during their next legislative sessions. Following protests by these three states, however, Congress—in the Highway Safety Act of 1976— prohibited the secretary from requiring helmet use laws. Moreover it suspended his authority to impose sanctions for other safety standard violations—pending a comprehensive review of all such standards—and it permanently amended the law to eliminate the more important sanction authorized under the 1966 act, loss of highway construction funds.[12][15] During the next eighteen months, twenty states repealed or watered down their helmet laws.

Between September 1966 and January 1977, NHTSA required the auto manufacturers to recall 52.4 million vehicles (43 percent of all those sold in this period) for repair of mechanical defects. The agency has also established a computer tracking system and

[12.] Congress had previously curtailed the secretary's power, in 1973, by prohibiting the issuance of new highway safety standards, or the amendment of any of those already in effect, without congressional consent.

nationwide hotline to enable subsequent purchasers of recalled vehicles to determine whether the repairs have been made. It has made no effort to require consumers to heed these recalls, however. It might, for example, have passed on its vehicle identification data to state inspection authorities, with a recommendation that they require the owners of recalled vehicles to take them in for free repairs prior to the next inspection deadline. Its failure to do so has apparently been due to its fear of a consumer and congressional outcry.[13]

Between 1969, when Czechoslovakia became the first nation in the world to require seat belt use, and early 1977, eighteen nations, two provinces of Canada, and Puerto Rico adopted mandatory seat belt use laws.[18] Peter N. Ziegler (of NHTSA) has recently reported comparable before and after data on seat belt usage for ten of these jurisdictions. Though enforcement almost everywhere has been weak and penalities light, seat belt usage rose considerably in every case.[14] (See table 7.11.)

Announcing a proposed rule on occupant crash protection in June 1976, Secretary of Transportation William Coleman stated that the enactment and enforcement of seat belt use laws would be the most cost-effective action the nation could take in the field of motor vehicle safety. Standards involving new technology, he noted, could not become effective for several years and then would enter the vehicle fleet at a rate of only 10 percent a year.

[13.] Consumers have tended to ignore all but the most serious recalls. For example, when Volkswagen recalled 3.7 million vehicles in 1972 because of the possibility of defective windshield wipers, only 0.5 percent of the owners brought their cars to dealers within a year. Even when General Motors recalled 1.2 million vehicles in 1974 because of a power brake defect that could result in a sudden and complete loss of braking ability, only 72 percent of the owners brought in their vehicles within nine months.[16]

Fortunately production defects do not appear to be a leading cause of serious accidents. An ongoing study at Indiana University's Institute for Research in Public Safety, sponsored by NHTSA, has exhaustively examined a large number of fatal accidents during the past several years. It has concluded that mechanical failures were the main cause of 5 percent of these accidents and a contributing cause of another 10 percent. In about half of these cases, however, the mechanical failure was maintenance related (for example, worn brake drums, bald tires) rather than assembly related.[17]

[14.] Leon Robertson (of the Insurance Institute for Highway Safety) reports, however, that fatality rate reductions are invariably less than might be expected on the basis of observed usage increases. He speculates that the primary reason for this disparity is that those who are disproportionately involved in major accidents are the least likely to comply. Additionally many people comply by wearing their belts very loosely, with the result that they realize little benefit when involved in accidents.[19]

TABLE 7.11
Effects of Safety Belt Laws

	Effective Date of Law	Penalty for Noncompliance	Enforcement[a]	Public Information Program	Belt Usage before Law Effective	Belt Usage after Law Effective
Australia	1/1/72	Max $20	1	Yes	1971 25%	1975 85%
New Zealand	6/1/72	Max $20	1		May 1972 30%	1975 83%
Puerto Rico	1/1/74	$10	0–1	Yes	July 1973 4%	July 1976 25%
Sweden	1/1/75	Max $100	1	Yes	36%	March 1976 79%
Netherlands	6/1/75	20¢–$120			Oct. 1974 Rural: 28% Urban: 15%	June 1975 Rural: 72% Urban: 58%
Finland	7/1/75	None	3	Yes	June 1975 9–40%	Dec. 1975 53–71%
Norway	9/1/75	None	0	Yes	Sept '73–'75 Rural: 37% Urban: 15%	June 1975 Rural: 61% Urban: 32%

Israel[b]	7/1/75	Max $110	3	Yes	June 1975 8%	July 1976 80%
Switzerland	1/1/76	$8	1–2	Yes	May 1975 35–50%	May 1976 87–95%
Canada Ontario	1/1/76	$20–100	1	Yes	Oct 1975 17%	June 1975 64%

Source: Peter N. Ziegler, "The Effect of Safety Belt Usage Laws Around the World," *Journal of Safety Research* 9, no. 2 (June 1977): 98.

[a] 0: essentially none; 1: when motorist stopped for another purpose; 2: strict (when observed not wearing belt); 3: only requested to "buckle up" by officer.

[b] Urban roads exempt.

By contrast, a seat belt usage rate of 70 percent might be achieved within a year or two, and would save as many lives annually as would an air bag standard after it had been in effect for a decade.[20]

Both Secretary Coleman and his successor, Brock Adams, however, rejected the mandatory seat belt strategy. Adams, in explaining his decision, pointed out that a recent national survey had shown two-to-one public opposition to seat belt use laws, that no state had seen fit to enact such a law, and that Congress in 1974 had denied funding to a proposed program that would simply have encouraged state enactment of such laws.[21] Thus the likelihood that Congress would approve a more vigorous federal program, such as the one threatening to withhold highway construction funds from states without such laws, appeared to be negligible.

Finally, there has been great resistance in most American states and localities to the strict enforcement of speed limits and other safety regulations, and to the imposition of penalties more severe than fines even for such major infractions as driving while intoxicated, hit-and-run driving, and negligent homicide with a motor vehicle.[15] Among the penalties generally considered more severe than fines are drivers' license suspensions. In most jurisdictions these are rare and almost invariably of brief duration.

Working within the framework of such constraints, NHTSA in 1968 articulated the goal of reducing the motor vehicle fatality rate from the current (1967) level of 5.5 per hmvmt to 3.5 by 1980. Rather inadvertently—as a consequence of the sharp drop in fatalities following adoption of the 55 mph speed limit, for reasons of energy conservation, in 1974—this target was achieved in 1975. As of mid-1977, NHTSA had not established any new target. Nor have any targets ever been articulated with respect to transit safety.

[15.] Statistical data are lacking on this point, but a recent illustration may convey something of its flavor. A Massachusetts driver, having been convicted of negligent homicide (two children), driving while intoxicated, and leaving the scene of an accident, was sentenced to a $250 fine and a brief suspended jail term. Deeming this penalty absurdly light, the mother of one of the dead children appealed successfully for an investigation by the chief justice of the state district court system. Concluding his inquiry in July 1977, the chief justice reported that no further action was warranted because the original sentence was "well within the range established by law."[22]

Innovations

Three categories of measures appear cost-effective as means of enhancing safety: business regulation to bring about the marketing of safer cars; consumer regulation to prevent the deactivation of passive restraint systems, to require high standards of vehicle maintenance, and to deter reckless driving; and low-capital highway safety improvements.

Business Regulation

The first standard issued under the Motor Vehicle Safety Act required that automobiles produced after January 1, 1968, have lap and shoulder belts for the two front outboard seating positions and lap belts for all other seating positions. Though 80 percent of American motorists neglect to use their safety belts, NHTSA estimates that those in use are currently saving 3,000 lives and preventing 39,000 moderate to critical injuries each year.[23]

Recently, controversy has focused around proposals to mandate the installation of protection devices that do not require any active precautionary behavior (such as the fastening of seat belts) by occupants. Two such systems, the air bag and the passive (or automatic) seat belt, have for several years been deemed fully operational by NHTSA.[16]

[16.] Air bags are fabric cushions that rapidly inflate with gas when a head-on crash occurs with sufficient force to register on a sensor device. The purpose is to cushion the occupant against collision with rigid features of the vehicle interior.

Passive seat belts are designed to adjust themselves automatically around occupants as they enter the vehicle. The only passive seat belt currently available, as an option on the Volkswagen Rabbit, consists of a shoulder harness attached to the rear edge of the front passenger door and to a retractor between the front seating positions. When the door is opened the belt pulls away from the occupant. When the door is shut the belt adjusts itself automatically around the occupant.

Neither of these systems is likely to meet NHTSA's passive restraint standard by itself—the air bag because it may fail to hold occupants in place during side collisions and the VW passive shoulder belt because it may fail to hold occupant torsos upright during head-on collisions. Thus, air bag systems will probably include supplemental lap belts, and passive shoulder belt systems will include either passive lap belts or (as in the case of the present VW system) impact absorbing material below the dashboard to protect occupant knees.

Finally, both systems are at present being considered only for front seat installation. The reason is that approximately 90 percent of all occupant fatalities (92 percent in 1975) occur to front seat occupants, and presumably even a higher proportion of those attributable to occupants colliding with rigid vehicle interior features.[24]

Ford and General Motors installed 1,831 air bags on fleet vehicles in 1972 and 1973 (831 1972 Fords and 1,000 1973 Chevrolets.) As of mid-1977, the air bags had deployed as expected in every case where they should have, and there had been no inadvertent deployments. General Motors also offered air bags as optional equipment on full-sized Buicks and Oldsmobiles in the 1974 through 1976 model years and sold about 10,000. As of mid-1977, those that had been involved in accidents had invariably performed as expected, though three had also deployed on the road in the absence of accidents. (In none of these did the driver lose control of the car. GM traced the problem in one case to a design flaw, since corrected, and in the other two to owner tampering.[25] Nonetheless, considering sales too meager, it discontinued this option at the end of the 1976 model year.[17])

Passive seat belts have been standard equipment since 1975 on the "deluxe" version of the Volkswagen Rabbit. By the end of 1977, about 90,000 had been sold. As the deluxe option package includes style and comfort elements, purchasers do not necessarily select it with safety in mind. Some, indeed, even disconnect the passive seat belts. But NHTSA surveys have found approximately 80 percent operative during the first year of ownership, with few owners of still-operative belts expressing dissatisfaction with them.[27] Notably, the owners of passive seat belts are not more likely than other Rabbit owners to fasten active seat belts when traveling in other cars. For example, 87 percent of the respondents in one survey who owned passive seat belts reported wearing them "almost always," but only 37 percent reported that they usually wore seat belts when driving other cars. Among those who reported that they "almost never" wore seat belts in other cars, 78 percent said that they "almost always" did so in their Rabbits.[28]

NHTSA has concluded that air bag and automatic seat belt systems are essentially equivalent in value, except that the latter are acceptable only with bucket seats—no way having yet been devised to protect more than two front seat occupants with them.[29] It estimates that air bags in mass production would cost $112, plus

17. As of early 1977, according to NHTSA, reported moderate, severe, and fatal injuries among occupants of the GM cars equipped with air bags were running 58 percent below the level that would otherwise have been expected.[26]

an average of $28 for operating costs over the life of each vehicle.[18] (The auto companies have put forward considerably higher estimates. GM testified in June 1977 that the average original purchase cost would be $193 and the operating cost $53. Ford testified in October 1976 that the purchase cost would be $235 and the operating cost $187.[30]) NHTSA estimates, with no discernible objection from the manufacturers, that passive seat belts would entail an average initial purchase price of $25 plus a lifetime operating cost of $5.[31] Offsetting these expenditures would be savings in insurance premiums, plus savings in uninsured losses. Various leading insurance companies and associations testified in 1977 that savings in the bodily injury portion of auto insurance bills would be in the range of 25–30 percent, and that savings would be realized as well in general health and life insurance premiums. In the testimony apparently found most persuasive by NHTSA, Nationwide Mutual Insurance Companies estimated that these savings would total $32.50 a year over the life of each insured car (constant 1977 dollars).[32]

In estimating the potential effectiveness of passive restraint systems, NHTSA has assumed that most occupants of cars equipped with air bags and lap belts would not bother to fasten the lap belts, and that a considerable proportion of the owners of cars equipped with passive seat belts would disconnect them. (NHTSA dismisses the possibility that Congress or the state legislatures might be persuaded to pass laws prohibiting the disconnection of passive restraint systems. Such laws could easily be enforced during routine safety inspections).[19] Thus, whereas NHTSA estimates that, with 100 percent usage of the lap belts, air bag systems would prevent 54 percent of all automobile occupant fatalities (13,700 lives in 1975), it judges that in fact only one-fifth of all occupants

[18.] The principal components of the operating cost estimate are new bags for cars that have been involved in accidents and the fuel penalty exacted by the slight weight of the air bag systems.

[19.] Responding to the hostility of Congress to federal safety actions impinging on traditional state-local prerogatives, the secretary of transportation in 1977 urged dropping even NHTSA's advisory guidelines for vehicle inspection programs. He also urged that twelve of the existing eighteen federal highway safety standards be dropped and that Congress eliminate his authority to impose sanctions on states in noncompliance with the remaining standards.[33]

would fasten their lap belts, reducing the saving to 33 percent (9,100 lives). Similarly, whereas passive belts would prevent 38 percent of occupant fatalities if no one disconnected them (10,400 lives), the agency assumes that two-fifths of all car owners would do so, reducing the saving to 25 percent (6,800 lives).[34] Both Secretary Coleman and Secretary Adams have maintained that unless passive restraints are adopted as standard equipment on all new cars, fatality and injury rates are likely to rise as the nation shifts toward lighter vehicles in order to conserve fuel.

Even in the face of these considerations, Secretary Coleman decided late in 1976 not to issue a passive restraint regulation for new cars. As the primary justification for this decision, he cited fear of a negative public reaction and repetition of the seat belt interlock experience.[35] Hopeful that it would prove a more acceptable strategy, Coleman negotiated voluntary agreements with the U.S. auto manufacturers to market 250,000 cars with air bags during each of the model years 1980 and 1981, and with Volkswagen to market 125,000 automatic seat belt systems during each of these model years. These large-scale demonstrations, he indicated, would provide an opportunity to generate consumer support for either a publicly imposed standard or a voluntary decision by the manufacturers to install passive restraint devices as standard equipment on all new cars.[36]

Seven months following Coleman's decision, his successor overturned it. Secretary Adams, encouraged by support for a passive restraint standard from the United Auto Workers union and most of the large insurance companies as well as consumer groups, issued a final order on June 30, 1977, mandating the inclusion of passive restraint systems as standard equipment on all new cars produced after September 1, 1983. The standard is to apply to full-size cars beginning two years earlier and to intermediate-size cars beginning one year earlier.[20]

[20.] The secretary explained that this long lead time was required for technical reasons and maintained that his decision to phase in the standard with large cars becoming subject to it first was also based on technical grounds. In order to provide space for air bag systems, he found, instrument panels would have to extend about four additional inches into the passenger compartment. This presented few problems in the design of larger cars but would require the redesign of small car instrument panels. For this reason, he noted as well, manufacturers might find automatic seat belt systems particularly attractive for the smaller cars.[37]

In explaining the secretary's optimism (which proved to be justified) that Congress would permit this standard to become effective, NHTSA administrator Joan Claybrook stressed that, unlike the earlier interlock standard, it would not impose any inconvenience on ordinary motorists. Asked to comment on the auto industry's expected effort to secure a congressional veto, she noted simply that it had never won a regulatory battle in Congress except when allied with organized labor.[38]

The passive restraint systems currently certified as operational by NHTSA by no means exhaust the potential for dramatically improving automobile occupant crash protection. Throughout most of its life, NHTSA has been supporting development work aimed at building safety into vehicle design in more comprehensive fashion. An early effort, initiated well before the fuel shortages and price increases of 1973–1974, produced an experimental safety vehicle that was close to indestructible but that also weighed more than 5,000 pounds. Further, it appeared certain to be extremely costly even in full-scale production.

Following the emergence of fuel economy as a key collateral objective, NHTSA initiated a new effort, labeled the research safety vehicle (RSV) project, aimed at designing the safest possible car weighing under 3,000 pounds and likely to carry a price tag suitable for mass marketing. Three prototype designs have been developed as of mid-1978, two in the subcompact and one in the full-size range. Though none has yet been tested, NHTSA has estimated many of their performance characteristics on the basis of engineering studies and analyses of component test results where these have been developed in other contexts. (See table 7.12.) Those for the Calspan vehicle are considered most reliable because it entails technically conservative modifications of an existing (Simca) design well known to automobile engineers. The two Minicars designs offer the promise of higher ultimate performance through the use of largely untried techniques.

Seventeen prototype versions of each of the two subcompact designs are due for extensive crash testing during late 1978 and 1979, and fuller engineering details are available on these than the larger RSV. Specific innovative features include the following:

TABLE 7.12
RSV Characteristics

	Subcompacts			Full Size	
	Typical 1977	Calspan	Minicars	1977 Impala (base vehicle)	Minicars
Occupant protection (passive) (mph)					
Frontal barrier	30[a]	45–50	50+	30[a]	40
Car-to-car side	15–20[a]	40–45	45+	20–25[a]	30
No-damage protection (mph)					
Front	5[b]	8	10	5[b]	10
Rear	5[b]	5	5	5[b]	5
60 MPH braking distance (feet)	165–190	153	131	180	160
Combined urban-rural EPA fuel economy (mpg)	11–44	29[c]	34[c]	19[d]	27.5[e]
Emissions (HC/CO/NO$_x$) (grams per mile)	1.5/15/2.0	.41/9/1.5	.28/2.4/1.2	1.5/15/2.0	.41/3.4/.4
0–60 MPH acceleration (secs.)	10–20	16–18	16	12.5	13.5
Passenger compartment volume (cubic feet)	66–87	83	100	122	122
Weight (lbs.)	2,500–3,000	2,637	2,150	3,800	2,850
Estimated cost in mass production (1977 dollars)	3,000–6,000	4,446	3,925	5,600	NA

Source: Subcompact data from National Highway Traffic Administration press release, "Status of the Research Safety Vehicle," June 9, 1977. Performance, weight, and cost of the 1977 Chevrolet Impala used as the full-size RSV base vehicle are from *Consumer Reports* 42, no. 2 (February 1977): 87. Crash performance of this vehicle has been estimated by Minicars, Inc. Full-size RSV data are from NHTSA news release and fact sheet "Large Research Safety Vehicle," April 20, 1978.

a Assumes restraint systems are worn.

b Damage to nonsafety related items allowed.

c Using present technology engines. The Calspan vehicle uses a 1,716 cc four cylinder gasoline engine currently in production in the Dodge Omni and Plymouth Horizon. The Minicars vehicle uses a 1,595 cc four cylinder stratified charge gasoline engine currently in production in the Honda Accord.

d Using standard 305 cubic inch V8 engine with three speed automatic transmission.

e Using a preliminary version of the turbocharged four cylinder Volvo gasoline engine with five speed manual transmission and Lambda-Sond emission control system.

• Passive seat belts in the Calspan vehicle that would inflate during crashes (on the same principle as air bags), providing much more of a cushion effect than conventional seat belts.

• Dual chamber air bags, telescoping bag mounts, and knee bolsters in the Minicars vehicle to dissipate "g" forces during a collision more effectively than conventional air bags.

• Impact-absorbing, though conventional, body in the Calspan vehicle sufficient to enable passengers restrained by seat belts or air bags to survive 45–50 mph barrier crashes.

• An innovative Minicars body employing foam-filled sheet metal panels and promising sufficient impact-absorption to enable re-strained occupants to survive barrier crashes of more than 50 mph.

• Impact-resistant fuel storage cells mounted against the rear fire wall to eliminate fuel leakage after collisions and rollovers (the primary cause of fires in the wake of accidents).

• Tires able to run for fifty miles at 50 mph after a puncture (to eliminate the risk of control loss during a blowout and the need to make repairs at roadside).[21]

• A small radar and microprocessor in the Minicars vehicle to warn the inattentive driver of impending hazards and to trigger the brakes automatically in cases of unavoidable high-speed collision (with the aim of reducing the crash impact speed to a level com-patible with the survival of restrained passengers.)[39]

NHTSA officials expect all three RSV designs to meet the 1985 fuel economy standard and at least one to meet all three of the ultimate Clean Air Act emission standards without further modifi-cation. The aims of the next stages of the RSV project will be to refine the current performance and cost estimates in the light of intensive prototype vehicle testing and to devise means of reducing the cost of RSV safety features. There is no expectation that NHTSA will ever mandate the marketing of RSV vehicles per se, but it is anticipated that the RSV project findings will be translated into specific performance standards during the years ahead.

[21] This feature also eliminates the need for a spare tire, thereby saving weight and per-mitting the achievement of luggage space comparable to all but the largest full-size cars.

In short, just as automobiles have not been designed until recent years with fuel economy and emission control as high priority objectives, they have not been designed with safety as a prime objective either. A paradoxical result in each case has been that the engineers, when finally turned loose on the problem, have been able to achieve apparent triumphs in the form of extremely rapid short-term progress.

Consumer Regulatory Measures

The Department of Transportation concluded in a 1976 review of available highway safety measures that the enactment and strict enforcement of seat belt use laws would save by far the most lives and would be the most cost-effective (in terms of dollar cost per death averted).[22] Its cost would be relatively trivial; it could affect the entire vehicle fleet very quickly (whereas the Adams passive restraint rule will not affect the entire fleet until pre-1984 cars are phased out in the middle and late 1990s); and it could save an estimated 89,000 lives over the decade 1977 through 1986.[23] [42] At least, so the highway safety experts judged. Both Secretary Coleman and Secretary Adams, on the other hand, judged that it

[22.] The report, prepared in response to a congressional directive, examined thirty-seven types of measures selected as most promising from an initial list of more than two-hundred.[40] It dealt only with measures eligible for assistance under Title 23, U.S. Code. These include construction, traffic enforcement, educational, emergency medical, and alcohol treatment programs but not the regulation of vehicle characteristics, which is authorized by Title 49. (Subsequent DOT analyses, however, have sought to compare the cost-effectiveness of passive restraint systems with actions to require the use of existing seat belts.)[41]

The task force that developed the report consisted of safety specialists from the Federal Highway Administration, the Office of the Secretary of Transportation, and NHTSA. A private contractor carried out an extensive review of available data. Officials of twenty-nine states and 593 localities were surveyed on the time and expenditures likely to be required for implementation of each measure under consideration, and a 103 member Delphi panel of experts was utilized to make informed judgments where data were lacking.

Although this report is clearly the most authoritative currently available on the cost-effectiveness of alternative highway safety measures, its estimates are based heavily on uncertain assumptions, extrapolations from fragmentary data, and professional judgments. If the estimates are frequently expressed in precise form, the reason is simply that these were the results generated by complex sets of calculations based on approximate and often quite shaky foundations.

[23.] The study team estimated that it would take two years fully to implement a mandatory seat belt usage program even if the necessary political decisions were made quite promptly, that seat belt usage would gradually rise under the influence of the program to 80 percent, and that when fully operational, the program would prevent 10,000 fatalities a year over and above those prevented by existing levels of seat belt usage.[43]

would be foolhardy to expect the widespread enactment of such laws in the United States, let alone effective enforcement and widespread compliance.

A similar attitude of defeatism about behavioral regulation has traditionally marked speed limit determination and enforcement. The standard practice has been to base speed limits on the eighty-fifth percentile speed observed under free-flow traffic conditions, leaving only 15 percent of drivers to be dealt with by law enforcement officials. The conventional wisdom has been that it would be self-defeating to strive for greater policy influence on driving behavior. Thus the *Transportation and Traffic Engineering Handbook* (which endorses the eighty-fifth percentile approach) comments: "The consensus of traffic engineers in the United States is that motorists usually adjust their speeds according to conditions on the road and not necessarily to posted speed limits. Hence, if unreasonably low limits are posted, the limit will be violated by large numbers of drivers. This leads to disrespect of other posted limits as well."[44]

Early in 1974, however, the 55 mph speed limit was adopted by Congress as an energy conservation measure, and during that year the fatality rate per hmpmt fell by 15 percent. By contrast, the declines in every other year since 1966 had ranged between 2 and 6 percent. Average vehicle speeds on rural interstate highways dropped from 65.0 mph to 57.6 mph, while those on urban interstates dropped from 57.0 mph to 53.1 mph, and interstate fatalities declined by 32 percent. (In contrast, local street fatalities fell by only 7 percent.)[45]

More recently average speeds have begun to creep back up, and enforcement has become increasingly lax. States must in theory enforce the 55 mph limit to remain eligible for federal highway aid. To date, however, federal officials have demanded no more than pro forma certification of compliance with this requirement. A *New York Times* survey early in 1977 reported that police in most states issued summonses only to vehicles exceeding the 55 mph limit by more than 10 mph, and that many state laws explicitly provided only trivial penalties for violations below the pre-1974 posted limit.[46] And the U.S. secretary of transportation reported to Congress in October 1977 that during the first half of the year not a single state had maintained an eighty-fifth percentile speed (on roadways with the posted national speed limit) as low as 55 mph. The actual range of eighty-fifth percentile speeds was 57–66 mph, and forty states registered *average* speeds in excess of 55 mph. Although average speeds remained well below those recorded prior to 1974, and only about 7 percent of observed vehicles exceeded 65 mph, Secretary Adams considered the trend ominous. Labeling the 55 mph speed limit "perhaps the most important safety measure in modern times," he urged that Congress require all states to achieve eighty-fifth percentile compliance by 1982.[24] [47] There is no prospect of early congressional action on this proposal.

Because the focus was on energy conservation, the potential for preventing accidents by reducing speed limits that were already at or below the 55 mph level was ignored even in 1974. It seems likely, however, that just as speeds of 65 and 70 on expressways entail a substantial risk increment over and above speeds of 55, speeds of 45–55 on many older roads entail significant risk increments above speeds in the range of 30–40. To our knowledge, however, no state has undertaken a review of these lower speed limits in response to the demonstrated safety benefits of the 55 mph limit, nor has the U.S. Department of Transportation sponsored any research on this question. Without the energy tie-in and the sharp prod of an oil embargo, this is another issue that safety officials view as beyond the political pale.

In DOT's 1976 survey of highway safety measures, one other class of consumer regulatory measure emerged as having substantial life-saving potential. The study team estimated that alcohol safety measures—consisting primarily of the use of specially trained alcohol enforcement patrols (especially nights and weekends), secondarily of alcohol treatment clinics—could save 13,000 lives over the decade 1977 through 1986.[49] It found this to be a relatively high cost strategy, however, ranking eighteenth in esti-

24. In its 1976 survey of available highway safety measures, DOT concluded that effective enforcement of the 55 mph limit offered the second most significant opportunity to avert fatalities over the 1977–1986 decade, right after mandatory seat belt use. The potential saving for the ten-year period was 32,000 lives and 415,000 personal injuries.[48]

mated cost-effectiveness among the thirty-seven measures examined. (The reason was the treatment element. NHTSA officials informed us off the record that they viewed alcohol treatment programs as nearly worthless in terms of direct contribution to highway safety but indispensable as means of bolstering the political acceptability of enforcement programs.) Whereas the estimated cost of mandatory seat belt usage was $506 per death forestalled and that of speed limit enforcement was $21,200, the alcohol safety package carried an estimated cost of $164,000 per death averted.[50]

How great a cost should have been deemed too high? NHTSA has estimated that the average cost per fatality in 1975 was $287,000 (making no allowance for pain and suffering, but including the present value of future earnings).[51] Additionally, measures that save lives also prevent nonfatal injuries and property damage. Thus the DOT safety report estimated that the alcohol safety package, in addition to preventing 13,000 fatalities in the decade 1977 to 1986, would avert 153,000 nonfatal injuries and 392,000 property damage accidents. If one placed a $5,000 value on each injury averted and a $1,000 value on each property damage accident averted, those benefits alone justified 54 percent of the cost of the alcohol package. Using this approach, measures were cost-effective in 1975 if their cost per death averted was less than about $600,000.[25]

Highway Improvements
The DOT safety report identified twelve road construction mea-

[25.] The ratio of fatalities to nonfatal injuries and property damage accidents averted did vary from one technique to another but not sharply. Thus the alcohol package ranked eighteenth in cost-effectiveness re fatalities, twenty-fourth re nonfatal accidents, and sixteenth re property damage accidents.

All of the benefit estimates reported thus far were for each technique if adopted in isolation. In a separate analysis, the DOT safety report estimated the incremental benefits that would accrue from each of the thirty-seven measures examined if they were adopted in order of cost-effectiveness. The results of this exercise, presented in table 7.13, suggest (if one accepts the $600,000 criterion) that the first twenty-five merited implementation. Surprisingly, an analysis that ignores the incremental feature—on the reasonable assumption that the most cost-effective measures, mandatory seat belt usage and effective speed limit enforcement, are among the least likely to be implemented—yields a similar conclusion. On this basis, the first twenty-eight in the DOT safety report ranking merited implementation.

TABLE 7.13
Cost-Effectiveness of Thirty-Seven Highway Safety Measures, Considering
Fatality Prevention Benefits Only

Measure (by Rank Order)	Incremental Fatalities Averted	Incremental Cost (millions of dollars)	Cost per Incremental Fatality Averted
1 (Mandatory seat belt usage)	89,000	$45	$506
2 (55 mph speed limit enforcement)	26,000	676	21,200
3-8 (combined)	10,000	329	32,900
9-16 (combined)	10,000	1,480	148,000
17-18 (combined)	14,000	3,140	224,000
19-25 (combined)	10,000	3,760	376,000
26-31 (combined)	10,000	12,270	1.23 million
32-37 (combined)	3,000	19,900	6.63 million

Source: DOT, *Highway Safety Needs Report*, figures 1, 2.

sures as likely to enhance safety at a cost per death averted of
$610,000 or less. Potential overlap aside, it estimated that these
measures would save 28,000 lives over the decade 1977 through
1986 in return for an expenditure of $4.2 billion, or an average
cost per fatality forestalled of $147,000. (See table 7.14.) As
actual expenditures for highway safety construction (all levels of
government combined) totaled $2.5 billion in 1975, this repre-
sented less than two years worth of spending at the current level.
The rate of cost increase beyond these twelve measures was quite
steep. The safety report estimated that the next three would save
1,600 lives over the decade at an average cost of $1.5 million each.

The measures listed in table 7.14 are all environmentally unobtrusive as well as very low cost by highway program standards. By
contrast the five heaviest construction measures examined, though
still rather low cost as highway construction activities go, were
ranked as the least cost-effective among the thirty-seven safety
measures considered. Together they offered a potential saving of
4,400 lives at an average cost of $4.4 million each. (See table 7.15.)

TABLE 7.14
The Dozen Most Cost-Effective Highway Construction Safety Measures Examined in the DOT Safety Report

Rank Among 37 Safety Measures	Technique	Estimated Fatalities Forestalled (1977–1986)	Estimated Cost (Millions of Dollars)	Cost Fatality Forestalled (Millions of Dollars)
2	Strict inspection of highway construction and maintenance practices by contractors, utilities, and others working in roadways	459	9	0.020
6	Upgrading or installation of regulatory and warning signs	3,670	125	0.034
7	Upgrading or installation of guardrails to redirect vehicles leaving the travel lanes	3,160	108	0.034
9	Improvement of pavement skid resistance at high accident locations	3,740	158	0.042
10	Installation of bridge guardrails as in (7)	1,520	70	0.046
11	Installation of wrong-way entry avoidance devices on divided highways	779	39	0.049
15	Installation of impact-absorbing devices (e.g., barrels) at fixed object locations where removal of the fixed object or the use of breakaway design is unfeasible	6,780	735	0.108
16	Systematic replacement of rigid sign and lighting supports adjacent to traveled ways with break-away supports	3,250	379	0.116

20	Upgrading and installation of median barriers to redirect vehicles that leave their travel lanes and would otherwise encounter serious collision hazards	529	121	0.228
24	Provision of clear recovery areas (at least 30 feet out from the pavement edge) at hazardous locations on expressways to enable drivers whose vehicles leave the travel lanes to return without injury	533	151	0.284
26	Clearing obstructions to improve sight distance at selected intersections	468	196	0.420
28	Upgrading and installation of traffic signals and systems	3,400	2,080	0.610
Totals		28,288	$4,171	0.147 (avg.)

Source: DOT, *Highway Safety Needs Report*, figures 1, 2.

TABLE 7.15
The Least Cost-Effective Highway Construction Safety Measures Examined in the DOT Safety Report

Rank Among 37 Safety Measures	Technique	Estimated Fatalities Forestalled 1977–1986	Estimated Cost (Millions of Dollars)	Cost per Fatality Forestalled (Millions of Dollars)
33	Improvement in access control by the construction of barrier-type medians, frontage road construction to eliminate driveway and minor street entrances, grade separations at crossings	1,300	3,780	2.91
34	Bridge widenings to equal the width of roadways and shoulders on either side; only on roads with speed limits over 35 mph	1,330	4,600	3.46
35	Railroad highway grade crossing improvements such as increases in sight distance, better geometrics and signals (automatic gates excluded)	276	974	3.53
36	Construction of paved or stabilized shoulders on roads with speed limits over 35 mph	928	5,380	5.80
37	Improvements in roadway alignment and gradient at high accident locations	590	4,530	7.68
Totals		4,424	$19,264	4.35 (average)

Source: DOT, *Highway Safety Needs Report*, figures 1, 2.

The safety report did not appraise new expressway construction as a potential safety strategy. Significant components of such an appraisal, however, might include the following. Fatality rates on the interstate system average 60 percent lower than those on streets and highways.[52] This suggests, if one ignores induced travel, that it will reduce the overall number of motor vehicle fatalities by about 12 percent (60,000 per decade at the current level of VMT and at current noninterstate fatality rates). The capital cost of the system will be in excess of $100 billion by the time it is finished. Over a decade, then, the cost per death averted will be about $1.7 million. New expressways have many other objectives in addition to safety, however, and they are extremely long-lived investments, so there is wide room for dispute about what proportion of the cost should be assignable to this purpose and what the period of amortization should be. Utilizing some premises, quite clearly, new expressways might appear to be highly cost-effective safety investments. On the other hand, the interstate system has (both directly and via its land use impacts) generated a great deal of traffic that would not otherwise have occurred. There are no consensual estimates of the magnitude of these induced travel effects, but if one assumes (illustratively) that the interstate program has generated increases of 30 percent in freeway VMT and of 10 percent in nonfreeway VMT, it emerges as having had no effect whatever on the number of motor vehicle fatalities. If one judges that the induced travel effect has been even greater, the program emerges as having added to the accident toll.

As new proposals for expressway construction are evaluated in the years ahead, at least two other factors merit consideration. First, the interstate cost figures cited above, which are nationwide and largely historic, doubtless understate the future costs of urban expressway construction by a wide margin. (This is quite apart from the fact that citizen resistance virtually precludes such construction in the developed portions of most American urban areas.) Second, by the time facilities now in the planning stage become operational, improved on-board protection systems will presumably, by saving many lives themselves, greatly reduce the life-saving potential of all other measures.

On balance, then, although interstate freeway fatality rates are remarkably low, the case for additional expressway construction as a safety measure is weak.

Summary

Forty-six thousand Americans a year are killed in motor vehicle accidents. The absolute number of fatalities per year peaked in 1972, but the fatality rate has declined continuously over the past half-century—from 18.2 per hundred million vehicle miles in the period 1923–1927 to 3.3 in 1976. The latter rate was the lowest of any major nation.

As of 1970, automobile occupancy averaged 2.2 per vehicle mile. Assuming that this figure still held in 1976, the nationwide fatality rate in that year was 1.5 per hundred million passenger miles of travel. The fatality rate on urban roads alone (less than half that on rural roads) was 1.0. Urban motor vehicle fatalities were divided about equally between occupants and nonoccupants, so the occupant risk of urban motor vehicle travel was about 0.5 per hundred million passenger miles. For those who drove only when sober, who obeyed speed limits, who regularly fastened their safety belts, and who avoided travel by motocycle, the occupant risk was probably in the range of 0.2 per hundred million passenger miles.

Bus and rail rapid transit have much lower occupant fatality rates (on a passenger mile basis) than private motor vehicles, but considerably higher nonoccupant rates. The combined rapid transit rate is approximately twice that for automobiles and trucks. Because transit vehicles have extremely high nonoccupant fatality rates per vehicle mile, service expansion programs that generate below-average load factors may entail higher accident risks per passenger mile than these nationwide average figures would suggest.

Until the mid 1960s, the motor vehicle accident toll was viewed as almost entirely attributable to poor driving, and the preferred remedy was driver training. Today multiple causation theories command general acceptance, and there is near-universal skepticism about the feasibility of altering driver behavior.

The most promising strategies for enhancing motor vehicle safety appear to be: regulation of the auto manufacturers to bring about vehicle design improvements; direct consumer regulation to prevent the deactivation of passive restraint systems, to require high standards of vehicle maintenance, and to prevent dangerous driving; and capital expenditures for relatively low-cost safety improvements to existing roads. Measures in the second category probably have the greatest technical potential for cost-effectiveness, but they have fared poorly to date in the American political arena. Measures in the first and third categories, by contrast, have stirred little public opposition so long as they have been unobstrusive from the standpoint of everyday motorist behavior.

Thus motor vehicle safety policy has focused overwhelmingly since the mid 1960s on accelerating the adoption of vehicle and roadway design improvements that make no demands upon motorists and which they easily ignore. This strategy appears to be quite cost-effective as far as it goes. Significantly, however, the most valuable safety measure of recent history has been a modest consumer regulation adopted in the first instance for other reasons entirely (and weakly enforced in the period since): the 55 mile per hour speed limit. While most now acknowledge the life-saving value of this measure, few public figures have been prepared to consider the incorporation of other consumer regulatory elements into the nation's motor vehicle safety strategy.

Nature of the Problem

The auto-dominant system of urban transportation has provided unprecedented levels of mobility for those able to take full advantage of it. A larger and larger proportion of the American people, moreover, are able to do so. From 1950 to 1975, the proportion of American households owning at least one car rose from 52 percent to 83 percent; the proportion of multiple-car households rose from 7 percent to 33 percent; and from 1950 to 1975 the percentage of adult Americans licensed to drive increased from 43 percent to 83 percent.[1]

For those without ready access to automobiles, however, the trend has been far less favorable. The majority shift from transit to motor vehicle travel has compelled sharp curtailments of transit service. From 1950 to 1970, vehicle miles of transit service nationally declined by 37 percent.[1] [2] During the same period, urbanized area population grew by 71 percent, and urbanized land area increased by 176 percent.[2] In consequence, there was a 77 percent decline in the density of transit service over the two decades, from 236 transit vehicle miles per square mile of urbanized area in 1950 to only 54 in 1970. Moreover, the nation's older, denser central cities, the places with the most fully developed transit services, have generally experienced both population and employment declines since 1950. All but one of the ten U.S. cities with the greatest transit ridership lost population between 1950 and 1973; several declined by as much as one-fifth.[5] Urban population growth was concentrated almost entirely in suburbs and in the newer central cities of the South and West that were characterized by low-density suburban life-styles..[3]

This chapter was jointly authored by John Pucher and Alan Altshuler, with research assistance from Chris Hendrickson.

[1.] This trend has been reversed since 1970. From 1970 to 1976, transit vehicle mileage increased by 7.6 percent.[3]

[2.] Urbanized area population increased from 69.2 to 118.4 million. Urbanized land area increased from 12,733 square miles to 35,081.[4]

[3.] Thus, among the twenty largest U.S. cities in 1973, those that had grown fastest since 1950 were Phoenix (495 percent increase from 1950 to 1973), Houston (121 percent), San Diego (127 percent), Dallas (88 percent), Memphis (66 percent), and Los Angeles (which grew by the largest absolute amount—770,000 people--but by only 39 percent).

Mobility is most usefully conceived in terms of the ease with which desired destinations can be reached. In the typical American city of 1850, almost all destinations were within walking distance for the average able-bodied adult. For example, the radius of settlement was only about two miles in Boston, then the fourth largest U.S. city. By 1900, electrified streetcars and commuter railroads had extended the outer boundaries of settlement by at least eight additional miles.[6] Though some urban workers lived as far as ten miles from the core, suburban development was almost entirely residential and was tightly clustered around rail stations and streetcar lines. Those insufficiently affluent to live in the suburbs had little reason to go there. It was still quite feasible—indeed the norm for all but the affluent—to make the vast majority of personal trips on foot. By contrast, those without ready access to automobiles today find themselves cut off from numerous destinations to which they may urgently desire access.

Most campaigns for improved equity in modern America focus on alleged failures to improve the relative circumstances of disadvantaged groups at sufficiently rapid rates. It is unusual to come across a situation in which the circumstances of the disadvantaged have deteriorated absolutely over a sustained period of time. For many Americans without cars and/or drivers' licenses, however, the absolute level of mobility has fallen sharply over the past several decades. Given the dramatic mobility improvements experienced by most Americans in this same period, it follows that the relative deprivation of those left behind has worsened acutely.

Concepts of Equity

An equitable arrangement may be understood as one that is just and fair. In modern America, where justice and fairness tend to be defined with reference to equality—of rights, opportunities, and claims to public service if not of income, employment, and status—perceptions of inequity generally focus on degrees of inequality. In evaluating calls for government action on equity grounds, however, public officials consider much more than the simple degree to which inequality is present. Most notably, they weigh: the significance of the item with reference to which inequality exists (access to medical facilities, for instance, by comparison with access to national parks); the extent to which the claimants are "deserving" of public assistance (the elderly, for example, versus those disabled by alcoholism); the degree to which they constitute a well-organized, intensely committed bloc of voters (veterans, for example, by comparison with welfare recipients); the risk that a favorable response would antagonize other groups; and the extent to which such a response would open the floodgates to massive new expenditure requirements.

Not surprisingly, they tend to respond most generously to groups that are well-organized, single-minded, widely viewed as deserving, and small. The preeminent such group in American society is veterans with severe service-connected disabilities. Thus the Veterans Administration stands ready to pay the full cost of any vehicle modifications that disabled veterans require in order to drive, and indeed to do so repeatedly as they buy new cars throughout their lives. The cost per car modified for quadriplegic veterans runs at times as high as $25,000.[7]

Three main concepts of equity uneasily coexist and compete for priority within the field of urban transportation:

1. Fee for service: to each according to his or her financial contribution.

2. Equality in service distribution: to each an equal share of public expenditure or an equal level of public service, regardless of need or financial contribution.

3. Distribution according to need: to each a share of public expenditure or service based on need as government has chosen to define it, preferably with the revenues drawn (by progressive taxation) predominantly from those in least financial need.

The first of these concepts is central to the private market system. It permeates a wide variety of government programs as well, but the trends of recent decades has been for government to act with increasing consistency to offset inequalities arising in the marketplace thus most government programs enacted since 1960 involve distribution in accord with equity concepts 2 and/or 3, and numerous older programs have also undergone adaptation in their distributional patterns to render them less sharply at odds with the ideologies of egalitarianism.[8]

Local governments still derive 15 to 20 percent of their revenues from user charges.[9] Until the 1960s the predominant view in this country was that mass transit should be financed entirely on the basis of user charges, and even today the contrary view remains controversial in some metropolitan areas with little dependence on transit and a conservative bent.

The fee-for-service concept continues to predominate in government highway programs, though there are numerous cross-subsidies within the highway revenue-expenditure system. Light vehicle users subsidize heavy-vehicle users, urban users subsidize rural users, off-peak users subsidize peak users, users of older streets and highways subsidize users of expensive new urban expressways, and so on.[10] Though efforts to measure these cross-subsidies are inevitably controversial (because joint costs constitute an estimated 85 percent of total costs), some of them appear to be sizable. An Urban Institute study for the U.S. Department of Transportation has recently concluded, for example, that autos and light-weight trucks together bore 98 percent of the highway user tax burden for joint costs during the two decades 1956–1975, although they accounted for only 91 percent of vehicle mileage and 80 percent of ton mileage.[4] If common costs are distributed according to vehicle mileage, the implicit cross-subsidy to heavier vehicles was $18 billion; if they are distributed according to ton-mileage, the cross-subsidy was $46 billion.[13] Similarly rural highway users enjoyed subsidies adding up to $67.5 billion during this period, whereas urban highway users paid $29.5 billion more in user taxes than they received in highway construction outlays.[14] Combined federal and state subsidies to rural highways users during these two decades were about five-fold those to urban mass transit users.[5]

These refer only to the direct flow of user tax payments and government expenditures. Additionally there has been a great deal of controversy in recent years about the indirect costs of the high-

[4] User tax payments by heavy and medium vehicles were, however, sufficient to cover fully the incremental costs occasioned by their special characteristics. The Urban Institute study estimates that such "occasioned" expenditures amounted to $62.1 billion, whereas user payments from heavy and medium vehicles totaled $68 billion.[12]

[5] Federal and state transit expenditures in this period totaled about $14 billion.[15]

way system. These include the health effects of air, noise, and water pollution attributable to motor vehicle travel, the disruption of neighborhoods and ecological resources by highway construction, and the value (over and above their market prices) of nonrenewable resources such as oil and prime agricultural land consumed for highway transportation purposes.

The distributional impacts of the highway finance system have also come in for increasing criticism. Lower-income groups are somewhat less likely to own cars than higher-income groups, and lower-income households with cars drive fewer miles per year. Thus they tend to contribute less in absolute terms to highway trust fund coffers than higher-income households. At the same time, they contribute more in relative terms—and the latter is central to the contemporary economic definition of tax regressivity.

Suggestions for reforming the system of highway finance may be classified as falling within the fee-for-service ideological framework or the distribution-according-to-need framework. Critics in the former group desire to perfect the system of user charges so that cross-subsidization will be reduced and external costs internalized. That is, they would like peak-hour users to pay more and off-peak users less; they would like the social costs of air pollution to be reflected in highway user charges; and so on. There are severe methodological obstacles to achieving a high degree of precision in the user charge system, but these have been far overshadowed by the political. While the alleged victims of the current system have displayed little concern, each proposal for change has evoked intense resistance from those fearing that it would harm them.

Critics in the egalitarian tradition are primarily oriented toward making the highway finance system more progressive. Their predominant objective in recent years has been to secure allocations of highway revenues for transit purposes, but they have also opposed increases in gasoline taxes (on the ground that revenue needs should be met with more progressive taxes), and they have argued that any gasoline tax increases should be offset by full cash rebates to low-income households.[6]

6. Thus, when the House of Representatives voted down a proposed five-cent increase in the gas tax as part of President Carter's energy bill in August 1977, the opposition con-

In the transit field, public debate has focused primarily on the distribution of benefits rather than costs, because public revenues for transit subsidization have been drawn from general funds that are typically fed by a wide variety of tax sources. Until the 1970s, most critics of transit distribution were content to argue that service within each metropolitan area should be distributed equally to sectors of like market potential—and, in particular, that low-income sectors should obtain their "fair share" of service. In recent years, however, they have increasingly pressed for service distribution according to need, focusing specifically on the mobility deficits of the physically handicapped, the elderly, and the poor.

Establishing the Extent of Deprivation

The mere fact that a group averages fewer trips per capita than the national norm by no means provides adequate evidence that its members suffer from mobility deprivation. Older and handicapped people, for example, may be more sedentary in their life-styles and less inclined than average to make trips even under conditions of equal travel opportunity. Both groups, moreover, have low rates of labor force participation and thus of trip making for work-related purposes.

If measurement of travel behavior alone provides an inadequate test, one may adopt the view that individuals are deprived if they are unable to make some of the trips that they would like. Travel desire not currently realized in behavior is generally termed latent travel demand. While undeniably of central importance, however, the concept of latent travel demand is extremely difficult to operationalize. Desire is largely a function of opportunity, and it adapts to altered opportunities over time. Even if one seeks merely a snapshot of desire at one moment in time, the problem is how to obtain it. Asked by a pollster what trips they would like to make,

sisted of Republicans, rural Democrats, and spokesmen for the poor. (The specific proposal that came to a vote differed substantially from that originally recommended by the president. Whereas he had recommended that the revenues be rebated to the public, the proposal voted on would have allocated half for mass transit and half for highway maintenance.) Congressman Ronald V. Dellums (Democrat of California), in leading that portion of the opposition concerned primarily about the poor, emphasized that any gas tax increase would entail great hardship for low-income workers needing to commute by automobile.[16]

some people will engage in flights of fancy, others will propose to emulate their more fortunate neighbors, and still others will respond in terms of their most basic needs. One can probe their implicit criteria (at substantial expense) with batteries of follow-up questions, but the result is to eliminate only part of the uncertainty. In fact, thorough studies based on such direct evidence of perceived deprivation are almost entirely lacking.[17]

A third approach is to equate low utilization of social services with transportation deficiencies.[18] The 1971 White House Conference on Aging, for example, concluded that inadequate transportation was a major cause of poor service utilization.[19] In fact, however, there is negligible evidence on this point, and some of that which is available runs counter to the thesis. For example, in the only survey dealing with this question, fewer than 5 percent of the elderly reported that they had ever foregone medical treatment due to lack of transportation.[20]

A fourth and extremely attractive approach, if adequate data were available, would be to analyze the results of experiments in which selected members of allegedly deprived groups had been afforded dramatically improved mobility opportunities—for example, taxi vouchers or new demand-responsive transit systems with low fares. While new services and subsidies have been provided to numerous groups in a wide variety of settings over the past dozen years, however, rigorous studies of their effects on personal travel behavior are almost entirely lacking.[21]

Finally, one may focus on the ease with which selected groups can utilize existing public transportation services. This approach, most notably as applied to the design of fixed-route transit systems, has been central to the claims of elderly and handicapped spokesmen in recent years, and it has been incorporated into numerous pieces of federal legislation. If relatively consensual and easy to operationalize, however, this final approach begs all the key questions. What is the overall degree to which those affected currently experience mobility deprivation? How relevant are fixed-route services, even if fully accessible, to alleviation of their mobility deficits? And how might alternative means of assisting them compare with design modifications of fixed-route transit systems in cost-effectiveness?

We shall return to these questions below. Let us now turn, however, to a review of available data on the current travel patterns of handicapped, elderly, and low income urban residents.

Mobility Problems of the Physically Handicapped

The most compelling claims for special mobility assitance are those made on behalf of the physically handicapped. There are major uncertainties, however, even about the number of Americans with mobility-related handicaps, let alone the severity of their mobility deprivation and the most cost-effective means of aiding them.

The Transportation Systems Center (TSC) of the U.S. Department of Transportation has estimated on the basis of national survey data that, as of 1970, 13.4 million individuals, 7 percent of the U.S. population, were handicapped in ways that rendered them "unable to use conventional transit or to use it only with difficulty." Of these 53 percent were also elderly. Presumably a good many were also poor, though data were not presented on this point.

Of the total handicapped group, 11 percent (1.4 million) were institutionalized and/or suffered from "acute" conditions; 17 percent (2.3 million) suffered from visual or hearing rather than motor impairments; and 6 percent (0.8 million) were confined to wheelchairs or walkers. The remaining two-thirds (8.8 million) were categorized under two very broad headings: "uses special aids" and "other mobility limitations."[22]

The National Center for Health Statistics (NCHS) of the Department of Health, Education and Welfare has estimated, on the other hand, that as of 1972, the number of individuals with "chronic mobility limitations" was 6.9 million—or roughly half the number judged by TSC to be handicapped in ways that impaired their ability to use mass transit.[7] NCHS found that 58 percent of those with chronic mobility limitations were elderly. Of the total handicapped group, 39 percent (2.7 million) were institu-

---

[7] The most important difference between the NCHS and TSC data bases was that NCHS asked whether respondents had trouble getting around, whereas TSC asked about objective (though very broadly defined) physical conditions and then made its own estimates of which were likely to impair mobility.

tionalized or confined to their homes. These included roughly half the elderly handicapped and one-quarter of the nonelderly handicapped. Another 25 percent (1.7 million) utilized special aids or required help from another person in getting around. The remaining 36 percent (2.5 million) simply reported that they had "trouble getting around alone."[23]

The best study available on the trip-making patterns of physically handicapped people was conducted by Abt Associates in Greater Boston during 1968.[24] It may have been atypical with reference to national conditions, however, because the Boston area is characterized by relatively high density and extensive transit service. Moreover the sample consisted of only persons who were in fact active (rather than confined to institutions or their homes). The Abt respondents made only about one-half as many trips per capita as·the general population. Of the trips they did make, 60 percent were by automobile and half of these were made as auto drivers; 24 percent were made by public transportation; and 14 percent were made by taxi. The most striking difference between the handicapped and the general population was in use of the taxi mode. The handicapped relied on taxicabs more than eight times as heavily (13.7 percent of all trips versus 1.6 percent), and made four times as many taxi trips per capita in absolute terms. Transit, on the other hand, accounted for virtually the same proportion of trips among the active handicapped as among the general population (24.6 percent versus 24.4 percent). (See table 8.1.) Those who said that they rarely or never used transit were asked why not. The principal reasons cited were structural obstacles and fear for safety. In contrast, the main reason cited by those who rarely or never traveled by taxi was cost.

The handicapped made only about one-third as many trips for commutation purposes as the general population, whereas they made almost two-thirds as many nonwork trips.[25] To some extent their lower labor force participation rate may have been transportation related. But one-third were elderly, and many of the others were doubtless kept from working by other than mobility factors. The Census Bureau has estimated that 11.2 nonelderly individuals were handicapped with respect to employment in 1970,

TABLE 8.1
Distribution of Trips by Mode, Greater Boston, 1970 (Excluding Walking)

	Percentage of Total Trips	
Mode	Handicapped	General Population
Auto Driver	30.5	46.0
Auto passenger	29.9	19.6
Taxi	13.6	1.6
Specialized taxi	1.0	
Bus	14.5	13.1
Subway	9.1	10.1
Train	.6	1.2
School bus and truck	1.9	8.4
Total daily trips per capita (all modes)	1.13	2.23

Source: Abt Associates, "Transportation Needs of the Handicapped: Travel Barriers, Cambridge, Massachusetts" (NTIS, PB-187-327, 1969), pp. 80–90.

nearly four times the number that NCHS estimated to suffer from chronic mobility limitations[26]

Mobility Problems of the Elderly
Ten percent of Americans in 1970 were over the age of sixty-five. According to the Nationwide Personal Transportation Study (NPTS), 66 percent of households with elderly members had automobiles available as of 1970, by comparison with 83 percent of all households, and 43 percent of the elderly were licensed to drive, by comparison with 74 percent of the general population sixteen years of age and older.[27] Of all trips made by the elderly, 94 percent were made by motor vehicle, just one percentage point below the national average for persons sixteen and older.

Overall trip making by the elderly was much less frequent than for other adults, however. Whereas the average American over the age of sixteen made 849 trips a year, the elderly averaged only 377 trips, less than half as many. (See table 8.2.) A fairly steady decline in trip making appears to set in after about the age of fifty. Those aged fifty to sixty-four in 1970 made about three-quarters as many trips as those thirty to forty-nine; those aged sixty-five to

TABLE 8.2
Trips per Capita and by Mode, 1970

Mode	Percentage of All Trips		Trips per Capita	
	Persons 65 & Over	All Persons 16 and Over	Persons 65 and Over	All Persons 16 and Over
Auto driver	53.4	62.6	201	531
Auto Passenger	35.9	25.7	135	218
Motorcycle		0.2		2
Truck (driver or passenger)	4.2	6.0	16	51
Subtotal: Private vehicle	93.5	94.5	352	802
Transit bus	4.3	2.8	16	24
Rapid transit	0.5	0.9	2	8
Commuter rail	0.1	0.2		2
School bus	0.6	1.2	2	10
Taxi	0.6	0.3	2	2
Subtotal: public transportation	6.1	5.4	22	46
Other (airplanes, etc.)	0.4	0.1	1	1
Total	100.0	100.0	375	849

Source: Federal Highway Administration, Nationwide Personal Transportation Study, report 6, "Characteristics of Licensed Drivers," (Washington, 1973), pp. 12–14, and FWHA, NPTS, report 9, "Mode of Transportation and Personal Characteristics of Tripmakers" (Washington, 1978), p. 31.

sixty-nine made about three-fifths as many trips as those fifty to sixty-four; those seventy and over made about two-thirds as many trips as those sixty-five to sixty-nine (and fewer than one-third as many trips as those thirty to forty-nine).[28]

Nationwide the elderly rely more heavily on transit and taxi travel than the general population does, but they do not account for a disproportionate share of transit and taxi patronage. Indeed they make fewer transit trips per capita than the national average. Their rate of taxi usage is just above average. (See tables 8.3 and 8.4.)

The falloff in travel with age seems attributable mainly to two factors: retirement from the labor force and deteriorating health.

TABLE 8.3
Comparison of Transit Use by Age Groups, 1970

| Age Group | Group as Percent of U.S. Population | Percentage of Age Group's Trips by Mode | | | Percentage of Mode's Patronage by Age Group[a] | | | | Annual Trips per Capita by Total Age Group |
		Bus	Rapid Transit	Total Transit	Bus	Rapid Transit	Bus	Rapid Transit	
5–65	81.8	2.7	0.7	3.4	92.0	96.0	92.8	92.8	830
Over 65	9.8	4.3	0.5	4.8	8.0	4.0	7.2	7.2	377

Source: Federal Highway Administration, NPTS, report 6, "Characteristics of Licensed Drivers," p. 31.

[a] NPTS did not count trips by children under the age of five. Thus transit patronage percentages have been adjusted as if all transit riders were five years of age or older.

TABLE 8.4
Proportion of Taxi Trips by Population Age Groups, 1970

Age Groups	Percentage of All Trips Made by Taxi	Total Personal Trips (millions)	Total Taxi Trips (millions)	Percentage of Total Taxi Trips by Age Group
5–13	0.2	21,020	42	11
14–15	0.2	5,271	11	3
16–20	< 0.05	15,527	–	–
21–25	0.3	14,652	44	11
26–29	0.4	10,046	40	10
30–39	0.3	23,905	72	18
40–49	0.2	24,070	48	12
50–59	0.3	16,685	50	13
60–64	0.7	6,391	45	11
65–69	0.8	3,236	26	7
70 and over	0.4	4,263	17	4
Total	0.3	145,066	395	100

Source: Federal Highway Administration, "Characteristic of Licensed Drivers," appendix C, table 1.

Note: In aggregate, 89.3 percent of the population was between the ages of 5 and 65 and made 89.1 percent taxi trips; 10.7 percent of the population was 65 or over and made 10.9 percent of taxi trips. NPTS did not count trips by children under the age of 5.

The latter is extremely resistant to measurement in the middle ranges, but it is clear at the extreme that numerous older persons are simply unable to travel. Nearly two million people over the age of sixty-five reported chronic disabilities in 1972 that confined them to their homes or to institutions.[29] This was roughly one-tenth of the elderly population, and it excluded those laid up at the time of the survey with nonchronic disabilities.

J. K. Markovitz has reported in detail on trip-making patterns of the elderly (disaggregated by income) in the New York metropolitan region as of 1963. Her data base was the Tri-State Home Interview Travel Survey conducted in that year. The tri-state elderly respondents averaged only 44 percent as many trips per capita as the total population. They made 76 percent as many noncommutation trips, however. Noncommutation trip making increased sharply as household income passed $3,000 a year, but only negligibly as it rose further. Even in the higher-income categories, total trip making among the elderly barely exceeded half that of the general population on a per capita basis.[30]

Elderly households were significantly smaller than the regional average (1.95 persons per household versus 3.09). Thus at any given household income level, elderly per-capita income was 58 percent higher. Yet elderly households in the over $10,000 income category made only about as many trips per capita as the regional average for households in the $3,000–6,000 income range.

By far the most significant indicator of mobility among the tristate elderly was possession of a driver's license. Drivers made four times as many trips as nondrivers. They even made about as many trips by mass transit as nondrivers, and drivers with household incomes over $10,000 made 44 percent more transit trips per capita than the average for nondrivers.[8] The four-to-one ratio of total trip making by drivers held even in the over $10,000 income category. Moreover the elderly drivers in this affluent income group made twice as many "taxi and other" trips as the nondrivers.[32]

These data suggest that a high proportion of the nondrivers were simply not in the market for significant amounts of travel. Without knowing how many were wholly or largely in this category, it is impossible even to begin to estimate the amount of deprivation that may have been felt by the nondrivers who did wish to travel more.

Mobility Problems of the Poor

There is no consensual definition of poverty, and it is in any event a matter of degree. Thus we shall speak mainly of relationships between income and mobility rather than of poverty per se. Refer

---

[8] In aggregate, the elderly made exactly the same proportion of their trips by transit as the general population (33 percent). Because of their lower absolute rates of trip making, however, the elderly made only 44 percent as many transit trips per capita as the general population.[31]

ences to poor or low-income households without further qualification, however, shall denote those with incomes below $5,000 in 1970 or below $7,500 in 1975. Personal income per capita rose by about one-half (51.2 percent) between 1970 and 1975, so these are roughly equivalent figures.[33]

Inequalities over the human life cycle and on a per-capita basis tend to be much smaller than inequalities among households at any given moment, it should be emphasized. Young people and old people, for example, generally earn less than those in the prime of life. The young are buoyed by their high expectations, however; they tend to have low child care costs and medical expenses; and they frequently have unreported income in the form of gifts and scholarships. The elderly have negligible child care expenses; they benefit from Medicare and other government programs; they live in small households; and they frequently have substantial accumulated capital (some of which, like equity in their homes, directly reduces their need for income).[34]

Utilizing U.S. government definitions of poverty (changing over time, and varying with family size and region of the country), researchers at the University of Michigan have recently reported on the experience of poverty among 16,000 representative Americans during the nine-year period 1967–1976. They found that whereas 12 percent of the sample had a poverty-level income during 1975, under 3 percent were poor in every one of the nine survey years; these were predominantly members of households headed by persons with one or more of the following characteristics: over sixty-five, little formal education, black, female, disabled.[35]

Finally, some of those who appear to be poor on the basis of reported cash incomes have substantial unreported incomes, receive thousands of dollars worth of benefits in kind (ranging from food stamps to free medical care), or live in rural circumstances which permit them to grow much of their own food and cut their own wood fuel.

Unfortunately, no studies seeking to relate travel patterns to income have ever adjusted for such factors, even the most obvious, such as household size and regional variations in the cost of living.

Thus there is considerable disagreement about what to make of the data that are available. What does emerge clearly, however, is that trip making tends to increase as a function of both income and automobile ownership. Within the same income categories, members of households that own automobiles make two or three times as many trips as the members of households without them. Within each category of automobile ownership (0-1-2-3 cars), there is a further tendency for trip making to increase with income, but it is significantly less pronounced.

Automobile ownership increases with income, so part of the increase in trip making associated with the former is reasonably attributed to the latter.[9] Equally striking, however, most households above the very lowest income levels do own automobiles and achieve rates of trip making at least four-fifths the national average. As of 1974, only 43 percent of households with incomes under $3,000 owned cars, but 61 percent of those in the $3,000–5,000 category and 76 percent of those in the $5,000-7,500 category did so. (See table 8.5.)

Notably, about 3 percent of households in the over $20,000 categories also had no cars. Applying this proportion to the total share of U.S. households without cars, one may reasonably estimate that about one-sixth of all carless households are so for reasons wholly unrelated to income. This approach also suggests, however, that income constraints account for 95 percent of carlessness among households with incomes below $3,000, and for 92 percent of that among households in the $3,000–5,000 income range.

Table 8.6 presents national data on household travel by automobile for all purposes, adjusted for both income and automobile ownership. As of 1970, households with incomes under $3,000 averaged roughly one-third as many auto trips as the population generally and roughly one-fourth the average for households with incomes over $10,000. Such low-income households, if they did not own a car, averaged only one-sixth as many trips as the overall population. If they did own a car, however, they achieved a trip-

[9.] The other side of the coin is that rates of car ownership are highly correlated with the number of adults, and particularly with the number of employed adults, per household. Thus one may view both income and car ownership as attributable to demographic characteristics and employment.

TABLE 8.5
Automobile Ownership by Household Income, 1974

Household Income	No Car	One or More Cars	One Car	Two Cars	Three or More Cars	One or More Light Trucks	One or More Motor Vehicles
Under $3,000	56.8%	43.2%	37.0%	5.5%	0.7%	7.8%	46.2%
$3,000–4,999	39.3	60.7	51.9	8.0	0.8	11.0	64.2
$5,000–7,499	24.0	76.0	60.4	13.6	2.0	14.3	79.4
$7,500–9,999	15.0	85.0	61.9	20.9	2.2	16.8	88.3
$10,000–14,999	8.3	91.7	54.9	32.4	4.4	22.2	93.9
$15,000–19,999	4.5	95.5	45.4	42.3	7.8	22.7	96.7
$20,000–24,999	3.1	96.9	36.8	46.9	13.2	19.2	97.4
$25,000 and over	3.3	96.7	29.5	45.7	21.5	17.2	97.2

Source: U.S. Department of Commerce, Bureau of the Census, *Consumer Buying Indicators, 1974 Survey of Purchases and Ownership,* in *Motor Vehicle Facts and Figures* (1977), p. 38.

TABLE 8.6
Auto Travel per Household by Income and Auto Ownership, 1970

Auto Ownership	Under $3,000	$3,000–3,999	$4,000–4,999	$5,000–5,999	$6,000–7,499	$7,500–9,999	$10,000–14,999	Over $15,000	All Incomes
Daily person trips									
None	1.1	2.2	2.2	2.4	2.9	3.2	2.8	3.3	1.7
One	3.5	4.8	5.8	5.3	6.5	7.3	7.0	6.1	5.9
Two	5.5	8.9	9.3	7.8	8.0	9.3	8.7	10.5	9.1
Three or more	NA	NA	12.0	12.3	10.6	12.8	12.1	13.0	12.4
Total	2.2	4.2	5.4	5.2	6.6	8.0	8.1	9.5	6.2
Daily person miles									
None	9.2	19.4	14.6	22.3	14.3	15.8	22.5	43.2	13.4
One	27.9	43.2	40.2	44.2	61.5	70.8	68.2	71.0	54.2
Two	64.9	82.8	93.3	79.5	68.3	102.2	98.1	113.0	96.6
Three or more	NA	NA	88.1	108.0	84.9	137.2	109.5	129.5	123.8
Total	17.8	34.0	41.3	46.6	55.8	81.0	84.2	102.9	60.6

Source: Federal Highway Administration, Nationwide Personal Transportation Study, report 11, "Auto Ownership" (Washington, 1973), table 26.

making rate more than half the national average, and they made more trips than carless households with incomes over $10,000. Households with incomes of $3,000 to $5,000 that owned a car achieved a trip-making rate four-fifths the national average, and those with incomes of $4,000 to $5,000 achieved a rate nine-tenths the national average.

As both low-income households and carless households consist disproportionately of those with few adult members, with heads over the age of sixty-five, and with heads who suffer from chronic mobility limitations, it seems reasonable to judge that a very large proportion of the low-income households are also in one or more of these other categories. We estimate, for example, that between one-quarter and two-fifths of carless housholds with incomes under $5,000 were headed by persons over the age of sixty-five.[10]

Households without cars tend to live disporportionately in central cities and to be relatively well served by mass transit. In 1974, 29 percent of central city households lacked cars, by comparison with 12 percent of suburban households.[38] In 1970, 82 percent of all SMSA households with incomes under $5,000 lived within six blocks of public transportation, by comparison with 58 percent of those with incomes over $15,000. (See table 8.7.) Given the more central locations of the poor, moreover, it seems probable that their nearby transit routes were more numerous and operated more frequently than those easily accessible to more affluent urbanites. In practice, individuals from low-income households relied on transit for 14 percent of their trips, whereas those with incomes over $7,500 used it for only 4 percent. Notably transit reliance did not decline as incomes increased beyond the $7,500–10,000 range. Indeed households with incomes above $15,000 relied on transit for 5.0 percent of their trips, by comparison with a 3.6 percent modal split for those in the $10,000–15,000 range. (See table 8.8.)

[10.] Roughly 15 percent of all U.S. households in 1970 were both in this income range and without cars.[36] About 9 percent of U.S. households were both headed by individuals over sixty-five and did not own a car.[37] Given that elderly-headed households are represented disproportionately among those with low incomes, and that on average the elderly without cars have considerably lower incomes than those who do own cars, it seems reasonable to assume that half to three-quarters of the elderly households without cars (comprising 4–6 percent of all U.S. households) also had incomes below $5,000.

TABLE 8.7
Transit Accessibility by Income, 1970

Annual Household Income Group	Distance to Nearest Public Transportation (in Blocks)				
	Less than 1	1-2	3-6	Over 6	None Available
Under $5,000	30.3%	34.5%	17.4%	9.2%	8.4%
$5,000-9,999	20.9	33.2	18.3	15.5	11.7
$10,000-14,999	15.5	29.3	18.3	20.6	16.3
Over $15,000	13.3	23.7	20.6	25.5	15.9
All households	21.3	30.8	18.6	16.6	12.4

Source: Adapted from Federal Highway Administration, Nationwide Personal Transportation Study, report 5, "Availability of Public Transportation and Shopping Characteristics of SMSA Households" (Washington, 1972), p. 11.

Although low-income travelers were much more dependent on mass transit than other groups, they also traveled much less frequently. In consequence, households with incomes under $5,000, which constituted 28 percent of all U.S. households, accounted for only 29 percent of transit patronage. (See table 8.9.)

Although the aggregate income profile of transit users was almost identical to that of the general population, this was far from the case on a mode-by-mode basis. Low-income households accounted for 34 percent of bus and streetcar ridership, 15 percent of rail rapid transit ridership, and zero percent of commuter rail ridership.

Since low-income households made fewer trips in aggregate than others, the income profile of all travelers was considerably above average. By comparison with the income profile of all travelers, that of rapid transit riders was just about average, that of bus riders was dramatically below average, and that of commuter rail riders remained far above average. (See table 8.9.)

The figures come into particularly sharp focus as one considers the proportion of all trips in each income category made by each mode. Low-income households made 12.2 percent of all their trips by bus or streetcar, whereas those with incomes over $7,500 made

TABLE 8.8
Modal Distribution for Urban Travel by Income Class, 1970

Income Class	Auto Driver	Auto Passenger	Bus or Streetcar	Subway or Elevated	Commuter Rail	Taxi	Total
Below $5,000	47.6%	37.8%	12.2%	1.5%	0%	.8%	100%
$5,000–$7,499	55.8	37.0	5.5	1.4	0.1	0.2	100
$7,500–$9,999	57.6	38.3	2.5	1.0	0.2	0.5	100
$10,000–$14,999	60.3	36.0	2.4	0.9	0.3	0.2	100
$15,000 or more	60.7	34.0	3.1	1.6	0.3	0.3	100
All incomes	57.3	36.6	4.4	1.2	0.2	0.3	100

Source: John Pucher, "Equity in Transit Financing" (Ph.D. diss., MIT, 1978), p. 28. The distributions were calculated from a computer tape of the 1970 Nationwide Personal Transportation Study supplied by the Federal Highway Administration, U.S. Department of Transportation.

Note: Each figure in the table represents the percentage of the total trips made by each income group accounted for by the indicated mode.

TABLE 8.9

Composition of Modal Usage for Urban Travel by Income Class, 1970

Group	Below $5,000	$5,000–$9,999	$10,000–$14,999	$15,000 or more
All households	28.4%	30.9%	23.0%	17.6%
All travelers	12.1	42.0	29.6	16.2
Auto drivers	10.1	41.6	31.1	17.2
Auto passengers	12.7	43.2	29.1	15.1
Bus or streetcar riders	34.1	37.8	16.4	11.6
Subway or elevated riders	14.9	42.8	21.2	21.1
Commuter rail riders	0	35.1	39.6	25.2
Taxi passengers	28.5	42.3	16.0	13.3
Public transportation users (Total, all modes)	27.6	37.1	18.0	17.7

Source: Pucher, "Equity in Transit Financing," p. 24. The figures on the distribution of all U.S. households by income class were calculated from U.S. Department of Commerce, Bureau of the Census, *1970 Census of Population*, vol. PC(1)-D1: *Detailed Characteristics, United States Summary* (Washington, D.C.: U.S. Government Printing Office, 1973), table 258. The aggregate public transportation income distribution was calculated from the NPTS by the FHWA and reported in Jose Gomez-Ibanez, "Federal Assistance for Urban Mass Transportation" (Ph.D. diss., John F. Kennedy School of Government, 1975), p. 210. The remaining statistics in the table were calculated by John Pucher from a NPTS computer tape supplied by the Federal Highway Administration. Local trips were defined as those of fifty miles or less. Overnight trips and school bus trips were excluded regardless of length.

Note: The first line displays the percentage of all U.S. households in each income group. Other lines display the percentage of the total riders of each mode accounted for by each income group.

2.6 percent of their trips by this mode. Low-income households made 1.5 percent of their trips by rapid transit, exceeding the 1 percent level that prevailed in the middle-income categories but about equal to that in the over $15,000 category. Low-income households made vanishingly few trips by commuter rail (0.0 percent with rounding), while those with incomes over $10,000 made 0.3 percent of their trips by this mode. (See table 8.8.) Low-income households relied on automobiles for 85 percent of all trips, by comparison with a 95 percent automobile modal split for those with incomes above $15,000. They were more likely to travel as passengers (44 percent of auto trips versus 36 percent), but the difference was considerably less than might have been anticipated. (See table 8.8.)

The distinctions were considerably sharper for commutation trips only. Fifty-four percent of low-income employees traveled to work by automobile, nearly two-fifths of them (20 percent) as passengers. By comparison 75 percent of those with incomes over $15,000 commuted by automobile, approximately one-fifth (16 percent) as passengers.[39]

Surprisingly the very poor—those with incomes under $3,000—relied on taxis for five times as high a proportion of their trips as the general population (1.6 percent versus 0.3 percent). Moreover travelers from households with incomes under $5,000 accounted for 29 percent of taxi usage. Only bus and streetcar riders had a lower income profile than taxi riders. (See table 8.9.)

Transport Deprivation as a Cause of Poverty

The idea that transport deprivation is a major cause of unemployment, and thus of poverty, enjoyed a brief vogue in the late 1960s. The McCone Commission on the Watts riots expressed the thesis most clearly: "Our investigation has brought into clear focus the fact that the inadequate and costly public transportation currently existing throughout the Los Angeles area seriously restricts the residents of the disadvantaged areas such as south central Los Angeles. The lack of adequate transportation handicaps them in seeking and holding jobs, attending schools, shopping, and fulfilling other needs."[40] There seemed reason to believe that the commission's diagnosis might have wide applicability. Many of the nation's central cities were declining absolutely as employment centers. Those that were not tended to be the newer cities of the South and West, characterized by low density, extreme automobile dominance, and minimal transit service.[11] In short, the vast majority of urban employment growth, whether central city or suburban, was at locations served poorly or not at all by mass transportation. It appeared, further, that blacks were particularly disadvantaged by the flight of employment from central locations, because discrimination tended to keep them confined to central residential locations.

During the several years following the McCone Commission report, the federal government sponsored fifteen demonstration projects intended to assist low-income (especially minority) urban residents to obtain employment at suburban locations. Eighty-three new transit routes were established, mainly on corridors between central city gettoes and very large suburban employment centers (or corridors).[42] Several attracted substantial patronage, but the vast majority did not.

The most striking successes were in Chicago and Los Angeles. The Chicago service was an express bus route from the end of a rapid transit line to O'Hare International Airport, where about 19,000 people were employed. The line, which provided the only transit link between the airport and downtown Chicago, was also of potential benefit to air travelers. As it turned out, the air travel market was essential to the success of the service. Seventy percent of the 1,100 daily passengers on the line were noncommuters. Of the commuters, 40 percent said that they had been hired subsequent to commencement of the service, and two-thirds of these claimed that they were dependent on the service for their jobs. In the year following the survey, however, half of this group stopped using the service. It was unknown what proportion of the lost riders had shifted to automobiles, as opposed to changing jobs.[43]

[11.] Between 1960 and 1970, the central cities of the nation's thirty-three largest metropolitan areas (all those with 1970 populations exceeding one million) declined overall by 2 percent. Those in the Northeast declined by 10 percent and those in the North Central region declined by 11 percent. By contrast, those in the South grew by 14 percent and those in the West by 12 percent. [41]

The Los Angeles experience was varied, but one route in particular (along Century Boulevard) attracted considerable patronage.
It connected Watts with a large General Motors plant at one end of
the line and with Los Angeles International Airport at the other,
as well as numerous other employment sites at points along the
way. The line attracted over 3,000 passengers a day, was estimated
to have helped 1,200 people find jobs during the three-year project life, and was retained as a regular transit route at the end of
the demonstration.[44]

More typical, however, were the experiences in Boston, East
Los Angeles, and Sacramento. The Boston service was designed to
assist ghetto residents in seeking employment and commuting to
jobs around circumferential Route 128, which had been a magnet
for Boston area employment growth since its completion in the
early 1950s. Accompanied by an intense publicity campaign, the
service was offered for six months. Patronage was meager, and the
operating deficit was $3.72 per trip. Only 42 responses were
obtained to the customer survey, of which twelve indicated that
the respondents would have to seek other employment if the service were discontinued.[45] The East Los Angeles service sought
to connect its low-income population with the City of Commerce,
an industrial enclave. In its second year, the service had a patronage of 130 per day and entailed an estimated operating subsidy per
passenger of $1.45. Fares covered only 10 percent of total
cost.[46] The Sacramento project sought to connect two low-
income neighborhoods with a variety of human service facilities,
shopping centers, colleges, and (via transfers) all of the employment locations served by other routes in the system. After two
years, the line carried 600 passengers a day but less than one per
bus mile.[47]

By 1970, the Urban Mass Transportation Administration
(UMTA) had lost interest in funding special employment services
for the poor. There seemed little more to demonstrate and UMTA
had no authority to provide routine operating subsidies. A shift in
national mood with reference to poverty issues was also occurring at this time, symbolized by the election of President Nixon.
Primarily, however, UMTA's loss of interest seems to have been

attributable to its sense that these demonstrations had produced only meager benefits. They may have helped several thousand people obtain jobs, but it was uncertain that the beneficiaries would have been unable to find jobs in the absence of the projects. A typical pattern, moreover, was that riders who used the special transit services to obtain jobs used some of their first earnings to purchase cars. Thus rider turnover tended to be high.

Labor market economists never attached much credence to the thesis that poor transit service was a significant cause of ghetto unemployment. At the height of UMTA's interest in special employment services (1968), the American Academy of Arts and Sciences sponsored a conference on poverty and transportation, the proceedings of which remain the single most important source on the subject. The task of reviewing available evidence on the causes of high ghetto unemployment fell to economist Peter Doeringer. He barely mentioned transportation. Instead he maintained that the primary causes were lack of education and training, poor and often disruptive work habits, deficiencies in labor market information, and employer unwillingness to hire low-productivity workers at wage rates prevailing for other employees.[48]

Bennett Harrison has noted more recently that the central cities, while losing both population and jobs in the postwar period, have been losing the former more rapidly. Thus although employment growth has been predominantly suburban, central city ratios of jobs to population have actually been rising. Like Doeringer, Harrison concludes that lack of job accessibility does not appear to be a significant cause of high ghetto unemployment.[49]

Finally, large numbers of inner-city poor people currently work at suburban locations. Most probably got to their original job interviews, if they did not already own a car, by borrowing one or obtaining a lift. The others probably took taxis or utilized the poor transit connections that were available. Once employed, presumably, the vast majority purchased cars or joined carpools. The serious policy question is how much, and at what expense, public policy can substantially improve upon this pattern.

Transit Subsidies: Who Benefits?
The beneficiaries of government transit expenditures include many

others in addition to transit patrons. To the extent, for example, that transit services facilitate the achievement of desired land-use patterns or reduced fuel demand and vehicle emissions, benefits are diffused widely among the general population. To the extent that they improve the relative accessiblity of core areas, they enable downtown real estate owners and businesses to reap more concentrated benefits in the forms of higher rents and more sales. And to the extent that subsidies enable transit agencies to spend money they would not otherwise have, they entail direct financial transfers to transit employees and suppliers.

Between 1970 and 1976, as transit subsidies increased seven-fold, the average real (inflation-adjusted) wages of transit workers rose at three times the average rate for the U.S. economy as a whole (13 versus 4 percent).[50] Including fringe benefits, the average U.S. transit worker earned $18,934 in 1976.[51] The recent gains of transit employees have been achieved, moreover, in the face of declining consumer demand for their output and of declining productivity on their own part. Passengers carried per employee fell by 18 percent from 1970 to 1976, and vehicle miles of service per employee declined by 9 percent.[52] By contrast, labor productivity in the rest of the urban economy rose by an estimated 10 percent over the same period.[53] Transit labor unions, fully cognizant of the benefits their members derive from public transit subsidization, have been among the most vigorous advocates of increased spending for this purpose.

Because the main nonrider beneficiaries of transit subsidies have substantially higher incomes on average than do riders, the overall distribution of transit subsidy benefits is less favorable to the poor than the distribution among riders alone. Available data permit quantification only of the latter distribution, however, and thus we shall focus on it in the following discussion.

If all transit trips were equally subsidized, low-income households would receive approximately average shares of transit expenditure benefits. In practice, however, they do considerably less well. There is a sharp inverse correlation between the level of subsidy per trip received by each transit mode and the degree of its usage by low-income people. As table 8.10 indicates, average per-trip subsidies (nationwide) in 1975 were: bus and streetcar, $0.21;

rapid transit, $0.36; and commuter rail, $1.11. Low-income travelers utilized buses and streetcars for 89 percent of their transit trips, rapid transit for 11 percent, and commuter rail for 0 percent. The comparable distribution for households with incomes above $22,500 was: bus and streetcar, 62 percent; rapid transit, 32 percent; and commuter rail, 6 percent. (See table 8.8.) Overall, if one assumes that all trips within each transit category were equally subsidized, low-income households received transit subsidy benefits about one-sixth lower than the average for all households. Accounting for 28.4 percent of all urban households (and for 27.6 percent of transit trips), they received 23.5 percent of transit operating subsidy benefits. Households in the next higher income category ($7,500–15,000) were the principal gainers. Accounting for 30.9 percent of all urban households, they received 38.9 percent of the operating subsidy. (See table 8.11.)

Insofar as trips within each mode were subsidized unequally, the net effects seem likely to have been to the disadvantage of the poor. Similarly recent trends in the expansion of fixed-route transit service appear likely to reduce the share of subsidy benefits received by low-income households. Specifically:

• With few exceptions, American transit systems charge flat fares or variable fares that fail to cover the full additional cost of longer trips (bearing in mind both the additional vehicle mileage required to serve them and the reduced load factors at the outer ends of routes). Because distance from the core tends to be associated with higher income in American urban areas, it has been widely hypothesized that the benefit of this practice accrues primarily to higher-income groups.

• Most recent transit service expansion appears to have been designed to serve peak-period travelers between CBDs and low-density residential neighborhoods developed since 1945 at considerable distances from the core. New services of this type tend to be regressive in their subsidy impact—as both CBD commuters and the residents of fringe areas tend to have above-average incomes. Peak-period service expansion tends more generally toward regressivity, because transit usage by low-income people (who have relatively low rates of labor force participation and high rates of

TABLE 8.10
U.S. Aggregate Transit Operating Statistics by Mode, 1973–1975 (in Thousands, Except for Ratios and Fares)

	Bus and Streetcar			Subway and Elevated			Commuter Rail		
	1973	1974	1975	1973	1974	1975	1973	1974	1975
Operating expense ($)[a]	1,698,749	2,290,461	2,621,004	837,390	948,912	1,084,892	413,161	495,350	571,256
Operating revenue ($)	1,283,532	1,437,899	1,510,910	514,108	501,801	491,460	250,364	262,584	283,389
Operating deficit ($)	415,217	852,562	1,110,094	323,282	447,111	593,432	162,797	232,766	287,867
Operating revenue/operating expense	0.76	0.63	0.58	0.61	0.53	0.45	0.61	0.53	0.50
Total passengers	4,946,000	5,209,000	5,269,000	1,714,000	1,726,000	1,668,000	238,766	254,417	260,476
Operating expense per passenger ($)	0.34	0.44	0.50	0.49	0.55	0.65	1.73	1.95	2.20
Average fare ($)	0.26	0.28	0.29	0.30	0.29	0.29	1.05	1.05	1.09
Operating deficit per passenger ($)	0.08	0.16	0.21	0.19	0.26	0.36	0.68	0.92	1.11

Source: Pucher, "Equity in Transit Financing," table 3.1, p. 40. The bus and streetcar figures were derived from APTA, *Transit Fact Book* (1976), pp. 28, 32. Trolley coaches are included in this category. The statistics for commuter rail and rapid transit were collected by Pucher from individual transit agencies in the twenty-six largest U.S. metropolitan areas. APTA's rapid transit passenger statistics which differed by about 10 percent from those collected by Pucher, were used in the table to achieve comparability with the bus figures.

aIncludes taxes, excludes depreciation.

TABLE 8.11
Distribution of Transit Operating Subsidies among Income Classes, 1975

Type of Subsidy	Below $7,500[a]	$7,500– $14,999[a]	$15,000– $22,499[a]	$22,500 or More[a]	All Incomes[b]
Bus and streetcar ($000)[c]	378,542	419,615	182,055	128,711	1,110,094
Rail rapid transit ($000)[c]	88,422	253,989	125,214	125,214	593,432
Commuter rail ($000)[c]	0	101,041	113,995	72,542	287,867
Total operating deficit, all transit modes ($000)	466,964	774,645	421,264	326,467	1,991,393
Percentage distribution of total deficit	23.5	38.9	21.2	16.4	100%
Percentage distribution of households	28.4	30.9	23.0	17.6	100%
Average subsidy per household ($)	36.94	54.17	36.95	35.01	41.77

Source: Pucher, "Equity in Transit Financing," p. 49. The distributions were calculated on the basis of the deficit data of table 8.10 and the income data of table 8.9.

[a] These categories are the 1970 income classes of the NPTS survey adjusted to account for the growth in personal income between 1970 and 1975.

[b] The sum of each row does not exactly equal the total subsidy to each mode due to rounding error.

[c] The amount of the deficit assigned to each income class equals the total deficit for each mode multiplied by the percentage of that mode's riders belonging to the indicated income class.

transit utilization for nonwork trips) is much less concentrated in peak periods than that of other groups.

Only fragmentary evidence bearing on these propositions is available, but on the whole it strongly supports them.

• A recent study of alternatives for the Washington Metro rapid transit system estimated that, at 1976 costs and currently projected fares, completion of the forty-one mile core of the system would entail an operating deficit of $0.13 per passenger trip. The next twenty-seven miles of planned expansion would entail, for each additional passenger attracted, a deficit of $0.73 per trip, and the remaining thirty miles of the planned system would entail a deficit per trip of $1.23.[12]

• A May 1975 survey revealed that whereas households with incomes under $7,000 comprised 33 percent of the population of the San Francisco BART district in 1970, they accounted for only 17 percent of BART ridership. By contrast, households with incomes above $15,000 accounted for 25 percent of population but 48 percent of ridership.[55]

• From 1972 to 1975 transit vehicle mileage increased nationwide by 13.3 percent. Total patronage rose in this period by only 5.8 percent.[56] While it by no means follows necessarily that the new vehicle mileage entailed longer trips and lower load factors than the old (perhaps patronage was dropping on old and new lines alike), most observers believe that this was in fact at least one significant cause of the load factor decline.

• As of 1970, the average employed person in U.S. metropolitan areas enjoyed an earned income of $7,557. Employees who lived in suburbs and worked in CBDs, however, had average incomes nearly two-fifths higher. And suburban commuters to CBDs by

[12.] The ninety-eight mile system was the plan officially adopted by Congress in 1969. The three stages were defined by the study team rather than in the plan itself. Its method was to identify three plausible ways to round out the system (which had originally been projected as more than self-supporting with reference to operations). Overall, though by no means in every specific route mile, each successive stage involved substantial increases in distance from the CBD. The capital costs of the system per incremental trip served were also expected to rise sharply with each successive stage (and to be borne entirely by the taxpayers).[54]

transit enjoyed even higher earnings than those who commuted by automobile: $10,589 versus $10,432. (See table 8.12.)

• Low-income households account for a much higher proportion of off-peak than for rush-period transit patronage. As of 1970, low-income households accounted for 25 percent of peak-period bus patronage but for 41 percent of off-peak patronage; they accounted for 9 percent of peak-period rapid transit patronage and for 23 percent of off-peak patronage. At the other end of the spectrum, households with incomes above $15,000 accounted for 16 percent of peak-period bus patronage and 9 percent of off-peak patronage; and they accounted for 26 percent of peak versus 15 percent of off-peak rapid transit patronage.[57]

Let us turn now to the distribution of capital subsidy benefits.

From the commencement of the federal transit program through fiscal year 1977, capital grants totaled $9.2 billion. State and local governments contributed an additional $4.0 billion, bringing the grand total to $13.2 billion. (See table 8.13. The total includes $2.0 billion in special grants for the Washington, D.C. Metro system, appropriated by Congress separately from the national program of mass transit assistance.)

Seventy-six percent of the cumulative total was earmarked for rail rapid transit and commuter rail improvements. (In 1975 the proportion was 68 percent. See table 8.14.) Because rail rapid transit and commuter rail account for only about one-quarter of aggregate transit patronage (table 8.10), and because the income profiles of their riders are considerably higher than those of bus and streetcar patrons (table 8.9), the resulting distribution of capital subsidy expenditures has been even less favorable to the poor than the distribution of operating subsidies. It is more difficult, however, to apportion capital subsidies among income groups than it is to apportion operating subsidies. Whereas the benefits of operating expenditures are realized during the year of subsidization, capital investments yield their benefits over many years; thus the relevant income distribution for capital subsidy assignment is that of future rather than current users.

The incomes of future transit riders cannot, of course, be fore-

TABLE 8.12
Average Annual Earnings of Workers Living in U.S. Metropolitan Areas with Population Above 100,000 by Mode Used for Journey-to-Work, Place of Work, and Place of Residence in 1970

Principal Mode Used on Journey-to-Work	All Workers Who Live in SMSAs	Workers Who Live inside CC and				Workers Who Live outside CC and			
		Work inside CC		Work in SMSA outside CC	Work outside SMSA of Residence[a]	Work inside CC		Work in SMSA outside CC	Work outside SMSA of Residence[a]
		in CBD	Elsewhere			In CBD	Elsewhere		
All Modes ($)[b]	7,557	7,375	6,402	6,998	8,097	10,468	8,386	6,991	9,326
Private Automobile ($)	7,598	8,370	7,089	7,384	8,397	10,432	8,515	7,427	9,111
Mass Transport ($)	5,982	6,386	5,099	4,312	7,267	10,589	7,998	4,011	12,692

Source: Adapted from Jose Gomez-Ibanez, "Federal Assistance for Urban Mass Transit," p. 218. Gomez-Ibanez based his calculations on data in U.S. Department of Commerce, Bureau of the Census, *1970 Census of Population*, vol. PC(1)-D1, *Detailed Characteristics, U.S. Summary*, (Washington, D.C.: U.S. Government Printing Office, 1973), Table 242.

Note: CC = Central City; CBD = central business district.

[a] Often these persons work in the central cities of adjacent SMSAs. For example, many persons who live in the Paterson-Clifton-Passaic, Newark, Jersey City, Stamford, or Norwalk SMSAs and work outside their SMSA of residence probably work in the New York City SMSA.

[b] Other modes besides private automobiles and mass transport include taxi, walking, and work at home.

TABLE 8.13
Transit Capital Commitments by Mode, Cumulative from 1965 to 1977 (in Millions of Dollars)

	Federal	State and Local[a]	Total
Rapid transit[b]			
Section 3	3,378.7	975.3	
Section 5	.7	.2	
Urban systems	69.9	17.5	
Interstate transfer	922.0	230.5	
Special D.C. Metro program	1,231.0	804.5	
Local BART funds (prior to federal match)	0	976.0[c]	
Total rapid transit	5,602.3	3,004.0	8,606.3 (65.3%)
Commuter rail			
Section 3	1,017.3	288.5	
Urban systems	11.9	3.0	
Interstate transfers	116.0	29.0	
Total commuter rail	1,145.2	320.5	1,465.7 (11.1%)
Bus[d]			
Section 3	2,332.5	641.2	
Section 5	79.8	20.0	
Urban systems	33.9	8.5	
Total bus	2,446.2	669.7	3,115.9 (23.6%)
Total, all modes[e]	9,193.7	3,994.2	13,187.9 (100.0%)

Source: John Pucher, "Equity in Transit Financing," p. 58. Calculated from: Urban Mass Transportation Administration, "Cumulative Capital Grants by Fiscal Year and Category, 2/1/65 through 9/30/77" (Washington, 1977); UMTA, "Multi-mode Capital Grant Commitments to Urbanized Areas, 2/1/65 through 9/30/77" (Washington, 1977); UMTA, "Transit Operating Performance and the Impact of the Section 5 Program" (Washington, 1977), p. 25. The Policy Analysis and Washington Metrorail Grant divisions of UMTA provided a considerable amount of additional, unpublished information.

[a] In general, the state and local amounts were estimated by assuming a one-third share until 1974 and one-fifth since then. Different matching shares were in effect for the special Washington Metrorail program and the pre-1964 BART program.

TABLE 8.13 (continued)

bIncludes light-rail lines.

cSome of the unmatched BART funds were assembled prior to 1965.

dIncludes trolley coaches but not streetcars.

eThis total does not include capital subsidies to ferries, personal rapid transit, inclines, or cable cars.

cast with any certainty. It seems most likely, however, that the relative incomes of bus and commuter rail patrons will remain about constant, because capital investments in these modes have focused mainly on the modernization of existing services. Approximately half of the rapid transit subsidy, on the other hand, has been devoted to the construction of new systems or lines, intended primarily to serve CBD employees who live in suburban or central city fringe areas. There has been considerable speculation that the patrons of these services will have higher incomes than the riders of older rapid transit systems.

Notwithstanding these complications, we have sought to apportion the benefits of 1975 capital subsidy expenditures by income class. In doing so we have utilized the income profiles of current riders, except that we have apportioned half of the rapid transit subsidy in accord with the income profile of BART riders in recognition of the portion of capital subsidy expenditures that has been utilized for the construction of new rapid transit lines. (We were suprised to discover that BART carries a greater proportion of low-income patrons than the older systems and that its overall ridership income profile differs only slightly from theirs.)[13]

[13.] Survey data are available on 1975 BART rider incomes. We have estimated the income distribution of riders on older systems by adjusting the 1970 NPTS findings to account for personal income growth between 1970 and 1975.[58] The ridership income profiles are as follows:

1975 **Income Distribution**

Income Class	Percentage of BART Riders	Riders on Older Rapid Transit Systems
Less than $7,500	19.4	14.9
$7,500–$14,999	32.1	42.8
$15,000–$22,499	23.0	21.2
$22,500 and over	25.4	21.1

TABLE 8.14
Transit Capital Grants by Mode, Federal Fiscal Year 1975 (in Millions of Dollars)

	Federal	State and Local[a]	Total
Rapid transit[b]			
Section 3	532.6	133.2	
Urban systems	10.0	2.5	
Interstate transfers	65.7	16.4	
Special D.C. Metro program[c]	126.9	106.3	
Total rapid transit	735.2	258.4	993.6 (57.3%)
Commuter rail			
Section 3	147.6	36.9	
Interstate transfers	0	0	
Total commuter rail	147.6	36.9	184.5 (10.6%)
Bus[d]			
Section 3	430.3	107.6	
Section 5	9.1	2.3	
Urban systems	5.7	1.4	
Total	445.1	111.3	556.4 (32.1%)
Total, all modes[e]	1,327.9	406.6	1,734.5 (100.0%)

Source: John Pucher, "Equity in Transit Financing," p. 58. Calculated from: Urban Mass Transportation Administration, "Cumulative Capital Grants by Fiscal Year and Category, 2/1/65 through 9/30/77" (Washington, 1977); UMTA, "Multi-mode Capital Grant Commitments to Urbanized Areas, 2/1/65 through 9/30/77" (Washington, 1977); UMTA, "Transit Operating Performance and the Impact of the Section 5 Program" (Washington, 1977), p. 25. The Policy Analysis and Washington Metrorail Grant divisions of UMTA provided a considerable amount of additional, unpublished information.

[a] Except for the Metrorail program, state and local amounts were estimated by assuming a one-fifth share, as provided by the Urban Mass Transportation Act of 1964 as amended.

[b] Includes light-rail lines.

[c] The special Metro category is in addition to section 3 and interstate transfer funds used for construction of this system.

[d] Includes trolley coaches but not light-rail lines.

[e] This total does not include capital subsidies to ferries, personal rapid transit (Morgantown, W. Va.), inclines, or cable cars.

Table 8.15 presents our estimated distribution. Low-income households (those with incomes below $7,500) obtained average benefits smaller than those received by any other income group and about one-fourth less than the nationwide average. Households in the $7,500–15,000 income category, on the other hand, received the greatest average subsidy, about one-fifth higher than the nationwide average.

A different pattern may be emerging in the face of rapidly rising transit costs and growing public resistance to increases in transit expenditure levels. UMTA's policy since about 1973 has been that new rapid transit systems must be developed in gradual stages. Whereas BART and the D.C. Metro were authorized from the start as large regional systems (71 and 98 miles respectively in length), recent UMTA approvals have been for much more modest first stages. The projected Atlanta, Baltimore, Miami, and Buffalo first-stage systems, for example, entail 14, 8, 21, and 6 route miles, respectively. (A $600 million commitment has also been made toward rapid transit in Detroit, but the precise system configuration has not been established.) Moreover, in a move to discourage the choice of high-cost heavy rail systems, UMTA has permitted the option of "trading down" on the committed heavy-rail funds for the construction of downtown shuttle systems and light-rail rapid transit instead.[59] The other key current pressure is to ensure that ghetto areas, conspicuously neglected in the initial planning of BART and Metro, receive substantial benefits. It bears mention, finally, that whereas suburban commuters to CBDs enjoy well above average earnings, central city residents employed in CBDs do not. Those commuting by transit, in particular, reported average earnings in 1970 15 percent lower than the average for all metropolitan workers and 40 percent lower than the average for transit commuters from suburbs to CBDs. (See table 8.12.)

In short, the distributive impact of transit capital expenditures must be determined with respect to the precise mix of investments undertaken. Whereas BART and Metro provide the poor with less than average benefits per household, some of the first-stage systems currently under design appear likely to provide low-income

TABLE 8.15
The Distribution of Transit Capital Subsidies among Income Classes, 1975

Type of Subsidy	Below $7,500[a]	$7,500–$14,999[a]	$15,000–$22,499[a]	$25,000 or More[a]	All Incomes[b]
Bus and streetcar ($000)[c]	189,700	210,300	91,200	64,500	566,400
Rail rapid transit ($000)[c]	170,402	367,135	219,089	231,012	993,600
Commuter rail ($000)[c]	0	64,760	73,062	46,494	184,500
Total capital subsidy, all transit modes ($000)	360,102	642,195	383,351	342,006	1,744,500
Percentage distribution of total subsidy	20.8	37.2	22.2	19.8	100
Percentage distribution of households	28.4	30.9	23.0	17.6	100
Average subsidy per household ($)	28.49	44.91	33.63	36.67	36.38

Source: John Pucher, "Equity in Transit Financing," p. 63. The distributions were calculated on the basis of the capital grant data of table 8.14 and the income data of table 8.9 and footnote 13.

[a] These categories are the 1970 income classes of the NPTS travel survey adjusted to account for the growth in personal income between 1970 and 1975.

[b] The sum of each row does not exactly equal the total subsidy to each mode due to rounding error.

[c] The amount of capital subsidy assigned to each income class equals the total subsidy for each mode multiplied by the percentage of that mode's riders belonging to the indicated income class. For rail rapid transit, half of the subsidy was assigned on the basis of the income distribution of riders of old rail rapid transit systems, and half on the basis of the incomes of riders of new rapid transit systems.

households with considerably greater benefits.[14] As most bus expenditures involve replacement and modernization rather than service expansion, it must be also assumed that low-income households receive more than equal shares of the benefits associated with this portion of the capital program.

Transit Subsidies: Who Pays?

It is widely believed that local governments—afflicted with declining tax bases, regressive tax structures, and large numbers of dependent residents—bear most of the transit subsidy burden. In fact, however, local governments bear only about one-third of the overall transit tax burden, and their share has been rapidly declining in recent years. Our bases for this estimate are as follows:

1. We have examined in detail the sources of operating subsidy · funds as of 1975 in the twenty-six largest U.S. metropolitan areas, which accounted for 73 percent of national transit patronage in that year and for 82 percent of the national operating deficit. Transit operating subsidies in these areas totaled $1.69 billion in 1975, including $0.85 billion (50 percent) raised locally. (See table 8.16.) The recent trend has been toward sharply increased participation by higher levels of government. Between 1973 and 1975, for example, while the overall operating deficit increased 90 percent, the local contribution rose by only 24 percent whereas the combined federal-state contribution grew by 267 percent.[15] [60]

2. As a rough approximation, we have estimated that operating subsidies in the nation's remaining metropolitan areas totaled $300 million and that these were financed similarly to those in the largest twenty-six.

3. We have estimated that transit capital obligations nationwide totaled $1.73 billion in 1975. (See table 8.14. Because no com-

[14.] This does not deal with the question of whether these systems will represent cost-effective ways of assisting them or even of dealing with their most serious problems of mobility deprivation. Our concern in this section is simply to identify the broad distributional pattern with respect to whatever benefits are produced, at whatever cost.

[15.] This statement refers to the twenty-three areas for which both 1973 and 1975 data could be obtained. Adequate 1973 data were unavailable from the District of Columbia, Denver, and San Francisco.

TABLE 8.16
Sources of Transit Operating Subsidy Funds in the 26 Largest U.S. Metropolitan Areas, 1975

	Amount (Thousands of Dollars)	Percentage of Total
Federal[a]	280,222	16.6
Individual income tax	156,924	
Corporation income tax	78,462	
Other	44,836	
State	435,142	25.7
Excise taxes	75,423	
Gasoline and motor vehicle taxes	12,776	
Unidentified excise taxes	62,647	
General sales taxes	209,018	
Business taxes	36,677	
Individual income taxes	114,024	
Local (including regional)	848,151	50.1
Gasoline and motor vehicle excise taxes	30,349	
General sales taxes	328,349	
Business taxes	45,322	
Individual income taxes	29,136	
Property taxes	345,363	
Payroll taxes	14,799	
Unidentified nonproperty taxes	54,833	
Bridge and tunnel tolls	105,853	6.3
Utility cross-subsidies	10,858	0.6
Freight cross-subsidies	11,166	0.7
Total, all sources	1,691,392[b]	100.0

Source: Pucher, "Equity in Transit Financing." (Ph.D. dissertation, MIT, 1978). Figures on the composition of state and local government revenues

TABLE 8.16 (continued)

were obtained from the *1972 Census of Governments, Government Finances,* vol. 4, no. 5, table 46, p. 122, and from the *1972 Census of Governments, Local Government in Metropolitan Areas,* vol. 5, table 12, p. 263. A detailed listing of transit subsidies in the twenty-six largest U.S. metropolitan areas disaggregated by type of tax and level of government can be found in Pucher, "Transit Operating Subsidies," MIT Center for Transportation Studies, 1976, table 2.

Note: Where taxes were not specifically earmarked for transit subsidization, the operating subsidy in each metropolitan area was distributed according to the composition of local general tax revenues in each specific area. The same procedure was followed at the state level. The state and local figures do not indicate any allowance for the federal contribution to general fund coffers by revenue-sharing grants. These accounted for about 4 percent of state-local revenues in 1975. Ultimately, therefore, federal taxes accounted for a higher proportion of total operating subsidies than shown in the table, and state-local taxes a lower percentage than indicated.

[a] There are no taxes at the federal level specifically earmarked for transit. Therefore amounts of specific taxes under this category reflect the composition of general revenues only, excluding payroll taxes for social security.

[b] This total excludes about $300 million in operating subsidies to transit in smaller metropolitan areas.

prehensive data were available on state-local expenditures, we have included only those required to match federal grants and assumed that these were split equally between the two levels of government. Additionally we have assumed that all three levels financed their respective capital subsidy contributions from the same sources utilized to finance operating subsidies.)

4. Combining these estimates, we find that transit obligations totaled $3.72 billion in 1975, financed 46 percent by the federal government. ($1.71 billion), 32 percent by localities ($1.19 billion), 18 percent by states ($0.67 billion), and 4 percent from other sources ($0.15 billion).

We have not been able to estimate the precise distribution of the tax burden among income classes by metropolitan area because the same taxes may have considerably different distributional consequences, depending on their specific provisions and geographic coverage in given local settings. We have made nationwide tax incidence estimates, however, based on national studies of the distributional effects of each type of tax at each level of government. These indicate that the transit subsidy tax burden was roughly proportional in 1975 at household incomes of up to $30,000 and significantly progressive above that level. Taxes for this purpose absorbed 0.36 percent of incomes up to $15,000, 0.33 percent of incomes between $15,000 and $30,000, and 0.51 percent of incomes over $30,000. (See table 8.17.) These figures indicate, of course, that high-income households paid much more than low-income households in absolute terms. For example, the average $6,000 household paid about $22 whereas the average $40,000 household paid $204.

As indicated in table 8.18, low-income households receive lower average transit subsidies than those in any other income category. Their disadvantage on the benefit side of the ledger, however, is considerably more than offset by their advantage on the tax side. Because the data bases for the benefit and tax analyses utilize different income categories, we have been unable to calculate the overall dollar flows among income classes associated with transit subsidization. By assuming that households were typical of their income categories in both tables, however, we have been able to estimate approximate dollar flows per household at specific income levels. As reported in table 8.19, these calculations suggest that the overall effect of transit subsidization has been significantly redistributive in absolute terms, though only because the overall tax system is redistributive.

As a whole, then, the transit finance system is redistributive but inefficiently so. Although the poor are more subsidized than taxed, they receive less than average per-household shares of the total transit subsidy. The poor make only about one-seventh of their urban trips by transit, they comprise only about two-sevenths of all transit patrons, and they receive less than one-quarter of transit subsidy benefits. By contrast, numerous programs designed explicitly for redistributive purposes concentrate virtually all of their benefits on the poor and near poor. It follows that the current transit subsidy program cannot be justified solely, or even primarily, as an instrument of redistribution.

TABLE 8.17
The Distribution of the Tax Burden for Transit Capital and Operating
Subsidies, 1975 (Taxes as Percentages of Total Money Income)

Level of Government	Under $8,000	$8,000–$14,999	$15,000–$29,999	$30,000 and Over	All Incomes
Operating subsidies[a]					
Federal	0.028	0.034	0.036	0.077	0.038
State and local	0.190	0.164	0.131	0.131	0.162
Total, all levels	0.218	0.198	0.167	0.208	0.200
Capital subsidies					
Federal	0.098	0.119	0.125	0.268	0.132
State and local	0.048	0.041	0.033	0.033	0.041
Total, all levels	0.146	0.160	0.158	0.301	0.173
Total transit subsidy					
Federal	0.126	0.153	0.161	0.345	0.170
State and local	0.238	0.205	0.164	0.164	0.203
Total, all levels	0.364	0.358	0.325	0.509	0.373

Sources: Adapted from Pucher, "Equity in Transit Financing," p. 89. The
operating subsidy distributions are based on the financing data of table 8.17
and unpublished estimates of nationwide tax burden incidence (on a money
income basis) in 1968 provided by Karl Case of Wellesley College. These tax
estimates were part of a larger study he undertook with Richard Musgrave
and Herman Leonard; related results of this study appear in "The Distribution of Fiscal Burdens and Benefits," *Public Finance Quarterly* 2 (July 1974).
The capital subsidy distributions were calculated on the basis of the capital
grant data of table 8.14 and the same tax incidence distributions as for operating subsidies.

Note: The operating distributions were calculated by weighting the general
tax incidence distributions by the percentage of the total operating subsidy
derived from each tax at each level of government and by adjusting the distributions to reflect the percentage of total money income in the United
States devoted to subsidizing transit operations in 1975. The corresponding
capital subsidy distributions were obtained in approximately the same manner.
Because data on capital subsidy financing were not available by specific tax
type, the weighting of these distributions was according to level of government only, necessarily assuming that the specific mix of state and local taxes
was the same as for operating subsidies. Due to the unavailability of more
recent nationwide tax incidence estimates, it was also necessary to assume

TABLE 8.17 (continued)

that the relative distribution of the tax burden did not change significantly from 1968 to 1975. Moreover the estimates are nationwide aggregates, which do not take into account the specific geographic coverage of state and local transit taxes. Finally, even as national estimates, the general tax distributions of Case, Musgrave, and Leonard, on which this table is based, depend crucially on a number of reasonable, although quite controversial, theoretical assumptions about the incidence of each type of tax.

[a] The nationwide operating subsidy ($1.99 billion) has been distributed in accord with the funding composition in the 26 largest metropolitan areas as reported in table 8.16.

Goals

Though advocacy groups call frequently for a national commitment to such goals as equal mobility for all Americans at a price that each can afford, Congress and most transportation analysts have taken a far more cautious approach to the determination of equity objectives.

Equity, like energy efficiency and clean air, has emerged as a significant objective of public policy in the field of urban transportation only since the mid-1960s. The federal highway program has never had improved mobility for the handicapped, elderly, and poor as a distinct policy objective, and its financing structure is still premised mainly on the fee for service concept of equity. Similarly the federal transit program commenced in 1964 with no specific commitment to the transportation disadvantaged. It attracted some support on the ground that transit was the mode of the poor, but its active political constituents—transit operators and labor unions, downtown business interests, transit suppliers—were motivated by other objectives than improving the mobility of the poor. They believed that the main concern should be service expansion to the lower-density areas to which so many former transit patrons had moved. They viewed transit as a means of generating downtown revival. They were anxious to attract support from the auto-reliant majority by demonstrating that improved transit could reduce traffic congestion. They were much taken with the analogy of new rapid transit systems to the interstate

TABLE 8.18
The Distribution of Operating and Capital Transit Subsidies among Income
Classes, 1975 (Subsidy Amounts in Millions of Dollars)

Type of Subsidy	Below $7,500[a]	$7,500–$14,999[a]	$15,000–$22,499[a]	$22,500 and More[a]	All Incomes[b]
Operating subsidy, total	467	775	421	327	1,991
Bus and streetcar	379	420	182	129	1,110
Rail rapid transit	88	254	125	125	593
Commuter rail	0	101	114	73	288
Capital subsidy, total	360	642	383	342	1,735
Bus and streetcar	190	210	91	65	556
Rail rapid transit	170	367	219	231	994
Commuter rail	0	65	73	46	185
Total transit subsidy	827	1,417	804	669	3,726
Bus and streetcar	569	630	273	194	1,666
Rail rapid transit	258	621	344	356	1,587
Commuter rail	0	166	187	119	473
Percentage distribution of total subsidy	22.2	38.0	21.6	18.0	100
Percentage distribution of all households	28.4	30.9	23.0	17.6	100
Average subsidy per household ($)	65.43	99.08	70.58	71.68	78.15

Source: Tables 8.11 and 8.15.

[a] These categories are the 1970 income classes of the NPTS survey adjusted to account for the growth in personal income between 1970 and 1975.

[b] The sum of each row does not exactly equal the total subsidy to each mode due to rounding error.

TABLE 8.19
Sample Calculations of Per-Household Transit Subsidies, Net of Tax Costs, for Selected Income Levels, 1975

Household Income	Transit Subsidy per Household ($)	Transit Tax per Household ($)	Net Impact per Household ($)
$5,000	65	18	+47
$12,000	99	42	+57
$20,000	71	65	+6
$35,000	72	178	−106

Source: Tables 8.17 and 8.18.

Note: The tables from which this table has been calculated report average experiences per household within fairly broad income categories. Considerable variations in average experience per household doubtless exist at various income levels within each category. Thus in developing this table, we have utilized income levels approximately in the mid-range of each category for which estimates are presented in tables 8.17 and 8.18.

highway system—both high-capacity new travel arteries imposed on preexisting patterns of urban development. They were attracted by the idea that modern, preferably automated, new systems might provide a means of offsetting spiraling labor costs. And, after all, the federal program was exclusively one of capital assistance (until November 1974). Thus it was only natural to focus on capital-intensive improvements. As it happened, though no one quite realized it at the time, there was a strong inverse correlation between degree of capital intensiveness and degree of benefit to the handicapped, elderly, and poor.

As reported previously, transit program administrators did give high priority in awarding demonstration grants during the late 1960s to projects designed to improve employment access to outlying areas by the central city poor. But the demonstration projects undertaken for this purpose absorbed less than 1.5 percent of transit program spending up to 1970 (and much less thereafter.)[16] The special problems of the transportation-disadvantaged were probably given even less priority at the local level.

[16.] George Hilton reports that the poverty demonstrations cost a total of $10.2 million.[61]

Since about 1973, however, a new wave of concern for the transportation disadvantaged has emerged—focused on the needs of elderly and handicapped people, mainly for noncommutation purposes, rather than on the commutation problems of the poor. The impact of this new concern has extended beyond the transit demonstration program to the capital grant program; Congress has mandated equal accessibility by the elderly and the handicapped as a key design objective for federally aided transit facilities. (As noted earlier, however, the reference is to the physical accessibility of the systems themselves rather than access by the elderly and handicapped to their most desired destinations.)

The Department of Health, Education and Welfare (HEW), moreover, has become a significant source of financial support for transportation of the disadvantaged to medical and social service centers. Though intended to assist with only one category of trip purpose, the HEW programs may potentially provide a core patronage base for services designed more generally to serve the elderly, handicapped, and poor.

In mandating these programs, Congress has explicitly or effectively adopted the following objectives with respect to the mobility of transportation-disadvantaged groups:

1. Handicapped people, including the elderly who suffer from physical enfeeblement, shall be provided mass transit service opportunities at least comparable to those available to other urban residents.

2. Eligible federal aid recipients shall be afforded all necessary assistance in securing access to federally supported medical and social services.

3. Some special efforts of a more general nature shall be made to facilitate the mobility of the elderly and handicapped.

Notably the poor receive mention in this set of objectives only with reference to the special problem of access to medical and social services.

The objective of comparable transit service opportunity may be met in principle either by designing conventional transit facilities to be fully accessible by those with physical disabilities or by providing alternative, demand-responsive services. The debate about which approach is preferable has become particularly intense since Congress, in the 1973 Federal-Aid Highway Act, mandated that transit facilities built with highway program assistance be fully accessible to the elderly and handicapped.[17] [62]

Spokesmen for handicapped groups, led particularly by Vietnam War veterans who have not been handicapped all their lives and who are determined to resist all forms of segregation based on their disabilities, have pressed hard for full accessibility rather than alternative service. Critics of this position have argued that the full-accessibility strategy is characterized by extremely high cost per trip served and distinctly limited value to the elderly and handicapped. The costs are particularly high insofar as the objective is wheelchair accessibility, which entails elevators at rail stations, special lifts on buses, and substantial delays whenever a wheelchair passenger boards or alights from a bus. The value is limited by two considerations: most of the trips that elderly and handicapped people wish to make are served poorly or not at all by conventional transit; and even where the service is quite good, potential handicapped patrons are likely to be deterred by the problems of getting to it from their origins and from it to their ultimate destinations. At any given cost, in this view, it is possible to provide the elderly and the handicapped with substantially greater mobility benefits by subsidizing taxi service or providing demand-responsive transit service in specially modified small vehicles (vans and minibuses). Transit operators and UMTA officials concerned with this issue maintain that most of the elderly and handicapped themselves seem to prefer this alternative service approach even though the most vocal spokesmen for handicapped interests reject it.[18]

[17.] The Architectural Barrier Act of 1968 (PL 90-480) clearly set forth the policy that all public facilities constructed with federal funds should be available and accessible to the handicapped. Since 1973, Congress has been firm in extending this policy to new fixed-rail systems. The debate has now shifted to the advisability of requiring that older rapid transit systems and all new transit vehicles be fully accessible.

[18.] Legal suits have been brought by handicapped individuals to force the purchase of fully accessible buses in a number of cities. To date the only case decided on the merits

The commitment to ensure access to medical and social services appears in numerous HEW statutes. For example, the Medicaid program requires that each state have a Medicaid plan, which must include provision for ensuring "necessary transportation of recipients to and from providers of (medical) services."[63] The eligible forms of transportation range from ambulance and taxi to private automobile and transit common carrier. The only requirement is that the mode be appropriate in each case. Similarly the Rehabilitation Act of 1973 provides that no handicapped person can be excluded from participation in any program receiving federal financial assistance.[64] Other HEW programs lack such ringing guarantees but do provide funding for transportation services. For example, the Older Americans Act, as amended in 1973, authorizes expenditures for "transportation services where necessary to facilitate access to social services." Similarly the Social Service Amendments of 1974, which consolidated numerous federal grant programs for state-administered social services, included provisions for the support of transportation to and from social service facilities.[65]

Without committing itself to the support of a specific level of mobility for the elderly and the handicapped, Congress has taken a number of explicit measures in recent years to authorize special transportation services for them. Several provisions of particular note were enacted in 1973 and 1974. Section 16 (b)(2) of the Urban Mass Transportation Act of 1964, as amended in 1973, authorizes capital grants to private, nonprofit organizations to assist them in providing special transportation services for the elderly and handicapped.[66] The Federal-Aid Highway Amendments of 1974 authorized a new program of rural public transportation demonstration projects, intended primarily for the benefit of the transit dependent.[67] This program is administered by the Federal Highway Administration (its first venture into the direct subsidization of mass transportation) and is financed primarily out

has been in Birmingham, Alabama. The federal district court found in this case that no fully accessible bus was reasonably available and that UMTA had carried on a good faith program of technical studies and demonstration projects to improve the state of the art with respect to bus design. Injunctive relief was denied.

of the Highway Trust Fund. The National Mass Transportation Assistance Act of 1974, which authorized federal transit operating assistance for the first time, set as a condition for the receipt of such assistance the establishment of reduced fares for the elderly and the handicapped during off-peak hours.[68]

In brief, then, the priority of equity as a transportation policy objective appears to have increased significantly in recent years. Congress has limited its goal articulation, however, to specific guarantees of access to public facilities and services and to more general probes in the direction of "doing something" to improve the mobility of elderly and handicapped individuals. The special mobility problems of the nonelderly, nonhandicapped poor have not received prominent attention during the 1970s.

One final point. Although it has not been reflected in specific statutory language, there has in practice been a substantial recent growth of awareness on the part of transit officials of the distributional consequences of their actions. Impassioned spokespersons for the elderly, the handicapped, and low-income neighborhoods have become highly visible figures during the 1970s in the transit policy arena. There are numerous divisions among the claimants, however, and their demands tend to carry high price tags. Moreover transit officials remain under pressure to provide improved service for suburban commuters, to relieve traffic congestion, to help revitalize CBD economies, and now to demonstrate that transit can save energy and reduce air pollution as well. At the same time, they are faced with spiraling costs and intense public resistance to fare and tax increases on the one hand, to service cutbacks on the other. In this setting, most transit operators see little near-term opportunity for a significant reorientation of service patterns to benefit the handicapped, the elderly, and the poor. As and when new services are added, however, the interests of these groups appear to command considerably more attention today than they did a decade ago.

Innovations

Of the measures under review throughout this book (see above,

p. 50) three seem particularly relevant to the interests of the handicapped, the elderly, and the poor: demand responsive transit, fixed-route transit improvement, and private ride sharing. Additionally we shall comment briefly on the transportation voucher concept, taxi deregulation, and subsidized car ownership.

Demand Responsive Transit (DRT)

Insofar as the ablebodied, the nonelderly, and the nonpoor use public transportation, they do so primarily for commutation purposes during peak periods in high-density radial corridors. Their overwhelming priorities are reliability and speed in these hours and corridors. At other times and for other trip purposes, they rely on their cars. The handicapped, the elderly, and the poor, by contrast, are far more reliant on transit for nonwork purposes. Being captive riders, they do not demand great speed, nor do their trips tend to be highly peaked. But their travel patterns are highly diverse, resembling those associated normally with automobile and taxi usage much more than those associated with fixed-route transit. And many of them find it difficult or impossible to get to fixed-route transit stops on their own (and from such stops to their final destinations), even when these access trips involve only a few blocks.

The transit industry has traditionally concentrated on meeting the demands of its commutation patrons. They are important economically; they are articulate politically; they generate high load factors, even if only for brief periods; they can most efficiently be served by the types of service the industry feels best able to provide; and they are the cheapest of all potential transit users to serve. By contrast the mobility-deprived tend to be unimportant from the standpoint of the regional economy; they have until recently been all but invisible politically; those who are spread out geographically and/or who are physically infirm generate very low load factors; and the cost of serving them is high.

It is scarcely surprising, .then, that transit administrators, hard pressed to hold down their rates of spending growth, have been slow to embrace the cause of DRT, or that the DRT pioneers have predominantly been human service agencies and small communities with little conventional transit service.[69]

Human service agencies have become involved in transportation as a means of ensuring access by clients to their facilities, and almost invariably their assistance is confined to trips for this purpose. Transportation expenditures incidental to the carrying out of health and social service missions are authorized under at least fifty federal programs.[70] Although these funds are utilized largely in support of transit and taxi travel (by user reimbursement or contracts with taxi companies), it seems apparent on the basis of state and local studies that several thousand agencies are providing special transportation services nationwide. Extreme fragmentation is the norm, with each agency endeavoring separately to meet the needs of its own clients, often operating only one or two vans and relying for driving services on volunteers or employees who also perform nontransportation duties.

No official or current estimate of transportation expenditures by human service agencies nationwide is available. Arthur Saltzman has projected on the basis of detailed local studies, however, that as of about 1973, expenditures were in the range of $340–564 million.[71] Because his high projection was based on findings in a region characterized generally by high social service expenditure rates (the San Francisco Bay area) and his low on findings in part of a state noted for the opposite (Texas), a mid-range estimate would seem most plausible. A similar mid-range estimate of the number of vehicles operated by human service agencies would be about 25,000. By way of comparison, the U.S. transit industry operated 49,000 buses in 1973.[72]

Additionally Congress has authorized several new transportation programs for the elderly and handicapped in recent years. Notably (and reflecting the widespread view that conventional transit operators cannot or will not perform aggressively in this field), section 16(b)(2) of the Urban Mass Transportation Act, enacted in 1973, provides for 80 percent federal funding of the capital cost of vehicles purchased by private nonprofit agencies to transport elderly and handicapped clients. Expenditures under this program in fiscal 1977 totalled $22 million.[73]

While it is obvious that special services confer nearly all of their benefits on mobility-deprived individuals, there is substantial evidence as well that DRT services offered to the general public are disproportionately utilized by the mobility-deprived. It is easy to understand why. The trips best served are of the types that most people are accustomed to making by automobile. Because of scheduling and route diversion complexities, moreover, the service tends to be quite slow. Reid Ewing, in a study of sixteen such systems, has recently found that their average door-to-door trip times (wait plus ride) ranged from three to ten times those attainable by private automobile, with a median DRT/auto ratio of six.[74] Thus the patrons tend to be those without ready alternatives. Ewing's findings on user characteristics, reported in table 8.20, indicate that nondrivers, members of households without cars, and the elderly have generally been represented far in excess of their population shares[19] —with the degree of such overrepresentation varying widely, however, in accord with the demographic characteristics of the areas served. The Columbus system, illustratively, was operated by the local Model Cities agency in an inner-city ghetto. The result: 69 percent of users were from households without automobiles and 82 percent were nondrivers. By comparison, in Ann Arbor, a relatively affluent university community, 26 percent were from households without cars (many of them presumably students) and 45 percent (nearly half of them under the age of sixteen) were nondrivers.

If DRT is potentially of great significance as an equity mode, clearly its potential achilles heel is high cost. Ewing found that DRT services operated by transit agencies typically cost far more than exclusive-ride taxi services in the same communities (for trips of equal length and occupancy). DRT fares were invariably well below taxi fares, but this was simply because the former were heavily subsidized.

[19.] These are overlapping categories. Unfortunately precise data on their population shares in these specific communities were unavailable, so our reference is to the comparison with national figures. It bears emphasis, however, that except in Columbus and Beverly-Fairfax (a section of Los Angeles) the service areas were all within small cities or suburbs. Thus one may reasonably assume that only 10–15 percent of households in them were carless.

Table 8.20
Characteristics of Demand-Responsive Transit Riders

	Date of Survey	Percentage of Users from Households with No Auto	Percentage of Users from Households with One Auto	Nondrivers (% of Users)	Youth, Percentage of Users Under 16	Elderly, Percentage of Users Over 64	Handicapped, Percentage of Users[a]
Ann Arbor, Mich.	2/75	26	35	45	20	4	0.6
Benton Harbor–St. Joseph, Mich.	11/74	41	38	64	9	17	unknown
Beverly-Fairfax, Calif.	2/76	unknown	unknown	unknown	unknown	89	2.0
Columbus, Ohio	8/72	69	15	82	15	22	unknown
El Cajon, Calif.	10/75	unknown	unknown	unknown	unknown	33	0.6
La Habra, Calif.	10/75	unknown	unknown	unknown	unknown	19	0.4
Ludington, Mich.	9/74	54	27	68	7	41	2.9
Merced, Calif.	unknown	unknown	unknown	unknown	unknown	unknown	unknown
Midland, Mich.	10/74	22	37	50	18	9	0.8
Niles, Mich.	5/75	58	28	unknown	13[b]	30	1.7
Oneonta, N.Y.	11/74	unknown	unknown	unknown	13	21	unknown
Rochester, N.Y.	6/75	23	41	57	11	7	0.7
Santa Clara County, Calif.	2/75	unknown	unknown	unknown	55[c]	3	unknown
Xenia, Ohio	7/75	unknown	unknown	65	33[c]	3	unknown

Source: Reid Ewing and Nigel Wilson, "Innovation in Demand-Responsive Transit," MIT Center for Transportation Studies (October 1976), table 10, pp. 28–29.

[a] Figures refer to the nonambulatory handicapped.

[b] No attempt was made to compensate for "no response."

[c] Figures were obtained through interpolation.

Potential strategies for reducing DRT costs include the following. Taxi rather than transit operators and employees can be utilized to provide service. Vehicles can be utilized to provide commuter subscription and/or school bus services during the hours when it is possible thereby to generate high productivities. Able-bodied passengers can be asked to walk to pickup points. Evening service can be avoided or limited to one or two nights a week. Service can be confined to weekdays. And notice of trip requests can be required from an hour to a day in advance.[75] But these strategies are often politically unfeasible, and even in the best of circumstances, DRT will normally entail a much higher cost per passenger mile than fixed-route bus service in high-density corridors. This will often be decisive as elected officials consider proposals that DRT be made widely available to the general public. When the beneficiaries are clearly identified as needy, on the other hand, high costs per passenger mile are likely to be viewed as far more tolerable. Thus human service agency expenditures for transportation have been growing rapidly with virtually no public comment. (If, as estimated above, these expenditures were in the range of $450 million as of 1973, this was equivalent to about one-half of the nationwide operating deficit incurred by conventional transit services.)

It bears note, moreover, that the costs per trips of DRT are often modest by comparison with the costs of some of the more expensive transit services offered the general public and some of the alternatives being promoted as means of assisting the elderly and handicapped. In fiscal 1976, for example, the average BART patron received a subsidy of $3.75 per trip.[76] And the U.S. Department of Transportation has recently estimated that full adaptation of the nation's fixed route transit systems for use by the handicapped would entail a capital cost of $1.7 billion and additional operating costs totaling $69 million a year at 1977 prices.[77] Local officials have charged that the actual costs would be several times higher and that the beneficiaries would be few. The New York and Chicago transit authorities have estimated, for example, that their combined capital costs would be about $3 billion and their additional operating costs in the range of $250 million per year. And they have noted that the Washington Metrorail system, which does meet full accessibility standards, carries only six wheelchair users per 100,000 patrons.

Recognizing that equity-related transportation expenditures—particularly for the elderly, the handicapped, and human service agency clients, even if not necessarily for the ablebodied poor—are almost certain to grow rapidly in the years ahead, urban transportation officials and analysts have become increasingly concerned since about 1975 with evaluating the cost-effectiveness of the options available. All require large amounts of money, at least relative to the number of trips served; it seems apparent that if these markets are to be served effectively at all, the costs per trip are bound to be very high by comparison with the costs of fixed route service for able-bodied commuters. Specifically, the main options appear to be:

● Making conventional transit vehicles and stations physically accessible to all, including those in wheelchairs.

● Expanding the current fragmented services provided by public and private nonprofit human service agencies for their clients.

● Developing integrated special service systems.

● Developing demand-responsive shared-ride systems (whether operated by transit agencies or taxi companies) that are open to the general public but with the largest subsidies reserved for those in specific eligible categories.[20]

● Transportation vouchers, which eligible recipients would be free to utilize for the purchase of taxi or transit services.

These are not, of course, mutually exclusive options, but they are competitors for resources. And while there is room for consider-

[20.] General use systems might be rendered fiscally feasible in some circumstances by enabling them to piggy-back on services justified in the first instance of their relevance to special service needs. In such circumstances, joint costs might be borne as a human service expense.

able disagreement about which of the four latter options is most cost-effective, all look quite attractive by comparison with the strategy of making conventional transit systems fully accessible.

Fixed Route Transit Service

Fixed route transit service improvements represent the primary instrument available for enhancing the mobility of the carless poor who live clustered in relatively high-density neighborhoods. Low-income travelers might themselves prefer DRT service, but the electorate is likely in most circumstances to oppose underwriting the high per-trip costs of DRT for the ablebodied poor.

Fixed route subsidies are likely to benefit the poor disproportionately only if they are carefully targeted to do so. It will be recalled, for example, that the members of low-income households are slightly overrepresented among bus patrons nationwide, that they are considerably underrepresented among rapid transit patrons, and that they are scarcely represented at all among commuter rail patrons (table 8.9). Yet bus patrons currently receive much lower per-trip subsidies than commuter rail and rapid transit users. A gradual reallocation of transit expenditures toward equalizing per-trip subsidies among the several transit modes would thus be of enormous benefit to low-income users in aggregate. The poor also make a greater proportion of their transit trips during off-peak hours and for relatively shorter distances than other groups. Thus a concentration of available funds on the maintenance of low off-peak fares and on low base fares within a zonal structure will normally provide them with greater benefits than utilization of the same dollar amount in support of an undifferentiated fare structure. (Time-of-day pricing would tend as well to improve transit efficiency by alleviating pressure for peak period service expansion and permitting greater utilization of existing off-peak capacity.) Finally, if obviously, the proportion of benefits received by the poor tends to vary with their population share along any particular route. Effective targeting for equity purposes therefore must be rooted first and foremost in a corridor-by-corridor understanding of local demography.

Single-minded efforts to target subsidy expenditures at the poor are likely to conflict with other objectives of the transit program. The effectiveness of transit subsidy dollars in conserving energy, reducing air pollution, and strenghtening central city economies is probably greatest, for example, when they are utilized to attract nonpoor weekday travelers to CBDs. This market includes large numbers of patrons with the option to drive, and it can generate higher vehicle load factors than any other. Per dollar expended, service improvements designed specifically for the poor are likely to attract fewer passengers than comparable expenditures in the service of core-bound travelers, and a much higher proportion of those attracted are likely to represent new trips with little or no effect on the central city economy rather than trips diverted from automobiles and/or from suburban centers of economic activity.

This is by no means to suggest, however, that the current allocation of transit expenditures represents a well-calculated effort to get the most return from each subsidy dollar. Some core-bound travelers (most notably commuter rail patrons) receive extremely high per trip subsidies. In general, moreover, since the elasticity of demand for rush hour transit service in high-density corridors is extremely low, fares for such service could be considerably increased (as a means of obtaining funds for equity reallocation) with little risk of substantial patronage loss. Finally the cessation of new rail rapid transit construction would free up about a billion dollars a year for reallocation at negligible cost in terms of other stated transit program objectives. In estimating the subsidies associated with new rapid transit systems and lines, it is essential to include capital as well as operating costs, because the former are not yet sunk. Projected on this basis, the per trip subsidies—predominantly to ablebodied, nonpoor commuters—are almost invariably in the DRT range or higher. Such an allocation of available subsidy funds is virtually impossible to justify even if one accepts the most optimistic estimates of the benefits accruing from rapid transit construction.

Increased Private Ride Sharing
Although most current ride sharing involves noncommutation

travel,[21] it is generally agreed that increases in ride sharing brought about by government and/or employer efforts are likely to involve only commutation. In practice, such efforts are unlikely to be undertaken on a wide scale for equity reasons;[22] but where they do emerge in response to other stimuli, low income employees are likely to participate and benefit disproportionately. (As of 1970 automobile commuters with household incomes under $5,000 were twice as likely to be passengers as those from households with incomes above $10,000. With the drivers included, average vehicle occupancies were 1.6 for the former group and 1.3 for the latter.[79]) It is not possible on the basis of current evidence to say much more than this.

Other Measures

The other potential instruments for relieving mobility deprivation

[21.] As of 1970 auto vehicle occupancies averaged 1.4 for commuter trips and 2.2 for nonwork trips. Three-quarters of all commuter vehicle trips involved only the driver. But those who commuted as automobile passengers were far more numerous than those who did so by public transportation. Nationwide 18.3 percent commuted as auto passengers, 7.5 percent as transit (including commuter rail) passengers. As the following table indicates, only the residents of cities larger than one million were more prone to commute by transit than as auto passengers.[78]

Place of Residence	Percentage of Commutation by Transit (All Forms)	Percentage of Commutation as Auto Passengers
Unincorporated areas and incorporated places under 100,000 (75% of all commuters)	3.3	18.7
Incorporated places 100,000–999,000 (16% of all commuters)	12.8	19.8
Incorporated places over one million (8% of all commuters)	35.0	11.5

[22.] As noted in chapters 5 and 6, recent government efforts to promote ride sharing have been stimulated by concerns about fuel demand and air pollution, while employer programs initiated independently of these public efforts have been stimulated by parking shortages at work sites and severe congestion problems on access roads to them.

are transportation vouchers, taxi deregulation, and subsidized car ownership.

Insofar as the problem of mobility deprivation arises from an inability to afford available transportation services, clearly the most straightforward solution is to augment the purchasing power of the poor. Economists tend to prefer unrestricted cash grants as the best method of alleviating deprivation that stems from inadequate purchasing power, but American governments in practice pursue a mixed strategy, supplementing unrestricted transfer payments with some restricted to use for the purchase of "merit" goods and services (such as food, medical care, and higher education) and also subsidizing many service providers on the ground that the benefits of their activities flow largely to the needy.

There are two obvious means available for increasing the share of government transportation subsidies received by the elderly, handicapped, and poor. The first is to target public transportation services for their benefit. The second, far more precise and certain (in view of all the other pressures on transit providers as they allocate service), is to distribute subsidies directly to members of the target groups in the form of vouchers for the purchase of service.

In considering vouchers, the first question that typically arises is whether they should be good only for the purchase of transit rides or usable as well for the purchase of private taxi services (and possibly even of vanpool services within the framework of organized ride-sharing programs). Many people are offended by the idea of vouchers being used to purchase "luxurious" door-to-door services, but it will be recalled that the poor already account for a much greater proportion of taxi patronage (29 percent) than of rapid transit or commuter rail patronage (15 percent and 0 percent respectively). Yet whereas rapid transit and commuter rail services are heavily subsidized, taxi operators are heavily taxed; and taxis are able to serve many of the nonradial and off-peak trips that the mobility-deprived are anxious to make far better than existing or prospective transit systems.

If a voucher program operated like the current food stamp program, recipients would presumably be eligible to purchase a given dollar value of vouchers at a price discount determined on the basis of such eligibility criteria as age, physical disability, and income. Alternatively (as President Carter has proposed with reference to the food stamp program itself), they might simply be given limited numbers of vouchers and left to pay market rates for additional purchases after these were exhausted each month. In either case recipients would have a strong price incentive to patronize cheaper services, but they would also be empowered to determine when higher priced options were more cost-effective from the standpoint of their own travel objectives.

One final note: although voucher programs might legitimately by justified on human service rather than transportation grounds, they would provide an important source of subsidization for transportation providers as well. Agricultural interests clearly recognize this in the case of the food stamp program, and indeed it has become relatively invulnerable politically because it so well unites agricultural with urban liberal interests in Congress.[80]

Virtually all analysts of taxi economic (as opposed to safety) regulation have concluded that its primary function is to protect current permit holders from increased competition and from threats to the resale value of their permits (originally acquired from the government at nominal cost). Where entry is free, low-income people reap a double benefit. As patrons, they benefit from lower fares and increased taxi availability. As relatively unskilled participants in the labor market, they benefit from increased job opportunities. Even without price decontrol, moreover, entry decontrol would tend to hold down fares by eliminating the need to earn a rate of return on inflated permit values, by forcing current operators to think about the extent to which successful fare increase petitions might draw in new competitors, and by encouraging disputes among the operators about fare strategy that would provide regulatory officials with good excuses for denying many increase petitions. (The other side of the coin is that price decontrol alone would often have little or no impact on fares.) In practice these benefits of free entry have long been readily observable in Washington, D.C., but its political history is unique. Elsewhere the militant resistance of current permit holders tends to make entry decontrol an untouchable issue politically.

A potentially valuable change that does not threaten the economic interests of current taxi operators is authorization for shared-ride services (already permitted in a small minority of jurisdictions). Current prohibitions of shared-ride service date to the 1920s and 1930s, when the transit industry was striving successfully to stamp out jitney competition[81] Today shared-ride restrictions are typically justified with reference to customer fear of crime, but in fact they seem largely to be sustained by inertia. Where permitted, ride sharing appears both to increase taxi service availability during rush hours and to curtail pressure for general fare increases. Patrons can be offered the option of specifying exclusive-ride service, moreover, in return for a higher fare.

Finally some observers have maintained that it would be cheaper as well as more helpful in many circumstances to assist mobility-deprived people in acquiring auto mobility than to provide them with public transportation services. In considering subsidized car ownership, it seems essential to distinguish between the poor and the handicapped as potential beneficiaries. Political opposition to such aid for the ablebodied poor would be overwhelming; and even if not, the task of detailed program design would be extremely forbidding. It would be impossible to determine who would lack cars in the absence of a subsidy program, so eligibility would have to be extended to all households with incomes below specified levels. Because the subsidies would themselves raise some recipients above the eligibility cutoff level, a sliding scale of allowances for those in the near-poor category would doubtless be necessary. Low-income households without licensed drivers would reasonably contend that they should be eligible for equivalent allowances to be used for the purchase of mobility by other modes, including taxi. The result would be an expensive program similar in most respects to a general increase in income assistance levels, and virtually impossible to justify as an alternative to such unrestricted aid.

We have previously noted, on the other hand, that veterans with service-connected disabilities are eligible for 100 percent assistance by the Veterans Administration in purchasing special equipment required to enable them to drive. Similar assistance, if perhaps with a lower matching ratio, might well be extended to some others among the handicapped. One format for the introduction of such aid might be to provide local governments with grants for the general purpose of mobility assistance to the handicapped, leaving them discretion to utilize the funds in any of several ways: to pay for transportation vouchers, to subsidize special DRT services for the handicapped, and/or to assist some eligible recipients in achieving independent automobility. Particularly in fringe areas and rural locales characterized by low density and great distances, the last might often by adjudged the most cost-effective method of assisting handicapped recipients who are (or can be rendered with mechanical aids) physically able to drive. Even in some higher-density communities, the aim of assisting handicapped recipients to become as independent as possible might dictate making transportation vouchers usable to cover certain automobile costs as well as for the purchase of transit, taxi, and vanpool services.

Summary

The auto-dominant system simultaneously affords the adult driving majority with unprededented mobility while actually reducing the effective mobility of those without ready access to cars. In contemporary urban regions most destinations are virtually unreachable, even by ablebodied adults, without a car. For those unable to walk substantial distances to and from transit stops, effective mobility is particularly limited. Moreover, current welfare standards are higher than in previous eras. And mobility-deprived groups, especially the elderly and handicapped, have become organized and outspoken in their pursuit of government assistance.

There are great uncertainties, however, as to the precise degrees of mobility deprivation suffered by the several main claimant groups. Older and handicapped people, for example, tend to have low rates of labor force participation and to be relatively sedentary in their life-styles even under conditions of equal travel opportunity. Significant numbers of them, moreover, are confined to their homes or to institutions and would be unable to travel in the best of transportation system circumstances. Finally, a large proportion of the elderly and poor do have cars and driver's licenses and seem to achieve mobility rates similar to those of other urban residents.

Clearly, however, there are substantial numbers of elderly, handicapped, and low-income people who suffer from acute mobility-deprivation that might be alleviated by transportation measures. And there is widespread agreement that their needs merit high priority in the allocation of government resources for urban transportation purposes. Prior to the 1970s, this agreement tended to be ritualistic, but it has taken on greatly increased significance during the past several years. No overall minimum mobility standards have been adopted, nor have comprehensive programs been undertaken to deal with the mobility-deprivation problem. Rather, government efforts have striven toward the limited objectives of making fixed route transit services fully accessible to those with physical handicaps and of enabling those eligible for publicly supported medical and social services to make all necessary trips incidental to the receipt of such services.

General transit subsidies as currently allocated do not confer disproportionate benefits on the handicapped, elderly, and poor. Indeed the members of these groups, on average, receive less than average benefits per household (though because they pay much lower than average taxes the net effects of government transit involvement have been redistributive in their favor). The implication is that, insofar as enhancing their mobility is a prime objective, careful targeting of transit subsidy expenditures is essential. Effective methods for achieving this purpose include the following: payment of subsidies directly to eligible individuals in the form of transportation vouchers or transit fare discounts; increasing the expenditure share devoted to DRT, particularly services restricted to usage by target groups and those serving low-income areas; assignment of priority in fixed route service design to serving the needs of low-income travelers; equalizing per trip subsidies as between bus and rail transit patrons; and structuring transit fares to favor short-trip and off-peak users.

Nature of the Problem

The term congestion denotes any condition in which demand for a facility exceeds free-flow capacity at the maximum design speed. In principle, it is applicable to all transportation modes. High levels of rapid transit demand require longer dwell times at stations than would otherwise be necessary, high levels of aircraft activity may impose significant waits for runway time slots, and so on. This chapter, however, shall focus exclusively on urban motor vehicle congestion.

In a society geared to organizing economic activity precisely around the clock, delay is perceived as inefficient as well as exasperating. The degree to which any particular level of congestion is perceived as a problem requiring public action, however, is largely a function of public expectations and of the perceived costs of remedial measures. Thus it is frequently observed that public concern about congestion appears to be at least as great in low-density urban regions of the American South and West as in the highest-density regions of the Northeast. Objective traffic conditions are far inferior in the latter, but expectations are also much lower and the perceived costs of remediation are much higher.

During the 1950s, when the concept of an urban transportation problem first emerged, and well into the following decade, it was viewed almost exclusively as one of street and highway congestion, to be addressed by the construction of additional highway capacity. More recently, widespread opposition has developed to large-scale urban highway construction, and congestion itself has come to be viewed as only one among numerous problems associated with the urban transportation system; but congestion relief remains almost everywhere one of the professed high priority objectives of urban transportation policy.

If there is widespread agreement on the inherent desirability of congestion relief, however, there is substantial disagreement or uncertainty about each of the following: whether progress has been made in the battle against congestion, what the precise consequences of congestion are (other than immediate user annoyance and time loss), what criteria of benefit should guide congestion relief activities, and which of the several methods available for relieving congestion should be viewed as acceptable.

History

The decade immediately following World War II was one of exploding highway travel demand, unaccompanied by any significant increase in the level of highway improvement activity. As of 1955, American motor vehicles traveled roughly three times as many miles as at the height of World War II (when gas and rubber rationing constrained private motor vehicle use) and roughly twice as many miles as in 1940.[1] President Eisenhower's Advisory Committee on a National Highway Program, which reported in January 1955, emphasized that the highway system was probably in worse shape than it had been in 1940. During World War II virtually no construction had occurred and road maintenance had been seriously neglected. Since 1945, highway expenditures had been well above their prewar levels and growing, but nearly all of the increase had disappeared when adjustment was made for inflation. On an inflation-adjusted basis, the committee found, the level of road investment was little above what it had been in 1940, when the amount of traffic had been half as great.[2]

No comprehensive measures of the degree of congestion relative to that of 1940 or 1945 were available, but a widespread sense existed that conditions were becoming much worse. This was, moreover, before the host of urban problems associated with race, poverty, and violent disorder moved to the forefront of national attention. Along with physical blight, congestion was viewed by many analysts as one of the two most significant threats to the prosperity and quality of life in urban America. Thus Wilfred Owen opened the most perceptive and widely quoted book of the 1950s on urban transportation by observing:

American cities have become increasingly difficult to live in and to work in largely because they are difficult to move around in. In-

[1] The official estimates were 302 billion vehicle miles in 1940, 208 billion in 1943, 250 billion in 1945, and 603 billion in 1955. Growth during the 1920s, it bears note, had been even more rapid, from 51 billion vehicle miles in 1921 (the first year for which estimates are available) to 206 billion in 1930.[1]

ability to overcome congestion and to remove obstacles to mobility threaten to make the big city an economic liability rather than an asset. . . .

The greatest transportation difficulties are experienced while commuting between home and work. . . . This movement is frequently accomplished with the most antiquated facilities and under the most frustrating conditions. The trip to work often cancels the gain from shorter hours on the job, and the daily battle with congestion is in sharp contrast to other improvements in modern working conditions. . . .

As congestion and blight have multiplied the difficulties and frustrations of urban life, there have been growing indications that in many places urban growth has passed the point of diminishing returns. . . . The threat of greater congestion has raised the question of whether a nation born of farms is destined to die of cities.[3]

Owen was far ahead of his time in certain respects. He advocated better land-use planning to reduce the need for travel, tolls and higher downtown parking charges to constrain peak period demand, and even the use of highway user revenues to subsidize mass transit. These were distinctly secondary themes, however. What placed his work in the mainstream were his treatment of the urban transportation problem as almost exclusively one of congestion, his certainty that it was worsening, his conviction that it ranked among the two of three most significant urban problems, his judgment that the main need was adaptation of urban places to the motor age, and his view that the predominant method of adaptation had to be limited access freeway construction. These central themes were already the essence of conventional wisdom about the urban transportation problem as Owen wrote in the mid-1950s, and they were to hold sway in the vast majority of urban areas for the next decade and a half.

In retrospect, there is substantial room for debate even about whether congestion was worsening during the 1950s. Traffic conditions were less favorable than they had been during the war, but it is questionable whether they had deteriorated by comparison with the prewar era. A variety of investment and traffic management innovations had gained wisespread adoption since the war—limited access highways, one-way street systems, staggered traffic signals, and so on—making the inflation-adjusted comparison of current highway expenditure levels with those of 1940 a tenuous one. Further the vast majority of traffic growth was occurring outside the most congested areas. Thus even if traffic conditions in the growth areas themselves were deteriorating, travelers on these roads may have been experiencing improvement relative to the conditions they had previously known in more central locations. Similarly there is reason to believe that most commuters who had shifted from mass transit to their automobiles were commuting at higher average speeds than previously, even if some of them were devoting more time to commutation because they had chosen to acquire homes more distant from their jobs.

As for trends on specific streets and highways, and between specific points, only the most fragmentary evidence is available even now. The one broad survey ever conducted of data on travel time trends in American cities, by Peter Koltnow, reports only a scattering of comparisons of prewar, wartime, and immediate postwar travel times with those prevailing in the mid-1950s.[4] Notably:

• On Fifth Avenue in Manhattan, the average travel speed was 7.6 mph in 1929, 14.5 mph in mid-1945 (just before the end of the war), and 8.7 mph in 1956.

• In Los Angeles, despite a tripling of motor vehicle registrations between 1936 and 1957, off-peak travel times between the central business district (CBD) and fourteen outlying locations declined from an average of thirty-three minutes to twenty-six minutes.

• In Boston motor vehicle traffic into and through the CBD increased by 80 percent from 1927 to 1960. Nonetheless average all-day speeds on nine major downtown streets compared in the two years increased by 27 percent from 10.5 to 13.3 mph.

• In Phoenix, where the population doubled between 1947 and 1957, average peak hour speeds on the region's main arterial streets increased—without the aid of significant new construction—from 24.7 to 29.6 mph. (In the following decade, as population tripled and the region's freeway program continued to lag, average peak hour speeds declined to 26.3 mph—still better than the 1947 level and quite good indeed by the standards of many older regions.)

In short the fragments of evidence available suggest that traffic conditions were significantly better in the mid-1950s than they had been during peacetime years in the previous couple of decades. Whatever the congestion trends, however, many more people were spending substantial amounts of time in automobiles —directly experiencing congestion—each day. Having purchased cars and adopted auto-reliant life-styles, they aspired to free-flow traffic conditions and were eager to believe that their growing annoyance with traffic delays reflected an intensifying objective problem rather than their own rising expectations.

Transportation anaylsts as well believed that traffic conditions were worsening, adding that they would continue to deteriorate unless highway supply were massively augmented. Traffic volumes, they projected, would inevitably grow at least as rapidly as gross national product. Thus the President's Advisory Committee on a National Highway Program labeled its estimate of a 46 percent increase in vehicle mileage from 1954 to 1965 "soundly conservative."[5] Traffic management improvements, though desirable, were viewed as trivial. The disposition of the time was to assume that significant increases in capacity would result only from new construction, most notably of limited access freeways.

Leaders of the automobile and related industries doubted that rapid sales growth could continue in the absence of a massive upgrading of the highway network. Among the leaders of business and labor generally, there was a near-universal belief that continued growth in the motor vehicle-related sectors of the economy, which already accounted for one-seventh of gross national product, was an essential condition of overall national prosperity. Public officials and downtown businessmen of the nation's central cities hoped that congestion relief might be an important part of the cure for their economic stagnation.[6]

Thus the circumstances were ripe for political mobilization in support of a dramatic program of congestion relief. The effort that in fact occurred placed great emphasis upon public relations and the media, and was remarkably successful in stamping its viewpoint upon the national consciousness as well as upon the statute books. As Gary T. Schwartz has recently noted, the liberal litany of the 1950s was "Better Schools, Better Hospitals, Better Roads," and editorial support for the interstate highway program spanned the gamut from the Hearst newspapers to the *New Republic*.[7]

The advocates of an expanded national highway program took for granted that traffic growth, economic progress, and an improved quality of life were inextricably linked. They assumed, consequently, that the path to congestion relief had to be capacity expansion rather than demand constraint. In the language of the highway movement, an adequate supply of highway capacity to serve peak levels of unconstrained traffic demand in smoothly flowing fashion was a "need," not simply a desirable objective. And in order to be sure that adequate capacity would be available when needed, it was essential to do much more than simply deal with current traffic jams. It was necessary as well to begin designing and building immediately for the traffic volumes anticipated a couple of decades hence.

In reviewing the history of this multiyear campaign, we have been as much struck by the paucity of data on which its arguments were based as by the apparent lack of controversy surrounding them. Thus the President's Committee, in arguing the case for completion within a ten-year period of the largest public works project in the history of the world, the interstate highway system, reported no data whatever on the magnitude of the congestion problem or the precise benefits that would flow from alleviating it. It merely noted that traffic had been expanding much more rapidly than the number of lane feet of highway, reported "competent" estimates that an adequate national highway system would reduce vehicle operating costs by "as much as a penny a mile," and noted that the accident fatality rate on modern limited access highways tended to be "only a fourth to a half as high as on less adequate highways."[8] Its report made no mention of the possibility that a vast highway program might encourage more

driving—and land use patterns that would require more driving—
nor did it mention such considerations as the social and environmental disruption that might be associated with a massive program
of highway investment. (Nor, indeed, did the highway program
even provide relocation payments for displaced residents and businesses until 1962.)[9] This pattern persisted throughout the
hearings on what eventually became the Highway Act of 1956,
and it characterized even the best scholarly writing of the period.

The Costs of Congestion

Surprisingly evidence about the extent and the costs of congestion
is almost as scarce today as it was in the mid-1950s. Consider, for
example, the relationship between congestion and safety. It is well
known that fatality rates per vehicle mile are only half as great on
interstate highways as on all other roads combined, but it is less
well known that overall fatality rates are lowest during peak commutation periods and highest during late night hours, when congestion is nonexistent.[2] More direct causal evidence on the conges-
tion-safety relationship is simply unavailable. Nor has any discernible progress been made in specifying the relationship between
congestion and aggregate economic activity—within any metropolitan area, let alone the nation as a whole.

A modest amount of technical literature has been produced in
recent years about motor vehicle energy consumption and emission levels under specified operating conditions (see appendix F).
But it is of limited value in estimating the costs of congestion even
where traffic conditions are known with a high degree of precision. It is of no value whatever in estimating the national costs of
congestion, because no data are available on the proportions of
national motor vehicle mileage occuring under various traffic conditions.

The most obvious cost of congestion remains traveler delay, and
more research has focused on this indicator of congestion cost

[2.] The fatality rate during the six peak commutation hours is 60 percent of the twenty-
four hour average, whereas that from 10 PM to 4 AM is 400 percent of the average.
Roughly six times as much vehicle mileage occurs during the commutation hours but
slightly fewer fatalities.[10]

than any other since the 1950s. Travel time savings have regularly served, moreover, as the single measure of benefit used to establish highway improvement priorities. But theory remains primitive about the degree to which highway improvements generate increased travel versus reduced travel time budgets. If, as many believe, good highways stimulate land use dispersal, with the result that urban residents end up traveling more miles in roughly the same amount of time, the central issue is not value of time. It is rather the value that may be placed on assisting people to live and work at lower densities—a very different and far more controversial issue.

Evidence that might permit rigorous testing of the theory of highway-induced dispersal is almost totally lacking, and qualified observers have arrived at opposite conclusions. Gary T. Schwartz, for example, has recently challenged the conventional wisdom that the interstate highway program has on balance been a force for urban dispersal. He notes that central city officials consistently maintained in the 1950s that improved highways were necessary to stem downtown decline, that in fact urban freeway construction did tend to enhance the relative accessibility of downtown areas, and that numerous downtowns experienced investment booms in the 1960s after languishing during the 1940s and 1950s.[11] (Virtually no interstate highways were opened to traffic in urban areas before 1960).

Gary Fauth, Gregory Ingram, and Eugene Kroch, on the other hand, have presented some evidence which, at very least, makes clear that improved highway networks do not translate simply into reduced travel time budgets for urban residents.[12] Comparing average weekday travel patterns in the Boston and Los Angeles regions as of 1970, they found that:

• Los Angeles residents made 32 percent more trips per capita than Boston residents (1.36 round trips per day versus 1.03), and 44 percent more trips per capita by automobile than Boston residents (1.34 round trips per day versus 0.93).

• The average trip length in Los Angeles was nearly twice as great as in Boston (19.1 versus 9.9 miles), but so was the average auto travel speed (36.5 mph versus 19.1 mph). Consequently the average auto trip took about the same amount of time in each region. And the average Los Angeles resident spent about 46 percent more time traveling by car each day than the average Bostonian (42.2 minutes versus 28.9).

• By contrast, Los Angeles residents devoted much less time to transit travel because they made only 1.6 percent of their trips by transit, whereas Bostonians made 10.4 percent of their trips by transit.

• The average door-to-door transit trip speed in Boston was 45 percent as great as the average auto trip speed. Comparable data were unavailable for Los Angeles, but on the premise that the Boston ratio held there as well we calculate that the average Bostonian devoted 7.2 minutes per day to transit travel, by comparison with 1.1 minutes for the average Los Angelino.

• Overall the average Los Angeles resident devoted 20 percent more time to travel than the average Bostonian (43.3 versus 36.1 minutes per day), even as the former reaped the benefits of a vastly superior highway system.

We are unable to judge whether Los Angeles residents travel so much more than their Boston counterparts because of the sprawling distribution of activities in their region or because they simply enjoy being on the move. What is most striking about the comparison, however, is that the relatively low travel speeds of Bostonians have by no means translated into high travel time budgets. Whether Boston's economy and quality of life have suffered by comparison with those of Los Angeles in consequence of its higher density and lower demand for travel is another matter, but it is a very different question indeed from that of the value to be placed on traveler time savings between fixed geographic points.

There is no question that highway improvements alleviate congestion and reduce travel times over the short run. The great uncertainties are the rate at which dispersal effects occur and the extent to which they ultimately dissipate the travel time savings. To complicate the task of estimation even further, it appears that regions may at times obtain substantial congestion relief without highway investment—as a result of congestion-induced (rather than highway-induced) dispersal. This can occur if a region previously contained excess road capacity in outlying areas and if locational decisions are geared (by public and/or private decision makers) to exploit it. Dispersal clearly spreads any givern amount of traffic more thinly over the landscape and greatly reduces peak period directional imbalances. Stated another way, urban sprawl, which is often portrayed as a primary cause of traffic congestion, may also be viewed as an important part of the solution.

In short, both congestion and highway improvements undertaken to relieve it may generate sprawl and the increases in travel that go with it. On balance, one would expect highway improvements to be a much stronger influence for dispersal, because congestion suppresses a good deal of travel demand and helps to sustain the viability of downtown-oriented transit even as it encourages sprawl in the location of new traffic generators that are strongly oriented toward motor vehicle access. Virtually no research has been done, however, on the magnitude of the difference.

Goals

Perspectives on Congestion Relief
It is possible to distinguish at least four conceptions of congestion relief optimization and some of the circumstances in which they may point toward divergent investment and traffic management strategies: achievement of free-flow conditions at whatever speeds facilities happen to be designed for; speed maximization (within legal limits); highway capacity maximization; and social welfare (or utility) maximization. The choice of which ought to predominate in planning and evaluating congestion relief programs is central in many circumstances to the definition of facility design objectives, the choice of traffic management strategies, and even the determination of whether a congestion problem exists at all.

The objectives of free-flow and speed maximization are so closely related that they are generally treated as identical. The technical measure of congestion, after all, is the reduction in average speed relative to that possible under free-flow conditions. Over the short run, their practical dictates are indeed the same; given a fixed highway supply, both point toward demand constraint to achieve levels of traffic compatible with free-flow operation. Over the longer term, however, as highway expansion options are considered, the policy dictates of these two conceptions may diverge more significantly. The objective of speed maximization is likely to point toward an emphasis on construction of new facilities with high design speeds, even at the cost of neglecting many opportunities to improve traffic flow on existing facilities with lower design speeds. In contrast the objective of free flow may point toward the design of new roadways with lower construction costs and lower design speeds, and toward allocation of a larger share of available resources to the improvement of flow on existing streets and highways.

Ultimately if strategies of demand constraint are considered unacceptable, the objective of free flow implies a definition of investment need adequate to ensure free-flow operation at all times for unconstrained levels of traffic demand. In practice highway officials have adopted this definition of need, and they have endeavored to satisfy highway needs with facilities designed for the highest speeds deemed compatible with safe operation.[3] At the same time they have recognized that considerations of cost and political feasibility more frequently require compromise of these objectives in urban than in rural areas.

These themes are well illustrated in *Policy on Design of Urban Highways and Arterial Streets,* published by the American Association of State Highway Officials (AASHO) in 1973.[4] This document, prepared by a committee of state highway engineers, notes explicitly that there is no scientific method for determining the

[3.] Safety is a relative concept. Many would argue that the highway engineers would have served the cause of safety better by designing for lower operating speeds, particularly on freeways, than they generally have. The imposition of the 55 mph speed limit on existing freeways in 1974 reduced the nationwide fatality rate on interstate highways by 20 percent.

[4.] The association has subsequently changed its name to the American Association of State Highway and Transportation Officials (AASHTO). Its members are the highway departments of the fifty states.

degree of anticipated future congestion to accept in designing a freeway and that motorist tolerance for congestion will vary with the perceived cost of alleviating it. Bearing these considerations in mind, it recommends the following guidelines to aid in arriving at sound professional judgments about freeway design in specific cases:

1. "The highway should be so designed that . . . traffic demand [twenty years after opening] will not exceed the possible capacity of the facility even during short periods of time. . . . Since traffic does not flow uniformly throughout a full hour, allowance should be made for peaking within the hour."[13] Stated another way, highways should be designed to serve peak hour demand, including the highest peaks within the peak hour.

2. The ideal of free-flow operation at all times will normally have to be compromised in urban areas. It should be compromised only minimally, however, in designing freeways that are intended to serve longer trips within metropolitan areas. Peak hour volumes in the design year on such facilities should not exceed 60 percent of theoretical capacity (versus 50 percent in rural areas). At this level of demand, the average peak hour running speed for all vehicles (fast and slow drivers combined) will be about 52 mph (versus 53 on highways designed to the ideal rural standard).

3. More substantial compromise will frequently be necessary in designing freeways to serve short urban trips (presumably near the core). A reasonable objective in such cases, taking financial constraints into account, is to design for peak period volumes in the design year of 75 percent of capacity. At this level of demand, an average peak hour running speed of 48 mph should be feasible.

4. If political and fiscal constraints mandate even more severe compromises, little more can be offered as guidance except the principle that stop-and-go traffic, even for brief periods during rush hours, should be viewed as intolerable.[14]

In short, free-flow traffic, even at the peak of the peak, at the highest "reasonable" design speed, is the ultimate ideal in highway policy. But the method of pursuing this ideal must be supply expansion rather than demand restraint, and political factors may necessitate design compromise in urban areas. Thus a minimum professionally acceptable design standard is articulated for the worst urban cases: avoidance of stop-and-go traffic.

If the objectives of speed maximization and free flow tend to guide highway officials in determining highway needs, especially for rural areas, the objective of capacity maximization tends to guide them in devising short-term traffic management policies wherever severe congestion exists and in establishing urban investment priorities. This objective points toward substantially less need than the previous two for demand restraint over the short run, and substantially lower estimates of needed expansion over the long run. Any given amount of highway supply will be able to accommodate many more vehicles when operating at maximum capacity than at free-flow capacity. Indeed capacity tends to be maximized at demand levels just below those at which stop-and-go traffic conditions begin to be experienced.

In distinguishing degrees of congestion, professional highway engineers refer to six "levels of service," labeled A through F. Though average operating speeds decline consistently from level A through level F, capacity tends to increase through level E. The traffic volume deemed compatible with level C performance is generally considered to be a highway's "design capacity." According to the *Highway Capacity Manual,* which was produced by a task force of federal highway engineers in cooperation with a committee of the Highway Research Board in the mid-1960s, the following volume-speed relationships may be anticipated on a modern six-lane freeway with a design speed of seventy miles per hour:

• At level A, with peak period demand in the range of 800 passenger cars per lane per hour (somewhat lower if trucks and buses are included in the traffic stream), the freeway will operate with stable speeds in the range of 60 mph.

• At level C, with demand in the range of 1200–1600 cars per lane per hour—depending on the precise configuration of the highway, local driving habits, and so on—it will operate with a stable average speed in the range of 50 mph.

• At levels D and E, which may be experienced at demand levels in the range of 1,400–2,000 cars per lane per hour, it will operate with growing instability at speeds in the range of 30–40 mph. The level E maximum—in this case, 2,000 cars per lane per hour—is defined as the freeways' capacity and represents a volume-capacity ratio (v/c) of 1.00.

• At still higher levels of demand (level F), operating speeds may range from zero (complete breakdown) to the highest level associated with level E. It will be essentially impossible, however, to move more vehicles than the level E maximum, even when driving conditions are ideal.[15] (For additional detail, see table 9.1.)

It is far more difficult to correlate specific traffic volumes with performance levels in dealing with arterial streets and nonlimited access highways. The performance of such roads depends primarily on intersection capacity and the number of disruptive turning movements that motorists wish to make rather than on the capacity of the roadway itself. Thus reliable estimates of street and highway performance at various levels of traffic demand can be made only on the basis of specific network analyses.[16] With respect to arterial streets as well as to freeways, however, the following can be said: increased demand above the level of free-flow operation involves some time loss for every user; increased demand above the level of design capacity (level C) adds the further penalty of reliability degradation even as average delays continue to increase; and at some further point increased demand also reduces the absolute number of vehicles that can be served during any unit of time.

American highway officials have always felt obliged—and in the context of American law and public opinion, they *have* been obliged—to serve all the traffic that happens to show up at any time as best they can. In this situation, the first rule of highway policy must be capacity maximization. Free-flow and speed maximization may be the ideals, but level F performance is the nightmare. In practice, moreover, if one assumes that demand is totally outside the influence of policy and that resources are generally inadequate to serve need, there is no conflict among the three objectives. The potential for conflict is realized only when one considers, as economists are prone to do, whether the benefits associated with a highway facility or network might be increased if some means could be found to reduce demand and thus improve the level of service.

The case for demand constraint is simplest and, in principle if not always in practice, least controversial when the objective is to maximize capacity. Economists have frequently maintained, however, that the objective should be social welfare (utility) maximization rather than capacity maximization and that in many circumstances this calls for demand reduction well below the level of maximum highway capacity. The economists' recommendations have been based on sophisticated arguments to the effect that the social, economic, and/or environmental benefits of such demand reduction (time savings for users, reduced pollution levels, and so on) would more than offset the harm done to those kept off the roads during peak demand periods. By contrast, demand restraint to maximize capacity can be defended in terms of permitting more people to utilize the road network than would otherwise be able to do so in a given period of time. The benefit of improved service quality may be viewed in this context as the frosting on the cake.

The principle of demand restraint to maximize capacity has in fact become widely accepted among highway officials since the mid-1960s, with the understanding that the method used must be queue management (for example, by metering access to freeways) rather than pricing. The egalitarian ideal of first come, first served has been viewed as a sacred tenet of American highway policy. The principle of demand restraint to maximize utility, on the other hand, has never commanded significant support outside the ranks of the economics profession.

Official Goal Statements

Rather remarkably, in view of the priority that congestion has commanded as a problem, virtually no specific objectives for its alleviation have been articulated over the years. Although the general direction toward which highway investment and traffic

TABLE 9.1 Levels of Service and Maximum Service Volumes for Freeways and Expressways under Uninterrupted Flow Conditions

Traffic Flow Conditions			Service Volume Capacity (v/c) Ratio[a]				
			Basic Limiting Value for Average Highway Speed (ahs) of 70 mph, for:			Approximate Working Value For Any Number of Lanes For Restricted Average Highway Speed of	
Level of Service	Description	Operating Speed[a] (mph)	4-Lane Freeway (2 Lanes/ Direction)	6-Lane Freeway (3 Lanes/ Direction)	8-Lane Freeway (4 Lanes/ Direction)	60 mph	50 mph
A	Free flow	> 60	< 0.35	< 0.40	< 0.43	—[b]	—[b]
B	Stable flow (upper speed range)	> 55	< 0.50	< 0.58	< 0.63	< 0.25	—[b]
Peak-hour factor (PHF)[c]							
C	Stable flow	> 50	< 0.75 × PHF	< 0.80 × PHF	< 0.83 × PHF	< 0.45 × PHF	—[b]
D	Approaching unstable flow	> 40		< 0.90 × PHF		< 0.80 × PHF	< 0.45 × PHF
E[f]	Unstable flow	30-35[e]		< 1.00			
F	Forced flow	< 30[e]		Not meaningful			

[a] Operating speed and basic v/c ratio are independent measures of level of service; both limits must be satisfied in any determination of level.

[b] Operating speed required for this level is not attainable even at low volumes.

[c] Peak-hour factor for freeways is the ratio of the whole-hour volume to the highest rate of flow occurring during a 5-min interval within the peak hour.

Maximum Service Volume under Ideal Conditions, Including 70-mph Average Highway Speed (Total Passenger Cars per Hour, One Direction)

4-Lane Freeway (2 Lanes One Direction)				6-Lane Freeway (3 Lanes One Direction)				8-Lane Freeway (4 Lanes One Direction)				Each Additional Lane Above Four in One Direction			
1400				2400				3400				1000			
2000				3500				5000				1500			
0.77	0.83	0.91	1.00^d	0.77	0.83	0.91	1.00^d	0.77	0.83	0.91	1.00^d	0.77	0.83	0.91	1.00^d
2300	2500	2750	3000	3700	4000	4350	4800	5100	5500	6000	6600	1400	1500	1650	1800
2800	3000	3300	3600	4150	4500	4900	5400	5600	6000	6600	7200	1400	1500	1650	1800
4000^c				6000^e				8000^e				2000^e			
						Widely variable (0 to capacity)									

[d] A peak-hour factor of 1.00 is seldom attained; the values listed here should be considered as maximum average flow rates likely to be obtained during the peak 5-min interval within the peak hour.

[e] Approximately.

[f] Capacity.

Source: Highway Research Board, *Highway Capacity Manual*, special report 87 (Washington, D.C.: Highway Research Board, 1965), table 9.1.

management programs should strive has been clear, the legislative approach to pursuing it has invariably been one of establishing fiscal and/or mileage ceilings, of ensuring that resources are spread equitably over the relevant political landscape (the entire nation, in the case of federal highway legislation), and then leaving the professionals to achieve the greatest degree of relief possible within this framework of policy.

The language establishing the interstate highway system, for example, provided that the system should "connect by routes, as direct as practicable, the principal metropolitan areas, cities, and industrial centers, and . . . serve the national defense."[17] The Federal Aid Highway Act of 1956, which established the interstate system as the nation's highest transportation funding priority, specifically included routes into as well around the principal cities, but the rationale for basic route selection remained connectivity. The urban extensions were justified as feeders to and distributors from the interregional system; routes intended principally to serve local traffic needs were ineligible for designation.[18] Thus, as Gary T. Schwartz writes, "The Miami map shows only one Interstate entering the city from the north and halting in midcity; Indianapolis, on the other hand, is rather thoroughly crisscrossed and encircled by [four] Interstates. This is entirely sensible in basic extension terms."[19]

Schwartz notes that the cities accepted the extension rationale because Congress was not, at the time, prepared to vote funds explicitly to deal with urban transportation needs. They did, however, secure adoption of the principle that, once routes had been selected, they should be designed with "equal consideration" to local needs along with those of interstate commerce.[20] (They were able to achieve this concession in practice, despite the ideological aversion of many congressmen to funding local transportation activities, because urban residents were going to contribute half or more of the tax revenues needed to finance the interstate system and the votes of their congressmen were essential to enactment of these tax provisions.) The central design issue pursuant to this provision was how many interchanges to provide. The more frequent the interchanges, the more useful would be the freeways for local trips, the more traffic they would attract, and in many circumstances the more lanes would be required. The Bureau of Public Roads officially estimated in 1958 that the "equal consideration" provision would add 63 percent to the cost of urban Interstate mileage.[21] The question of precisely how many interchanges to provide was in practice resolved in each case by negotiation among federal, state, and local officials. What bears emphasis here is that the statutory objective was not to achieve some specified degree of urban congestion relief; it was rather to facilitate the utilization by urban residents of expensive facilities built primarily to serve interregional travel.

The one specific service goal established by the 1956 act was that interstate highways should "be adequate to accommodate" forecast levels of traffic twenty years from the date of final approval of the plans for their construction. The act did not, however, define the concept of adequacy or distinguish between peak and off-peak service levels. Instead it directed the secretary of commerce, in cooperation with the state highway departments, to develop design standards. Initial standards were promulgated in July 1956 and have since been updated periodically. The current standards provide that interstate segments shall be adequate to handle design year traffic in the peak hour, defined as the thirtieth highest hourly volume in the year.[22] They do not specify the level of service that must be provided during this hour, however. In fact, Federal Highway Administration engineers routinely consult AASHTO's *Policy on the Design of Urban Highways and Arterial Streets*—which, it will be recalled, urges that level C service be provided on urban highways during the peak hour if possible, but notes that inferior levels of peak hour service may have to be accepted in many urban circumstances.[23]

No new goals with respect to congestion relief have received official sanction since 1956. In effect, moreover, the original goals have explicitly been downgraded in priority over the past decade as numerous constraints have been placed on the program in the name of citizen participation, environmental protection, and so forth.[24] And Congress has explicitly recognized the primacy of local objectives in providing the justification for some urban interstate segments by a series of actions since 1967. In that year it authorized route substitution at the initiative of a state, subject to the following constraints: certification by the U.S. secretary of transportation that the substitution would not imperil completion of a "unified and connected" interstate system "including urban routes necessary for metropolitan transportation;" limitation of the federal contribution to the level that would have been required for implementation of the original project at 1967 cost levels (the official 1968 interstate cost estimate); and limitation of the total mileage that might be added nationally to the Interstate System under this provision to 200.[25]

In 1973 the national limit on interstate mileage that might be added in this manner was raised to 500. Far more significantly, however, states were authorized to substitute mass transit projects for interstate highway projects that they no longer wished to construct; the local governments affected by any proposed withdrawal and substitution were accorded significant roles in the decision process; and costs were frozen for all future substitutions at the 1971 cost level (1972 interstate cost estimate).[26]

In 1976 the provision was amended again, this time to authorize the substitution of local street and highway projects as well as mass transit and alternative interstate highway projects for deleted interstate segments. On a retroactive basis, moreover, all substitute projects remaining to be implemented were authorized to receive inflation adjustments in the same manner as interstate projects that were continuing to go forward. In calculating these adjustments, the plans for the deleted segments (rather than those for the substitute projects) were to continue to be utilized.[27]

In short Congress has now adopted the principle that, as long as the essential integrity of the national system is not sacrificed, virtually any other local transportation projects can be substituted for interstate projects.[5] It follows that the vast majority of urban interstate projects remaining to be implemented are more accurately viewed as federal funding commitments to the metropolitan areas in question—to be used for any of a wide variety of

[5.] The test of interstate system integrity has proven invariably to be connectivity. Federal officials have never found that an interstate route found nonessential by state

transportation purposes at state and local discretion—than as elements of a national plan.

Turning from the statute books to broader statements of urban transportation policy, one finds even less evidence of commitment to specific congestion relief goals. In 1975, for example, the U.S. secretary of transportation issued the nation's first comprehensive *Statement of National Transportation Policy*. Its clearest statement of broad objectives for domestic transportation policy read as follows:

The Transportation sector should contribute substantially to an improved quality of life by:
(1) Attaining high standards of safety;
(2) Protecting our air and water from pollution, reducing excessive noise and supporting sound land use patterns and community development;
(3) Bringing people together and closer to the variety of benefits that our culture and economy offer;
(4) Minimizing the waste of human resources that results from *congestion*, inadequate transportation service and inefficiency in transport operations;
(5) Providing the lowest cost services to the consumer consistent with safety, a reasonable rate of return on capital, a sound government fiscal policy and other public interests;
(6) Promoting the most efficient use of scarce, finite and costly energy supplies;
(7) Creating and maintaining employment and capital opportunities.[28]

Its section on highway transportation elaborated on these general objectives with statements such as:

• Interstate commerce and national security require that a high level of performance be maintained on our Nation's major highway systems; . . .
• Completion of the Interstate System is a top Federal priority,

and local officials was in fact "necessary for metropolitan transportation." Connectivity can be achieved in many instances, moreover, by incorporating existing noninterstate mileage as part of the interstate system. This was the strategy adopted in Boston, for example, when $671 million worth of interstate segments were withdrawn in 1974. Interstate connectivity was preserved by redesignating existing state circumferential route 128 as part of interstate 95. So long as such designations do not entail any federal funding commitment, they do not fall under the 500 mile limitation on substitute mileage that may be added to the interstate system.

especially where connective intercity links are concerned.[6] *Where links are proposed that principally serve local needs, we will expect State and local officials to justify these expenditures carefully.*

• The initial planning of most of today's highways was undertaken when energy was cheap, considered in plentiful and unlimited supply, and environmental considerations were not as prevalent. Now, *we encourage State and local communities to rethink some of the highway planning already done so as to determine if a particular highway still offers the best transportation alternative.* Where it does, we urge that it be built as soon as possible; where it does not, we urge policies that do not place any undue disincentive on the alternative.

• *The special problems of urban areas require an intermodal approach, utilizing the option to transfer Federal highway funds to mass transit, where appropriate. . . .*

• Since large segments of the Nation's highway structure are now in place, we must address the future requirements for and utilization of the Highway Trust Fund. [30]

In short the federal policy priority in highway transportation remains the connective intercity links; many of the highways projected years ago, before energy conservation and environmental protection became major national priorities, should be reevaluated; and we should proceed on the policy assumption that most of the nation's ultimate highway infrastructure is already in place. Any further suggestions for urban highway building should be subjected to close scrutiny, with emphasis on the alternative of mass transportation.

The section of the *Statement* on urban transportation concluded with nine specific statements of policy direction, none of which included mention of congestion as a problem or highway

---

[6.] This was by no means to suggest that the interstate system would be completed soon. The comptroller general estimated in 1975 that if the rate of construction cost inflation averaged 5 percent and the rate of spending totaled $3.25 billion a year, the system would be completed in 1990 (at a total cost from the beginning of the program of $113 billion). If the inflation rate averaged 10 percent, the system would be completed in 2009 (at a total cost of $184 billion).[29] Congress could accelerate the completion date by increasing the authorized spending level, but the recent trend has been to target increased spending for mass transit and the noninterstate highway programs even while paying lip-service to the priority of interstate system completion. There has even been serious talk in recent years of "declaring the Interstate System complete" at an early date and folding the program into a more general system of transportation revenue sharing.

construction as a solution.[31] The messages, again, seemed to be clear: congestion no longer ranks among the highest priority problems of transportation, and the era of urban expressway construction is essentially over.

Innovations

Five of the eight categories of innovations here under review (see above, p. 50) appear to have significant potential as means of alleviating congestion: highway capacity expansion, preferential traffic management, private ride sharing, direct consumer regulation, and price disincentives. Additionally we shall discuss fixed route transit improvements because these are widely believed to be effective instruments of congestion relief.

Highway Capacity Expansion

Having discussed the effects of highway capacity expansion at some length above, we shall confine ourselves here to reviewing several key points. It is vital to distinguish between travel time savings between specific points (speed increases) and changes in personal travel time expenditures. New highway capacity does tend to alleviate congestion and raise average travel speeds at least over the short run, but it also tends to induce additional travel. Although there is general recognition that the induced travel effect is a real phenomenon, little is known of its precise rate, magnitude, or dependence on other circumstances (such as rate of metropolitan growth and local zoning policies).

What does seem clear is that, even over the long run, areas that invest heavily in road capacity seem to maintain higher travel speeds than those that do not. Their main arteries may in time become heavily congested during peak hours, but they will normally continue to operate at higher speeds than older, unimproved roads. Congestion on many Los Angeles freeways is severe during peak hours, for example, but average peak-period highway travel speeds in the Los Angeles area remain substantially higher than those in Boston. Where land ·use densities are lower than in Los Angeles and the ratio of freeway capacity to population is higher, congestion may be almost entirely avoidable. Thus in Houston as of 1969, the average commuter making a thirty-minute freeway trip from the core during the peak averaged 51 mph.[32]

It is far less apparent that highway capacity expansion generates reductions in personal travel time expenditures. The fragmentary evidence available suggests that increases in average speed are followed relatively quickly by increases in travel mileage that negate any time savings. Indeed, in the Boston-Los Angeles comparison reported above it was the Los Angelinos who spent 20 percent more time traveling. The implication is that urban residents have historically purchased reductions in land use density with their highway expenditures far more significantly (and durably) than they have purchased travel time savings.

The highway expansion approach to congestion relief tends as well to be cost-ineffective from an energy standpoint. The fuel-saving benefits of congestion relief are equally available if it is achieved by means other than road construction, and they are likely—at least in cases involving new expressway development—to pale in any event beside the energy costs of construction, induced travel, and high travel speeds.[33]

Finally congestion tends to be greatest where development is most intense; and it is precisely in such areas that highway construction entails the most severe community disruption, the most intense public controversy, and the highest dollar cost. Thus the highways with the greatest congestion relief potential are also the least feasible to construct. Spending on urban highway construction by all levels of government combined fell 37 percent in constant dollars between 1971 and 1975. (See table 9.2.) A more specific indicator of the decline in capacity expansion in developed corridors is the rate of residential dislocation attributable to federally aided road construction.[7] This rate fell by 79 percent between 1969 and 1976: from roughly 5,300 to 1,100 people a month. (See table 9.3.) These figures suggest that most current highway construction activity in the built-up sectors of urban areas is confined to improvements on existing rights-of-way. New

[7.] Figures on dislocation attributable to state and local construction undertaken without federal aid are unavailable. The number of such dislocations is almost surely trivial, however.

TABLE 9.2
Government Expenditures for Urban Highway Construction, 1956–1975 (in Millions of Constant 1975 Dollars)

| | System | | | |
	Interstate	Federal Primary and Secondary	Other	Total
1956	533	1,557	1,262	3,352
1960	2,222	1,753	1,600	5,575
1965	3,223	1,825	1,783	6,831
1970	2,832	2,078	2,046	6,956
1971	2,847	2,443	1,953	7,243
1972	2,776	2,122	1,828	6,726
1973	2,201	1,849	1,682	5,732
1974	2,010	1,449	1,287	4,746
1975	1,583	1,610	1,340	4,533

Source: Kiran Bhatt et al., *An Analysis of Road Expenditures and Payment by Vehicle Class (1956–1975)* (Washington: The Urban Institute, 1977), table 1.4.

TABLE 9.3
Relocations per Month Caused by Federal Aid Highway Construction

Period[a]	Dwellings	Persons
3/30/65–9/30/68	2,071	
10/1/68–12/31/69	1,834	5,331
1/1/70–12/31/70	1,654	4,807
1/1/71–12/31/71	1,591	4,362
1/1/72–6/30/72	1,204	3,944
7/1/72–6/30/73	897	2,438
7/1/73–6/30/74	838	2,057
7/1/74–6/30/75	717	1,764
7/1/75–9/30/76	670	1,105
Total	104,148	305,334

Source: Federal Highway Administration, "Relocation Statistical Assistance Report" (unpublished, 1976).

[a] The figures are expressed in relocations per month although the periods reported by FHWA are of varying length.

roads continue to be built, but mainly in the less-developed sectors of urban areas and primarily with the aims of connecting up existing links, providing improved circumferential routes, and opening up new areas rather than alleviating severe congestion. Early prospects for a change in this pattern appear to be negligible.

Improved Traffic Management

Prior to the interstate program the predominant task of highway engineering in developed urban areas had always been traffic management—the art of optimizing the use of a fixed network of streets and highways. During the heyday of urban expressway construction, from the late fifties through the early seventies, the prosaic tasks of management tended to be eclipsed by those of expansion. As the viewpoint has won general acceptance in the mid-1970s, however, that future opportunities for capacity expansion by construction in developed corridors will be few, a striking revival of interest in traffic management has occured.

It is essential to distinguish three separate purposes of traffic management: the maximization of vehicle-carrying capacity, the maximization of people-carrying capacity, and the promotion of amenity and safety by assigning some roadway space predominantly or exclusively for pedestrian use. It is essential further to distinguish between management approaches that entail the channeling of traffic and those that entail reductions in the overall volume of traffic.

Until the past several years, virtually all traffic engineers have viewed their main task as the maximization of vehicle-carrying capacity. This objective was particularly ascendant in the years following World War II, a period characterized by street widening (at the expense of sidewalk narrowing) on a massive scale in urban areas and by the elimination of transit reservations on many arterial streets as streetcars gave way to buses. By contrast, the distinguishing feature of the recent traffic management revival has been the emphasis placed on management for other objectives in congested urban corridors and zones—most notably for the maximization of people-carrying capacity on overloaded roadways during peak periods and for the maximization of pedestrian amenity on the main shopping streets of downtown areas.

Traffic management is unquestionably a powerful instrument for the maximization of vehicle throughput. As measures undertaken with this aim in mind tend to benefit all motorists equally, moreover, they are typically noncontroversial—at least among motorists. What conflicts are encountered generally involve choices between the interests of through travelers and those of adjacent land users. Business people, for example, frequently resist one-way street systems and curb parking restrictions on the ground that these will impair access to their establishments, and residents typically prefer a predominant emphasis on safety, quiet, and pedestrian amenity in the management of their streets. Traffic engineers recognize these concerns as legitimate, but they often find themselves embroiled in conflict with business and neighborhood associations over the precise balance among objectives to be struck.

Specific techniques for maximizing vehicle throughput on local street networks include traffic-actuated signal systems, one-way street patterns, turn restrictions, on-street parking prohibitions, and truck loading restrictions. On major highways the primary technique of management is access control; and indeed the expressway concept itself emerged from a recognition that uncontrolled access to through arteries tended to degrade their traffic-carrying performance severely. Even where access is confined to specially designed ramps, however, traffic demand exceeds freeway design capacity at times. The most potent technique that traffic engineers have devised to deal with this problem is ramp metering (the use of traffic signals on entrance ramps to keep vehicle input and freeway capacity in balance). This technique entails the deliberate creation of entrance ramp queues, but ramp delays are in general far more than offset by travel time savings on the main roadway.[34]

Generalization about the power of individual techniques is difficult because a great deal depends on such site-specific characteristics as traffic volumes on cross-streets, the extent of local compliance with traffic regulations, and the potential for expressway ramp queues backing into adjacent local streets.[35] Documented illustrations, however, include the following:

• A one-way pattern established on north-south streets in Manhattan produced a 22 percent reduction in travel time for north-south travelers, a 40 percent travel time saving for cross-town travelers, and a 20 percent reduction in pedestrian accidents.[36]

• On Fullerton Avenue in Chicago, ten intersections were improved by signal modernization, channelization, and widening to provide turning lanes. The average travel speed in the peak-flow direction increased by 42 percent during the morning peak and 43 percent during the afternoon peak, and the accident rate fell by 51 percent.[37]

• A complex of traffic management measures in the Canton, Ohio central business district—traffic-actuated signals, two new one-way streets, channelization, bus turnout lanes, and removal of some on-street parking—reduced overall vehicular delays by 37 percent and the number of traffic accidents by 10 percent.[38]

• Freeway ramp metering brought about an average increase in the average peak period speed on Dallas' expressways from 14 mph to 30 mph and on the Los Angeles Harbor Freeway from an estimated 15–20 mph before metering to a measured 40 mph after.[39]

In sum, then, although there is much uncertainty about the precise additive value of specific techniques in any given set of circumstances, it seems clear that management strategies can bring about dramatic increases in the vehicle-carrying capacity of existing roadways in a wide range of circumstances. As we turn to management techniques aimed at the maximization of people-carrying capacity, however, the picture is significantly more clouded. The question is not whether such techniques can produce improved service for favored categories of users, but whether there are many settings in which they can produce net benefits for favored and nonfavored users in aggregate.

The distinguishing feature of management techniques aimed at maximizing people-carrying capacity is preferential treatment for high-occupancy vehicles (HOVs). Such techniques may be applied on both streets and freeways, but we shall concentrate on the latter—first, because the claimed benefits of freeway priority techniques are generally far more dramatic, and second, because virtually no thorough studies of HOV priority schemes on local streets (reporting the costs for non-HOV travelers as well as the benefits for HOV users) have been carried out.[40]

There are four major categories of HOV priority techniques on freeways: preferential access within the context of ramp metering for all traffic, exclusive HOV lanes physically separated from the regular travel lanes, reserved regular travel lanes in the predominant flow direction ("with-flow" lanes), and reserved regular travel lanes in the off-peak direction ("contraflow" lanes).

As noted above, access metering can be a highly effective technique for maximizing freeway capacity during periods of potential overload. Where queue delays on the metered access lanes are substantial and where means can be found to enable HOVs to bypass the queues, metering can also provide HOV travelers with benefits substantially greater than those reaped by other users. On some California access ramps, for example, queue delays as long as eight or nine minutes are regularly experienced at the peak of the peak, and one study of such a ramp in Los Angeles concluded that HOV preference had stimulated the formation of 80–100 carpools.[41] It is typically difficult and expensive, however, to construct special HOV access ramps in highly congested areas, and the reservation of one lane on a typical two-lane access ramp for exclusive HOV use will frequently cause the non-HOV queue to back up into nearby streets, stalling traffic on them. Elsewhere queue delays on metered freeways are generally brief for all vehicles, and thus preferential HOV treatments can provide only minor time savings for HOV travelers relative to other users.

HOV access preference can also be provided on the multilane approaches to toll facility collection stations. The best-known application of this technique is on the inbound approach to the San Francisco-Oakland Bay Bridge. Since December 1971 three approach lanes, about one mile in length, have been designated for

HOV use between 6 A.M. and 9 A.M. each weekday. Additionally, since March 1974 a metering system has regulated the flow of non-HOV vehicles through the toll plaza to prevent overload of the main bridge travel lanes, and since March 1975 HOV vehicles have been exempt from the fifty-cent bridge toll. The combined effect of these measures has been an increase in average peak-period auto occupancy on the bridge from 1.33 to 1.45. Although no claim is made that this increase in occupancy has been accompanied by a reduction in vehicle mileage, the Bay Bridge experience is widely considered to be a great success.[8]

Let us turn now to the several types of exclusive HOV travel lane treatments. Physically separated HOV lanes provide the highest levels of service to users. To date, moreover, they have entailed service improvement for non-HOV along with HOV users because they have been implemented only as net additions (by new construction) to the number of lanes available. Those not qualifying for use of the HOV lanes, consequently, have benefited from the removal of HOV vehicles from the general traffic lanes.

It is difficult to justify the construction of physically separated HOV lanes, however, except where three requisite conditions are simultaneously present: sufficient potential demand to ensure that each HOV lane will carry more people, at least during peak periods, than the average general traffic lanes; sufficient congestion to ensure that the HOV vehicles will achieve significant time savings relative to those in the general traffic lanes; and sufficient room within the existing right-of-way to permit construction of the HOV lanes without substantial new land takings. There are in practice few corridors in which all of these conditions prevail, and at

[8.] After so many years, it is impossible to say what the pattern of bridge usage would be in the absence of the HOV lanes. Shortly after these lanes commenced operation, however, bridge officials noted that whereas the number of carpools had nearly doubled, the number of non-HOV vehicles had remained approximately constant. They speculated that most of the new carpools may have been attracted from other routes, but they did not conduct any surveys to test this hypothesis.[42] The only measure to alleviate congestion, parenthetically, appears to have been the metering of non-HOV vehicles through the toll plazas. This was, of course, simply a version of general ramp metering.

The Bay Bridge HOV preference measures have led to several imitations on the West Coast. Notably a one-mile stretch of lane has been reserved on the Evergreen Point toll bridge in Seattle, and toll exemptions for HOV vehicles during the morning and evening peak hours have been implemented on the San Mateo-Hayward and Dunbarton bridges in the San Francisco Bay Area.[43]

present there are only two separated HOV roadways in the United States: the Shirley Highway and San Bernardino Freeway busways, in the Washington, D.C., and Los Angeles areas, respectively. Both are considered highly successful. The Shirley busway, for example, which cost $43 million (in 1972 dollars) for eleven miles, brought about an increase in bus patronage during its first five years from 1,900 to 11,500 per day in each direction, with half the new riders being drawn from the ranks of automobile drivers.[44] But there are no indications that the pace of diffusion of this innovation is about to accelerate.

With-flow and contraflow reserved lanes involve negligible or no new construction, but they do entail difficult problems of enforcement, safety, and access-egress between the special lanes and general traffic lanes. Contraflow lane use is almost always confined to buses because the potential for head-on collision with oncoming traffic is such that extremely careful driving is considered imperative. Despite the risk, contraflow lanes have generally been more acceptable because they do not reduce the number of lanes assigned to general traffic and they are much easier to enforce (since access and egress are possible at only a few points).

The most notable example of a contraflow lane has been on the I-495 approach from New Jersey to the Lincoln Tunnel in the New York region. This 2.5-mile lane, which functions for two hours during the morning peak each weekday, commenced operation in 1970. It carries more than 800 buses in an average morning and has carried as many as 1,100. These normally carry about 34,000 passengers, but the total has approached 47,000 on occasion; and the bus lane typically carries ten times as many passengers during its hours of operation as each of the regular tunnel-bound auto lanes.[45] The bus passengers save eight to ten minutes on normal days and up to twenty-five minutes on days when the general-purpose lanes are more tied up than usual. The removal of so many buses from the general traffic stream has also generated substantial time savings for other peak-directional (eastbound) motorists without discernibly affecting travel times for motorists traveling in the off-peak (westbound) direction.[9] [46]

[9.] Virtually none of the traffic relief has been attributable to modal shifts. Only 4 percent of the bus patrons on the I-495 contraflow lane were diverted from automobiles;

Such potential bus volumes are unique in the United States to the New York region, however, and indeed probably unique to the specific corridor in question. A similar contraflow lane on the Long Island Expressway, for example, had to be limited to approximately 100 buses per hour because of concern on the part of city officials about the capacity of Manhattan streets to accommodate larger volumes.[47] Buses utilizing the Lincoln Tunnel, on the other hand, have direct access from the tunnel exits on the Manhattan side to the vast, multilevel Port Authority Bus Terminal.

Outside of the two New York contraflow bus lanes, the best-known application of this concept has been on Boston's severely congested Southeast Expressway. Though it has produced significant benefits for bus patrons, this example illustrates the difficulty of attracting large bus volumes in most American circumstances. The Southeast Expressway contraflow lane is in operation two and a half hours each weekday morning for about seven months each year. (It is teminated during the months when daylight arrives late because of concern about the safety of putting down traffic cones during the hours of darkness.) As of 1972, it attracted an average of only twenty-six buses during each hour of operation.[48]

Contraflow lanes generally have very modest startup and operating costs. If they are to produce net time savings, however, they must be on suitably configured roadways with relatively modest levels of traffic in the off-peak direction and substantial levels of bus transit demand in the peak-flow direction. Herbert Levinson has recently estimated that on a well-configured six-lane freeway (all entrances and exits to the right of the through traffic lanes) carrying 4,500 vehicles in the peak-flow direction and 2,700 in the off-peak direction, 86 full buses per hour on the contraflow lane would be required to produce a net time saving for all users in aggregate.[49]

Such analyses have generated a good deal of interest in opening

this figure includes former passengers as well as drivers. The same factors that made it possible to generate such high bus volumes had persuaded the vast majority of Manhattan-bound commuters even before implementation of the bus lane to leave their cars at home.

preferential lanes to other high-occupancy vehicles—most notably passenger cars with three or more occupants—along with buses. Fearing head-on collisions at high speeds, however, highway and law enforcement officials have been unwilling to implement the broadened HOV concept on contraflow lanes; the result has been serious consideration for the first time of with-flow reserved lanes.

The most significant effort thus far to implement the with-flow reserved lane concept was the so-called diamond lane experiment on a 12.5 mile segment of the Santa Monica Freeway in Los Angeles (March 15–August 9, 1976).[50] The Santa Monica Freeway, eight lanes wide for most of its length, runs between downtown Los Angeles and the city's heavily populated west side. It is the most heavily traveled freeway in California. The demonstration project consisted of three main elements: the allocation of one lane in the peak-flow direction for vehicles with three or more occupants during the hours of 6:30–9:30 A.M. and 3–7 P.M. each weekday;[10] improvements in the ramp-metering system, which had been operational for some time and which included preferential access for buses and carpools at twelve of the thirty access ramps on the freeway segment in question; and a quintupling of bus service (from approximately 35 bus runs per day to 180).

Results during the first two months of the project were almost uniformly negative. In the ninth week, the freeway was still carrying 10 percent fewer peak period travelers than during a comparable base period one year earlier. Vehicle occupancies were up—from an average of 1.23 in the base period to 1.31—but not nearly enough to compensate for the 16 percent reduction in the number of vehicles utilizing the freeway during the seven peak hours. Transit patronage was triple the base period level, but it had failed to grow in step with the quintupling of service, and transit still carried only 3 percent of all peak period freeway users. Meanwhile traffic volumes on parallel streets were 11 percent higher than during the base period. And accident rates were up sharply. Despite the reduced traffic volume on the freeway, the average number of peak period accidents on it per week during the first

[10.] The designated lanes were marked by painted diamonds on the road surface—hence the label by which the project came to be known.

ten project weeks was three and a half times the base period level.[51] Senior officials of the California Department of Transportation (Caltrans) continued to insist throughout this period that the project was a success, but no one else visibly supported them, and they were subjected to an overwhelming barrage of public and media criticism.

Results did improve as the months passed. Notably peak period person volume on the freeway exceeded the base period level for the first time during the twenty-first (and final) project week. Parallel street volumes fell below the base period level in the eighteenth week. And the accident rate stabilized at twice the base period level during the last five project weeks. Finally transit patronage and carpooling continued to rise slowly, though average vehicle occupancy never exceeded 1.36 and transit patronage never exceeded 3 percent of peak period travel. (Carpooling tripled during the course of the project, accounting for 5 percent of peak period freeway usage during the base period and 14 percent in the final project week, but no data were collected on the proportion of carpools on the freeway during the demonstration period that had simply been attracted from other routes.)[52]

On August, 9, 1976, a federal district judge enjoined the diamond lane component of the demonstration project on the ground that it should have been preceded by an environmental impact statement. Rather than prepare an impact statement, Caltrans chose to terminate the demonstration at this point (though it retained the ramp metering elements as permanent improvements). It did, though, prepare a final evaluation report in which it concluded that the diamond lane project in its final weeks had provided significant (though not precisely measured) benefits to HOV users during peak periods without adversely affecting users of the general traffic lanes and adjacent parallel streets.[53]

The detailed study findings bear out this conclusion but suggest as well that most of the project's benefits were attributable to its ramp metering features rather than to the diamond lane component. These involved the installation of demand responsive metering systems on two access ramps and fine-tuning of the meter rates at all other access points to maximize throughput.[11] In consequence of these improvements, the nonpreferential freeway lanes carried 11 percent more vehicles, and at slightly higher average speeds, in the final project week than during the base period. (Average freeway travel times for non-HOV vehicles were essentially unchanged by comparison with the base period, however, because the line-haul increases in speed were offset by increased ramp delays.) Except for the non-HOV volume gains, which were wholly attributable to the metering components of the demonstration, and for illegal use of the diamond lanes themselves by about one thousand non-HOV vehicles per day, peak period person-volume in the final week would have been 4 percent below the base period level rather than 3 percent above it.[54] HOV occupants as well saved considerably more time in consequence of the access than of the diamond lane elements. Average diamond lane speeds were only about 9 mph higher than those in the non-HOV lanes during the morning peak (50 versus 41) and 4 mph higher during the afternoon peak (50 versus 46). Therefore even HOV travelers who utilized the entire 12.5 mile length of the diamond lanes saved only 3.5 minutes in the morning and 1.5 minutes in the afternoon. By contrast, those who utilized ramps offering preferential HOV access realized average time savings of between 5 and 11 minutes.[55]

A less eventful demonstration incorporating the with-flow HOV lane concept occurred in the Miami area during 1974. This effort, sponsored by the Florida Department of Transportation and Dade County, has received far less attention than the diamond lane experiment, though in some respects it was more ambitious technically and it achieved far greater acceptance politically. (The lack of furor may well account for the lack of attention.) The demonstration included both a contraflow bus lane and a with-flow carpool lane on a 5.5-mile stretch of U.S. 1 extending south from the Miami CBD. Additionally it entailed an expansion of transit service from one to six routes and an increase in service frequency on the preexisting route. According to the final evaluation report,

[11.] Demand responsive meter systems make continuous traffic signal adjustments in response to data on the level of freeway congestion; other meter signals are preset.

peak period bus ridership increased by more than 400 percent during the nine months of the demonstration, and average auto occupancy rose from 1.30 to 1.45. Overall the highway carried 2,400 more people during the hours of operation (7–9 A.M. and 4–6 P.M.) in 350 fewer vehicles than a year earlier, and travelers in the reserved lanes saved an average of 6–8 minutes. But drivers in the unreserved lanes experienced average 15-minute time losses, and reported accidents in the demonstration period were 64 percent more numerous than during the base period.[56] These results can scarcely be interpreted as positive from the standpoint of congestion relief, but they were in practice viewed as positive by public officials because of the increases in transit usage and carpooling. [Subsequent to the demonstration period the contraflow lane was eliminated for reasons of economy—the cones setting it off had to be put down and taken up manually—but the with-flow lane, now utilized by both buses and carpools, continues to operate as of mid-1978. Dade County officials judge that the addition of buses to the with-flow lane had only a slight adverse effect on their average speeds and no discernible effect at all on average carpool speeds.]

Summing up, it seems clear that reserved lane treatments can provide significant benefits for HOV users in numerous circumstances where overall congestion is severe, that new exclusive lanes (because they represent expanded capacity) will normally provide significant congestion relief for both HOV and non-HOV travelers, and that contraflow lanes can in some circumstances also provide congestion relief for both general purpose and HOV travelers. New lanes and contraflow lanes are plausible instruments, however, in very few corridors. By contrast, with-flow reserved lane treatments are potentially applicable in a great many corridors but entail degradation of service for non-HOV travelers at least over the short run, and there is considerable doubt as to whether they can produce net time savings in many circumstances even over the long run.

Private Ride Sharing
As traffic volumes approach roadway capacities, small changes can

have disproportionate effects on the level of congestion. There is little doubt, consequently, that significant commuter shifts from drive-alone to carpool or vanpool travel would provide dramatic congestion relief. The problem is that such shifts seem to occur only when employers actively promote and facilitate them and that relatively few employers feel motivated to do so. Having treated this subject in chapter 5, we shall say no more about it here.

Consumer Regulatory Measures

The main regulatory measures that might alleviate congestion are commuter parking restrictions and gasoline rationing. As the impact of rationing would presumably be similar to that of gasoline price increases, which are discussed in the next section, we shall focus exclusively in this section on parking restrictions.

The most frequently proposed targets of regulation are for-hire parking facilities, particularly in CBDs, but the limited evidence available suggests that only the most draconian restrictions on for-hire parking alone would significantly affect peak period traffic volumes. As of 1970, 93 percent of American employees who drove to work parked for free, and most of the remainder, even in large central cities, paid very little.[57] In Washington, D.C., for example, a survey of auto commuters on a major radial freeway in 1972 revealed that 56 percent parked for free at work and another 24 percent paid less than a dollar a day. At this time the price of commercial parking in downtown Washington ranged from two dollars a day on up.[58] In Pittsburgh, when a three-day strike in 1972 closed down 93 percent of downtown for-hire parking spaces (23,600 of 25,400), peak period traffic volumes on streets within the CBD did fall by 24 percent.[59] But a 25 percent sales tax on for-hire parking in San Francisco, levied from 1970 to 1972, had no discernible impact at all on traffic, though it had very substantial effects on for-hire parking demand. Damian Kulash, in a study of the effects of this tax, estimated that it had generated a reduction of 10 percent in the number of vehicles utilizing for-hire spaces each day, and a significant decline as well in the average duration of occupancy, but that this had translated into no more than a 2 percent reduction in the number of vehicle trips occurring within the city. In practice, Kulash found it impossible to document that even this modest reduction has occurred. Though commuters cut back their usage of for-hire parking much more sharply than short-term parkers, for example, no comparable reduction showed up in an analysis of traffic trends on the Golden Gate Bridge.[60] The most likely explanation was that many commuters who stopped using for-hire spaces may have simply switched to spaces excempt from the tax—for example, on-street spaces at greater distances from their jobs than they had previously chosen to walk.

More severe restrictions on downtown parking could, of course, yield quite significant congestion relief benefits, but only at the cost of great inconvenience to many commuters and at the risk of providing a major additional spur to employment dispersal. Concern about the latter effect led EPA, in devising its transportation control plan for Greater Boston (pursuant to the Clean Air Act Amendments of 1970), to substitute a regionwide commuter parking restriction scheme for an earlier proposal focused on the core alone.[61] The effect was to expand greatly the number of outraged citizens in the region, and no effort was ever made to implement this scheme. It bears mention, however, that given the opportunities for on-street parking in suburban areas, and for crowding more cars on given amounts of parking lot area (if, for example, the method of enforcement had been to rope off sections of existing lots), effective implementation would have been possible only with the vigorous cooperation of local law enforcement agencies. As the proposed restrictions enjoyed negligible support among state and local officials, it seems probable that such cooperation would have been spotty at best. On the reasonable assumption that enforcement would have fallen off sharply with distance from the core, the burden of the restrictions would, despite EPA's intent, have been borne primarily by downtown commuters.

General Increases in the Variable Price of Auto Travel
To the extent that the overall demand for automobile travel is

price elastic, general price increases—those affecting all travel by automobile rather than simply travel on congested routes—would yield some congestion benefit. The available evidence suggests, however, that the travel reduction in each case would be quite minor relative to the scale of the price increase, that commuter travel would be curtailed less than other travel, and that the traffic volume reduction would be highly vulnerable to dissipation over time.

As discussed in chapter 5, most studies of the short-run elasticity of demand for gasoline estimate it to be in the range of -0.2, and indicate that work-trip elasticity is significantly lower than nonwork trip elasticity. It is generally thought, moreover, that over time the predominant effect of gasoline price increases would be to induce price-sensitive consumers to purchase cars with better fuel economy rather than to curtail their travel.[62] In brief, then, whereas demand elasticity for gasoline itself is considerably higher over the long term than the short term, that for automobile travel with reference to the price of gasoline is much lower over the long term than the short term.[63] As it is travel that generates congestion, the implications of these findings are: that gas price increases would have to be very large to bring about appreciable reductions in peak period automobile travel, and that fresh increases would be needed periodically in order to maintain the short-term congestion-relief impact of the initial increase.

Congestion Pricing

Though general increases in the variable cost of automobile travel would have surprisingly meager effects on congestion, there is every reason to believe that surcharges aimed at congested facilities, zones, and time periods would yield dramatic congestion-relief benefits. The reasons are simple. First, many motorists have substantial flexibility in their choices of route and travel time even for commutation trips. Second, it might be feasible to impose much higher charges if these were confined to specific facilities and relatively brief time periods than if they were to be collected from all motorists on all roads at all times (as, for example, a gas tax increase would be).

More generally, economists have long viewed the congestion problem primarily as one of inefficient allocation rather than of inadequate supply. Where the price of travel is the same on all roads at all times, the incremental dollar cost of using facilities when they are congested is zero. Motorists who travel in congested periods do incur time delay costs, but they have no reason to consider the costs of the delays that they impose on others. And when travel demand on any facility exceeds the level compatible with free-flow operation, the aggregate delay imposed by each incremental vehicle on others far exceeds the delay experienced by its own occupants.

Thus, economists maintain, where the monetary cost of highway travel is invariant, a substantial amount of congestion is inevitable. Even where substantial excess capacity is available in a corridor twenty or twenty-two hours a day, congestion is likely to be experienced during the remaining hours unless tolls (or other rationing mechanisms) are employed to increase the temporal spread of peak demand. Thus even those highway supply additions most successful in relieving total congestion tend to do so much more by reducing the duration of the peak than by reducing the severity of congestion at the peak of the peak. The reason is simple. Congestion does not suppress much travel demand in aggregate, but it does induce some motorists to travel at times that are less than optimal for them. As it is relieved, they are enabled for any given congestion penalty to travel at more preferred times. Thus it is far easier to build highways that will be very lightly traveled during off-peak periods than it is to build highways that will have excess capacity at the peak of the peak.[64]

Though the potential effectiveness of congestion pricing is generally recognized, there has been intense controversy about whether it is equitable, its likely effects on land use and urban form, the practical feasibility of levying charges that relieve congestion without also constraining travel on underutilized road segments, and what the major objectives of pricing schemes should be.

The main equity argument against pricing is that any system of congestion tolls would favor use of the roads—a public good—by affluent consumers during periods of heavy demand. Economists point out in rebuttal that excessive demand tends to dissipate the value of highway facilities for all users, that low-income people choosing to travel by bus would benefit significantly from the congestion relief, that carpools as well as buses might be exempted from the tolls, and that congestion toll revenues might be used to subsidize mass transit or to pay for other measures of particular benefit to the poor.

The land-use argument against congestion tolls is that they would be a force for urban dispersal, thus further weakening the competitive position of downtown areas and—over the long run—public transportation as well. The basic premises underlying this viewpoint are that congestion tolls would normally apply only to core-oriented travel and that the tolls would reduce the total volume of core-bound travel. Virtually all economists and planners accept the first of these premises as valid, but there is substantial disagreement about the second. Some maintain that the elimination of severe congestion would in fact make downtown areas *more* attractive. Efficient congestion tolls would spread traffic more evenly over time, would enable travelers to avoid the delays and frustrations associated with stop-and-go traffic, would induce some shifts (by price-sensitive commuters) from drive-alone to transit and carpool travel, would provide a source of revenue for transit service improvement, and would divert many peak-period through travelers (who make no contribution to its economic life) around the core. The value of decongestion for core-bound travelers (taken as a group) would far outweigh the cost of their toll payments, with the result that overall travel demand to the core would actually increase. One economist who has recently expressed this viewpoint is John Kain.[65] Others argue more cautiously that congestion pricing would benefit the core if it were part of a larger package including improved transit service.[66]

Still other analysts, however, including some advocates of congestion pricing, conclude that congestion tolls would in most cases be a force for dispersal. Illustratively, a British interagency planning group in 1974 developed a plan for levying congestion fees on cars entering the London core during the day on weekdays. Although it estimated that the impact of this scheme would be slightly to encourage the relocation of economic activities outside the restricted area, its attitude toward this finding was one of complete equanimity. In principle, it judged, if an area is congested, the relocation of traffic-generating activities out of it should be viewed as desirable, and if policy makers wish to discourage some activities from relocating, they can utilize some of the congestion fee revenues to provide them with direct inducements to stay.[67]

In a similar vein, Gerald Goldstein and Leon Moses have argued that most U.S. urban households seek to hold down their commutation costs while continuing to avoid public transportation, carpooling, and high density living. Thus, they contend, the primary land use effect of measures raising the price of auto commutation to the core would be to increase the attractiveness of suburban enterprises as employers. Goldstein and Williamson discount the potential increase in core area attractiveness that other economists think would flow from the decongestion itself.[68]

All of these analyses are based predominantly on speculation; empirical data on the land use impact of congestion tolls are almost entirely lacking. Except for the London analysis, moreover, they all deal with congestion pricing as a generic concept rather than with specific pricing proposals. There is good reason to believe, however, that different pricing schemes might have sharply different land use consequences.

In the simplest possible case—the use of pricing to achieve capacity maximization at a single bottleneck point—the argument that congestion pricing would increase the overall attractiveness of destinations requiring access through the bottleneck point is quite persuasive. William Vickrey, for example, the most prominent advocate of congestion pricing throughout the two decades in which the idea has received serious intellectual attention, postulates a case in which the following conditions prevail:

• a bottleneck point has a maximum capacity of 3,600 vehicles per hour;

• 7,200 commuters, each driving one to a car, wish to pass through the bottleneck point on an evenly distributed basis between 8 A.M. and 9 A.M. each morning;

• there is no additional traffic demand during the second hour required to clear all 7,200 vehicles past the bottleneck point;

• commuters value additional time that they might spend at home before departure at the rate of $1.20 an hour, time spent at the work site before they have to be there at $.60 an hour, and delay time making them late for work at $2.40 an hour. (For the purpose of this analysis, it does not matter what value is assigned to travel time itself, so Vickrey assigns it an arbitrary value of zero.) In the absence of pricing, Vickrey writes, the equilibrium condition under these assumptions will be as follows: a queue will build up linearly from zero minutes waiting time at 7:20 A.M. to 40 minutes waiting time at 8:40 A.M. It will then decline linearly again to zero at 9:20 A.M.[69]

The ideal toll in this situation, assuming no change in travel demand due to the toll itself, would be one that rose and fell linearly during the two-hour peak period, from zero at 7:20 to $.80 at 8:40 and back to zero at 9:20. Such a toll pattern would enable the same number of vehicles as previously to pass the bottleneck point during the two-hour period, but without the need for any to spend time queueing. The revenue could be utilized to reduce other taxes. In addition to saving all peak period travelers some time, the pricing approach would maximize consumer freedom. Those placing a higher value on time could, by paying for the privilege, travel at the peak without wasting any time on queues. Those placing a lower value on time could avoid all or most of the toll by traveling earlier or later. The toll mechanism would also provide a dramatic improvement in peak period bus service, a reduction in peak period bus operating costs, an incentive for modal shift to transit and carpooling, and an inducement to stagger work hours.[12] If shifts in the time and/or mode of travel reduced peak period vehicle demand by one-eighth, to 6,300 vehicles, the new equilibrium situation would involve

---

12. We are indebted for the last point to George Hilton rather than Vickrey, but of course it reinforces Vickrey's argument.[70]

tolls for only one and three-quarter hours, from 7:30 to 9:15, with a maximum toll of $.70.[71]

Few cases are so simple, however. Congestion pricing is rarely proposed for a single bottleneck point or with the objective of maximizing vehicle throughput. It is much more frequently proposed for congested core areas taken as a whole and with multiple objectives in mind that would entail some reduction in traffic flow. Thus, the pricing scheme proposed for Central London in 1974 (which was ultimately rejected by Greater London Council in the face of public opposition) entailed imposition of a flat congestion charge for street use anywhere in inner London from 8 A.M. to 6 P.M. each weekday. Similarly the only congestion pricing scheme implemented anywhere in the world to date (in Singapore) involves a flat charge for automobile use anywhere in the CBD during the hours it is in effect (7:30–10:15 A.M. each weekday).

The Singapore scheme, inaugurated in June 1975, illustrates both the potential power of congestion pricing and some of the difficulties of fine-tuning. The fee is very high (U.S. $1.30 a day), particularly considering the earnings of Singapore residents. It applies to passenger cars entering the restricted zone with three or fewer occupants. Two months after its imposition, traffic flow into the restricted zone during the hours of operation by vehicles in the tolled category was down by 74 percent. Overall traffic flow was down by 40 percent. During the afternoon peak, however, traffic volumes were down by only 3–4 percent. Through traffic, diverted around downtown in the morning peak period, returned to its normal routings later in the day; some commuters brought their cars downtown at lunchtime; others who came in by transit or carpool in the morning arranged to be picked up by other household members at the end of the day.[71] In such complicated situations it is impossible to say whether congestion pricing will increase or reduce the overall attractiveness of the core area.

The practical impediments to the effective implementation of congestion charges (given a basic policy decision to utilize them) are typically stressed by government highway officials and disparaged or ignored by economists. These include the virtual impossibility of fine-tuning the tolls so as to alleviate congestion without also constraining motorists who would like to use available excess capacity, and the difficulty of adjusting toll schedules over the months and years as experience accumulates regarding their effects.

Traffic conditions on any given facility, at any given time of day, generally vary sharply from one day to the next. And average traffic conditions vary widely from street to street within any congested zone. Thus any price schedule—even one providing for adjustments every few mintues, as in Vickrey's example—that effectively relieves congestion when and where it would otherwise be severe will also lead to substantial increases in the amount of unused capacity on other days and other streets. One might, of course, as a matter of policy determine that the amenity and time-saving benefits associated with a specified degree of congestion relief outweighed the inconvenience associated with discouraging the use of excess capacity. In practice, however, urban motorists tend to accept moderate degrees of congestion with relative equanimity, to resent efforts to restrict their access to roads with spare capacity, and to view the idea of congestion pricing with intense hostility. So it would be difficult to arrive at such a policy determination by a democratic process.

Assuming for the moment that congestion pricing might be acceptable to alleviate severe stop-and-go congestion—that is, to maximize capacity—the question arises: how prevalent is stop-and-go congestion? The answer, apparently, is that except on the streets of, and some of the least adequate approaches to, a few of the nation's very largest and densest downtowns, it is a relatively infrequent phenomenon. For the most part, motorists avoid creating stop-and-go traffic jams by adjusting their routes and/or travel times. When traffic does break down, it is generally on very short stretches of roadway and/or because of special circumstances (for example, more vehicles than usual converge on a given point at a particular moment, slippery road conditions develop, an accident or breakdown occurs). It makes more sense, the opponents of congestion pricing maintain, to deal with such irregular sources of congestion by putting out radio traffic bulletins than to implement a complex system of demand restraint every working day of the year.

In short, a toll schedule geared to average conditions, even at a single bottleneck point, would leave substantial excess capacity much of the time (when driving conditions were ideal) and would fail to eliminate stop-and-go congestion much of the remaining time (when conditions were particularly adverse). A shift in the toll schedule to eliminate one of these problems would aggravate the other. Further, the consequence of such a toll would normally be to increase congestion on alternative routes. Assuming that motorists had previously arrived at an equilibrium distribution of traffic over the several routes that minimized their collective travel time, the likely consequence of such a diversion would be to increase total travel time delays.

In the case of a toll imposed upon entry into a congested subarea, the problem of simultaneous congestion and excess capacity would be severely compounded. In this situation, the two conditions would normally coexist at each moment rather than simply alternate over time. Careful analysis might demonstrate, moreover, that the point of total network capacity maximization was at or very close to the existing untolled equilibrium. At very least, it can be said that no subarea toll has yet been proposed with the claim that it would increase the total throughput of the street network. There are doubtless extreme circumstances in which a street network is so congested overall that an area toll would increase throughput. It seems probable, however, that such circumstances are very rare.

Finally it is not feasible to vary tolls every few minutes, as Vickrey recommended. Given the congestion pricing technologies that are currently available (most notably, window stickers that motorists would purchase in advance), such complexity would unduly burden both motorists—who make many trips on the spur of the moment, and whose regular trips are often made at variable times from day to day—and law enforcement personnel. At some point in the future, technologies than can accommodate variable pricing (with periodic billing by mail) will doubtless become cost competitive.[73] Even if these are adopted, however, there will doubtless be intense public pressure for simple toll schedules.[13] Motorists will want to be able to estimate, as they start out on trips, what toll charges they are likely to incur. Further, there is little point in precisely calibrating the charges if the schedule is too complicated for the average motorist to keep clearly in mind.

In consequence of such considerations, all current and proposed toll schedules involve minimal temporal variation. Bridge, tunnel, and turnpike authorities have resisted even suggestions that they economize on collection costs by eliminating tolls during their periods of very light demand, making up the difference by charging a bit more the rest of the time. The Singapore and proposed London schemes each involve a limited period of restriction, but a flat daily charge for central area street use during the restricted period.

Yet much of the case for congestion pricing, at least as an instrument for maximizing capacity, breaks down if flat charges are levied. Thus Vickrey writes: "It is important to note that a flat toll undifferentiated by time of day would have a much less salutary effect. The [carpool incentive] effect might be somewhat similar to that of the differentiated toll, but much of the resulting reduction in queuing *would come from a reduction in total daily traffic,* which might be even more wasteful [than the lack of any toll at all]."[74] In short a flat toll will have no effect on demand peaking. It will reduce congestion only by reducing the overall level of demand. This will be least true of a scheme like Singapore's, which involves a levying of charges for only a few hours each weekday morning, but even a toll so limited will have no effect on the intensity of peaking within the restricted period (Vickrey's example). A major unintended effect of the Singapore scheme, additionally, has been a great deal of waste motion: numerous downtown employees make special trips during the day to collect their cars from storage points outside the restricted zone; other household members make special trips to pick up employees at the end of the working day; through travelers utilize

---

[13.] While technically impressive, such technologies would be triply controversial: as instruments of congestion pricing, as threats to personal privacy, and as sources of inconvenience for motorists who were not tied into the metering and billing system.

circuitous routes during the morning peak period that they had previously rejected (presumably with time considerations in mind) and that they continue to reject during the rest of the day. Thus the time savings of some travelers have been significantly (and perhaps more than) offset by time losses for others.

Government, when it does employ price as a policy instrument, almost always does so in highly inefficient fashion. Because price increases are politically controversial, public agencies tend to utilize price as a rigid instrument rather than an infinitely adjustable one. Initial price levels, moreover, are generally dictated more by political and legal considerations than by rational planning considerations. Economists tend to treat such irrationalities as accidental features of specific case examples. Highway officials, on the other hand, most of whom spend their lives working for government agencies, tend to view them as fundamental characteristics stemming from the very nature of the political process.

Thus even in Singapore—a small, firmly governed, one-party state—the government has to date treated its initial price level decision as unchangeable despite the fact that results have been substantially different from those forecast. As noted above, morning-only congestion charges have proven to have a negligible impact on afternoon traffic volumes. This appears to be of less immediate concern, however, than the fact that traffic flow during the restricted period has fallen by 40 percent rather than the desired 25–30 percent. Peter L. Watson and Edward P. Holland of the World Bank comment as follows: "This fact, together with the deserted downtown streets, . . . indicates that the price was set too high, leading to severe underutilization of existing capacity, which is economically inefficient. . . . The government must choose between reducing the fee to achieve a more efficient solution, or leaving it too high to avoid future increases and to promote the broader goal of modifying motorists' attitudes toward the use of the car. Singapore chose the latter alternative."[75] Stated another way, Singapore has opted for rigid adherence to a price level determined initially on the basis of erroneous estimates in order to avoid the unpleasantness of having to consider price increases in future years. Presumably government "face" has also had something to do with the refusal to admit a miscalculation.

Writing with reference to American experience, Vickrey finds that "where tolls actually exist, the pattern is more often than not, perverse from the standpoint of optimum routing of traffic. Because of commuter discounts, the average tolls levied in peak periods are typically lower than in off-peak periods. And toll differentials frequently encourage travelers to seek out *more* congested rather than less congested routes. For example, motorists from the west side of Lower Manhattan to Brooklyn can pay a toll to use the Brooklyn-Battery Tunnel or cross Canal Street to contribute to some of the heaviest congestion in New York to reach the free Manhattan Bridge. Instances of this sort can be multiplied. " [76]

Because Vickrey's concern is to prescribe ideal policy rather than to explain the roots of actual policy, he passes over these examples without further comment. The implication is that they have nothing to do with systemic characteristics of American government that might impair the effectiveness of congestion pricing once it was properly understood by senior officials. In practice, however, each of Vickrey's examples well illustrates the inertial characteristics of the American policy process. Each is rooted in political and legal commitments undertaken reasonably, though in piecemeal fashion, during earlier periods rather than in any recent policy judgments. The current system of highway finance, for example, with tolls on only a miniscule proportion of the total system, reflects the perspectives, priorities, and technologies that prevailed during the formative years of the automotive era. Local streets had historically been laid out as part of the development process and maintained at the expense of the property owners to whom they provided access. There seemed no way to toll them in any event. In rural areas the primary purpose of highway investment was to end the market and cultural isolation of low-income farmers, a general welfare objective. Given rural incomes and traffic volumes, few road improvements could have been financed on a toll basis, and tolls would have interfered with the social objective of encouraging use. Moreover toll collection costs were extremely high relative to what might be collected except where traffic had to pass through a bottleneck point, as in crossing a river or bay.

Not only has this basic pattern proven extremely resistant to change, but decisions to toll individual facilities have likewise manifested strong tendencies toward permanence. Such decisions have generally been based on a reluctance to impose taxes, even conventional highway user taxes, for construction of the facilities in question and on a finding that they could be financed with revenue bonds. Having become accustomed to tolls on these facilities, the public has generally accepted their continuance after the bonds were paid off in passive fashion. By the same token, having become accustomed to the lack of tolls on other facilities, the public has reacted to talk of their imposition with intense hostility.

One may choose for economic modeling purposes to consider these inertial characteristics of the governmental system accidental, highway officials conclude, but they are in fact of its essence. Thus they ought to receive thorough consideration by anyone who would predict the likely effects of congestion pricing in practice.

We have written about congestion pricing thus far exclusively as an instrument of congestion relief to the point of capacity maximization. To the economist, however, unlike the highway engineer, the optimal solution is by no means necessarily to maximize physical throughput. It is rather to maximize the differential between benefit (travel time saved by any given degree of congestion relief) and cost (inconvenience to those motorists induced by the congestion toll to modify their travel behavior.) The cash payment itself is ignored, because economists postulate that it is just a transfer payment from one set of taxpayers to another and that it probably permits holding down some other taxes.

Putting aside for the moment that no one is able to specify monetary values for the stated parameters of benefit and cost with any precision, one may theorize as follows:

1. Each motorist should pay a price based on the marginal cost to all motorists combined of adding more vehicles to the traffic stream at any moment.

2. The equilibrium situation may be viewed as that which would emerge in successive iterations if direct cash transfers were arranged between those with a strong relative preference for time and those with a strong relative preference for money. Eventually a demand level would be found at which the price all remaining users were willing to pay equaled the price the last traveler was willing to accept in order to get off the road.

3. The equilibrium situation might in principle be anywhere between completely free-flow (level A service) and maximum stable capacity (level C). The precise equilibrium point would be a function of the distribution of preferences among users as between time and money.

Though this formulation leaves out such utility considerations as the possible preference of the larger public for energy conservation and cleaner air, it is indeed more elegant intellectually than the idea that traffic management should focus on maximizing vehicle throughput. It is subject in principle, moreover, to the incorporation of any additional externalities that can be assigned dollar values.

On the other hand, whereas vehicle throughput can be measured, personal utility gains and losses cannot be. It is not feasible to ration highway space by arranging for direct cash transfers between actual and potential users. It is impossible to achieve a public consensus on the social value of either the utility gained by those enabled to drive more quickly or the disutility imposed on those induced by the toll to modify their travel behavior. Nor is it feasible to secure wide acceptance of the premise that the toll payments should be left out of the cost-benefit calculation on the ground that they are only transfers among groups of taxpayers. Motorists and elected officials have an overwhelming disposition to view them as costs, and to discount severely the prospect of benefits to be obtained as the revenues are expended.

Although the economic analysts of congestion have been unable to specify optimal toll schedules, they have been able to specify two practical implications of the foregoing: first, it is a serious error to take congestion as a clear economic signal that capacity should be expanded; and second, even in the absence of precise utility measures, price might play an important role in urban traffic management if political decisions, based upon careful planning analyses, could win recognition as acceptable surrogates.[14] The first of these points has become an important part of the arsenal of antihighway groups, budget officials, and others desirous of holding down the level of highway capital expenditures. The second has attracted considerable interest among transportation planners in recent years. They are comfortable with the idea that policy must be based ultimately on the judgments of policy makers rather than on scientific measurements of utility, and they recognize as well that price can be a powerful instrument for the modification of human behavior.

Taking note of this development, Charles Hedges, a senior Department of Transportation economist, has written of the shift among those concerned with congestion pricing from "normative economics concerned with the conditions of achieving an optimal allocation of resources" to practical transportation system management concerned with the means of pursuing politically determined objectives. More specifically, Hedges argues: "Experience has shown that providing alternatives to the private automobile is a *necessary* but not a *sufficient* condition to induce a significant proportion of automobile commuters to abandon (or share) their cars, or change their time of travel. Thus, the most pragmatic reason for charging motor vehicles higher prices is to permit the transportation system management plan to *succeed*."[77]

In sum, congestion tolls represent an instrument of enormous potential power for the alleviation of congestion. There are serious questions, however, about whether congestion pricing would in practice generate overall time savings for travelers or otherwise

[14.] The predominant view among economists is that supply should be expanded only when traffic demand exceeds road capacity even in the presence of a toll schedule high enough to finance the capacity expansion. A key problem is how to determine this point in the absence of tolls. Estimates of the average value of traveler time do not supply an answer because the elasticity of demand is a function of the distribution of values rather than the average value. Moreover, estimates of the value of time leave open the question of how much disutility is involved when motorists alter their schedules or in other ways find close substitutes for their former behavior that do not involve greater travel time expenditures.

enhance the public welfare. When one adds to these uncertainties the intensity of current public hostility to road pricing, it is easy to understand why elected officials have to date viewed this technique as beyond the political pale.

Fixed Route Transit Improvements

Investments in transit service expansion, particularly new rapid transit systems, are regularly promoted on the ground that they will relieve congestion; and it is widely believed that they attract support even from confirmed motorists who hope that better transit service will induce others to get off the road.[78] In practice, however, fixed route transit improvements appear rarely to be effective instruments of congestion relief.

Over the short run, at least, most new transit services draw a large majority of their patrons from those who were already transit users, new travelers, and previous auto passengers. Although they do attract some auto drivers, their impact on highway traffic volume is normally very small. There are notable exceptions, such as the Shirley Highway busway, but the experiences of the Dan Ryan rapid transit line in Chicago, the Quincy rapid transit extension in Boston, and the Bay Area Rapid Transit (BART) system in San Francisco appear to be more typical.

Nine months after the 1969 opening of the Dan Ryan line, a survey was conducted of passengers boarding at the terminal station. Only 8 percent of the new patrons had previously made the trip as auto drivers. Eighty percent had been attracted from other bus and rail transit routes, 6 percent had previously made the trip as auto passengers, and 6 percent had not previously made the trip at all.[79]

The Quincy extension began service in September 1971. Vehicle counts several months later on all major road facilities in its corridor revealed that whereas traffic had previously been increasing by about 4 percent a year, it was now up about 7.5 percent from the year earlier figure. Although no one attributed the acceleration of traffic growth to the transit opening, there was certainly no basis for contending that it had produced any congestion relief.[80]

The early impacts of the BART system have been studied more thoroughly than those of any previous transit improvement. BART commenced transbay service in September 1974. Six weeks later the system was carrying 25,000 passengers a day in each direction. A survey of those traveling in the inbound direction revealed that 13,000 had previously traveled by bus, 2,000 had not previously made the trip, and 2,000 had previously traveled as auto passengers. The remaining 8,000, or one-third, had previously traveled as auto drivers. This proportion, though very high by comparison with most other new transit services, was similar to that attracted by the Lindenwold rapid transit line in Philadelphia, the nation's only other rapid transit route completed in the postwar period for which data are available.[81]

The impact of BART on transbay auto travel, however, proved to be far less than the 8,000 diversion figure would suggest. Fully 7,000 new vehicle trips had appeared each day on the San Francisco-Oakland Bay Bridge (the transbay highway facility from which nearly all the auto trips replaced by BART had been attracted). After considering many possible explanations, the BART impact analysts found only one to be plausible: that congestion on the bridge had previously suppressed a good deal of potential travel demand. As BART relieved the congestion, many potential trips became actual trips.[82]

The congestion relief impact of BART was apparently greatest in the first three weeks of service, and it was gradually dissipated by induced travel growth over the following three months. At the end of three months, volume appeared to be roughly level with the year earlier figure (having been down 6 percent in the first week of BART service), and the period of heavy congestion on the inbound approach to the bridge toll plaza was judged to be about as long as it had been prior to the commencement of BART service.[15] [83]

BART's success in attracting a high proportion of previous auto commuters was doubtless attributable to the severe congestion and high parking charges that they encountered when driving. This

[15.] The oil embargo and gasoline price increases during the winter of 1973–1974 significantly complicated the task of appraising BART's impact on transbay auto travel. Traffic

should not be taken to suggest, however, that it would have attracted even a greater proportion of former motorists had these factors been operating more powerfully. BART's situation may in fact have been near optimal from the standpoint of attracting motorists. Had the previous deterrents to driving been stronger, those sensitive to congestion and parking costs would have already switched in greater numbers to transit. Illustratively, during the first year of New Jersey's contraflow bus lane on the approach to the Lincoln Tunnel, only 4 percent of bus patrons on the route reported that they had previously been automobile drivers or passengers. Ninety percent had previously commuted by bus, 3 percent had switched from rail transit, and 3 percent had not previously made the trip.[84]

Over time, it does seem probable that successful fixed route transit improvements, by attracting high-density clusters of jobs and residents to the vicinity of transit stations, gradually attract an increasing proportion of trips that would otherwise have been made by automobile. (The measurement of such long-term effects is extraordinarily difficult because one cannot rely on passenger surveys to determine what travel patterns would otherwise have occurred.) By the same token, however, such increases in density entail parallel increases in person trips per unit of land area. In general, it appears that although the transit share increases with density, so does the ratio of motor vehicle travel demand to street capacity. Thus the world's most transit-oriented cities tend also to be characterized by the most severe traffic congestion.

Summary

During the 1950s and 1960s the urban transportation problem was

volumes throughout the San Francisco region were significantly lower in the fall of 1974 than would have been anticipated in the absence of these developments. The BART impact analysts therefore sought to factor out their impact.

Prior to the embargo, traffic on the Bay Bridge had been increasing by roughly 2 percent a year. Traffic on two other transbay bridges deemed to be unaffected by BART had been increasing at rates of 6 percent and 7 percent respectively. (These were the San Mateo-Hayward Bridge and the Richmond-San Rafael Bridge.) During the second month of BART service, at a time when Bay Bridge traffic was down 2 percent from the year earlier level, traffic on the other two bridges was down 1 percent and 6 percent respectively. In short, Bay Bridge traffic was 4 percent below the level that would have been forecast on the basis of previous trends, but traffic on the other two bridges was 7 percent and 14 percent below the trend projection levels.

viewed almost exclusively as one of street and highway congestion, to be addressed by the construction of additional capacity. Widespread community and environmental opposition have dramatically curtailed large-scale urban highway construction in the present decade, however, and congestion itself appears to have receded significantly as an urban transportation policy priority.

Congestion is a problem mainly to the extent that it causes time losses for travelers. Available data indicate that it is not a significant cause of increased energy use, air pollution, or accident rates. Fragmentary evidence suggests, moreover, that even the time losses attributable to congestion may be more apparent than real—insofar as the alternative is highway capacity expansion. Historically capacity expansion measures appear to have contributed signnificantly to the decline of urban densities, and consequently to the need for additional travel mileage (even if at higher speeds). It may be, therefore, that the primary function of capacity expansion over the long term is to facilitate low-density development rather than to reduce the amount of time that urban residents must spend traveling.

Urban motorists almost surely experience less congestion (as a proportion of total travel) today, and achieve substantially higher average speeds, than their counterparts of several decades back. These gains have been achieved only in part as a direct consequence of highway improvement measures. More significantly, they are attributable to the diffusion of population and economic activity, both within and between metropolitan regions. The proportion of travel occurring in low-density settings with little congestion has been rapidly growing throughout the postwar period. (The diffusion of activity has itself been facilitated by highway improvements, of course; the implication is that their indirect effects may have been as significant as their direct in alleviating congestion.)

Among potential relief measures, the most cost-effective are typically those in the traffic management category. These usually involve relatively minor expenditures and negligible community or environmental disruption. Their advantages are particularly striking in the densest cities, where congestion problems are most severe and the obstacles to new highway construction most intense. Traffic management measures are fairly noncontroversial insofar as they benefit all motorists alike or as they benefit high occupancy vehicle (HOV) users without imposing any new costs on other travelers. Preferential measures that entail additional congestion for non-HOV travelers, however, remain highly controversial. They are most feasible where a constituency of adjacent land users supports them, as in some central retail districts, but they have to date been politically unacceptable on arterial streets and highways.

Although parking restrictions and roadway use price systems could theoretically be designed to bring about any degree of congestion relief desired, they have provoked intense and overwhelming opposition wherever they have been proposed in this country. Roadway use pricing systems, additionally, are quite difficult in practice to fine-tune.

Similarly, dramatic increases in private commuter ride sharing would significantly relieve congestion, but the types of measures that might generate such changes appear themselves to be politically unfeasible.

Fixed route transit improvements have to date produced little or no congestion relief, even over the short term. Over the long term, moreover, insofar as they stimulate higher density development than might otherwise occur, such improvements are properly charged with part of the responsibility of increased congestion.

Nature of the Problem

It is axiomatic that travel and land use patterns are in large part functions of one another. There is little certainty, however, about the strength of their mutual influence relative to the many other forces that bear upon each, and particularly upon land use. And while there is increasing agreement that policy makers should consider the land use consequences of transportation decisions, there is no consensus on the degree to which they should endeavor to shape development trends or indeed on the directions of development that they should consider desirable.

In short run, the direction of influence is predominantly from land use to travel. That is, trip-making patterns, volumes, and modal distributions are largely a function of the geographic distribution of activities. (That there is room for variation, however, within the framework of a relatively fixed land use pattern was best illustrated during the 1940s—first as gasoline and rubber rationing severely constrained auto use during World War II, then with rapidly increasing auto ownership in the immediate postwar period.) What is more relevant in the present context, however, is that accessibility—both immediate and as estimated over the economic lives of real property investments—is a vital consideration as locational decisions are made. Thus, over time, transportation is a significant factor in shaping land use.

The influence of available transportation technologies, services, and infrastructure patterns upon urban form is most obvious as one takes the very long view. Thus, in cities one hundred years ago, when most travel was on foot, densities were extraordinarily high, commerce and industry were highly centralized, and the radius of settlement rarely extended more than two miles from the core even in the largest urban areas. The development of electrified streetcar and rail rapid transit during the late nineteenth and early twentieth centuries permitted significant decentralization, clustered along the transit lines, and the radius of settlement gradually extended to eight or ten miles in large urban areas. Small numbers of urban residents, utilizing commuter railroads, traveled to work from even greater distances. Settlement continued, however, to be concentrated within walking distance of stations. More recently the coming of the automobile and truck, combined with dramatic improvements in street and highway systems, has permitted a filling in of the spaces between transit lines, a radical deconcentration of commerce and industry along with residential settlement, and a further extension of the settlement radius as large numbers of urban residents have found employment in the suburbs and beyond.[1]

Prior to the 1950s, most commentators on urban issues viewed high densities as a source of social pathology and associated progress with enabling urban dwellers to enjoy less crowded living conditions. During the 1950s, a parallel concern developed about the deterioration of central cities, but few of those who advocated central city renewal addressed the issue of urban form directly. Rather central city officials pressed for renewal assistance as one more distributive program among the many affecting urban areas, most of which continued to facilitate urban sprawl. Over time, as interest developed in metropolitan planning and in achieving improved coordination among the proliferating variety of grant-in-aid programs, the federal government began to require comprehensive analyses of the potential land use impacts of transportation decisions.[1] But federal support for the consideration of land use impacts did not imply any federal preferences among potential land use outcomes. It rather reflected judgments that comprehensive planning was beneficial, that the disparate mix of federal aid programs should be forged into a coherent policy

---

[1.] The key statutory provision requiring analysis of the interrelationships between land use and transportation is section 134(a) of Title 23, U.S. Code, enacted as part of the Federal Aid Highway Act of 1962. Section 134(a) requires that federally aided transportation investments be based on a coordinated, comprehensive, continuing planning process. The term *comprehensive* is defined to include economic factors, population, land use, transportation facilities, travel patterns, terminal and transfer facilities, traffic control, zoning, financial resources, and social and economic value factors. The evolution of regulations pursuant to this requirement, and vigorous enforcement, gathered momentum in the early 1970s; prior to then, many observers judged that the requirement was more window dressing than reality.[2] In recent years it has become a central factor in urban transportation planning, however.[3]

Section 134(a), especially as interpreted in the Federal Highway Administration's Policy and Procedural Memorandum 90-2, remains the basic requirement in federally aided transportation planning. It has been supplemented by numerous provisions in other statutes, however, most notably section 102 of the National Environmental Policy Act of 1969 and section 4(f) of the Department of Transportation Act of 1966, as interpreted by the courts.[4]

for each metropolitan region, and that if this task were to be performed within the context of American federalism, it could be done only by state and local officials acting cooperatively at the metropolitan scale. Stated another way, federal officials hoped that their own piecemeal actions could somehow be transformed into consistent, clearly articulated policies by the state and local officials of each metropolitan area, despite the lack of any strong governmental institutions at the metropolitan scale.[5]

The federal hope that comprehensive metropolitan planning would become a vigorous reality and a major influence on decision making in urban areas has largely been disappointed. What is more significant here, though, is that no clearcut public consensus has yet emerged in any metropolitan area in support of high-density development as a preferred outcome of land use and transportation policy decisions. The region that has probably come closest— and that has achieved a great deal of national publicity for doing so—is Minneapolis-St. Paul, Minnesota. The Metropolitan Council of the Twin Cities region has delineated a Metropolitan Urban Service Area (MUSA) and specified that major investments in urban facilities to 1990 should be confined within this area. The MUSA boundaries leave a great deal of room for continuing urban dispersal, however, and indeed they are defended by the council as a guide to orderly rather than concentrated development. The council's development framework states explicitly that "development should occur in a variety of densities and community forms" to provide as much consumer choice as possible.[6]

If consensus is lacking on the objective of high urban density, this is not to suggest that there is any discernible support for deliberate government action to promote low-density development. Rather there is continuing predominant support in virtually all American regions for letting market forces and consumer preferences—constrained by zoning and environmental regulations, to be sure, but not guided in any more positive planning sense—determine the evolution of urban form. Those who adhere to this view generally argue that transportation investment decisions should strive mainly to accommodate existing and projected travel patterns. They rarely dispute that it is appropriate for transportation policy to serve a variety of other objectives as well—ranging from energy conservation to the successful implementation of local renewal plans. Where they invariably draw the line, however, is at establishing the promotion of higher land use density as a general criterion for the evaluation of transportation alternatives.

Consumer Preferences and Demographic Trends

As Daniel Elazar has noted, Americans have always striven within the constraints imposed by their incomes and by available transportation technologies to combine as much of the rural life-style as possible with their urban occupational roles.[7] They have expressed this preference consistently and clearly both in their behavior as consumers and in their answers as public opinion survey respondents.

A national survey in 1971, for example, found 53 percent of those polled preferring to live in a rural area or small town, 33 percent preferring a small urban center, and only 13 percent preferring a large urban center. Only 2 percent of those who currently lived in rural areas or small towns and 6 percent of those who currently lived in small urban centers wished that they could live in a large urban center. By contrast, 34 percent of those who currently lived in large urban centers wished that they could live in a rural area or small town, and another 26 percent said that they would prefer to live in a small urban center.[8]

William Michaelson reported in 1968 on a similar set of findings with respect to housing type preferences. The Survey Research Center of the University of Michigan surveyed the residents of thirty-two large metropolitan areas. (New York City was left out of the sample as sui generis.) Ninety-five percent of the respondents said that they would prefer living in single-family homes. Those who expressed this preference included two-thirds of all current apartment dwellers, 91 percent of young couples with no children, and 80 percent of older couples with no children. Additionally, 85 percent of the respondents said that they preferred a noncentral location, explaining most frequently that they desired ample outdoor and indoor space and that they disliked noise, confusion, and crowding.[9]

In practice, despite widespread fears that single-family homes have become too expensive for most Americans, the recent trend has been away from multifamily construction.[10] Whereas 44 percent of all private housing starts were multifamily from 1968 to 1973, only 24 percent were multifamily from 1975 through mid-1977, the lowest level since 1961.[2] [11]

Further, the rate of population dispersal sharply accelerated during the first half of the 1970s. The recent trend is not simply for the largest central cities to experience substantial out-migration but for the largest metropolitan areas as a whole to do so. The Census Bureau reported in 1977 that the nation's eight largest metropolitan areas, which had absorbed a net in-migration of 2.4 million people during the 1960s, experienced a net out-migration from 1970 through 1976 of 1.8 million.[12] Overall (including natural increase), the nation's thirty-five metropolitan areas with populations larger than one million grew at only half the national rate (2.5 versus 4.8 percent) from 1970 through 1975, with all of the increase occurring in the sun belt.[3] By contrast, metropolitan areas larger than one million grew more rapidly than the nation as a whole during the 1960s (16.9 versus 13.4 percent).[13] Even more strikingly, whereas the largest metropolitan areas grew four times as rapidly as nonmetropolitan counties during the 1960s (16.9 versus 4.4 percent), they grew only two-fifths as rapidly during the first half of the 1970s (2.5 versus 6.6 percent).

In brief, then, the forces of dispersal—within, between, and from metropolitan areas—appear massively predominant; and they seem to be in harmony with the life-style preferences of the

[2.] These are national figures, excluding mobile homes. The multi-family proportion was considerably lower, of course, during the forties and fifties than at any time since. From 1945 through 1957 it ranged between 5 and 11 percent. Over the following six years it rose to 34 percent, and thereafter never dipped below 33 percent until 1975.

[3.] The fastest growing were Phoenix, Tampa-St. Petersburg, Anaheim, San Diego, Houston, Miami, Denver-Boulder, Atlanta, and San Jose. These nine accounted for 91 percent of total growth among the thirty-five.

Among the nation's thirty-five largest central cities, all but eight declined in population from 1970 to 1975. The entire group, which gained 5.1 percent in population during the 1960s, declined by 4.3 percent from 1970 to 1975. The central cities experiencing growth in the first half of the 1970s were Houston, San Diego, San Antonio, Memphis, Phoenix, Jacksonville, San Jose, and Omaha.[14]

American people. Why, then, should government consider doing battle with these forces?

The Critique of Sprawl

Those who advocate vigorous public efforts to promote higher land use densities tend to argue from a critique of urban sprawl as it has occurred since the end of World War II. The main elements of this critique are as follows:

Urban sprawl entails the prodigal conversion of land from agricultural and other vital life-supporting uses (such as forest and wetland) to urban and transportation uses. Between 1940 and 1969, this conversion process absorbed 23 million acres in the forty-eight mainland states, three times the amount converted during the previous thirty years—raising the total proportion of U.S. land in urban and other built-up areas from 2.0 to 3.2 percent (37 to 60 million acres).[4] [15]

The numbers may appear small as a proportion of total U.S. land area, but if so they are misleading. A great deal of American land is barren and virtually unpopulated. Urban sprawl has consumed some of the most valuable American farmland, along with very precious wetland and forest resources, since World War II.[5] Given the growing value of agricultural production capacity in a hungry world and the nation's growing environmental consciousness, this has been an extremely high price to pay for the luxury of market dominance in the allocation of land.

[4.] These data are from the U.S. Census of Agriculture, which defined urban places as "areas occupied by towns and cities of 1,000 or more population" and "other built-up areas" as including rural road rights-of-way, airport and railroad property, and other public institutional uses.[16]

As of 1969, rural built-up uses accounted for 26 million of the 60 million acres in "urban and other built-up areas." It was not possible on the basis of the published data to break out acreage within urban places that remained in nonurban uses.

[5.] Of the acreage converted in the most recent decade for which data are available, 1959–1969, about 40 percent (3.0 million of 7.3 million acres) had recently been in productive agricultural use.[17]

Though only fragmentary data are available, moreover, the prime culprit in the conversion of farmland appears to be low-density residential sprawl. A 1971 Department of Agriculture survey of ninety-six counties in twelve northeastern states established that 85 percent of their acreage converted from agriculture during the 1950s went for new residences, with an average density of two units per acre. Development at townhouse densities of nine units per acre would have cut the acreage required by three-fourths.[18]

Urban sprawl is wasteful of energy. The two studies cited most frequently in support of this point are by the New York Regional Plan Association (RPA) and the Real Estate Research Corporation (RERC). RPA found that per-capita energy consumption for all purposes combined in the New York region was 32 percent below the national average; consumption in the city itself was 45 percent below average.[6] The RERC study, carried out for the U.S. Council on Environmental Quality and published in 1974 as *The Costs of Sprawl,* was the most elaborate effort yet made to isolate the variable of density from its usual correlates of age, obsolescent design, and low-income population, thereby to measure some of the most important consequences of urban form per se.[20] Its method was to make detailed estimates of the energy, environmental, capital, and operating costs associated with six hypothetical new communities—each containing 10,000 dwelling units, each housing an "average" urban fringe population mix, and each constructed in a "typical" environmental setting. The six communities varied along two dimensions: density (high, medium, low) and community design (optimal, typical). At the extremes were an optimally designed high-density community (19 units per net residential acre) and a "typical" low-density community (3.5 units per acre).[7] *The Costs of Sprawl* concluded that the well-designed high-density community would be optimal with reference to all four key indicators examined, and that the typical low-density community would be least desirable with reference to all four. Its treatment of energy utilization dealt only with residential heating and air conditioning and with automobile usage, but it found with respect to these components of overall consumption that the well-designed high-density community would require up to 44 percent less energy than the typical low-density community.[21]

[6.] Net energy consumption per capita was 255 trillion Btu's nationwide, 172 trillion in the New York region, and 139 trillion in New York City itself. The region as defined by RPA included thirty-one counties and 19.8 million people. Consumption per capita in that portion of the region outside New York City averaged 194 trillion Btu's per capita.[19]

[7.] The high-density community consisted 40 percent of high-rise apartments (30 units per acre), 30 percent of walk-up apartments (15 per acre), 20 percent of townhouse units (10 per acre), and 10 percent of clustered single-family homes (5 per acre). The typical low-density community consisted 75 percent of detached single-family homes (3 per acre) and 25 percent of clustered single-family homes (5 per acre).

Urban sprawl is environmentally harmful. The authors of *The Costs of Sprawl* concluded that the air pollution generated by a residential community was primarily a function of its energy consumption for residential heating and for automobile travel. They judged, consequently, that their well-designed high-density community would generate 45 percent less air pollution than their typical low-density community.[22]

Urban sprawl is economically wasteful. The authors of *The Costs of Sprawl* found that the total capital cost (public and private combined) of their well-designed high-density community would be 44 percent less than that of the typical low-density community. The largest proportionate cost savings in the high-density community were in the development of roads and utilities (55 percent), but the largest absolute saving was in the residential construction itself.[23]

Operating costs varied primarily with the number of people served rather than with density or cummunity design features. Nonetheless the aggregate estimated operating cost of the well-designed high-density community was 11 percent below that of the typical low-density community.[24]

Urban sprawl tends to impose hardship on those without ready access to cars. With declining densities, fewer and fewer locations are accessible on foot or by transit, and reduced transit patronage tends to force the absolute contraction of transit service. RPA has estimated in a recent study of land use density and urban travel demand that, holding all other factors constant, neighborhoods with fifteen dwelling units per acre typically generate about 30 percent fewer auto trips per capita and twice as many transit trips as neighborhoods with five dwelling units per acre. This impact of higher density on urban travel is roughly comparable to that of gasoline and rubber rationing in World War II, which cut urban auto usage by an estimated 25 percent and increased transit patronage (from a much higher base, of course, than that existing today) by about 55 percent.[25] RPA found, moreover, that neighborhood density had less to do with the level of transit usage than the size of the region's downtown employment concentration, the distance of the neighborhood from downtown, the shape of the density gradient (are densities consistently high in the corridor between the neighborhood and downtown?), and the shape of the city (how constrained is motor vehicle access to the core?).[26]

Taken together these findings suggest that a land-use policy aiming to increase transit availability should focus simultaneously on at least three aspects of urban density: the amount and regional share of employment located in the downtown core, the number of residential units per acre in neighborhoods, and the degree of proximity between the core and the neighborhoods. They suggest as well that a policy which effectuated sharp increases in density over time with reference to all three measures might have a very striking impact on urban travel patterns.

Urban sprawl has tended to limit access to employment by the poor, especially the black poor. Conclusive evidence that job dispersion has reduced the employment opportunities of low-income central city residents is unavailable, but the widespread impression that it has seems plausible. To the extent that jobs are distant from low-rent neighborhoods and are accessible only by car, it stands to reason that they will be less obtainable by people who have no cars or unreliable older cars.

Urban sprawl has accentuated class and race segregation. The significant consequences of sprawl include enabling affluent people to live far from poor people, enabling most whites to live far from concentrations on nonwhites, and leaving those local jurisdictions with the greatest responsibility for serving the poor with little wealth (particularly of a residential nature) to tax.

The Defense of Market Dominance

Such, at least in broad outline, is the critique of urban sprawl and of any transportation policy that does not seek to combat it. In responding, the advocates of market dominance generally take off from the premises that most Americans like low-density living and are willing to pay a significant premium for it, and that government intervention to override such preferences can be justified only where their social costs are clearly very high. Continuing, they maintain not that sprawl is costless but that its opponents tend drastically to overstate its costs. Their most significant arguments, which respond directly to the critique outlined above, are as follows:

Fears of a cropland shortage are unwarranted. The estimated cropland loss of 3 million acres during the decade 1959–1969 constituted only half of one percent of total U.S. acreage deemed suitable for cultivation. As of 1973, moreover, only 401 million of the 631 million acres deemed suitable for cropland use were actually in cultivation. In practice, the amount of acreage in cropland use is primarily responsive to price and policy incentives rather than to any current or potential shortage of land. Thus, as George E. Peterson and Harvey Yampolsky of the Urban Institute have recently commented, "Between 1972 and 1973, . . . more than twenty-eight million acres (or almost a full century of retirements for urban use at recent conversion rates) were added to cropland use as a result of higher farm product prices and the elimination of federal payments for keeping land out of production."[27]

Low-density urban development does absorb more land than high-density development, but the advocates of high density typically exaggerate both the magnitude and ecological significance of the difference. Low-density need not entail chaotic sprawl. The Twin Cities Development Framework, cited previously, provides an excellent illustration of a plan designed to prevent the needless expansion of urban uses into what are at present rural areas without mandating high residential densities. The primary objective of the development framework, one that commands wide public support in the Twin Cities region, is to economize on public infrastructure and service requirements of a regional nature (such as highway, transit, and trunk sewer connections). Secondarily, it aims to prevent the absorption of rural land while large amounts of usable land remain undeveloped within the Metropolitan Urban Service Area. But it carefully skirts the question of the densities at which Twin Cities residents should live and work. In short, the term *sprawl* denotes both disorderly and low-density development, and one may quite reasonably oppose the former alone.

Low-density residential development tends, moreover, to leave most land in open space uses—for lawns, gardens, trees, and children's play areas. Though not available in normal times for agricultural production, this open space does serve other key environ-mental values (such as water runoff, oxygen production, and recreation).[8] Nor should it be forgotten that in periods of acute need such land can be drawn quickly into agricultural production. A 1951 British study (conducted during the final phase of postwar austerity) found that in typical London neighborhoods, with twelve dwelling units per residential acre, the market value of food production per residential acre (in domestic gardens) averaged 94 percent of that on typical British farm land. Though comparable data for the World War II period were unavailable, the fragmen-tary data that did exist indicated that food production in domestic gardens had then been substantially higher.[29] The 1951 result was achieved with only 14 percent of residential acreage being used for food cultivation. It was possible because the gardens were cultivated with an intensity that could not be justified in commer-cial agriculture.

Finally it bears repetition that the rate of urban population growth has slowed dramatically in recent years, and that virtually all current urban growth is occurring in low-density regions that seem irretrievably committed to auto dominance. The first of these trends suggests that the rate of land conversion to urban uses has probably been much slower in the 1970s than in the previous three decades. The second suggests that there is only a negligible prospect of altering the postwar pattern of gearing new urban development to the requirements of auto accessibility. Insofar as this prognosis is accurate, increases in the average density of new residential construction will have disproportionately small effects on the total amount of land required for any given increment of urban population. New commercial developments, for example, will still be arranged in the suburban pattern—along major roads,

[8.] Auto dominance has probably entailed a significant reduction, parenthetically, in the proportion of urban land devoted to transportation rights-of-way. Before the automo-bile, as it was extremely inconvenient to walk around large blocks, many streets were needed. Karl Moskowitz has reported that the portions of Sacramento, California, laid out originally in 1850 devoted 38 percent of total land area to streets and sidewalks. The portions laid out between 1900 and 1930 devoted 21 percent to these purposes, and those laid out after World War II devoted 15 percent to them.[28] This calculation does not address the question of land usage per capita for transportation purposes, nor does it include the impact of the automobile on land required off-street for parking, but it does serve to refute a common misconception.

with ample parking space, in low-rise buildings. Only if large numbers of people could be induced to live at densities similar to those in the older central cities (fifty per residential acre and up) would this be likely to change significantly.

Most of the alleged evidence that high densities entail large energy savings disolves upon close examination. The New York Regional Plan Association (RPA), it will be recalled, found that per-capita energy usage in the New York region as of 1970 was 32 percent below the national average. Jumping to the obvious conclusion (which quickly became general among those aware of the RPA study), the *New York Times* headlined its front-page story on the report, "Metropolitan Area Relatively Efficient in Its Use of Energy."[30] In fact, however, nine-tenths of the New York advantage was attributable to the fact that energy-intensive industries were virtually absent from the region. Its per-capita energy usage for industrial purposes was 82 percent below the national average. Eliminating industrial consumption from the equation, energy usage per capita in the region was only 5 percent below the national average.[31]

The remaining New York advantage was in the transportation sector. On a regionwide basis, its per-capita energy consumption for transportation purposes was 29 percent below the national average. (In New York City alone transportation energy usage was 53 percent below the national level; in the rest of the region it was 13 percent below.)[32]

Residential energy usage, on the other hand, was 16 percent above the national average. The reasons for this were unclear, but comparisons within the region provided little support for the view that high residential densities and low residential energy usage inevitably go together. On a per-capita basis, residential energy usage in New York City itself was only 3 percent lower than in the remainder of the region. On a residential floorspace basis, Manhattan ranked tenth in energy efficiency among the thirty-one counties in the region. The most efficient county by this measure, paradoxically, was exurban Sullivan, which also had the lowest population density of any county in the region. (See table 10.1.)

TABLE 10.1
Residential Energy Consumption in the New York Region, 1970

County	Gross Population Density (Pers./Sq. Mi.)	Residential Energy Usage (Thousand Btu per Sq. Ft. of Floor Space)	Efficiency Ranking in Order of Increasing Energy Intensiveness
Manhattan	69,965	138	10
Brooklyn	37,531	176	23
Bronx	35,066	134	8
Queens	18,293	191	26
Hudson	13,479	115	4
Essex	7,291	135	9
Union	5,273	144	11
Richmond	5,120	200	29
Nassau	4,790	229	31
Bergen	3,845	158	20
Passaic	2,467	148	14
Westchester	2,058	206	30
Middlesex	1,866	150	17
Mercer	1,336	146	12
Rockland	1,288	191	26
Suffolk	1,256	192	28
Fairfield	1,253	182	25
New Haven	1,224	179	24
Monmouth	969	146	12
Morris	820	153	18
Somerset	646	148	14
Ocean	326	122	7
Dutchess	272	148	14
Orange	267	153	18
Putnam	241	118	5
Warren	205	112	3
Hunterdon	160	119	6
Litchfield	153	165	21
Sussex	147	107	2
Ulster	124	167	22
Sullivan	53	83	1

Source: Regional Plan Association and Resources for the Future, *Regional Energy Consumption: Second Interim Report* (New York: Regional Plan Association, 1974), p. 9.

Finally, commercial and public facility energy usage per capita in the New York region exceeded the national average by 24 percent. This may simply have reflected New York's preeminence as a commercial center, but doubt is cast on this interpretation by the fact that usage per capita was considerably lower in the city than the suburban portions of the region. Even in New York City itself, however, energy consumption for commercial and public purposes was 11 percent above the national average.[33]

Similarly the energy savings attributed by *The Costs of Sprawl* to high density require substantial qualification. First, the aspects of energy consumption that it examined—residential space heating and air conditioning plus automobile travel within the residential community itself—account for only about one-fifth of total urban energy consumption.[34]

Second, its claim of a 41 percent saving in energy usage for space heating and air conditioning rested primarily on the fact that it postulated different indoor space standards for the several types of dwelling units, and hence for the several types of communities, it compared. At the extremes, it assumed that single-family households would require 1,600 square feet of indoor living space whereas households occupying high-rise apartments would require only 900 square feet. Overall the high-density community had 34 percent less residential floor space than the low-density community, and this accounted for five-sixths of the claimed energy saving.[35]

Third, *The Costs of Sprawl* credited the high-density community with requiring 49 percent less energy for travel purposes than the low density community. This claim was based on a simple error of calculation, however. The text of the report noted correctly that the opportunities for travel saving were confined to convenience shopping, school, and other trips of a very local nature. In the calculations, however, credit was taken for a reduction in all types of travel. Thus the report estimated that the average household in the high-density community would travel only 9,900 miles per year, whereas the average household in the low-density community would travel 19,700 miles per year.[36] Precise data are unavailable, but it seems reasonable to assume that, at most, 20 percent of annual household auto mileage is for intraneighborhood travel. If one utilizes the 20 percent assumption, four-fifths of the claimed saving in automobile energy consumption for the high-density pattern evaporates.

Fourth, the report stated that high density would facilitate the substitution of mass transit for some automobile travel. It apparently took credit for the saving in auto fuel consumption, but it failed to provide any estimate of mass transit fuel requirements. (We are unable to calculate the precise impact of this oversight because the report did not include any specific estimate of modal shift or transit vehicle mileage.)

If one holds dwelling unit size constant and allows only 20 percent of the claimed auto travel saving (but still levies no charge for mass transit energy usage), the energy demand differential between the well-designed high-density community and the typical low-density community shrinks from 44 percent to 14 percent. If one compares the well-designed high-density community with the report's well-designed low-density community, moreover, the differential narrows to 6 percent.[37]

These percentages, moreover, are relative to the share of total energy consumption accounted for by the uses under consideration, roughly one-fifth. In short, the estimated saving in total urban energy consumtion attributable to the shift from low-density sprawl to optimally designed high density is about 3 percent, and that attributable to the density factor alone is about 1 percent. Considering that the postulated increase in residential density needed to achieve this 1 percent saving is 443 percent (3.5 to 19 units per acre) and that the actual impact of any regionwide or national policy to promote density would surely be far more modest, the conclusion would seem to follow that the promotion of high residential density is a relatively unpromising source of energy savings. This conclusion might require modification it if could be shown that increases in residential density would have dramatic multiplier effects with reference to other aspects of urban land use and energy consumption. But the authors of *The Costs of Sprawl* made no effort to estimate such effects.

The estimates in *The Costs of Sprawl* of air pollution reductions attributable to high density were direct functions of the energy saving estimates and hence must be deflated in similar degree. Moreover the harmful effects of air pollution are a function of concentration and human exposure rather than of emissions per capita. Thus even as the authors of *The Costs of Sprawl* claimed that an area developed at 30 units per net residential acre (10 per gross acre) would generate only half the emissions per capita of an area developed at 3 units per net residential acre (2 per gross acre), they were compelled to note that air pollution per acre—which is to say, pollution exposure per capita—would be more than twice as great in the high-density community.[9] [38]

The residential construction cost and community service economies claimed in The Costs of Sprawl *as benefits of high density were mainly attributable to dubious assumptions employed by the authors.* They estimated, for example, that the capital cost of constructing each dwelling unit would be only half as great in the high-density as in the low-density community ($16,000 versus $32,000); but two-thirds of the saving was attributable to their premise that the high-density community would have 34 percent less floor area. Most of the remaining advantage it enjoyed was attributable to its walk-up apartment and townhouse rather than to its high-rise apartment elements. The report found that walk-up apartments would cost 40 percent less per square foot to build than single-family homes, townhouses 32 percent less, and high-rise apartment units 12 percent less.

Turning to public facility costs, evaluation becomes more speculative because the authors neglected to calibrate the results of their prototype analysis against the experience of actual communities. They estimated, however, that the high-density community would require public facility capital investments one-third smaller than the low-density community ($11,000 versus $16,500 per dwelling unit), and annual operating expenditures 11 percent lower ($1,870 versus $2,110).[39]

In arriving at these estimates, the authors simply ignored the

[9]. Though noted in the *Detailed Cost Analysis* volume of *The Costs of Sprawl*, this point was omitted from the *Executive Summary* volume and we have never seen reference to it in documents citing *The Costs of Sprawl* as a source, indeed as *the* authoritative source, on the subject of density and air pollution.

long-standing controversy about whether, and the extent to which, density affects the level of resident demand for public services. They merely postulated, in order to simplify the task of cost estimation, that the impact was nil. Other analysts have judged on the basis of data from actual communities, however, that the residents of high-density communities do seem to require and/or demand more expensive packages of community services than those who live at low densities. Thomas Muller has recently published an excellent brief survey of this literature, concluding that while the causes are not fully understood density appears on balance to be a force for higher public expenditures.[40]

Key reasons for the typical correlation of high density with high expenditure levels in actual communities, even when age and population mix are held constant, appear to be as follows. Residents of low-density communities are frequently contented without sidewalks, with utility lines above rather than below ground, and with street lights only on main thoroughfares. They may be satisfied as well with less professional fire protection because fires are less prone to spread where structural densities are low. With less shared community space, they are likely to require fewer paid maintenance services. Thoroughly committed to auto reliance, they are prone to resist high levels of spending for mass transit. Less dependent generally on public services than the residents of high-density communities, they tend to be more supportive of officials who stand firm in dealings with public employee unions, even taking strikes on occasion; the results are likely to include less union dominance in labor-management relations and lower unit costs of public services.

Even within the framework of its own assumptions, however, the analysis of community service operating costs in *The Costs of Sprawl* contained numerous surprising omissions. Although it assumed, for example, that residents of the high-density community would make substantially greater use of public transit than residents of the low-density community, it did not include any estimate of mass transit expenditures. Although it estimated that the high-density community would have two and one-half times as much vacant land as the low-density community—65

percent of total land area versus 24 percent—it neglected to estimate any expenditures for policing and maintaining this additional
acreage.[41] And although high-rise apartment buildings normally
require paid staffs to provide security and tend their shared spaces
(hallways, lobbies, elevators, and so on), it omitted any estimates
of the cost of such personnel.

In brief, then, while there are some potential economies associated with higher residential densities, the likely savings in residential construction cost are clearly much smaller than estimated in
The Costs of Sprawl (except as residents are induced to accept
floor space reductions), and all of the projected community
service economies hinge on the dubious assumption that residents
of high- and low-density communities would make the same
service demands.

*While it is true that low-density development entails some hard-
ship for those without ready access to cars, it scarcely follows
that the majority should be compelled to adopt a life-style intended for the convenience of the minority.* It would seem more
reasonable to ask the majority to take specific steps to alleviate
specific hardships (for example, to subsidize improved transit services for the mobility disadvantaged) than to urge reorganization
of the entire pattern of urban settlement.

Further, no policy aimed at increasing residential densities
would be likely to produce major benefits for those without cars.
High-density new construction would, in all probability, consist
mainly of townhouses and garden apartments with substantial
parking and open space around them, rather than of high-rise concentrations with densities of 10,000 to 20,000 per square mile.
The residents of such new developments would continue to rely
overwhelmingly on the automobile for their mobility—in part because aggregate neighborhood densities would continue to be fairly
low, but even more significantly because the forces that have made
for dispersal of their employment, recreational, and other destinations would continue to operate, and because each year's increment to the urban area would be scarcely noticeable. (This projection is most likely to be realized insofar as the developments in
question are financed in the private marketplace and must therefore be marketed to relatively affluent people.)

It is far from certain that urban sprawl has adversely affected the employment opportunities of the central city poor. Bennett Harrison has made a careful study of the hypothesis that it has, and found it contrary to the evidence. He notes, first, that the rate of population and job dispersion from the central cities has been relatively constant since the late nineteenth century. It slowed during the Depression and World War II and then accelerated for a time right after World War II, but it has otherwise been remarkable for its consistency. Second, he finds that population has been leaving the central cities much more rapidly than jobs, including jobs with low skill requirements. In a sample of eight large central cities, for example, the ratio of jobs to population increased from 0.45 to 0.50 between 1960 and 1967.[42] Other things being equal, this trend should have translated into an improvement in the job opportunities of central city residents.

The question that remains is why central city unemployment rates are in fact so high relative to the rates experienced elsewhere. Harrison himself concludes (but does not demonstrate) that the answer lies in racial discrimination. Others would contend that his figures on job-population ratios are misleading because they fail to take account of the growing ease of auto commutation from the suburbs to central city jobs or to specify the nature of the jobs available in central cities. Still others would maintain that the primary cause of high unemployment in central cities lies in the socialization patterns of many central city neighborhoods (reinforced by the economic incentives associated with welfare programs and illicit slum businesses), which render large numbers of people unwilling to take the low-paying jobs for which their skills fit them and so disruptive or unreliable when they do obtain jobs that employers quickly fire them.

Even if one assumes, however, that high unemployment rates among the central city poor are due in significant part to urban dispersal, it seems doubtful that any conceivable programs to increase urban densities would do much to alleviate them. The forces making for dispersal are so powerful, and the programs would almost surely be so modest, that at best the results would be some curbing of leapfrog development and some minor increases in the density levels of new suburban construction. The likelihood that such programs would substantially affect the level of investment or the number of jobs available in central city core areas would appear to be extremely small.

This serves to highlight a related point. *Although government highway, housing, and tax policies favorable to motor vehicle dominance and single-family residential development have doubtless increased the rate of urban land absorption in the postwar period, it seems unlikely that they have greatly affected the rate of departure from central cities.* Harrison's data indicating that the rate of dispersion has been relatively constant for almost a hundred years, taken together with more general analyses of consumer motives in leaving central cities, suggests that even without these policies the pace of suburbanization would probably have been about what it has been, though it would have occurred in somewhat more compact fashion. Absolute physical distances between the classes and races would probably be less had these policies not been implemented, but there is little reason to believe that psychological, economic, and political distances would be any less.

In brief, then, the charge that low-density urban development entails excessive energy, environmental, economic, and social costs remains the subject of heated controversy. The consequence in the public arena, with rare and localized exceptions, has been avoidance of the issue. In the field of transportation, this has meant a predominant orientation toward serving land development and travel behavior trends rather than trying to shape them. In serving these trends, of course, transportation programs have unavoidably facilitated them. The question remains, however: How much leverage with respect to land use outcomes can transportation policy provide in the future, now that the American people have made such a massive commitment to low-density, auto-reliant land use patterns and life-styles?

Innovations[10]

Though it is apparent that major changes in urban transportation

[10.] Each of the previous five chapters, focused like this one on a "problem" of urban

technologies and infrastructure patterns have in previous generations played highly significant roles in the evolution of urban
form, there is far less certainty about the potential of transportation policy as an instrument for shaping land use in the contemporary urban environment. The primary sources of doubt are as
follows.

First, the transportation changes that have most affected land
use to date have all entailed technological improvements that offered consumers and businesses greater locational flexibility than
they had previously enjoyed. No successors to the automobile and
truck that offer enhanced mobility appear to be on the horizon,
however; and indeed most current proposals for change would
constrain mobility by rendering motor vehicle travel more expensive and/or by shifting significant amounts of personal travel from
the auto-driver to slower and less flexible modes (ranging from organized carpooling to fixed guideway transit).

Second, there is at present in nearly all U.S. urban areas an extraordinary amount of street and highway capacity relative to current or foreseeable demand. To be sure, there is congestion during
peak hours, particularly on the main arteries carrying commuters
to and from downtowns; but there are also enormous amounts of
highly accessible land in suburban and exurban areas. The increments in transportation capacity conceivable in most urban areas
over the next several decades, moreover, will be quite marginal.
They may indeed increase the attractiveness of specific locations,
particularly for shopping center and high-rise development, but
they are unlikely to influence the overall density pattern.

Third, central area employment, the main generator of peak
period congestion, tends to be static or declining—and this is particularly so in the older metropolitan areas that have both the
worst congestion and the most heavily patronized transit systems.
Thus failure to expand transportation capacity on the approaches
to core areas will not bring about dramatic increases in congestion,

transportation, contains a section on goals. This chapter does not, because we have been
unable to identify national goals, or even major public debates about what they might
be, with respect to urban form. Public controversy to date has focused on general calls
for stronger land use regulation and for better planning rather than on substantive goal
proposals.[43]

at least not unless there are further large shifts among downtown commuters from transit to automobiles.

Important questions remain, however. What about those few urban areas that may be able to implement massive projects, such as new rapid transit systems? May they reasonably hope to alter development trends significantly? Suppose the nation chooses to conserve energy by adopting gas rationing or by steeply increasing the gas tax? Of the innovations under consideration in this volume, these appear to be the only ones that might plausibly be thought to have significant potential as shapers of urban form. Thus, let us turn now to an examination of the available evidence on their likely impacts.

Rapid Transit

By facilitating long-distance commutation, major transit service improvements have tended historically to be forces for urban dispersal. At the same time, they have played a central role in the servicing of central business districts and they have induced high-density clustering around some stations. In estimating the precise nature as well as magnitude of impact that any new rapid transit system (or extension) would have, it is essential to consider the following: what reasons there are to believe that improved transit access would induce significant numbers of employers who might otherwise locate elsewhere to opt for the core, whether zoning policies would tend to reinforce or counteract the transit potential for generating high density clusters adjacent to stations (outlying as well as downtown), and whether the specific configuration of the proposed system is such that it might facilitate still longer distance commuting by core area employees.

As recognition has grown among urban transportation professionals in recent years that transit improvements are unlikely to save much energy, to yield substantial air quality benefits, or to relieve congestion noticeably, advocates of new rapid transit systems have placed increasing emphasis on their potential roles as instruments of "central city revitalization."[11] [44] In support of

[11.] There is no support among reputable economists for the view that surface transportation improvements can attract development to a metropolitan region that would

the view that transit can be a major catalyst for central city renewal, advocates of rapid transit investment have pointed mainly
to historical studies of land use effects during the first great era of
rapid transit construction (pre-1920) and to the apparent postwar
successes of new rapid transit lines in Toronto, Philadelphia, and
San Francisco as generators of property value increases and new
construction.[12]

The consulting firm of De Leuw, Cather & Co. has recently carried out a review of available evidence on rapid transit land use
effects for the U.S. Department of Transportation.[47] Its conclusions may be summarized as follows:

• Historical studies of New York, Chicago, and Boston indicate
that rapid transit often had major effects on the location of residential development prior to 1920. The effects appear to have
been greatest where population growth was extremely rapid, economic conditions were favorable to new housing investment, and
the lines extended into open land.

• The documented effects of rapid transit were all of a decentralizing, density-reducing nature and had to do with residential

not otherwise have occurred there. Transit advocates nonetheless frequently make such
claims. The official "Composite Report," for example, which was widely distributed to
San Francisco Bay Area voters during the 1962 BART referendum campaign, anticipated
that the rapid transit system would enable the region to "attract a larger share of the
nation's future growth."[45] Following an extensive search for evidence that might support this claim, two key economic consultants to the federally financed BART Impact
Program have recently concluded:

There is no evidence from this research that any industry moved to the Bay Area because
BART or BART's service influenced the corporate decision-making process. There is no
evidence of even the perception that BART improved the economic viability of the region, or the efficiency with which the region's resources could be utilized.

These findings suggest that the level of transportation service which is considered
essential to economic viability has been reached with the combined resources for intraurban travel provided by existing highways and transit networks. . . . Rapid transit, if
introduced to a region, may have impacts on the locational decisions of business, commerce, or industry *within* the region. But these impacts. . . do not bear on the competitive advantage of the region itself in gaining a larger share of the nation's future
growth. . . . [In effect, they] represent shifting piles of sand within a region.[46]

[12.] New rapid transit systems have also been developed or are currently being built in
Montreal, the District of Columbia, Atlanta, and Baltimore; and the Urban Mass Transportation Administration has given preliminary federal aid approvals for new starts in
Miami, Buffalo, and Detroit. Careful studies of land use effects in these areas are as yet
unavailable, however.

development. None of the evidence deals with rapid transit effects on commercial or industrial location.

• None of the conditions that enabled transit to have massive impacts on land use prior to 1920 currently exist, and no such impacts since 1920 have been persuasively documented. The most notable change, of course, is that the automobile has become ubiquitous since 1920. Additionally urban work places are today highly dispersed and the pace of metropolitan growth has slowed dramatically.

• The popular view of the Toronto experience is based on two factors: rapid growth along the route of its initial (Yonge Street) subway line in the decade after that line opened in 1955, and undocumented assertions by several enthusiasts that the development occurred almost entirely because of the subway. The leading publicist of this viewpoint claimed indeed that by 1964 the line had generated enough new tax revenue to cover its annual amortization charges.[48]

More careful studies have shown that property values did increase more rapidly along the Yonge Street route in its first decade than elsewhere in the city of Toronto (slightly more than twice as fast during the decade 1954-1964), but none have shown that the line attracted any development to the city—let alone to the region—that would not otherwise have occurred there. Nor have any shown that it affected the mix or density of new housing constructed in the city during this period.

Two more recent studies have sought respectively to measure the effects on property values of an extension opened subsequent to the initial Yonge Street line and of the entire system during the period 1965-1972. The first found a very minor increase in relative property values near the extension in question. The latter found no impact of the system whatever during the 1965-1972 period.[49]

• All studies of the Philadelphia Lindenwold line (opened in 1969), which merely added to an extensive preexisting rail network in the Philadelphia region, agree that it has had no discernible effect on the downtown area and that it had a small one-time positive effect on property values elsewhere along the route. [50] Individual studies have concluded in addition that the gross magnitude of the property value impact along the route was in the range of $33–51 million, that this increase was probably at the expense of other corridors in the same sector of the metropolitan region, and that the line may have pulled some office functions out of downtown Camden, which was already declining, to other locations in the vicinity of stations.[51] None of the studies, apparently, have considered whether the line affected the mix and density of new construction, as opposed to its precise location.

• Studies of the San Francisco BART system have indicated that it was one among a number of significant factors—whose individual contributions cannot be disaggregated—helping to fuel that area's downtown office construction boom during the 1960s and early 1970s, and that its effects on suburban property values have ranged from small to invisible.[52]

In summary, then, the De Leuw, Cather review suggests that the clearest impacts of recent rapid transit construction have been with respect to the precise locations of new development within the sectors of regions containing the transit corridors (for example, the New Jersey portion of the Philadelphia region); that evidence is lacking as to whether rapid transit lines have affected the mix and density of that development; and that serious claims to the effect that rapid transit has strengthened the core vis-à-vis the suburbs are based entirely on the case of San Francisco.

Two more detailed analyses of the land use impacts of BART— one by Melvin M. Webber, the other by Michael V. Dyett and Emilio Escudero—have recently concluded that BART has not had any discernible effect on the distribution of employment among subareas within the San Francisco region.[53] The three counties served by BART (of nine in the region) accounted for 64 percent of regional employment in 1960 but for only 53 percent in 1975. Between 1965 and 1975, the BART counties experienced a 13 percent growth in employment, by comparison with 49 percent growth in the remainder of the region. Even within the three counties there was no evidence of BART impact. Employment growth during the decade was 13 percent both in the BART corridor and in the remainder of the three-county area.[54]

How do these findings square with the fact that a remarkable downtown building boom occurred in the wake of the decision to construct BART? From 1964 through 1975, thirty-five high-rise office buildings with 18.5 million square feet of floor space were completed in the San Francisco CBD, and another seventeen buildings (10.0 million square feet) were scheduled for completion by 1981.[55] Webber, Dyett, and Escudero discount BART as a major cause of this boom. The San Francisco core, they note, was in the midst of a building boom even prior to the BART referendum (1962), and the city as a whole continued to decline relatively as an employment center even in the postreferendum period. From 1965 to 1975, indeed, it ranked last among the nine Bay Area counties in employment growth, and its rate of increase was only one-fifth that of the rest of the region: 6.7 percent versus 34.1 percent.[56] Dyett and Escudero add that even by the single measure of office construction and rehabilitation, BART has failed to have a discernible impact:

According to building permit data, neither San Francisco nor Oakland have increased their share of regional office construction during any portion of the BART period. Informants identified four office buildings which might have located in a different part of the Bay Area except for BART, but none were in San Francisco. Two were in Oakland and two were in Richmond, indicating that whatever small redistribution might be BART-induced has reinforced older cities other than San Francisco.[57]

Webber points out that whereas BART officials now like to claim credit for the San Francisco office boom, the original advocates of BART maintained that it was needed to accommodate forecasts of major downtown office employment growth. Downtown San Francisco, as an extremely attractive headquarters center within one of the fastest-growing regions in the nation, had been booming since early in the postwar period. Moreover, during the period 1964–1975, a number of other downtowns in the West, Midwest, and Southwest enjoyed office construction booms comparable to that of San Francisco, even though they did not build new rapid transit systems. Whereas San Francisco added 4,200 square feet of high-rise office space per thousand population in its metropolitan area, Houston added 5,500, Chicago 4,500, and Dallas 3,500; and Phoenix, Denver, and Seattle all experienced growth in the range of 3,000 square feet per thousand population.[58]

Webber concludes that the San Francisco office boom was a product of multiple factors, and that it is impossible to sort out BART's specific contribution. What one can say, he writes, is that the basic prerequisite was the city's powerful, preexisting attraction (as part of a larger, even more booming, region) in the private marketplace and that some transportation improvements were doubtless necessary if the full market potential for growth were to be realized. Did it matter significantly that the Bay Area chose to make these transportation improvements in the form of BART— rather than, for example, by expanding bus services, by implementing preferential bus treatments on its streets and highways, and/or by otherwise improving its road system. Webber sees no evidence that, apart possibly from the promotional effect of BART, it did.[59]

Stated another way, Webber views BART as a transport investment in the classic mold, designed essentially to accommodate market forces rather than to reshape them, and to do so by heavy infrastructure investment rather than by improving the utilization of existing infrastructure. This interpretation leaves room for a finding that BART, as a symbol of public commitment and as one among several available options for improving access to the core, further strengthened the preexisting market forces. But it suggests as well that the strengthening effect might have been achieved at less expense by other means, and that the San Francisco experience provides no support for those who would use rapid transit as a primary technique for the "revitalization" of core areas that are currently stagnant or declining.[13]

[13.] For analytic purposes the federally sponsored BART Impact Program has hypothesized a No-BART Alternative (NBA), which entails the bus service improvements deemed likely to have evolved had the decision to construct BART not been made in 1962. The capital cost of the NBA involved only fifteen buses over and above those actually in ser-

If BART has failed to stem the overall tide of land use dispersal in the Bay Area, it does appear to have encouraged a clustering of development along the BART corridor within downtown San Francisco. Dyett and Escudero write:

San Francisco's business district has experienced a definite redirection of office building to Market Street (location of the BART line) and south of Market area. This redirection, while coincident with BART's development, was not directly caused by BART in the sense that it would not have occurred if BART had not been built. Nevertheless, BART was cited as one of several factors influencing timing and location—but not density—decisions on seven major projects, representing about 10 percent of total office space built or under construction in San Francisco since 1965. Apart from BART's *direct* influence, approval of the 1962 BART bond issue helped to promote the Market Street [urban renewal] Project, which in turn attracted new office development to Market Street.[61]

Outside of downtown San Francisco, however, the clustering effects have been meager. Webber writes that "most suburban stations stand in virtual isolation from urban development activity in their subregions, seemingly ignored by all except commuters who park their cars in BART's extensive lots. A few apartment buildings have been built within one-mile radii of a few stations . . . [and] two modest-sized office buildings were erected, in Berkeley and Walnut Creek, close to the stations. . . . In general, however, the transit stations have not attracted higher density suburban developments."[62] He adds that in a few places suburban zoning regulations have been changed in order to prevent commercial and/or high-density construction near stations. (Similar suburban resistance has materialized in other regions developing or extending rapid transit lines during the 1970s as well, and as zoning is everywhere a local government function, federal and regional

vice during the mid-1970s. (Half of BART's patrons, accounting for 8 percent of region-wide transit patronage, would presumably have been lost to transit in the absence of BART.) Most of the patrons thereby shifted to buses would have been utilizing the transbay route, which has remained profitable for its operator, AC Transit, despite the competition of BART. Overall, therefore, it is estimated that the NBA would have reduced the taxes required for bus transit subsidization, even as it wholly averted the need for taxes to cover the debt service and operating subsidy requirements of BART.[60]

transit officials have been powerless to do anything about it.)

If San Francisco was prospering well before the decision to construct rapid transit, Detroit seems likely to provide an acid test of the urban revitalization thesis. The population of the city of Detroit dropped by nearly one-third (1.85 to 1.27 million) from 1950 to 1977. Whereas the rate of loss from 1950 to 1970, moreover, was about 1 percent a year, the rate from 1970 to 1976 was about 2.5 percent a year.[63] From 1970 through 1976, as employment in the Detroit suburbs grew by more than 150,000 jobs, central city employment declined by 55,000.[64] Whereas motor vehicle access to downtown San Francisco is severely constrained, moreover, Detroit has one of the most elaborate freeway networks in the country; and whereas 15 percent of Bay Area residents commuted to work by transit in 1970 (prior to the opening of BART), only 8 percent of Detroit area residents did so.

In approving an initial federal commitment of $600 million toward the cost of the proposed Detroit rapid transit system in October 1976, U.S. Secretary of Transportation William Coleman emphasized that the primary objective would be central city revitalization. Indeed he stipulated that the federal commitment was contingent upon the receipt of private sector commitments of equal magnitude to undertake new office, commercial, and residential development in the city.[14] [65]

Subsequent to the secretary's announcement the Urban Mass Transportation Administration granted funds to the city of Detroit for a study of the potential economic impacts of alternative rapid transit configurations. Reporting in March 1977, the city's consultant made the following estimates:

1. The most favorable rapid transit configuration—a two-corridor rapid transit system wholly within the city—would, over the fourteen year period 1977–1990, generate a 22 percent increase ($1.05 billion at 1977 prices) in the amount of investment projected for the city if transit service remained unchanged. In the categories

14. He did not specify, however, that the private sector commitments had to be for investments that would not otherwise have occurred in the city; nor did he specify a time frame; nor did he say that the investments had to be along the transit route. The city's economic consultant subsequently estimated that, even in the absence of any transit improvements, private sector investment in the three development categories mentioned by the secretary would total $1.2 billion between 1977 and 1990.[66]

specified by Secretary Coleman, the projected increase was 70 percent ($0.85 billion).[15] All of this development would be attracted
from Detroit's own suburbs—something of a political problem in
view of the need for regionwide financing of the rapid transit
system.[67]

2. To the extent that suburban transit service was improved along
with that inside the central city, the development impact within
the city would be diminished.[68]

3. The projected development effects were contingent upon the
transit service improvements being on fixed guideway. Even an
express bus system, supplemented by an extended (four-mile)
downtown people-mover on fixed guideway, would draw only
one-fifth as much private investment into the city as would the
rapid transit system.

These estimates, although presented in detailed quantitative
form (107 tables), were entirely judgmental. And while the consultant's judgments were informed by discussions with local public
officials and developers, they do not appear to have been based on
any systematic review of experience elsewhere. Thus the Detroit
report merits little credence as an indication of what would in fact
happen if one or another of the transit options examined were in
fact implemented. The Coleman decision and this report taken together, however, are of great interest as illustrative (a) of current
public rhetoric with respect to the potential of rapid transit as an
instrument of central city revitalization and (b) of the study procedures typically relied upon by federal, state, and local officials
to justify large-scale investments with which they are anxious to
proceed. The Detroit consultant study, moreover, was superior to
the vast majority of those in UMTA's files.

What, then, can be said by way of summary about the potential
of rapid transit as a shaper of land use in the contemporary urban
environment? The evidence seems clear that, in a growth environ-

[15.] Of the investment dollars drawn into the city by rapid transit, 42 percent were projected to be for housing, 28 percent for hotel and retail uses, 17 percent for industrial
uses, and 12 percent for offices. The lion's share of total investment, with or without
rapid transit, was projected to be industrial—74 percent if no transit improvements
occurred, 64 percent of the larger total if rapid transit configured optimally from the
city's standpoint were implemented.

ment, rapid transit can induce significant clustering of new development in the vicinity of downtown stations. On the basis of the San Francisco experience, moreover, a plausible case (but no more) can be made that, whether other factors are conducive to downtown growth, rapid transit can provide a modest additional fillip. There is no evidence otherwise, however, that rapid transit can affect the distribution of investment among sectors of regions—let alone among regions themselves—and even clustering effects within sectors appear generally to be negligible outside of CBDs.

If the land use effects of rapid transit seem remarkably weak, the reason is largely, it may be argued, that American policy makers have failed to accompany rapid transit expenditures with strong land use and travel regulatory measures to bring about high levels of usage. There is a good deal to be said for this view, and it highlights an even more critical point: that rapid transit construction makes sense in the current period only as an accompaniment of far more powerful instruments for shaping land use (zoning, property taxation, and so forth). If policy makers were prepared to implement broad strategies for the achievement of very high density urban development, rapid transit might indeed play an effective supportive role. To say that high-density urbanization requires high capacity (though not necessarily fixed guideway) transit is far from saying, however, that high capacity transit can do much by itself to bring about high-density urbanization.

Other Measures

While the predominant effects of major postwar highway investment have doubtless been of a decentralizing nature, it is essential to ask about specific proposed highway investments to which sectors of the region they would provide improved accessibility. As Gary T. Schwartz has noted, central city officials demanded radial and inner circumferential expressways during congressional consideration of the interstate program—and they were probably quite right (in terms of their economic development objectives) to do so. [69] They reasonably believed, after all, that suburban freeway construction would go forward regardless. It bears repetition in this context that most of the rapidly growing downtowns in recent years have been in highly motorized regions of the Sun Belt; it seems highly doubtful that they would have done as well if postwar expressway improvements had been confined to the suburbs.

The other side of the coin is that major suburban highway improvements do indeed seem to be significant forces for dispersal. Thomas Muller and several colleagues have recently compared the experiences of three medium-sized regions with beltways and three without them. They concluded that the beltways had significantly harmed downtown retail sales. Prior to beltway construction, the trend of CBD sales relative to overall SMSA sales had been similar in both sets of regions. In the decade 1963–1972, however, following construction of the three beltways, the ratio of CBD to total SMSA sales fell by 56 percent in the beltway cities versus 43 percent in the nonbeltway cities. Although both sets of regions experienced comparable growth rates in total SMSA sales, CBD sales in the nonbeltway cities rose in absolute terms by 18 percent over the decade whereas CBD sales declined by 7 percent in the beltway cities.[70]

Improvements in automobile fuel economy, increases in private ridesharing, and expansion of demand responsive transit service all appear supportive of low-density urbanization, though not significant as independent forces for dispersal. Fuel economy improvements reduce the cost per vehicle mile of driving. Private ridesharing tends to thrive on long trips, and it is as common a form of commutation in rural as urban areas. It might have a significant role to play within the framework of broader strategies aimed at bringing about high density (since it can dramatically increase the person-carrying capacity of street and highway systems), but there is no case whatever to be made for the view that ridesharing is naturally conducive to high density. Like private ridesharing, demand responsive transit is characterized most significantly by its capacity to serve the diffuse travel patterns associated with low density land use. While it might in theory be utilized in support of a high-density strategy, in practice it tends to be most attractive in communities with little or no conventional transit service.[71]

Summary

Government highway expenditures and the wide diffusion of automobile ownership have doubtless been major contributors to postwar urban decentralization. In considering future policy options, however, it is essential to ask two further questions: How clear is it that the trend toward lower urban densities should be viewed as a negative development? and What is the likelihood that urban transportation measures, if undertaken explicitly with this purpose in mind, might be able to stem the tide?

The evidence seems overwhelming that most Americans prefer low-density living. To our knowledge, moreover, no American state or region (let alone the national government) has adopted increased urban density as a policy goal. More tangibly, low-density development does absorb substantial amounts of land, it does entail hardship for those without cars, and it does involve somewhat greater energy usage than high density patterns. It is far from clear, however, that it need be more expensive, more damaging environmentally, or very much more costly in terms of energy consumption.

It seems improbable that moderate increases in residential densities would save a great deal of land or significantly alter the circumstances of those without cars. Dramatic reductions in land requirements and in automobile reliance would depend on the achievement of much higher densities than anyone has seriously proposed for mass consumption, or than could possibly be achieved without a virtual revolution in American housing and land use regulatory policies. Given national migration patterns, moreover, this revolution would have to occur primarily in urban areas that are now among the lowest density and most auto-reliant in the nation.

There appear to be few current circumstances, finally, in which transportation measures alone can have a significant impact on metropolitan patterns of land development. Highway access is already ubiquitous throughout and well beyond American urban areas. In this bountiful highway environment, even a total cessation of new highway construction would have virtually no impact on development for many years to come, and transit improvements can generally enhance the relative accessibility of locations served in only quite modest degree. Where a considerable potential for core area development exists, and where numerous government policy instruments (including strong land use controls) are being deployed to help fulfill this potential, transit improvements will normally have a significant supporting role to play. To act on the premise that they can do more than perform such a supportive role in an otherwise favorable environment, however, is simply to invite disappointment.

III THE OPTIONS

Our concern throughout this volume has been with the interplay of politics, problem perceptions, and policy innovations in urban transportation, but the spotlight thus far has been on the first two of these dimensions. In part I we reviewed the postwar history of urban transportation politics and policy development, and we theorized about the factors that appear to bear most significantly on the political feasibility of proposals for change. In part II we sought to identify the major problems of urban transportation and to appraise the cost-effectiveness of eight broad types of innovations as potential means of alleviating them. We shall endeavor in this concluding part and chapter to complete the picture. Our primary aim will be to discern which of the main candidate innovations appear to combine in high degree both political feasibility and cost-effectiveness with reference to the most salient problems of urban transportation. Recognizing that policies are often undertaken for reasons other than alleviating these problems, we shall consider additional arguments for implementation where they appear significant as well.[1]

By way of background, we shall begin by summarizing our previous discussions of the key factors bearing on political feasibility in the current period, of the main 'problems' in urban transportation, and of the other criteria frequently called upon as justifications for public activity in this field.

Determinants of Political Feasibility

Political feasibility, we have argued, tends to vary inversely with the degree of private inconvenience that any given proposal would entail and with the visibility of the connection between the public action and private discomfort. It matters a great deal to elected officials whether the linkage is clear and immediate or blurred and deferred. At the same time it bears emphasis that public attitudes, and thus governmental priorities, are fluid. Many people were genuinely concerned in the 1950s about whether it was proper for

---

[1] Where evidence referred to in this chapter has been presented earlier, the documentation will not be repeated. We believe the index is adequate to enable readers interested in this documentation to locate it easily.

the federal government to become involved in such apparently local matters as the financing of mass transit and the control of air pollution, but these inhibitions evaporated during the 1960s. There was a great reluctance to consider regulating the automobile companies until the mid-1960s, matched by an easygoing acceptance of the disruption of neighborhoods and public open spaces to make way for expressways, but these priorities were completely reversed during the subsequent decade. The issue of congestion commanded more attention than all others combined in the field of urban transportation during the 1950s and 1960s, but it has been relegated to the back-burner during the 1970s. And whereas the predominant atmosphere was one of fiscal abundance from the 1950s through the early 1970s, with the result that policy focused overwhelmingly on capacity expansion, the predominant tone since about 1973 has been one of scarcity—fiscal, energy, and ecological—with the result that attention has focused increasingly on means of improving the utilization of existing capacity.

The great constant, though, has been an extreme reluctance to interfere directly with widespread patterns of voter (consumer) behavior. Until the mid-1960s, there was no disposition even to try to influence urban travel behavior. The emphasis, rather, was entirely on accommodating market trends—most notably, the trend of ever-increasing motor vehicle traffic. More recently a variety of government policies have sought to lure motorists into high-occupancy vehicles and to ensure their use of safer, less polluting, more energy-efficient automobiles. The methods have been promotion, service provision, and regulation of the auto manufacturers, however, rather than direct constraints upon individual travel behavior.

With these features of the political system in mind, we have suggested that innovative options can usefully be categorized and ranked in order of acceptability as follows:

1. The most feasible innovations are those that consumers will buy in the private marketplace, at prices high enough to cover their production costs. Where such innovations require public implementation, it greatly helps to be able to contend that decisions on

use are voluntary and that public expenditures are financed by user charges.

2. Among measures that do entail some compulsion, the most attractive are those that alleviate widely perceived problems at little or no cost (fiscal, social, or environmental) and that either (a) operate in the first instance upon corporate enterprises rather than individual travelers or (b) entail the exercise of traditional governmental powers in relatively unobtrusive ways. An example in subcategory a would be new-car fuel economy standards that involved direct regulation only of the auto manufacturers, and that resulted in unchanged or even lower lifetime costs for automobile owners. An example in subcategory b would be traffic signal systems giving priority to buses.

3. Among measures that entail significant public or private cost for the benefits they confer, the most feasible are those that do so in ways that permit substantial diffusion or deferment of the blame. Spending decisions are frequently in this category, particularly when revenues are growing rapidly at constant tax rates, when there is widespread acceptance (as in the 1960s and early 1970s) of growing deficits, or when expenditures can be bonded. (From the standpoint of state and local officials, spending decisions are also in this category whenever large portions of the cost are to be borne by higher levels of government.) Decisions to tax are generally separated quite widely in the governmental process, moreover, from decisions to spend. Some regulatory decisions are in this category as well. The most obvious examples are new-car performance standards that lead, years after enactment (or executive rulemaking), to automobile price increases. Few motorists tend to associate these increases with government actions; fewer still are likely to associate them with specific legislative votes. At the time of adoption, moreover, it is frequently plausible to hope that the costs will prove trivial. Even if they do not, the companies may be able to offset them in large part by making other economies. If, finally, the companies do announce price increases out of line with the general rate of inflation, and if they choose to stress government regulation as an important contributing factor, it may

still be plausible to attack them for seeking to blame their own "greedy" and "irresponsible" price decisions on others.

In practice the companies recognize that airing disputes with public officials in the media tends to be a losing game for them. Thus while they stress potential inflationary effects in opposing proposed new requirements prior to adoption, they rarely stress government regulations in explaining actual price increases. On the whole, moreover, they have been able to keep their prices from rising more rapidly than the overall consumer price index, so the issue has been relatively moot.

4. The least acceptable innovations are those that entail substantial costs or interference with widespread patterns of behavior, imposed in such a manner that the blame is likely to fall squarely upon the public officials who adopt the innovation. Examples include gasoline tax increases, parking regulatory and surcharge measures, and seat belt use laws. Even within this category, the extent of political resistance will tend to vary with such factors as the degree of inconvenience, of public support at any given moment for the objective, and of recognition that the method chosen is the most appropriate way to serve it. Thus a small gas tax increase to provide revenue for highway maintenance and construction tends to entail little inconvenience, to be for a long-accepted public purpose, and to be viewed as the appropriate method of securing revenue for this purpose. By contrast, proposals for large increases to constrain demand entail the prospect of quite substantial inconvenience, in the service of a very new public purpose, and by a highly controversial method for implementing that purpose. The importance of shifts in public concern about an objective is well illustrated by the history of the 55 mile per hour speed limit. Adopted at the height of the Arab oil embargo, it would clearly have been unfeasible a few months earlier; and even in this crisis atmosphere more powerful conservation measures—which would have entailed greater inconvenience—were rejected. Given the intense action mood that existed at the time to do something meaningful about energy conservation, the attraction of the speed limit reduction lay largely in the fact that it was the mildest measure

available (and among the most easily explainable) that might fit the bill.

Overall, then, measures tend to be more acceptable as the restraints they entail seem relatively trivial, as they fit comfortably within existing fields of public jurisdiction, as they are inexpensive, and as action moods prevail in problem areas with reference to which their efficacy has been established beyond controversy. Resisting cognitive dissonance the public strives, moreover, to evaluate measures consistently with reference to all of these criteria. Thus measures entailing the provision of improved services, to be used or not by consumers on a purely voluntary basis, tend to win relatively easy acceptance as cost-effective. (This is particularly the case insofar as they fit comfortably within the framework of existing agency mandates and staff capabilities. Such measures have ready-made sales staffs and constituencies, and few—except possibly taxpayers—have any reason to oppose them.) At the other extreme, where measures entail significant new elements of constraint on personal travel behavior, the media and the public tend to seize upon all negative evidence while ignoring or expressing distrust of most positive evidence as to their efficacy. The ignition interlock and Los Angeles diamond lane experiences well-illustrate this phenomenon.

One final point. The bounds of feasibility are constantly evolving. Constraints that seem new and outrageous today may seem commonplace a few years hence. The most striking change of recent years has been the growth in acceptance of business regulation to shape product performance characteristics. Mandatory insurance and safety inspection laws, together with traffic management innovations such as preference for high-occupancy vehicles and downtown pedestrian malls, indicate, moreover, that direct regulation of the motoring public is not impossible. This is the area in which politicians proceed with greatest trepidation, but we nonetheless expect continued policy evolution in the years ahead. The most likely candidates for early adoption appear to be inspection and maintenance requirements with reference to the new-car air pollution standards adopted in recent years, and more aggressive approaches to traffic management preference for high-occupancy vehicles. The least likely candidates for early adoption appear to be gas tax increases, parking restrictions, seat belt use laws, and other measures aimed at changing the daily behavior of large numbers of motorists.

The Problems of Urban Transportation

In chapter 4 we identified nineteen criteria that are frequently mentioned as bases for evaluating the current system of urban transportation and strategies for improving it. All entailed aspects of personal mobility or external effects directly related to the functioning of the urban transportation system. We explicitly omitted pork barrel criteria (such as the volume of jobs and contracts generated by transportation expenditures) from the list, on two grounds. First, such effects bear only an incidental relationship to the urban transportation system. Second, the inclusion of pork barrel effects as genuine benefits will almost always lead to the conclusion that public expenditures should be increased—since, by definition, they yield their worth in payrolls and profits, in addition to whatever other benefits they produce. Given that this is a clear recipe for public make-work, and that virtually all economic activities (private as well as public) entail payrolls and profits, it seems appropriate to treat the objectives of short-term economic stimulation and of a praiseworthy urban transportation system as quite distinct.

We judged that seven of the nineteen criteria were problems in the sense that many people viewed current system performance with respect to them as inadequate and viewed these inadequacies as high priority justifications for public remedial action. The seven were energy consumption, air quality, equity, safety, congestion, land use impact, and noise. The last of these, noise, we treated only briefly because it has commanded little attention in urban transportation policy debates. We examined the others at substantial length, however, arriving at the following summary conclusions with respect to their essential characteristics:

1. The energy demands of the current system are indeed profli-

gate by international standards, and they entail the following major consequences: large and rapidly growing dollar outflows for oil imports, high vulnerability to the threat of a future oil embargo, and reduced national capacity for independent decision making in world (especially Middle Eastern) affairs. The monetary outflows in turn tend to weaken the dollar internationally, to reduce the American standard of living, and to compound domestic inflation. It appears probable, moreover, that all of these consequences will become more severe in the middle or late 1980s as world oil demand begins to press hard against limits on production capacity. In short, the national interest in curbing oil import requirements is acute. Urban transportation usage is only one component of this much larger problem, but it is a highly significant one that has reasonably been targeted by national policy makers for a major conservation effort.

2. Air pollution is primarily a health problem. There are major unresolved questions, however, about the health consequences associated with current air pollution levels in American metropolitan areas, about the appropriate targets toward which public policy should aim, and about the urgency with which these targets should be pursued. Current national policy is to strive toward the goal of perfectly safe air quality: levels of air pollution so low that no one, however feeble, will suffer any ill effects, however minor. A comparable goal in the field of safety would require an absolute prohibition on travel. No other nation has adopted such an ambitious objective nor claimed that it knew how to translate it into precise ambient air quality standards. The United States, moreover, has clearly had second thoughts since adopting this goal, along with a set of standards and tight deadlines, in a mood of high enthusiasm in 1970—with negligible heed for considerations of dollar cost or of tradeoffs with other values. To date the goal and the standards have proven firmly resistant to change;[2] but the deadlines have proven highly flexible and policy instruments that

---

[2.] Congress did in 1977 relax one of the target new-car emission standards, that for oxides of nitrogen. The other emission standards have remained unchanged, however, since their enactment in 1970, as have all the ambient air quality standards since their 1971 promulgation by the EPA administrator in accord with the perfect safety criteria specified in the 1970 legislation.

would directly constrain individual consumer behavior have been put aside. In brief, then, little of a precise nature can be said about the severity of the health consequences associated with current levels of air pollution, and the national commitment to air quality improvement is far weaker than it appears to be on the surface.

3. The core of the safety problem is that 46,000 people a year are killed in motor vehicle accidents. Additionally, large numbers suffer serious injuries and property damage costs are high. While there has long been a clear consensus on the general objective of reducing this toll, controversy has been endemic on the questions of who should be blamed for it and what methods should be deemed permissible in seeking to ameliorate it. Until the mid-1960s, the automobile industry's contention that the source of the problem was the "nut behind the wheel" faced little serious competition. More recently, however, multiple causation theories have achieved wide acceptance, and the focus of attention has shifted toward identifying levers of intervention that are both effective and politically acceptable. These much more frequently involve vehicle and roadway modifications than changes in driver behavior.

4. The nub of the equity problem is that the auto-dominant system simultaneously affords the adult driving majority with unprecedented mobility while actually reducing the effective mobility of those without ready access to cars. We have defined mobility as ease of access to desired destinations. In the compact pre-automobile city, most desired destinations could be reached on foot or for the price of a transit fare. In the dispersed urban regions of the automobile era, numerous destinations are virtually unreachable—even by ablebodied adults—without a car. For those unable to walk substantial distances to and from transit stops, or who have difficulty with stairs (into buses and/or rapid transit stations), effective mobility is particularly limited. Moreover current welfare standards are higher than in previous eras. And mobility-deprived groups, especially the elderly and handicapped, have become organized and outspoken in their pursuit of government assistance.

There are great uncertainties, however, as to the precise degrees of mobility deprivation suffered by the several main claimant groups, and even greater uncertainties about the extent to which these are remediable by transportation system changes. Older and handicapped people, for example, tend to have low rates of labor force participation and to be relatively sedentary in their life-styles, even under conditions of equal travel opportunity. Significant numbers of them, moreover, are confined to their homes or to institutions and would be unable to travel in the best of transportation system circumstances. Finally a large proportion, particularly among the elderly and poor, have cars and driver's licenses and seem to achieve mobility rates quite similar to other urban residents.

Clearly, however, there are substantial numbers of elderly, handicapped, and low-income people who suffer from acute mobility deprivation that might be alleviated by transportation measures, and there is widespread agreement that their needs merit significant consideration and priority in the allocation of government resources for urban transportation purposes. Prior to the 1970s, this agreement tended to be ritualistic, but it has rapidly taken on increased significance more recently. No overall minimum mobility standards have been adopted, nor have comprehensive programs been undertaken to deal with the mobility-deprivation problem. Rather government efforts have striven toward the limited objectives of making fixed-route transit services fully accessible to those with physical handicaps and of enabling those eligible for publicly supported medical and social services to make all necessary trips incidental to the receipt of such services. Additionally a variety of new programs designed to enhance the mobility of elderly and handicapped people have been undertaken, and it seems apparent that equity considerations receive far more attention in general transit service planning today than they did in previous decades.

If urban transportation equity objectives tend to lack specificity, the primary reasons are doubtless as follows. First, while there is general agreement on the desirability of doing something about the problem of acute mobility deprivation, there is intense controversy about precisely which claimants are deserving, how much it would be appropriate to assist them even if resources were unlimited, and what priority their claims should receive in the actual environment of scarce resources. Second, there is significant disagreement about the extent to which problems of resource deprivation should be dealt with by the provision of specific services as opposed to general income assistance. In practice the United States tends to pursue a mixed strategy, but this leaves the question of the degree to which mobility deprivation should be viewed as a transportation problem very much open. Third, the mobility problems of elderly, handicapped, and poor people do not threaten national security, prosperity, or public health. Ameliorating them is primarily a matter of ethics insofar as the driving majority and most transportation providers are concerned, rather than one of self-interest. Not surprisingly, it has tended to be more difficult to reach agreement on ethical imperatives than on paths of self-interest, and, having agreed, to secure resources for their implementation. The major change of recent years has been the upsurge of political organization and militancy among the elderly and the handicapped, providing many elected officials, even if not the motoring majority more generally, with a motive of self-interest in responding to their concerns.

5. During the 1950s and 1960s, congestion was widely perceived as the main problem of urban transportation. It is unquestionably a source of annoyance to motorists. Conventional wisdom has it, moreover, that a great many other costs are associated with congestion: time losses for motorists, economic losses for businesses (due to delays), increased energy consumption and engine emissions, and higher accident rates. Our analysis failed to confirm the conventional wisdom. Little solid evidence on the costs of congestion is in fact available. That which does exist, however, suggests that the primary correlate of congestion is high density. Where travel speeds are low, people arrange to travel less. It follows that, at least over the long term, the primary benefit flowing from congestion relief is the opportunity for low-density living rather than time savings for motorists. Insofar as congestion relief measures facilitate increased travel and travel at higher speeds, their energy and air pollution benefits tend likewise to be vitiated. As for

safety, the most striking bits of evidence available are that fatality rates are considerably lower in urban than rural areas and that temporally they are lowest during peak commutation hours.

Evidence on congestion trends is even harder to come by than evidence on the costs of congestion. Several points are clear, however. The vast majority of current urban growth is occurring in relatively new, low-density regions with minimal congestion; and in the older regions the vast majority of growth is occurring in low-density suburban areas. Congestion is most severe on the approaches to major downtown areas. Travel to these downtowns tends to be increasing very slowly or not at all. Further, the classic instrument of congestion relief (highway construction) is least applicable in their vicinity, and they rely heavily on transit systems that would lose most of their patronage if congestion were suddenly eliminated.

In brief, then, we found no reason to judge that congestion is in fact a major urban transportation problem. This is not to argue that congestion relief efforts should be abandoned, any more than it is to argue that families should give up their aspirations for more luxurious cars. But it is to distinguish sharply between congestion and the more consequential problems associated with the contemporary American system of urban transportation.

6. The wide diffusion of automobile ownership and government highway expenditures have doubtless been among the major contributors of postwar urban sprawl. In judging whether transportation system impacts on land use constitute a significant current problem, however, it is essential to ask two further questions: What is the basis for viewing the trend toward lower urban densities as a negative development? and What is the likelihood at this late date that transportation policy shifts, if designed explicitly to stem the tide of urban dispersal, would be able to do so?

In response to the first of these questions, the evidence seems overwhelming that Americans prefer low-density living. If they could, about two-thirds of current apartment dwellers would live in single-family homes, whereas almost none of those living is single-family homes would opt for apartments. Similarly about 85 percent of large metropolitan area residents indicate that they would prefer to live in noncentral locations. To our knowledge, no American state or region (let alone the national government) has adopted increased urban density as a policy goal. Specific programs have indeed been adopted to facilitate central city renewal, but these fragmentary initiatives have been more than offset by other programs supportive of dispersal. Local zoning has focused overwhelmingly on holding densities down. And at the regional scale virtually all American officials have been content to let overall density outcomes be determined in the marketplace.

While admitting that low-density living is a luxury most Americans seem anxious to purchase, recent critics have argued that the objective costs of sprawl are in fact much higher than generally recognized, so high indeed that the nation can no longer afford the laissez-faire policies that have prevailed to date.

Our own review of the evidence suggests that the picture is far less dramatic. Low-density development does absorb substantial amounts of land, it does entail hardship for those without cars, and it does involve somewhat greater energy usage than high-density patterns. It is far from clear, however, that it need be more expensive, more damaging environmentally, or very much more costly in terms of energy consumption. Likewise, it seems improbable that moderate increases in residential densities would save a great deal of land or significantly alter the circumstances of those without cars. Dramatic reductions in land requirements and in automobile reliance would depend on the achievement of very high densities indeed, much higher than anyone has seriously proposed for mass consumption, and much higher than could possibly be achieved without a virtual revolution in American housing and land use regulatory policies. As long as most new housing is financed in the private marketplace, developers will aim to satisfy the desires of relatively affluent urbanites, those who have traditionally been most determined and best able to express their taste for low-density living. The obstacles to achievement of a sharp increase in the average density of new urban development would seem particularly severe, moreover, in a period when most new urban development is occurring in the nation's lowest density metropolitan areas.

Overall, then, it seems more plausible to concentrate on alleviating the specific harmful effects of sprawl than to launch a full-scale assault on low-density living itself. The worst excesses of leapfrog development, poor site planning, poor home insulation, and inadequate mobility alternatives for those without cars are all susceptible to very significant amelioration without forcing new development into patterns reminiscent of the preautomobile era.

In response to the second question, it does not appear that transportation measures alone can have a major impact on land development patterns in the current period. Highway access is already ubiquitous throughout (and well beyond) American metropolitan areas, and there is so much spare capacity in suburban and exurban areas that even a total cessation of new highway construction would have virtually no impact on development for many years to come. In this bountiful highway environment, transit improvements can have only a modest impact on the relative accessibility of the locations served. In a few selected locations, where a high market potential for core area development exists and where numerous government policy instruments are being deployed to help fulfill this potential, transportation improvements will normally have a significant supporting role to play. To act on the premise that transportation improvements can do more than play a supporting role where other conditions are favorable to development, however, is simply to invite frustration.

Other Evaluation Criteria

Urban transportation policy decisions frequently hinge on other considerations than effectiveness in ameliorating the "problems" associated with the current system. These include, most typically, impacts on other criteria among the nineteen we have identified as bases for substantive evaluation of the system and pork-barrel effects.

As noted in the previous section, we categorized seven of our nineteen substantive criteria as problems—in the sense that many people consider them priority candidates for remedial attention. We categorized the remaining criteria as follows:

• Those with respect to which system performance in the steady state tends to be grudgingly accepted, but which frequently become major foci of controversy when potential improvement actions threaten, as by-products, to generate significant increases in their magnitude: public dollar costs, user dollar costs other than tax payments, and neighborhood and environmental disruption.

• Those with respect to which current system performance is generally considered good, at least from the standpoint of the adult majority with a high degree of automobility: reliability, speed, convenience, flexibility, personal security, comfort, consumer freedom, privacy, and recreation.

The central distinction between these and the problem criteria is not one of intrinsic significance; it is rather between those aspects of current system performance that are widely considered candidates for remedial attention and those that are not. As attention turns to the appraisal of remedial options, it is only to be expected that impacts on the nonproblem criteria will at times outweigh those on the problems themselves.

As explained above, we view pork-barrel effects as irrelevant to overall substantive evaluation of the urban transportation system and of alternative improvement strategies. They are certainly of great political relevance, however, and they are central to substantive evaluation from particular microperspectives—those, for example, of contractors, suppliers, organized construction workers and transit employees, state and local jurisdictions, and particular government agencies. Not surprisingly, those with the most to gain tend also to be the most active politically and to exercise disproportionate influence on public decision-making processes. (The losers, by contrast—taxpayers and claimants who would prefer government allocations of greater immediate benefit to themselves —tend to be diffusely affected by any particular decision, and thus to be much less active.) In brief, then, whatever weight one thinks they deserve on the merits, pork-barrel effects are clearly central to any understanding of how public officials in fact appraise program options.

Innovations

We have labeled innovative any policies or service concepts that, if widely implemented, would significantly alter the performance characteristics of the urban transportation system. Our focus, in short, has been on potential impact rather than on intellectual originality. Thus we have treated major increases in highway capacity and fixed route transit service as innovative even though, from another standpoint, they would simply involve "more of the same." By the same token we have emphasized that nearly all current activities are noninnovative, in that their aims are to provide for the maintenance, operation, and routine expansion (to accommodate development trends) of the existing system—in short, to reinforce it—rather than to change it in any fundamental respects.

We have delineated eight broad types of innovative measures for consideration:

1. Highway capacity expansion.

2. Fixed route transit service expansion.

3. Demand responsive transit (dial-a-ride, shared-ride taxi).

4. Government efforts to promote increased private ridesharing (carpooling and vanpooling).

5. Traffic management techniques giving preference to high occupancy vehicles.

6. Business regulatory measures concerned with product performance characteristics (such as automobile fuel economy).

7. Regulatory measures aimed directly at consumers (e.g., gasoline rationing, seat belt use laws).

8. Price, including tax, increases designed to bring about reductions in vehicle miles of travel (VMT) and/or in gasoline consumption.

Some of these measures may be more effective and politically acceptable in combination than individually. Consumers are more likely to respond to vanpool promotional efforts, for example, if they also face parking restrictions at their employment sites; such restrictions in turn are likely to be more platable if high-quality alternatives to single-occupant automobile commutation are made available. While noting such interactive effects where they appeared to be of particular significance, we have sought for the most part to analyze the separate additive impacts of the individual measures under review in typical applications.

The first four, it bears note, predominantly involve the distribution of benefits, to be taken up or not by travelers and transportation providers on a voluntary basis. The last three, by contrast, entail the imposition of constraints. The fifth, preferential traffic management, combines elements of both, though as implemented to date it has almost invariably entailed new benefits for high occupancy vehicle users far more noticeably than the imposition of new constraints on other travelers. The exceptions, such as the Los Angeles diamond lanes, have tended to be few and short-lived.

Classification along this dimension becomes more complicated when costs borne by others than travelers and providers (such as, taxes and disruptive neighborhood impacts) are brought into the equation. It is highly instructive to begin, however, as most politicians do, by examining the likely consequences of innovative options for travelers and providers. On the whole, only those that survive this initial screening are evaluated seriously with reference to their other potential impacts.

Highway Capacity Expansion

We have explicitly focused on the dimension of highway capacity expansion rather than on that of highway program expenditure. Substantial increases in highway spending may well be necessary in the years ahead simply to provide for maintenance and for the reconstruction of long-neglected older facilities (especially bridges). These will not be innovative as here defined, however, because their predominant aim will be to perpetuate current performance characteristics of the urban transportation system in the face of threatened deterioration, rather than to bring about significant improvements.

In practice, we have judged, capacity expansion does not have much potential for improving system performance with reference to any of our problem criteria. One might expect it to appear promising at least as an instrument of congestion relief. In the very corridors where congestion is most severe, however, the social, environmental, and dollar costs of new construction tend to be most prohibitive, and citizen opposition tends to be most intense. Combined, these factors have brought major capacity expansion efforts virtually to a halt in densely settled urban areas during the 1970s. And in our view quite properly so; the costs of such construction almost invariably outweigh the potential benefits.

Where substantial highway capacity expansion is feasible in urban areas—most notably on the fringes—the major benefits tend to be speed increases (due less to congestion relief than to improved connections between specific points and higher design speeds) and improvements in the accessibility of land along the affected corridors. The land use effect tends to be an additional fillip to sprawl. Given that highway construction is an energy-intensive activity and that capacity expansion tends to induce additional travel, the energy consequences appear to be negative. The new roads are generally safer than the old per mile of travel, but much of this benefit is likely to be vitiated if they facilitate high speeds and to be further diluted over time as they induce additional travel mileage. Additionally, there are a wide variety of more cost-effective ways to enhance motor vehicle safety—including some that involve highway investment—than capacity expansion.

Although there seems little to be said on behalf of highway capacity expansion from a cost-effectiveness standpoint, it ranks extremely high on the political feasibility dimension. Specific projects that would impose concentrated costs on the residents of established neighborhoods or that would significantly disrupt the natural environment have become unfeasible during the 1970s in most urban areas, but a great deal of capacity-expanding highway construction is possible (particularly in low-density regions and outer suburban areas) without violating these constraints. And on a more general plane—when it comes to enacting program authorizations and appropriating funds—highway construction continues to be relatively noncontroversial.

The most striking political assets of highway construction are the force of inertia and its pork-barrel effects. More specifically:

• Highway construction fits perfectly within an existing institutional framework; indeed, it would involve far more political inconvenience to drop the program than to continue it.

• Large numbers of people—militant, well organized, well financed, and spread throughout every congressional district—have become accustomed to earning their livelihoods building highways. And they have enjoyed considerable success in persuading public officials that government has an obligation to keep them fully employed in this activity.

• It seems obvious to most people that with the vast majority of urban travel occurring on highways, with a good deal of congestion observable at peak periods, and with overall traffic volumes continuing to grow by several percent a year, a highway construction program must be necessary.

• State and local officials find it enormously attractive (so long as projects do not stir up intense neighborhood and environmental opposition) to distribute contracts, construction jobs, land development opportunities, and user benefits financed by a combination of federal aid and long-term state bonds. The benefits are clear and immediate; the costs are widely diffused and, at the state level, predominantly deferred.

This combination is so attractive that where opportunities exist to increase a state's share of federal highway aid allocations, extraordinary goldplating is likely to occur. The interstate program, which since 1956 has been the main locus of highway expansion activity (and which entails a 90–10 matching ratio) provides such an opportunity. Congress has chosen to express the long-term ceilings on the interstate system in terms of mileage rather than dollars, and each state's annual dollar allocation (within a fixed appropriation ceiling) is based on the ratio of its estimated cost of interstate system completion to the national total. Thus states have a powerful incentive to make each miles as expensive as possible.

The full inflationary potential of the interstate decision process has become apparent only in the 1970s, as state highway officials have come under increasing pressure to avoid community and environmental disruption. The challenge has been to remain in business without causing such disruption—and the most ingenious have recognized that neither costs nor any need to provide transportation benefits need significantly constrain them. The most expensive projects, and the least cost-effective from a transportation standpoint, have been developed in the densest urban settings, where ordinary expressway construction was halted years ago. Thus, instead of reconstructing the old West Side Highway in Manhattan or getting along with an at-grade arterial on the same alignment, New York designed the Westway, a depressed and (predominantly) covered freeway with an estimated cost of $1.2 billion for four miles. Simultaneously, Massachusetts proposed depressing its Central Artery in downtown Boston at a cost of $1.0 billion for three miles. Like their state counterparts, federal highway officials have been predominantly disposed to build whatever they can in urban areas. To reinforce this favorable predisposition, state officials—in cooperation with highway contractors, suppliers, and construction labor unions—have brought intense pressure to bear through their congressional delegations. And to date they have achieved an unblemished record of success.

Despite these political assets, the federal-aid highway program has declined in real (inflation-adjusted) terms since the early 1960s. Moreover the proportion of total spending devoted to capacity expansion—as opposed to environmental amenities, relocation payments, safety, and the reconstruction of existing facilities—has dropped sharply over the years. The consequences of these developments have been most apparent in the interstate program, whose estimated completion date has been extended from 1972 to sometime after the turn of the twenty-first century.

Nor is there significant pressure today for increases in the level of highway expansion activity. In pursuing budget growth, highway officials themselves have come in the 1970s to focus on deferred maintenance rather than capacity expansion needs. Their construction-oriented constituents have recognized, furthermore, that from a pork-barrel standpoint repair and reconstruction programs may be preferable (on a dollar-for-dollar basis) to capacity-expansion programs. They can support projects in many more legislative districts during any given time period; they entail negligible controversy; they can bring projects quickly from initial conception to the point of contract-letting; and they minimize the use of highway program dollars for such "frills" as land taking, relocation, environmental impact analysis, and legal representation.

It appears probable, then, that even if total urban highway spending rises more rapidly than the cost of living in the years ahead, little or none of the increment will be devoted to capacity expansion. Indeed unless some increases (for maintenance purposes) do occur, deterioration of the existing highway network may well merit attention as a significant problem of urban transportation during the 1980s.

Fixed Route Transit Service Expansion

In thinking about transit performance characteristics, it is vital to distinguish between current averages and those that would be associated with new service increments. After decades of explosive sprawl, only a small proportion of urban travel is concentrated along corridors in volumes and patterns with substantial potential for generating high transit load factors. After decades of service contraction, most transit vehicle mileage is currently in these corridors. The core of the potential transit market, in short, is already being served. As transit service is extended into less promising markets, or as service frequencies are increased in the corridors already served, the percentage growth in patronage will generally fall far short of the percentage increases in cost and vehicle mileage.

Our analysis has suggested that transit service expansion will normally provide negligible benefits, if any, with respect to energy, air quality, safety, or congestion. Properly targeted, however, it might be quite central to strategies aimed at improving the equity characteristics of the urban transportation system. And, where other circumstances are favorable, transit service improvements may at times play a significant supporting role in strategies aimed at promoting core area investment. Political factors, however, have tended to minimize the extent to which transit service improvements have been able to perform these equity and land use functions in practice.

In estimating the effects of particular expansion options on energy consumption and air quality, the key factors to bear in mind are as follows: the incremental load factor (the increase in passenger mileage divided by the increase in vehicle mileage); the time and capital cost required to bring the new service to the point of carrying passengers; the changes in prospect over the next couple of decades with respect to automobile fuel economy and emission characteristics;[3] the proportion of new transit patrons drawn from the ranks of automobile drivers (as opposed to automobile passengers, pedestrians, and individuals utilizing the new service to increase their total amount of travel); the extent to which access to the new service will be by car (the first few miles of auto travel after cold starts are by far the least energy efficient and the most polluting); and the likelihood that temporary congestion relief as some drivers shift to transit will call forth new automobile trips previously suupressed by the congestion itself.

In general, we found, the type of service expansion most likely to yield energy and air quality benefits is express bus service in corridors where automobile commuters experience severe congestion delays and the buses can avoid these delays by utilizing special lanes, access ramps, and/or preferential traffic signal systems. Insofar as the special lanes or ramps require new construction, however, the energy costs of the construction itself must be taken into account. And if the preferential measures entail a worsening of congestion for other traffic, increases in energy consumption and air pollution due to this congestion effect must be entered in the ledger. Express bus services in congested corridors, however, do often have the potential to attract high load factors, drawn largely from the ranks of automobile drivers. On the negative side, there appear to be relatively few corridors in which congestion is

---

[3.] The improvements likely with respect to transit fuel economy and emissions are, by comparison, relatively meager.

severe, express transit service is currently lacking, and ready opportunities exist to provide major time savings for express bus patrons without substantially inconveniencing other highway users. Thus, despite a sprinkling of widely publicized successes, the number of cases nationally in which express buses have been afforded significant time advantages over other vehicles in congested corridors remains small enough to be counted on one's fingers.

A transit energy-saving measure that might be far more widely applicable, at least in principle, is fare elimination (or sharp reduction) *not* accompanied by service expansion. This strategy would entail significant service degradation for current riders, however, in the form of intensified crowding, and probably no more than one-quarter of the new patrons attracted would be former drivers. Thus the tax cost per barrel of oil conserved would be very high, even assuming that transit operators firmly resisted all entreaties to relieve overcrowding by providing more services. Insofar as they responded to these entreaties, of course, the dollar cost would rise even as the energy savings dissolved.

Broad regional strategies of bus service expansion, and most rapid transit construction projects,[4] are likely to entail increased energy consumption. In the former case, the reason is simply low incremental load factors. The latter case is far more complicated and will vary widely with the details of specific proposals. Key elements that frequently point toward increased energy usage, however, include the following: projects that involve substantial tun-

---

[4]. The potential exceptions are those involving at-grade improvements on existing rights-of-way in circumstances where high patronage volumes can reasonably be anticipated. The prototype example to date is Philadelphia's Lindenwold Line, which involved quite modest improvements on an existing rail right-of-way in a severely congested corridor radiating from one of the nation's largest concentrations of downtown employment. Even the Lindenwold Line does not seem actually to have *saved* energy, however. What can be said is that it has significantly enhanced mobility and facilitated development in its corridor while roughly breaking even in energy terms.

Some rapid transit advocates claim that up to a dozen Lindenwold-type opportunities are available elsewhere in the United States. We are quite skeptical. There may indeed be a dozen corridors that are comparable in terms of right-of-way availability and traffic potential. What seems less likely is that designs of the Lindenwold type will be brought forward as serious proposals in more than a couple of them. The Lindenwold Line was developed by a revenue bond authority without federal aid or substantial citizen involvement, and prior to the enactment of most current environmental laws. No rapid transit proposals of the 1970s have evolved in circumstances comparably conducive to parsimony.

neling are likely to incur, as BART did, up to half the energy cost (and probably air pollution cost as well) of their initial half-century during the construction period, before they ever carry a revenue passenger; by the time new rapid transit lines currently in the planning stage become operational, automobile fuel economy and emission characteristics will be dramatically improved relative to the mid-1970s; long-term patronage forecasts based on estimates of residential and employment patterns several decades hence are intrinsically uncertain, and forecasts based on hopeful assumptions that long historic trends (for example, toward dispersal), currently operating with undiminished force, will be reversed during such a time period are particularly error-prone; most patrons of new systems typically arrive by car; and the only studies available, of the BART transbay and Lindenwold lines, indicate that drivers shifting to the new rapid transit services were almost instantaneously replaced on the highways by new drivers. The last is a particularly counterintuitive finding, but less surprising on reflection than at first glance. The rapid transit (like the express bus) potential for auto diversion is greatest in severely congested corridors, and it is well known that such congestion normally suppresses a certain amount of potential traffic demand. As even the most successful new transit services have induced fewer than 10 percent of motorists to switch, and as these have been in extraordinarily congested corridors, it is perhaps not so remarkable that the motorists in question have proved to be quickly replaceable.

Even at their most successful with reference to energy and air quality objectives, moreover, transit improvements are trivial and cost-ineffective instruments for achieving these objectives. The reason is primarily that the current base of transit patronage is so small. Even a doubling of transit patronage, with the increment drawn entirely from the ranks of automobile drivers, would reduce automobile VMT in urban areas by less than 3 percent. In practice, at least half the new patronage would probably be drawn from other sources, and transit vehicle mileage would have to be vastly increased. Thus, the automobile travel reduction would be under 1.5 percent, and it would be largely offset by increased transit energy consumption and emissions. The dollar cost of such a strategy would under the most optimistic assumptions have been about $6.7 billion a year in 1975. By 1990, when automobile fuel economy and emission characteristics are sharply improved, it would not only cost far more but it might even—unless the transit load factors were extremely high or some unexpected break-through had occurred with respect to bus fuel economy and emission characteristics—have negative energy and air quality consequences.

Transit service expansion likewise has negligible potential with reference to safety, and the primary reason again is that it has so little potential for reducing automobile passenger mileage. Additionally motor vehicle fatality rates are lowest during peak commutation hours, and transit fatality rates per vehicle mile are several times greater than those for private motor vehicles.[5] The latter finding suggests that increased transit patronage attracted at the cost of low incremental load factors (and these largely composed of others than former automobile drivers) might well involve a slight increase in the urban transportation accident toll.

Transit has often been sold as a means of reducing congestion; and it is true that in corridors where the transit share of peak hour travel is currently high a cessation of transit service would severely intensify congestion. There is little evidence, however, that transit service expansion can significantly reduce congestion. This apparent paradox is explainable as follows. The present transit share is high mainly on the approaches to the nation's largest, most concentrated, downtown employment centers. These have developed over many decades, premised on the availability of good transit access. Peak period congestion on the approaches to them is severe. On the one hand, this congestion serves to sustain transit patronage; on the other, it signifies the existence of a great deal of latent highway travel demand, ready to be expressed as and when additional highway capacity becomes available. Except in such cor-

[5.] The overall transit bus and rail rapid transit fatality rates per vehicle mile in 1975 were 3.7 and 6.0 times as great, respectively, as the urban automobile-truck rate. Considering nonoccupants alone, the bus and rapid transit fatality rates were 7.3 and 11.7 times the automobile-truck rate per vehicle mile.

ridors, new transit service generally has negligible potential to attract automobile drivers from their cars. And in such corridors, when it does attract them, they tend to be quickly replaced on the highways, as noted above with respect to the BART and Lindenwold studies.

To the extent, moreover, that transit improvements induce higher density development over the long term than would otherwise have occurred, they will normally bring about an increase in traffic congestion. Congestion is a function of the ratio of traffic demand to road system capacity. As density increases within any area, the transit share tends also to increase, but so does the absolute level of highway traffic demand per unit of road capacity. By comparison, land use dispersal has the opposite effects; transit shares decline, but so does the absolute level of highway traffic demand per unit of road capacity. The results are so readily observable that it is something of a wonder anyone can propose transit service expansion seriously as a long-term congestion relief measure. The nation's (and the world's) highest density cities are invariably characterized by severe traffic congestion as well as by high transit modal splits. In contrast, at any given population scale the lowest-density urban areas tend to be characterized by the least congestion as well as by the least reliance on transit. Insofar as congestion is the problem, it has been aptly remarked, diffusion is the simplest solution.[1]

Transit service expansion can significantly ameliorate mobility deprivation, particularly among the carless poor who live at reasonably high densities. Unless carefully targeted for this purpose, however, transit improvements are likely to produce quite meager equity benefits. To date they have rarely been targeted for this purpose.

The primary needs of the carless poor are not for improved high speed, peak period, downtown-oriented commuter services. Their mobility deprivation applies overwhelmingly to other types of trips. It can best be ameliorated by off-peak and crosstown service improvements. Such improvements, however, typically attract very low incremental load factors and almost no automobile drivers. Rather they reduce waiting and walking times for existing low-income transit users; they afford new trip-making opportunities; they reduce the dependence of carless individuals on others for automobile "lifts"; and they replace some burdensome walking trips. Politically such improvements attract no support from downtown business interests; they generate no construction jobs or contracts; they do not expand the base of transit system support (typically weakest in the suburbs); they cannot plausibly be sold as instruments of congestion relief or as spurs to core area development; and they are entirely lacking in technological excitement. In short, they have neither glamour nor significant pork-barrel value; the benefits are hard to measure; and they typically come at rather high cost per trip served.

It is scarcely surprising, then, that the great preponderance of recent transit service expansion has aimed at serving the potential transit markets of least relevance to the problem of mobility deprivation. The prime target clientele has been suburban commuters to downtown jobs, a group characterized by income and auto-mobility levels well above average. This strategy is quite comprehensible in terms of other policy and political objectives, but it has served to minimize the equity value of transit service expansion.

Evidence bearing on the transit potential for shaping land use in the current period is both sparse and ambiguous, but it suggests that the land use impact of even the most massive improvements (new rapid transit systems) will rarely be more than marginal. Where service extends well out into the suburbs, moreover, the predominant direction of impact may be toward dispersal rather than concentration.

It is important to distinguish between concentration and clustering. *Concentration* refers to the proportion of development occurring near the regional core; *clustering* refers to the precise configuration of development within any sector of the region. In practice, new rapid transit systems often generate intense clustering around their downtown (though rarely their suburban) stations, but they do not seem to have substantial concentration effects. It is readily understandable why this might be so. Given the ubiquity of highway access throughout contemporary urban regions and certain inherent limitations of transit (either the vehicles must stop frequently and travel on local streets, or the average patron must expend considerable time and effort reaching the stops that do exist), transit improvements can have only a modest impact on the relative accessibility of even the best-served locations. Given all the other factors that go into location decisions by investors, this impact will rarely tip the balance between locating downtown and locating elsewhere. Having once decided to locate downtown, however, investors are likely to be quite strongly influenced by considerations of transit accessibility as they evaluate specific alternative sites.

Major transit investments appear most likely to have significant concentration effects in circumstances where numerous other factors as well are highly conducive to downtown investment, and then to do so primarily because of their symbolic value—as tokens of government commitment to the future of downtown. The San Francisco case, often cited in support of the view that transit investment can touch off a downtown investment boom, illustrates these points. The San Francisco core was experiencing a construction boom even prior to the BART referendum (1962), and BART in practice has had only a modest impact on downtown accessibility (since excellent bus services were already available in the corridors it serves). The public commitment to construct BART undoubtedly reinforced the confidence of potential investors in the future of downtown San Francisco. But there is wide latitude for debate about whether BART made more than a slight difference and about whether a vigorous program of bus service improvements on existing streets and highways might have yielded comparable benefits at a fraction of BART's cost. What does seem indisputable is that BART played a supporting rather than a leading role, and in a setting where the preexisting market potential for downtown investment was extremely strong.

There is another side of the coin as well, however, in estimating the long-term impacts of transit service improvements—like BART —extending far into the suburbs. People who commute to downtowns do so because that is where they earn their livelihoods. If long-distance commutation is difficult, many of them will choose to live relatively close in. Dramatic transit service improvements will not induce large numbers of downtown workers to move farther out immediately, but they are indeed likely to have some effect in this direction over time. Thus whereas the most notable short-term effect of transit improvements serving distant suburbs may be to attract some commuters who already live there out of their cars, a longer-term effect may be to induce more commuters to live there. It is not difficult to imagine circumstances in which the dispersal effect would be stronger than the concentration effect. The key variables, probably, are the inherent attractiveness of the downtown and the specific configuration of the rapid transit system. Thus consultants to the city of Detroit have recently argued (correctly, in our view) that a rapid transit system there would do the city little good if it extended substantially into the suburbs.

Transit might be most effective in promoting high density as part of a comprehensive policy package including moratoria on public facility improvements in the suburbs, zoning and property tax policies driving investors toward the core, metropolitan school districts, and concentration of the transit improvements themselves in the inner portions of the region. But there is virtually no political constituency in any region for such a policy package. Moreover a key objective of central city and transit agency officials in recent years has been to secure regionwide transit financing; and the price of suburban tax contributions has been promises of improved suburban service. Local transit proponents themselves have generally deemphasized the objective of high density, recognizing it as one of the least consensual values that might be served by transit. They have sought (successfully) to present transit investment as one among many distributive policies (financed, moreover, predominantly by higher levels of government), not as part of a comprehensive package involving moratoria on other popular programs and new regulatory constraints.

Transit service improvements may also be justified, finally, with reference to the modest aim of improving the quality of life for current users. We have stressed above that the existing system of urban transportation provides extremely high quality service from the standpoint of those with ready access to automobiles. From the standpoint of most transit users, one need scarcely add, its service characteristics are distinctly inferior.

Turning from substantive to political analysis, the most puzzling question is how a mode with such a narrow patronage base, concentrated in such a small proportion of the nation's congressional districts, and of such dubious value in serving the main objectives that have typically been cited to justify increased spending on it, could have enjoyed such a run of funding growth as transit has during the 1970s. From fiscal 1970 to 1978 (estimated), federal transit aid obligations rose thirty-fold. As of fiscal 1978, the transit share of federal spending for urban transportation purposes is expected to be 52 percent, whereas the transit share of urban personal travel is under 3 percent and its share of freight travel is 0 percent.

The keys to the recent political successes of transit, in our judgment, have been as follows: First, the intense negative reaction stirred by the interstate highway program in some quarters during the late 1960s and early 1970s provided a vital source of mobilizing energy. Second, the antihighway movement needed a positive as well as a negative ideology and program—an alternative strategy for providing improved mobility, attracting federal aid to urban areas, and (where rapid transit was remotely plausible) generating construction jobs and contracts. Third, the decline of transit was perceived by downtown business interests and central city officials as a severe threat to their investments and tax bases, brought on in significant part by the "imbalance" of massive federal and state highway investment combined with a near-total neglect (until the late 1960s) of transit. Fourth, mass transit proved to be a program with extremely wide ideological (even if not market) appeal, able to attract support from such disparate interests as the central city poor, downtown businessmen, environmentalists, and construction workers, and stirring negligible opposition once the basic idea gained acceptance that urban transit was a public service of national concern rather than simply a local business. Fifth and finally, the combination of antihighway sentiment, urban area demands for increased transit funding, and continuing support in many other quarters for highway funding generated a political marriage of highway and transit program supporters in the Congress (commencing in 1973) and in numerous states with large urban areas. The essential terms of this marriage were a cessation of generalized attacks on the highway program by transit program advocates, in return for large-scale increases in transit funding and substantial flexibility for urban areas to use their highway aid allocations for transit purposes.

In brief, then, transit has proven to be a distributive, unifying policy capable of being incorporated into the much larger highway (now highway-transit) coalition. But at the same time its fiscal appetite has proven to be quite voracious, and the absolute level of transit spending has now reached a point at which large percentage increases also involve large amounts of money in absolute terms. There has been a dramatic shift of predominant national mood since the early 1970s, moreover, from one of fiscal abundance to one of austerity, and there has been a gradually spreading recognition that transit may not be a cost-effective instrument for pursuit of many of the objectives associated with it by its more enthusiastic advocates. Thus it seems probable that the period of transit service expansion, brief and modest though it has been, is drawing to a close. The predominant concern among state and local elected officials, and among transit labor union leaders, is now to secure additional operating subsidy assistance for the maintenance of existing service levels. The elected officials are anxious to avoid tax increases, fare increases, service cutbacks, and labor turmoil; the labor unions hope to achieve wage and fringe benefit increases and to avoid layoffs. These objectives are far more immediate and compelling than any associated with service expansion.

In practice the fiscal pressures are such that service cutbacks have already occurred in numerous metropolitan areas during 1976 and 1977, and most of those that had previously been aggessive in expanding service are no longer doing so. The transit prospect, in short, much resembles that in the highway field. The challenge of the next few years is more likely to revolve around avoidance of system deterioration than a new round of expansion. Two important differences, however, bear note. First, users respond more immediately to transit service cutbacks because they are more visible (at least over the short term) than cutbacks in highway maintenance. Second, the transit fiscal pressures are more severe; transit appears to require larger percentage increases in spending each year to maintain current service levels, and it is in direct competition with all other claims on general revenues; the highway maintenance fiscal crisis, on the other hand, could probably be resolved with a penny or two increase in the gas tax every few years.[6]

Demand Responsive Transit (DRT)

The key dimensions of transit service responsiveness are spatial and temporal. Spatially, DRT may at one extreme be as flexible as exclusive-ride taxi service; at the other, it may simply offer slight deviations from fixed routes. Temporally, DRT operators may strive for instant response to individual trip requests, they may condition their acceptance of individual demands by requiring substantial advance notice, or they may serve only recurrent trips on a subscription basis. Our concern has been primarily with DRT services at the more responsive end of the spectrum—those involving doorstep service (or a close approximation thereof) between a wide variety of points and responding to individual trip requests.

Not surprisingly, vehicle productivities (trips served per hour of operation) tend to decline as the degree of responsiveness increases and as the density of demand drops.[7] Costs, in turn, are a function both of vehicle productivities and of costs per vehicle hour. Because DRT is a highly labor-intensive service, the overwhelming determinant of cost per hour is the nature of labor arrangements— including wages, fringe benefits, and work rules. DRT combines conventional taxi and transit service concepts, and it can be provided at least as well by taxi as by transit organizations. In general,

[6.] Until the oil crisis of 1973–1974, such increases were routine at the state level. Since then, however, elected officials have been extremely skittish about actions that might lead voters to view them as one of the causes (and the one most vulnerable to retaliation) of gasoline price inflation.

[7.] Demand density—the number of trips per square mile per hour—varies with a wide range of factors in addition to land use density. These include the demographic characteristics of the population served, restrictions on service eligibility, service quality, the fare level, hours of service, and the characteristics of any competitive transit and taxi services in the same area.

taxi rates of labor compensation (including fringe benefits) are less than half those of transit employees, and taxi work rules are considerably more flexible. The result is not simply that DRT service normally costs less than half as much when provided by taxi companies; it is also that highly responsive DRT (many-to-many, nonsubscription) provided by transit agencies typically costs more per passenger mile than exclusive-ride taxi service in the same locales. This is not to say, of course, that fares are higher; in practice, subsidized fares have frequently been comparable to those for fixed route service. But it is to emphasize that the public costs of DRT, and particularly of transit agency-provided DRT, tend to be extremely high.

DRT may be approached as primarily an instrument for enhancing the equity of the urban transportation system or as a community luxury. In the former case, the emphasis will typically be on serving the handicapped, the carless elderly, and the carless poor who live at densities too low to make fixed route service a plausible option for relieving their mobility deprivation. In the latter case, the emphasis is likely to be on serving children, on taking commuters to and from fixed route transit stops, and on otherwise relieving household members of the need to chauffeur one another about.[8]

Both equity and convenience objectives can frequently be served by the same DRT system, but their relative weights are likely to have a determining influence as choices are made with respect to service area boundaries, patterns of operation, eligibility and fare policies, degree of advance notice required, system scale, and predominant sources of financing. An equity-oriented system, for example, is likely to concentrate on serving human service facilities and low-income neighborhoods, to require advanced notice as a means of facilitating the grouping of trips, to restrict eligibility for service (or at least for heavily subsidized fares) to selected mobility-deprived groups, to hold down the number of vehicles even if this entails significant sacrifices with respect to wait and travel times, and to rely heavily on contracts with human

[8.] Doubtless the best-known example of this type is the Westport, Connecticut, DRT system. Westport is one of the most affluent commuter suburbs of New York City, and its reported motives for supporting DRT are almost entirely of the convenience rather than the equity variety.[2]

service agencies rather than more conventional sources of transit funding.

Given the very high cost of DRT service, it is difficult to justify as a federal, state, or regional funding priority except for the purpose of aiding mobility-deprived groups who cannot effectively (or at any lower cost) be aided with fixed route strategies. Affluent localities, on the other hand, may reasonably choose to finance convenience-oriented DRT systems as community amenities. Other communities may find that they can add many convenience features to DRT systems that are justified basically on equity grounds at quite tolerable incremental cost. And in practice a certain number of low-density communities are likely to find themselves with federal and state aid allocations for which they have no other plausible use; a high proportion of the systems implemented to date have apparently been stimulated in this manner.[3]

Because most of the mobility deprived are handicapped, enfeebled by age, and/or resident in low-density neighborhoods that are unsuitable for blanketing with fixed route transit service, DRT must be viewed as an extremely promising instrument for enhancing urban transportation system equity. Additionally DRT may be utilized to provide superior service at no greater cost than fixed route transit in certain areas of moderate and high density during late evening hours and on weekends; and most of those who utilize tranist during such periods are mobility deprived. The central questions are how to hold down costs and how to finance the high per-trip subsidies that are bound to remain in the best of circumstances. The answers are fairly obvious but often difficult to implement politically.

A central element of any cost-minimization strategy must be to rely on taxi companies or other private contractors rather than public transit agencies to provide the service; but transit labor unions and many public transit officials oppose this tactic (the latter mainly to keep peace with the former). Yet unless DRT is able to operate at costs per vehicle hour more closely approximating taxi than transit operations, its future appears dim. Those concerned with transit budgeting are likely to conclude that its costs are absurdly high for any but the most compelling equity purposes, and that even these can be met more cheaply by purchasing conventional taxi service.

The bright side of the picture is that equity-oriented DRT services have the potential to thrive even in the midst of more general transit austerity. The elderly and the handicapped in particular have long been neglected by transit policy makers, and their recent lobbying efforts have evoked positive responses from most elected officials. Additionally, insofar as DRT funding comes from human service agency sources (or from specially earmarked federal and state transit aid appropriations), it may be relatively insulated from the broader urban and transit fiscal crises. In order to capitalize effectively on these fiscal opportunities, DRT service planners will have to concentrate on serving the elderly, the handicapped, and human service recipients more generally, and they will have to demonstrate that their costs are reasonable by comparison with exclusive-ride taxi service.

DRT does not, finally, appear to have any potential for alleviating other urban transportation problems than equity. Operating with very low load factors and serving high proportions of new (along with former pedestrian) trips, DRT service expansion generally entails increased energy consumption and emissions. Operating mainly in low-density areas and serving few commuter trips, it is irrelevant to the problem of congestion. Nor does it seem likely to have any noticeable impacts on safety or land use.

Increased Private Ride Sharing

Private ride sharing refers here to all motor vehicle travel in which the driver is accompanied by at least one passenger, the driving function is uncompensated (or compensated in only nominal fashion), and the vehicle is owned or leased by an individual for personal use or by an institution for the use of its employees. So defined, ride sharing is already the predominant mode of American travel. The average automobile occupancy per vehicle mile is 2.2. And although occupancies are considerably higher for non-work than for commutation trips (2.5 versus 1.6), many more people carpool to work—indeed many more ride as passengers in carpools—than commute by transit. (Nationally 18.3 percent commute as auto passengers, 7.5 percent as transit riders. Considering urban areas alone, the figures are 18.2 percent and 10.4 percent.)

The question, then, is not whether large numbers of people will ride share, but whether much can be done to increase the amount of ride sharing—and particularly to increase the proportion of private motor vehicle users traveling as passengers. If so, one would expect the potential to be greatest with respect to commuter trips, which currently involve both the lowest occupancies and the greatest bunching of trips in time and space.

If in fact large numbers of additional commuters could be induced to ride share, significant benefits would accrue with respect to energy consumption, emission levels, and congestion. As ride sharing became more prevalent and formally organized, moreover, disproportionate benefits would accrue to carless employees, who would now find it both more feasible and socially less awkward to enter into ride-sharing arrangements. The quality of service would be extremely high by comparison with transit: doorstep service and a seat for every passenger. And costs would be very low. Indeed private commutation costs would be significantly reduced. Public costs, it has generally been assumed, would be confined to publicity, technical assistance (to employers), and the provision of matching services. Unlike fixed route transit, finally, private ride sharing seems at least as applicable in low-density as high-density areas.

In practice, however, current patterns of travel behavior are quite firmly rooted in the circumstances and preferences of individual travelers, and apparently it will take a great deal more than government promotional efforts and matching services to bring about significant increases in ride sharing. Those who now ride as passengers include very high (though not precisely known) percentages of individuals who cannot drive and/or who are members of the same households as their carpool drivers.

As one considers strategies for inducing large numbers of commuters who presently drive alone to ride share, it is essential to bear in mind that although ride sharing is cheap monetarily it is far from costless. It involves travel time delays due to route circuity and waits for other passengers. It is extremely rigid temporally—much more so than transit, let alone single-occupant auto travel. It is highly resistant to intermediate stops (such as for shopping on the way home from work). It involves social relationships, possibly including agreements on cost sharing, that many find unpleasant. And it typically requires frequent search costs, because individual pool members are changing jobs, shifts, residential locations, and modal choice preferences all the time.

These costs are easy to overlook—and are in fact relatively insignificant—when ride sharing is spontaneous, when the typical pool is small (two or three people), and when most sharing is among people with close personal ties. They rapidly become conspicuous, however, as organized efforts are made to generate major increases in ride sharing, predominantly among strangers and in relatively large pools.

To date, substantial increases in ride sharing have been achieved only where employers have played vigorous promotional and organizing roles. By contrast, regionwide publicity campaigns and offers of free matching service aimed directly at commuters have been virtually without impact. It is unclear precisely why employer commitment should make such a difference, but it seems likely that the key variables have been to make ride sharing somewhat fashionable within a relevant social setting and to provide social reinforcement for precise clock-watching, which might in other circumstances be frowned upon by supervisors. Additionally, some employers have organized vanpool services—an activity that has involved them in purchasing and insuring vehicles, screening drivers, and deducting fares from paychecks—and many more have set aside desirable parking locations for carpools. (The latter is likely to be significant only where parking is in very short supply or where much of it is remote from the work site.)

A central question, then, is how to obtain vigorous employer commitments to ride sharing. No ready answers are available. The vast majority of effective employer efforts, and all the spectacular cases that are regularly cited to demonstrate the great potential of ride sharing, were undertaken for compelling business-related reasons. Several large employers have faced severe impending parking shortages due to expansion on a constrained site; one constructed a nuclear power plant at a location with severely limited road access; still another moved from Manhattan to New Jersey, leaving many employees with no ready means of getting to work.

A limited number of major employers face such problems each year, and with these precedents before them they are likely in the future to consider undertaking ride-sharing programs. Even if they all decide positively, however, the regionwide and national effects of their decisions will be trivial. And there appear to be fairly significant deterrents to involvement by very many other employers. Ride-sharing programs, especially those that include vanpooling, typically involve substantial hidden subsidies in the form of staff services; they are likely to absorb significant amounts of top mangement energy; most employers feel that they have much higher priority concerns than telling their employees how to commute; and they fear that any deployment of truly powerful incentives—such as reductions in parking space availability for single-occupant commuters—would generate adverse employee reactions. Additionally, many employers prefer to have their employees free to stay beyond normal quitting time when necessary to complete items of work, and they are reluctant to take on a responsibility for providing backup transportation service home whenever employees do so.

On the whole, then, we judge that government promotional and technical assistance efforts by themselves are unlikely to bring about significant increases in private ride sharing, increases large enough, for example, to show up in national surveys of commutation travel behavior. Indeed, as the incidence of automobile ownership continues to grow and (probably) average household size continues to decline, the normal expectation would be that the incidence of ride sharing will continue its long historic decline.[9]

[9.] National data on automobile occupancies over time are unavailable. The New York Port Authority has periodically collected occupancy data on vehicles utilizing its trans-Hudson bridges and tunnels since the 1920s, however. These indicate that the average passenger car had 2.50 occupants in 1925, 2.40 in 1940, 2.18 in 1950, 2.04 in 1960, 1.88 in 1970, and 1.83 in 1972. The Nationwide Personal Transportation Study reported an average occupancy of 1.9 in 1970.

These figures, parenthetically, include weekend travel, whereas regional transporta-

At the same time, we view ride sharing as the nation's major backup transportation system for dealing with any acute oil shortage that may occur abruptly (due to embargo or war) in the next several decades. The shortage would apparently have to be more severe than that experienced during the winter of 1973–1974, when the vast majority of motorists coped simply by cutting back on noncommutation travel. In a crisis that threatened economic paralysis, however, the level of ride sharing could be quickly and sharply increased. By contrast with mass transit, furthermore, ride sharing could serve the most dispersed as well as the most concentrated employment sites; it could do so without requiring new vehicles, or subjecting commuters to intense overcrowding, or forcing them to give up doorstep service; and it would actually save a considerable amount of money. (As congestion disappeared, some commuters would even save time.)

Short of such an oil crisis, the most likely strategy for bringing about increased ride sharing would be government restrictions or surcharges on employee parking, but the political appeal of ride sharing to date has been premised on the assumption that it is a purely distributive strategy—entailing benefits for those choosing to avail themselves of the technical assistance and matching services made available by government, but no coercion. There seems no likelihood that the use of auto-disincentive measures to stimulate ride sharing will become feasible in the near future. Thus far there has even been an unwillingness to consider subsidy strategies, on the substantive ground that cost is not among the principal barriers to increased ride sharing and on the political ground that there is no constituency for such a new subsidy program. Even the companies most involved in ride sharing have judged that the political and bureaucratic complications associated with a subsidy program (for example, to cover the capital cost of vans) would surely outweigh any benefits.

tion surveys are almost invariably of travel on average weekdays. A large majority of the latter have found occupancies in the range of 1.45–1.65. The trans-Hudson weekday figure in 1972 was 1.64.

A number of urban areas have conducted surveys of internal trips at more than one point in time during the postwar period. These have invariably found occupancies declining or essentially unchanged.[4]

Preferential Traffic Management

Traffic management provides the illustration most frequently cited to explain how all the members of a society can enhance their effective freedom by accepting certain constraints. Prior to the interstate program, moreover, virtually all expansion of highway capacity in developed urban settings occurred by traffic management innovation. And, after two decades in the shadow of that ambitious effort to expand capacity by brute force (and massive spending), traffic management has again won recognition in the middle and late 1970s as the main instrument for dealing with urban highway problems. One may usefully divide traffic management measures into three categories.

• Those that benefit all vehicle users more or less equally.

• Those that discriminate in favor of high occupancy vehicle (HOV) users without imposing noticeable costs on other travelers.

• Those that discriminate in favor of HOV users and/or pedestrians at some obvious cost to other travelers.

Prior to the 1970s, the overwhelming focus of traffic management, as of urban transportation policy generally, was on measures in the first category. Insofar as exceptions were made, they were to recognize certain claims of pedestrians and adjacent landowners: to be able to cross streets safely and to have certain residential streets free of through traffic. Other trade-offs had to be made between vehicle users themselves at times—most notably between through travelers and those desiring to park—and occasional parkways were declared off-limits to heavy vehicles (including buses). But the primary objective was clear: to improve traffic flow for all vehicles equally. During the first two postwar decades, moreover, even the other values traditionally recognized by traffic engineers were very much on the defensive. Faced with an apparently inexorable tide of rising traffic, highway officials strove insofar as possible to narrow sidewalks and eliminate parking on through streets, to resist neighborhood demands for through-traffic disincentives (such as frequent stop signs), and so on. They also thought little of cutting swaths through neighborhoods to provide optimal paths for new expressways.

In the 1970s, as major new construction has ground to a halt in the developed portions of most urban areas, the focus of attention has returned to the question of how to get the most from existing streets and highways. Widespread consensus has developed, moreover, around the following propositions: that traffic management should focus on optimizing person flow rather than simply vehicle flow; and that in some circumstances it should give higher priority to such values as neighborhood and pedestrian amenity, air quality improvement, and the encouragement of HOV travel than even the optimization of person flow.

Our primary concern in this book has been with measures giving preference to HOV vehicles—usually just buses, sometimes carpools and vanpools as well—in congested traffic streams. The primary measures in this category are exclusive lanes and preferential signal systems. The most dramatic successes have been achieved in several situations where it has been feasible to develop new or contraflow HOV lanes on severely congested freeways without imposing any obvious costs on non-HOV travelers. Indeed where the HOV volumes have been high—as on the I-495 contraflow lane approaching New York's Lincoln Tunnel and the Shirley Highway busway in Washington, D.C.—other travelers in the peak-flow direction have actually reaped significant congestion-relief benefits.

The opportunities to provide major time savings for HOV users without imposing costs on other travelers are extremely limited, however. The construction of new HOV lanes in severely congested corridors typically involves great expense and may involve considerable disruption as well. And contraflow lanes are extremely difficult to justify except in corridors with very high peak period bus volumes.[10] There are many more circumstances in which substantial HOV benefits might be provided by reallocating with-flow lanes currently in general traffic service, but such measures, involving obvious and substantial reductions in highway capacity for already-congested general traffic streams, remain highly controversial.

[10.] It is generally considered unsafe to open contraflow lanes to carpools along with the buses; their operating costs—for putting down and taking up lane markers each day—are relatively high; they typically impose slight additional congestion costs on travelers in the off-peak direction; and traffic engineers worry that when bus frequencies are low, some oncoming motorists are likely to forget the existence of the contraflow lane.

The best-known example to date of an effort to reassign with-flow lanes for HOV use was the diamond lane experiment on the Santa Monica Freeway in Los Angeles. The diamond lanes were introduced with substantial accompanying publicity to the effect that they were intended both to increase total peak-period person flow and to enable bus and carpool users to avoid congestion entirely. Before the experiment was terminated, its main sponsor (the California Department of Transportation) claimed that these objectives had in fact been achieved. During the early weeks, however, as travelers adjusted to the new arrangement, general traffic congestion was sharply intensified, accident rates were up as well, and overall person flow was down. Public and media reaction took firm shape during this period, and in retrospect the experiment is generally viewed by traffic officials accross the country as a modest technical success but a great political fiasco.[11]

By contrast, more limited preferential measures—such as special access ramps or lanes for HOV vehicles onto metered freeways—have aroused little controversy. These do not reduce the amount of highway capacity available for general traffic; they simply provide some temporal preference for HOVs (rarely more than a few minutes) in gaining access to this capacity. There is, further, increasing acceptance of the view that much stronger restraints on general traffic are probably justified on downtown shopping streets and in residential neighborhoods than on major traffic arteries. Numerous cities have implemented pedestrian malls, transit-pedestrian streets, and exclusive bus lanes on downtown streets in recent years. And, with vigorous federal encouragement, some are currently designing more extensive auto-restricted zones. The predominant aims are to enhance pedestrian amenity (creating something of the ambience of the suburban shopping mall downtown) and to facilitate transit operations. Meanwhile neighborhood residents in many locales have made substantial headway during the 1970s pressing the view that child safety and quiet should take near-total precedence over through traffic demands in the management of residential streets.

[11.] In fact, even the technical claims of success are weak. The eventual time savings associated with the diamond lane project were attributable mainly to its ramp metering components rather than to the diamond lanes themselves.

This serves to highlight a key political point: there are activist constituencies for traffic restriction in residential neighborhoods and (at least a few) downtown shopping areas, and these consist of adjacent land users. HOV users, on the other hand, have never to our knowledge mobilized on a traffic management issue. Thus preferential traffic management on expressways and arterial streets remains a technocratic initiative. The main supporters are professional transportation officials, and—since traffic management measures are generally cheap and nondisruptive—they can often implement their ideas even without an active constituency. Whenever their proposals do arouse substantial opposition, however, elected officials—sensing the lack of politically relevant support—tend quickly to run for cover.

In considering the cost-effectiveness of traffic management measures, the most important fact to bear in mind is that their costs (social and environmental as well as fiscal) tend to be extremely low. Additionally they can be implemented quickly and, if necessary, reversed easily. Thus even where benefits are modest, they may easily justify their cost; and even where cost-effectiveness in uncertain, there may be little risk in experimenting.

We emphasize these points in order to underline our judgements both (a) that preferential traffic management measures have a high potential for cost-effectiveness with reference to a wide range of important objectives and (b) that they have little potential for substantially alleviating any of the main problems of urban transportation.

In selected circumstances, for example, preferential treatments in highly congested corridors may induce as many as several thousand commuters to shift from driving to riding as HOV passengers. The opportunities to generate such diversions are relatively few, however, and even the most spectacular successes in the nation to date have reduced regionwide automobile travel by only a small fraction of 1 percent. It is difficult to imagine how even the full range of measures likely to be feasible in any urban area during the foreseeable future could bring about an aggregate reduction of more than 1 percent. Thus the potential of preferential traffic management as a method of conserving energy and of reducing air pollution on a regionwide basis would appear to be meager. Auto-restricted zones, on the other hand, may provide a highly effective technique for reducing pollution concentrations on particular downtown streets with heavy pedestrian volumes (and thus high rates of human exposure).[12]

Preferential measures can provide dramatic congestion relief for HOV occupants in many settings, but this will often be at the expense of other travelers except where the HOV vehicles are utilizing new (or previously underutilized) lane capacity. Particularly where existing with-flow lanes are reserved, however, time losses for non-HOV travelers are likely to exceed time savings for HOV occupants unless the HOV volumes are high. And even where new lanes are constructed, they might frequently provide greater congestion relief if assigned for general traffic use; the issue again turns on the volume of HOV usage.[13]

There is also a certain equity appeal about giving priority to people over vehicles in the allocation of scarce highway capacity. But the main beneficiaries thus far have been downtown commuters, in general an affluent and ablebodied group. The major equity issues in urban transportation, of course, revolve around the types and amounts of service that should be provided the carless poor and the physically handicapped rather than marginal differences in travel time for specific categories of peak period highway users.

Pedestrian amenities on downtown shopping streets are likely to have some positive impact on downtown sales, but no one has suggested that they are likely to have a substantial impact on overall development trends. Similarly traffic restrictions in residential

[12] The price of this site-specific benefit, it should be noted, will normally be a slight increase in regionwide motor vehicle travel. Although they may induce a few core-bound travelers to leave their cars at home, auto-restriction schemes will also in most cases force large numbers of motorists to take more circuitous routes to their destinations than they would have chosen themselves. Additionally, unless measures are implemented to increase capacity on the bypass routes around the zone, it must be anticipated that they will become more congested.

[13] Nonpreferential traffic management measures (such as one-way street systems, freeway metering, traffic-actuated signal systems, and channelization) are, by contrast, able to yield significant congestion relief in a much wider range of settings. The primary reasons are simply that they do not require large HOV volumes or sufficient lane capacity to segregate types of traffic in order to yield their potential benefits.

areas may significantly improve pedestrian safety and reduce noise within them. As long as the streets to which traffic is diverted have little amenity value to begin with, the net quality-of-life gain may be very worthwhile. But annoyance with traffic on residential streets is not generally considered to be one of the primary reasons why urban residents have been abandoning the central cities in such vast numbers during recent decades.

Finally preferential traffic management can make a significant contribution to holding down transit costs by reducing bus congestion delays. But it is hard to imagine even the most aggressive regionwide program of preferential traffic management achieving more than a several percentage point reduction in transit operating costs.

To sum up: the potential benefits of preferential traffic management and of traffic restriction in the interest of adjacent land users are significant, varied, and frequently available at low cost. We anticipate that the bounds of feasibility with respect to these concepts will continue to be pressed outward in the years ahead. Their greatest potential, however, appears to be with reference to enhancing pedestrian and residential amenity at the microscale. We see little evidence that measures in this category can substantially improve the aggregate performance of the urban transportation system with reference to any of the problem criteria on which we have focused in this book.

Business Regulation
The predominant scholarly view is that business regulation, by impeding market entry and by placing a heavy burden of proof on those proposing to compete in new ways, has tended to retard the pace of technical and service innovation.[5] Our concern in the present study, however, has been with a special and relatively new type of regulation: aiming explicitly to accelerate the pace of innovation with reference to selected product performance characteristics.

Such regulation dates only from 1965 in the field of urban (or, more precisely, motor vehicle) transportation. But since then, it has been by far the most significant locus of policy innovation in this field. While there is room for substantial controversy about the degree to which it has in fact accelerated the pace of technical progress, there seems little question that it has profoundly affected the research and product design priorities of the regulated businesses (most notably the auto manufacturers, secondarily the oil refiners) and sharply accelerated the pace at which relevant technical developments have reached and become standard in the consumer marketplace.

We have stressed that the American political system is strongly oriented toward reliance on benefit distributing rather than constraint strategies wherever possible. As action moods have developed around the issues of safety, air quality, and energy during the 1960s and 1970s, however, there has been a widespread recognition that distributive strategies were unlikely to affect them more than tangentially. It has gradually become apparent to elected officials, moreover, that as constraint strategies go, product performance regulations are among those entailing the least risk of voter backlash. Those constrained directly, and most obviously, are a few large companies rather than large numbers of voters. And since the initial battle over safety (1965), the companies themselves have resisted each extension of the scope of regulation far more tepidly than might have been expected. Accepting the basic decisions to regulate as nearly inevitable, they have concentrated primarily on heading off "unrealistic" technical demands (with respect to deadlines, standards, and enforcement procedures) and on making clear that all costs would ultimately be borne by consumers. The consumers themselves have been all but invisible in the key (legislative and administrative) decision-making arenas. Thus where pressure from the media or from activist groups for regulatory action has been intense, countervailing opposition has been surprisingly weak.

The companies and other critics of performance standard regulation have made much of the fact that all costs are ultimately borne by consumers. But in practice these costs tend to be uncertain, blurred, and deferred—characteristics that minimize their potential for evoking voter backlash. It is rarely implausible at the time standards are adopted to hope for technological breakthroughs and/or dramatic economies as existing prototype technologies move into mass production. Increased new-car purchase prices may be offset by reductions in other dollar expenditures (for gasoline, medical care in the aftermath of accidents, and so on). The mandated costs may simply substitute for others that would have been incurred in the absence of regulation (for example, safety versus annual style changes, fuel economy versus horsepower). When and if the costs do appear, they are invariably mixed in with many other causes of inflation. And there is always room for dispute about whether the companies have exaggerated in estimating the costs of regulation in order to minimize their own responsibility for price increases. Finally, these costs generally appear, if at all, quite a few years after the publicized decisions of elected officials. If, indeed, they appear too great as deadlines approach, the requirements can be relaxed. The public mood will almost surely be quite different by this time. Meanwhile several elections will have intervened, and those who voted for the original legislation will have reaped the benefits of allying themselves with the action mood when it was most intense.

From a consumer standpoint, the degree of perceived constraint associated with performance standard regulation has typically been mild, and seems likely to remain so.[14] The typical consumer, after all, has long been accustomed to choosing from among the range of options available in dealer showrooms. Few have spent much time grousing about the lack of still other options. With performance standard regulation the companies continue to stress the differences among models, trying to focus consumer attention on the choices that are available. It seems probable that they will continue to succeed about as well as they have in the past, especially since the predominant effect of regulation will be to shift the range of options rather than to narrow it. Cars with fuel economies of less than about 20 miles per gallon in combined city-

[14.] The main exception was the ignition interlock requirement, which entailed behavioral as well as hardware regulation. (The interlock system prevented ignition until front seat occupants had fastened their seat belts.) This regulation encountered little opposition until the first interlock-equipped cars appeared in the marketplace. But criticism was intense thereafter, and many owners found ways to disconnect their interlock systems. The regulation was withdrawn by an act of Congress about a year after it first became effective.

highway driving are likely to be taxed off the market by the late 1980s, for example, but the range of fuel economies available will probably be greater than that available prior to 1975, when regulatory targets were first enacted. Similarly all cars will come equipped with air bags or automatic seat belts; but prior to the enactment of safety regulation in 1966, occupant restraint equipment was itself unavailable.

Additionally it bears emphasis that even distributive programs generally entail constraints—eventually, even if not immediately—in the form of taxes. And most regulatory programs involve hidden taxes in the form of higher prices. So long as consumers retain a wide range of choice about how much to spend on auto transportation and what features to spend it on, and so long as the add-on costs of mandated equipment remain a small percentage of the total cost of auto travel, it seems unlikely that many voters will focus on government-imposed product performance standards as among the more onerous constraints on their own behavior.

If product performance regulation has proven to have surprising political appeal, it has also gained increasing recognition as an instrument of great substantive power. Around 1970, indeed, there was a tendency in many quarters—illustrated by the Clean Air Act Amendments of that year—to believe that the companies could achieve virtually any target by any deadline. It subsequently became apparent that their actual capacities were far from unlimited, and there has been a constant tug-of-war between public and company officials in the years since over precisely what these capabilities are. But the companies have in fact made remarkable strides toward improving fuel economy, emission control, and safety. These performance criteria have two notable features in common: they largely involve characteristics of individual vehicles as mechanical systems rather than more complex interaction effects, and they had long been neglected by the auto manufacturers until recent years. The significance of the latter feature is that the companies have been able to exploit substantial backlogs of available technologies and promising ideas accumulated during the long years of neglect.

Though business regulation is in fact a powerful instrument, it also lends itself to the enactment of "morality plays" in which politicans strike antibusiness postures and proclaim grand accomplishments while skimping on effective enforcement and reliable monitoring.[6] The most blatant case has been that of air pollution control. Compliance by the manufacturers has been judged exclusively on the basis of tests performed on prototype, professionally maintained cars. Though the average vehicle life is slightly over ten years, the testing procedure assumes a "useful life" of five years or 50,000 miles, whichever comes first; and—astonishingly—the companies have been permitted to replace deteriorating control equipment as needed during the test so long as they have also called for such replacement in the manuals provided vehicle purchasers. Though performance degradation of on-the-road vehicles is known to vitiate most of the benefit of new-car emission control standards, inspection and maintenance have to date been almost totally neglected.[15] Despite all of these facts, most official forecasts have been premised on the assumption that vehicles will perform in accord with official new-car standards throughout their actual (10+ year) lives.

The bases for this morality play syndrome are easily comprehensible. The media and activist citizens' groups focus overwhelmingly on one or two policy symbols with respect to each performance criterion, of which the most notable are the new-car standards. The companies, on the other hand, actively lobby with respect to every implementation detail. Public officials, for their part, find it convenient to make some concessions to the companies on matters about which only they seem actively concerned, to avoid mandating the cost and inconvenience of lifetime maintenance so long as there is little public awareness or concern about on-the-road degradation, and to claim as much accomplishment as they can reasonably hope to get away with.

Thus it is easy in some circumstances to exaggerate the benefits of performance standard regulation—most notably, with respect to components that degrade substantially over time in the absence of

[15.] The Clean Air Act amendments of 1977 do look toward the implementation of inspection and maintenance programs in regions expected to remain in violation of ambient air quality standards after 1982, but they are vague as to when such programs may become operationsl.

maintenance, whose levels of performance can be determined only with expensive testing equipment, and whose failures predominantly entail external costs rather than adverse consequences for vehicle owners themselves. These factors are extremely significant in the case of emission control but much less so in the cases of safety and fuel economy. Even with respect to emission control, however, performance standard regulation stands out as by far the most powerful and cost-effective approach available. And it seems likely to become much more powerful over time—as the manufacturers shift to emission control technologies less prone to degradation and/or as environmental groups turn their attention to the inspection and maintenance issue. It seems reasonable to assume, finally, that the federal government will require less degradation-prone technologies as it becomes clear they are available at reasonable cost, and that the companies feel under substantial pressure to deal with the degradation problem before it becomes (as it easily could) a hot public issue.

Direct Consumer Regulation and Price Disincentives
Both of these last two categories of policy instruments involve constraints imposed directly on large numbers of individual travelers. Regulatory measures prohibit and penalize specific types of behavior; pricing measures leave consumers free to allocate their own resources but reduce the incidence of disfavored behavior by increasing its dollar cost.

Our concern has been primarily with measures intended to reduce overall VMT and/or gasoline consumption. But we have also considered a wide range of more limited constraints, ranging from peak period congestion tolls on specific routes to mandatory seat belt use laws to requirements for the periodic inspection and maintenance of emission control equipment.

All of the consumer regulatory and pricing measures examined in this book have proven to be politically unfeasible thus far. Motorists have accepted a variety of other direct constraint measures (such as driver licensing, mandatory insurance, and periodic safety inspection) with relative equanimity over the years, however, and thus it would be rash to assume that the current bounds of feasibility are fixed. In seeking to estimate where the next breakthroughs are likely to occur, we judge that the variables on which to concentrate are the following:

• *To what extent would the proposed constraint require changes in daily behavior?* Clearly strategies that aim at curtailing VMT require more behavioral change than those designed to ensure near-universal seat belt usage, which in turn require considerably more change than inspection and maintenance requirements.

• *To what extent does the policy objective command acceptance as a critical public need—particularly on national security, health, or safety grounds?* Gas rationing has been accepted in wartime, and public opinion polls indicate that it would be again if the nation were faced with a prolonged oil embargo. Safety inspection laws have presumably won acceptance as a legitimate public safety measure, and emission control inspection laws are likely to do the same as, when, and where the public becomes persuaded that the violation of ambient air quality standards involves substantial adverse health effects.

• *How obvious is the linkage between the actions by elected officials and the inconvenience or discomfort perceived by travelers?* President Carter's 1977 proposal for a gasoline surtax met instant, all but unanimous, Congressional rejection. His proposed crude oil tax, on the other hand, received House approval and was accorded a serious chance of enactment until the final stages of the conference committee deliberations on the president's energy package. The crude oil tax, like other business taxes (and costs attributable to regulation), would have reached consumers as an indistinguishable component of private sector prices rather than as a clearly labeled tax. The difference appears trivial when so described. Considering, however, that popular debates almost invariably proceed from the assumption that business tax and regulatory costs fall on stockholders, and that as of mid-1977 fewer than half of all American adults knew that the nation imported any oil at all, elected officials may be forgiven for judging that a little sleight of hand can go a long way.[16]

[16.] Only 48 percent of the respondents in an August 1977 national poll carried out by CBS News and the *New York Times* knew that the United States had to import oil, and

• *How vulnerable is the proposed measure to charges of unequal impact, particularly in such a way as to discriminate against low-income people and/or against the residents of whole states or regions of the country?* Numerous polls have indicated that the public would prefer gas rationing to large gas tax increases as a means of limiting demand in a crisis, though virtually all serious analysts view rationing as an administrative nightmare that would eventually entail far greater bureaucratic, economic, and even equity costs than a well-designed tax disincentive system. To the average voter, it seems apparent that a tax system would discriminate against the poor, against residents of nonurban areas, and against others with a legitimate need for above-average fuel consumption, whereas a rationing system would be at the same time more egalitarian and sensitive to special needs. In practice, a rebate system such as that proposed by President Carter in 1977 can make a tax program redistributive in favor of the poor, and the Carter proposal might easily have been adjusted as well to provide higher rebates for rural residents. The claims of special need, moreover, are what eventually turn rationing systems into administrative jungles. But these arguments have never carried much weight politically, and the nation's standby plan for any future acute oil shortage is to impose rationing.

Political feasibility aside, regulatory and pricing measures have enormous potential for ameliorating the main problems of urban transportation at relatively modest cost. Specifically:

1. Gasoline rationing and taxation are relatively interchangeable as effective means of curtailing fuel consumption, with the following qualifications. Rationing is a blunter and more expensive instrument, but it is also more certain—particularly insofar as quick and/or sharp cutbacks in usage are sought. If combined with an effective program of supply curtailment, rationing can bring about whatever reduction in usage is desired, and it can do so virtually overnight. The elasticity of demand, by contrast, is much greater over the long term than the short, and it is considerably

little more than one-third of these knew that the United States currently imported more than 40 percent of the oil it consumed. Only 38 percent of the respondents believed that in fact there was a real oil shortage; 49 percent believed that the claims of an oil shortage were simply a ploy to enable the oil companies to charge higher prices.[7]

more uncertain where large price changes are concerned—as virtually all available estimates are based on studies of the impacts of quite modest changes. The other side of the coin is that the administrative costs and economic distortions associated with rationing tend to grow over time, whereas these costs, slight to begin with, tend to diminish over time insofar as price disincentives are utilized. In short, taxation appears to be a preferable method where only modest and/or gradual reductions in demand are sought, and when it is anticipated that the program of demand curtailment will be long-lived.

If increases in the relative price of gasoline tend over time to become more powerful in their effect on fuel demand, they tend to become less powerful in their effect on VMT. The reason is simply that consumers can, and do, respond over time by purchasing more energy-efficient vehicles. Congress has already enacted legislation requiring average new-car fuel economy to double from 1974 to 1985, and it seems clear that a tripling would be feasible if absolutely required. Thus even assuming a long-term elasticity of demand for gasoline in the range of unity (which is about what most economists do estimate), price increases would have to be extraordinarily severe to bring about significant long-term reductions in VMT.

Only a small proportion of the VMT reduction occurring in response to supply curtailment and price disincentive measures, it bears note, would be translated into increased transit patronage. Motorists tend to give up or consolidate certain trips, particularly of a recreational and personal business nature, before they shift to transit. The New York Regional Plan Association (RPA) has estimated that even during World War II, when transit was relatively ubiquitous in the areas of urban settlement, only 37 percent of the reduction in urban automobile passenger mileage (nationwide) was translated into transit patronage growth. With transit service now much more inferior to auto travel for the vast majority of trips that people wish to make in urban areas, the elasticity of transit demand in response to constraints on automobile travel is doubtless much lower than during World War II. It is impossible to test this proposition rigorously in the absence of constraints comparable to those of the war period. Far milder constraints did bring about a reduction in auto travel between 1973 and 1974, however, and RPA estimates that the transit capture rate during this episode was only 7 percent. (See table 11.1.)

2. Regionwide restrictions or surcharges on employee parking would, if effectively enforced, doubtless have a substantial impact on commutation VMT, on air pollution in the immediate vicinity of major employment sites and travel arteries, and on congestion. Because their impact would be confined to commutation travel, however, and because many of the cars left at home would be used during the day by other household members, the impact on fuel consumption and regionwide air pollution would be far less notable.

There are, it should be noted, substantial enforcement problems associated with parking restriction. It is usually possible to crowd a great many more cars on any given amount of parking lot space than is currently the norm at employment sites, and it is often possible for employees to find off-site parking spaces within walking distance of their jobs. Thus simple enforcement actions like roping off portions of employer parking lots (the EPA proposal in Boston) might have negligible effect. A more complex enforcement program, involving frequent on-site inspections and strong measures to deter off-site parking by employees, would be considerably more expensive as well as more onerous from the standpoint of commuters.

Core area parking restrictions are easier to defend politically, since transit service is normally best to the core and air pollution is worst within it. Typically fewer than 10 percent of regional employees work in the central business district, however, and a substantial proportion of these already arrive by transit. (Where the CBD share of employment is higher, so generally is the proportion of CBD workers commuting by transit.) Thus the impact of such restrictions on regionwide emissions and fuel consumption would tend to be extremely modest. Additionally, core area parking disincentives would tend to have a decentralizing land use effect by encouraging those with choices to satisfy their travel objectives at other locations. Restrictions directed solely at employees would

TABLE 11.1
Billions of Passenger Miles of Travel by Mode

	1940	1944	Change 1940–1944	1973	1974	Change 1973–1974
Commuter rail	3.997	5.344	+1.347	4.245	4.692	+.447
Rapid transit	15.245	17.037	+1.792	11.998	12.082	+.084
Trolley	14.858	23.790	+8.932	0.621	0.450	−.171
City bus	11.932	27.200	+15.268	14.217	15.177	+.960
Total: urban transit	46.032	73.371	+27.339	31.081	32.401	+1.320
Urban auto	291.339	217.630	−73.709	962.850	943.418	−19.432
Transit capture rate			37.1%			6.8%

Source: Boris Pushkarev and Jeffrey Zupan, *Public Transportation and Land Use Policy* (Bloomington: Indiana University Press, 1977), pp. 8–9.'

tend to have the least dispersal effect, but even these might stimulate employment shifts over time. Little is known about the precise magnitude of these potential land use effects; in the absence
of certainty that they would be nonexistent, however, central city
officials and downtown business people can be expected to argue
with particular passion against parking restrictions confined to the
core. If, on the other hand, these dispersal effects did prove substantial, the most significant long-term result of core area parking
restrictions might be additional VMT regionwide.

3. All components of mechanical systems deteriorate with extended usage, and this is particularly so with respect to components that involve moving parts and/or chemical reactions. Insofar
as policy makers are concerned with the lifetime performance
characteristics of motor vehicles, rather than simply with new-car
performance, they must give serious consideration to inspection
and maintenance (I/M) requirements. It is possible to implement
such requirements as pure business regulations by requiring the
manufacturers to provide lifetime warranties. Such warranties
would tend in some cases (most notably, emission control) to have
a major impact on new car prices, however, and they would still
require motorists to expend time and energy arranging for the I/M
work. Additionally, the warranties would normally leave the companies free to deny free service where the motorist had neglected
some routine maintenance or operated the vehicle improperly. The
longer the warranty, the higher the proportion of motorists who
would find, to their dismay, that it failed to cover their own cases.
If, on the other hand, the warranty provisions did not include requirements for proper maintenance and vehicle operation, owners
would have little incentive to avoid the need for warranty repairs,
and the original cost of the warranty provision would have to be
that much higher. The price, finally, would entail substantial cross-
subsidization from the careful to the careless.

The I/M issue is most urgent with respect to air pollution. EPA
surveillance studies indicate that the performance of emission control systems degrades rapidly in the absence of I/M. Illustratively,
actual carbon monoxide and hydrocarbon emissions after one full
year of operation were essentially unchanged from the 1971 to

the 1974 models, though the new-car standards called for reductions on the order of one-third between these two model years.[8] After only about a half-year of operation, on average, 63 percent of the 1975 models tested in five cities were in noncompliance with at least one of the three standards for that year.[9] And an EPA study of 1974 models concluded that whereas the new-car standards for that year called for carbon monoxide and hydrocarbon emission levels about 60 percent below the 1970 standards, in practice they would achieve lifetime reductions of only about 20 percent in the absence of I/M.[10]

Congress in 1977 specified that air quality control regions expected to be in violation of ambient air quality standards after 1982 would have to file schedules for the implementation of I/M programs. It did not specify what these timetables should be, however. And while it mandated stiff penalties for regions neglecting to file them, it provided only minor penalties for regions neglecting to implement them.

Given that the ambient air quality standards have been set at levels intended to protect even the most feeble from the most trivial adverse health effects, it does appear sensible to confine I/M programs to regions in violation of the standards. At the same time, because most current forecasts are based on the assumption that new-car standards will be maintained over actual vehicle lifetimes, many more regions will actually be in violation during any specific future year than current official forecasts anticipate. At some point it seems likely that environmental organizations will seize upon this anomaly and that the political system will begin coming seriously to grips with the I/M issue.

Even without government I/M programs, most owners are likely to take corrective action to deal with major performance degradation of safety and fuel economy control systems. Further, most states already have safety inspection programs and require in connection with them that automobile mufflers (which are important safety as well as noise control devices) be in good working order. Even so a Department of Transportation safety study has recently estimated that more intensive brake and tire I/M requirements would probably save a considerable number of lives.[11] Estimates are unavailable of the extent to which maintenance neglect may threaten realization of the full potential of the federal new-car fuel economy program; this would certainly appear to merit high priority as a topic for future research.

4. The Department of Transportation study cited in the previous paragraph concluded that, aside from vehicle modifications, the most cost-effective measures that might be taken in the field of automobile safety were the adoption and enforcement of mandatory seat belt use laws (even with quite modest fines and infrequent enforcement checks), strict enforcement of the 55 mph speed limit, and alcohol safety countermeasures (including the use of special enforcement patrols to detect and arrest alcohol-impaired drivers during high-risk periods). Additionally it ranked mandatory helmet use laws for motorcyclists as among the most cost-effective safety measures available. The study did not even consider such stronger measures as jail sentences for alcohol-impaired drivers (imposed in some other countries) and reduced speed limits on older roads that were unaffected by adoption of the 55 mph expressway speed limit in 1974; but it seems reasonable to assume that the neglect of these measures was attributable to the fact that they seemed so far beyond the American political pale rather than that they appeared cost-ineffective.

5. Finally, road use pricing and core-area supplementary licensing schemes have enormous potential for alleviating congestion, because the elasticity of demand for travel on particular roads at particular times is much higher than the overall elasticity of motor vehicle travel demand. Contrary to most economists, we judge that the average motorist, even after trying road use pricing, would continue to express a preference for congestion. If the only problem of concern were congestion, however, it would be difficult to imagine a quicker or more cost-effective solution. And even with all complexities considered, we judge it far superior to highway construction as a method of relieving congestion in high-density urban areas. (This is by no means to suggest that one or the other ought to be chosen; our own first preference in the vast majority of cases would be to do neither.)

In brief, then, consumer regulatory and price disincentive measures have great technical potential for alleviating most of the significant problems of urban transportation in cost-effective fashion. For the most part, however, they are viewed by elected officials as politically untouchable. We anticipate that inspection and maintenance requirements, helmet use laws, stricter speed limit enforcement, modest indirect price disincentives like the rejected wellhead tax on crude oil, and other constraint measures that entail very little behavioral change for most people will become gradually more feasible in the years ahead. But the most obvious and direct forms of consumer restraint—large gas tax increases, parking restrictions, congestion tolls, and so forth—seem likely to remain beyond the pale for many years to come.

Concluding Remarks

The current American system of urban transportation, we have emphasized, is not itself a problem. From the perspectives of the vast majority of American adults—those who are licensed to drive and who live in car-owning households—it can more appropriately be labeled a resounding success. It affords them an unprecedented range of residential, employment, and other locational choices at prices that most appear quite willing to pay in the marketplace. These prices include some modest hidden subsidies—mainly in the form of adverse external effects for which no payment is made— but the attractions of the system are such that the full internalization of these costs would have only the most trivial impacts upon urban travel behavior.

At the same time, there are a number of important problems associated with this system. Our own judgment, and that of the political system as well, appears to be that four of these command the highest priority for remedial attention: the high energy requirements of the system, its air pollution impacts, the large number of motor vehicle fatalities and serious injuries associated with it, and the equity issues posed by the fact that substantial numbers of handicapped, elderly, and very poor urban residents are unable to achieve high levels of "auto-mobility."

In seeking to ameliorate these problems, we have noted, it is essential to bear a number of key political constraints in mind.

The American governmental system is highly resistant to measures that directly constrain voters to alter their behavior, that threaten to disrupt sectors of the economy, or that involve the repudiation of ongoing programs with well-organized clienteles. Since about 1970, it has also been highly resistant to measures that threaten neighborhood and environmental disruption. Prior to the mid-1970s it was relatively receptive to spending proposals but several factors have joined to make fiscal ceilings another key constraint during the past several years. First, voter resistance to tax increases has severely intensified. Second, a number of techniques for incurring large expenditure increases without having to consider tax increases, which were extremely important during the 1960s and early 1970s, are no longer available.[17] Third, the costs of existing services have been rising more rapidly than revenues at constant tax rates. In consequence of these factors in combination, the fiscal resources available (or likely to become so in the near future) are severely strained simply to maintain current service levels. Indeed it seems more likely that the next few years will witness cutbacks in existing services than that substantial resources will become available for new or expanded services.

Our analysis has suggested, in any event, that only one of the four main problems of urban transportation—inequity—is susceptible of effective attack by spending measures. Fixed route and demand responsive transit services are the most likely instruments for enhancing the mobility of those without ready access to automobiles. We have emphasized, however, that transit service improvements are likely to yield major equity benefits only if they are carefully targeted to do so. Most transit improvement efforts to date have focused on the travel demands of downtown commuters—an ablebodied group with above average incomes on the

[17.] These fell into two main categories. At the federal level, the triumph of Keynesian economic theory permitted a dramatic increase in the annual gap between revenues and expenditures during the late 1960s and early 1970s. By the mid-1970s, however, economists were generally agreed that still higher budget deficits would be extremely inflationary. At the state and local levels, borrowing increased even more dramatically from the 1950s through the mid-1970s, despite the fact that operating budgets were generally required to be balanced each year. In the wake of the New York City fiscal crisis, however, state-local accounting and borrowing practices became subject to extremely close scrutiny by investors, taxpayer associations, and the media, with a consequent dramatic slowdown in the rate of debt increase.

whole—rather than on those of the mobility deprived. The resultant services, on the whole, have done little or nothing to enhance system equity.

The most promising strategies for curtailing energy consumption, air pollution and the motor vehicle accident toll all entail business regulation aimed at improving the performance characteristics of automobile hardware. Such regulation entails constraint, but in a manner that is not particularly noticeable from the standpoint of the average consumer. It taps the technological and organizational resources of the private sector more effectively than even government contracting (since it leaves incentives for cost control and for competitive technical approaches intact). And its potential is particularly great where a performance criterion has—like the three in question—long been neglected by the industry. In these circumstances there is likely to be a substantial backlog of available and almost-available technology ready to be applied within a relatively few years.

In the case of emission control, most of the benefit of regulation to ensure improved new-car performance apparently tends to be lost in the absence of effective lifetime maintenance. Owners have negligible incentive, moreover, to carry out such maintenance in the absence of public regulation. Thus inspection and maintenance requirements are the obvious next step in regions with air pollution problems that would otherwise remain significant through the 1980s and beyond.

The cause of fuel economy might be pursued as effectively by pricing and/or rationing measures as by business regulation, but these are extremely unpalatable politically. Similarly the cause of safety might be pursued in highly effective fashion by such measures as mandatory seat belt and (for motorcyclists) helmet use laws, by strict speed limit enforcement, by tough measures to keep alcohol-impaired drivers off the roads, and by the application of more stringent brake and tire inspection standards. While several of these are doubtless more acceptable than gas taxation or rationing to curtail demand (some states, after all, do have helmet use laws and relatively strict speed limit enforcement), the disposition of political decision makers has been to view rapid progress in the use of such direct consumer regulatory measures as unfeasible.

In brief, then, effective attacks on the major problems of urban transportation must necessarily entail constraint strategies (in three cases) and transit improvement priorities sharply different from those that have traditionally prevailed (in the fourth). In the first three cases, however—energy, air pollution, and safety—there are opportunities for dramatic progress by applying the constraints directly to only a few large corporations, challenging them to achieve the policy targets by technical innovation and to recoup their costs incurred along the way in the private market place. Though never applied prior to the 1960s, this particular category of constraint measures has proven to combine great problem-solving power with high political acceptability. In the fourth case—equity—the measures called for arouse no discernible opposition in principle. But they are expensive, they are unglamorous, and the competition for transit resources is likely to be particularly fierce during the years immediately ahead. If it were not for the effective recent mobilization efforts of the elderly and handicapped, and the accompanying evidence of high receptivity to their claims by elected officials, we would severely doubt the likelihood of much equity-oriented service expansion in the near future. Even as it is, we consider this a matter of extreme uncertainty.

What does seem clear is that the major problems of urban transportation can be effectively addressed without significant behavioral change. A prolonged embargo or war-induced oil shortage may, of course, at some point require dramatic short-term behavioral adaptation (mainly, we judge, by the curtailment of nonessential auto travel and by private ride sharing). But aside from such unforeseeable crises of a political nature, there do not appear to be any developments on the horizon that would require urban Americans to alter their patterns or volumes of automobile travel.

APPENDIX A
URBAN FREIGHT TRANSPORTATION

Goods movement, conducted almost entirely by truck, accounts for a significant share of urban vehicle miles of travel (VMT) and for a considerably larger proportion of the energy, air quality, safety, and noise problems associated with urban transportation.[1] Medium and heavy trucks, for example, accounted for only 6 percent of urban VMT in 1975 but for 14 percent of combined auto and truck fuel consumption.[1] In the same year, tractor-trailer trucks accounted for 4 percent of nationwide VMT but for 7 percent of highway fatalities.[2] EPA reported in 1973 that heavy vehicles, which accounted for about 10 percent of nationwide VMT, were responsible for 18 percent of combined auto and truck particulate emissions, 19 percent of hydrocarbon emissions, 24 percent of nitrogen oxide emissions, and 18 percent of carbon dioxide emissions.[3] Finally, trucking accounted for nearly one-third of total urban transportation expenditures (public and private combined) in 1975. (See table 2.2.)

Despite these considerations and the central importance of goods movement in the urban economy, the freight component of urban transportation has rarely attracted significant policy attention. In seeking to account for this apparent oversight, we have found ourselves drawn to the following hypotheses.

First, while they have joined in general campaigns for road improvement, truckers have generally not pressed very hard for public solutions to their special problems—most notably, street congestion in terminal and warehouse areas. Rather they have concentrated in recent decades on relocating freight-handling facilities to sites relatively free of congestion and with ample space for off-street loading and unloading. Illustratively, Wilbur Smith, Inc., found in a 1966 study that, even as the number of truck terminals in the Chicago region increased slightly (from 541 to 544) between 1950 and 1960, the number in the Loop declined by one-third (from 185 to 122) and the percentage within 4.5 miles of it declined from 77 to 54 percent.[4]

[1.] The growing utilization of light trucks and vans for personal travel makes a precise accounting of commercial truck use quite difficult. Federal policy makers have in recent years classified trucks weighing more than about 8500 pounds, however, as heavy-duty commercial vehicles. See appendix C for a brief discussion of the rapid growth of light truck and van use for personal travel purposes in recent years.

Second, ideological critics of motor vehicle dominance have generally excluded intraurban trucking from their attacks, recognizing the lack of any viable alternative. Whereas it has been fashionable in some quarters to speak of the national "love affair" with the automobile and to call for increased mass transit usage, it has been readily apparent that these concepts were inapplicable to the motor freight component of the urban transportation system.

Third, few voters (or media consumers) appear to be interested in the subject of urban goods movement. Thus where public authorities have adopted measures of benefit to both auto and truck users, they have invariably stressed the former in their public statements. And where they have taken steps of benefit primarily to truck users, these have generally proceeded with little fanfare.

Fourth, there is little peaking associated with freight transportation, and indeed the morning commuter hours tend to be a period of particularly light commercial truck movement. Consequently popular campaigns for measures to relieve congestion have typically portrayed it as quite simply an auto-induced phenomenon. Had such campaigns focused more on local street congestion, especially during off-peak hours, they would necessarily have paid far greater attention to trucking; but for a variety of reasons (including the lack of obvious remedies) they have not.

Finally, the absolute contributions of motor freight to the energy, air quality, and safety problems of urban transportation are decidedly secondary by comparison with those of light passenger vehicle use. Truckers have successfully capitalized on this fact in arguing for a concentration of public regulatory energy on light duty vehicles. While medium and heavy trucks have been subjected to some modest safety and emission regulations (about equivalent, as of 1978, to those specified for 1971 autos), they have escaped fuel economy regulation altogether. (Congress has accepted the truckers' argument that their own economic interests will drive them to adopt all reasonably cost-effective fuel conservation techniques.)

The one area in which medium and heavy trucks have been singled out for public remedial action is noise. Noise control advocates have successfully maintained that an initial emphasis on light vehicle regulation would be wholly inappropriate. Even here, though, the regulations adopted have required only hardware modifications (as opposed to changes in use patterns) and have been drawn with respectful attention to industry arguments about lead time requirements and the importance of holding down costs.

It seems likely that medium and heavy trucks will attract increasing regulatory scrutiny as the auto and light truck contributions to major problems associated with the urban transportation system are reduced. A federal interagency task force estimated in 1976, for example, that if all current EPA standards were successfully implemented, medium and heavy trucks would by 1990 generate hydrocarbon emissions nearly equal to, nitrogen oxide emissions slightly greater than, and carbon dioxide emissions more than twice those of the entire light vehicle fleet.[5] There is little indication, however, that the general pattern of viewing the urban transportation system almost exclusively in terms of its personal travel component is about to be broken.

Table 2.1 is based on the following sources and calculations:

1. Automobile and truck capital and operating costs (other than automobile insurance), school bus and other bus costs, and taxi revenues are as reported in Transportation Association of America, *Transportation Facts and Trends,* 13th ed. (August 1977), pp. 4, 5.

2. Auto insurance costs have been estimated for 1975 by averaging the Federal Highway Administration estimates for 1974 and 1976, Cf. FHWA, Highway Statistics Division, "The Costs of Operating an Automobile," 1974 and 1976 ed. (Washington: U.S. Government Printing Office).

3. Public highway expenditures attributable to auto and truck use have been calculated from Kiran Bhatt et al., *An Analysis of Road Expenditures and Payments by Vehicle Class (1956–1975)* (Washington: The Urban Institute, 1977), p. 62, appendixes 1, 8. The estimated amounts include the following subtotals: capital ($3.3 billion attributable to autos, $1.2 billion to trucks), maintenance ($1.0 billion auto, $1.0 billion truck), administrative costs of highway agencies and traffic police ($0.7 billion auto, $0.1 billion truck), and police and judicial system costs attributable to auto-related crimes and tort actions ($2.5 billion auto, $0.5 billion truck).

4. Rail rapid and bus transit revenues are as reported in American Public Transit Association, *Transit Fact Book,* 1976-1977 ed. (Washington: APTA, 1977), table 4. Operating subsidies have been calculated from tables 4 and 5.

5. Commuter rail revenues are as reported in *Transportation Facts and Trends,* p. 5. Commuter rail operating subsidies are as reported in John Pucher, "Losses in the American Transit Industry, 1973-1976," New Perspectives on Urban Transportation Project (Center for Transportation Studies, MIT, May 1977), table 2-1.

6. Transit capital expenditures are as reported in table 8.14.

In the course of developing table 2.1, we have also reviewed the data available on highway user tax receipts and on general revenues expended for highway purposes in urban areas. As indicated in table B.1, highway user tax receipts in urban areas are more than sufficient to cover the public costs of the urban highway system. In practice, however, about three-fifths of the highway user tax revenues raised in urban areas are expended outside them, and about three-fifths of urban highway costs are covered by general revenues.

TABLE B.1
Urban Highway Tax Receipts and Public Expenditures, 1975

| Vehicle Class | Receipts | | Expenditures[a] |
	User Receipts Collected in Urban Areas	General Revenues	
Autos	8.1		7.5
Trucks	3.3		2.8
Total	11.4	6.1	10.3

Sources: User receipts allocated by vehicle type have been calculated from Kiran Bhatt et al, *An Analysis of Road Expenditures and Payments by Vehicle Class (1956–1975)* (Washington: Urban Institute, 1977), appendixes I and II. General revenues allocated for capital, maintenance, and "conventional" administrative costs are as reported in FHWA, *Highway Statistics*, 1975 ed. (Washington: U.S. Government Printing Office, 1977), sect. 3, table UF-1, p. VIII-7. General revenues allocated for "additional" administrative costs are as estimated in Bhatt et al., *loc. cit.*, p. 112.

Note: A considerable percentage of general revenues are from such quasi-user charges as local auto property taxes and state sales taxes on auto purchases. The available data do not permit distinguishing these from other general receipts with any precision, however, so we have simply included them in the general revenue category. The data likewise do not permit distinguishing urban from rural collections of those general receipts utilized to pay "additional administrative costs;" thus we have contented ourselves with the rough estimate that urban receipts and expenditures for this item are in balance.

There has been much debate as to whether general revenue contributions to the highway sector should be viewed as subsidies to motorists. The alternative viewpoint is that they are payments in recognition of the pedestrian and local property access functions of streets and highways.

[a] From table 2.1.

The passenger mileage estimates presented in table 2.2 were derived as follows:

1. Transit passenger mileage was calculated separately for bus, rail rapid, and commuter rail. Trip length estimates of 3.93 miles for bus and 6.57 miles for rail rapid transit were obtained from U.S. Department of Transportation, *1974 National Transportation Report: Urban Data Supplement* (Washington: U.S. Government Printing Office, 1976), tables D-23, D-30. These estimated trip lengths were then multiplied by the American Public Transit Association's estimates of total unlinked trips for each year by mode: *Transit Fact Book, 1976-1977 Edition*, p. 26. Commuter rail passenger miles for 1975 are from Association of American Railroads (AAR) "Operating and Traffic Statistics, Class I Line-Haul Railroads in the United States," O.S. series no. 217 (1975). Commuter rail passenger miles for other years have been estimated from AAR's *Yearbook of Railroad Facts,* 1977 ed. p. 32.

2. Auto passenger mileage was derived for each year by multiplying FHWA's estimate of auto vehicle mileage in urban areas by 2.2, which represents average occupancy per urban vehicle mile as reported in the Nationwide Personal Transportation Study (NPTS). Cf. FHWA, *Highway Statistics* (Washington: U.S. Government Printing Office, various years), table VM-1, and NPTS, report 1, Automobile Occupancy, (Washington: FHWA, 1972), p. 7.

Regrettably the estimates contain several probable sources of error, which we have been unable to quantify. On balance, it appears that correction of these errors would modestly reduce the transit modal shares indicated in table 2.2. specifically:

1. NPTS is the only nationwide source for estimates of urban auto occupancy and is available for only 1969-1970. Thus we have assumed a constant occupancy throughout the period covered, though fragmentary data indicate that average auto occupancies have been declining over time. Correction for this factor would tend to raise the auto travel estimates for the years prior to 1970.

2. The *National Transportation Report,* which examined transit trip lengths as of 1971, is the only source for nationwide esti-

mates. Thus we have assumed constant trip lengths throughout the period covered, though it seems clear that average transit trip lengths have been increasing over time. Correction for this factor would tend to depress the transit travel estimates for earlier years.

3. Commuter rail passenger mileage estimates prior to 1971 involve considerable uncertainties because of the passenger classifications ("commutation and multiple ride," "coach," and "parlor and sleeping car") used by the Interstate Commerce Commission. The Association of American Railroads has for many years summed the data on numbers of passengers using discounted "commutation" tickets reported by the individual railroads and has presented this total as commutation patronage. However, when AMTRAK assumed almost all intercity service in 1971, it became clear that a considerable number of commuter rail patrons were riding on single-trip tickets. In 1975, for example, single-trip passengers accounted for 23 percent of commuter rail passenger trips and 22 percent of commuter rail passenger miles. We have assumed that this pattern prevailed in earlier years as well.

4. The auto estimates do not include personal travel by light truck and van because precise estimates of such usage are unavailable. Indisputably, however, such travel has increased rapidly during the 1960s and 1970s. Illustratively the proportion of trucks and vans used "primarily for personal transportation" (urban and rural combined) rose from 25 percent in 1963 to 41 percent in 1972, suggesting that it may be in the 50 percent range as of 1978. Meanwhile, the truck/van proportion of total motor vehicle registrations rose from 16 percent in 1965 to 21 percent in 1975. The average truck used primarily for personal transportation was driven 9,800 miles in 1972 (compared with 10,200 miles for the average auto). Thus it appears that correction for this factor would add 8–10 percent to the auto passenger mileage figures presented for 1970 and 1975. The upward adjustment in earlier years would be considerably smaller, but it is impossible to say (even approximately) how much smaller with any confidence.[1]

Noise is unpleasant sound, and appraisals of given sounds vary widely both among individuals and, for any specific individual, among circumstances (by activity, time of day, and so on). There is ample room for disagreement, consequently, about how multidimensional sound readings should be translated into policy-relevant measures of noise. And in practice there are numerous contenders for recognition as the most useful noise scale. The simplest of these is the decibel (dB) scale, which measures the physical intensity of sound waves in the air, and virtually all others build upon it.[1] The most commonly used for regulatory purposes is the A-weighted decibel (dBA) scale, which weights decibel readings to accommodate the finding that most people judge high- and low-pitched sounds to be louder than sounds of equivalent intensity in the middle range of pitches. The dBA scale is the basis for all equipment standards under the federal Noise Control Act.

Most progress in motor vehicle noise abatement until recently came from the manufacturers, who recognized that noise loud enough to distrub residents and pedestrians would be offensive as well to potential buyers. Their remedy was the development of low-cost mufflers that reduced the noise of automobile engines to relatively unobtrusive levels. Where prospective purchasers were deemed indifferent to noise (as with respect to trucks), however, or positively attracted by it (as with motorcycles), little or no abatement was achieved.

Through the mid-1960s, motor vehicle noise regulation was confined to state and local requirements that original equipment mufflers be replaced more or less in kind as they wore out. During the late 1960s, however, in the context of the general environmental awakening, several states (including New York and California) enacted decibel-based noise standards. In 1970 Congress directed EPA to conduct a comprehensive study of the effects of noise on public health and welfare and to develop recommendations for

---

[1.] The decibel is a nonlinear measure, being ten times the logarithm of a sound's physical intensity. A logarithmic scale is employed to permit compression of the extraordinary range of sound intensities detectable by the human ear to a manageable size. On the dB scale zero is the threshold of hearing, 140 the average threshold of physical pain. The key points to bear in mind are that a three decibel increment equals a doubling of physical sound intensity, while a ten decibel increment is perceived by the average listener as approximately a doubling of loudness.

federal legislative action. EPA's consequent 1972 report was quickly translated into the Noise Control Act of that year.[1] Although the authors of this report were unable to document hearing loss or psychological illness due to excessive noise in non-occupational settings, or to determine whether overall urban noise levels were increasing, they found substantial evidence that large numbers of Americans were annoyed by transportation noises, particularly those emanating from commercial airports and urban freeways.[2] Given the action mood then prevailing on environmental issues, and a growing preference by the manufacturers themselves for uniform national standards rather than varying state standards, the focus during the 1972 congressional session was on choosing among alternative bills rather than on whether to enact national standards at all. The hearing record indicates that the greatest concern of noise control advocates was jet aircraft noise (ultimately dealt with in separate legislation) and that motor vehicle noise was addressed as much at the urging of equipment manufacturers as of environmentalists. Indeed the major dispute about motor vehicle noise was about whether the federal government should preempt the field of new-car noise regulation. The environmentalists maintained that the states should be left free to enact more stringent standards than the federal government chose to mandate nationwide, whereas the manufacturers argued the reverse. The latter eventually prevailed.

Patterned after the 1970 Clean Air Act Amendments, the Noise Control Act directed EPA to develop ambient noise standards low enough to preclude any harm to human health or welfare and source emission standards that, when fully achieved, would reduce noise levels throughout the nation below the ambient standards. Unlike the clean air legislation, however, it left EPA complete discretion in determining appropriate compliance schedules and

[2]. Subsequently, a 1973 nationwide survey conducted by the Bureau of the Census found noise mentioned most frequently among undesirable neighborhood conditions about which residents were concerned. Forty-four percent of homeowner respondents and 48 percent of renters expressed concern about undesirable noise levels (from all sources) in their neighborhoods. By comparison, only 11 percent of owners and 17 percent of renters mentioned crime. Not surprisingly, concern about noise was greatest in central cities, where 52 percent of owners and 50 percent of renters reported annoying neighborhood noise levels.[2]

TABLE D.1
Ambient and Motor Vehicle Emission Noise Standards

A. Ambient Standards

Primary (to protect against health damage, defined as any loss of hearing): Weighted average of 75 dBA during an 8 hour period or 70 dBA during a 24 hour period.
Second (to protect against harm to the public welfare, defined as general annoyance and speech interference): Weighted average of 55 dBA outdoors and 45 dBA indoors during a 24 hour period.

B. Emission Standards

Type of Vehicle	Maximum Noise Level[a]	Effective Date	Projected Additional Cost per Vehicle[b]	Additional Cost as a Percentage of Purchase Price[b]
Medium and heavy trucks	83	Jan. 1, 1978	$35–$426	0.6–5.8%
	80	Jan. 1, 1982	$180–$850	2.2–11.5%
	reserved for future determination	Jan. 1, 1985	NA	NA
Street motorcycles	83	Jan. 1, 1980	NA	NA
	80	Jan. 1, 1982	NA	NA
	78	Jan. 1, 1985	NA	5–13%
Buses (interior)	86	Jan. 1, 1979	NA	NA
	83	Jan. 1, 1983	NA	NA
	80	Jan. 1, 1985	NA	1.8–8.8%
(exterior)	83	Jan. 1, 1979	NA	NA
	83	Jan. 1, 1983	NA	NA
	77	Jan. 1, 1985	NA	1.8–8.8%

Source: Environmental Protection Agency, "Noise Emission Standards for Transportation Equipment: Medium and Heavy Trucks," *Federal Register* (April 13, 1976): 15544; EPA, "Noise Emissions Standards for Transportation Equipment: Buses," *Federal Register* (September 12, 1977): 45777, 45780; and EPA, "Noise Emission Standards for Transportation Equipment: Motorcycles," *Federal Register* (March 15, 1978): 10823, 10833.

[a] At at distance of fifty feet perpendicular to the center line of travel with the vehicle operated in its noisiest mode, generally full throttle acceleration.

[b] Costs vary with type of engine and vehicle weight (medium weight gas powered vehicles are considerably cheaper to muffle than heavy diesels) and with the size of manufacturer (since a larger production run allows research, development, and tooling costs to be spread over more vehicles).

interim standards. It neglected to authorize any form of behavioral regulation (such as night-time bans on truck traffic in residential neighborhoods). It directed EPA to take cost into account when setting interim standards (rather than simply to mandate the use of best available technologies).[3] And it failed to provide any government funding for research to accelerate the pace of technical progress. In brief, then, the central premise of the Noise Control Act was (and is) that noise regulation should follow behind the ordinary advance of technology in the private sector, ensuring simply that hardware improvements deemed cost-effective by EPA are universally adopted within a short while after they become available.

Transportation products identified to date as "major sources" of excessive noise are trucks weighing more than ten thousand pounds, buses, and motorcycles. EPA does not plan to require further improvements in the muffling of automobile engines, judging that trucks, buses, and motorcycles are so much noisier than cars at present that there is little point to devoting regulatory energy to the latter until sharp reductions have been achieved in emissions by the former. By way of illustration: if a traffic stream consists of one heavy truck emitting 84 dBA and nine cars emitting 69 dBA each (both figures being about average today at moderate cruising speeds), the combined noise level is about 85 dBA. Even if all the automobiles are removed, the sound level does not fall below 84 dBA; but if the truck sound is reduced to the automobile level, the combined emission from the ten vehicles falls to 79 dBA (perceived by most listeners to represent a 30 percent noise reduction from 84 dBA).[4]

The ambient and motor vehicle emission standards thus far promulgated by EPA pursuant to the Noise Control Act are shown in table D.1.

Proven reserves are current estimates of the amount of oil that can be obtained from fields already discovered at current prices and with current technology. Estimates of proven world reserves vary, but a widely accepted one is that proven reserves in the entire non-communist world totaled 555 billion barrels at the end of 1975. This total was distributed geographically as follows: Saudi Arabia, 27 percent; the other Middle Eastern OPEC nations (including Libya and Algeria), 43 percent; the non-Middle Eastern OPEC nations (most notably, Nigeria, Venezuela, and Indonesia), 10 percent; the United States, 6 percent; and the rest of the world (most notably, Canada, Mexico, Brazil, and Egypt), 14 percent.[1] The U.S. proven reserve was less than six years worth of current consumption, and more recent estimates place proven U.S. reserves at the end of 1976 as equal to only five years worth of current consumption.[2]

Total oil consumption by the noncommunist nations in 1976 totaled 17.6 billion barrels, or 3.2 percent of proven reserves.[3] Potential future additions to reserves are thought to exceed current proven reserves by a factor of about two. This is far from saying, however, that adequate supplies will be available in a time frame sufficient to maintain level or growing consumption over the next several decades. Most future discoveries are expected to be of relatively small fields, often in locations from which recovery (if undertaken at all) will be extremely expensive. For example, the most recent large discoveries outside the Middle East have been under the North Sea and in remote sections of Alaska. Some future discoveries are likely to be under ocean floors beyond the continental shelves and Antarctica.[4] Thus the prospect is that new additions to proven reserves will fall off gradually, even as consumption increases in the coming decades. The Workshop on Alternative Energy Strategies, a multinational research project sponsored by the Massachusetts Institute of Technology, has made the following range estimates of future additions to noncommunist world reserves in billions of barrels added per year:[5]

1975-2000   10-20
2000-2010   8-12

2010-2020   6-7
2020-2025   3-4

Assuming that average annual additions in each period will be in the middle of the estimated ranges, total additions during the fifty-year period will be 608 billion barrels. Combined with current proven reserves of 555 billion barrels, these figures suggest that world oil consumption might continue for sixty-five or seventy years at the 1976 level. (Both the production and consumption figures are for the noncommunist world only.)

If one assumes, however, that demand will grow at 3 percent a year (versus the 1940-1976 rate of 6.6 percent), consumption in the year 2000 will be slightly more than twice the 1976 level.[6] In this scenario, consumption during the twenty-five year period 1976-2000 totals 642 billion barrels, whereas additions to proven reserves total 375 barrels. At the end of the year 2000, remaining proven reserves are equal to 8.0 years of consumption at the then-current rate. By comparison, proven reserves in 1975 equalled 31.5 years at the current level of consumption. Carrying this scenario forward a bit further, if one assumes level demand after 2000, proven reserves reach zero in the year 2012.

The above scenario would obviously be impossible to play out to anywhere near its end, but it does serve to dramatize the fact that world oil consumption will have to peak and begin declining well before 2000.

This is far from the end of the story, however. It is only the end insofar as oil extraction by currently economic techniques (mainly natural pressure) from conventional wells is concerned. Such techniques generally yield about 25 percent of the oil actually in the reservoirs being tapped. Technologies already exist (though they are not economic in many circumstances) to extract oil from other sources than wells (oil shale, tar sands, and coal). Further a variety of techniques exist for creating oil substitutes and additives from wood and other agricultural products. The key question is thus, How quickly will these alternative sources become commercially attractive and, where environmental problems currently exist, environmentally acceptable? The rate at which they become commercially attractive will be a function both of world oil prices (relative to prices overall) and of the rate at which extraction technologies improve.

The Federal Energy Administration has estimated that U.S. oil shale reserves alone may eventually supply 1,800 billion barrels of oil, more than all the oil expected ever to be recoverable from conventional fields. This amount is equivalent to about three hundred years of U.S. consumption at the 1976 rate. As of 1977, the estimated cost of oil shale production was about twice the world price of oil ($25–30 a barrel versus $13.50). And there are severe environmental problems associated with oil shale production. But significant progress is anticipated with reference to both of these obstacles in the decades ahead.

In short the world will not run out of oil in the next several generations. The relative price of oil is likely to increase fairly sharply during the 1980s and 1990s, however, and supplies may be tight during the latter half of this period. Precisely how tight they are will depend on the following factors: the rate at which demand increases, the extent to which the OPEC nations (and particularly Saudi Arabia) choose to increase their production capacity, the world price (since higher prices will tend to depress demand and to stimulate investment in new extraction technologies), the net oil trade balance of the communist world, and the rate at which new sources of oil are brought into production. The predominant view is that the last will play a minor role until about the year 2000, but much less attention has been paid to this topic than to conventional oil forecasting.

It is quite possible, then, that oil and close oil substitutes will be in relatively ample supply by sometime in the twenty-first century, though at substantially higher prices than Americans have been accustomed to paying. Such long-term forecasts are necessarily quite speculative, however. The shorter-term, more certain prospect is that the final decades of the twentieth century will be a period of rapidly intensifying pressure for oil conservation.

APPENDIX F
ASSUMPTIONS EMPLOYED IN ESTIMATING POTENTIAL ENERGY SAVINGS FROM INCREASED VANPOOLING, CARPOOLING, AND MASS TRANSIT USE

A rather wide variety of estimates have been advanced of the energy that might be saved if large numbers of current automobile commuters could be induced to vanpool, carpool, or use mass transit. Many of these estimates appear to have been developed on the basis of a few rough assumptions, however; some have been developed by officials or trade associations with specific program or modal axes to grind; and none have been published with a full and systematic statement of the assumptions on which they rest. Thus we have deemed it necessary to develop estimates of our own (presented on pages 154–158), based upon explicit assumptions in which we felt reasonable confidence. Our purpose here is to set forth these assumptions.

Vanpool Energy Savings

Our estimates of the contributions to energy conservation that might be made by various levels of vanpooling are based on the following assumptions:

1. The U.S. automobile fleet in 1975 averaged 14.9 miles per gallon (mpg) and in 1980 will average 16.1 mpg. The 1975 figure is an EPA estimate.[1] The 1980 forecast is FEA's, based on a projection of EPA figures for past years and an assumption that new car performance will progress smoothly toward compliance with the standards mandated in the Energy Policy and Conservation Act of 1975. The act requires that 1978 model cars average 18 mpg, that 1979 model cars average 19 mpg, and that 1980 model cars average 20 mpg.

2. Vans averaged 10 mpg in 1975 and will average 12 mpg in 1980. The 1975 estimate is based upon the actual experience of the 3M Company.[2] The 1980 estimate is little more than a guess. There appear to be two primary means by which van fuel economy can be improved over the next several years. Ignition system improvements seem likely to improve the mileage of gasoline-powered vans, which all of those on the road now are, by about 5 percent. More significantly, the introduction of diesel-powered vans will potentially improve fuel economy by 40–50 percent. The

great uncertainties are when diesel-powered vans will become available and how quickly thereafter their market shares will grow.

3. Vanpool users will be drawn disproportionately from the ranks of those living substantial distances from work. Current national experience is that ride sharing increases with average commutation trip distance. The average auto commutation trip nationally was 9.4 miles in 1970 (8.4 miles in incorporated areas, 11.1 miles in unincorporated areas).[3] The average 3M vanpool patron lives an estimated 15 direct driving miles from work. We have assumed that the average vanpool patron, at levels of diversion up to 15 percent of those currently commuting by automobile, will live 12.0 direct driving miles from work. For scenarios that involve even higher levels of diversion, we have assumed a more typical commutation trip mix, with an average direct driving distance of 10.0 miles.

4. Vanpool users will be drawn disproportionately from the ranks of current carpoolers, but not at all from the ranks of current transit patrons. This, again, is based on the 3M experience. It bears mention, however, that 3M has not offered van service to areas from which transit service is readily available. The national average auto occupancy for commutation trips in 1970 was 1.39.[4] For scenarios involving levels of diversion up to 15 percent of present auto commuters, we have assumed an average occupancy of 1.6 for the autos from which vanpool users will be attracted. For scenarios involving higher levels of diversion, we have assumed a previous auto occupancy of 1.5.

5. The vans will average 11 riders each (including the driver, who will be making his or her own commutation trip). Each van, therefore, will replace 6.9 auto trips at levels of diversion up to 15 percent and 7.3 auto trips at higher diversion levels.

6. In order to achieve their average occupancy rate of 11.0, the vans will have to be routed rather circuitously. Whereas the average 3M vanpooler lives 15 direct driving miles from work, the average van travels about 25 miles each way. Thus we estimate that average van driving distance will be about two-thirds more than the average distance that each patron would drive if he or she

commuted to work by car alone. In short, if the average direct commutation distance is 12 miles, the average van route will be 20 miles. This averages out to 0.8 miles attributable to each patron other than the driver.

7. The average automobile previously driven to work also required some circuitous mileage in order to achieve its average occupancy of 1.6. If we assume that auto driving distance was increased 0.8 miles for each passenger, that the average auto occupant lived 12 miles direct driving distance from work, the average auto vehicular trip at an occupancy of 1.6 was 12.5 miles.

8. The average automobile formerly used for commutation was driven to work, we assume, 230 days a year. When commuters were ill, out of town, or on vacation, the vehicle was left home. By contrast, the van must operate every working day. Thus we assume that it will be driven 250 days a year.

9. Twenty percent of the fuel saved directly as a result of the modal shift from autos to vanpools will be lost due to additional driving of the vehicles left at home by other households members. This figure is lower than those recently estimated by two consultants studying the energy-saving potential of carpooling. Cambridge Systematics, Inc., in a study prepared for FEA, has estimated that 35 percent of the energy saved by additional carpooling would be lost as a result of additional household driving.[5] Gregory Ingram, Gary Fauth, and Eugene Kroch of Harvard University, in a study prepared for the U.S. Department of Transportation, have estimated that the loss would be in the range of one-third.[6]

We have reduced these estimates, for the following reasons. First, both studies assumed that the new carpoolers had previously driven only the national average distance to work. We have assumed that vanpoolers will be drawn disproportionately from among those living at a greater than average distance from work— and there is no reason to assume that additional household driving will increase as a function of average commutation trip length. Second, it seems likely that some vanpool patrons would, as they became confident of the reliability of vanpool service, sell their second and third cars. Few would do so, presumably, just because they had joined a carpool; but vanpool reliability should be extremely high, and vanpooling would not require any patrons to use their own cars.

10. The total employed work force in the United States as of 1975 was 87.0 million. By projecting the 1970–1975 rate of growth in the total labor force (including the unemployed) and assuming a constant rate of unemployment, we have anticipated that the number of employed in 1980 will be 96.0 million.

11. As of 1970, 15 percent of employed individuals worked at home, walked to work, or had no fixed place of employment.[7] Of the remainder, 83 percent commuted to work by automobile, 8 percent by truck, 7 percent by mass transit (bus, streetcar, and rapid transit), and 2 percent by other means (railroad, school bus, taxi, motorcycle, and "all other").[8] We have assumed that these proportions will remain unchanged in the absence of a major increase in vanpooling and that the universe from which vanpool patrons might be drawn is the group currently commuting by automobile. The potential vanpool market, as thus defined, totaled 61 million in 1975 and will total 68 million in 1980.

Carpool Energy Savings

Our guiding assumptions in estimating the potential energy saving impact of increased carpooling have been as follows:

1. The auto fleet averaged 14.9 mpg in 1975 and will average 16.1 mpg in 1980.

2. Carpooling, like vanpooling, will tend disproportionately to draw commuters who live relatively long distances from work. For scenarios that involve an increase in average auto commutation occupancy from 1.39 to the range of 1.6, we have assumed that the average trip attracted would have entailed a direct driving distance of 12.0 miles. For scenarios that involve even higher levels of occupancy, we have assumed a more typical commutation trip mix, with an average direct driving distance of 10.0 miles.

3. Each carpool member riding as a passenger is assumed to add 0.8 miles to average vehicular trip length. (At any level of average occupancy, the number of passengers will be the same regardless

of the precise mix of vehicular occupancies on which the average is based.)

4. We postulate that the average auto with one occupant is driven to work 220 days a year, that an auto with two occupants is driven to work 235 days a year, and that an auto with three or more occupants is driven to work 250 days a year. As a carpool with three members (driver plus two passengers) will require a vehicular trip every workday, additional passengers will not increase the number of vehicular trips required in the course of a year. We have assumed that one-fifth of all carpool passengers are in the category requiring no additional vehicular trips.

5. Because our immediate concern is with the energy saving impact of shifting auto drivers to the passenger category, we have ignored the possibility that regionwide carpool incentive programs might attract significant numbers of commuters from mass transit.

6. Twenty-five percent of the fuel saved directly as a result of additional carpooling will be lost due to additional use of the vehicles left at home by other household members. We have assumed an offset loss of only 20 percent, it will be recalled, with respect to vanpooling. Our higher estimate with reference to carpooling is based on three considerations. First, there will be a considerable number of days when the average carpool fails to operate; thus carpoolers who can afford it will want to have backup commutation options. Second, most carpool arrangements will be based on reciprocal driving arrangements which will require members to have cars available. Third, carpool members will tend to arrange their schedules so as to leave cars at home when other household members need them most; thus additional household driving per day that each car is left at home will tend to be somewhat greater than if the same cars were left home every day of the week.

7. The total U.S. employed work force was 87 million in 1975 and will be 96 million in 1980.

8. Seventy-one percent of employed individuals commuted to work by automobile in 1970: 55 percent as drivers and 16 percent as passengers.[9] We have assumed that these proportions will

remain unchanged to 1980 in the absence of a major increase in carpooling.

Transit Energy Savings

In calculating the potential energy conservation impact of shifts to mass transit usage, we have built upon the following findings and assumptions:

1. The 1975 auto fleet averaged 14.9 mpg, and the 1980 fleet will average 16.1 mpg. These are combined urban-rural figures, however. As such, they are appropriate when considering carpooling and vanpooling because these are not specifically urban in character. But they are inappropriate when considering the energy that might be saved by diverting urban travelers to mass transit. Thus we have assumed that the average fuel economy for auto trips diverted to mass transit would have been 80 percent of the national average: 11.9 mpg in 1975 and 12.9 mpg in 1980. These estimates are more favorable to transit than those contained in a group of scenarios recently published by a UMTA staff economist in the American Public Transit Association's *Journal*.[10] She assumes that urban auto fuel economy was 12 mpg in 1974, that it will rise to 14 mpg in 1980 on the basis of present trends extended, and that it could rise to as high as 17 mpg in 1980 under conditions of intense energy stringency and high prices.

2. Between one-quarter and one-half of the new transit patrons will be former auto drivers. This range will doubtless strike some readers as too low, but it is consistent with the limited evidence available. The 50 percent estimate, moreover, is approximately that utilized by UMTA's staff economist. Her projection is that if transit ridership increases at a rate of 3 percent a year to 1980 (present trends extended), 53 percent of the new transit patrons would otherwise be drivers; at a 6 percent rate of increase, however (intense pressure to conserve energy scenario), only 46 percent of the new patrons would otherwise be drivers.[11]

Our own estimate is based primarily on two sources of evidence. First, Atlanta brought about a 28 percent increase in transit ridership during 1972 and 1973 by reducing the fare from $.40 to $.15 and by expanding service. Of the new patrons, 42 percent were previous auto drivers. (Twenty-two percent were previous auto passengers, 21 percent were induced trip makers, 5 percent had formerly walked, and the remainder fell into several miscellaneous categories.)[12] Second, the Lindenwold rapid transit line in the Philadelphia region, which commenced operation in 1969, was carrying 30,000 passengers a day as of 1973. Forty percent of these were former bus patrons, and so do not count as new transit patrons. Twenty-eight percent, or slightly fewer than half of the remainder, were former drivers.[13]

3. New transit patrons will be attracted by means of additional service on existing rights-of-way. (This assumption permits us to ignore the large amounts of energy needed to construct new rapid transit and commuter rail facilities.) Because most of the new patronage is likely to result from improved service on outlying route segments that are now served poorly or not at all, we have assumed that average trip lengths for new riders will be one-third longer than those for the average rider in 1975. Our estimates of 1975 trip lengths for bus and rail rapid transit (from DOT's *1974 National Transportation Report*) are 3.93 and 6.57 miles, respectively.[14] Our commuter rail trip length estimate is 22.68 miles in 1975 (calculated from Interstate Commerce Commission data summarized in the Association of American Railroad's *Yearbook of Railroad Facts* and in its publication "Operating and Traffic Statistics: Class I Railroads.")[15] Thus we estimate that new transit patrons attracted between 1975 and 1980 will have average trip lengths of 5.24 miles for bus, 8.57 miles for rail rapid transit, and 30.24 miles for commuter rail.

4. 1975 fuel consumption per vehicle miles for transit (in miles per gallon of gasoline equivalent) is estimated to be 4.1 mpg for buses, 1.9 mpg for rail rapid transit, and 1.1 mpg for commuter rail.[16] Bus fuel economy is assumed to improve by 10 percent between 1975 and 1980 while rail rapid transit and commuter rail remain constant. We have adopted the position of UMTA's staff economist on the question of bus fuel economy gains in order to avoid any appearance of antitransit bias; but we confess to strong

skepticism about it. (She projects, as we do, no improvement in rail fuel economy over this period.)[17] The reason we are skeptical is that the recent trend is precisely the reverse. From 1973 to 1975, as the number of bus miles operated rose 11.5 percent, nationwide fuel consumption for bus transit increased by 20.2 percent.[18] As rapid transit vehicle mileage rose 2.0 percent, rapid transit energy consumption increased by 13.5 percent. In brief, then, it appears that the newer transit vehicles pay in part for their improved amenity features (such as air conditioning) with worse fuel economy than their predecessors.

5. Thirty percent of the direct energy saving attributable to increases in transit modal split will be lost to a combination of additional driving of vehicles left home, transit access trips via auto by commuters diverted to transit for the major portion of their trip, and additional passenger mileage (compared with travel by auto) due to indirect transit routings.

6. Each of our 1980 scenarios compares base case fuel consumption in that year with probable consumption under the conditions specified in the scenario. Our 1980 base case assumes that the overall rate of growth in urban passenger mileage from 1975 to 1980 will be 4 percent a year. Transit is assumed to maintain its modal share at 2.8 percent during this period. Thus transit passenger mileage will increase 4 percent a year and transit patronage will increase 3 percent (because of the greater average trip lengths of new transit patrons by comparison with old). This translates to a 22 percent increase in mileage, and a 16 percent increase in patronage, in the 1980 base case relative to 1975.

APPENDIX G
THE ENERGY AND AIR POLLUTION COSTS OF CONGESTION

The major costs commonly attributed to congestion are traveler time delays, loss of economic production, increases in the traffic accident rate, increases in fuel consumption, and increases in vehicle emissions. The first three of these have been discussed in chapter 9, so we shall concentrate here on the alleged energy and air pollution costs of congestion.

It is impossible to estimate the nationwide costs of congestion because no data exist on the proportion of national traffic mileage that occurs in circumstances of any congestion, let alone in specified degrees of congestion. Thus it is possible to review only what is known about the energy and air pollution costs of motor vehicle travel as a function of speed and speed changes. Higher and more stable speeds may be taken as indicative of the absence of congestion, lower speeds and more frequent speed changes as indicative of its presence. This procedure is far from satisfactory, but it is the only one with respect to which data are available.

A further point to bear in mind is that congestion remedies tend not only to affect the level and constancy of traffic speeds but also to affect the number of vehicle miles traveled (VMT). In general, highway improvements generate increases in VMT while demand restraint strategies generate reductions. Exceptions abound, however. Central area congestion pricing schemes, for example, are likely to generate increases in VMT if they induce large numbers of through travelers to detour around the tolled area. Similarly parking restrictions may generate increases in VMT if they encourage large numbers of trips to be made for the sole purpose of dropping off other household members.

Because the direction of VMT change is problematic for some remedies, and because in any event the magnitude of change associated with any particular remedy will be site specific, the following discussion will deal only with the effects of altering average travel speeds and the frequency of speed changes.

Fuel Consumption

The two most authoritative studies of automobile fuel economy, each conducted by driving a small fleet of instrumented vehicles on a test track, are by the Federal Highway Administration and by Paul J. Claffey and Associates.[1] With respect to constant speed travel the two studies, though based on slightly different vehicle mixes, report similar results (table G.1). Their main finding, in short, is that constant speeds in the range of 30–40 mph appear to be most fuel efficient.

What is much more complicated than determining fuel consumption as a function of constant speed is determining fuel consumption as a function of average speed and level of congestion. Claffey and Associates conducted a number of tests in which instrumented vehicles were driven in actual traffic. They hypothesized that the amount of fuel consumed was a function of the driver's attempted speed as well as his actual speed. Drivers attempting to move faster than the stream of traffic by weaving and passing were hypothesized to burn more fuel than those content to flow along with the stream. The experimental results confirmed the hypothesis, but the test procedure did not supply any information about the actual distribution of driver attitudes and attempted speeds. The findings with respect to travel on a six lane expressway at level grade (for a mix of vehicles deemed representative of those on the road in 1969) are shown in table G.2.

These figures indicate that congestion, up to the point of severe stop-and-go traffic, has only a negligible impact upon the fuel consumption of automobiles whose drivers are content to travel at 45 mph. The fuel consumption impact on vehicles whose drivers are anxious to travel at substantially higher speeds, however, is quite significant. Of possibly greater relevance is the finding that drivers who are satisfied with lower speeds obtain far better fuel economy, even under level F conditions, than do those who are anxious to travel at higher speeds under level A conditions. As most drivers tend to travel at about the same speed as the traffic stream, it would appear that average fuel economy is probably better in conditions of moderate congestion than in conditions of free flow. The fuel penalties associated with speed variations are more than offset by the savings attributable to lower average speeds.

When congestion becomes severe, however, fuel consumption

TABLE G.1

Constant Speed in mph	Miles per Gallon	
	FHWA	Claffey
10		13.9
20		20.0
30	21.05	22.7
40	21.07	21.7
50	19.49	19.2
60	17.51	17.2
70	14.93	14.9

Source: Federal Highway Administration, "The Effect of Speed on Automobile Gasoline Consumption Rates" (Washington: Federal Highway Administration, 1973), table 1; and Paul J. Claffey and Associates, *Running Costs of Motor Vehicles as Affected by Road Design and Traffic*, National Cooperative Highway Research Program Report III (Washington: Highway Research Board, 1971), table 6.

is likely to increase rapidly due to idling time and extreme speed variations. Claffey and Associates calculated the fuel penalties associated with a variety of speed change cycles (deceleration to achieve a specified speed reduction, followed by acceleration back to the former speed). (See table G.3.) Correlating these data with those presented in table G.1 for fuel consumption at constant speeds, one finds that a vehicle averaging 30 mph with four speed change cycles per mile of 10 mph each will consume the same amount of fuel as a vehicle traveling at a constant 60 mph. It can easily be imagined that extreme congestion, with average speeds of only 5-10 mph and numerous speed changes per mile, involves quite significant fuel penalties. It appears that lesser degrees of congestion, however, are neutral or even mildly positive in their fuel economy impact.

Air Pollution

David Curry and Dudley Anderson of the Stanford Research Institute have conducted the leading study of relationships between

TABLE G.2
Fuel Consumption on a Six-Lane Expressway at Level Grade, 1969

Level of Service	Volume per Hour—One Way	Miles per Gallon at Attempted Speed	
		45 mph	60 mph
A	0–2,400	20.4	17.2
C	4,000–4,400	20.4	16.3
D	4,800–5,200	20.3	16.0
E	5,600–6,000	20.3	15.8

Source: Claffey and Associates, *Running Costs of Motor Vehicles*, table 6C.

TABLE G.3
Excess Gasoline Consumed (Gallons) by Amount of Speed Reduction before Accelerating Back to Speed

Speed (mph)	Speed Reduction					
	10	20	30	40	50	60
20	0.0032	—	—	—	—	—
30	0.0035	0.0062	—	—	—	—
40	0.0038	0.0068	0.0093	—	—	—
50	0.0042	0.0071	0.0106	0.0140	—	—
60	0.0051	0.0090	0.0130	0.0167	0.0203	0.0243

Source: Claffey and Associates, *Running Costs of Motor Vehicles*, table 8.

emissions per vehicle mile, average speeds, and numbers of speed changes.[2] As they carried out their study with 1968 automobiles, the magnitudes of impact that they found were clearly unrepresentative of vehicles marketed during the past several years. It appears highly probable, however, that the directions of change that they found still prevail. These were as follows: carbon monoxide (CO) emissions per vehicle mile drop continuously with increasing speed, when the number of speed change cycles is held constant; hydrocarbon (HC) emissions per vehicle mile decline with speed increases up to about 35 mph, but increase thereafter; nitrogen oxide (NO_x) emissions per vehicle mile increase steadily with speed; and CO and HC emissions increase as a function of the number of speed change cycles. Curry and Anderson did not estimate the impact of speed change cycles on NO_x emissions.

Utilizing the Curry-Anderson data, one finds the following. Emissions on a one-mile highway segment carrying 1,000 vehicles per hour at an average speed of 30 miles per hour, with two complete stops per vehicle per mile, would total 0.73 pounds of HC per hour and 60 pounds of CO per hour. If some congestion remedy made it possible to carry the same traffic at a constant speed of 60 miles per hour, HC emissions would increase slightly to 0.77 pounds per hour but CO emissions would fall by nearly two-thirds, to 22 pounds per hour. In short, assuming any fixed amount of VMT, congestion relief will normally bring about significant reductions in CO emissions. The impact on HC emissions will tend to be minor, with the direction of change depending on the specific circumstances.

NOTES

Notes to Chapter 1

1. Ralph Nader, *Unsafe at Any Speed* (New York: Grossman, 1965).

2. Alan Altshuler and Robert Curry, "The Changing Environment of Urban Transportation: Shared Power or Shared Impotence?" *Urban Law Annual* (1975): 21–41.

3. Cf. Roger W. Cobb and Charles D. Elder, *Participation in American Politics: The Dynamics of Agenda-Building* (Boston: Allyn and Bacon, 1972), chap. 5; and Anthony Downs, *Inside Bureaucracy* (Boston: Little, Brown, 1967), chaps. 14, 16.

4. *New York Times*, January 5, 1977, p. 10.

5. Ibid., October 22, 1977, p. 22; October 24, 1977, p. 9; November 1, 1977, p. 64.

6. Cf. K. H. Schaeffer and Elliott Sclar, *Access for All: Transportation and Urban Growth* (Baltimore: Penguin Books, 1975), chaps. 7, 8; Jane Jacobs, *The Death and Life of Great American Cities* (New York: Vintage Books, 1961), chap. 18; John Burby, *The Great American Motion Sickness* (Boston: Little, Brown, 1971), esp. chap. 3; A. Q. Mowbray, *Road to Ruin* (Philadelphia: Lippincott, 1969), esp. chaps. 5, 6; Ben Kelley, *The Pavers and the Paved* (New York: Donald W. Brown, 1971), chaps. 5–8; and American Public Transit Association, "Urban Transportation Policy Statement," *Passenger Transport*, November 18, 1977, pp. 1, 3.

7. Cf. B. Bruce-Briggs, *The War Against the Automobile* (New York: E. P. Dutton, 1977); J. R. Meyer, J. F. Kain, and M. Wohl, *The Urban Transportation Problem* (Cambridge: Harvard University Press, 1965), chaps. 5, 6, 13, 14; and Michael Kemp and Melvyn Cheslow, "Transportation," in William Gorham and Nathan Glazer, eds., *The Urban Predicament* (Washington, D.C.: The Urban Institute, 1976), pp. 281–356.

8. Cf. Downs, *Inside Bureaucracy*, chaps. 8, 16, 17; James Q. Wilson, *Political Organizations* (New York: Basic Books, 1973), chap. 14; and Cobb and Elder, *Participation*, pp. 7–8.

9. For a particularly colorful account of the obstacles to implementation even when policies themselves are consensual, see Jeffrey L. Pressman and Aaron B. Wildavsky, *Implementation* (Berkeley: University of California Press, 1973).

10. Cf. Aaron B. Wildavsky, *The Politics of the Budgetary Process* (Boston: Little, Brown, 1964), pp. 11–18, 136–138, and Robert Behn, "The False Dawn of the Sunset Laws," *The Public Interest* (Fall 1977): 103–118.

11. Cf. Alan A. Altshuler, *The City Planning Process: A Political Analysis* (Ithaca: Cornell University Press, 1965), pp. 299–332.

12. Cf. Peter Bachrach and Morton Baratz, *Power and Poverty* (New York: Oxford University Press, 1970), pp. 3–63.

Notes to Chapter 2

1. Theodore J. Lowi, "American Business, Public Policy, Case Studies, and Political Theory," *World Politics* 16 (July 1964): 677–715.

2. Boris Pushkarev and Jeffrey Zuppan, *Public Transportation and Land Use Policy* (Bloomington: Indiana University Press, 1977), pp. 8–9.

3. Cf. Daniel Elazar, "Are We a Nation of Cities?" *The Public Interest*, no. 4 (Summer 1966): 42–58; Edward Banfield, *The Unheavenly City Revisited* (Boston: Little, Brown, 1974), chap. 2; and Bennett Harrison, *Urban Economic Development* (Washington, D.C.: The Urban Institute, 1974), chap. 3.

4. Cf. Raymond Vernon, *The Myth and Reality of Our Urban Problems* (Cambridge: Harvard University Press, 1962); Boris Yavitz, "Technological Change," in Eli Ginzberg et al., *Manpower Strategy for the Metropolis* (New York: Columbia University Press, 1962), chap. 2; and John Meyer, John Kain, and Martin Wohl, *The Urban Transportation Problem* (Cambridge: Harvard University Press, 1965).

5. The 1950 urbanized area population and land area from U.S. Bureau of the Census, *Census of Population: 1950*, vol. 1, *Number of Inhabitants* (Washington, D.C.: U.S. Government Printing Office, 1952), pp. 1–26; 1970 figures from U.S. Bureau of the Census, *1970 Census of Population*, vol. 1, *Characteristics of the Population*, pt. A, sec. 1, pp. 1–74.

6. Charles Abrams, "The Housing Order and Its Limits," *Commentary* 35 (January 1963): 10–14.

7. George Peterson, *Federal Tax Policy and Urban Development* (Washington, D.C.: The Urban Institute, forthcoming).

8. Robert Wood, *1400 Governments; The Political Economy of the New York Metropolitan Region* (Garden City: Doubleday, 1964), pp. 93–104.

9. Cf. Gary T. Schwartz, "Urban Freeways and the Interstate System," *Southern California Law Review* (March 1976): 406–513, for a superb political analysis of the origins of the interstate program and particularly of its urban elements.

10. Federal Highway Administration, *Highway Statistics, Summary to 1965* (Washington, D.C.: U.S. Government Printing Office, 1967), pp. 75–76.

11. *Fortune* (May 1977): 366.

12. Motor Vehicle Manufacturers Association, *Motor Vehicle Facts and Figures '77* (Washington, D.C.: Motor Vehicle Manufacturers Association, 1977), p. 72.

13. Schwartz, "Urban Freeways and the Interstate System," pp. 479–480.

14. American Public Transit Association, *Transit Fact Book, 1976-1977 Edition*, tables 4, 6, 7.

15. Schwartz, "Urban Freeways and the Interstate System," pp. 427–439, 466–468.

16. Fiscal 1970 obligations from Executive Office of the President, *Budget of the United States Government: Appendix, Fiscal Year 1972* (Washington, D.C.: U.S. Government Printing Office, 1971), p. 761; fiscal year 1978 estimate from Executive Office of the President, *Budget of the United States Government: Appendix, Fiscal Year 1978* (Washington, D.C.: U.S. Government Printing Office, 1977), p. 707.

17. Fiscal 1974 obligations from Executive Office of the President, *Budget of the United States Government: Appendix, Fiscal Year 1966* (Washington, D.C.: U.S. Government Printing Office, 1965), pp. 260-269; fiscal 1978 estimate from Executive Office of the President, *Budget of the United States Government: Appendix, Fiscal Year 1978*, pp. 680-687; consumer price data from Council of Economic Advisors, *Economic Report of the President* (1978) (Washington, D.C.: U.S. Government Printing Office, 1978), table B-47; and highway construction price data from Federal Highway Administration, "Price Trends for Federal-Aid Highway Construction" (Washington, D.C.: Federal Highway Administration, mimeo.), fourth quarter 1964 and fourth quarter 1977.

18. Percentage of federal highway aid spent in urban areas calculated from Kiran Bhatt, Michael Beesley, and Kevin Neels, *An Analysis of Road Expenditures and Payments by Vehicle Class (1956-1975)* (Washington, D.C.: The Urban Institute, 1977), table 1.3, p. 95. (Table is based on unpublished FHWA data.)

19. Cf. David W. Jones, Jr., "Urban Highway Investment and the Political Economy of Fiscal Retrenchment" (typescript, Institute of Transportation Studies, University of California at Berkeley, 1978).

20. Cf. for example, Robert Wood, *Suburbia: Its People and Their Politics* (Boston: Houghton Mifflin, 1969); William Whyte, *The Organization Man* (New York: Simon and Schuster, 1956); and Wilfred Owen, *The Metropolitan Transportation Problem* (Washington: Brookings Institution, 1956).

21. Urban Mass Transportation Administration, Office of the Associate Administrator for Transit Assistance, unpublished tabular materials on transit capital grants.

22. National Mass Transportation Assistance Act of 1974, PL 93-503.

23. Cf. James Q. Wilson, "Planning and Politics: Citizen Participation in Urban Renewal," in Wilson, ed., *Urban Renewal: The Record and the Controversy* (Cambridge: Harvard University Press, 1966), esp. pp. 409-410. On the relocation issue more generally, see ibid., pt. 4. Data on highway program residential takings are presented in table 9.2 of this work.

24. Cf. Bernard J. Frieden and Marshall Kaplan, *The Politics of Neglect* (Cambridge, Mass.: MIT Press, 1975), pp. 19-54.

25. American Public Transit Association, *Transit Fact Book, 1976-1977 Edition*, tables 4, 5. These totals are for bus and rail rapid transit only. Additionally, commuter rail operating subsidies totalled $500 million in 1975 but comparable estimates for earlier years are unavailable.

26. Council of Economic Advisors, *Economic Report of the President* (Washington, D.C.: U.S. Government Printing Office, 1978), table B-47; and Tax Foundation, *Facts and Figures on Government Finance* (1977), table 5.

27. Urban highway expenditure rate calculated from Kiran Bhatt, Michael Beesley, and Kevin Neels, *An Analysis of Road Expenditures and Payments by Vehicle Class (1956-1975)* (Washington, D.C.: The Urban Institute, 1977), p. 114.

28. American Public Transit Association, *Transit Fact Book, 1976-1977 Edition*, table 10.

29. Ibid., table 13.

30. Reid Ewing, "Case Study: Portland, Oregon," Transit Finance Project technical memo 3 (Center for Transportation Studies, Massachusetts Institute of Technology, November 1977).

31. Alan Altshuler, "The Federal Government and Para-Transit," in Transportation Research Board, *Para-Transit*, special report 164 (Washington, D.C., 1976), pp. 87-104 (esp. 97-102).

32. 40 USC 276a(1)-276a(5).

33. William Tye, "The Economic Costs of the Urban Mass Transportation Capital Grant Program" (Ph.D. diss., Harvard University, 1969), pp. 138-144; George Hilton, *Federal Transit Subsidies: The Urban Mass Transportation Assistance Program* (Washington, D.C.: American Enterprise Institute, 1974), pp. 56-59.

34. Sec. 5 of the Urban Mass Transportation Act is the statutory basis for the formula program; sec. 3 is the statutory basis of the discretionary capital grant program.

35. 49 USC sec. 1604m.

36. Federal budget deficits and fiscal 1977 GNP from Council of Economic Advisors, *Economic Report of the President* (Washington, D.C.: U.S. Government Printing Office, 1978), tables B-1, B-71; fiscal 1963-1972 GNP from U.S. Dept. of Commerce, *National Income and Product Accounts of the United States* (Washington, D.C.: U.S. Government Printing Office, 1976), table 1.22; fiscal 1973 GNP from U.S. Dept. of Commerce, *Survey of Current Business* 56, no. 9 (September 1976), table 1.22; fiscal 1974-1976 GNP from U.S. Dept. of Commerce, *Survey of Current Business* 57, no. 8 (August 1977), table 1.22.

37. Tax Foundation, *Facts and Figures on Government Finance* (1977), tables 61, 63.

38. Ibid., table 10.

39. 23 Code of Federal Regulations 450.

40. Ibid., appendix.

41. Amitai Etzioni, *Comparative Analysis of Complex Organizations* (New York: Free Press, 1975).

42. Ronald Kirby et al., *Para-Transit: Neglected Options for Urban Mobility* (Washington, D.C.: The Urban Institute, 1974); and Transportation Research Board, *Para-Transit*, special report 164 (Washington, D.C.: Transportation Research Board, 1976).

43. James P. Womack, "Para-Transit and the Journey to Work: A Status Report" (paper prepared for the Transportation Research Board, San Diego Para-Transit Conference, December 1977), p. 20.

44. Urban Mass Transportation Administration, "Service and Methods Demonstration Program Annual Report" (Washington, D.C.: U.S. Department of Transportation, April 1977).

45. Chris Hendrickson with Anthony Palmere, "An Analysis of Existing and Consolidated Transportation Services Provided by Human Service Agencies in Massachusetts" (mimeo., Center for Transportation Studies, Massachusetts Institute of Technology, November 1977).

46. U.S. Department of Health, Education and Welfare, Office of the Regional Director (Atlanta), "Transportation Authorities in Federal Human Services Programs" (March 1976).

47. Arthur Saltzman, "Special Service Transportation Systems Which Serve the Transportation Disadvantaged: Current Operations and Future Projections" (mimeo., Transportation Institute, North Carolina Agricultural and Technical University, 1976), pp. 2-13.

48. Kenneth Mericle, "Collective Bargaining in the Transit Industry and Its Impact on Para-Transit Innovation" (mimeo., Center for Transportation Studies, Massachusetts Institute of Technology, October 1976), chap. 2, pp. 2-6, 2-7.

49. Altshuler, "Federal Government and Para-Transit," pp. 93-95, 98.

50. Transit wages calculated from American Public Transit Association, *Transit Fact Book, 1976-1977 Edition*, table 11, on the assumption that the average transit employee worked 1,870 hours per year. Average wage income per hour on this basis was $4.94. This includes pay during the year at overtime and holiday rates, but this does not invalidate the comparison since the reported taxi rate also includes all days of the year and hours of the day. Taxi wage data are from A. L. Webster, E. Weiner, and J. D. Wells, "The Role of Taxicabs in Urban Transportation" (Washington, D.C.: U.S. Department of Transportation, 1974), table 1.

51. Reid Ewing, "Demand-Responsive Transit: Problems and Possibilities" (Ph.D. diss., Massachusetts Institute of Technology, 1977), pp. 249-251.

52. Reid Ewing and Nigel Wilson, "Innovations in Demand-Responsive Transit" (National Technical Information Service, 1976), table 14.

53. Norman Kennedy, James Kell, and Wolfgang Homburger, *Fundamentals of Traffic Engineering*, 8th ed. (Berkeley: Institute of Traffic and Transportation Engineering, 1973), pp. 1–2.

54. Arthur A. Carter, Jr., "Increasing the Traffic Capacity of Urban Arterial Streets" (Washington, D.C.: Bureau of Public Roads, 1962); and William L. Mertz, "Transportation System Management from the Federal Highway Administration Perspective," in Transportation Research Board, *Transportation System Management*, special report 172 (Washington, D.C.: Transportation Research Board, 1977).

55. Norbert Tieman, "Heading in the Right Direction," in Transportation Research Board, *Transportation System Management*, p. 18.

56. John Crain and Associates, "Actions to Reduce Vehicle Use in Congested Areas," in Transportation Research Board, *Transportation System Management*, pp. 77–79; and Organization for Economic Cooperation and Development, "Better Towns with Less Traffic" (proceedings of a conference April 14–16, 1975, Paris, OECD, 1975).

57. Tieman, "Heading in the Right Direction," pp. 17–19.

58. Michael Meyer, "A Review of Transportation System Management Plans Submitted in Response to New Federal Policy," Center for Transportation Studies working paper 76-3 (mimeo., Center for Transportation Studies, Massachusetts Institute of Technology, October 1976).

59. American Public Transit Association, *Transit Fact Book, 1976–1977 Edition*, table 7.

60. Robert H. Salisbury, "The Analysis of Public Policy: A Search for Theories and Roles," in Austin Ranney, ed., *Political Science and Public Policy* (Chicago: Markham, 1968), p. 167; and Roger Teal and Alan Altshuler, "Economic Regulation: The Case of Aviation," *Policy Studies Journal* 6, no. 1 (Autumn 1977): 50–62.

61. Cf. Marver Bernstein, *Regulating Business by Independent Commission* (Princeton: Princeton University Press, 1955).

62. Charles L. Schultze, *The Public Use of Private Interest* (Washington, D.C.: Brookings Institution, 1977), pp. 7–11; William Lilley III and James C. Miller III, "The New Social Regulation," *The Public Interest* 47 (April 1977), pp. 49–61; and Eugene Bardach, "Reason, Responsibility, and the New Social Regulation" (mimeo., Graduate School of Public Policy, University of California at Berkeley, 1977).

63. These are fiscal year comparisons. Data on social programs and total spending are from Tax Foundation, *Facts and Figures on Government Finance* (1977), tables 18 and 5, respectively. GNP data are from Council of Economic Advisors, *Economic Report of the President* (1960, 1977).

64. Schultze, *Public Use of Private Interest*, p. 12.

65. The Motor Vehicle Air Pollution Control Act was PL 89-272. The National Traffic and Motor Vehicle Safety Act was PL 89-563.

66. Ralph Nader, *Unsafe at Any Speed* (New York: Grossman, 1965).

67. Mark Nadel, *The Politics of Consumer Protection* (New York: Bobbs-Merrill, 1971); James L. Sundquist, *Politics and Policy* (Washington, D.C.: Brookings Institution, 1968), pp. 377-381.

68. For a classic discussion of why the same people may express different preferences when confronted with collective (public policy) as opposed to individual market choices, see James Buchanan, "Individual Choice in Voting and in the Market," *Journal of Political Economy* 62, no. 4 (August 1954): 334-343.

69. Charles O. Jones, *Clean Air: The Policies and Politics of Pollution Control* (Pittsburgh: University of Pittsburgh Press, 1975), pp. 62-66; J. Clarence Davies III and Barbara S. Davies, *The Politics of Pollution* (Indianapolis: Bobbs-Merrill, 1975), pp. 47-48; and Harold W. Kennedy and Martin Weeks, "Control of Automobile Emissions—California Experience and the Federal Legislation," *Law and Contemporary Problems* 33, no. 2 (Spring 1968): 298-301.

70. Davies and Davies, *Politics of Pollution*, p. 48; Sundquist, *Politics and Policy*, pp. 367-371.

71. PL 91-604 and 94-163, respectively.

72. Jones, *Clean Air*, chaps. 7, 8; and Howard Margolis, "The Politics of Auto Emissions," *The Public Interest* (Fall 1977): 3-21.

73. Quoted by Jones, *Clean Air*, p. 186.

74. Quoted by ibid., p. 201.

75. PL 95-95, sec. 201.

76. Bernard Asbell, "The Outlawing of Next Year's Cars," *New York Times Magazine*, November 21, 1976, pp. 126-131.

77. *Natural Resources Defense Council v. Environmental Protection Agency*, 543 F 2d 359, (1973).

78. Joel Horowitz and Steven Kuhrtz, "Transportation Controls to Reduce Automobile Use and Improve Air Quality in Cities: The Need, the Options, and Effects on Urban Activity" (Washington, D.C.: Environmental Protection Agency, Office of Air and Waste Management, 1974), pp. 5-7, 11; and Daniel Balz, Richard Corrigan, Arthur Magida, and Linda Demkovich, "America Faces Turning Point in the Long Love Affair with the Automobile," *National Journal*, January 3, 1976, p. 12.

79. Horowitz and Kuhrtz, "Transportation Controls," pp. 27-28.

80. *Congressional Quarterly 1973 Almanac*, pp. 682-697.

81. *Congressional Quarterly 1974 Almanac,* pp. 727-732.

82. PL 94-116, sec. 407.

83. Oil import percentage from U.S. Department of Energy, *Monthly Energy Review,* March 1978, p. 8; oil import value from U.S. Department of Commerce, *Survey of Current Business,* June 1977 and March 1978, table 3; "U.S. Merchandise Trade" balance of trade data from *Survey of Current Business* (June 1977 and March 1978), table 1, "U.S. International Transactions."

84. U.S. Treasury Department estimate reported in *New York Times,* November 25, 1877, p. D2.

85. International Monetary Fund, *International Financial Statistics* (Washington, D.C.: International Monetary Fund), March 1977 and *Wall Street Journal,* October 20, 1978, p. 37.

86. *New York Times,* March 3, 1975, p. 1.

87. Ibid., June 12, 1975, pp. 1, 38.

88. U.S. Department of Labor, *Monthly Labor Review* (March 1977): 108-114.

89. Cf. John Kenneth Galbraith, *A Theory of Price Controls* (Cambridge: Harvard University Press, 1952).

Notes to Chapter 3

1. Cf. American Public Transit Association Task Force on Para-Transit, "Para-Transit in the Family of Transit Services," *Transit Journal* (May 1976): 20-21.

2. Alan Altshuler, *The City Planning Process* (Ithaca: Cornell University Press, 1965), pp. 257-258, 267-290.

3. Cf. Alan M. Voorhees, Inc., "A Proposal for Auto Restricted Zones and Multi-Use Auto Systems," TSC/230-0078-ES (Cambridge, Mass.: Transportation Systems Center, April 1975); Institute for Environmental Action in association with the Columbia University Center for Advanced Research in Urban and Environmental Affairs, "American Urban Malls—A Compendium," HUD-PDR-192-4 (1976), and "Banning the Car Downtown—Selected American Cities," HUD-PDR-192-3 (1976).

4. Cf. Mel Scott, *American City Planning Since 1890* (Berkeley: University of California Press, 1969), pp. 188, 258-260; and James Dahir, *The Neighborhood Unit Plan: Its Spread and Acceptance* (New York: Russell Sage Foundation, 1947), pp. 16-26.

5. Cf. Scott, *American City Planning,* pp. 335-342.

6. American Institute of Planners and Motor Vehicle Manufacturers Association, *Urban Transportation Fact Book* (Washington, D.C.: American Institute

of Planners, 1974), vol. 1, table I-26. On the planning of the Atlanta rapid transit system, see Office of Technology Assessment, *An Assessment of Community Planning for Mass Transit: Atlanta* (Washington, D.C.: Office of Technology Assessment, March 1976), vol. 2.

7. John Pucher, "Transit Operating Subsidies in the 26 Largest U.S. Metropolitan Areas," New Perspectives Project Technical Memorandum no. 3 (Center for Transportation Studies, Massachusetts Institute of Technology, May 1977), table 3-1.

8. For a detailed treatment of the factors militating in favor of this orientation, see Alan Altshuler and Robert Curry, "The Changing Environment of Urban Development Policy—Shared Power or Shared Impotence?" *Urban Law Annual* 10 (1975): 3–41.

9. Cf. Institute of Traffic Engineers, *Transportation and Traffic Engineering Handbook* (Englewood Cliff, N.J.: Prentice-Hall, 1976), pp. 853–864.

10. Cf. Martin Wohl, "Increasing the Taxi's Role in Urban America," *Technology Review* (July–August 1976): 45–53; Douglass Lee, Jr., "Economic Evaluation of Taxicab Regulation," Technical Report 70 (Institute of Urban and Regional Research, University of Iowa, 1976); Ross Eckert, "Regulatory Commission Behavior: Taxi Franchising in Los Angeles and Other Cities" (Ph.D. diss., University of California at Los Angeles, 1968); James P. Womack, "Metropolitan Taxi Regulation in Toronto and Montreal," New Perspectives Project Technical Memorandum (Center for Transportation Studies, MIT, 1977); and Alan Altshuler and James Womack, "Potential Taxi Demonstration Concepts for Dade County, Florida," New Perspectives Project Technical Memorandum (Center for Transportation Studies, MIT, 1977).

11. Cf. Alan Altshuler, "The Federal Government and Paratransit," in Transportation Research Board, *Para-Transit*, special report 164 (Washington, D.C.: Transportation Research Board, 1976), pp. 97–102, and Jefferson Associates, "Administration of Section 13(c)—Urban Mass Transportation Act" (Washington, D.C.: U.S. Department of Labor, 1972).

Notes to Chapter 4

1. Roger Bezdek and Bruce Hannon, "Energy, Manpower, and the Highway Trust Fund," *Science* 185 (August 23, 1974): 669–675, table 1.

2. Cf. section 4(f) of the Department of Transportation Act of 1966, 23 USC 138(1970) and 49 USC 1653(f) (1970); National Environmental Policy Act of 1969, 42 USC 4321-47 (1970) as amended, 42 USCA 4332(2)(D), pamphlet 5 (1975); and the Uniform Relocation Assistance and Real Property Acquisition Policies Act of 1970, 42 USC 4601 ff.

3. Alan Altshuler and Robert Curry, "The Changing Environment of Urban Development Policy—Shared Power or Shared Impotence?" *Urban Law Annual* 20 (1975): 3–41, treats these themes at greater length. Also see Martin

Convisser, "Transportation and the Environment," *Policy Studies Journal* 6, no. 1 (Autumn 1977): 40-49.

4. Michael A. Johnson, "The Influence of Basic Preference Attitudes on Choices Between Auto and Transit Travel," working paper 7701 (Institute of Transportation Studies, University of California, Berkeley, January 1977), table 6, pp. 19, 38, 40.

5. David Hartgen, "Attitudinal and Situational Variables Influencing Urban Mode Choice: Some Empirical Findings," *Transportation* 3 (1974): 377-392.

6. Rex Wallin and Paul Wright, "Factors Which Influence Modal Choice," *Traffic Quarterly* 28 (1974): 274, 277, 283.

7. H. J. Bauer, "A Case Study of a Demand-Responsive Transportation System" (Warren, Mich.: General Motors Research Laboratories, 1970), p. 19.

8. Martin Wachs, "Consumer Attitudes Toward Transit Service: An Interpretative Review," *Journal of the American Institute of Planners* 42, no. 1 (January 1976): 96-104.

9. Reid Ewing, "Demand-Responsive Transit: Problems and Possibilities," (Ph.D. diss., Massachusetts Institute of Technology, 1977), pp. 95-97.

10. A table summarizing the findings of the leading studies appears on p. ix of Nail Cengiz Yucel, "A Survey of the Theories and Empirical Investigations of the Value of Travel Time Savings," staff working paper 199 (International Bank for Reconstruction and Development, February 1975).

11. Cf. C. A. Barnett and P. D. Saalmans, "Report on County Hall Journey to Work Survey, 1964," (London: Greater London Council, January 1967). See also Ian G. Heggie, "A Diagnostic Survey of Urban Journey to Work Behavior," in Ian Heggie, ed., *Modal Choice and the Value of Time* (Oxford: Clarendon Press, 1976), pp. 39-41.

12. The nonwork trip share of total person trips has been derived from table A-10 of report 8 and table 11, appendix C of report 9, Federal Highway Administration, Personal Transportation Study (Washington, D.C. 1973).

13. Wachs, "Consumer Attitudes," pp. 98-99.

14. Ibid., p. 99.

15. Johnson, "The Influence," pp. 19, 43.

16. Ewing, "Demand-Responsive Transit," p. 105.

17. Ibid, p. 104, table 3.4.

18. Ibid., pp. 116, 121.

19. Wachs, "Consumer Attitudes," p. 101; and Kathleen Soloman, Richard Soloman, and Joseph Sullivan, *Passenger Psychological Dynamics: Sources of Information on Urban Transportation* (New York: American Society of Civil Engineers, 1968).

20. Bauer, "A Case Study," p. 24.

21. Wachs, "Consumer Attitudes," p. 101.

22. Ewing, "Demand-Responsive Transit," pp. 95–97.

23. See, for example, B. Bruce-Briggs, "Mass Transportation and Minority Transportation," *The Public Interest* 40 (Summer 1975): 45.

24. Ibid., p. 44.

25. Federal Highway Administration, "Social and Economic Effects of Highways" (1976 edition), p. 45.

26. Johnson, "The Influence," table 1.

27. Ibid., table 4.

Notes to Chapter 5

1. B. Bruce-Briggs, "Gasoline Prices and the Suburban Way of Life," *The Public Interest* (Fall 1974): 131–136.

2. *New York Times*, April 18, 1977.

3. Ford Foundation Energy Policy Project, *A Time To Choose: America's Energy Future* (Cambridge, Mass.: Ballinger, 1974), p. 5.

4. Executive Office of the President (EOP), *The National Energy Plan* (Washington, D.C.: U.S. Government Printing Office, 1977), p. 3.

5. Richard L. Goen and Ronald K. White, "Comparison of Energy Consumption Between West Germany and the United States" (Menlo Park, Calif., Stanford Research Institute, June 1975) (also available from the National Technical Information Service, PB-245 652). The material in this paragraph is based on chapters 2 and 3.

6. Ibid., p. 31.

7. Authors' calculation based on ibid., tables 12, 13.

8. Federal Energy Administration (FEA), *Monthly Energy Review* (March 1977): 44, 49.

9. John Pollard, David Hiatt, and David Rubin, "A Summary of Opportunities to Conserve Transportation Energy" (U.S. Department of Transportation, Transportation Systems Center, August 1975), p. 5–4. Direct transportation uses in 1967 accounted for 25.3 percent of U.S. energy consumption versus 25.9 percent in 1976.

10. Federal Highway Administration (FHWA), *Highway Statistics, 1974 Edition* (Washington, D.C.: U.S. Government Printing Office, 1975), p. III-2.

11. Cf. Eric Hirst, "Energy Intensiveness of Passenger and Freight Transport Modes: 1950-1970" (Oak Ridge National Laboratory, National Science

Foundation Environmental Program, 1973). It is estimated there that local trips, defined as trips of thirty miles or less, account for 55 percent of auto and truck mileage combined, and for 63 percent of motor vehicle fuel consumption. Note that only 43 percent of truck mileage occurred in urban areas as of 1975.

12. EOP, *National Energy Plan*, p. 14.

13. 1970 import percentage from FEA, *National Energy Outlook* (Washington, D.C.: U.S. Government Printing Office, 1976), p. 2; 1977 figure from FEA, *Monthly Energy Review* (March 1978): 8.

14. FEA, *Monthly Energy Review* (March 1977): 2, 26.

15. The 1970 import volume is from the Congressional Budget Office (CBO), *President Carter's Energy Proposals: A Perspective* (Washington, D.C.: U.S. Government Printing Office, June 1977), p. xiv; 1977 import volume from FEA, *Monthly Energy Review* (March 1978): 8; and 1970 and 1977 import dollar values from the U.S. Department of Commerce, *Survey of Current Business* (June 1977 and March 1978), table 3.

16. U.S. Central Intelligence Agency (CIA), *International Energy Biweekly Statistical Review*, November 30, 1977, pp. 13, 14.

17. U.S. Bureau of the Census, *Statistical Abstract of the United States* (1976), p. 396; U.S. Department of Commerce, *Survey of Current Business* (April 1977): 12.

18. Estimate of OPEC investments in the United States is from the U.S. Department of the Treasury, as reported in "Arab Investments in the U.S. Slacken; Changing Market Conditions Cited," *New York Times*, November 25, 1977, pp. A1, D2. These are very rough estimates since most OPEC banking is done by intermediary bankers who are secretive as to the source of the funds they are investing. The estimate of the portion of OPEC's oil purchased by the United States is from the CIA, *International Energy Biweekly Statistical Review*, November, 30, 1977, pp. 2, 5.

19. European and Japanese production and consumption estimates are from the CIA, *The International Energy Situation: Outlook to 1985* (Washington, D.C.: Library of Congress Photoduplication Service, April 1977), p. 15.

20. U.S. Department of Commerce, *Survey of Current Business* (March 1978), table 3.

21. Cf. for example, Marc J. Roberts, "Is There an Energy Crisis?" *The Public Interest* (Spring 1973): 17-37.

22. EOP, *National Energy Plan*, pp. 16, 63.

23. Ibid., p. 16. Cf. also *Newsweek*, June 25, 1977, p. 71.

24. For an excellent review of the issues associated with coal conversion, see *Congressional Quarterly*, June 19, 1977, pp. 1211-1220.

25. All data are from EOP, *National Energy Plan*, figure IX-2, except the low coal estimate, which is from CIA, *International Energy Situation*, p. 8.

26. The low estimate applies the low production estimate to the *National Energy Plan* estimate of total consumption without new conservation measures. The high estimate applies the high *National Energy Plan* estimate of total consumption if its recommended conservation measures are adopted.

27. EOP, *National Energy Plan*, p. 95.

28. CIA, *International Energy Situation*, p. 8.

29. *New York Times*, June 19, 1977, sec. 3, pp. 1, 2, is the source on both the 1975 and 1977 estimates of 1985 nuclear capacity. The figure of sixty-three plants in operation as of early 1977 is from EOP, *National Energy Plan*, p. 71.

30. EOP, *National Energy Plan*, p. 95.

31. Workshop on Alternative Energy Strategies (WAES), *Energy: Global Prospects 1985-2000* (New York: McGraw-Hill, 1977); and CIA, *International Energy Situation*.

32. CIA, *International Energy Situation*, table 5.

33. EOP, *National Energy Plan*, p. 15.

34. CIA, *International Energy Situation*, table 5.

35. Ibid.

36. FEA, *Monthly Energy Review* (August 1977): 84.

37. Cf. Nazli Choucri with Vincent Ferraro, *International Politics of Energy Interdependence: The Case of Petroleum* (Lexington, Mass.: D. C. Heath, 1976).

38. CIA, *International Energy Situation*, p. 18.

39. Ibid., p. 16; cf. also p. 18.

40. Calculated from WAES, *Energy*, p. 136.

41. Authors' calculation based on ibid., p. 127, using the middle of the estimated range; and CIA, *International Energy Situation*, as cited previously on actual 1976 demand.

42. CIA data from *International Energy Situation*, p. 18; WAES data from *Energy*, table 3-5, 3-8, pp. 133-139.

43. WAES, *Energy*, pp. 97, 246.

44. "The President's State of the Union Message, Including Economy and Energy," Office of the White House Press Secretary, January 15, 1975.

45. FEA, *National Energy Outlook*, p. 40.

46. PL 94-163.

47. CBO, *President Carter's Energy Proposals*, pp. 63, 72.

48. EOP, *National Energy Plan*, pp. 14, 95, 96.

49. Ibid., p. 96.

50. Ibid.

51. CBO, *President Carter's Energy Proposals*, p. 22.

52. EOP, *National Energy Plan*, p. 38; CBO, *President Carter's Energy Proposals*, p. 60.

53. CBO, *President Carter's Energy Proposals*, p. xviii.

54. Ibid., pp. 63–67.

55. The Phelps and Smith article in the *Wall Street Journal*, "The Flaw in the Crude Oil Tax," September 28, 1977, p. 26, touched off a debate in the media on the merits of the crude oil tax. Cf. Anthony Parisi, "Carter Wellhead Tax: Does It Make Sense?" *New York Times*, October 11, 1977, and responding letters in the *Times* from E. R. Heydinger of the Marathon Oil Company and John Savoy of the Sun Company, on October 24. The Phelps-Smith thesis had actually been published in January 1977 ("Petroleum Regulation: The False Dilemma of Decontrol," Santa Monica, Rand Corporation, Rand Report R-1951-RC) but had attracted little attention prior to the *Wall Street Journal* article.

56. CBO, *President Carter's Energy Proposals*, p. 67.

57. Ibid., pp. xviii, 65.

58. Adam Clymer, "Energy Conferees Conditionally Back 'Gas Guzzler' Tax," *New York Times*, December 8, 1977, pp. 63, 67.

59. *Congressional Quarterly Weekly Report* 35, no. 21 (May 21, 1977); p. 955, reported, in summarizing initial congressional actions on the Carter energy package, "On May 17, Carter's own Secretary of Transportation, Brock Adams, suggested at a House Ways and Means Committee hearing that the first nickel of the proposed gasoline tax—which would generate about $6 billion per year—should be spent to improve mass transit, energy research, and road repairs instead of being rebated to consumers. Though Adams said he had cleared his proposal with the White House, presidential press secretary Jody Powell later insisted that the President remained committed to his rebate plans."

60. FHWA, *Highway Statistics* (Washington, D.C.: U.S. Government Printing Office, various years), table VM-1.

61. National Highway Traffic Safety Administration (NHTSA), "The Second Annual Report to Congress on the Automobile Fuel Economy Program" (January 1978), table 3.

62. Federal Task Force on Motor Vehicle Goals Beyond 1980, *Report on Motor Vehicle Goals Beyond 1980*, vol. 2, *Task Force Report* (Washington, D.C.: U.S. Department of Transportation, September 1976), p. 1-1.

63. Ibid., vol. 1, "Executive Summary," p. 27.

64. Ibid., vol. 2, p. 8-22.

65. Ibid., p. 14-9.

66. Ibid., vol. 1, p. 16.

67. Ibid., vol. 2, chaps. 9, 10.

68. William Stevens, " 'Big Car' of 1985 Is Expected to be a V-6 Weighing 3,000 lbs.," *New York Times*, May 4, 1977, p. B9; and William Stevens, "Auto Makers Generally Endorse Energy Proposals but GM Terms 'Guzzler' Penalty Tax 'Simplistic,' " *New York Times*, April 22, 1977, p. B6.

69. NHTSA, "Second Annual Report," table III.

70. U.S. Environmental Protection Agency, "1978 Gas Mileage Guide" (Washington, D.C.: U.S. Government Printing Office, 1977), p. 19.

71. NHTSA, "Second Annual Report," table 3, for data on overall imported car fuel economy.

72. Federal Task Force, "Motor Vehicle Goals," pp. 8-16, 8-24.

73. Paul A. Samuelson, *Economics*, 8th ed. (New York: McGraw-Hill, 1970), pp. 359-365; and Edwin Mansfield, *Principles of Microeconomics* (New York: Norton, 1974), pp. 136-139.

74. John Pucher and Jerome Rothenberg, "Pricing in Urban Transportation: A Survey of Empirical Evidence on the Elasticity of Travel Demand" (Center for Transportation Studies, Massachusetts Institute of Technology, September 1976) (also available from the National Technical Information Service).

75. Federal Task Force, "Motor Vehicle Goals," vol. 2, pp. 17-9, 17-10.

76. Pucher and Rothenberg "Pricing in Urban Transportation," pp. 55-59.

77. Federal Highway Administration, Nationwide Personal Transportation Study, report 8, "Home-to-Work Trips and Travel" (Washington, D.C., 1974) table A-10.

78. Ibid.

79. Robert Hemphill, "Statement Before the Subcommittee on Surface Transportation, Committee on Public Works and Transportation, U.S. House of Representatives" (mimeo., September 17, 1975), pp. 7-8. As of mid-1977, the FEA ride-sharing staff stood by these estimates.

80. Trip length and VMT data from Federal Highway Administration, Nationwide Personal Transportation Study, report 8, "Home-to-Work Trips and Travel," tables 19 and 20. Occupancies calculated from Federal Highway Administration, Nationwide Personal Transportation Study, report 1, "Automobile Occupancy" (Washington, D.C., 1972), table 4.

81. James P. Womack, "Overcoming Barriers to Increased Ride Sharing" (Center for Transportation Studies, Massachusetts Institute of Technology, September 1976), pp. 13-15.

82. Ibid., pp. 58-59.

83. Ibid., pp. 59-61; Roger Teal, "Para-Transit Innovation in Urban Transportation: A Political-Organizational Analysis" (Ph.D. diss., Tufts University, May 1978), chap. 4.

84. James P. Womack, "Para-Transit and the Journey to Work: A Status Report" (delivered at the Transportation Research Board's Conference on Para-Transit, San Diego, December 1977), p. 18.

85. John Attanucci, "Analysis of Carpooling Behavior and the Formulation of Carpool Incentive Programs" (Master's thesis, Massachusetts Institute of Technology, 1974), cited by Womack, "Overcoming Barriers," p. 63.

86. Calculated from Terry Atherton, John Suhrbier, and William Jessiman, "The Use of Disaggregate Travel Demand Models to Analyze Carpooling Policy Incentives" (prepared by Cambridge Systematics, Inc., for the Federal Energy Administration and presented at the Transportation Research Board meeting, Washington, D.C., January 1976).

87. Ibid., p. 33.

88. Womack, "Overcoming Barriers," p. 55.

89. Ibid., p. 45.

90. Lew Pratsch et al., "Vanpooling: An Update" (Washington, D.C.: Department of Energy, March 1978).

91. Womack, "Overcoming Barriers," pp. 42-44, 51.

92. Robert Hemphill, "Statement Before the Subcommittee," pp. 7-8; Eric Hirst, "Transportation Energy Conservation Policies," *Science,* April 24, 1976, pp. 15-20.

93. American Public Transit Association (APTA), *Transit Fact Book, 1976-1977 Edition,* tables 7, 11.

94. Mayo Stuntz, "Mass Transit and Energy Conservation" (Federal Energy Administration internal memo., March 5, 1975); and Robert Hemphill, "Statement Before the Subcommittee," p. 11.

95. Skidmore, Owings, and Merrill, Inc., and Systems Design Concepts, Inc., *Energy, the Economy and Mass Transit: Executive Summary* (Washington, D.C.: Office of Technology Assessment, June 1975), p. 40.

96. APTA, *Transit Fact Book, 1976-1977 Edition,* tables 7, 11.

97. Skidmore, Owings and Merrill, *Energy, the Economy and Mass Transit,* p. 37.

98. APTA, *Transit Fact Book, 1976-1977 Edition,* table 15.

99. Timothy J. Healy, "Energy Requirements of the Bay Area Rapid Transit (BART) System" (California Department of Transportation, November 1973).

100. Charles Lave, "The Negative Energy Impact of Modern Rail Transit Systems" (mimeo., Department of Economics, University of California at Irvine, 1976), pp. 2-9, 16-18.

101. Ibid., pp. 9-10, 18.

102. Amory Lovins, *Soft Energy Paths: Toward a Durable Peace* (Cambridge, Mass.: Ballinger, 1977), pp. 67, 133-136.

103. The APTA estimates are from the *Transit Fact Book, 1975-1976 Edition*, table 17. We have made our own estimates on the basis of APTA, *Transit Fact Book*, tables 6, 10, and the trip length estimates utilized in table 2.2 of this book.

104. Hemphill, "Statement Before the Subcommittee," exhibit 6.

105. Jack Faucett Associates, Inc., *A Study of Alternative Metro Rail Systems* (Washington, D.C.: Congressional Research Office, Library of Congress, January 15, 1976).

106. CBO, "Urban Transportation and Energy: The Potential Savings of Different Modes," prepared for the U.S. Senate Committee on Environment and Public Works (Washington, D.C.: U.S. Government Printing Office, September 1977), tables B-1, B-2.

107. James P. Curry, "Case Studies of Transit Energy and Air Pollution Impacts" (Environmental Protection Agency, May 1976) (also available from the National Technical Information Service, report EPA-600/5-76-003).

108. Ibid., p. 122.

109. Ibid., p. 6.

110. Ibid., pp. 6, 89-96.

111. Ibid., pp. 125-139.

112. Ibid., pp. 112-122.

113. Ibid., pp. 78-84.

114. Ibid., pp. 6, 104-108.

115. The traffic impact of BART is discussed in greater detail on pp. 369-371.

116. Ibid., pp. 151-159.

117. Mayo Stuntz and Eric Hirst, "Energy Conservation Potential of Urban Mass Transit," conservation paper 34 (Washington, D.C.: Federal Energy Administration, 1975).

118. Curry, *Case Studies*, pp. 92, 133, 156.

119. Reid Ewing and Nigel Wilson, "Innovation in Demand-Responsive Transit" (National Technical Information Service, 1976), table 4; and CBO, "Urban Transportation and Energy," table 7, A-1, A-2.

120. Ewing and Wilson, "Innovations," table 4A.

121. Ibid., table 7.

122. Stuntz and Hirst, "Energy Conservation."

123. For additional detail, see pp. xxx and appendix G.

124. Regional Plan Association and Resources for the Future, "Regional Energy Consumption" (New York: Regional Plan Association, 1974), p. 7.

125. Roger Bezdek and Bruce Hannon, "Energy, Manpower and the Highway Trust Fund," *Science* 185 (August 23, 1974): 670.

126. Charles River Associates, "Energy Impact of Federal Capital Grant Programs for Transportation" (Federal Energy Administration, July 1976), p. 3.

Notes to Chapter 6

1. Howard Margolis, "Another View of the Politics of Auto Emissions Control" (Center for International Studies, Massachusetts Institute of Technology, August 1977). A somewhat abbreviated version of this paper appeared as "The Politics of Auto Emissions," *The Public Interest* (Fall 1977): 3-21.

2. National Academy of Sciences, Committee on Medical and Biologic Effects of Environmental Pollutants, *Nitrogen Oxides* (Washington, D.C.: National Academy of Sciences, 1977), p. 4.

3. U.S. Department of Transportation, Federal Highway Administration, *Highway Statistics, 1973 Edition* (Washington, D.C.: U.S. Government Printing Office, 1974), p. 75; U.S. Federal Highway Administration, *Highway Statistics, Summary to 1965* (Washington, D.C.: U.S. Government Printing Office, 1967), pp. 1-12; and Barry Commoner, *The Closing Circle* (New York: Alfred Knopf, 1971), pp. 166-168.

4. U.S. Council on Environmental Quality, *Environmental Quality: The Fourth Annual Report of the Council on Environmental Quality* (Washington, D.C.: U.S. Government Printing Office, September 1973), p. 266.

5. Frank P. Grad et al., *The Automobile and the Regulation of Its Impact on the Environment* (Norman: University of Oklahoma Press, 1975), p. 49; Commoner, *Closing Circle*, p. 65.

6. Commoner, *Closing Circle*, pp. 68, 69.

7. HC, NO_x, and CO emissions data from U.S. EPA, "1973 National Emissions Report" (Research Triangle Park, EPA, 1976). Lead data from Environmental Protection Agency, "Air Quality Criteria for Lead" (Washington, EPA, 1977): 5-6.

8. *South Terminal Corporation* v. *Environmental Protection Agency*, 504 F.2d 662-665 (1974), cited by Michael E. Padnos and Edward Selig, "Transportation Controls in Boston: The Plan That Failed" (typescript, June 1976), pp. 84-86.

9. Environmental Protection Agency, "National Air Quality and Emissions Trends Report, 1975" (Washington, D.C.: EPA, 1976), p. 47.

10. 1940 data from U.S. Council on Environmental Quality, *Environmental Quality: The Fifth Annual Report of the Council on Environmental Quality* (Washington, D.C.: U.S. Government Printing Office, December 1974), chap. 3, table 5, 9, 15, 16, 17. 1975 data from EPA, "National Air Quality," p. 47.

11. Grad et al., *Automobile*, pp. 48-49.

12. Ibid., pp. 43-46; Commoner, *Closing Circle*, p. 71; EPA, "Fuel Regulations: Control of Lead Additives in Gasoline," *Federal Register*, December 6, 1973, pp. 33734-33741.

13. Daniel Balz, Richard Corrigan, Arthur Magida, and Linda Demkovich, "American Faces Turning Point in Its Long Love Affair with the Automobile," *National Journal*, January 3, 1976, p. 9.

14. Margolis, "Another View," p. 14. The OECD quotation is from *Report of the Committee of Experts on Automobile Pollution* (Paris: OECD, 1972), p. I-2.

15. J. Clarence Davies III and Barbara Davies, *The Politics of Pollution*, 2d ed. (Indianapolis: Bobbs-Merrill, 1975), p. 225.

16. This account is based primarily on Charles O. Jones, *Clean Air: The Policies and Politics of Pollution Control* (Pittsburgh: University of Pittsburgh Press, 1975), pp. 25-28, 31-35, 62-69, secondarily on Davies and Davies, *Politics of Pollution*, pp. 25-28, 45-49, and Margolis, "Another View," p. 9.

17. U.S. Public Health Service, "Motor Vehicles, Air Pollution, and Health," House Doc. 489, 87th Cong., 2d sess., June 1962, p. 54, quoted in Jones, *Clean Air*, p. 62.

18. U.S. Senate, Committee on Public Works, Report by Special Subcommittee on Air and Water Pollution, "Steps Toward Clean Air," 88th Cong., 2d sess., 1964, pp. 2 5, as cited by Jones, *Clean Air*, p. 63.

19. The quotation is from sec. 6(a) of the Act, as cited by Jones, *Clean Air*, p. 63.

20. PL 89-272.

21. Margolis, "Another View," p. 9.

22. Jones, *Clean Air*, pp. 65-66.

23. Margolis, "Another View," table 1.

24. This section is based on ibid.; Jones, *Clean Air*, pp. 145-210; and Davies and Davies, *Politics of Pollution*, pp. 52-66.

25. Margolis, "Another View," p. 11.

26. John C. Esposito, *Vanishing Air* (New York: Grossman, 1970), p. 289.

27. Cf. Jones, *Clean Air*, pp. 152-154.

28. Margolis, "Another View," p. 24.

29. Ibid., p. 23.

30. Jones, *Clean Air*, p. 176.

31. Margolis, "Another View," p. 17.

32. Ibid., pp. 21–32.

33. Alan A. Altshuler and Robert W. Curry, "The Changing Environment of Urban Development Policy—Shared Power or Shared Impotence?" *Urban Law Annual* (1975): 21–38, esp. pp. 30–31.

34. *Sierra Club* v. *Ruckelshaus*, 344 F. Supp. 253 (D.D.C. 1972).

35. *Natural Resources Defense Council* v. *Train*, 545 F.2d 320, (1976).

36. Calculated from Margolis, "Another View," table 1.

37. Environmental Protection Agency, "Regulation of Fuels and Fuel Additives: Control of Lead Additives in Gasoline," *Federal Register* 41, no. 189 (September 28, 1976): 42675–42677.

38. Sections 108–110 of the Clean Air Act as amended in 1970.

39. U.S. Environmental Protection Agency, "Ambient Air Quality Standards," *Federal Register* 37, no. 84 (April 30, 1971).

40. Grad et al., *Automobile*, p. 35.

41. Ibid., p. 34.

42. National Academy of Sciences, Coordinating Committee on Air Quality Studies, *Air Quality and Automobile Emission Control: Summary Report* (Washington, D.C.: U.S. Government Printing Office, September 1974), vol. 1, p. 1.

43. Grad et al., *Automobile*, p. 32.

44. Joel Horowitz and Steven Kuhrtz, "Transportation Controls to Reduce Automobile Use and Improve Air Quality in Cities: The Need, the Options, and Effects on Urban Activity" (Washington, D.C.: U.S. Environmental Protection Agency, Office of Air and Waste Management, November 1974), p. 5.

45. Ibid., pp. 6–7.

46. David Burnham, "Cars Said to Fail Pollution Rules," *New York Times*, July 4, 1975, pp. 1, 36.

47. Interviews by Alan Altshuler with EPA officials, Washington, D.C., August 20, 1975.

48. Horowitz, "Transportation Controls," p. 11; Balz et al., "Love Affair with the Automobile," p. 12.

49. Horowitz, "Transportation Controls," pp. 27–28.

50. Ibid., p. 28.

51. Cf. EPA, "Boston Transportation Control Plan," *Federal Register* 40 CFR 52.1134, November 8, 1973; and Padnos and Selig, *Transportation Controls*, pp. 52-53.

52. *Brown* v. *EPA*, 521 F.2d 827 (9th Cir., 1975); *State of Maryland* v. *EPA*, 530 F.2d 215 (4th Cir., 1975).

53. *District of Columbia* v. *Train*, 521 F.2d, 971, 988 (C.A. D.C. 1975).

54. The quotations in this paragraph are from sections 172(b)(2) and 172(b) (11)(A) of the Clean Air Act as amended in 1977.

55. Ibid., secs. 176(a) and 176(b).

56. U.S. Department of Transportation et al., "An Analysis of Alternative Motor Vehicle Emission Standards," tables 1, 2.

57. Ibid., p. 2.

58. For a summary of the House and Senate debates on emission controls, see *Congressional Quarterly Almanac* 33 (1977): 638, 642.

59. Bernard Asbell, "The Outlawing of Next Year's Cars," *New York Times Magazine*, November 21, 1976, pp. 128-131.

60. *Congressional Quarterly Almanac* 32 (1976): 131, 133, 137, 140, 141.

61. On the 1970 Nixon proposals, cf. Margolis, "Another View," pp. 11, 12, 24, 25, 27.

62. *Federal Register* 42, no. 101 (May 25, 1977): 25742. (40 CFR 85.)

63. EPA, "Emission Control System Performance Warranty Regulations— Short Test Establishment" *Federal Register* 42, no. 101 (May 25, 1977): 26742-26768.

64. EPA, "Control of Air Pollution from New Motor Vehicles and New Motor Vehicle Engines" *Federal Register* 42, no. 204 (October 21, 1977): 56298.

65. Ibid., pp. 56298-56302.

66. David Harrison, Jr.. "Controlling Auto Emissions: How to Save More Than a Billion Dollars per Year and Help the Poor Too," discussion paper D76-11 (Department of City and Regional Planning, Harvard University, October 1976).

Notes to Chapter 7

1. U.S. Department of Transportion, National Highway Traffic Safety Administration, *Traffic Safety '76: A Report on Activities Under the National Traffic and Motor Vehicle Safety Act of 1966 and the Motor Vehicle Information and Cost Savings Act of 1972* (Washington, D.C.: U.S. Department of Transportation, 1977), table A-2; and Barbara M. Faigin, "1975 Societal Costs of Motor Vehicle Accidents" (Washington, D.C.: National Highway Traffic Safety Administration, 1976), tables 2, 23, and pp. 2-27.

2. Passenger mileage has been estimated by multiplying the Federal Highway Administration's 1975 estimate of vehicle miles of travel (1.3 trillion) by the Nationwide Personal Transportation Study's estimate of average occupancy per vehicle mile (2.2). FHWA estimate from *Highway Statistics*, 1975. (Washington, D.C.: U.S. Government Printing Office, 1977), sec. 3, p. III-2, table VM-1. NPTS estimate from Federal Highway Administration, Nationwide Personal Transportation Study, report 1, "Automobile Occupancy" (Washington, D.C., 1972), p. 8.

3. U.S. DOT, *Traffic Safety '76*, table A-17, pp. A-39–A-47.

4. Leo Bogart, "The Automobile as Social Cohesion," *Society* (July–August 1977): 12.

5. Ralph Nader, *Unsafe at Any Speed* (New York: Grossman, 1965).

6. Bogart, "Automobile As Social Cohesion," p. 12.

7. U.S. Department of Transportation, *The Secretary's Decision Concerning Motor Vehicle Occupant Crash Protection* (Washington, D.C.: U.S. DOT, 1976), pp. 15–16. NHTSA was originally termed the National Highway Safety Bureau.

8. FHWA, NPTS, report *Automobile Occupancy*, p. 8.

9. U.S. Department of Transportation, National Highway Traffic Safety Administration, *Traffic Safety '74* (Washington, D.C.: U.S. DOT, 1975), p. 19.

10. National Safety Council, *Accident Facts, 1974* (Chicago: National Safety Council, 1974), p. 55.

11. National Safety Council, *Accident Facts, 1976* (Chicago: National Safety Council, 1976), p. 48.

12. U.S. DOT, "Final Rule, Federal Motor Vehicle Safety Standard 208 (Passive Restraints)" (Washington, D.C.: U.S. DOT, June, 1977), p. 53.

13. National Safety Council, *Accident Facts, 1976*, p. 76 for 1970–1975; and National Safety Council, "Accident Facts: 1977 Preliminary Condensed Edition" (Chicago: National Safety Council, 1978), p. 2 for 1976 figure.

14. PL 93-492, sec. 109.

15. U.S. Department of Transportation, *Report to the President on Compliance with the 55 MPH Speed Limit* (Washington, D.C.: U.S. DOT, 1977), pp. I-1, II-10. The act was PL 94-280.

16. National Highway Traffic Safety Administration, "Motor Vehicle Safety Defect Recall Campaigns," 1972, p. 68; 1973, p. 76; 1974, pp. 24, 75.

17. Indiana University Institute for Research in Public Safety, "Tri-Level Study of the Causes of Traffic Accidents: Interim Report II" (Washington, D.C.: U.S. DOT, August 1976).

18. Peter N. Ziegler, "The Effect of Safety Belt Usage Laws Around the World," *Journal of Safety Research* 9, no. 2 (June 1977): 97–99; H. George

Johannesson and Charles H. Pulley, "Safety Belt Use Laws in Europe—A Positive Initiative for Saving Lives," Society of Automotive Engineers Paper 770152 (1977), p. 2.

19. Leon S. Robertson, *Automobile Seat Belt Use in Selected Countries, States and Provinces with and without Laws Requiring Belt Use* (Washington, D.C.: Insurance Institute for Highway Safety, 1977).

20. William T. Coleman, "Notice of Proposed Rule Making," *Federal Register* 41, no. 115 (June 14, 1976): 24075; cf. also U.S. DOT, *The National Highway Safety Needs Report* (Washington, D.C.: U.S. DOT, April 1976), p. 8.

21. U.S. DOT, "Final Rule," pp. 13, 14.

22. *Boston Globe*, July 12, 1977, p. 3.

23. U.S. DOT, "Final Rule," p. 53.

24. National Highway Traffic Safety Administration, "Fatal Accident Reporing System 1975 Annual Report," p. 53, table E-3.

25. U.S. DOT, "Final Rule," pp. 29-30.

26. Ibid., p. 19.

27. U.S. DOT, *Passive vs. Active Safety Belt Systems in Volkswagen Rabbits: A Comparison of Owner Use Habits and Attitudes* (Washington, D.C.: National Highway Traffic Safety Administration, 1976), pp. vii, 6.

28. Ibid., pp. 4-5.

29. U.S. DOT, "Final Rule," p. 34.

30. Ibid., p. 54.

31. Ibid., p. 21.

32. Ibid., pp. 23-25.

33. U.S. DOT, National Highway Traffic Safety Administration, *An Evaluation of the Highway Safety Program* (Washington, D.C.: U.S. DOT, July 1977), pp. vii, viii.

34. U.S. DOT, "Final Rule," p. 53, plus calculations by the authors of estimated saving with 100 percent usage.

35. U.S. DOT, "The Secretary's Decision Concerning Motor Vehicle Occupant Crash Protection" (Washington, D.C.: U.S. DOT, December 6, 1976), p. 6.

36. U.S. DOT, "Final Rule," p. 7; *New York Times*, December 7, 1977, p. 1.

37. U.S. DOT, "Final Rule," pp. 37-43.

38. *Boston Globe*, July 14, 1977.

39. Calspan Corporation, "Design, Development and Testing of Calspan/Chrysler Research Safety Vehicle—Phase II," vol. I (Washington, D.C.: NHTSA, 1977), p. 5-3; and Minicars, Inc., "Research Safety Vehicle—Phase

II," vol. 2 (Washington, D.C.: National Highway Traffic Safety Administration, 1977) chap. 3.

40. U.S. DOT, *National Highway Safety Needs Report* (Washington, D.C.: U.S. DOT, April 1976).

41. Coleman, "Notice of Proposed Rule Making," pp. 24070-24079.

42. U.S. DOT, *Highway Safety Needs Report*, p. 5.

43. Ibid., p. VI-5.

44. Institute of Traffic Engineers, *Transportation and Traffic Engineering Handbook* (Englewood Cliffs, N.J.: Prentice-Hall, 1976), p. 854.

45. U.S. DOT, *55 MPH Speed Limit*, table 4.

46. Ben A. Franklin, "Truckers Plan National Slowdown to Protest 55-MPH Speed Limit," *New York Times*, January 30, 1977, p. 22.

47. U.S. DOT, *55 MPH Speed Limit*, pp. 5, 21, and p. 2 of Secretary Adams's cover memorandum to President Carter.

48. U.S. DOT, *Highway Safety Needs Report*, figs. 6.2, 6.4.

49. Ibid., fig. 5.4.

50. Ibid., table 6.4.

51. Faigin, "Societal Costs," table 2.

52. U.S. DOT, *Highway Safety Needs Report*, p. IV-5.

Notes to Chapter 8

1. U.S. Bureau of the Census, *Statistical Abstract of the United States* (1976), p. 27; Motor Vehicle Manufacturers Association, *Motor Vehicle Facts and Figures, 1978* (Detroit, 1978), p. 39; Motor Vehicle Manufacturers Association, *Automobile Facts and Figures, 1952* (Detroit, 1953), p. 15.

2. American Public Transit Association, *Transit Fact Book, 1976-1977 Edition* (Washington, D.C.: American Public Transit Association, 1977), p. 30.

3. Ibid., p. 36.

4. U.S. Bureau of the Census, *Statistical Abstract of the United States* (1975), p. 17; U.S. Bureau of the Census, *County and City Data Book* (1972), table 4.

5. U.S. Census, *Statistical Abstract* (1976), pp. 22-24.

6. Sam Bass Warner, *Streetcar Suburbs* (New York: Atheneum, 1974), p. 14.

7. Sandra Rosenbloom and Alan Altshuler, "Equity Issues in Urban Transportation," *Policy Studies Journal* (Fall 1977): 37.

8. Ibid., p. 36.

9. J.R. Aronson and Eli Schwartz, eds., *Management Policies in Local Governments* (Washington, D.C.: International City Managers Association, 1975), p. 146.

10. Kiran Bhatt et al., *An Analysis of Road Expenditures and Payments by Vehicle Class (1956-1975)* (Washington, D.C.: The Urban Institute, 1977); J. R. Meyer et al., *The Urban Transportation Problem* (Cambridge: Harvard University Press, 1965), pp. 60–74.

11. Bhatt et al., *Analysis of Road Expenditures,* table 18.

12. Ibid., tables 18, 19.

13. The total cross-subsidy figures were derived by Pucher from ibid. and from table 13 of Bhatt et al., *Congressional Intent and Road User Payments* (Washington, D.C.: The Urban Institute, 1977), p. 66.

14. Bhatt ct al., *Analysis of Road Expenditures,* table 2.

15. APTA, *Transit Fact Book, 1976-1977 Edition,* pp. 20, 22, 23; Urban Mass Transportation Administration (UMTA), "Cumulative Capital Grants by Fiscal Year and Category, February 1, 1965 Through September 30, 1977" (unpublished memorandum, 1977); John Pucher, "Equity in Transit Financing," (Ph.D. diss., Massachusetts Institute of Technology, 1978), figure 4.1, table 6.3. Of the $14 billion total, $10 billion was for capital and $4 billion for operations. In making these calculations, we assumed that states and localities split the nonfederal share of federally aided capital projects equally. State operating assistance was calculated on the basis of actual amounts after 1972 and an assumed equivalent proportion of the total operating subsidy prior to 1973.

16. Steven Rattner, "House Rejects Efforts to Raise Tax on Gasoline," *New York Times,* August 5, 1977, pp. A1, D13.

17. Several of the most useful, though still very partial and preliminary, studies that have been carried out are: J. A. Miller, "Identification and Definition of the Mobility Requirements of the Handicapped and the Elderly" (Ph.D. diss., Northwestern University, 1975); J. Gillan and M. Wachs, "Lifestyles and Transportation Needs Among the Elderly of Los Angeles County" (paper presented at the Transportation Research Board meeting, January 1976); F. Carp, "Transportation and Retirement," *Transportation Engineering Journal* (November 1972).

18. Rosenbloom and Altshuler, "Equity Issues," pp. 34–35.

19. 1971 White House Conference on Aging, *Recommended Action: Transportation* (Washington, D.C.: U.S. Government Printing Office, 1971).

20. Frances Carp, testimony before the U.S. Senate Special Committee on Aging, *Hearings: Transportation and the Elderly, Part I,* February 25, 1974 (Washington, D.C.: U.S. Government Printing Office, 1974), p. 68; Marjorie

H. Cantor et al., "Dial-a-Ride: The New York City Experience" (New York: Office of the Aging, May 1975).

21. Rosenbloom and Altshuler, "Equity Issues," p. 35.

22. U.S. Department of Transportation, Transportation Systems Center, *The Handicapped and Elderly Market for Urban Mass Transit*, PB-224-821 (Washington, D.C.: National Technical Information Service, 1973).

23. National Center for Health Statistics, *Limitation of Activity and Mobility Due to Chronic Conditions*, series 10, no. 96 (November 1972), table 2.

24. Abt Associates, "Transportation Needs of the Handicapped: Travel Barriers, Cambridge, Massachusetts," PB-187-327 (Washington, D.C.: National Technical Information Service, 1969).

25. Ibid., table VI-1, p. 80.

26. U.S. Bureau of the Census, *General Characteristics of the Population, 1970, U.S. Summary*, vol. 2 (Washington, D.C.: U.S. Government Printing Office, 1973), table 220.

27. Federal Highway Administration, Nationwide Personal Transportation Study, report 6, "Characteristics of Licensed Drivers" (Washington, D.C., 1973), p. 14.

28. Federal Highway Administration, Nationwide Personal Transportation Study, report 9, "Mode of Transportation and Personal Characteristics of Trip Makers" (Washington, D.C., 1973), p. 31.

29. National Center for Health Statistics, *Limitation of Activity*, table 2.

30. J. K. Markovitz, "Transportation Needs of the Elderly," *Traffic Quarterly* 24 (1971): 240.

31. Ibid., p. 245; Tri-State Regional Planning Commission, *Measure of a Region* (New York: Tri-State Regional Planning Commission, 1967), p. 21.

32. Markovitz, "Transportation Needs of the Elderly," table 4, p. 250.

33. U.S. Bureau of the Census, *Statistical Abstract of the U.S.* (1977), table 694, p. 431.

34. Irving Kristol, "Taxes, Poverty, and Inequality," *The Public Interest* (Fall 1974): 3–28.

35. Survey Research Center, Institute for Social Research, University of Michigan, unpublished estimates cited by Robert Reinhold, "Poverty Is Found Less Persistent but Wider Spread Than Thought," *New York Times*, July 17, 1977, pp. 1, 36. The estimates are tentative and are currently being revised.

36. Federal Highway Administration, Nationwide Personal Transportation Study report 11, "Auto Ownership" (Washington, D.C., 1973), table 3.

37. Automobile Manufacturers Association, *Automobile Facts and Figures*,

1972 (Detroit, 1973), p. 30; U.S. Bureau of the Census, *Statistical Abstract of the U.S.* (1976), p. 27.

38. Motor Vehicle Manufacturers Association, *Motor Vehicle Facts and Figures, 1977,* p. 38.

39. Federal Highway Administration, Nationwide Personal Transportation Study, report 8, "Home-to-Work Trips and Travel" (Washington, D.C., 1973).

40. John Kain and John Meyer, "Transportation and Poverty," in American Academy of Arts and Sciences, *Conference on Poverty and Transportation* (Boston, 1968), p. 1.

41. American Institute of Planners and Motor Vehicle Manufacturers Association, *Urban Transportation Factbook* (Washington, D.C.: American Institute of Planners, 1974), table I-10.

42. George Hilton, *Federal Transit Subsidies* (Washington, D.C.: American Enterprise Institute for Public Policy Research, 1974), pp. 25-30.

43. Ibid., pp. 29-30; Committee for Economic and Cultural Development, *The O'Hare Express: An Employment Access Demonstration Project,* PB-212-677 (Washington, D.C.: National Technical Information Service, 1972).

44. Hilton, *Federal Transit Subsidies,* pp. 26-27.

45. Ibid., pp. 25-26.

46. State of California, Business and Transportation Agency, "Transportation Employment Project, South Central and East Los Angeles," Project CAL-MTD 12 (Washington, D.C.: U.S. Department of Transportation, 1971), p. 18.

47. Hilton, *Federal Transit Subsidies,* pp. 28-29.

48. Peter Doeringer, "Ghetto Labor Markets—Problems and Programs" (paper presented at the Conference on Transportation and Poverty, American Academy of Arts and Sciences, Boston, June 1968).

49. Bennett Harrison, *Urban Economic Development* (Washington, D.C.: The Urban Institute, 1974), pp. 42-46.

50. John Pucher, "Equity in Transit Financing," p. 14. Pucher's calculations are based on data in APTA, *Transit Fact Book, 1976-1977 Edition,* p. 34; U.S. Bureau of the Census, *Statistical Abstract of the U.S.* (1977), tables 667, 771; and U.S. Department of Commerce, Bureau of Economic Analysis, *Survey of Current Business* (July 1977), table 6.9.

51. APTA, *Transit Fact Book, 1976-1977 Edition,* p. 34.

52. Ibid., pp. 26, 30, 34.

53. U.S. Bureau of the Census, *Statistical Abstract of the U.S.* (1977), table 658.

54. Jack Faucett Associates, "Washington Area Metro Rail System: A Current

Perspective and a Preliminary Appraisal of Alternatives," prepared for the Congressional Research Service of the Library of Congress (Washington, D.C., 1976), p. 82.

55. Melvin M. Webber, "BART's Outcomes: An Early Appraisal," monograph 26 (Institute of Urban and Regional Development and Institute of Transportation Studies, University of California, Berkeley, October 1976), table V. A somewhat shorter version, without the table, appeared in *The Public Interest* (Fall 1976): 79–108.

56. APTA, *Transit Fact Book, 1975–1976 Edition*, tables 6, 10.

57. John Pucher, "Equity in Transit Financing," p. 33.

58. Ibid., pp. 60, 61.

59. This information was obtained from Cynthia Burbank, Policy Analysis Division of UMTA, U.S. Department of Transportation.

60. John Pucher, "Equity in Transit Financing," table 6.1, as revised by excluding Denver, San Francisco, and Washington from the 1975 total.

61. Hilton, *Federal Transit Subsidies*, p. 28.

62. PL 93-87, sec. 165.

63. Social Security Amendments of 1967 (PL 90-248), Title XIX; the specific requirements and authorizations cited derive from the regulations established by HEW, the department responsible for administering the act.

64. PL 93-112, sec. 504.

65. Older American Act, Pl 89-73, sec. 101 as amended by sec. 102 of the 1973 Comprehensive Services Amendments (Pl 93-29); and the Social Services Amendments of 1974 (PL 93-647), sec. 2002.

66. The Federal-Aid Highway Act of 1973 (PL 93-87) contained Title III, "The Urban Mass Transportation Act of 1974 Amendments." Sec. 301(g) amended sec. 16(b) of the 1964 Act by adding paragraph 2, which allowed grants to nonprofit agencies.

67. PL 93-643, sec. 103 amended sec. 147 of the Federal-Aid Highway Act of 1973 (PL 93-87).

68. Pl 93-503, sec. 103 revised sec. 5 of the Urban Mass Transportation Act of 1964.

69. APTA Task Force on Paratransit, "Paratransit in the Family of Transit Services," *Transit Journal* (May 1976): 5–26; Roger Teal, "Paratransit in Urban Transportation: A Political–Organizational Approach" (Ph.D. diss., Tufts University, 1977); Arthur Saltzman, "Special Service Transportation Systems Which Serve the Transportation Disadvantaged: Current Operations and Future Projects" (unpublished draft report, Alan M. Voorhees and Associates, 1977); U.S. Department of Transportation, Urban Mass Transportation Administration, *Demand-Responsive Transportation: State-of-the-Art Overview* (Washington, D.C.: UMTA, 1975), appendix A.

70. U.S. Department of Health, Education and Welfare, *Transportation Authorities in Federal Human Service Programs*, SHR-0000739 (Washington, D.C.: National Technical Information Service, 1976).

71. Saltzman, "Special Service Transportation," pp. 5-13.

72. APTA, *Transit Fact Book, 1975-1976 Edition*, table 12; estimate includes trolley coaches.

73. The figure was obtained from Cynthia Burbank, Policy Analysis Division of UMTA, U.S. Department of Transportation.

74. Reid Ewing and Nigel Wilson, "Innovations in Demand-Responsive Transit" (Center for Transportation Studies, MIT, October 1976), p. 62.

75. Reid Ewing, "Demand-Responsive Transit: Problems and Possibilities" (Ph.D. diss., MIT, 1977), chap. 5.

76. Calculated on the basis of tables 2 and 7 of Webber, "BART Outcomes."

77. U.S. Department of Transportation, "Nondiscrimination on the Basis of Handicap in Federally Assisted Programs and Activities," *Federal Register* 43 (June 8, 1978): 25018.

78. Auto occupancy data are from U.S. Department of Transportation, Nationwide Personal Transportation Study, report 1, "Automobile Occupancy," (Washington, D.C.: U.S. DOT, 1972), table 3; percentage of commutation by transit and as auto passengers has been calculated from Federal Highway Administration, Nationwide Personal Transportation Study, report 8, "Home-to-Work Trips and Travel" (Washington, D.C., 1973), table A-10.

79. Calculated from FHWA, NPTS, report 8, "Home-to-Work Trips and Travel," table A-14.

80. *Congressional Quarterly Almanac* 32 (1976): 607-619; *Congressional Quarterly Weekly Reports* 35 (July 16, 1977): 1447-1451, (July 30, 1977): 1565-1566.

81. E. W. Kitch, M. Isaccson, and D. Kasper, "The Regulation of Taxicabs in Chicago," *Journal of Law and Economics* 14 (1971): 285-350. This article provides the best history of taxi and antijitney regulation nationwide as well as in Chicago.

Notes to Chapter 9

1. U.S. Bureau of the Census, *Historical Statistics of the United States: *Historical Times to 1957* (Washington, D.C.: U.S. Government Printing Office, 1960), p. 463.

2. President's Advisory Committee on a National Highway Program, *A Ten Year National Highway Program, A Report to the President* (Washington, D.C.: U.S. Government Printing Office, 1955), p. 10.

3. Wilfred Owen, *The Metropolitan Transportation Problem* (Washington, D.C.: Brookings Institution, 1956), pp. 1, 4, 21.

4. Peter Koltnow, *Changes in Mobility in American Cities* (Washington, D.C.: Highway User's Federation for Safety and Mobility, 1970), pp. 6–10, 19–20.

5. President's Advisory Committee, *Ten Year Program*, pp. 8–9.

6. Alan A. Altshuler, *The City Planning Process* (Ithaca: Cornell University Press, 1965), pp. 17–83.

7. Gary T. Schwartz, "Urban Freeways and the Interstate System," *Southern California Law Review* (March 1976): 479–480.

8. President's Advisory Committee, *Ten Year Program*, pp. 8–11.

9. Schwartz, "Urban Freeways," pp. 483–484.

10. Calculated from FHWA, Nationwide Personal Transportation Study, report 1, "Automobile Occupancy" (Washington, D.C., 1972), table 1 and NPTS, report 10, "Purposes of Automobile Trips and Travel" (Washington, D.C., 1974), table A-14. See table 7.9 for additional details.

11. Schwartz, "Urban Freeways," pp. 501–507.

12. Gary R. Fauth, Gregory K. Ingram, and Eugene Kroch, "Cost and Effectiveness of Emission Reduction and Transportation Control Policies," *International Journal of Transport Economics* (April 1975): table 1.

13. American Association of State Highway Officials (AASHO), *A Policy on the Design of Urban Highways and Arterial Streets* (Washington, D.C.: AASHO, 1973), p. 295.

14. Ibid., pp. 296–298.

15. Highway Research Board, *Highway Capacity Manual*, special report 87 (Washington, D.C.: Highway Research Board, 1965).

16. Donald Dewees, "Congestion Costs in Urban Motoring: Some Toronto Estimates," research paper 71 (Center for Urban and Community Studies and Department of Political Economy, University of Toronto, January 1976), p. 13.

17. Federal Aid Highway Act of 1944, ch. 626, sec. 7 (58 Stat. 842), as excerpted in Schwartz, "Urban Freeways."

18. U.S. Bureau of Public Roads memorandum, June 9, 1955, quoted in Schwartz, "Urban Freeways," pp. 425, 469.

19. Schwartz, "Urban Freeways," p. 470.

20. Federal Aid Highway Act of 1956, ch. 462, sec. 116(b), (70 Stat. 385), codified at 23 USC 101 (b) (1970), as quoted in Schwartz, "Urban Freeways," pp. 470–471.

21. Schwartz, "Urban Freeways," 474–475.

22. 23 Code of Federal Regulations 625.3(a) 14-15.

23. American Association of State Highway Officials, *Policy*, p. 310.

24. Alan A. Altshuler and Robert W. Curry, "The Changing Environment of Urban Transportation: Shared Power or Shared Impotence," *Urban Law Annual* (1975); Schwartz, "Urban Freeways," pp. 464-465.

25. Federal Aid Highway Act of 1967 (signed into law January 2, 1968), (81 Stat. 772), codified at sec. 103(e)(2) (1970).

26. Federal Aid Highway Act of 1973, sec. 137(a)(1), 137(a)(2), and 137(b), codified at 23 USC 103(e)(2), 103(e)(4).

27. Federal Aid Highway Act of 1976, sec. 110(a) and 111 (90 Stat. 425), codified at 23 USC 103(e)(2).

28. *A Statement of National Transportation Policy by the Secretary of Transportation* (Washington, D.C.: U.S. Government Printing Office, 1975), p. 4.

29. Schwartz, "Urban Freeways," p. 451.

30. *National Transportation Policy*, pp. 9-10.

31. Ibid., p. 8.

32. Peter Koltnow, *Changes in Mobility in American Cities* (Washington, D.C.: Highway User's Federation for Safety and Mobility, 1970).

33. On the energy requirements of highway construction, see pp. 168-169. On the relationship between speed and fuel demand, see appendix F.

34. Interplan Corp., *Transportation System Management: State of the Art* (UMTA and FHWA, February 1977), pp. 5-8.

35. Dewees, "Congestion Costs," p. 13.

36. Interplan, *State of the Art*.

37. Federal Highway Administration, *1974 Annual Report on Urban Area Traffic Operations Improvement Programs (TOPICS)* (Washington, D.C., 1973), pp. 30-31.

38. Ibid., pp. 38-39.

39. Interplan, *State of the Art*, pp. A-7.

40. Ibid., pp. 33-40.

41. Ibid., p. 8.

42. Ibid., p. 41, and conversations with Leonard Newman of the California Department of Transportation in August 1976.

43. Interplan, *State of the Art*, p. 41.

44. James T. McQueen et al., "Evaluation of the Shirley Highway Express-Bus-On-Freeway Demonstration Project: Final Report" (Washington, D.C.: Urban Mass Transportation Administration, 1975), pp. 1-4.

45. Interplan, *State of the Art*, table 8.

46. Alan M. Voorhees, Inc., *Status of the Urban Corridor Demonstration Program* (Washington, D.C.: U.S. DOT, 1974), pp. 45–54.

47. R. H. Pratt Associates, Inc., *Low Cost Urban Transportation Alternatives*, vol. 2: *Results of Case Studies and Analysis of Busway Applications in the United States* (Washington, D.C.: U.S. Government Printing Office, 1973), p. 40.

48. Ibid., pp. 43–53.

49. Herbert S. Levinson et al., NCHRP 155, *Bus Use of Highway Planning and Design Guidelines* (1975), pp. 74, 75, table 39.

50. State of California, Department of Transportation, "Evaluation Report on the Santa Monica Freeway Diamond Lane Project After 21 Weeks of Operation" (September 1976).

51. Ibid., pp. 6, 28, 32, 33.

52. Ibid., pp. 6, 8, 23.

53. Ibid., pp. 35, 36.

54. Ibid., pp. 5, 6, 16, and calculations by the authors.

55. Ibid., pp. 21–25.

56. Harry Rose and David Hines, "U.S. 1-South Dixie Highway Contra-Flow Bus Lane and Carpool Lane Demonstration Project" (Dade County Office of Transportation Administration, 1976, mimeo.).

57. Federal Highway Administration, Nationwide Personal Transportation Study, report 8, "Home-to-Work Trips and Travel" (Washington, D.C., 1973), p. 46.

58. Raymond H. Ellis, "Parking Management Strategies," special report 172 (Transportation Research Board, 1977), p. 62.

59. L. A. Hoel and E. S. Roszner, *The Pittsburg Parking Strike*, U.S. Department of Transportation report UMTA-Pa-11-0011-72-2 (Transportation Research Institute, Carnegie-Mellon University, December 1972), p. 10.

60. Damian Kulash, *Parking Taxes as Roadway Prices: A Case Study of San Francisco Experience* (The Urban Institute, December 1973), pp. 25–28.

61. Michael Padnos and Edward Selig, "Transportation Controls in Boston: The Plan That Failed" (American Bar Foundation and the National Academy of Sciences, 1976).

62. Burke K. Burright and John Enns, *Econometric Models of the Demand for Motor Fuel* (Santa Monica: Rand Corporation External Publication R-1561-NSF, April 1975), p. 48.

63. John Pucher and Jerome Rothenberg, "Pricing in Urban Transportation:

A Survey of Empirical Evidence on the Elasticity of Travel Demand," pp. 17, 18.

64. Anthony Downs, *Urban Problems and Prospects*, 2d ed. (Chicago: Rand McNally, 1976), chap. 9; Paul T. McElhiney, "Evaluating Freeway Performance in Los Angeles, *Traffic Quarterly* 14, no. 3 (July 1960): 296-312.

65. John F. Kain, "Toward Better Urban Transport Pricing: Using What Is Known and Exploring What Is Not Known," in Transportation Research Board, *Urban Transportation Pricing Alternatives* (Washington, D.C.: Transportation Research Board, 1976).

66. Kiran U. Bhatt, "Session II Summary," in *Urban Transportation Pricing Alternatives*, p. 4.

67. Greater London Council, "The London Supplementary Licensing Study," *A Study of Supplementary Licensing* (London: Greater London Council, May 1974), pp. 44-45.

68. Gerald Goldstein and Leon Moses, "Transport Controls, Travel Costs, and Urban Spatial Structure," *Public Policy* (Summer 1975): 355-380.

69. William Vickrey, "Current Issues in Transportation," in Neil W. Chamberlin, ed., *Contemporary Economic Issues* (Homewood, Ill.: Richard D. Irwin, 1973), pp. 200-201.

70. George Hilton, *Federal Transit Subsidies: The Urban Mass Transportation Assistance Program* (Washington, D.C.: American Enterprise Institute, 1974), pp. 114-115.

71. Ibid., pp. 201-203.

72. Peter L. Watson and Edward P. Holland, "Congestion Pricing—The Example of Singapore" in *Urban Transportation Economics*, Transportation Research Board special report 181 (Washington, D.C.: TRB, 1978), pp. 27-30. This article previously appeared in *Finance and Development* 13, no. 1 (March 1976): 20-24.

73. Kiran U. Bhatt, "What Can We Do About Urban Traffic Congestion: A Pricing Approach" (Washington, D.C.: The Urban Institute, February 1975), pp. 22-28.

74. Vickrey, "Current Issues in Transportation," pp. 202-203.

75. Watson, "Congestion Pricing," p. 7.

76. Vickrey, "Current Issues in Transportation," p. 204.

77. Charles Hedges, "The Role of Price in the Urban Transportation Market," in TRB, *Urban Transportation Pricing Alternatives*, p. 6.

78. Andrew Marshall Hamer, *The Selling of Rail Rapid Transit* (Lexington, Mass.: Lexington Books, 1976).

79. Hilton, *Federal Transit Subsidies*, pp. 67-68.

80. Max Kaplovitz, "Interim Report, South Shore Extension Effect on Southeast Corridor Travel Pattern" (Massachusetts Department of Public Works, March 1972), esp. p. 2.

81. Hamer, *Selling of Rail Rapid Transit*, p. 24.

82. Peat, Marwick, Mitchell & Co., *Immediate Travel Impacts of Transbay BART* (Springfield, Va.: National Technical Information Service, May 1975), pp. 34–37.

83. Ibid., p. 43. Cf. also Alistair Sherret and Joel Markowitz, "Effects of BART on Work Journeys in the Bay Area" (paper presented at the Annual Meeting of the American Society of Civil Engineers, October 1977) (available from the Metropolitan Transportation Commission, Berkeley, California).

84. R. H. Pratt Associates, *Low Cost Urban Transportation*, p. 27.

Notes to Chapter 10

1. Seymour Mandelbaum, *Community and Communications* (New York: W. W. Norton, 1972), chap. 2; John Meyer, John Kain, and Martin Wohl, *The Urban Transportation Problem* (Cambridge: Harvard University Press, 1965), pp. 9–24; Wilfred Owen, *Cities in the Motor Age* (New York: Viking Press, 1959), chap. 1; Jean Gottman, *Megalopolis* (New York: The Twentieth-Century Fund, 1961), chap. 1; Edward C. Banfield, *The Unheavenly City Revisited* (Boston: Little, Brown, 1974), chap. 2; and Leon Moses and Harold F. Williamson, Jr., "The Location of Economic Activity in Cities," in Matthew Edel and Jerome Rothenberg, eds., *Readings in Urban Economics* (New York: Macmillan, 1972).

2. Cf. Thomas A. Morehouse, "The 1962 Highway Act: A Study in Artful Interpretation," *Journal of the American Institute of Planners* 35, no. 3 (May 1969): 160–168.

3. Cf. Alan A. Altshuler and Robert Curry, "The Changing Environment of Urban Development Policy—Shared Power or Shared Impotence?" *Urban Law Annual* (1975) (Washington University School of Law, 1976), pp. 1–43, esp. pp. 11–21.

4. Ibid., pp. 21–38.

5. Ibid., pp. 11–21; Melvin Mogulof, *Governing Metropolitan Areas: A Critical Review of Council of Governments and the Federal Role* (Washington, D.C.: The Urban Institute, 1971); U.S. Advisory Commission on Intergovernmental Relations, *Improving Urban America: A Challenge to Federalism* (Washington, D.C.: U.S. Advisory Commission on Intergovernmental Relations, 1976), chap. 1; and Noreen Lyday, *The Law of the Land: Debating National Land Use Legislation, 1970–75* (Washington, D.C.: The Urban Institute, 1976).

6. Metropolitan Council, "Metropolitan Development Framework, Transportation Chapter" (Minneapolis: Metropolitan Council, July 1976), p. 45.

7. Daniel Elazar, "Are We a Nation of Cities?" *The Public Interest* (Summer 1966): 47–48.

8. Sara Mills Mazie and Steve Rawlings, "Public Attitudes Toward Population Distribution Issues," in Sara Mills Mazie, ed., *Population Distribution and Policy*, vol. 5 of research reports prepared by the U.S. Commission on Population Growth and the American Future (Washington, D.C.: U.S. Government Printing Office, 1973), p. 605; see also James L. Sundquist, *Dispersing Population* (Washington, D.C.: Brookings Institution, 1975), pp. 24–30.

9. William Michaelson, "Most People Don't Want What Architects Want," *Trans-Action* 5, no. 8 (July–August 1968): 37–43.

10. Bernard J. Frieden and Arthur P. Solomon, "The Nation's Housing: 1975–1985" (Cambridge, Mass.: Joint Center for Urban Studies, April 1977), pp. 99–116.

11. Data for 1961–1973 from Robert Schafer, *The Suburbanization of Multi-family Housing* (Lexington, Mass.: D. C. Heath, 1974). Data since 1974 from U.S. Bureau of the Census, *Housing Starts* (monthly), various issues.

12. U.S. Bureau of the Census, "Current Population Reports," series P-26 (Washington, D.C.: U.S. Bureau of the Census, 1977).

13. U.S. Bureau of the Census, "Current Population Reports," series P-26.

14. Ibid., series P-25.

15. U.S. Department of Agriculture, Economic Research Service, *Major Uses of Land and Water in the United States: Summary for 1959*, Agricultural Economic Report 13 (Washington, D.C.: U.S. Government Printing Office, 1962), p. 11, table 7; U.S. Department of Agriculture, Economic Research Service, *Major Uses of Land in the United States: Summary for 1969*, Agricultural Economic Report 247 (Washington, D.C.: U.S. Government Printing Office, 1973), p. 38, appendix table 10.

16. Department of Agriculture, *Uses of Land and Water*, pp. 11, 42.

17. George Peterson and Harvey Yampolsky, *Urban Development and the Protection of Metropolitan Farmland* (Washington, D.C.: The Urban Institute, 1975), p. 6.

18. U.S. Department of Agriculture, "Urbanization of Land in the Northeastern United States," Economic Research Service Miscellaneous Publication 485 (August 1971), cited by ibid., p. 12.

19. Regional Plan Association and Resources for the Future, *Regional Energy Consumption: Second Interim Report* (New York: Regional Plan Association, 1974), p. 7.

20. Real Estate Research Corporation, *The Costs of Sprawl, Detailed Cost*

Analysis (Washington, D.C.: U.S. Government Printing Office, 1974), pp. 3, 6, 35, 90-92.

21. Ibid., p. 147.

22. Ibid., pp. 102, 132-136.

23. Ibid., pp. 93-97.

24. Ibid., pp. 93-98.

25. Boris Pushkarev and Jeffrey M. Zupan, *Public Transportation and Land Use Policy* (Bloomington, Ind.: Indiana University Press, 1977), pp. 8-9.

26. Ibid., chap. 2.

27. Peterson and Yampolsky, *Urban Development*, p. 6. Cf. also Earl O. Heady, "The Agriculture of the U.S.," *Scientific American* (September 1976): 106-127.

28. Karl Moskowitz, "Living and Travel Patterns in Automobile Oriented Cities," in *The Dynamics of Urban Transportation* (Automobile Manufacturers Association, 1962) cited by John Kain, "Urban Form and the Cost of Urban Services," discussion paper 6 (Program in Regional and Urban Economics, Harvard University, 1967), pp. 26-28.

29. Lewis Keebel, *Principles and Practices of Town and Country Planning* (London: Estates Gazette, Ltd., 1959), chap. 14.

30. "Metropolitan Area Relatively Efficient in Its Use of Energy," *New York Times*, May 2, 1977, pp. 1, 5.

31. Regional Plan Association, *Regional Energy Consumption*, p. 7.

32. Ibid., p. 7.

33. Ibid., p. 9.

34. U.S. Federal Energy Administration, *Project Independence Final Report* (Washington, D.C.: U.S. Government Printing Office, 1974), p. A-123, estimates that residential space heating and air conditioning account for 16 percent of U.S. energy consumption and that auto usage accounts for slightly less than 20 percent. We have estimated below that only about one-fifth of auto usage is for intraneighborhood travel. Thus total consumption for these three purposes is about 20 percent of the urban total.

35. RERC, *Costs of Sprawl, Detailed Cost Analysis*, p. 37.

36. Ibid., p. 147.

37. Ibid.

38. Ibid., p. 23.

39. Ibid., p. 89.

40. Thomas Muller, *Fiscal Impacts of Land Development* (Washington, D.C.: The Urban Institute, 1975), pp. 21-24; Kain, "Urban Form and the Cost of

Urban Services," pp. 51-53; Harvey Brazer, "City Expenditures in the United States," occasional paper 66 (mimeo., National Bureau of Economic Research, 1959); and Robert C. Wood, *1400 Governments* (Cambridge: Harvard University Press, 1961), pp. 32-41.

41. RERC, *Costs of Sprawl, Detailed Cost Analysis,* p. 92.

42. Bennett Harrison, *Urban Economic Development* (Washington, D.C.: The Urban Institute, 1974), chap. 3, esp. table 20.

43. Noreen Lyday, *The Law of the Land* (Washington, D.C.: The Urban Institute, 1976).

44. C. Kenneth Orski, "The Role of the Federal Urban Mass Transportation Program in Urban Economic Development and Revitalization" (address to the National Council for Economic Development, Washington, November 18, 1977).

45. Richard Grefe and Angus McDonald, "The Regional Economic and Fiscal Impacts of BART," revised (mimeo., Berkeley, BART Impact Program, October 1977), p. 16.

46. Ibid., pp. 16, 17.

47. De Leuw, Cather and Company, "Land Use Impacts of Rapid Transit: Implications of Recent Experience" (Washington, D.C.: U.S. DOT, August 1977).

48. G. Warren Heenan, "The Economic Effect of Rapid Transit on Real Estate Development," *Appraisal Journal* (April 1968): 213-224, cited by ibid., pp. 42-43.

49. Donald Dewees, "The Effect of a Subway on Residential Property Values in Toronto" (mimeo., Toronto, University of Toronto Institute for Policy Analysis, 1975), and Alan Abouchar, "The Analysis of Property Values and Subway Investments and Financing Policies" working paper 7306 (mimeo., Toronto, University of Toronto Institute for the Quantitative Analysis of Social and Economic Policy, 1973), both cited by De Leuw, Cather, "Land Use Impacts," pp. 43-44.

50. De Leuw, Cather and Company, "Mid Project Review Materials on Land Use Impacts of Recent Major Rapid Transit Improvements in the United States and Canada" (mimeo., November 1976), p. 4; Foh-tsrang Tang, "Detection and Estimation of Transportation Impact with Models of Suburban Residential Property Sales Prices" (Ph.D. diss., University of Pennsylvania, 1975); and Richard Mudge, "The Impact of Transportation Savings on Suburban Residential Property Values" (paper presented at the North American Regional Science Conference, November 10, 1973, Atlanta, Georgia).

51. Chin Ming Yan, "Impact of a Rapid Transit Line on Suburban Vacant Land Values" (Ph.D. diss., University of Pennsylvania, 1976); and Jeffrey Platt, "Residential Property Value Gradients and Urban Transportation Impacts" (Ph.D. diss., University of Pennsylvania, 1972); Mudge, "Impact of

Transportation Savings;" Colin Gannon and Michael Dear, "The Impact of Rapid Transit Systems on Commercial Office Development: The Case of the Philadelphia-Lindenwold Line" (University of Pennsylvania Transportation Studies Center, 1972); and Colin Gannon and Michael Dear, "Rapid Transit and Office Development," *Traffic Quarterly* (1975): 223-442, all cited by De Leuw, Cather, "Land Use Impacts," pp. 91, 93.

52. Douglass, B. Lee, Jr., *Market Street Study*, BART Impact Studies Final Report Series (Berkeley: University of California, 1973); and Douglass B. Lee, Jr., *Key Informant Interviews*, BART Impact Studies Final Report Series (Berkeley: University of California, 1973), both cited in De Leuw, Cather, "Land Use Impacts," pp. 71-85.

53. Melvin M. Webber, "The BART Experience—What Have We Learned?" monograph 26 (Institute of Urban and Regional Development and Institute of Transportation Studies, Berkeley: University of California, October 1976). A somewhat shorter version of this monograph appeared in *The Public Interest* (Fall 1976): 79-108; and Michael V. Dyett and Emilio Escudero, "Effects of BART on Urban Development" (paper presented at the Annual Convention of the American Society of Civil Engineers, San Francisco, October 1977).

54. Dyett, "Effects of BART," pp. 8-10.

55. Webber, "The BART Experience," p. 12.

56. Ibid., table 1, and calculation by the authors.

57. Ibid., p. 14.

58. Ibid., pp. 13-14.

59. Ibid., p. 15.

60. Grefe and McDonald, "Regional Economic and Fiscal Impacts of BART," pp. 10-11, 15-16.

61. Dyett, "Effects of BART," p. 15.

62. Webber, "The BART Experience," p. 15; and Dyett and Escudero, "Effects of BART," pp. 14-15.

63. American Institute of Planners and the Motor Vehicle Manufacturers Association, *Urban Transportation Fact Book, Vol.* 2 (Washington, D.C., 1974), p. 32; and Hammer, Siler, George Associates, "Transit Generated Private Investment, Detroit, Michigan" (March 1977), p. 21.

64. Hammer, Siler, George, "Transit Generated Private Investment," pp. 3-4.

65. Secretary of Transportation William Coleman to Michigan Governor William G. Milliken and Detroit Mayor Coleman Young, October 19, 1976.

66. Hammer, Siler, George, "Transit Generated Private Investment," p. 165.

67. Ibid., pp. 51, 165.

68. Ibid., p. 105.

69. Gary T. Schwartz, "Urban Freeways and the Interstate System," *Southern California Law Review* (March 1976), pp. 470, 506.

70. Tom Muller, Kevin Neels, John Tilney, and Grace Dawson, "The Economic Impact of I-295 on the Richmond Central Business District" (Washington, D.C.: The Urban Institute, 1977), p. 36.

71. Reid Ewing, "Demand-Responsive Transit: Problems and Possibilities" (Ph.D. diss., Massachusetts Institute of Technology, 1977), p. 6.

Notes to Chapter 11

1. Cf. B. Bruce-Briggs, "Mass Transportation and Minority Transportation," *The Public Interest* 40 (Summer 1975): 43–74.

2. Westport Transit District, "Summary of Service and Methods Demonstration of Integrated Conventional Transit and Paratransit Services" (April 1977).

3. Reid Ewing, "Demand Responsive Transit: Problems and Possibilities" (Ph.D. diss., Massachusetts Institute of Technology, 1977), chap. 1.

4. The New York Port Authority data on Trans-Hudson automobile occupancies come from Boris Pushkarev and Jeffrey Zupan, *Public Transportation and Land Use Policy* (Bloomington, Ind.: Indiana University Press, 1977), exhibit 0.2. The auto occupancy estimates from surveys in various metropolitan areas are reported in Federal Highway Administration, "Estimating Auto Occupancy" (Washington, D.C.: FHWA, 1972), tables 2, 3. The Nationwide Personal Transportation Study (NPTS) occupancy estimate is from FHWA, NPTS, report 1, "Automobile Occupancy" (Washington, D.C., 1972) table 1. The NPTS survey was almost unique in that it distinguished among trips by length; it found that average occupancy per vehicle mile was 2.2.

5. Cf. James Q. Wilson, "The Dead Hand of Regulation," *The Public Interest* (Fall 1977): 39–58.

6. Bruce Ackerman has previously referred to the politics of clean air as a morality play. Cf. his article, "Clean (Cough) Air," *New York Times*, August 20, 1977, p. 21.

7. Anthony Parisi, "Poll Finds Doubt on Energy Crisis," *New York Times*, September 1, 1977, pp. 1, 58.

8. Alan P. Berens and Michael Hill, *Automobile Exhaust Emission Surveillance Analysis of the FY 1974 Program*, prepared for the Environmental Protection Agency, EPA-460/3-76-019 (September 1976), pp. 5, 12.

9. Ibid., p. 8.

10. David Burnham, "Cars Said to Fail Pollution Rules," *New York Times*, February 4, 1975.

11. U.S. Department of Transportation, *The National Highway Safety Needs Report* (Washington, D.C.: U.S. Department of Transportation, 1976), p. 5.

Notes to Appendix A

1. Kiran Bhatt, Michael Beesley and Kevin Neels, *An Analysis of Road Expenditures and Payments by Vehicle Class (1956–1975)* (Washington, D.C.: The Urban Institute, 1977). Calculated from appendix 2 and p. 121. Bhatt et al. define "medium and heavy trucks" as those with more than four wheels.

2. National Highway Traffic Safety Administration, *Fatal Accident Reporting System, 1975 Annual Report* (Washington, D.C.: U.S. Department of Transportation, 1976), p. 103 for tractor-trailer truck fatalities. Federal Highway Administration, *Highway Statistics, 1975 Edition* (Washington, D.C.: U.S. Government Printing Office, 1977), table VM-1 for tractor-trailer VMT.

3. U.S. Environmental Protection Agency, "1973 National Emissions Report" (Research Triangle Park, North Carolina, EPA, 1976), calculated from "United States Summary," p. 1. "Heavy trucks" are those weighing more than 8,500 pounds. VMT is authors' estimate.

4. Wilbur Smith, Inc., *Transportation and Parking for Tomorrow's Cities* (Washington, D.C.: Automobile Manufacturers Association, 1966), p. 263.

5. U.S. Energy Resources Council, *Interagency Study of Post-1980 Goals for Commercial Motor Vehicles* (Washington, D.C.: U.S. Government Printing Office, 1976), p. 15.

Notes to Appendix C

1. Data on truck use are from U.S. Bureau of the Census, *1972 Census of Transportation*, volume 2; *Truck Inventory and Use Survey* (Washington, D.C.: U.S. Government Printing Office, 1973), table 1. Data on truck registrations from Motor Vehicle Manufacturers Association, *Motor Vehicle Facts and Figures*, 1976–77 ed., p. 35. Data on average miles driven per year for personal use trucks from *Census of Transportation*, volume 2, table 2; data on average miles driven per year by autos calculated from *Highway Statistics, 1972 Edition*, tables MV-1, VM-1.

Notes to Appendix D

1. Environmental Protection Agency, *Report to the President and Congress on Noise* (Washington, D.C.: U.S. Government Printing Office, 1972). The Noise Control Act of 1972 is Public Law 92-574.

2. U.S. Bureau of the Census, *Annual Housing Survey: 1973*, Part B, "Indicators of·Housing and Neighborhood Quality" (Washington, D.C.: U.S. Government Printing Office, 1975), table A-4.

3. Section 6(c)(1) of the 1972 Noise Control Act states that product noise standards shall be "requisite to protect the public health and welfare, taking into account the magnitude and conditions of use of such product. . . ., the degree of noise reduction achievable through the application of the best available technology, and the cost of compliance."

4. Calculated by the authors from EPA, *About Noise* (Washington, D.C.: U.S. EPA, 1976), figure 5.

Notes to Appendix E

1. Workshop on Alternative Energy Strategies (WAES), *Energy: Global Prospects 1985-2000* (New York: McGraw-Hill, 1977), p. 136, is the source of the OPEC and total estimates; U.S. estimate is from Federal Energy Administration, *National Energy Outlook* (Washington, D.C.: U.S. Government Printing Office, 1976), p. 54; estimate for other major countries from WAES, *Energy*, p. 238, and Central Intelligence Agency, *International Energy Situation: Outlook to 1985* (Washington, D.C.: Library of Congress Photoduplication Service, April 1977), pp. 10, 11, 15.

2. Executive Office of the President, *The National Energy Plan* (Washington, D.C.: U.S. Government Printing Office, 1977), p. 14, and *Newsweek*, June 27, 1977. The latter places reserves at the beginning of 1977 at 4.8 years.

3. CIA, *International Energy Situation*, table 5. Translation from barrels per day to barrels per year by the authors.

4. WAES, *Energy*, pp. 115–116.

5. Ibid., p. 126.

6. Executive Office of the President, *National Energy Plan*, p. 15.

Notes to Appendix F

1. T. C. Austin, R. B. Michael, and G. R. Service, "Passenger Car Fuel Economy Trends Through 1976," paper 750957 (Society of Automotive Engineers, October 1975), p. 18.

2. Robert Owens and Helen Sever, "The 3M Commute-a-Van Program: Status Report" (Washington, D.C.: Federal Highway Administration, 1974), p. 15.

3. Federal Highway Administration, Nationwide Personal Transportation Study, report 8, "Home-to-Work Trips and Travel," (Washington, D.C.: U.S. FHWA, 1973), table 6.

4. Federal Highway Administration, NPTS, report 1, "Automobile Occupancy," (Washington, D.C., 1972), table 3.

5. John Suhrbier, Terry Atherton, and William Jessiman, "The Use of Dis-

aggregate Travel Demand Models to Analyze Carpooling Policy Incentives," prepared by Cambridge Systematics, Inc., for the Federal Energy Administration (presented at the Transportation Research Board Meeting, January 1976), p. 33.

6. Gregory Ingram, Gary Fauth, and Eugene Kroch, *TASSIM: A Transportation and Air Shed Simulation Model*, vol. 1: *A Case Study of the Boston Region* (Washington, D.C.: U.S. Department of Transportation, 1974.)

7. FHWA, NPTS, report 8, "Home-to-Work Trips and Travel," table A-14.

8. Ibid.

9. Ibid.

10. Cynthia J. Burbank, "Transit Energy and Energy Conservation Programs: Vitally Linked," *Transit Journal* (May 1976): 62–64.

11. Ibid., p. 63.

12. J. P. Curry, "Case Studies of Transit Energy and Air Pollution Impacts," prepared by De Leuw, Cather and Co. for the Environmental Protection Agency, March 1975, cited by Eric Hirst, "Transportation Energy Conservation Policies," *Science* (April 1976): 15–20.

13. D. E. Boyce, K. Nguyes, T. Noyelle, and V. R. Vuchic, "Impact of Rapid Transit on Fuel Consumption and Cost for the Journey to Work," prepared for the Federal Energy Administration, June 1975, cited by ibid.

14. U.S. Department of Transportation, *1974 National Transportation Report: Urban Data Supplement* (Washington, D.C.: U.S. Department of Transportation, 1976), tables D-23, D-30.

15. Association of American Railroads, *Yearbook of Railroad Facts* (Washington, D.C.: Association of American Railroads, 1977), p. 32; Association of American Railroads, *Operating and Traffic Statistics: Class I Line-Haul Railroads in the United States* (Washington, D.C.: Association of American Railroads, 1976).

16. Congressional Budget Office, *Urban Transportation and Energy: The Potential Savings of Different Modes* (Washington, D.C.: U.S. Government Printing Office, 1977), p. 55.

17. Burbank, "Transit and Energy Conservation Programs," p. 64.

18. American Public Transit Association, *Transit Fact Book, 1976–1977 Edition*, tables 10, 16.

Notes to Appendix G

1. Federal Highway Administration, "The Effect of Speed on Automobile Gasoline Consumption Rates" (Washington, D.C.: Federal Highway Administration, 1973); and Paul J. Claffey and Associates, *Running Costs of Motor*

Vehicles as Affected by Road Design and Traffic, National Cooperative Highway Research Program, report 111 (Washington, D.C.: Highway Research Board, 1971).

2. David A. Curry and Dudley G. Anderson, *Procedures for Estimating Highway User Costs, Air Pollution, and Noise Effects* (Washington, D.C.: Highway Research Board, 1972).

INDEX